Michael Pye
Strategies in the Study of Religions

Religion and Reason

Founded by Jacques Waardenburg

Edited by
Gustavo Benavides and Michael Stausberg

Volume 52

De Gruyter

Michael Pye

Strategies in the Study of Religions

Volume Two: Exploring Religions in Motion

De Gruyter

ISBN 978-1-5015-1319-0
e-ISBN 978-1-61451-191-5
ISSN 0080-0848

Library of Congress Cataloging-in-Publication Data

A CIP catalog record for this book has been applied for at the Library of Congress.

Bibliographic information published by the Deutsche Nationalbibliothek

The Deutsche Nationalbibliothek lists this publication in the Deutsche Nationalbibliografie; detailed bibliographic data are available in the Internet at http://dnb.dnb.de.

© 2013 Walter de Gruyter GmbH, Berlin/Boston

Printing: Hubert & Co. GmbH & Co. KG, Göttingen
∞ Printed on acid-free paper

Printed in Germany

www.degruyter.com

Foreword to Volume Two

The present volume of *Strategies in the Study of Religions*, subtitled *Religions in Relation and Motion*, takes us forward into a variety of studies with comparative and theoretical implications. These include: Part Four: Comparing and Contrasting, Part Five: Tradition and Innovation and Part Six: Transplantation and Syncretism. In conclusion, Part Seven meshes the study of religions, as an academic discipline, with a number of problem areas of wide social interest and concern: Identity, Plurality, Dialogue, Education and Peace. The contents of Volume One, subtitled *Approaches and Positions* are presupposed here, and so readers are therefore requested to refer back to them as the context requires. The Preface and the General Introduction to both volumes of *Strategies in the Study of Religions* are to be found in Volume One. For convenience however, we repeat here the contents page for both volumes, the Editorial Note immediately below, the overview of publications and the general index.

Editorial Note

The papers selected for inclusion in these volumes have arisen over the course of many years and have appeared in extremely varied places. Here, the central intention is to present each one as it was conceived at the time, and in most cases hardly any changes have been made during the compilation and editing process. Typological errors have been corrected, the orthography of non-English terms and names has in general been up-dated, and occasionally a sentence has been polished for greater clarity without changing the sense. In a few cases, an article has been abbreviated to avoid too much overlap with others, and this is signaled. Since there are thirty-nine articles in all, not counting the introductions, a certain amount of cross-referencing between the articles has been added, which is of course new. Another difference is that the bibliographical style has been unified to the "author-date" system throughout the two volumes and in some cases the details have been improved or completed. This bibliographical streamlining, which reduces the length and number of footnotes, means that the individual articles no longer look like photocopies of the originals. In addition, there will occasionally be found a clearly marked "retrospective footnote" with some special information or signposting. Nevertheless, in spite of these editorial activities, no substantial revisions have been undertaken. Consequently, thought sequences across the forty years from 1972 up until 2012 will be reliably discernible for any readers who are interested in that aspect. While any one article can be read in its own right, as originally intended, the coordinated arrangement over seven parts maps the author's understanding of various options and opportunities in the study of religions.

Contents

Volume I: Exploring Methods and Positions

Preface VII
Editorial Note VIII
General Introduction 1

Part One   Methodological Strategies

1.1 Introduction to Part One 9
1.2 Methodological Integration in the Study of Religions 15
1.3 Field and Theory in the Study of Religions 33
1.4 Philology, Fieldwork and Ephemera in the Study of Japanese
     Religions 50
1.5 Participation, Observation and Reflection: An Endless
     Method 69
1.6 Getting into Trouble with the Believers: Intimacy and
     Distance in the Study of Religions 86

Part Two   East Asian Starting Points

2.1 Introduction to Part Two 109
2.2 An Asian Starting Point for the Study of Religions 115
2.3 Tominaga Nakamoto and Religious Pluralism 126
2.4 Three Teachings (Sānjiào) Theory and Modern Reflection on
     Religion 136
2.5 Modern Japan and the Science of Religions 144

Part Three   Structures and Strategies

3.1 Introduction to Part Three 173
3.2 Studies of Religion in Europe: Structures and Desiderata ... 178
3.3 Intercultural Strategies and the International Association for
     the History of Religions 196

VIII   Contents

3.4 Memories of the Future: Looking Back and Looking Forward
    in the History of Religions 208
3.5 Political Correctness in the Study of Religions: Is the Cold
    War Really Over? 223
3.6 Difference and Coherence in the World-wide Study of
    Religions 244

Author's Publications Cited in the Present Work 263

Consolidated Index to Volumes I and II 277

Volume II: Exploring Religions in Motion

Foreword to Volume Two V
Editorial Note VI

Part Four Comparing and Contrasting

4.1 Introduction to Part Four 3
4.2 On Comparing Buddhism and Christianity 11
4.3 Comparative Hermeneutics: A Brief Statement 32
4.4 Shintō and the Typology of Religions 40
4.5 Soteriological Orientations in Religion 51
4.6 'Polytheism' and 'Monotheism' as a Problem in the Typology
    of Religions 62
4.7 Prayer and Meditation as Comparative Concepts 72
4.8 Purification and Transformation in Comparative Perspective. 88

Part Five Tradition and Innovation

5.1 Introduction to Part Five 105
5.2 Religious Tradition and the Student of Religion 108
5.3 Ernst Troeltsch and Gerardus van de Leeuw on Tradition .. 117
5.4 Elements of a General Theory of Innovation in Religion ... 130
5.5 New Religions in East Asia 152
5.6 Won Buddhism as a Korean New Religion 179
5.7 Aum Shinrikyō. Can Religious Studies Cope? 202

5.8 Distant Cousins: Transmitting New Japanese Religions to Brazil 218

Part Six   Transplantation and Syncretism

6.1 Introduction to Part Six 243
6.2 The Transplantation of Religions 247
6.3 Syncretism and Ambiguity 253
6.4 Syncretism versus Synthesis 264
6.5 Buddhism and Shintō on One Island 278
6.6 Syncretism in Chinese Temples of South-East Asia and Taiwan 287

Part Seven   Some Contextual Questions: Identity, Plurality, Education, Dialogue, Peace

7.1 Introduction to Part Seven 309
7.2 Religion and Identity: Clues and Threads 314
7.3 Christian Churches and Political Change in Eastern Europe . 327
7.4 Reflecting on the Plurality of Religions 342
7.5 The Study of Religions and the Dialogue of Religions 352
7.6 Presuppositions of an Integrative Religious Education 376
7.7 Peace in the Dialogue of Religions 391

Author's Publications Cited in the Present Work 402

Consolidated Index to Volumes I and II 415

Part Four
Comparing and Contrasting

4.1 Introduction to Part Four

The time is long since past when specialists thought that the purpose of comparing religions was only to find out their common features, or even some kind of essence common to them all. Yet this idea has lived on rather persistently in the public mind, and it is conceivably out of sheer embarrassment over this and other meanderings in the history of "comparative religion" (cf. Sharpe 1986) that some researchers into religion try to ignore questions of comparison altogether. They would prefer them not to be posed at all, it seems. Students are less squeamish and sometimes seek to write lengthy essays or dissertations on a comparative topic. Unfortunately such essays often go wrong because it is so difficult to achieve a philological balance, or to give equal treatment to apparently similar themes in widely differing linguistic and cultural contexts. When examiners are satisfied with one part, they may be dissatisfied with the other. It is remarkable however that while philologically oriented scholars may adopt an expression of severe scorn, social scientists are not at all averse to setting up very widely ranging typologies which seem to have little basis in local fieldwork or in precise historical studies. In between these extremes we frequently find implied, but un-argued and unrefined comparisons in the writings of historians and cultural scientists dealing with one particular culture, but using terminology which would at least seem to have a meaning beyond its confines. This can come close to the oversimplification met with in public discourse. Because of all this it is very desirable that specialists in the study of religions make at least some efforts in the direction of comparative work.

The papers below are essays, along selected lines only, which arose in the course of other studies. They do not provide the details of a comprehensive system. Nevertheless the rudiments of a comprehensive perspective will be visible at various points. We should distinguish here between morphological questions, i.e. a view of the shape of any or various cases of religion, and typological questions, that is, the sorting of particular religious systems into leading types. Morphologically speaking, the four main aspects of any religious system are: the conceptual, the behavioural, the social and the subjective or attitudinal, as stated in the writer's *Comparative Religion* (Pye 1972a).[1] None of these four should be regarded as having any kind of normative priority over the others. These "aspects" correspond approximately to "dimensions" as put forward by Ninian Smart over many years and elaborated particularly in his *Dimensions of the Sacred* (Smart 1996), where as many as seven are named. The selection of a single term for each of these aspects is of course rather difficult. However, the view taken earlier, and here, is that such aspects must be sufficiently generally formulated to include all known cases, and sufficiently sharply defined to avoid overlaps and redundancy. Thus "religious behaviour" is to be preferred to "ritual" because some religious behaviour is not ritualized and some ritual behaviour might arguably not be "religious". The category "religious concepts" is to be preferred to "doctrine" because many religious concepts, including myth and legend of various kinds, occur in non-formalized patterns; religious concepts include both doctrine and myth. Such options are discussed further in "Religion: shape and shadow" (Pye 1994b, not included here). Identifying these aspects in a disciplined manner is the first step in the morphology of religion. Since Buddhism and Christianity are both would-be universal religions, they can be compared relatively easily with regard to their various aspects, and this is sketched out in the article "On comparing Buddhism and Christianity" (4.2 below). The fact that the term "dimensions" is used there is not intended to change the argument. However, the aspect or dimension of dynamic movement in religions may be added to the basic four aspects, as pointed out below, lest these be misunderstood as static.

Equally important is the question of a general typology of religions. A major typological distinction may be drawn between primal religion and critical religions. While newly founded religions are in some way or other inherently critical of ordinary life, seeking to go beyond it or resolve its tensions quite radically, primal religious systems are above all experienced as securing and reinforcing regular patterns of natural life. In the article just mentioned, this distinction was set out (referring to Buddhism and Christianity as "universal" religions (a term later replaced by "critical religions")) with respect to the rites which are strikingly typical of each type.

---

1   Otherwise stated: religious concepts, religious states of mind, religious action, religious groups, the sequence of these four being immaterial, such that they can be presented in a circular diagram (Pye 1972a: 12).

In "Shintō and the typology of religion" (4.4 below), for example, the focus shifts to the features of primal religious systems, while taking account of dynamic adjustments made during historical processes. As with most portmanteau designations for particular religions the reference of the term Shintō has frequently been contested, and this is not surprising because while there are many continuities the character of "Shintō" has changed considerably in the course of history. In this article it is argued that while Shintō may be regarded in a most general sense as a primal religion (rather than a critical one), it has been considerably adapted in accordance with the pressures of history, and is hence better characterised as an "adjusted primal religion." To a marked extent, historic Shintō has become so elaborate and specific, that the substratum of primal religion in Japan has found more general patterns of its own – a subject too complex to be set out here in detail.[2] In spite of this far-reaching displacement, such soteriology as is offered in the context of Shintō shrines continues to be inner-worldly, that is, dealing mainly with matters of the present life, and in this it differs from the main objectives of founded religions such as Buddhism and Christianity.

The overall typology of primal and critical religions or religious systems was further pursued in "Soteriological orientations in religion" (4.5 below). Here the notion of "critical religions" is further differentiated into religions of salvation, of guidance, and of awareness and gnosis. Yet the overall ritual distinctions between the two main categories remain. As to the soteriological orientations under discussion, the key point is that primal religious systems typically make room for the resolution of temporary, this-worldly problems (such as the healing of illness) but in a manner which is consistent with the ordinary course of life, while critical religions offer, or seek, some kind of transcending solution either as an alternative or very frequently in addition to the temporary solutions. It is not surprising therefore that new religions quite commonly offer healings of specific illnesses, while at the same time commending the perspective of a transcending salvation in their own specific terms. This range is covered by the terms proximate soteriology and ultimate soteriology.

The distinction between primal and critical religious systems is relevant to more themes in the study of religions than are considered in this part. Attention was already drawn to the task of identifying the pri-

---

2   See however Pye 1996e, Pye 2004a and Pye 2009c (not included in the present volumes).

mal religious patterns of Japanese culture, given that Shintō has long been so adjusted and adapted that it by no means monopolises this ground. Looking ahead to Part Seven of the present volume, the fundamental distinction is correlated with questions about identity in "Religion and identity: clues and threads" (1994 and 7.2). The main argument at that point is that the crossovers between the main types can be very significant when it comes to particular issues such as identity creation and reinforcement. While that paper was focused on South Africa, similar considerations were advanced in "Shintō, primal religion and international identity" in the first issue of the internet journal *Marburg Journal of Religion* (Pye 1996e).

It is with such overall morphological and typological patterns in mind that the general orientation of the pieces in this part can be understood. However there is also another strand to be considered. It will be seen that "On comparing Buddhism and Christianity" (4.2) is by no means a would-be normative or final statement about the relative truth or value of these substantial and very complex traditions; it seeks to set a certain framework in which further comparative reflections maybe fruitful. Immediately following it below is a short piece entitled "Comparative hermeneutics: a brief statement" (4.3) which seeks to show how the delicate problems of following through internal lines of interpretation within specific traditions can be brought into the light of comparative study. A more substantial essay on this subject, too long for inclusion here, had introduced a work edited with Robert Morgan in which parallel questions and procedures in the interpretation of Buddhism and Christianity, i. e. hermeneutical matters, were considered comparatively (Pye and Morgan 1972). This represents a move consistent with the acceptable features of the phenomenology of religion, but one which highlights the dynamics of tradition as a process (on which see further in Part Five), which the major representatives of the phenomenology of religion had largely ignored in favour of a more or less timeless synchronicity.

Further in Part Four below, a small number of thematic comparisons are taken up, each with accompanying theoretical reflections which may help to show how any comparisons can be made to work in the study of religions. In three cases the subjects themselves were set by external request. It will be noticed that the previously mentioned "Soteriological orientations in religion" (4.5) was conceived for and appeared in connection with a dialogue between religions involving the Japanese religion Tenrikyō (The Teaching of Heavenly Wisdom) and

Catholic partners.³ The paper entitled "Prayer and meditation as comparative concepts" (4.7) arose in connection with a dialogue between Tenrikyō and (mainly) Lutheran theologians, and the same applies for "Purification and transformation in comparative perspective" (4.8). In each of these cases non-theological specialists were present, of whom the present writer was one. It is not without interest that in a context created by a particular religious organization, Tenrikyō, still regarded as a "new religion," contributions were sought in this way from non-affiliated specialists in the study of religions. The sponsorship was in fact indirect, since the events were arranged through associated universities. The other main parties to the dialogues also had direct or indirect religious affiliations – except for the non-theological students of religions.[4] The language of these papers was purposely set at a level suitable for oral communication and reading by non-native users of English from various quarters, and therefore does not reflect the heavier style of some kinds of "scientific" dissertations. Nevertheless the intention is no different.

Interleaved among these papers, for general thematic reasons, is a contribution which addresses a somewhat traditional topic in the comparative study of religions, namely concepts of divinity, the title being: "'Polytheism' and 'monotheism' as a problem in the typology of religions" (4.6). A simple note of warning may be attached to this article, as it may prove to be irritating for some readers who are used to thinking of Christianity as "monotheism." It often happens, when comparative studies are undertaken, that believers get upset, as was already discussed in "Getting into trouble with the believers..." in Part One (1.6). However this cannot always be avoided. It is so often the case that believers do not wish to know that their religions are somehow like other religions. It can also happen that students of religion can unwittingly share a commonly held view on religions, e.g. about the presumed monotheism of Christianity. The intention of the paper however is, of course, not to draw theological controversy, but in words from its rather sedate conclusion, to "...illuminate questions which arise where religious systems prove to be diverse, both when we compare re-

---

3   Cf. an interview in Japanese about the nature of this symposium in the booklet Tenrikyōdōyōsha 1998: 97–8.
4   On the relations between the study of religions as a discipline (that is, not theology) and various forms of interreligious dialogue see further in "The study of religions and the dialogue of religions" at 7.5 below.

ligious systems with each other, and when we compare different versions of a religion which bear a single name and somehow seem to be part of a wider common tradition." At the same time the argument may seem to some to be troubling, for above all it seeks to *de*construct the two key notions "monotheism" and "polytheism" and replace them with alternative categories which are more appropriate for comparative purposes.[5]

The themes introduced in this part are admittedly no more than examples of the many others such as "mysticism" or "pilgrimage" which have attracted attention, including by the present writer, but which cannot all be pursued here. Comparison is an inevitable and a desirable aspect of the study of religions, and it should not be scorned, as is easily done. Distinctions should be respected however between (a) morphological considerations (which in the first instance seek generic simplicities), (b) typological considerations (which tend quite justifiably to emphasise difference as well as similarity) and (c) thematic explorations which, while elucidating ever more fascinating materials, should aim at careful working definitions which may be of use for further studies. About pilgrimage for example, the writer has advanced the following summary definition in various places: "Pilgrimage is the deliberate traversing of a route to a sacred place which lies outside one's normal habitat." A similar but slightly more complicated definition of mysticism is argued for in "Shinran as a mystical religious thinker" (cf. Pye 2004c).[6] The key points are: (i) an intensive subjectivity which goes beyond that of daily, functional religiosity, (ii) a relationship to the relevant tradition which is at once loyal and in critical tension to it, and (iii) the integration of various forms of experience which may otherwise seem to be in some kind of opposition (life and death, good and evil, gender polarity etc.). Shinran (1173–1262), the founder of Jōdo Shinshū, a major de-

---

5   Unfortunately, the phrase "need to be deconstructed" of the original manuscript was replaced in the first published version (with no proof-reading opportunity) by its very opposite: "need to be constructed." As a result the argument was stood on its head, confusing readers and reviewers.
6   The English original, dating from 2001, was made available with limited circulation in the conference handbook of the 10th Biennial Conference of the International Association of Shin Buddhist Studies (Ōtani University August 2–4 2001), 1–16; however, in the German translation (Pye 2004c) see especially pages 324–5.

nomination of Japanese Pure Land Buddhism,[7] is not usually thought of as a mystic (the "tension with believers factor" appears again here, complicated by a linguistic misunderstanding), but precisely for this reason we can see how careful analysis and definitions can help to shed more appropriate light on well-known cases.

Further relevant papers which refer to comparison in certain ways will appear in the rest of the present volume, notably in "Ernst Troeltsch and Gerardus van de Leeuw on tradition" (5.3), "Elements of a general theory of innovation in religion" (2012 and 5.4), and in a broad sense the whole of Part Six which deals with syncretism. It is important to reflect on the merits and failings of older attempts at "comparative religion," especially as undertaken by phenomenologists such as Gerardus van der Leeuw, Friedrich Heiler or Mircea Eliade. These are often uncritically quoted by the representatives of other disciplines who seem to think that the study of religions has simply stood still for half a century or more. However we should not be locked into their works, even if they are regarded in some quarters as classics. While being aware of not a few pitfalls, which can more easily be seen in retrospect, the writer believes that a seriously critical attempt to study religions comparatively can bring precise insights which are "scientifically" viable, at least in the sense of being heuristically useful for continuing research. Since comparative reflections are evidently unavoidable, it is better to make them explicit and try to achieve progress step by step.

Bibliographical references

Dobbins, James C. 1989. *Jōdo Shinshū. Shin Buddhism in Medieval Japan.* Bloomington and Indianapolis (Indiana University Press).
Pye, Michael 1972a. *Comparative Religion. An Introduction through Source Materials.* Newton Abbot, England (David and Charles) and New York (Harper and Row).
– 1991c. "Reflections on the Treatment of Tradition in Comparative Perspective, with Special Reference to Ernst Troeltsch and Gerardus van der Leeuw" in: Kippenberg, Hans G. and Luchesi, Brigitte (eds.) *Religionswissenschaft und Kulturkritik.* Marburg (Diagonal-Verlag): 101–111.
– 1994b. "Religion: Shape and Shadow" in: *Numen* 41 (1): 51–75.

---

7   For presentations of this tradition, see Dobbins 1989 and anthologies drawn from the pages of *The Eastern Buddhist* (Pye 2011, 2012, etc.).

- 1996e. "Shintō, primal religion and international identity" in: *Marburg Journal of Religion 1/1:* (virtual pages). <http://www.uni-marburg.de/fb03/ivk/mjr/pdfs/1996 /articles/Shintō1996>.
- 2004a *The structure of religious systems in contemporary Japan: Shintō variations on Buddhist pilgrimage. (Occasional Papers 30).* Marburg (Centre for Japanese Studies).
- 2004c "Shinran als mystischer religiöser Denker" in: Schönemann, Friederike and Maaßen, Thorsten et al.(eds) *Prüft Alles, und das Gute behaltet! Zum Wechselspiel von Kirchen, Religionen und säkularer Welt. Festschrift für Hans-Martin Barth zum 65. Geburtstag.* Frankfurt am Main (Otto Lembeck): 309–35. (Translated from the English of 2001 by Gerhard Marcel Martin.)
- 2009c "Leading patterns in everyday Japanese religion" in: *Sphinx, Yearbook 2008–9* (Societas Scientiarum Fennica): 45–53.
- 2011 (ed.). *Beyond Meditation. Expressions of Shin Buddhist Spirituality* (Eastern Buddhist Voices 1). London (Equinox Publications).
- 2012 (ed.). *Listening to Shin Buddhism. Starting Points of Modern Dialogue* (Eastern Buddhist Voices 2). London (Equinox Publications).

Pye, Michael and Morgan, Robert (eds.) 1973. *The Cardinal Meaning. Essays in Comparative Hermeneutics: Buddhism and Christianity* (Religion and Reason 6), The Hague (Mouton).

Sharpe, Eric 1975 (1986). *Comparative Religion: a History.* London (Duckworth).

Smart, Ninian 1996. *Dimensions of the Sacred. An Anatomy of the World's Beliefs.* London (HarperCollins).

Tenrikyōdōyōsha (eds.) 1998. *Tenrikyō to Kirisutokyō no Taiwa. Rōma Tenrikyōten.* Tenri (Tenrikyōdōyōsha).

4.2 On Comparing Buddhism and Christianity

This paper was written in response to a request during an extended visiting appointment at Tsukuba University, Japan (1979–80). The full title of the periodical in which it appeared can be translated as "Collection of Studies from the Academic Section for Philosophy and Thought of Tsukuba University" and is referred to simply as "Studies" in English. The present text has been very slightly edited, e.g. with the provision of details for references, but is in all important respects unchanged.

Introduction

The modern historical consciousness now prevalent in east and west alike has created new tasks and new opportunities in the interpretation of Buddhism and of Christianity. This consciousness has two fundamental implications for both traditions which cannot be escaped by anybody who seriously reflects on them. The first is that historical criticism of the authoritative reference points of faith, especially of the origins of each of the two faiths, has long made it impossible to find there any absolute refuge, however important those reference points may continue to be in locating the meaning of tradition. The second is that elementary knowledge of the history of culture makes it impossible to maintain an intellectually viable interpretation of one religious tradition in grand isolation, as if it were sealed off from the influence of all others and as if it had no structural analogies with others. The result is that the sense of religious superiority frequently enjoyed and communicated by teachers within Buddhism and Christianity is no longer excusable. To say this is not to preclude the possibility of preferential judgments in the long run. Nor is it to overlook that cluster of problems still remaining for both traditions which may initially be referred to as the question of absoluteness (as in Ernst Troeltsch's *Die Absolutheit des Christentums* (Troeltsch 1902). It is merely to assert that the base-line for contemporary and future interpretations of either Buddhism or Christianity, or both, must be a recognition of the full availability of both traditions, and indeed of other religious traditions and general features of human experience.

If two traditions or more are held in view while interpretation proceeds, some kind of comparative reflection becomes inevitable. Yet this all too easily turns into over-simplified rejection of the tradition least accessible to the interpreter, or in some cases to a naive acclamation of what is alien. Persons attending to these matters may be unduly affected by chance features in their own personal development, or they may be constrained to adopt certain attitudes because of official positions which they hold in religious organisations. All too often like is not compared with like. Monologues pass each other in the wind. There seems to be a need therefore for some charting of a framework for relaxed comparison, some attention given to an appropriate structure for reflection, some indication of the range of features which need to be considered. The purpose of this paper is to suggest an outline which may be useful in this connection and which at least may be thought to have some validity in terms of the study of religions as an academic pursuit.

Relations between Buddhism and Christianity have usually been rather guarded, when not actually polemical. The oldest polemical writing is probably the Japanese work *Ha Daiusu* (i. e. *Contra Deum*) written in 1620 by the ex-Christian convert Fabian Fucan, and it remains instructive.[1] Since then eirenic works have also been written, but the sense of rivalry has not altogether departed. Influential Christian theologians such as Karl Barth and Paul Tillich have reacted to the existence of Buddhism in ways consistent with their theologies, but without really grasping the significance of Buddhism in a positive way. For their part Buddhist writers not infrequently make passing references to Christianity which pick on some isolated feature, yet betray inadequate understanding of the real tensions and strengths in the Christian tradition. For example, it is sometimes supposed that the Buddhist teaching of *anātman* (Japanese *muga* 無我) is a refutation of a presumed central Christian doctrine of the soul, while in reality Christian doctrines of the soul or the self are by no means as straightforward as may first appear, especially if one reckons that early borrowings from Greek thought are not necessarily essential equipment for Christians in later centuries.

It might be thought that the best way to get over inadequate and unduly argumentative relations at the conceptual level would be to abandon them altogether and to shift the meeting of the two traditions on to the level of religious practices. One thinks here of shared meditation programmes, shared efforts to maintain or develop moral standards

---

1   For a study and a translation see Elison 1973.

or shared efforts to secure world peace. There is clearly some merit in this course, but only some. The conceptual problems will in fact remain as long as humans have heads. Not only that, religious practice or even *jissen* (実践 'actually putting into practice'), undisputed though its priority may be as an existential concern, almost always is found to come trailing ideas, both in Buddhism and in Christianity. It is sometimes thought that Buddhism does not have this characteristic, but in reality Buddhist meditation cannot be separated from a Buddhist perception of the way the world is, as *is* clear from the classic Buddhist meditation instructions. Conceptual reflections such as these present ones should therefore be recognised as a form of mental work which is in some way relevant to religious practice, and which is indeed at least as necessary in its own way as the physical construction of buildings for religious purposes. In short, what might at first seem like a pure reliance on religious practice may be a form of self-deceit, though not dishonourable, and may represent a form of escapism from difficult but real conceptual questions.

If such escapism is disallowed, some coherent framework is needed which permits the meaning conveyed by each of these two complex traditions to come to light at one and the same time. The present argument suggests a framework which is illustrated by incidental discussion of some of its features. The reader will realise that substantive discussion cannot really go beyond suggestions and pointers in the space of one article. In any case it must be admitted that the writer is still reflecting on many of the sub-issues which press for treatment in the context of the overall framework, and indeed he will probably never achieve the competence to deal with them adequately.

In terms of the relations between intellectual disciplines it is proposed that the key discipline for developing an even-handed approach to the interpretation of Buddhism and Christianity is neither Christian theology nor its Buddhist equivalent but the historical and comparative study of religion. Taken together, the historical and comparative study of religion are the central elements of the scientific study of religion/s, or *Religionswissenschaft,* to which of course various other disciplines contribute in varying degree. This discipline proceeds phenomenologically in the sense that it treats the experience of the believer as its primary datum, without being sociologically or psychologically reductionist, nor yet adopting *a priori* positions about the truth or falsity of any particular belief system. Thus the historical and comparative study of religion, as an intellectual discipline, is able to play a mediating role between the Buddhist and Christian traditions, taking each with full seriousness, and providing a basis of knowledge, and indeed of understanding, on which renewed interpretative essays can build. Naturally the usefulness of this basis will depend on the correctness and judiciousness with which it is developed, so that prior reflection over a wider comparative field is also of some significance.

While academic writing on the nature and structure of religion has suggested many variations, the present writer considers that the simplest while most comprehensive view of any religious phenomena recognises four interrelated dimensions which together constitute the believer's religious experience. These have already been discussed elsewhere (Pye 1972a),[2] but in brief they are the conceptual (including symbolic, mythic, etc.), the behavioural (including both ritual and moral action as the case may be), the social (that is, the social extension of the religion as perceived and experienced by its members) and the psychological (here in the limited sense of the attitudinal profile and the state of mind and sensibility of the believer). Of course the sociological and the psychological study of religion also have a major task of functional explanation, but that is secondary to the study of religion phenomenologically conceived. These four dimensions are all of equal importance and it is misleading to give priority to any one of them. In particular it is unsatisfactory to regard either belief systems or ritual and practice systems as the main focus of "religious experience" as is commonly done. Neither should the dimension of sensitivity or feeling be simply equated with "religious experience," as was done in the work of William James, Rudolf Otto and Joachim Wach. This error represents a protestant emphasis on the value of subjective feeling, and no doubt illustrates a fundamentally healthy reaction to what the Protestant tradition has perceived as the ritualism and scholasticism of Catholicism. It is of course not without significance when religious believers or practitioners themselves stress the importance of one or other of these four dimensions; but at the same time they may not themselves be analytically aware of the way in which their experience is conveyed through the other three. For the observer it is methodologically important to maintain all four in steady view and to see the religious experience of the believer as constituted in some way or other by them all.

---

2   Retrospective note: the term "aspects" was however preferred to "dimensions."

In addition to these four major dimensions, in terms of which any example of religion can be characterised without undue stress, there is what might be considered a fifth dimension, namely the extension of the four basic dimensions through time, with the resultant patterns and routines which can be observed running through the traditions as historically known to us. It is this fifth dimension, which the believer views as tradition and where the observer tries to perceive patterned dynamics, which provides the main springboard into new, creative interpretations. If this fifth dimension is clearly perceived and fully used by the practitioners of religion, many of the problems caused by an inordinate sense of modernity subside into insignificance. It is only when the routines of intermediate tradition are ignored that a religious message seems to have to make a gigantic leap from the time of the origins of the faith, or from some presumed age of archaic experience, forward to the consciousness of modern man. Even when such leaps are encouraged, as in the work of a Rudolf Bultmann or of a Mircea Eliade respectively, the relation of the first meaning to its reception by modern man remains extremely problematic. At the same time it could well be argued by theologians and their Buddhist conterparts that the values and meanings most deeply required by humanity today or at any time have all been carried forward in one way or another by the complex traditions of Buddhism and Christianity, which have themselves in many ways adopted modernity and even contributed to it. Thus it is surprising that the importance of the workings of tradition, or the dynamics of religion through time, has not yet been widely recognised in the literature of the science of religions. This fifth dimension of religion is indeed the link between the deep past and the present, between messages lost and messages transmitted, between those who have in the past perceived the central meanings offered by the religions and those who may do so in the future. Yet this is already to flex the springboard for further interpretations, and before enthusiasm disturbs the picture unduly it is desirable to take a sober view of the four elementary dimensions of religion as these appear in Buddhism and in Christianity. In order to illustrate the procedure in outline some reflections will now be offered on each of these dimensions in turn. Depending on the point of view and experience of the reader some of the points made will no doubt seem quite elementary and perhaps over-simplified; yet that is one of the unavoidable characteristics of a comparative approach which seeks to achieve a degree of even-handedness with respect to two traditions.

Social dimension

Christianity belongs to a family of religions, consisting mainly of Judaism, Christianity and Islam, which are all strong in consciously intended social meaning. One of the keynotes of Israelite and thence Jewish religion has always been Torah; law, that is, in the special sense of a law for the people of God which they are bound, in a covenant with God, to maintain. Torah provided stipulations for all aspects of social life, and it represents such a strong identification of religious consciousness with the social life of the Jewish people that in modern times it has been considered possible by some to maintain Jewishness while being agnostic or even atheistic, in matters of belief. In the Muslim faith an almost equally strong emphasis on the ordering of social life, based on the Qur'an and subsequent Islamic law, can be seen as a follow-through to the Jewish heritage with an opening of the divinely sanctioned order to diverse peoples.

As to Christianity, the New Testament had already suggested a complex attitude towards Torah. This is seen both in the Gospels, where Jesus is portrayed as challenging rigid and repressive applications of Torah which failed to meet human realities and needs, and also in the epistles of Paul, where Torah is seen as something which binds humanity in sin so that man's condition needs to be transformed by grace. Nevertheless the growing Christian Church maintained the Old Testament containing the Torah, along with the New Testament, as a revelation of God's will, and not only was the Church seen as the people of God or as the "true Israel," but eventually there were attempts to order whole societies in accordance with God's law, the most famous being the theocracy of Calvin's Geneva. Even when the Christian churches have not held politically dominating positions, they have frequently displayed strong social concerns, right up to the Industrial Missions of modern times, which seek not individual conversions but the Christianisation or sanctification of the very structures of industry. The reason for this social concern, whatever form it takes, is that it is a central presupposition of Christianity to place a high value on open, loving relations between persons deemed to be equal before God. Thus the Church, as the caring community of the elect, seeks to transform society at large into a moral and caring community on a wide scale.

It is easy to contrast these tendencies in Christianity with a picture of Buddhism which emphasises impersonality and plays down relations between persons, hence attaching little importance to community. Paul Tillich argued that this was a major difference between the two traditions, and even went so far as to say that as a result democracy could not be expected to thrive in Buddhist countries. Such a view is probably faulty. It has arisen no doubt partly because of some real features of Buddhist teaching which may have received more emphasis among western observers than they enjoy in practice among Buddhists, and partly because of a strong assumption that it is the community of monks alone (the Sangha) which contains Buddhists. On this basis it is easy to see Buddhists as a series of individuals seeking enlightenment more or less independently from each other, and forming a Sangha only out of convenience. Yet such a view overlooks the real social forms of Buddhism. The presuppositions and ideals of Buddhist social forms are indeed different from those of Christianity but that does not mean that they are non-existent. Disciples of the Buddha are in fact supposed to aid each other on the path to enlightenment, following the example of their teacher, and this mutual support takes its main social form in the arrangements for regulating the Sangha. The arrangements include, in theory at least, the possibility of expulsion, which indicates the serious intent of the provisions. A significant feature in the early period and still today in Theravāda Buddhism is the regular *uposatha* meeting for self-examination at which members' minds are concentrated on the goal which they share.

Mutual interdependence on the path towards Buddhahood is however a much wider concept than it would be if it pertained to the Sangha alone, for it extends right through the whole natural community which supports the Sangha. The support of laity was amost certainly elicited and received during the Buddha's own lifetime, as all ancient sources agree, and certainly the Buddhist religion emerged very early as a civilisational force and not just a matter to interest a few miscellaneous individuals. This civilisational impact has been written up with particular emphasis by Trevor Ling in his work *The Buddha* (Ling 1973) which, though containing very little about the Buddha himself, gives prominence to the political compacts which took classical form in the Asokan model.[3] Indeed from the early legends onwards right through the later history of Buddhism it is possible to see a tripartite relationship between Sangha, king and people in which the Sangha legitimates the monarchy, the king rules the people benevolently, while the people in their turn give support to the Sangha. This is expressed diagramatically (and in more detail) in the present writer's own short work *The Buddha*

---

3   The sub-title is, appropriately, *Buddhist Civilization in India and Ceylon.*

(1979). A similar pattern was reflected in the Japanese Buddhism of the time of Shōtoku Taishi (574–623) and indeed again in the recent aspirations of the Nichiren Shōshū Sōka Gakkai which has taught of a 'third civilisation' (*daisan bunmei* 第三文明) and, although politics and religion are constitutionally distinct in Japan, of a "mysterious union between king and Buddha" (*ōbutsu myōgō* 王仏妙合).

However the social extension of Buddhism among the people is not just a question of some kind of social or political compact. It has another feature centering on the relationship between the Sangha and the people, which can be seen as a complex network of karmic relationships, binding together whole families and generations as they progress towards enlightenment and nirvana. For this reason aspects of Buddhism sometimes known as "popular Buddhism," "household Buddhism" or "funeral Buddhism" should not be written off as being merely the performance of necessary social functions. On the contrary this extension of Buddhism should be appreciated as a meaningful social dimension of Buddhist experience. Of course not everybody who takes part in a routine Buddhist activity is doing so because of an individual intention to achieve enlightenment in the near future. Social obligations undoubtedly play a much larger part in the minds of those concerned. Nevertheless there is also usually a real sense of a karmic connection linking all those who take part. Indeed it is probably correct to say that social connections are seen in this perspective as being *at the same time* karmic connections. In the case of Japanese Buddhism one may see here a conflation between the connections obtaining between one particular social group within society which is essentially limited, and the universalist karmic perspective of Mahāyāna Buddhism in general. It is one of the points at which the social experience of Buddhism syncretises with the elemental forces of Japanese society. Similar arguments could be advanced with respect to other Buddhist countries.

Thus the social dimension of Buddhism should be characterised positively on at least three levels: relations within the Sangha, relations between the Sangha and the socio-political order, and the sense of karmic continuity, dependence and responsibility which pervades the Buddhism of the people. It is only on such a basis that a comparative view of the social dimension of Buddhism and Christianity should build. The comparative approach should not be developed on the negative basis of pointing out what one tradition lacks in terms of the other, but, initially at least, by characterising positively what each tradition does entail in its own terms. Equally, this social dimension should not be treated in either case as a *mere* social function, but should be recognised as a value-bearing dimension of experience for those involved. The importance of this becomes especially clear if one considers its close relation to the behavioural or ritual dimension in which the believer may be caught up at many points in his life.

Behavioural dimension

Religious action can be loosely divided into formal rites of various kinds and religiously patterned behaviour performed in the context of life in general. The former is more specific, more evident, more structured, while the latter merges imperceptibly into the total range of human behaviour. Both are of considerable importance in both Buddhism and Christianity, so that in a broad sense it is possible to compare like with like.

The overt rites of Buddhism and Christianity have a major underlying similarity in that they are the rites of a universal religion of salvation or release which has made itself at home in a whole range of natural societies. In unmixed form the rites of such universal religions are quite different from the rites of primal religions which have a single social basis. Bearing in mind that both universal and primal religions have (1) rites which centre on individuals and (2) rites in which the whole group is the main focus, the range of rites can be expressed diagramatically as follows:

	(1) individual focus	(2) group focus
(P) Primal	rites of transition	seasonal rites etc.
(U) Universal	rites of initiation	rites of reinforcement

Rites in the P/1 category are Arnold Van Gennep's well known rites of transition (*rites de passage*) which see the individual through birth, adolescence, marriage and death. Naturally these are also social rites in the sense that they enable a society to manage changes in the relative position of the individuals within it. However they take place when the life-stage of specific individuals requires it. By contrast the rites in the P/2 category are the new year, spring-time and harvest festivals, rites connected with special occupations, and any others which rehearse the needs and aspirations of a single society. In a pure state, a universal religion of salvation or release also has two kinds of rite. Those which centre on the need of an individual, in category U/1, are above all the rites of initiation such as baptism and confirmation in Christianity and receiving the precepts (Japanese *jukai* 受戒) in Buddhism. The so-called initiations of primal religion are quite different since they mark the transition from childhood to adulthood and are more or less inevitable for all the members of a given society, whereas initiation in a religion of salvation or release implies voluntary entry into a group distinct from the natural society of which the person is also a member. The fact that in many situations these two are conflated will be referred to again below. In category U/2 may be placed rites which strengthen the select body or celebrate its central concerns. In early Buddhism this was above all the *uposatha,* though other rites now come into this category too depending on the sect, while in Christianity the main rite in this category has been in some form or other the Eucharist or Lord's Supper. These rites may be called rites of reinforcement in that they consolidate the position of members in their faith and discipline. Naturally this four-fold analysis of rites has a very wide application and many other specific examples and variations could be adduced.

The picture becomes interestingly more complex however when we consider the overall history of Buddhism and Christianity, for the simple reason that, as these extremely adaptable religions spread, from region to region and from age to age, they shared to a varying extent in the functions of primal religion. Thus Christianity rapidly developed a religious framework for birth, adolescence, marriage and death, infant baptism becoming a birth rite and confirmation becoming an adolescence rite. Similarly Buddhism became of great importance as a funeral religion in various countries, while in Theravāda Buddhism ordination took on a partial role as an adolescent rite for boys or young men involving them in separation from society, temporary monkhood and then a return to adult household life. In the more dominantly social category P/2 Buddhism and Christianity also took on a seasonal form. Christmas marked the winter solstice, and Easter marked spring with a popular emphasis on natural regeneration evidenced by bulbs, eggs, and so on. Christianity also provided agricultural rites in the form of Rogation-tide and Harvest Festival. Buddhism developed less in this respect, leaving more room for existing religious systems such as, in the Japanese context, Shintō. However Buddhism has become strongly affected by the sense of calendricity running throughout Japanese religion in general. One has only to think of the 108 soundings of the temple bells at midnight on New Year's Eve (*joya no kane* 除夜の鐘), signalling the passing of the old year, or of the two and a half million folk who make their New Year's visit (*hatsumōde* 初詣) not to a Shintō shrine, or not only to a Shintō shrine, but also to the famous Buddhist Temple Sensōji, at Asakusa in Tokyo.

The most common comparative reflection on this state of affairs is that Buddhism has usually effected some kind of compromise with the natural religions of its host countries, while Christianity, like Islam, has swept away indigenous religious practices to dominate the whole of life by itself. While there is some truth in this, it should not be overlooked that Christianity has in fact ingested much regional lore and custom in a complex indigenisation process, while the same is true of Islam, especially in Indonesia. Indeed, since Christianity has if anything produced a greater range of rites than Buddhism to suit the primal level of religious needs, the matter could be stated quite conversely, though unfashionably, namely that it is Christianity which has shown the more comprehensive adaptability, while Buddhism on the whole has maintained a more severe distance as a religion of separation and release. However that may be, it should be recognised in long-term discussion that the ritual dimension of both Buddhism and Christianity represents a complex interplay between rituals which facilitate the soteriological meaning of the religion over against natural life, and rituals which in various ways accommodate to the requirements of natural society. Not only that, but most Buddhist and Christian rituals display both of these aspects, so that they can only be properly understood in terms of a syncretistic and ambiguous function.

The second main area of religious behaviour is the less formal one of religiously motivated action within the believer's total range of ordinary action. On this matter reference must be limited here to the question of the status of ethical action in the two traditions, which is often misunderstood in both cases. In the case of Christianity it is often presumed that the religious sanction for ethics is rigidly authoritarian. However this is a misleading view which fails to do justice both to New Testament materials and to much of later Christian practice. The whole thrust of Christian ethics in the New Testament was towards (a) the interiorisation of law, and (b) the universalisation of law, that is, of course, of religious and ethical law. Jesus is recalled in the Gospels as relating divine law to human needs and by no means as simply reasserting the Jewish religious law in some new authoritarian fashion. In the case of Buddhism it is frequently supposed that ethics are secondary or even irrelevant and that Buddhism is essentially an amoral religion. This impression is sometimes reinforced by Buddhists themselves, especially in the Zen tradition, who stress that Buddhist enlightenment lies beyond the distinction between good and evil. Since the western observer usually feels obliged to be interested in enlightenment he may easily overlook the fact that the vast majority of Asian Buddhists do not expect early enlightenment. Yet for Buddhists in a pre-enlightenment condition, or a pre-nirvanic condition, karmic differences do matter, and hence moral guidance is not insignificant. There is indeed the broad difference between the two traditions that in Buddhism moral effort is essentially a preliminary, while in Christianity it is usually considered to be contemporaneous with and essential to the spiritual life. Nevertheless this difference can be exaggerated.

The above problem about the status of ethics in the two traditions may arise in part simply because ethics are frequently considered as an independent and coherent category in their own right. In reality ethics merge into wider questions about the assumptions and values of daily life, attitudes towards family life, work, society, and so on. Therefore it might be more fruitful to begin with a more comprehensive characterization of what might be called the *meaning-in-life* of Buddhism and of Christianity, including reference to ethically conceived behaviour but also to a wider range of behavior which is less formally but no less importantly inspired by religious values and attitudes. For the present the main point to be noted is that the comparison of Buddhism and Christianity should not have built into it from the very beginning an artificial and misleadingly rigid view of ethics. It is not necessary to expatiate on the intimate connections which this dimension of religion clearly has with the psychological and conceptual dimensions to which we now proceed.

Psychological dimension

Although this is called the psychological dimension for convenience it should be recalled that the expression is used in the limited sense of the states of mind, attitudinal profile and sensibility of the believer. Just as the social dimension considered earlier referred to the social extension of the religion as perceived and experienced by the believer, so too does the psychological dimension in this sense refer to the subjective extension of the believer's awareness or sensibility. We are not concerned at this point with functional explanations of religion which would correlate religious experience with non-religious factors such as neurosis or sexual repression, etc.

This dimension is particularly difficult to deal with because, while each of the four dimensions is in constant relation to the other three, it is in practice all but impossible to discuss it at all without speedy reference to the conceptual dimension. Another difficulty is that it is often all too rapidly assumed that it is this dimension which itself alone constitutes religious experience. However it is erroneous and misleading to restrict "experience" to the subjective sensibilities of religion, as is implied in the title and content of William James' extremely influential work *The Varieties of Religious Experience* (1902). The "experience" of the believer is more appropriately seen as pervading *all four* of the dimensions currently being considered. However these notes of caution do not mean that the religious consciousness or state of mind is not open to consideration. Indeed it would be superficial to ignore it.

With this dimension too the comparative picture is not as simple as might at first appear. The main constitutive feature common to most phases of Christian sensibility is probably a sense of trusting dependence. This has found prominent expression in the work of protestant theologians such as Friedrich Schleiermacher, but the feeling of which he wrote has a long heritage and many variations among Christians of almost all persuasions. Connected with this feeling are representative Christian values such as respect for personhood, desire for truthful speech, love, and so on. For Buddhism the main constitutive feature of spirituality can probably be declared to be a sense of detachment. This means that religiously directed feeling ranges over the experience of passions and the experience of the cooling of passions. It may not be inappropriate to say that while Christianity involves an acceptance, through suffering, of created existence, which in the last analysis is positively affirmed through the sense of resurrection, Buddhism by contrast leads to a withdrawing away from facticity or from the specific variety of ordinary life, at least in so far as passion-directed attachment is involved.

In such a brief statement some doctrinal signposts are inevitably drawn into play to indicate these dominant attitudes. However, it may be that the kind of language in which the attitudes or perceptions are most easily set forth does not do justice to the kind of subtlety required for a comparative consideration. For example, second thoughts obviously arise with respect to the above brief statement if one considers the nature of faith in Pure Land and True Pure Land Buddhism. The term *tariki* 他力 after all does mean other-power, and it is sincere reliance on the power of the Original Vow of Amitābha Buddha which is given centrality in these cases. It may be said that this sense of reliance on *tariki* is really untypical, while it is the *jiriki* 自力 of Zen Buddhism which is more truly Buddhist. However the reality is that both of these principles are widespread throughout Buddhism as a whole. The starkly accentuated contrast between *jiriki* and *tariki* represents a tension found in the *de facto* attitudes of most Buddhists, though usually it is more softly drawn. Thus some modification of the picture first drawn above is probably necessary at least from the Buddhist side.

The characterization of Christian feeling probably also needs modification. Above all, while a sense of dependent creaturely existence may be viewed as the elementary form of Christian sensitivity, the presumed resting place at the end of the Christian way (δδός –a New Testament term) is not life under its present empirical forms, but post-resurrection life, which is essentially mysterious. This mystery should not be underestimated as a factor in Christian sensitivity. Even when it is said that resurrection is a reaffirmation of creation, the manner of reaffirmation remains mysterious. Moreover since in this mystery finitude is overcome, presumably so too are the conceptual discriminations which belong to finitude, at least that is, such conceptual discrimination which Buddhists regard as an aspect of ignorance in the technical sense.

Further features of Buddhist and Christian feeling which demand careful reflection are the attitudes to the self and to the external world (both touched on in principle above), the attitude to reason and the role which reason is supposed to play in the religious consciousness, and so on. Of course all such reflections tie in closely with the problem of making comparisons of a conceptual kind, to which we now turn.

Conceptual dimension

The conceptual dimension of religion includes doctrinal statements and formulae but also much more. It refers to all mythical and symbolic projections of religious consciousness, including their expression in art of all kinds. In terms of ideas it includes both those which are unthinkingly carried over from previous cultures and those which are consciously selected and emphasised in new religious initiatives. Therefore it is not possible to light upon two clear-cut sets of doctrines and compare them item by item. Many doctrines in both Buddhism and Christianity, if not all, have a complex status because they arise in the context of myth, in the assumptions and arguments of a particular time, in symbolic presentation, and so forth.

Two further elementary cautions should be made. Firstly, literalistic interpretations should not be fastened on to religious concepts which the believers themselves consider subtle or mysterious. This danger is particularly important with regard to the various forms of Japanese Buddhism, some of which at first sight appear simplistic and even un-Buddhist to western observers. It is also particularly important with respect to some central doctrines of Christianity such as the doctrines of God, creation, incarnation and resurrection. The last is an especially instructive case, for the New Testament narratives on the resurrection of Jesus are themselves contradictory, or as some would say, complementary, in treating the resurrection at once as a physical wonder and as a mystery. Thomas can feel the wounds of Jesus with his own hands, *and* Jesus can stand among his disciples without entering a room in the normal way. Secondly it should not be lightly assumed that there is or even ought to be a simple unity of view maintained within one religious tradition. Admittedly this may be called for at times by representatives of one of the traditions. Thus in theory the Buddhist Sangha is supposed to agree about whether or not a particular dialogue or set of sayings represents the teaching of the Buddha, as may be inferred from the teaching on authority in the *Mahāparinirvāṇa Sūtra*. Christianity too is supposed to be a religion of unity, and schismatic divisions are reckoned by almost all to be a scandal, while yet from some points of view necessary to preserve true doctrine. The unity of the Church is also strongly symbolised by the body of Christ partaken in the Eucharist. The reality is however that quite different emphases are possible within each tradition even while they remain clearly Christian or Buddhist. Nor do these emphases necessarily contradict the kind of unity which is proper to each tradition. For example, Buddhism in one phase may emphasise separation from the world, following the Buddha as a model of nirvana, while in another phase it might emphasise immersion in ordinary life on the basis of recognising the Buddha-nature of all existence. Christianity may be understood essentially as a theocentric faith with Christ playing a secondary role in the action of divine providence, but then again it might be understood as radically christocentric, with human knowledge of God being formed mainly through an experience of Christ.

Such strong cautionary remarks may make the activity of comparison seem too hazardous to be worth undertaking. Yet it should not be overlooked that the very applicability of these remarks to the two traditions in question itself indicates some fundamental similarities. Other basic parallels combine to make comparison unavoidable, even though pitfalls abound. To start at bedrock, both are universal systems for the realisation of meaning in life. Both assume that man has a fundamental problem and offer ways of solving it which include at some point statements about the way the world is. This in turn means that both systems are in principle open to some kind of philosophical testing, even though both systems have well tried defence habits against the probes of independent reason. However, the application of philosophical tests of consistency and meaning goes beyond the initial comparison which can be made on a historical and phenomenological basis. Though the statements "about the way the world is," to use the common philosophers' phrase, may not always be immediately obvious, and the religious person himself, especially on the Buddhist side, may even claim that he does not make such, nevertheless there is a sense in which each religion points to what is presumed to be the ultimate nature of reality. Furthermore both religions propose rather mysterious conclusions about man's destiny, even while allowing less mysterious pictures thereof to communicate these mysteries to the majority. This point was already made with respect to the Christian concept of resurrection, but it, applies equally to related concepts such as "the kingdom of God" and "eternal life," which both break into ordinary life and go beyond it. The nature of life with God, just like the nature of God, can only be approached with the greatest of care, and negative terms are frequent. For Buddhism the nature of a Buddha's existence after nirvana, if indeed "after" is the right word, remains an undetermined question. Even a bodhisattva, still active in the world of ordinary life, "does not take his stand anywhere" (to use Edward Conze's regular phrase), and indeed cannot do so without forfeiting the freedom from attachments which enables him to release others. Similarly the Son of Man was said to have nowhere to lay his head.

Such ideas may all seem remarkably diverse if closely regarded, yet comparison is always partly a question of scale and focus. They may seem much more similar to each other when jointly contrasted with quite different systems such as the Shintō religion or rationalist or political ideologies. In so far as there are similarities it may be preferable to approach them by means of a neutral structure of some kind, for example by elucidating each system in terms of the pattern: man's present condition, the condition seen as a goal or aspiration, and the route or method for realising the aspired condition. It is however very difficult to devise such a structure which does not already imply some kind of doctrinal nuance. It would be helpful to move through a series of focuses, some of which are right for the broader scale of comparison but known to be deficient in some respects, and others of which are suitable for attending to the comparison of more detailed points but which run the danger of overlooking major similarities.

Whatever the scope of a comparative reflection the conceptual dimension of religion should always be recognised as containing a wide range of conceptual activity including philosophically refined doctrine, myth and symbol, semi-explicit assumptions and popular belief-systems which in one way or another convey, or betray, the central concerns of the tradition in question. It should also be remembered that the conceptual dimension of religion constantly moves together with religious feeling or spiritual stance, with some kind of socio-religious extension experienced by the believer, and with religious action of various kinds. It is not really possible specifically to refer to all of these at once, simply because of the limited nature of speech or writing. However reflection on one dimension should never proceed in such a way that it performs an injustice with respect to another. Furthermore all four of these dimensions are subject to change, as a matter of course, which leads to consideration of the fifth dimension.

The fifth dimension

Since religion is subject to the passage of time religious leaders and believers are forced to respond to ever-lengthening perspectives. In particular the transmission of religion from one culture to another, whether geographically or chronologically, means that new cultural elements are introduced to the tradition and new demands are made upon it. Two of the strongest religious drives relevant to such shifts of tradition are (a) mission, and (b) reform. Though both of these concepts have played a classical role in the way in which the history of the Christian Church has been perceived, they are both equally relevant to Buddhism. Both of these drives are more or less widely present at the level of conscious reflection among teachers and preachers in the two religions, and to a lesser degree among the believers generally. Less clearly understood, though no less important for an understanding of the nature of religious tradition, are (a) the way in which the elements of one religious tradition coexist, from time to time, with other religious and cultural elements of various kinds (see syncretism, below), and (b) the procedures by which the available resources of a tradition are selected and interpreted by its exponents (see hermeneutics, below). It is thought that these four categories together, though not all of quite the same provenance or status, may be adequate to aid the discernment of those patterns in religious change and religious consistency which can summarily be described as the dynamics of religious tradition.

As to the categories of mission and reform, it may be held that these are not appropriate to Buddhism, and indeed it is regrettable that both are drawn from common use in the history of Christianity. If more neutrally derived alternatives can be produced, so much the better. Nevertheless the facts of religious history are that both Buddhism and Christianity have been in principle missionary religions. Indeed this arises from their very nature as universalist religions of salvation or release. In Christianity man is commonly viewed as bound by sin and therefore needing to be brought to a renewed and rectified relationship with God, while in Buddhism man is viewed as bound by karma and ignorance and therefore in need of teaching and other help to be brought to a state of release or nirvana. Hence those involved in either religion are called upon to receive, and to transmit. That Christianity requires this is clearly indicated in the New Testament (e.g. *Matthew* 28:18–20 and *John* 20:23, the latter being a commission to forgive sins). It is less commonly realised among observers that there is a canonical basis for such involvement in transmission in Buddhism too, though of a rather different kind. It lies in the Buddha's very decision to teach anybody at all, for at first he was apparently inclined not to. This decision, described in legendary form in the *Mahāvagga* of the Pāli Books of Discipline, provides a theoretical beginning for the outward spread of Buddhism based on the Buddha's own resolve. The legend was taken up again in the early Mahāyāna *Lotus Sūtra*, with interesting glosses on the degree of understanding to be expected from his hearers and the modifications which the teaching would therefore require.

It is also quite clear that Buddhism as well as Christianity has been subject to reform movements, which seem to be more or less universally evident in founded religions. Again there is a strong inherent drive, even to the point of religious competition, to seek a correct and effective statement of the presumed original faith. While reformation is closely linked with Protestantism in the minds of historians of Christianity, perhaps more consideration should be given to reform motivation in the development of Catholicism. In the case of Buddhism reform has been paradoxically linked with development in the case of the origins of the Mahāyāna as a distinct movement. This is also true for later exponents of Mahāyāna, perhaps the most striking cases being the exponents of Zen Buddhism and the fiery Japanese Nichiren, who is certainly better seen as a reformer than as a "prophet" (*contra* Anesaki 1916).

There are no doubt many features of both mission and reform which deserve detailed comparative study, but the point being made here is that the two together have a tremendous impact on the overall pattern of each tradition. Both lead to new elements becoming a part of the overall tradition, so that the sorting and selection process becomes ever more complex for later generations. This developing richness of the traditions eventually demands more widely based theoretical analyses (a) of the manner in which religious and other elements are correlated with each other, and (b) the procedures by which the meanings of the traditions are elucidated.

For the first of these a proper analysis of syncretism is required. The main points of such an analysis have already been broached by the present writer (see "Syncretism and Ambiguity," 6.3 below), and the matter has been taken up rather differently by others such as Carsten Colpe (1977). Although the matter remains rather confused in the available literature, it does seem evident that a good theory of syncretism is needed to make sense of a range of interconnected problems. These include questions about indigenisation and acculturation (including the acquisition by universalist religions of rites otherwise provided in primal religions, discussed briefly above) and also questions about the linking and dropping of diverse religious and other elements, the formation of new religions, and so on.

An understanding of the dynamics of religious tradition with the help of such concepts can lead the observer very close to the interests and aspirations of the believers and exponents of the tradition. However even if the above were to be systematically achieved it would still be possible to come one step closer. This would be by sharing in the analysis of the procedures of interpretation employed by religious persons themselves, not forgetting that the latter are nowadays more than ever before sophisticated observers of themselves. This understanding of the work of the interpreters is called hermeneutics, though the term also has a history of extension to the practice of interpretation itself; an attempt to broach this kind of study in a comparative way has also been made elsewhere with special reference to Buddhism and Christianity (Pye and Morgan 1973). At such points the comparative study of religion can easily become a springboard for sharing in the interpretative efforts of today and tomorrow. At the same time the autonomous integrity of historical and comparative study should be carefully maintained, for otherwise the very value of the analysis will be lost.

Conclusion

It is hoped that the overall pattern of analysis set out above may be useful in providing a sufficiently simple, yet comprehensive and integrated framework for more sustained and detailed comparative work. The specialist reader will no doubt detect many points at which the argument is indebted to others, even where issue is taken, and this debt is gratefully acknowledged. It seemed important however not to obscure the structure of the argument with numerous references, since the argument is essentially a general one. Similarly the reflections offered under the five dimensions perceived are illustrative and often cautionary in intent. They suggest the kind of agenda appropriate to the discussion of each dimension, and, incipiently, the relations which should obtain between the various phases of comparison. Ideally each dimension is linked with all the others, but this is difficult to exhibit constantly. In particular it should be noted that the fifth dimension, that of the dynamics of religious tradition, is linked all the time to the other four, which together should be seen dynamically. It is an understanding of the dynamics of religion which brings the observer closest to the value forming character of contemporary religious experience.

Bibliographical references

Anesaki, Masaharu 1916. *Nichiren: The Buddhist Prophet.* Cambridge Massachusetts (Harvard University Press).
Colpe, Carsten 1977. "Syncretism and Secularisation: Complementary and Antithetical Trends in New Religious Movements?" in: *History of Religions* 17 / 2: 158–76.
Elison, George 1973. *Deus Destroyed. The Image of Christianity in Early Modern Japan.* Cambridge Massachusetts (Harvard University Press).
Ling, Trevor 1973. *The Buddha. Buddhist Civilization in India and Ceylon.* London (Temple Smith).

Pye, Michael 1972a. *Comparative Religion: An Introduction through Source Materials*. Newton Abbot (David and Charles) and New York (Harper and Row).
- 1979a. *The Buddha*. London and Dallas (Duckworth).

Troeltsch, Ernst 1902. *Die Absolutheit des Christentums und die Religionsgeschichte*. Tübingen (Mohr/Siebeck).

Van Gennep, Arnold 1960. *The Rites of Passage* (originally: *Les Rites de Passage*, Paris 1909). Chicago (University of Chicago Press).

First published in *Studies (Tsukuba Daigaku Tetsugakushisōgakkei Ronshū)* 5 (1980), 1–20.

4.3 Comparative Hermeneutics: A Brief Statement

This "statement" is partly based on a paper entitled "Comparative hermeneutics in religion" for a conference at the University of Lancaster, England, in January 1972 and published in a work jointly edited with Robert Morgan in 1973 (details below). A related lecture was given at a comparative religion seminar at the University of Tokyo in May 1973.

Analogies in interpretative procedures

Today it is necessary to admit that the plurality of religious traditions is part of the context to be recognized during the interpretation of any one tradition.[1] It is therefore of particular interest to approach the question of possible analogies between the interpretative procedures of diverse religious traditions, and it is this that reflection under the category "comparative hermeneutics" is intended to achieve. The discernment of such analogies may eventually provide a new basis for understanding the relations between at least some religions. Just over five years ago an attempt was made to introduce the concept of "comparative hermeneutics" as a matter of concern both for the general study of religions and for Christian theology. Since several relevant publications have appeared since then, these paragraphs are offered as a brief statement of the main points in the argument.[2]

The term "hermeneutics" is intended here to refer only to problems *about* interpretation, or to "theory of interpretation". The expectation is that people of differing cultural and religious traditions might agree

---

1   Cf. "Ernst Troeltsch and the end of the problem about 'other' religions" (Pye 1976), which challenges Christian theology to accept this requirement.
2   "Comparative hermeneutics in religion" is the lead essay in *The Cardinal Meaning, Essays in Comparative Hermeneutics: Buddhism and Christianity,* (Pye and Morgan 1973). The concept of a comparative science of hermeneutics mediating between the science of religion and various constructive and interpretative theologies was previously advanced in Pye 1971b and Pye 1974. Cf. also S.D.B. Picken's "The hermeneutical problem of Buddhist and Christian origins" (Picken 1974).

about certain theoretical aspects of the process of interpretation, without necessarily agreeing about what one particular religion means. Interpretation itself is the normal activity of a representative of a tradition, e.g. a Christian theologian, a Muslim theologian, or a Buddhist scholar-monk. Hermeneutics on the other hand may be used to refer to the procedures which such interpreters employ. Sometimes the term "hermeneutics" has been used to refer to the act of understanding and interpreting itself, but the present usage is meant to be restricted to procedural questions only. In so far as stress is laid on the comparative study of such problems, it is hoped that significant similarities may be found between the procedures used in the interpretation of religions whose contents may be quite different. For example, there may be some theoretical similarities with respect to procedures and criteria of interpretation in Buddhism and Christianity, even though the meaning of these two religions may finally be quite distinct.

Troeltsch on "essence" talk

The nature of hermeneutics thus theoretically conceived may be illustrated by reference to the important essay by Ernst Troeltsch on the nature of the problem about the "essence" [*Wesen*] of Christianity.[3] Other theologians such as Harnack and Loisy had offered arguments about what the "essence" of Christianity is, but Troeltsch attempted to analyse the *procedure* involved in any attempt to reformulate the "essence" of a religion.

Troeltsch argued that any attempt to formulate or convey the "essence" of Christianity would have three aspects.

(i) First, it would be critical in the sense that it would seek to distinguish between that which corresponds to the essence (of Christianity) and that which is contrary to it.

(ii) Second, it would be a developmental principle, with an inner, living flexibility, taking into account the variety of different forms which the religion has taken since its beginning down to the present.

---

3   See the collected works of Ernst Troeltsch (Troeltsch 1913). The essay "Was heißt 'Wesen des Christentums'?" was however first published in *Die Christliche Welt* 1903. For an English translation of the essay see Morgan and Pye 1977.

(iii) Third, it is not a mere abstraction from the past, though it depends on historical work, but it is also an "ideal" or value-bearing conception corresponding to the cultural possibilities of the present and the future. He wrote: "To define the essence is to shape it afresh".[4] It is not necessary to agree exactly with Troeltsch's analysis to see it as a clear statement of a modern hermeneutical problem within the Christian tradition.

The relevance of Troeltsch's analysis is however not restricted to Christianity. He himself saw it as a problem which arises in the attempt to characterise and bring out the meaning of any cultural or religious tradition. This is simply due to the fact that every such tradition is located in human history, and because it is no longer possible for modern man to take a naively miraculous view of revelation or of any equivalent dogmatic term. Although he did not apply it to the case of Buddhism in any detail, it is strikingly clear that his analysis would be relevant to the way in which European scholars, from Rhys Davids to Lamotte, have studied and interpreted Buddhism. Some scholars have worked like Harnack did, emphasising the purity of selected aspects of "original" Buddhism. Others, such as Lamotte, stress rather the total development of Buddhism as being the key to its meaning. However the application of Troeltsch's analysis to the work of European interpreters of Buddhism does not need detailed discussion here.

Parallel procedures in Buddhism

What is more important is that this same analysis finds parallel manifestations in the writings of oriental Buddhism itself. This can be illustrated in various ways, and special attention has been paid to the concept of "cardinal meaning" as it occurs in the *Platform Sutra* and elsewhere.[5] First, there is a critical or polemical aspect to the attainment of "the cardinal meaning" in so far as certain attitudes towards Buddhist practice and teaching are discarded as being impediments. Second, there is a dependence upon the conceptual and spiritual tradition of Buddhism as a whole down to the time in question. Third, Hui-neng's grasp of the

---

4   Troeltsch 1913: 431; Eng.trans.162. This is possibly Troeltsch's shortest sentence: "Wesensbestimmung ist Wesensgestaltung."
5   The expression is Philip Yampolsky's translation of *dà-yì* 大意 in *The Platform Sutra of the Sixth Patriarch*, (Yampolsky 1967).

meaning is seen in the *Platform Sutra* as opening a new chapter in the transmission, and eventually a new corpus of traditional materials to be added to those which need to be taken into account. Perhaps we may add Ui Hakuju's definition of the term based on general usage within the *Daizōkyō* (the Chinese Buddhist scriptures, – a vast collection), namely: "the general meaning; a statement which draws out and binds together the meaning of the whole, from the beginning to the end".[6] This is a formulation which would surely have pleased Troeltsch. The idea of drawing out the meaning involves a perceptive, even critical grasp of what is essential and what is not.[7] The rest of the sentence emphasises sufficiently the importance of an overall understanding of relevant tradition.

It must be admitted that there is a subsidiary question about the antiquity of this Buddhist conception and how it can be related to historical presuppositions of a distinctly modern kind. However it does seem that there is a way of thinking about the procedures of interpretation within Buddhism, which on the one hand has very definite roots within the tradition itself and which on the other hand has easily been linked with the kind of modern historical consciousness which has emerged in the eighteenth, nineteenth and twentieth centuries in Japan.

Japan is a country where the historical and comparative study of religion has flourished early and is now firmly established. This is no doubt partly due to the early development of historical and scientific attitudes towards religious tradition among the scholars of the Tokugawa Period (1603–1868). Such attitudes may be found already among Neo-Confucianists such as Itō Jinsai (1627–1705), Itō Tōgai (1670–1736) and Ogyū Sorai (1666–1728), all of whom began to see the Confucian tradition as one built up by human effort and subject to the effects of historical and social change.[8] The best example however is Tominaga Nakamoto (1715–1746), who tried to take a systematically critical attitude towards three religious traditions, Confucianism, Buddhism and Shintō, and yet at the same time to bring out their positive meaning. [See Part Two above] We do not need to share Tominaga's conclusions, which are very out-of-date, in order to retain his presuppositions, which

---

6   Ui 1965, *ad loc.*
7   The term "grasp" is used in this way in the context of Christian theology by my colleague Robert Morgan (and co-editor of *The Cardinal Meaning*) in his essay "Expansion and criticism in the Christian tradition" (Morgan 1973).
8   See various extracts in Tsunoda et al. 1958.

remain very modern. Thus it seems quite possible to argue that the question about the "essence" of Buddhism is not just some western importation, but that it is a thoroughly Buddhist and Asian question, although of course it has been expressed in slightly different ways and in different terminology.

Skilful means as a hermeneutical control

So far the argument itself has moved from a western analysis to an eastern religion. There is no reason however why it should not be carried out the other way round. For example, a hermeneutical concept in Buddhism might be found to be helpful in the analysis of western religions. Troeltsch invites us to distinguish between that which is essential, that which is inessential and that which is contrary to the essence (*wesenswidrig*). Mahāyāna Buddhism however, if the dialectics involved in the term *hōben* (c.f. Sanskrit *upāya* etc.) may be so very briefly stated, seems to say that all items of doctrine are both essential and dispensable, and that whether any item is contrary to the essence depends entirely upon the spiritual condition of the person concerned. The concept of "skilful means" is a hermeneutical control (see for example its use in the *Lotus Sūtra*), and it may therefore be that the way in which it is used in Buddhism could lead to the discernment of important aspects of interpretative procedures found in other religions, such as Christianity, which in these other cases have not yet been properly clarified.[9]

Of course there are major problems involved in any such move, whichever the direction in which it is made. Perhaps the most important danger to avoid is that of unwittingly importing from one religion to another a metaphysics which is closely linked to a hermeneutical concept but which may be quite foreign to the other religion. On the one hand, it is crucial to be clear that Troeltsch is using the term "essence" as a term in the philosophy of history. It has to do with the abstracting of coherent meaning from a mass of otherwise random data, that is to say, with a procedure which cannot now be avoided by anyone who wishes to interpret any religious tradition at all (though most people do it badly). As Troeltsch used it in this context it did not have anything to do with the structure of the universe and had no connection with spec-

---

9   A systematic attempt to state the meaning of this concept in Mahāyāna Buddhism will be found in the writer's *Skilful Means* (Pye 1978a).

ulative ontologies of which Buddhists would disapprove. On the other hand the Buddhist concept of "skilful means" is closely linked with the Mahāyāna doctrine of *śūnyatā* and also with the teaching of two kinds of truth, the provisional and the real. These in turn are about the way in which Mahāyānists claim *not* to be advancing ontological propositions such as those held by their opponents within and without Buddhism. Thus there would be a problem about whether the use of the term "skilful means" to elucidate interpretative procedures within other religions such as Christianity would not in fact lead to the importation of a fundamental spirituality, a kind of anti–metaphysics (if the claim of the Mādhyamika not to be advancing a position be given temporary credence), of a sort not in the end consistent with Christianity. However it may be possible to isolate the function of the term "skilful means" as a hermeneutical tool, and then to use it in a comparative context.

These problems show how important it is, if progress is to be made, to distinguish between questions about procedures of interpretation in religion (for which the term hermeneutics is here consistently reserved) and questions about the substantial contents or meanings of religious traditions.

Prospects

In sum the thesis still being proposed is that it is desirable to study the way in which religions are interpreted, on a comparative basis, and that such a study has natural roots within at least two historic religions, Buddhism and Christianity. One might hope thereby to develop a more stable framework for the consideration of such questions than is possible on the basis of the study of one religious tradition alone. This hope does not imply that all religious traditions work in exactly the same way. Nor does it imply that there is nothing to be learned about procedures of interpretation from other fields such as literature, political ideology, or law. It is assumed however that there are special analogies between religions and between their procedures of interpretation, and that it would be fruitful to explore these analogies more systematically. Some other problems which would come under the heading of "comparative hermeneutics" are: problems about demythologisation; problems about how traditions are shaped or how their shape changes; criteria for evaluating new forms of a religious tradition;[10] correlation theory; nature and function of religious language; the relationship between historical criticism and popular interpretations; and of course problems touching the approach to central religious concepts such as "transcendence" or "satori" and the relation of these to other ways of understanding the world.

Finally it should be stressed again that the comparative study of hermeneutics is not intended to displace the work of the interpreter of a religion, that is to say of the theologian or of the scholar-monk. The work of such persons is itself a religious work, and as such it forms the raw material for the study of comparative hermeneutics. Observed procedures are the material for reflections made on a comparative basis. It may be that these reflections will in some way be of service to those whose task it is to be directly engaged in the interpretation of a religion. It may also happen that such reflections do not turn out to be particularly useful. Comparative hermeneutics is not in itself intended to decide questions about the ultimate truths of religion or of life. One might say that it is "phenomenological" rather than theological, or buddhological, in the sense that it does not presuppose the falsity or the truth of any particular religious beliefs, while at the same time it takes the meaning of a religious system for its participants very seriously indeed. On this basis it should be possible for comparative studies to be done together by persons who may be drawn from various religious traditions. They should be able to study together on a comparative basis what is going on when religions are interpreted, and how those who interpret religions tend to deal with problems which arise. These same persons may also discuss and disagree about the truth or falsity, value or otherwise of their religions, but that would be, so to speak, on another day.

Bibliographical references

Morgan, Robert 1973. "Expansion and Criticism in the Christian Tradition" in: Pye and Morgan 1973: 59–101.
Morgan, Robert and **Pye, Michael** (eds.) 1977. *Ernst Troeltsch: Writings on Theology and Religion.* London (Duckworth) and Atlanta (John Knox).
Picken, S.D.B. 1974. "The hermeneutical problem of Buddhist and Christian origins" in: *Japanese Religions* 8 (2): 56–76.

---

10 Special attention is given to this problem in the papers by David Bastow, David Pailin and Karel Werner included in *The Cardinal Meaning* (Pye and Morgan 1972).

Pye Michael 1971a. "Syncretism and Ambiguity" in: *Numen. International Review for the History of Religions* 18 (2): 83–93.
- 1973b. "Comparative hermeneutics in religion" in: Pye and Morgan 1973: 1–58.
- 1974. "Problems of method in the interpretation of religion" in: *Japanese Journal of Religious Studies* 1 (2–3): 107–23.
- 1976. "The end of the problem about other religions" in: Clayton, John P. (ed.), *Ernst Troeltsch and the Future of Theology*. Cambridge (Cambridge University Press): 172–95.
- 1978a. *Skilful Means. A Concept in Mahayana Buddhism*. London (Duckworth) and (2nd edition 2003, Routledge).

Pye, Michael and Morgan, Robert (eds.) 1972. *The Cardinal Meaning. Essays in Comparative Hermeneutics: Buddhism and Christianity* (Religion and Reason 6), The Hague (Mouton).

Yampolsky, Philip 1967. *The Platform Sutra of the Sixth Patriarch*. New York and London (Columbia University Press).

Troeltsch, Ernst 1913 (and 1922). *Gesammelte Schriften* II. Tübingen (Mohr and Siebeck).
- 1913. "Was heißt 'Wesen des Christentums'?" in: Troeltsch 1913: 386–451.
- 1977. "What does does 'essence of Christianity' mean?" (English translation of "Was heißt 'Wesen des Christentums'?" 1913) in: Morgan and Pye 1977: 124–181.

Tsunoda, Ryusaku, de Bary, Wm.Theodore and Keene, Donald (eds.) 1958. *Sources of Japanese Tradition* (Introduction to Oriental Civilizations LIV, edited by Wm.Theodore de Bary). New York and London (Columbia University Press).

Ui, Hakuju 1965. *Bukkyō Jiten*, Tokyo (Daitō Shuppansha).

This article was first published in: *Japanese Journal of Religious Studies* 7/1 (1980) 25–33.

4.4 Shintō and the Typology of Religions

This paper was first presented at the Thirty-first International Congress of Human Sciences in Asia and North Africa, Tokyo 1983, and a summary published in the proceedings. The full text was first published in 1989 under the title "The place of Shintō in the typology of religion" and here it has been very slightly edited, notably with the addition of headings.

Typologies of religion

The typology of religion has been attempted by various authors at two distinct levels which may be termed the analytic and the holistic respectively. An analytic typology seeks to identify various elements which occur in different religious systems and to give these names such as myth, priest, prayer, purification ritual, and so on. A holistic typology seeks to consider whole religious systems or traditions as unities in themselves and to classify them in accordance with some overarching concepts. Popular categories here have been prophetic religion, mystical religion, revealed religion, nativistic religion, state religion, higher religion, or (with the anthropologists) great tradition, little tradition, and such like. In a well-founded and comprehensive approach neither the analytic nor the holistic typology should take priority but there should be some interdependence between the two. It seems possible to say, for example, without being finally committed to the concepts currently in wide use, that religions of salvation (holistic typology) do not in their initial form offer or require rites of transition (analytic typology). Cases which seem to count against this should be considered in terms of their diachronic development, for rites of transition may be brought into use as an accommodation to the needs of society. Primal religions, however (see further below on this concept), would normally be expected to provide rites of transition for the societies in which they function. For this reason the character of the juxtaposition between primal religion (which is not existentially critical) and salvation religion (which is) can be appraised in a given social context in terms of the provision of transition rites (cf. Pye 1980, also at 4.2 above).

It is easy to be critical of the analytic typologies proposed in the now classic works of Gerardus van der Leeuw, Friedrich Heiler and others, but it is difficult to make viable alternatives. As far as Shintō is concerned, it is for example remarkable that van der Leeuw's seven hundred pages in *Religion in Essence and Manifestation* contain not a single reference to it (Van der Leeuw 1933, 1938). One might of course argue in his defence that a really successful typology ought not to be required to have references to specific religions anyway. This would however be a remarkably optimistic line of thought. In fact, it has to be admitted that van der Leeuw's typology refers to many specific religions but at the same time cannot easily be related to the specific case of Shintō. In Heiler's *Erscheinungsformen und Wesen der Religion* (Heiler 1961) there are by contrast a number of specific references to aspects of Shintō. Yet this massive work is also negatively instructive in that it illustrates how such scattered references can get lost in the mass of varied details with the result that the real spirit or character of Shintō is lost. In spite of the difficulties evident from these famous examples, the need for comparative categories in the systematic study of religion remains, and these must in part take the form of an analytic typology. If not consciously attended to, such categories will only be brought into specific studies in an uncritical way, as so often happens when studies of religion are carried out by specialists in other disciplines. The elaboration of the required categories on a truly intercultural basis is still in its infancy. This paper, however, is more concerned with the problem of typology at the second, holistic level. Here too it is easy to be critical of widely current concepts but difficult to propose viable alternatives. While difficulties abound, it would nevertheless seem unavoidable in the systematic study of religion to attend to questions of holistic typology in order to provide a reasonably stable framework for attempts at comparison. The argument below consists of a proposal with respect to the place of Shintō in the holistic typology of religion, without, however, seeking to advance a comprehensive typology at this level.

Shintō in the typology of religion

It is difficult to think of any of the terms mentioned above as quite fitting the case of Shintō. It is also notable that none of them arose in connection with a consideration of the place of Shintō among the religions of the world. This need not matter in itself, for as with an analytic typology a truly viable holistic typology ought to be applicable to hitherto unconsidered religions. Nevertheless the plain fact is that is that here too we still have not got very far in the elaboration of the required categories on a truly intercultural basis. Moreover common sense suggests that in attending to this question it is desirable to take well-known specific religions into account. Hence the present argument seeks to contribute to the overall articulation of a holistic typology by attending, however briefly, to the specific case of Shintō, and conversely to say something definite about the place of Shintō among the religions of the world while bearing in mind the as yet still inadequately systematised wider discussion.

In considering Shintō itself in this context there are three major perspectives which should not be overlooked. Though obvious in themselves they need to be linked firmly to the discussion about the place of Shintō in the typology of religions. The first of these is the difficulty of getting a clear, central definition of Shintō, the second is the political or national import of Shintō, and the third is the recognition of the historical depth of Shintō.

The difficulty about getting a clear, central definition of Shintō should not ultimately be considered a difficulty in our understanding of it. This is because resistance to conceptual summarization pertains to its character as a religion in the first place. To recognize this is part of the act of understanding it. This does not mean that leading notions such as *matsuri* (festival), *kegare* (impurity), or *harae* (purification) should not be considered as helpful indicators of the nature of Shintō. They are however notions pertaining to a very large number of acts during which a very low value is placed on conceptual activity. This feature, resistance to conceptual summarization, is further illustrated by the tendency of those giving an account of Shintō to adduce a list of fields of tradition which together make it up, e.g. Shrine Shintō, Imperial Household Shintō, Folk Shintō, Domestic Shintō, Sectarian Shintō, etc.[1] Of course it may be possible to quote unifying statements such as that Shintō is humanity's response to the divine. Such statements however do justice neither to the Japanese-ness of people and gods alike nor to the diversity given within the Japanese framework. Hence one should not presume that Shintō is a religion which is relatively easy to grasp. In some ways of course it is easier to grasp than say, Nagarjunian or Thomist arguments about the nature of reality. Yet the nearer one comes to Shintō

---

1 For a typical list of this kind by a modern Japanese scholar see Ono 1973: 763.

the more difficult it is to grasp it in conceptual summary. One might say that it is anthropologically mysterious. This means that one is eventually confronted with the mystery of humans behaving in a Shintō-patterned manner as opposed to some other randomly chosen manner.

The second major perspective is the already adumbrated national dimension of Shintō. It is remarkable that the political aspect of Shintō was largely ignored in western accounts of the religion even while it was at the height of its modern political influence, with the notable exception of the works of D. C. Holtom.[2] This lesson appears to have been only half learned and there remain considerable obscurities. After disestablishment and constitutional separation it seems to be widely assumed that there is no political aspect to Shintō, even though there was a former political misuse. At the same time there are many points at which Shintō is related to or identified with national consciousness. One only has to think of the whole string of nationally prominent shrines, especially Ise Jingū, Meiji Jingū and Yasukuni Jinja, and of course the matter could be elaborated. Political misuse there may have been, disestablishment there was also, but there still remains a relationship between the Shintō religion and the Japanese people and nation. Admittedly this cannot easily be defined in a modern democratic constitution. Admittedly not all Japanese people have the same opinions on the subject. Admittedly it is difficult to distinguish between a more sharply political aspect and a more vaguely national aspect. Nevertheless this dimension cannot be subtracted from the self-understanding of Shintō religion at most of the points at which it can be observed. Just as Shintō shares a common area with folk religion, and just as it shares a common area with some of the sectarian developments which have become independent religious juridical persons, so too it shares a common area with the set of values and symbols which together make up the Japanese national feeling or identity.

The third major perspective is the historical depth of the Shintō religion. There do not seem to have been any attempts to do justice to the historical complexity of Shintō while assessing its place in the overall pattern of religious phenomena. The various phases through which it has passed have of course been described and documented. Thus we have Early Shintō, Ryōbu Shintō, and Sannō Ichijitsu Shintō, Yuiitsu Shintō, Kokugaku, Fukko Shintō, State Shintō, and Shrine Shintō, to name but the most salient. However, the fact that Shintō has passed

---

2   On these vagaries of western interpretation see Pye 1981.

through such phases has not really been taken into account in considerations of the nature of this religion. Shintō is usually lent a more or less timeless quality. Admittedly this is partly right, for it is part of the sense of a shrine that the *kami* (i. e. the divinity or divinities) are there now as they were (in some cases) before the shrine was built. Yet this is not the full complexity of Shintō. Since the Kokugaku scholars at least (eighteenth century), the Shintō tradition in its fullness has combined naiveté with historical sophistication. Nor are these two in conflict with each other, within the tradition. While not all who participate in Shintō activities are historically sophisticated, those who are, again since the Kokugaku School, are able to enjoy the rough, archaic elementariness of much of the religion while fully knowing that they do so from a historically advanced and adjusted standpoint.

In recent years this historically deepened standpoint has been supplemented by a sociological awareness transmitted by leading Japanese scholars of religion with an interest in Shintō (e. g. Yanagawa Keiichi, Sonoda Minoru). In principle the broadly Durkheimian flavour of such awareness is consistent with all three of the above mentioned perspectives.

Primal religion and adjusted primal religion

So far this argument has reflected, very briefly, on broad strategy in the typology of religion and on certain salient perspectives in the interpretation of Shintō. The next move is to consider the possible appropriateness of the term "primal" in linking these two interests. Is this an adequate term with which to locate Shintō in the typology of religion?

The term "primal" as referring to religion appears to have come into use first of all in the context of African religion, but its reference has been consciously widened by Harold W. Turner. In his words, "'Primal' is used in the sense of 'basic' or 'fundamental,' and to refer to those forms of society or religion, or those forms of comprehensive reference-systems, which are associated with what are commonly called tribal peoples or cultures." (Turner 1973: 3) The term is meant to gather up phenomena for which a wide range of names of varying dubiousness has been used in the past, including, to give Turner's list: "pre-literate, primitive, pagan, animistic, primordial, native, ethnic, tribal and traditional." (Turner 1973: 3)[3] Turner's perception of the need for such a term seems unexceptional and his general orientation is accepted. To save argumentation over detail however, which would be a distraction, the following is independently formulated to bring it to bear on the subject in hand.

The main intention of the term "primal" is to avoid the negative connotations of terms such as "primitive" while at the same time positively recognizing that the phenomena in question are in the main not the result of major developmental sequences in world cultural history. Putting it more sharply, in so far as these phenomena are communicated to us, they come in spite of the development of literary tradition and conscious historical perspectives. Primal religion is not necessarily preliterate. It may be post-literate, in which case it may be expected to be, at least on occasion, contra-literate. An example of this in the Japanese context would be the anti-sinification trend among the Kokugakusha, although it must be admitted that this movement was already an intellectual search for the elemental. More significant, for Shintō, is the usual emphasis on ritual as opposed to conceptualization. Needless to say, in complex societies this form of religious awareness is not always easily accessible and therefore in modern times we have seen various attempts to reach for these substrata of human experience. If Motoori Norinaga was in this sense a modern, it is even clearer in the case of the European Romantic movement. More recently the work of Lévi-Strauss and of Eliade has shown the same fundamental interest, though it emerges in different ways.

The phenomena with which all such interpreters are concerned have in common that they are discoverable in many quarters yet they are, for themselves, particularistic. That is, they all have to do with specific people, specific communities, and specific places. Names are very important. The religious phenomena with which they may be contrasted have in common that they are not discoverable everywhere and yet they are, at least latently, universalistic. These are the various religions of salvation or release which were more or less consciously founded or set in motion. Such religions have a time before and a time after, a sense of significant time through developing tradition, relevant rules for interpretation and for the maintenance of consistency, and so on. The distinction here may seem easy enough and has many forerunners. How-

---

3   For Turner's position see also Turner 1977: "The primal religions of the world and their study."

ever it is usually seen from the standpoint of the universalistic traditions. If the primary phenomena are viewed positively in themselves, yet without drawing them into some overriding Lévi-Straussian or Eliadian scheme, then some implications emerge which are not always noticed. And these are particularly relevant in the case of Shintō.

If we are to try to characterize the quality of religious awareness in primal religion more closely, we might say that it has the following features. It is socially inclusive within a defined geographical or kinship range. It accepts and celebrates the normal processes of life, conception, growth, harvest (or in non-agricultural economies hunt and capture) as being worthwhile. This is the basis of *matsuri* in the Japanese case. It seeks to protect and maintain this positive quality of life by avoiding or disarming disease, pollution and disaster. This is the basis of the concepts of *kegare* and *harae* in the Japanese case. It views life as something given, in a cosmic frame which is self-authenticating and supportive of its parts. Ritual action linked to life-processes is regular and satisfying.

To these features may be added some negative descriptors. In primary religion speculative questions are, in so far as they are raised, either given a mythological escape route (e. g. the activities of the god Susanoo for the problem of destructive forces in nature) or just left aside. Equally, the existence of exogenous social groups is not recognized in act or idea. In Shintō contexts, the normal reaction to the appearance of an occasional extraneous individual is to invite him or her to participate (in a marginal role).

As applied to Japan, we find that this basic quality of religious awareness is located in communities of ever-widening reference until we reach the national scale where various leading shrines, notably Ise Jingū, play their part. Yet it would be too simplistic to say that this, then, is primal religion. The special feature in the Japanese context, and perhaps in others, is that primal religion is present within modern life. This means that it is present in immediate association with its own historical depth and in immediate association with all the changes in economy, polity, and consciousness which have occurred, in particular during the last two or three hundred years. For this reason it seems appropriate to propose a new, associated category, which we may designate *adjusted primal religion*. For this, Shintō, in modern Japan, is a paradigmatic example.

To illustrate, when Motoori praised the Japaneseness of Japanese myth he did so on the basis that culture in the form of Chinese writing and philosophy had intervened. Innocence had been lost. Furthermore, the demographic results of the vast economic changes in modern Japan mean that the ideal relationship between *ujigami* (clan god) and *ujiko* (clan-child or clan member), which once reflected relatively stable small-scale communities, is today in large part fictitious. This does not prevent people from identifying with particular shrines. But again, innocence is lost.

The situation can best be understood by considering the reality of a large modern Shintō festival (*matsuri*) with its extensive range of participants. At the top end of concentrated religiosity are the religious specialists, the Shintō priests who officiate mainly within the shrine by reciting *norito* and performing purifications. The *norito* are prayers whose contents certainly match the main concerns of primal religion as described above, but which are hardly understood or even heard by the majority of the people. If the Shintō priests emerge, it is for a slow, formal walk to and from various points in the ritual, or to perform some ceremonial function in the festival, such as firing one arrow at a target, etc. Then come the participants who because of their important position in the community or in the festival arrangements themselves also enter the *haiden*, where worship is carried out. They will usually be dressed in their best clothes and greet each other solemnly. Thirdly come the actors in the procession or event which gives the festival its colour, the historical personages in period costume, or the sweating, sake-laden young men, heaving and pushing and pulling, banging drums, playing flutes and so on. These participants have a non-conceptualised feeling for their role. Fourthly come all those who feel drawn by kinship and custom to help prepare others for the activities, to stand by and follow along, to admire, to laugh, and generally to make a day of it. Here the local residents merge imperceptibly with the tourists, the mediating group being those who return from other places (returners) and their companions. Fifthly come the shop-keepers and temporary stall-holders (many of them more or less itinerant), the café-owners, hoteliers and transport agents who make their living by keeping everybody going. Sixthly come the cameramen, the poetasters and travelling Japanese Japanologists, and the *gaijin* (foreigners).

The point about this hierarchy of participation is that the central emphasis of primal religion remains, even while the complex social make-up and the media-informed awareness of the various participants mean that a change has taken place. There is now a modern knowledge that something is being done with the awareness of the past, for the sake of the present. There is a realisation that the celebration of primal value is our present responsibility. The typical epiphenomenon of this modern manner of being primal is the *hozonkai* (preservation society). For all its constructedness (and the construct, which is also throw-away, is a regular feature of Japanese primal religion) this adjusted primal religion has, unlike the yearnings of pan-symbolists and structuralists, a real relationship to its own history.

Shintō as adjusted primal religion

From this understanding of the place of Shintō in the typology of religion two implications may be noted at this stage. Their recognition may at least assist in the avoidance of errors in the interpretation of Shintō and of related religious matters in the future.

First, Shintō understood as adjusted primal religion, precisely because it has the historical depth and reflectiveness to adjust, remains essentially particularist. It seems unpromising to try to argue that modern Shintō has universalistic traits, as is sometimes done. The specific community, for all its modern demographic untidiness at sub-national levels, remains the essential locus of celebration and protection. It is notable that the universalistically inclined sects of Shintō derivation have become, admittedly in part because of political developments incidental to the development of religion itself, precisely that: sectarian movements or institutions which are separate from the main tradition of Shintō, which is now centrally focused through the Association of Shintō Shrines. This is not to deny that many Shintō leaders show a remarkable degree of international goodwill and respect for the traditions of other countries, which is of course (speaking for the moment at a human rather than a scientific level) most welcome. Nevertheless the fact remains that the Shintō tradition taken as a whole has, through the forms of adjustment briefly described above, maintained its particularism.

Second, the assessment of Shintō as adjusted primal religion provides an interesting reference point for the wider understanding of religion in the modern, industrialised and highly urbanised world. Clearly the presence or absence of religion so characterised must be an important factor in theories about secularisation, the persistence of religion and so on. Such theories must turn in part on the characterization of what it is whose ebb and flow is being considered. It may be possible to argue that other societies too have their own adjusted primal religion. There is not even a *prima facie* case for presuming this category to be uniquely relevant to the Japanese situation. At the same time there are also societies where one could only argue for the existence of such a form of religion with great difficulty, even though sociologists are hunting for something like it. The history of religions in those societies has simply been different. It is therefore not possible to transfer theories about religious change from societies without such a form of primal religion in their midst to those with it, or indeed the other way round.

There is certainly room for further discussion of both of these implications, both of which relate not only to the interpretation of Shintō but also more widely to the assessment of the part played by religion of various kinds in modern society. What seems clear however is that the Shintō religion should be typologized as "adjusted primal religion" and that it provides a clear and instructive model for this category in the comparative study of religions.

Bibliographical references

Hayes, Victor. C. (ed.) 1977. *Australian Essays in world Religions.* Sydney (Australian Association for the Study of Religions).
Heiler, Friedrich 1961. *Erscheinungsformen und Wesen der Religion.* Stuttgart (Kohlhammer).
Ono, Sokyō 1973. *Shintō no Kiso Chishiki to Kiso Mondai.* Tokyo (Jinja Shimpō Sha).
Pye, Michael 1980a. "On Comparing Buddhism and Christianity" in: *Studies (Tsukuba Daigaku Tetsugakushisōgakkei Ronshū)* 5 (1979 issue): 1–20.
– 1981. "Diversions in the interpretation of Shintō" in: *Religion.* 11: 61–74. (Republication of Pye 1978).
Turner, Harold W. 1973. "The Wholeness of Human Life" in: *Study Encounter* 9/4: 1–20, 3.
– 1977. "The primal religions of the world and their study," in Hayes 1977: 27–37.
Van der Leeuw, Gerardus 1933. *Phänomenologie der Religion.* Tübingen (J. C. B. Mohr).
– 1938. *Religion in Essence and Manifestation.* London (Allen & Unwin) (English translation from Van der Leeuw 1933).

This article was first published in: *Method & Theory in the Study of Religion* 1/2 (1989), 186–95. A summary had been published in: T. Yamamoto (ed) *Proceedings of the Thirty-first International Congress of Human Sciences in Asia and North Africa, Tokyo 1983,* (Tokyo (Institute of Eastern Culture) 1984, 1055–56, under the title, "The Place of Shintō in the Typology of Religion." A Japanese version was published as "Kaigaikara mita Shintō" 海外から見た神道 in Kōdō Izu (ed) *Gendai shintō kenkyū shūsei* Vol.10, Tokyo (Jinja Shinpōsha) 2000, 627–634.

4.5 Soteriological Orientations in Religion

This paper was prepared for the conference on "Tenrikyō-Christian dialogue" held at the Gregorian University in Rome, March 1998, and should be read in that light. It addresses the topic of "salvation" from the point of view of the comparative study of religions, without adopting the standpoint of one religion or another.

Introduction

"Salvation" has been regarded as the central function of religion in most forms of Christianity, and it is mainly from here that the word has entered the vocabulary of comparative religion. At the same time the resonance in many other religions is strong. Numerous newly founded religions offer "salvation" in some sense, whether it is so called or not. Indeed it is difficult to imagine an example of a "revelation" which does not imply a message of salvation. This is clearly true in the case of Tenrikyō, the Teaching of Divine Wisdom, which is understood by its followers to be a message of universal salvation for the whole of humanity on the basis of the revelation of God the Parent. Since other papers will be presenting the meaning of "salvation" from the point of view of these two religions, my purpose here is simply to propose a framework for comparative reflection on this subject. Such a framework should, if possible, provide room for the whole range of religions which in some way or other offer a teaching or a path of "salvation." even if it is not always called by this name. This perspective, in so far as it has any validity in the scientific study of religions, may provide a reference point for discussions between the representatives of any particular religions.

It is one of the functions of the comparative study of religions to draw attention to phenomena which are broadly analogous to each other, even though they may be known by different names in the religions themselves. First then, in order to lead into the subject matter, a major analogy in the history of religions will be considered, namely that between Buddhism and Christianity. Second, two major types of religion will be explained, namely primal religions and critical religions. Third, the most important soteriological orientations in religion will be presented against that

A major analogy in the history of religions

It is notable that while the term "salvation" is an important word in the Christian tradition, it does not occur in the formative stages of Buddhism. Nevertheless both Christianity and Buddhism provide their characteristic resolutions to the problems of human existence. In each of these religions human life as naturally experienced is understood to be problematic, whether characterised by "original sin" as in Christianity or by "ignorance" as in Buddhism. And each of these religions provides assistance in leading people away from the problematic situation in which they find themselves to another situation which in a spiritual sense is more satisfactory. Thus, broadly speaking, these two major religions are analogous, even though they vary in their assessment of the human situation and in the way in which the situation is to be resolved.

Broadly speaking, we might be tempted to say that Buddhism and Christianity place a different emphasis on the question as to whether human beings can work out their own salvation or are dependent on the action of a transcendent divine being for salvation. Nevertheless we should not forget that both of these aspects are present in Buddhism and Christianity alike, even though in a different balance. Though the simple words "Buddhism" and "Christianity" are not without meaning, they both refer to extremely complex traditions. Indeed, each of them might almost be thought of as large families of religions in which different emphases about important matters such as "salvation" can be documented (cf. Smart 1958 and 1997). The relation between what human beings can do for themselves, and in what sense they are dependent on the guidance, the assistance or the intervention of superior powers, takes extremely varied forms both in Buddhism and Christianity.

Consider the Buddhist case in just a little more detail. Here the early, underlying idea was that each individual should make the required effort to achieve a state of being "worthy," that is to say, to reach the stage of the *arhat* who can then enter the state of nirvana when the residues of karma have been exhausted. And yet people were invited to embark on this process, modelling themselves on the Buddha himself, through a process of being ordained, taught and guided. Of the "three refuges" in Buddhism, one is the rather abstract body of teaching known as *dham-*

ma (Skt. *dharma*) but the other two refer to other beings, namely the Buddha himself and the *saṃgha* (Skt. *sangha*), that is, the corporate body of ordained persons. Ordination was originally based on the simple yet profound words of the Buddha: "Come, monk" (and later also "Come, nun"), which amount to an act of far-reaching spiritual leadership by the Buddha, accepted in turn by the novice. The taking of "refuge", even by the laity, implies a readiness to accept assistance in a spiritual sense. Moreover, depending on progress made, it was a commonplace assumption that a series of further existences would probably still be necessary. Such individual existences, moreover, were understood to be part of an interactive pattern of mutual interdependence. Consequently there was plenty of room for the idea of assistance being provided by those in a relatively advanced stage, namely the great bodhisattvas, and thus in a sense for paths of salvation within the context of Buddhism. This came to full flowering in the various forms of Mahāyāna, or Great Vehicle Buddhism, in which spiritually advanced bodhisattvas and buddhas came to be regarded as having supernormal and salvific powers.

Let us now return to the analogy between Buddhism and Christianity. While the "salvation" aspect has usually been dominant in Christianity, the believers have usually been expected to make a considerable moral and spiritual effort on their own part. Conversely, in Buddhism the self-help aspect has been important from the beginning, but the recognition of the possibility of assistance by spiritually advanced or higher beings soon began to play an important role. Thus we can see even from this one analogy, which is a major datum in the history of religions, that a spectrum of forms of "salvation" could be envisaged, in which the various religions would be located according to their specific forms of teaching and practice. This spectrum should be located and differentiated, however, in an overall understanding of the morphology of religion. Only in such a perspective can the phenomena be correlated in a balanced manner.

Two major types of religion: primal and critical

In a consideration of the place of "salvation" in the general morphology of religion it is necessary to take one step back so that a more general theoretical pattern can come into view. It has been widely perceived that the distinguishable religious systems known in history can initially, and fundamentally, be classified into two major types, namely (i) those which uncritically reflect, support and affirm complete societies into which people are born, and (ii) those which regard human existence as in some sense problematic and offer a path of release or salvation from the normal situation. Though there are various names for these I call them "primal" and "critical" religions respectively, as also in "Religion and identity: clues and threads" (1995a, also at 7.2 below). Some may prefer to call the critical religions "salvation religions," or "soteriological" religions. The disadvantage of these latter terms is that they may obscure some of the other emphases which are found in critical religions, and to which I will refer later. Moreover, proximate soteriology is also a feature of primal religion.

In the detailed history of religions the distinction between these two main groups is not always easy to maintain, for two reasons. First, the critical religions have often arisen from within the context of the primal religion of a particular society, Christianity from within Judaism, Buddhism in the context of Brahmanism, the Ramakrishna Mission and Krishna Consciousness from within Brahmanism/Hinduism. Consequently there are shared characteristics. To put it another way, primal religions sometimes begin to develop the characteristics of critical religions. An example of this in the Japanese context would be the religion known as Kurozumikyō, which began with the teaching of Shintō priest Kurozumi Munetada in the year 1814. Second, and conversely, critical religions which achieve institutional success often take on some of the functions of "primal religion" in the societies in which they exist. This also leads to an overlap of characteristics. Both Buddhism and Christianity, for example, have taken on the role of providers of rites of transition for particular life stages, though they did not originally have this role. I refer to these socially and religiously very significant phenomena as "cross-overs" (Pye 1995a).

Nevertheless, the fundamental distinction between primal and critical religions can be maintained, especially if the self-understanding of specific religions is taken seriously. Which religions belong to which category depends on a range of characteristics. However the main question is whether those identified with a religion from their own point of view regard themselves as forming a natural society by virtue of birth or as an optional or selected society, that is to say an "elect" or "saved" society. Participation in a primal religion is usually regarded as a matter of obligation, whether one "believes" in it or not. Belonging to a "critical" religion, on the other hand, is usually regarded as being in principle voluntary, even if has become a matter of convention and habit in many cases. In modern pluralist societies, any of the above mentioned religions and many others are sometimes all regarded as so many optional faiths. However such a view fails to do justice to their different orientations. Krishna Consciousness is optional for individuals in western societies. Judaism however, also in the context of complex western societies, is not usually regarded as optional for those who are born into it.

The size of a particular religion has nothing to do with where it belongs typologically. The notion of "world religions" is therefore worthless from a theoretical point of view. As to primal religions, both the smallest and the largest human societies are sure to have one in some sense. In complex societies we find state religions and civil religion as variations of primal religion, depending on the political situation. As to critical religions, since they have a distinct historical beginning in the form of an experience of revelation, enlightenment, etc. they all begin as small religions, but some expand to become major traditions as time goes by.

The characteristics of the two major types of religion can be worked out further with respect to various features, such as ritual or other forms of religious behaviour.[1] However this is not the subject of discussion just here, and therefore I will turn specifically to the further delineation of "critical" religions under the aspect of "salvation" and its analogies.

"Salvation" in the general typology of religions

It has already been hinted that "salvation," though a dominant concept in some religions, may not be the best word to cover all relevant variations. Some dissatisfaction with it has also been expressed by Shimazono Susumu, who has proposed an additional category named "new spirituality movements." "The shift from salvation religion to new spirituality movements is a reflection of a radical individualism," he writes, "that is necessitated by the affluence and information-oriented nature of contemporary society." (Shimazono 1997) However it is not so clear that this is necessarily a historical shift from one kind of religion to another. It may be, rather, that the specific notion of "salvation" is not sufficiently comprehensive by itself to include the whole family of comparable religions. Within the overall range of critical religions, therefore, I would like to position those other orientations which need to be recog-

---

1 Retrospective note. See however "On comparing Buddhism and Christianity" (4.2 above), where typical forms of ritual are correlated with the same typology.

nised within the spectrum. In the title of this paper I have referred to all of these as "soteriological orientations," because the concept of "salvation" is being addressed particularly at the present conference. The point to note however is that the analogies, and indeed the differences between the various religions may emerge more clearly if the full range of "critical" orientations is considered.

What religious orientations are there which resolve the problematic character of human existence? Undoubtedly the concept of "salvation" is widespread, though the saviours differ. However, in addition to those religions in which the emphasis is on salvation through external action there are also others, like Buddhism, Jainism, Gnosticism, in which the main thread is awareness or special knowledge. In Buddhism, awareness in its complete form amounts to "enlightenment." The question therefore arises as to whether salvation on the one hand and awareness, enlightenment or gnosis on the other hand amount to two mutually exclusive types. Undoubtedly there are differences between religions, and it is not easy to see how these can easily be reconciled when the specific features of different religions are taken seriously. However, the spectrum of types within the general class of "critical" religions may be both greater and more coherent than is sometimes imagined. For example, there are various degrees of awareness which are available to followers of the Buddha who do not yet understand themselves to be enlightened. These are dependent on the authoritative teaching of the Buddha, who therefore is accepted as a leader of cosmic significance and thereby a kind of saviour, although this word is not used in Buddhism. At the same time, the working out of salvation in Christianity is usually related in a strong sense to the imitation of Christ as an exemplar.

To emphasise still further the coherence in the spectrum of critical religions (in the sense of overlapping family resemblances) I would like to draw attention to a major sub-type of religions which might be called "guidance religions." To indicate the origin of the term, it should be mentioned that it is drawn from the Japanese term *michibiki* which is commonly translated as "guidance," and which literally means "showing the way." The word *michibiki* is used to characterise an important mediatory activity in some Japanese religions such as Konkōkyō (founded in 1859). However it seems to me that the term is very useful in characterising a large number of religions including Buddhism, Upanishadic Hinduism, Daoism, Sufism, and many others which are less well known. The religions which Shimazono had in mind when referring to "new spirituality movements" also seem to belong here. On this basis the spectrum of varieties within "critical religions" could be mapped out using three guiding concepts, namely "salvation – guidance – awareness." In this formulation "awareness" includes "enlightenment" or "gnosis" in appropriate cases. Which religions belong under which of these categories is a matter for discussion, and some religions may appropriately be considered under more than one heading. For example, Buddhism is both a guidance religion and an awareness religion, and in some cases is understood as a salvation religion.

Another sub-question in the typology of critical religions is the relation between proximate and ultimate salvation. Proximate salvation refers to such matters as the healing of illness, rescue from tragic life-situations, or the avoidance of disaster. These positive effects are widely claimed by the believers of many religions. A concern with healing, for example, is apparently typical of the diverse elements making up the so-called New Age movement (Frisk 1997). Ultimate salvation is a more comprehensive and long-lasting understanding of the situation which is granted to the believer, a salvation which reaches to the very foundations of existence critically perceived, and which may therefore transcend finitude or death. In critical religions these two kinds of salvation are often closely associated with each other. I understand that this is true for the case of Tenrikyō, when we think of the idea of *sazuke* which accompanies the idea of *tsutome* in the overall idea of salvation. This is set out for example by Sawai Yuichi in a contribution to the compendium *The Theological Perspectives of Tenrikyō*[2]. It is also true for the case of Catholic Christianity, for which it will suffice to cite the example of the healings famously believed to take place at Lourdes.

There is a further, interesting complication in the overall typology in that proximate salvation is also found in the context of primal religions. That is to say, there are cases where "soteriological" effects are sought by means of traditional routines, without the fundamental basis of social existence being questioned and without any requirement for the individual to adopt a new, specialised social identity. The apparently very widespread, archaic layer of shamanistic culture usually has provision for this, and where this is not directly available, the gap is often filled by the appearance of religious practices which do not necessarily promote a radically new or comprehensive revelation. At the same time critical religions, with their radical review of human existence, do not necessarily exclude forms of proximate salvation, which may be very important to the believers. It ap-

---

2 Tenri (Oyasato Research Institute) 1986, 256 ff.

pears therefore that proximate salvation may be provided in the context both of primal and of critical religions.

On the basis of the above reflections, which have been stated with utmost brevity, the main features of a typology of salvation in religions can be mapped out as in the diagram.

Primal religion
(which secures the integrity of society and is in principle obligatory)

regular features:

	social coherence	identity celebration rites
	economic effectiveness	hunting rites
		fertility rites
		industrial rites
	protection	avoidance rites (social)
	positioning of individual	individual life rites (including social initiation)

soteriological features:

	proximate salvation	healing rites, etc.
		avoidance rites (individual)

Critical religion
(which provides solutions to the critical nature of human existence and is in principle voluntary)

proximate salvation		healing rites, etc.
		avoidance rites
ultimate salvation	}	
	}	{ initiation into special community
guidance (*michibiki*)	}	
	}	{ reinforcement rites
awareness/gnosis	}	

It will be seen from the table that primal religion takes account of the need to integrate the individual human being within any one natural society. Individual life rites are not merely there for the sake of the individual but even more so for the sake of the society, which is why they have so effectively been characterised as "rites of transition." In the complexities of the modern world, societies overlap at many points, and religion has therefore become one of the important indicators of the boundaries of any one society. As to the critical religions, it is of interest to note that the range of varieties can also be understood along a scale from religious heteronomy to religious autonomy. The simplest acceptance of religious authority is correlated with proximate salvation, while the most subtle, internalised relationship to religious authority is correlated with awareness or gnosis.

Conclusions

Taken with reference to the arguments presented, the table shown here provides a comparative guide to the variety of soteriological orientations in religion which can be widely documented in the history of religions. In conclusion it may now be asked where the particular cases of Tenrikyō and Christianity would be included in the above perspective. In the case of Tenrikyō it will be fairly clear to those familiar with its teaching and practice that it falls under the category of "critical religion" and is focused on both proximate and ultimate salvation. As to Christianity, it must be noted that the historical complexity is far greater than in the case of Tenrikyō, so that a one-to-one comparison is not possible. In general however, and considered in terms of its origins, Christianity also falls under the category of "critical religion."

What about the more detailed location within the category of critical religion? It seems correct to say that in the case of Tenrikyō there is a claim to ultimate salvation for the whole of humanity summed up in the word *tsutome* and a concern for matters of proximate salvation, especially healing, summed up in the word *sazuke*. A complication in the case of Christianity is the varying degree to which there is an expectation of proximate salvation. It might be said to have played at least a subordinate role during the time of Christian origins, as may be seen for example in the healing stories and in the provisional raising of Lazarus from the dead. Indeed there has been an interest in miracles which benefit people in their present lives all the way down through the history of Christianity. The Protestant churches are diverse in this regard. The major established denominations tend to place little emphasis on the forms of proximate salvation, but on the other hand there is a widespread interest in healing among fundamentalist and pentecostalist groups. As regards Catholic

Christianity it may be said that here, viewed overall, there is a clear focus both on proximate and on ultimate salvation.

A major practical difference resulting from the historical complexity of Christianity is that, in not a few regions of the world and at different periods of history, it has taken on at least some of the functions of "primal religion" for particular societies. As a result the rites of initiation into the Church, namely baptism, first communion (in Catholicism) and confirmation, have often served a double purpose as rites of transition for the natural society. In addition, marriage and funeral rites are provided, though these are not in themselves necessary for participation in a voluntary body of the elect. In this we can perceive the "cross-over" phenomenon referred to earlier. This has not yet happened significantly for Tenrikyō, though to some extent it might be considered to be applicable for family generations in which membership is, so to speak, inherited. It is also relevant in the context of the ethnically conditioned transplantation of Tenrikyō to other parts of the world. Nevertheless, the central practice or "reinforcement rite" of Tenrikyō, the sacred dance, is clearly focused on ultimate salvation, both for the individual and as a cosmic event transcending natural societies. The same is true for the central reinforcement rite of Christianity, namely the Mass or Eucharist.

Bibliographical references

Frisk, Liselotte 1997. "Vad är New Age? Centrala begrepp och historiska rotter" in: *Svensk Religionshistorisk Årsskrift* 6: 87–97.
Oyasato Research Institute (eds.) 1986. *The Theological Perspectives of Tenrikyo*. Tenri City (Tenri University Press).
Pye, Michael 1995a. "Religion and identity: clues and threads" in: De Gruchy, J.W.and Martin, S (eds.) *Religion and the Reconstruction of Civil Society (Papers from the founding congress of the South African Academy of Religion, January 1994)*. Pretoria (University of South Africa): 3–17.
Shimazono, Susumu 1997. "On contemporary salvation religion" in: *Tenri Journal of Religion* 25: 41–57.
Smart, Ninian 1958. *Reasons and Faiths*. London (Routledge and Kegan Paul).
1997. *Buddha and Christ. Lights of the World*. Bangalore (Dharmaram Publications).

This article was first published in: Tenri Organizing Committee of Tenrikyo-Christian Dialogue (eds), *Tenrikyo-Christian Dialogue*, Tenri City (Tenri University Press) 1999, 99–113; and in Japanese translation as "Shūkyō ni okeru kyūsaironteki shikō" (宗教における救済論的志向) in:-

Tenrikyō to Kirisutokyō no taiwa, Tenri City (Tenri University Press) 1998, 123–141. A related interview with the author in Japanese about the symposium appeared in a booklet entitled *Tenrikyō to Kirisutokyō no Taiwa. Rōma Tenrikyōten*, edited by Tenrikyōdōyūsha, Tenri 1998, 97–98.

4.6 'Polytheism' and 'Monotheism' as a Problem in the Typology of Religions

This paper was first presented at the 2nd congress of the European Association for the Study of Religions (EASR) held in Paris at the Collège de France, in September 2002, on the subject "Le monothéisme: diversité, exclusivisme ou dialogue?"

Introduction: current public assumptions

In recent months there has been an increasing public interest in "monotheism," regarded by some commentators as a causal factor in conflict. This interest may even have been a factor in the selection of the theme for this conference and for some of the contributions to it. The idea current among the public seems to be that a "monotheistic" belief system, presumed to be present in Judaism, Christianity and Islam, supports a set of attitudes including intolerance, exclusivism, arrogance and the will to dominate others, thus causing conflicts threatening world peace such as those between Arabs and Israelis, or the American Christian Right and radical Islamists. Against this background I was asked recently on radio to comment on the supposed relationship between monotheism and fundamentalism. The assumption behind the question was evidently that "fundamentalism," perceived as a social evil, has its roots in "monotheism." My answer was quite disappointing to the interviewer, I believe, because I explained that it is possible to find "fundamentalism" in many religious contexts including Hinduism, Buddhism or Shintō, none of which are normally categorised as "monotheist." At the same time, within the religions normally regarded as "monotheist," there is usually a wide range of attitudinal and conceptual options which includes very divergent fundamentalist and liberal variants. This can be seen not only in the context of the three so-called "Abrahamic" religions, which themselves are significantly different from each other in other respects, but very clearly in the most interesting case of Sikhism, which should normally also be regarded as a "monotheistic" religion, if indeed this category makes any sense at all. However it is precisely the notion of monotheism and the accompanying notion of polytheism which need to be deconstructed[1] if the popular misunderstandings and misleading media images are to be avoided. The main trend of this paper is therefore deconstructivist.

The history of religions and the inheritance of philosophical theology

It is evident from the history of religions, and from the history of this discipline, that it is almost impossible to have any kind of discussions about "monotheism" without taking note of the alternatives to it. This too is reflected in the present conference. Although the main theme of the conference is "monotheism," most of the contributions are, at least additionally, about presumed alternatives such as "polytheism" or "dualism." This is natural, if only because in the real history of religions the concept of "monotheism" arose in a dialectical relationship to "polytheism" and "dualism." Moreover, at the level of philosophical religious reflection, the concept of "monotheism" has been maintained and developed for centuries over against these and other generalised notions such as pantheism, monism and panentheism.

It must therefore be recognised that there has been a heavy theological investment in "monotheism" over against "polytheism" in particular. The assumption has often been, in the western world, that "monotheistic" religions are somehow able to view the world as a whole, and as having a unified purpose and a unified history and future destiny. Indeed there is some truth in the idea that such a perspective has been carried over into the sense of historical destiny found, in secularized form, both in Marxist socialism and in the secularized sense of mission characteristic of the civil religion of the United States of America. Both of these ideological perspectives have demanded, in their heyday, a globalized fulfilment. Even in theological terms, in modern times, such a perspective is felt to have some kind of kinship with scientific rationality, whereas polytheism by contrast is supposed to be pre-rational. If "God" is great, how can he be plural? Secondarily, the idea summed up in the word "henotheism" has been regarded as a conceptual advance on polytheism in the direction of rationality. Thus the Jewish religion,

---

1 Note that in the published conference proceedings this word was misprinted as "constructed" so that the sense was negated.

at a certain stage in its history, is denoted as having been somehow internally henotheistic, in that the worship of one God only was permitted, while at the same time this God was not yet perceived to be the God of all humankind and only later appropriated as such by others under the heading of monotheism.

Immediately above in the question "How can he be plural?" I used the word "he" for God. This is in line with the traditional speech forms of the leading "monotheistic" religions. The resistance to a dual gender for God is partly connected to the idea of "his" singularity. If God is "one," how can "he" have two genders? Concepts of divinity in which two genders are accommodated have commonly come to be regarded as polytheist, as in the case of Shintō with its divine pair Izanagi and Izanami. Concepts of divinity in which *no* gender at all is postulated for the ultimate divinity (even metaphorically) are regarded as "monist," as in the case of Vedantic Hinduism. In traditional western theologies, i. e. Jewish, Christian and Islamic, "monism" is also regarded as a failure to recognize the singularity of God in distinction to the creation.

But are all these distinctions satisfactory? I fear not. They are weighted in favour of a particular, very deeply ingrained and influential theological perspective. To get over this problem it is desirable to move towards a more satisfactory typology which takes account of the full morphology of religion in its four main aspects and their correlations. Such a typology should be independent of theological positioning in favour of the one or other concept which can be extracted from a preferred tradition. Polarised views, such as a contrast between polytheism (regarded as irrational) with monotheism (regarded as rational, or at least more rational), should be avoided.

Multiple agency and sole agency

We have learned from cognitive scientists that the brains of human beings work in such a way that we can recognize "agents" and that such agents may be empirical beings such as parents or animals or metaphorically conceived beings such as spirits or gods. This view, while plausible as far as initial learning processes are concerned, and apparently novel and exciting to a number of specialists in the study of religions, fails to explain the diversity of religious systems in the wider field. We have also learned from post-modernists, who are not usually the best friends of cognitive scientists, that the actors making use of various religious systems do so in order to negotiate their own positions in various ways. This too is a valuable insight for those who were not already aware of it. However the word "agency" which has been used in the excited phase of both of these theoretical movements, may be helpful in clarifying our thoughts about divinities. Even a simple reflection along these lines will have the effect of putting different things into different categories, which after all is the task of the typology of religion. Provisionally, therefore, let us regard "polytheism" as *perceived multiple agency*. And on the other hand let us provisionally regard "monotheism" as *perceived sole agency*. Of course I am referring here to the metaphorical level of discourse typical of religious systems. Questions about whether such divine agents or principles in some sense "exist" outside the minds of human beings are not of interest in a clearly delimited scientific enquiry.

Sanitising and replacing the vocabulary

We still have the problem that the element "-theism," as in monotheism, is heavily loaded with the image of a personalised, creating, historically acting God, and that this image is not appropriate in all contexts known to us in the history of religions, notably but not only in Buddhism. In other words there is a specific content implied by "-theism" which is not necessarily helpful in the development of a viable typology because it leads in a particular direction. However it is difficult simply to remove the concept of "-the/ism" from the traditional terms because it would just leave "poly...ism" and "mono...ism." During the drafting of this paper, therefore, I initially considered proposing two sets of complementary alternatives. The first set is *polydeism* and *monodeism*. These terms may remind some of us of "deities," a term which has more neutral associations than "theism." However it may remind others of "deism," which itself has a contrastive association against "theism," i.e. in suggesting a philosophically necessary but historically inactive God. Probably for this reason it was selected for the phrase *deus otiosus*, the lazy God, as opposed to a historically active *theos*. Indeed, nobody ever heard of a lazy *theos*. As a further alternative therefore I proposed a second set of new terms, namely *polydivinism* and *monodivinism*. These refer to conceptual patterns of religious systems which include many divinities (*polydivinism*) or one divinity (*monodivinism*) respectively.

However, since the paper was first drafted, Dr. Kazimiera Mikoś (of the Jagellonian University of Kraków) suggested to me that we replace *polydivinism* and *monodivinism* with *polydeitism* and *monodeitism* respectively. These terms are devised from *deity* (rather than *divinity*) but at the same time avoid the the associations of "deism." This suggestion seems to me to be entirely acceptable, and the new terms have therefore been gratefully adopted in the rest of the text below. The terminological development is recorded so that the sequence of ideas can be followed. Of course, the terms *polydeitism* and *monodeitism* sound peculiar, and the reason for that is that they are not some kind of faith-language but technical terms in the study of religions.

Recategorising known phenomena

With terms such as these in mind we may continue to think about divinities or deities as multiple or sole agents. The meaning of "henotheism" lies in the perception of a *preferred* single agency, –preferred, that is to say, from among various divinities which are otherwise known about. The other divinities may then be decried as immoral, weak, completely powerless, and eventually non-"existent." However they are in principle not regarded as unknown. That is, they play a role in the recognition and selection of potential agency. For this reason "henotheism" falls within the category of polydeitism. The same applies to "dualism," especially when personified agents are involved. Satan is a metaphorical agent and systems in which he occurs are therefore polydeitist. Were Satan to be regarded as the sole agent, we would have an example of monodeitist Satanism, but in Satanism itself Satan is usually regarded has having one or more opponents. Indeed it is the presumed struggle of powers which makes Satanism attractive to some people, who use the system to act out their own social and cultural discontents.

Thinking in a similar way about monodeitism, we may reserve this term for systems in which only one, sole metaphorical agency is supposed to play any role. It is of course not necessary to suppose that this "agent" does anything very much. He/she/it may or may not be regarded as passive, active or hyperactive. Incidentally, one of the main difficulties with the writings of cognitive scientists on religion is that they exaggerate or oversimplify the significance of the perceived "agents," rather as if people thinking religiously were always expecting "somebody," that is, an agent, to "do something." Often however, they may be perceived as being somehow there, but more or less inactively. Monodeitism includes not only examples such as Islamic "monotheism" on the one hand but also Vedantic monism on the other hand. At a certain level of religious thought, monodeitism may also include "Buddhism" and "Daoism," but of course these religious systems can *also* be considered as polydeitist. It all depends which presentations of these religions are being considered. These examples illustrate that any particular religious system (and we should remember that at some point it is whole religious systems which are the subject of the study of religions) may be at one and the same time polydeitist and monodeitist. Terms such as "Buddhism," "Hinduism" and "Daoism" should not be used naively, of course. This has been pointed out *ad nauseam* in recent times. Moreover we should also beware of falling into the grave danger of "essentialism" (of which the writer has been accused, misleadingly). Indeed the names used immediately above refer to a number of overlapping "systems," which not only are associated with each other in the sense of "family resemblances" but also interact with each other internally. The same applies to "Christianity," so that we may regard "Christianity" as being in some cases monodeitist (e.g. in the case of the Quakers, the Unitarian Church or the Universalist Unitarian Church) and in other cases as being polydeitist, which most of the historic churches are, especially Catholicism as widely practised. The fact that this idea may not appeal to theologians attempting to defend "monotheism" is completely irrelevant in this analysis, though of course it is an interesting phenomenon in itself.

If monodeitism includes both "monotheism" and "monism" it also includes what we might call monodaoism. "Dao-ism"(i.e. Way-ism) means any system unterstood to be based on a Way, including not only Daoism itself as a religious system, but also Confucianism and a variety of independent foundations of later date, which see themselves as offering methods following the "great way" or the "true way." It is important for such systems that the Way is a unified, integrated principle. At the same time the term "monism" would not be a very accurate way of designating them: hence the need for the term dao-ism (which here only is shown with a hyphen to highlight the distinction from the specific religious system or systems known as Daoism). The specific religion known as Daoism is some cases monodaoistic and therefore monodeitist, and in other cases polydeitist. To sum up, monodeitism is a wider term which includes monotheism, monism and monodaoism.

Interactions between the two main categories

As the above examples and much more historical and comparative observation which might be adduced show us, the two fundamental categories are not at all mutually exclusive when it comes to named religious systems. The interactions may be understood in terms of the idea of "cross-overs" between the two main types of religious system, namely primal religions and critical religions (that is soteriological, gnostic or guidance religions).[2] Because primal religions are related to specific social groups, as well as for other related reasons, the conceptual features are normally polydeitist. Since critical religions provide solutions for individuals and so, for that very reason, are theoretically universalizable for all human beings, they are normally monodeitist (whether monotheistic, monist or monodaoistic). However, primal religions are not only religious systems in their own right but also the matrix in which critical religions emerge, e.g. Buddhism in the context of Brahmanism, Christianity in the context of Judaism, or Kurozumikyō in the context of Shintō, so the ways in which these become monodeitist vary from case to case. Moreover universalizing religions, once successfully established, soon come to provide at least some of the necessary features of primal religion (or, variantly, civil religion) in the societies where they predominate. These developments, in both directions, may be regarded as "crossovers" which do not weaken the value of the typology but provide further, useful differentiation.

Relations between the main aspects of religion, and conclusions

The most economical morphology of religion regards any specific systems under four aspects, namely: conceptual, behavioural, social and emotional. These terms may be varied or accompanied by others: e.g. the emotional aspect may be referred to as the attitudinal aspect, if this is preferred in a particular context. This view of religious systems under four main aspects, each worthy of specific study by specialists in ritual studies, sociology, psychology of religion, etc., is to be preferred

---

2   These concepts are set out briefly in and in Pye 1995a "Religion and identity: clues and threads" (7.2 below) and Pye 1999b "Soteriological orientations in religion" (4.5 above).

to more miscellaneous lists of dimensions. Some of the more well-known enumerations simply leave out major aspects such as the social aspect, or misleadingly regard one or other of the four aspects as somehow being the essential locus of "religious experience," as I have argued elsewhere. In other cases misleading subdivisions, such as a distinction between myths and symbols (which all belong to the conceptual aspect) are given priority, or limitations are brought in as when religious behaviour is limited to "ritual,", as if this is somehow more "religious" than some other forms of behaviour such as ethical endeavour. Taking the four main aspects of religion into consideration, therefore, it would appear that the distinctions made above with regard to the conceptual realm can be correlated in various ways with the other aspects. It should be noted that we are only discussing certain details of the conceptual aspect, which itself is much more complicated. The typology of *polydeitism* and *monodeitism* is highlighted here because of the theme of the present conference, and it in no way exhausts the comprehensive exploration and analysis of the conceptual aspect of religions which includes much more than notions pertaining to "divinities." It is therefore rather by chance that the notion of perceived "agents" came to play a role in this discussion. Nevertheless, we may ask how the typology of *polydeitism* and *monodeitism* sits with the other aspects.

As regards the social aspect of religion, first, it may be argued that primal religions, relating to a delimited society, are more likely to be polydeitist. This is partly because primal religion has a sequence of functions for which different agents are presumed to be responsible, and partly because there is an awareness of potential (metaphorical) agents who have a realm of competence *outside* the system. To illustrate, representatives of the Shintō religion usually assume that people living in other parts of the world, not in Japan, have their own gods and spirits who are the equivalent of the Japanese *kami* (divinities). The invention of a more universalist message from within the context of a primal religion goes hand in hand with the development of monodeitist (including monodaoistic) concepts. This in turn can lead to religious communities which transcend primal social boundaries.

Religious behaviour can be read accordingly. In brief, I suggest that the rituals of polydeitist systems relate to the security of the society and the economy in question, to individual life-rites and to this-worldly soteriologies as occasion demands. They may be reinforced by ethical perspectives, usually defined by the boundaries of the group in question. Monodeitist systems give a stronger place to subjectively internalized, non-ritual behaviour/s and their rituals are expected to be consistent across different cultures (even though they usually come to vary somewhat over the course of time). Typically they provide a once and for all accession rite (for joining) and a repeated reinforcement rite. In Christianity these are baptism and the Eucharist. But other rites are developed when they take over the functions of primal religion, e.g. life-rites (birth and adolescence rites, marriages, funerals) and occasional this-worldly soteriological rituals, e.g. for healing or protection. The latter go hand in hand with the development, or the redevelopment, of polydeitism within the critical system. This is particularly evident in the case of saint cults where the supernatural agents are presumed to have particular competences. Parallels can easily be documented in the Buddhist systems of East Asia, where monodaoism is regularly complemented by the polydeitism of the various bodhisattva cults as well as by other relations with gods and goddesses who have a home within the overall system, such as Benzaiten in Japan.

This leaves the question of correlations with the emotional or attitudinal aspect of religions. Again, there are endless details which might be considered here. As an example of a positive correlation, I would suggest that there is a greater awareness of the possibility of inner self-development in monodeitist religions (the point is highly summarized), while there is a greater readiness to show pragmatic reliance on external (metaphorical) agents in polydeitist religions.

Finally however, let us reconsider the media-led question with which we began, that is, whether a particular conceptual type, "monotheism," is or may be connected to a particular attitudinal type, "fundamentalism," regarded here as an emotional force. At certain times in history both Hinduism and Shintō, while predominantly polydeitist, have been interpreted or, one might argue, reinvented, in a fundamentalist mode. The term "fundamentalist" is taken here to mean a simplificatory reliance on supposed roots which create a primal identity. It might be expected therefore that a polydeitist religion is just as likely to be correlated with fundamentalist attitudes and emotions as a monodeitist religion. And indeed this corresponds to the documentable phenomena of the history of religions. So we conclude that there is no intrinsic connection between "monotheism" and "fundamentalism."

Apart from addressing this specific question, which is "out there" in the public mind, I hope that I have also succeeded in showing by this example that typological work at the level of religious systems continues to be possible, and indeed extremely desirable. It can illuminate questions which arise where religious systems prove to be diverse, both when we compare religious systems with each other, and when we compare different versions of a religion which bear a single name and somehow seem to be part of a wider common tradition.

Bibliographical references

Pye, Michael 1995a. "Religion and identity: clues and threads" in: De Gruchy, J.W.and Martin, S (eds.) Religion and the Reconstruction of Civil Society (Papers from the founding congress of the South African Academy of Religion, January 1994). Pretoria (University of South Africa): 3–17. (Text at 7.2 below.)
– 1999b. "Soteriological orientations in religion" in: Tenri Organizing Committee of Tenrikyo- Christian Dialogue (eds), Tenrikyo-Christian Dialogue, Tenri City (Tenri University Press): 99–113. (Text at 4.5 above.)

This paper was first published in: Charles Guittard (ed), *Le Monothéisme: Diversité, Exclusivisme ou Dialogue. (Actes de l'Association Européenne pur l'Étude des Religions (EASR) Congrès de Paris, 11–14 Septembre 2002)* Paris (Editions Non Lieu) 2010: 25–32.

4.7 Prayer and Meditation as Comparative Concepts

This paper was a keynote lecture for a symposium on "prayer as interaction" held in Marburg, Germany in 2006 which brought together Evangelical (Lutheran) theologians and members of the Japanese religion Tenrikyō, with additional participation by specialists in the study of religions. Slight corrections have been made to the version published in the proceedings.

Introduction

To give an account of "research on prayer in the contemporary study of religions"[1] is almost like being asked to describe the horns of a turtle. The subject has been badly neglected. Prayer simply has not been a favoured theme in recent times. Ritual may be a widely studied theme, but "prayer" is not. Why is this? In general, the reason is that fashionable trends in the contemporary study of religions often owe more to ideas drawn from other disciplines than to the systematic analysis of religious systems themselves. Colleagues often hurry to identify themselves as post-modernists, post-colonial ethnologists, cultural scientists, or cognitivists: in fact, anything but as specialists in the study of religions or *Religionswissenschaftler*. The subject of "prayer" is therefore left aside as something very old-fashioned, the kind of thing with which the old school of the phenomenology of religion concerned itself, and which is nowadays best left to theologians or just "believers." I do not share this attitude.

In spite of various problems with the older approaches to the subject, easily recognisable with the hindsight of several decades, and in spite of its relative neglect in recent years, it must be said that in most religious systems "prayer," with its many names, and in its many variations, simply does play a significant role for believers and practitioners. There is therefore no reason why prayer should not be considered as a theme in the historical and comparative study of religions, just like other matters such as pilgrimage, myth, iconography, and so on. How this particular theme should be delineated for purposes of study is of course

---

1   The original title of the paper, as requested by the conference organizers.

Introduction 73

a complex matter which will be considered further here. It has been recognised for very many years now that the "Study of Religions" (*Religionswissenschaft*) should not begin with normative or essentialist definitions.[2] Rather, in this discipline we seek to adumbrate, or that is, sketch out an area of interest for further exploration and analysis with the appropriate methods.[3] With regard to any particular theme there are some important strategic matters to consider before going into details. What is to be included in the field of enquiry, or excluded, is of great import. This is particularly the case for "prayer."

In this contribution I will comment first on some of the ways in which prayer has been presented and discussed in writing which appears to represent the "study of religions." Then I will make some rather different proposals about the way in which this particular part of the field should be sketched out for further exploration. To anticipate, it will be argued that we should work with a somewhat wider perception of prayer than is often found. Our perception of this theme should *include* both (a) non-verbal prayer, which is typical of, but not exclusively related to mysticism, and also (b) a close association with the overlapping phenomenon of meditation, whether verbalised or not. Prayer should not be regarded as consisting only of messages to "counter-intuitive," supernatural beings. This is a simplistic cognitivist error (see further below). A little more complicatedly, while the frequently criticised error of logocentrism should be avoided, so that words alone are not regarded as the "be all and end all" of religion, we should also avoid the trap of tumbling over into an excessive emphasis on ritual practice. This tendency, expressed most radically in the phrase "rules without meaning" (Staal 1996), implies that words on the one hand and subjective attitudes on the other hand are of no real importance. While such a view may be tempting in respect to highly routinized ritual situations, it leads away from serious understanding of the subject, as may easily be seen in studies of the ritual use of the *Heart Sūtra* in Japanese Buddhism.[4]

---

2   This was clearly argued by the writer in the introduction to *Comparative Religion. An Introduction through Source Materials* (Pye 1972a) and in various later articles [see Part One in Volume One above]. Occasional critiques of my work for having "essentialist" tendencies are based on an entirely superficial reading of certain essays and, significantly, are nowhere documented with precise quotations.
3   See further, for example in 1.2 above (Volume One).
4   A manuscript in which I argued this in detail with slides was unfortunately stolen on Frankfurt railway station. It described a particular event in which a re-

Some publications examined

It is probably as a result of the external influences mentioned above that, in recent times, we find very little discussion of "prayer" in publications which represent "the study of religions" (*Religionswissenschaft*). For example, the relevant entry in the *Metzler Lexikon Religion*,[5] is entitled "Gebet/Fluch" (i. e. "prayer/curse"), as if "prayer" were somehow mainly the same kind of thing as a curse. The article begins with the simplistic assertion: "Prayer is one of the typical forms of religious communication," and goes on to propose a structure of "address, petition and vow," thereby making petitionary prayer central. This is a surprisingly limited conception which is hardly worthy of further attention. It will be interesting to see if the planned English translation of this lexicon also leaves "prayer" in this blind alley.[6]

More substantial is an article on "*Gebet*" (prayer) by Rainer Flasche in another recent German reference work entitled *Handbuch religionswissenschaftlicher Grundbegriffe* (Cancik et al. 1990–1998). Flasche went to great lengths to criticise Friedrich Heiler's well-known and substantial work of 1919 (dissertation 1917), which only goes to show how little had happened since. It is indicative that the most recent works referred to by Flasche are Kurt Goldammer's *Die Formenwelt des Religiösen* (1960), Hampp's *Beschwörung, Segen, Gebet. Untersuchungen zum Zauberspruch aus dem Bereich der Volksheilkunde* (1961), and Scheele's *Opfer des Wortes. Gebete der Heiden aus fünf Jahrtausenden* (1961). Flasche's own contribution is a series of questions about the "who, what, how, when, where, why, for what and whither" of prayer, all with typological sub-sections. These are intended as categories for further research.

Of course, everybody looks back, usually critically, to the famous work by Friedrich Heiler, *Das Gebet. Eine religionsgeschichtliche und reli-*

---

    ligious group performed ascetic rites under a forceful waterfall in Tochigi Prefecture, Japan, and argued that it certainly was possible to discern the "meaning" of the rite for the participants! For another attempt to describe this event, in spite of the loss, see Pye 1997c. The role of the *Heart Sūtra* in the transformatory, and hence (of course for the pilgrims) meaningful process of circulatory Buddhist pilgrimage (*o-meguri*) is also extremely relevant in this regard, as explained elsewhere.

5 Auffarth et al. 2000. The entry referred to here, by Thomas Oberlies, is in Vol.1: 442–6.

6 This English edition has since appeared, apparently with not a few changes from the original, but it was not immediately available for inspection.

gionspsychologische Untersuchung (1919), translated into English, with some abbreviations, relatively soon after its appearance.[7] At the same time, the reader of today may be surprised, even shocked, by the assumptions and style of this work. It is now, after all, more than eighty years old. However, while criticism is necessary (see below and in other contributions to this symposium), we should beware of brushing aside older achievements in *Religionswissenschaft* simply because they are unfashionable. Of positive value in Heiler's work are the beginnings of a typology which ranges from petitionary prayer to the mystical experience of the presence of God. This was not in itself particularly original, because it corresponds in general to the way in which prayer has long been taught in the major Christian traditions. To give but one example, such a perspective is found in *The Elements of the Spiritual Life. A Study in Ascetical Theology*, by F.P Harton, Warden of the Sisters of Charity at Knowle near Bristol (London 1932). This wide range is important. There is really no excuse for researchers today, as often happens, to treat "prayer" as if it were exclusively or mainly petitionary. Such a view is an expression of ignorance or prejudice. In view of the breadth of Heiler's treatment, it is all the more strange that Heiler thought it necessary to publish a *separate* work on meditation immediately afterwards entitled *Die buddhistische Versenkung. Eine religionsgeschichtliche Untersuchung* (1918). This separation of the two themes, prayer and meditation, does not seem to me to be at all justified (as will be explained further below). Another problem with the work, looking back over several decades, may be seen in Heiler's enthusiastic essentialism. In his presentation, prayer is the *central* component of all religion, especially the religion of "great souls." Indeed in parts the work is little more than a series of edifying quotations from such "religious geniuses," with little serious analysis. This is what happens when something called ""religious experience" is regarded as central to the understanding of "religion" or religious systems, as was common in those days. "Religious experience" is of course itself a highly problematic concept, typical of studies of religion in the Protestant tradition[8], but quite apart from that, Heiler was personally much too close to religious life to achieve the necessary de-

---

7   There was a second German edition and subsequently two English translations and a French translation. It would be an interesting and perhaps instructive task to compare the differences between all of these, but time does not permit.
8   Cf. my critique of Joachim Wach in Pye 1972a (Introduction).

tachment required for clear analysis.[9] This does not mean that the researcher in the field of religion must be personally non-religious. It is widely understood among specialists in this discipline, that the researcher may be religious, or not, and this is widely *mis*understood by representatives of adjacent disciplines.

The above criticism of Heiler is related to that advanced by Rainer Flasche who writes, in the article already quoted, that Heiler's underlying assumption is, as he puts it, "mono-religious," being based on the Judaeo-Christian paradigm. The wealth of detail provided from various areas in the "history of religions" should not be underestimated, but Flasche's point is that these are drawn into a unifying perspective which is dominated by a particular religious perspective. This "mono-religious" assumption was continued, he argues, by Scheele (1961), even though the latter was writing about the prayers of "heathens" (*Heiden*). Flasche rightly argues that the emphasis on "religious geniuses" does not do justice to the whole range of ordinary believers, and that the latter should be considered with equal interest by researchers into religion. However, while giving vent to very forthright criticism, he does overlook the sheer breadth of Heiler's concept of prayer within the Judaeo-Christian range, in particular the opening to mystical religion, where petitionary prayer becomes insignificant (though in a later context Flasche himself admits that the lines become blurred in this context (461). On the other hand, consistently enough, he follows Heiler in clearly separating prayer and meditation. This is because he himself defines prayer as "verbal communication with a power, of whatever kind, which lies beyond our own power of disposition."[10] With this starting point, Flasche could begin a new career among the cognitivists![11] However as Harton wrote, of course from within a living

---

9 For my own general appraisal of Heiler's work and position(s), see Pye 1997d.
10 Retrospective note. This is my own paraphrasing translation of "verbale Kommunikation mit einer wie auch immer gearteten Unverfügbarkeit," in which the unusual word *Unverfügbarkeit* means something which lies outside one's own competence to appropriate, direct or control. If a single word were sought, *eine Unverfügbarkeit* could be matched by the equally unusual expression "an unmanageability," i.e. something which one cannot oneself direct or control. Of course, this reflects the radical theological concept of a God whom we feeble humans are not in a position to manage. At the same time, many religious rites apparently involving various kinds of prayer, precisely do seek to make divine powers manageable in our own interests, or are, in German, *verfügbar*.
11 Retrospective note. Sadly, Rainer Flasche (of Marburg) passed away recently and I could not discuss these matters further with him.

tradition of prayerful life: "Never let us teach people to say prayers, but always teach them to pray..."[12] For the *Religionswissenschaftler* this is simply a reminder that the phenomenon of prayer is not only verbal.

Two substantial and very influential encyclopaedias may be mentioned at this point. The first is the *Encyclopaedia of Religion and Ethics* edited by James Hastings, which through coincidence appeared in 1918, at exactly the same period as Heiler's *Das Gebet*. The second will be the *Encyclopedia of Religion* published under the chief editorship of Mircea Eliade in 1987. In volume X of the Hastings *Encyclopaedia* there is a collection of nineteen articles on prayer in the context of various religions by different authors, beginning with "Introductory and Primitive," followed by "American" (meaning American Indian), "Babylonian," "Buddhist," and so on, and ending with "Teutonic" and "Tibetan." The order of these contributions is alphabetical. The opening article, by E.N. Fallaize, apparently an anthropologist, tells us that: "In its simplest and most primitive form prayer is the expression of a desire, cast in the form of a request, to influence some force or power conceived as supernatural."[13] Interestingly he adds that the modern usage of the term "connotes spiritual communion." The rather lengthy section on "Christian, Theological," by C. F. D'Arcy, is written in the same vein as Heiler's work, though not in dependence on it. He certainly regarded prayer as being more than verbal, as when we read "Prayer is, in general, communion of the human soul with God."[14]. At the same time the author spends considerable space on a spirited defence of the efficacy of petitionary prayer, arguing that while miracles are rare, "Answers to prayer occur every day"[15], though of course not necessarily in an evident manner. The articles on prayer in various other religious fields, e. g. by M. Anesaki on Buddhism or by Th. W. Juynboll on Islam (referred to as "Prayer, Muhammadan") are less religiously argumentative and more descriptive in the sense of the "history of religions," though in some details outdated of course. The relatively substantial article on prayer in Judaism, by Felix Perles, is also mainly descriptive, but contains the interesting comment that "mysticism...has exercised a most harmful influence, since the end of the 12th century, on both the conception and the content of prayer," that is, in worship in the synago-

---

12   Harton 1931: 230.
13   Hastings 1918 X: 154.
14   Hastings 1918 X: 171.
15   Hastings 1918 X: 177.

gue.¹⁶ This simply reflects the fact that as regards prayer there has been a long-standing tension, or range of options, between the verbal and the non-verbal and between the subjective and the overtly ritual. There is no overall systematisation which shapes these articles in the Hastings Encyclopaedia, but there are many scattered starting points for typological treatment, including some of the questions later formulated by Flasche as mentioned above.

The article on prayer in the *Encyclopedia of Religion* edited by Mircea Eliade, another landmark publication which appeared some 70 years later, may be said to illustrate the decay of the field in the minds of specialists in the study of religions. By contrast with the earlier detailed treatments there is one single article of five pages, by Sam D. Gill, who writes that "the general study of prayer is undeveloped and naïve." Of course, this depends on the point of view. One might also say that many who believe that they are setting the agenda for today in the study of religions have themselves a naïve view of the matter. This is not a criticism of the article as such, for the author tackles it bravely and informatively. What seems a little unsatisfactory is the "schema" consisting of prayer as (i) "text," i.e. "a collection of words that cohere as a human communication directed toward a spiritual entity," (ii) "act," including both communication and performance, and (iii) "*subject*, that is, as a dimension or aspect of religion, the articulation of whose nature constitutes a statement of belief, doctrine, instruction, philosophy, or theology."¹⁷ With the third of these he wishes to indicate that there is a massive literature in the religions themselves which reflects on prayer, a kind of "meta-prayer" as he calls it. Of course this is part of it, but it should be related to a wider discussion about how many, or what "dimensions" or "aspects" of religion there are, and this would lead us away from our present subject.¹⁸ The positive value of this article lies in its attempt to take account of more modern trends in ritual studies and of the idea that prayer can be "performative" as well as "communicative." In other words, while he is still worrying

---

16 Hastings 1918 X: 195.
17 Eliade 1987 XI: 489.
18 Ninian Smart was increasing the number of "dimensions" in his later years, while I have been trying to keep them limited to four. It is seriously confusing to bring in what Gill calls "meta-prayer" as a separate aspect of the phenomenon of religion, when, as far as the general morphology of religion is concerned, it can easily be included in the wider range of religious conceptuality. It is just a part of religious thinking.

about Heiler even after all these years, it is somehow recognised that there has to be some relation between the older, wide interest in the general history and phenomenology of religion/s and the (relatively) more recent studies about ritual acts or peformances of any kind including speech. Moreover the short paragraph on Buddhism as a "test case" for studies of prayer is very well conceived. He concludes: "It would be more valuable to comprehend specifically the similarities and differences of the various forms and functions of these Buddhist speech acts compared with prayer acts of theistic traditions. In their similarities lies the nature of religion, in their differences lies the distinctiveness of Buddhism among the religious traditions."[19] In spite of these positive aspects of the entry, it is nevertheless surprising that the editors did not require a more extensive treatment of this subject in the new encyclopedia which after so long has displaced the Hastings *Encyclopedia*, itself reprinted in the nineteen-seventies.

In recent research on religion the approach of cognitive analysis has been rather important and is also quite relevant to our subject, as has already been hinted. A writer who has recently offered an introductory account of the general relevance of this approach is Armin Geertz[20] who is selected for mention because he has also used "prayer" in a wider discussion of categorization in the study of religions.[21] Another recent discussion of "prayer" from the point of view of cognitive science is that by psychologist Justin Barrett in a collective volume edited recently by Veikko Anttonen and Illka Pyysiäinen.[22] In general it may be said that cognitive science has introduced some valuable insights to the study of religions, while at the same time making a dramatic reduction in the range of the field being studied.[23] Prayer is a case in point. By writers adopting the cognitivist approach such as Armin Geertz it seems

---

19 Eliade 1987 XI: 491 f.
20 Geertz 2004. This is not the place for a general discussion of the merits and demerits of the currently very fashionable "cognitive science" approach to the study of religions, or of its older starting points.
21 Geertz 2006.
22 Barrett 2005.
23 This comment should *not* be misunderstood. The point made here is *not* about "reductionism" versus "essentialism" or some kind of religious position. It means that the cognitive approach has simply reduced the range of social, cultural and historical phenomena which specialists in the study of religions are otherwise expected, quite rightly, to study.

to be regarded as being entirely verbal.[24] Moreover, even within the range of verbality prayer is regarded almost entirely as consisting of communication with a presumed supernatural being or beings, who are described with heavy anthropomorphism, as by Justin Barrett. As a result of these narrow perceptions, there is a heavy emphasis on petitionary prayer, that is, prayer which expects or beseeches a supernatural agent to do something. This is then carried forward into the questions posed by researchers.[25] One interesting positive result arising from Barrett's research is that when the gods are regarded as relatively unreliable, or fickle, the ritual needs to be very exact. Such divinities are described as "dumb" (that is, in American English, "stupid," rather than "silent," which is what this word means in British English). On the other hand, when a divinity is presumed to be more intelligent or wise, it does not matter, in the minds of religious persons, if the ritual is less accurate. So we can see that specialists in cognitive research are able to produce some helpful analyses. In general however, they seem to be unaware that the promotion of the child's recognition of external agents as a feature of mental development into a general "explanation" of religion leads into a fatal, and often arrogantly defended diminution of the field which they are supposedly researching into. Thus "prayer" is conceived of as a mode of address to spiritual beings, while these beings are presumed by the cognitive scientists to be non-existent and therefore "counter-intuitive." Prayer therefore appears mainly as an example of how religion is based on the propensity of human beings to regard "counter-intuitive" spiritual beings as "agents" in their experience (because the brain is set up in such a way that infants seek to understand the world as populated by agents with whom they have dealings). Consequently, the *varieties* of prayer, or its complexity as a field, are of little interest for cognitive science.

It will go too far afield to survey the innumerable studies in which the various cultural and behavioural sciences have paid attention to ritual, under which prayer is frequently subsumed. Allow me simply to refer to a general problem here, namely that ritual behaviour lends itself to explanatory analyses, whether ethnological or psychological, which do not pay regard to the intentions of the participants. Of course, the analysis of ritual is fascinating. However we must beware of the widespread but ultimately misleading assumption that what people *do* is more

---

24 See Geertz 2006.
25 See for example Barrett 2005: 97.

important than what they *say*. The main problem with this is that it is a half-truth. For one thing, to "say" something is in itself to "do" something. In other words, as has frequently been noted, "prayer," at least when verbal, not infrequently has a performative function. For another thing, the intention of the ritual is very often reflected in the words which accompany it. Indeed, words used, especially when repeated over and over again, themselves influence the way people think and feel. Finally, when intentionality is neglected, the phenomenon of prayer is not understood. It is the recognition of this intentionality which was one of the enduring strengths of the phenomenology of religion, even though in many cases it was fatally flawed by being too closely associated with precisely that intentionality.

Having regard to this very divergent literature relating to prayer, we can see that the subject has suffered from the way in which the study of religions has been promoted in an unbalanced way from various directions.

Some requirements concerning the field

As stated already, adumbration of the field is of prime importance. A limited view of the field may arise because a particular theory is already being held in mind. At this point therefore I would like to emphasise two areas which definitely should not be excluded from consideration if a balanced view is to be achieved.

First, prayer is often not a matter of words but of silence. This is often overlooked in explanatory theories of religion which find it convenient to reduce "prayer" to the petitionary prayer typical of primal religious systems. Of course, prayer frequently takes the form of an address, as in the well-known words "Our Father who is in heaven. Hallowed be your name. Your kingdom come..." (which is also discussed in Geertz 2006). Yet as is also well known, St. Paul emphasised that it is not Christian believers who pray, but the Spirit (i. e. the Holy Spirit) within them. Of course, it is a matter of historical fact that there is a long tradition of petitionary prayer in Christianity, both within the context of ritual and separate from it, and this typically involves words which specify what is requested, as in petitionary prayer. For example: "O God, please let it not rain today!" At the same time there is also a long tradition of silent prayer in Christianity, whether in a ritual context or not. There is the on-going prayer of the individual who participates in liturgy, whether

Catholic, Orthodox, or other. The liturgy involves words, some of the time, but the individual is not always using words. There is also the on-going, if frequently interrupted prayer of the individual through life, sometimes known as "the practice of the presence of God."

Second, *non*-petitionary prayer has a complex relationship to what is widely referred to as meditation. This is not just a matter of silent prayer being in some sense "meditative," as this is known in the Christian tradition. In a quite different area of the history of religions, namely in Mahāyāna Buddhism, we find the phenomenon that ritualized words, i.e. recitations, are used as a form of meditation. These can take on varied features which are otherwise characteristic of much prayer, for example, repetition, self-reflection or confession (in Japanese Buddhism: *sange*), in some cases a certain mode of address, and so on. Two well-known examples in Japanese Buddhism are the *nenbutsu*, addressed to Amida Buddha, and the *daimoku*, apparently addressed to the *Lotus Sūtra*. These will be explored in more detail below. The sustained recitation of the sūtras in general is also relevant here. This is also standard practice in Theravāda Buddhism. The sūtras are commonly recited in the presence of or "before" a focus of devotion such as a Buddha image. But while an external Buddha image may have various interrelated functions, so that one might think that some kind of interaction is taking place, it is frequently also understood as a symbol of the Buddha within every living being. All this recitation is complementary to the tradition of silent meditation otherwise typical of Buddhism (as in *zazen*) and indeed to the exploratory forms of meditation which are widely, if irregularly used in the major Christian traditions. As practised by the Quakers at "Meeting," meditation amounts to a liturgical form in its own right, even though the concept of "liturgy" is formally rejected by Quakers (the Society of Friends), and the meditation is not formally known as meditation.

We must therefore take into account that prayer has a subtle relationship both to language and silence, as well as to ritual practice –as will be explored later by others. However prayer also has a complex relation to meditation, and since no other paper is planned on this aspect a few more words will be said about it now. In particular I would like to include a few details about the relationship between repetitive recitation and prayer. Just mentioned was the well-known example of the *nenbutsu*, found in Pure Land and True Pure Land Buddhism (Shin Buddhism). This may be said in isolation or be repeated as "*Namu Amida Bu(tsu), Namu Amida Bu(tsu), Namu Amida Bu(tsu)*." Historically the *nenbutsu* has been uttered with the most varied of intentions, e.g. to pacify troubled spirits.

It has also been repeated innumerable times. Superficially, Amida Buddha is regarded as a superior being, an "agent" to be addressed. However the meaning of addressing Amida Buddha, who after all is widely understood to be a projection of the human mind, lies in the identification of oneself with the potential Buddha-nature of all living beings who are able to achieve Nirvana following rebirth or "birth" in the Pure Land. In the particular case of Shin Buddhism, it is not regarded as strictly necessary to say or recite the *nenbutsu* at all, but if one does, then the practice is regarded as an expression of *shinjin* (usually left untranslated, but meaning approximately "believing mind," or "mind of faith"). It is often overlooked that the *nenbutsu* is just one of such formulations which are well known in Mahāyāna Buddhism. Many are found, for successive recitation, in the *Sūtra of Buddha Names* (Japanese: *Butsumyōkyō*). A related formulation is the honoured title of the *Lotus Sūtra*, which runs in Japanese *Namu Myōhō Rengekyō* and as mentioned above is known as the *daimoku*. Note the expression *namu* which occurs again here, and which stems (via Chinese) from the Indian word *namas* (via the *sandhi* form *namo*). This implies a form of reverential address. But what is being addressed? It is the sutra itself, rather than any particular supernatural being. Moreover the repeated formula again has the purpose of identifying oneself with, or placing oneself inside the embracing meaning of the sutra, the "Lotus Sūtra of Wonderful Dharma." It is therefore meditational. In the context of popular lay movements such as the Sōka Gakkai it is also petitionary in so far as this-worldly benefits (*genzeriyaku*) are anticipated. However this is secondary to the main understanding common to the *Lotus Sūtra* tradition as a whole.

In fact the whole tradition of repeated reverential expressions is well known in Buddhism, being based on the Indian idea of the *stotra*, a hymn of praise. Nāgārjuna began his profound verses about nothingness with a hymn of praise:

> No arising and no ceasing
> No permanence and no severance
> No identity and no difference
> No arriving and no departing
> To the one who can expound this matter of causality
> And completely extinguish all sophistries
> I bow my head in reverence:
> The Buddha, greatest of all teachers.[26]

---

26 This is Brian Bocking's translation of the opening stanzas of the *The Middle Treatise* (Bocking 1995: 103).

Here we see a combination of reverential *address* with a view of existence which, it must be said, is not exactly based on a superficial, childish, or non-rational belief in supernatural beings.

Moreover, we should not think that this range of phenomena is peculiar to Buddhism alone. Consider the concept of *dhikr* in Islam. This has been wonderfully presented, with special reference to its interpretation by Al-Ghazāli (1058–1111, western calendar), by Nakamura Kōjirō of the University of Tokyo in his work *Ghazali on Prayer* (Nakamura 1973). He writes: "The word *dhikr* (from the verb *dhakara*) literally means 'to remember, recall' and 'to mention, to utter,' that is, both man's mental activity and vocal communication."[27] Now, as Nakamura pointed out elsewhere, this is extremely reminiscent of the *nenbutsu* in East Asian Buddhism. We should consider the character used for the *nen* of *nenbutsu* here, namely: 念, the upper and lower parts of which signify "now" and "mind" respectively. It means holding the Buddha, or God, in mind, *now*. This is exactly what the Muslim is supposed to do, not only, but especially in the mystical tradition represented by Al-Ghazāli.

Apart from translating the ninth, relevant part of Al-Ghazāli's *Ihyā' 'Ulūm al-Dīn*, entitled "The Book of Invocations and Supplications," Nakamura goes on to reflect on five aspects of the use of the term *dhikr* in his thought, and clearly links verbal invocation as for example in the form "Glory to God, and praise be to Him" (*Subhāna 'llāh wa-bi-hamdi-hi*) with inner meditation. Moreover, for Al-Ghazāli, any external merits which the recitation of such prayer might be thought to bring about are of little significance compared with "the special inner state which is induced in the heart of the Sūfī by its repeated utterance" (Nakamura 1973: 14). We can see from this example that verbal prayer may be a necessary stage in the development of a mystically orientated Muslim, but it is certainly of little importance in the later stages. Similar things may be said about the fundamental statement *La ilāha illa 'llāh* ("There is no god but God"). This is prayerful meditation, but not primarily communication.

Why is it that in some cases the petitionary structure of prayer is so important, and in others much less so? There are two explanations for this. The first lies in the general typology of religion. This leads into the correlation of divergences in types of ritual and so on with different types of religion in general. In particular, there is a different range of ritual activity in primal religions and in critical religions. The ritual activity

---

27 Nakamura 1973: 10.

of primal religions is related to the maintainance of the society in question and to occasional proximate soteriology. The ritual activity of critical religions on the other hand, initiates individuals into a saved or transformed community and reinforces their faith in the context of a new life (cf. Pye 1999b, also at 4.5 above). The second reason is that people's perception of the meaning of their religious orientation changes over time in accordance with their mental and psychological development. Thus, with the passage of the years literalism may in many cases recede while other appraisals of the nature of the world and one's place in it come to the fore. It is therefore not necessarily appropriate for prayer as verbal communication to be given pre-eminence; and in particular the observer is ill-advised to explain it as a mode of communication with supernatural beings who may not be thought to exist in the sense presupposed.[28] It is necessary therefore, in studies involving statistics, to take longitudinal studies into account, and this is not often done. It may be hypothesized that with increasing maturity, prayer is likely to be less understood as "asking for things" and more likely to be understood as a meditative process, with or without reference to any particular kind of supernatural beings.

Conclusion

The theme of this symposium has been formulated as "prayer as interaction," but without specifying with whom or what? Of course prayer is often presumed by believers or practitioners to be a kind of "interaction," or even a transaction. They act and speak accordingly. On the other hand, in the study of religions, while we may observe the practitioners' participation in a presumed interaction, we cannot posit that there is any responsive interaction from the other side, that is, on the part of "spiritual beings" or "God," "God the Father," "God the Parent," the Buddha, etc.. In other words, prayer may be understood as interaction, but we should not forget that this depends on the believer or participant and upon his or her conception of God, Buddha, etc. After all, what kind

---

28 The developmental psychology of Jean Piaget was particularly instructive in this regard (cf. Pye 1972), and indeed this aspect is most important for a good understanding of religious education. There is no reason why religious education cannot be a process which leads from simplistic views of religion, such as might be held by a child, into maturity.

of response is expected? In some cases, divine intervention would be appreciated. In many cases however, this is not expected. It is commonly taught that the "answer" to prayers may not correspond to the prayers, though this various from religion to religion. In primal religions, or adapted primal religions such as Shintō, petitionary prayer, especially as a ritual act, is more typical, and it is usually hoped that this will be somehow effective. Moreover, since there is also a significant relationship between prayer and meditation as themes in the study of religions, it is probably better not to over-emphasize the concept of "interaction," but to regard it as a specific sub-theme. In sum, it is important for a fully developed study of religions not to accept the simplistic view that the presumption of the existence of a supernatural or divine being, who will "do something," is a necessary constitutive element of prayer. This would be to fail to perceive the full field of "prayer."

Modern studies of "prayer" can be summarised under three main headings: (1) essentialist, phenomenological studies which are close to religious thought or theology (Heiler), (2) cognitivist or other sociometric studies which limit "prayer" to the simplistic pattern of petitions to supernatural beings, regarding it as verbal (Geertz, Barrett), and (3) wide-ranging typologies of prayer (Gill, Flasche). Of these, only the third approach seems likely to provide any basis for worthwhile further research. However, the typology needs to be extended to include the significant areas of non-verbal and non-communicational prayer, and meditation. Particularly in this further area, definitions and methodologies may not seem easy to define. This, however, is the challenge for the future.

Bibliographical references

Auffarth, C., Bernard, J. and Mohr, H. (eds.) 2000. *Metzler Lexikon Religion. Gegenwart – Alltag – Medien.* Stuttgart (J.B.Metzler).

Barrett, Justin L. 2005. "Dumb gods, petitionary prayer and the cognitive science of religion" in: Anttonen, V., and Pyysiäinen, I. (eds.) *Current Approaches in the Cognitive Science of Religion*, London and New York (Continuum): 93–109.

Bocking, Brian 1995. *Nāgārjuna in China, A Translation of the Middle Treatise.* Ceredigion (Scholars' Press).

Cancik, H., Gladigow, B. und Kohl, K-H. 1990–98. *Handbuch religionswissenschaftlicher Grundbegriffe.* Stuttgart/Berlin/Köln (Kohlhammer).

Eliade, Mircea (ed.) 1987. *Encyclopedia of Religion.* New York and London (Macmillan).

Geertz, Armin 2004. "Cognitive Approaches to the Study of Religion" in: Antes, P. Geertz, A.W. and Warne, R. (eds.) *New Approaches in the Study of Religion. Volume 2: Textual, Comparative, Sociological, and Cognitive Approaches.* Berlin (de Gruyter): 347–399.
– 2006. "Etude comparée des religions: Réflexions sur la science, les universaux et la condition humaine" " " in: Burger, M., Calame, C. (eds.) *Comparer les comparatismes. Perspectives sur l'histoire et les sciences des religions*, Paris and Milano (Etudes de Lettres): 75–111.
Goldammer, Kurt 1960. *Die Formenwelt des Religiösen.* Stuttgart (Alfred Kröner).
Hampp, Irmgard 1961. *Beschwörung, Segen, Gebet. Untersuchungen zum Zauberspruch aus dem Bereich der Volksheilkunde.* Stuttgart (Silberburg Verlag).
Harton, F.P. 1932. *The Elements of the Spiritual Life. A Study in Ascetical Theology.* London (SPCK).
Hastings, James (ed.) 1918. *Encyclopaedia of Religion and Ethics* Edinburgh (T. and T. Clarke).
Heiler, Friedrich 1919 (dissertation 1917) *Das Gebet. Eine religionsgeschichtliche und religionspsychologische Untersuchung.* München (E. Reinhardt).
– 1918. *Die buddhistische Versenkung. Eine religionsgeschichtliche Untersuchung.* München (E. Reinhardt).
Nakamura, Kōjirō 1973. *Ghazali on Prayer.* Tokyo (Institute of Oriental Culture, University of Tokyo).
Pye, Michael 1972a. *Comparative Religion: An Introduction through Source Materials.* Newton Abbot (David and Charles) and New York (Harper and Row).
– 1997c. "Perceptions of the body in Japanese religion" in: Coakley, Sarah (ed.) *Religion and the Body.* Cambridge (Cambridge University Press): 248–261.
– 1997d. "Friedrich Heiler (1892–1967)" in: Michaels, A. (ed.) *Klassiker der Religionswissenschaft. Von Friedrich Schleiermacher bis Mircea Eliade.* München (Beck): 277–289 and 399–400 (footnotes).
– 1999b "Soteriological orientations in religion" in: Tenri Organizing Committee of Tenrikyo-Christian Dialogue (eds.), *Tenrikyo-Christian Dialogue*, Tenri City (Tenri University Press): 99–113.
Scheele, Paul-Werner 1960. Opfer des Wortes. Gebete der Heiden aus fünf Jahrtausenden. Paderborn (Schöningh).
Staal, Frits 1996. Ritual and Mantras: *Rules Without Meaning.* Delhi (Motilal Barnasidass).

This paper was first published as "Research on prayer in the contemporary study of religions" in: Hashimoto, Taketo (ed.) *Prayer as Interaction. (Tenri University and Marburg University Joint Research Project September 2006).* Tenri (Tenri University Press) 2007: 3–28.

4.8 Purification and Transformation in Comparative Perspective

This paper was a keynote lecture for a joint Tenri/Marburg symposium on the theme "Purification: Religious Transformations of Mind and Body" held at Tenri University, Japan, in September 2010. It appears here in slightly reduced and modified form. The paper was originally entitled "Conceptual patterns in the analysis of religious transformations."

Conceptual orientation

The title of the symposium, *Purification: Religious Transformations of Mind and Body*, suggests an extremely rich subject matter, and it will surely be easier if we begin with some systematic orientations and conceptual clarifications. Even if not all who are present agree on these in detail, the points of reference may be useful for the articulation of debate. With this in mind, this introductory lecture is broadly based and will have just a few examples to illustrate the intended perspective.

First let me note that our main term "purification" has been used for a long time with a wide spectrum of associations, starting at one end with release from ritual pollution, and suggesting at the other end an entirely spiritualised ideal of perfection. There are many cases which fall somewhere in between, depending on the context of various religious systems. Let us look first at the two opposite ends of the spectrum of usage.

The concept of purification has a long history in conjunction with opposing terms such as pollution or taboo (*tapu*). In this sense it has played a widespread, if not universal role in the study of "primal religions" or, as some prefer, "indigenous religions," terms which will receive further comment below. Most generally stated, in these cases it is ritual separation which is above all important. The objective, in summary characterization, is to identify and secure an area or a realm of ritual purity, and hence of ritual security and ritual effectiveness.

Any visit to a Shintō shrine will illustrate this, because the first thing which visitors to the sacred area do is to rinse their mouth and their hands with water at the *temizuya*, just inside the entrance to the grounds. If the visit is a more formal one, that is, if a family or some other group are led in offerings and prayer by a priest inside the prayer hall, then the first thing the latter will do is to ask the assembly to bow their heads for the performance of *o-harae*. This is a ritual purification symbolised by the waving of a wand to which large strips of white paper are attached. In such cases, the whiteness symbolises purity. For a similar reason, the ends of beams used in the construction of Shintō shrines are sometimes painted in white.[1] The sacred area, or as one may equally say, the taboo area, is also separated off as a pure area, marked by various kinds of boundary symbols such as the *torii* (symbolic gateway) or the *shimenawa* (a rope of symbolic separation suspended above the shrine entrance), to which white strips of paper (*gohei*) are usually affixed. Thus, as far as purification is concerned the main conceptions in the context of Shintō are clearly concerned with separation, a common feature of primal religion. Shintō, as we now know it, is a primal religious system which has been adapted to modern times.[2] Though it no longer has a complete claim on Japanese society at large, it continues to have a broad social base, and more significantly, claims to have one.

The concept of ritual purification is extremely wide-spread in the history of religions and scarcely needs specific documentation here. Suffice it to recall the extreme detail of purification procedures in historically complex religions such as Judaism, notably in the book of Leviticus, and in Zoroastrianism, which is an even more complex case in that the concept of purification itself leads into major questions of spiritual attitude and development.

To a certain extent the same intention can also be seen in liturgies which were developed much later, while drawing on ancient religious custom to a certain extent. In the Anglican churches for example, before the priests or deacons enter the church area set aside for liturgical use, they will usually wash their hands, put on a white cloak (alb), possibly sound a gong, say a short introductory prayer in private, and only then become visible to the assembled congregation. So they are enacting *a visualised separation* from the profane world from which they came, before carrying out their specific functions within the liturgy. We should

---

1 This does not imply that white always has this connotation in the Japanese context. It can also symbolise death as in the shirts of pilgrims who are provisionally dead to the world.
2 Cf. Pye 1989c (and 4.4 above).

notice however that "purification" as such is here no longer the dominant theme. Rather, it is a matter of mental preparation, and of indicating to others that this mental preparation has been carried out in order to create confidence in the wider assembly.

Moving along to the other end of the spectrum, we may notice that taken literally the term "purification" implies an *action*, as is evident from its etymology. Now it is one thing to purify a separate, restricted space, or those who enter it. But if we take purification in conjunction with "transformation," as in "transformations of mind and body" (the symposium theme) the locus of meaning shifts considerably. The term can then take on meanings which are related less to ritual demarcations, which are above all socially significant, and more to a process of individual religious development. It is one thing to purify by means of ritual separation or exclusion. It is a very different thing personally to seek a kind of spiritual purification, in mind and body, as a religious process in the experience of the individual. I would therefore like to propose that these are two very different kinds of "purification". Not surprisingly, these two main kinds of "purification" can be linked to the wider typology of religions. Moreover, just as in the general typology of religious systems, there are in-between cases which require careful elucidation.

Purification and the wider typology of religions

These matters may seem rather evident to some, but it still sometimes seems to be necessary to point out that there are two main types of religion, of which the characteristics vary accordingly. Attention is drawn here a table which was first shown at the "Tenrikyō-Christian dialogue" held at the Gregorian University in Rome in March 1998. This table, included in Pye 1999b (and 4.5 above) sets out the two main types of religion, primal religion and critical religion, but without specific reference to purification. To understand the relevant positioning of purification in relation to these categories, the table should be consulted.

First a few general comments may be permitted. Although it has not become widely popular, I stand by the term "primal religion". It is intended to be more precise than merely referring to "folk religion", for example, or more recently "common religion", etc. Reader and Tanabe rejected the term "primal religion" on the grounds that "primal" could be confused with "primitive".³ It is difficult to see how we can make theoretical progress when different words are wilfully confused! It is quite acceptable if some authors prefer other terminology, but on the other hand expressions such as "common religion" or "indigenous religion/s" are inherently ambiguous. The expression "common religion" can either mean "vulgar" in the sense of "of the people" or it can mean "shared by" various parties. It is therefore fatally unclear. As to "indigenous religions," recently promoted by James Cox with special reference to the African context, the expression seems to have a sociological ambiguity in that new religions which significantly differentiate themselves from an underlying religious pattern in any one society could also be regarded as indigenous by outsiders to that society.⁴ In the Japanese context for example, we might say that Kurozumikyō or Konkōkyō are indigenous new religions, for they are not imported from outside. However, they are typologically quite distinct from the primal religion of the country. They distance themselves in their own specific ways from the underlying generality of Japanese religious culture. Because of such difficulties, I prefer the term "primal religion" for the latter.⁵

The main types referred to above are of course ideal types, to use the phrase of Max Weber, and while they can sometimes be seen in a very clear form, we also have to reckon with a certain "crossing over" of characteristics.⁶ I prefer not simply to say "mixed types" since this would be an admission that the typology does not work properly. For example, as debated by James Dator, is the Sōka Gakkai a "sect" or a "cult" or both?⁷ On the contrary, the crossing over of characteristics occurs for particular reasons in the dynamic context of historical developments. The apparent complexities do not affect the validity of the "types" but simply mean that we have to think about the characteristics carefully.

---

3   Reader and Tanabe 1998:27. The espousal of the term "common religion" here seems to go back to the usage of Robert Towler at Leeds, England, who was trying to find an alternative for "popular religion," cf. Towler 1974: 149.
4   For a spirited espousal of the expression however see Cox 1977.
5   For a presentation of the key features of Japanese primal religion see Pye 2004a and 2009c.
6   On the notion of cross-overs between the main types see Pye 1999b (and at 7.2 below).
7   Dator 1969.

In terms of these two main types, with consequential differentiations, how does "purification" fit in? Or rather, how are practices and processes associated with purification to be correlated with the overall typology? In fact, this is not so difficult to see. We have a determining starting point in the differentiation of ritual types, and the range of actions and attitudes which falls under "purification" quite naturally spreads across the same pattern of differentiation.

For example:

(i) Purification for demarcation and the creation of identity and security (with or without water, e.g. Orthodox house rite for protection against malign influences from the four quarters)
(ii) Purification as proximate salvation (in both primal and critical religion)
(iii) Purification in the rites of initiation to a soteriological community (baptism in Christianity being an obvious case) which is a once-only matter.
(iv) Purification in reinforcement rites (Zoroastrian purification rites and Mandaean repeated baptism, adducing John the Baptist). Standing under waterfalls in the Japanese Shugendō is thought of not just as arduous but also as purificatory of the "six roots" of karma (*rokkon shōjō*).

Japanese examples

Again, it is relevant here to provide specific examples of relevant Japanese terminology. In view of the above typological considerations, it is not at all surprising that, while some kind of "purification" is a major concept in several religious traditions of Japan, there are different words for it and indeed different understandings of it. The *harae* or *kiyome* of Shintō ritual is something which is usually performed *for* one, often by a priest who is in charge. It just takes place, to the satisfaction of the priest himself, for it is he (or rarely she) who is responsible for the purity of the demarcated, taboo place. Relatively little attention is paid to the attitude of the other participants. Of course, they are expected to be respectful, and some will no doubt feel moved in some way, mentally set at peace for a short time, and brought into a state in which they will not disturb the ritual purity.

By contrast, consider the expression *rokkon shōjō* or "purification of the six roots", referred to above, which is current in some of the Buddhist traditions of Japan, especially in the esoteric Shingon denominations. This definitely refers to the matter of one's own personal discipline and achievement. The idea of the purification of the six roots is also widely current in the context of the Shingon-related Shugendō, the semi-Buddhist tradition of mountain asceticism where there is a general assumption that hard practice, *shugyō*, will surely lead to transformatory results. Emphasis on such a process has been part of the long-term indigenisation process of Buddhism in Japan.

Somewhere between politics and folklore there is a wide area of religious activity and orientation in contemporary Japan which can fairly be referred to as "Shintō". But what is Shintō? One way of working out an answer to this question is to take the "shrines" (*jinja*, etc.) as a basic starting point, and indeed this is a firm assumption in the Shintō world itself. Since there are very many shrines throughout the whole country which are recognisable institutions and which are grouped together in associations, notably the Association of Shintō Shrines (Jinja Honchō), it is quite a reasonable approach to start here. However Shintō is not just a question of institutions. In connection with a pilgrimage around the shrines of Shimozuke (in eastern Japan), the leaflet containing all the information about them also has a short statement on "how to visit shrines", and this gives some indication of the meaning which is considered to underlie the practice, a meaning which is espoused by the institutions. Though typical, it is just a little more explicit than the statements which are sometimes seen, common though they are. So how does one visit a shrine or, that is, perform *o-mairi*[8]? What is one's appropriate attitude towards a divinity or *kami*?

> "Here is a simple explanation of how to do *o-mairi*. First purify your hands and mouth at the water stand (*temizuya*) and proceed to the front of the main shrine[9]. Offer a coin and ring the bell. The bell has the meaning of attracting the attention of the *kami-sama* and of cleanly purifying oneself. Making your petition within your breast, do two bows, two claps and one bow. In bowing deeply twice, clapping the hands twice, and at the

---

8 That is, here, to perform a visit to a Shintō shrine, although the word is also used more widely in various religious contexts.
9 The *honden*. Usually the building before which individual prayers are offered is known as the *haiden*, behind which a smaller *honden* is situated. In some larger shrines it is also possible to walk round and stand in front of the *honden*, where the *kami* is presumed to reside.

end making one more bow and then withdrawing, it is most important, above all, to do *o-mairi* with a grateful heart."

Clearly a dominant level of meaning is to be seen in the wish to receive, and ensure this-worldly benefits. These are often set out in detail. However the opportunity is also taken to instruct visitors in the correct manner of visiting a Shintō shrine. Moreover it is emphasized that, above all, the visit should be carried out with a sense of gratitude. That is to say, even while the mood of the visitor may be one of expectation, the complementary attitude of gratitude for favours received is presented as being even more important. Note however that "gratitude" is a value which is also generally current, in Japan, in what is usually referred to by observers as civil religion. The specifically Shintō note is added by the emphasis on ritual and inner purity.

While an emphasis on purity is clearly promoted by the Shintō purification rituals (*harae* or *kiyome*) the "purification" of the heart, or of one's being, is an intention which is not restricted to Shintō alone. Indeed the *yamabushi* 山伏 and related mountain traditions which are conveyed within and between Buddhism and Shintō (i. e. Shugendō) are known for their emphasis on the "purification of the six roots" (*rokkon shōjō* 六根清浄) mentioned above. In this expression the "six roots" refer to the six sense organs, traditionally listed (in Buddhism) as eye, ear, nose, tongue, body and mind. By "body" is meant the physical basis of all sensory perception, i. e. physical feeling, which escapes further definition, and by "mind" is meant the organ of conceptual perception, this usually being regarded in Buddhist analyses as the sixth of six senses. It is possible to take *rokkon shōjō* as an entirely Buddhist notion. However it just happens to fit conveniently also with the Shintō concept of purity, while leading one somehow beyond it into the Buddhist area. This probably accounts for its widespread use not only in Shingon Buddhism and among the *yamabushi* of Shugendō, but also among groups of Shintō-oriented pilgrims, for example on the three mountains in northern Japan known as Dewa Sanzan (Haguro-san, Gassan, and Yudono-san).[10] The full phrase recited is *zange zange rokkon shōjō* 懺悔懺悔六根清浄 i. e. "penitence, penitence, purify the six roots".

In part because of this motivation and impetus towards personal transformatory processes within the Buddhist tradition, we may also re-

---

10 Cf. Pye and Triplett 2007; and for an illustration of such pilgrims see Pye 2004a, frontispiece.

mark shifts of emphasis in the wider field of religious activities influenced by Shintō. As with other primal religious systems, so too has Shintō provided a matrix for the appearance of new and independent soteriologies, religious options which answer to a sense of dissatisfaction with the on-going life as usually experienced at the level of primal religion. Normally, within Shintō, there is no need for religious "enthusiasm", no need for personal conversion or transformation, no need for any special kind of spiritual development beyond normal psychological maturation. Precisely this however is offered by various new religions which include ideas and routines of purification in their activities. The group of religions known as World Messianity (Sekai Kyūseikyō) for example, focuses on a daily practice of mutual *jōrei*, a distinctive term usually left untranslated within the group itself in communication with its foreign members, and so highlighted as a special one.[11] It means approximately "purification of the spirit" although it is also considered to bring physical benefits to the sick.

Hardly known today, but a thoroughly relevant example for typological consideration, is the religion known as Misogi-kyō, which means nothing less than "The Teaching of Purification." This was a movement for enthusiasts who engaged in multiple washings of the body in order to experience a sense of religious concentration, a transformation of their being from its state in ordinary life. In 1973 it was possible to see a place just outside Ise Shrine (usually thought of as the most important of all Shintō shrines), very close to the main bridge which forms the entrance through which all must pass, where such ablutions were possible. There was a lowered area in which the practitioners could stand and where the water which they used would run off. All around were large wooden ladles, rather like those used in a traditional bath house. This arrangement has not survived however. The whole area before the shrine, outside the sacred area, has been steadily redeveloped as a tourist road. On recent visits informants have consistently claimed complete ignorance of any such religion as Misogi-kyō, or its facilities just outside the shrine. Clearly the group had been eased away from the area by pressure from the shrine authorities. This in turn illustrates that a separate, special transformatory process for just some individuals who think of themselves as special is not regarded as appropriate in relation to Shintō as such.

---

11 The spelling *johrei* will also be found in publications by this religious group.

On the other hand, the previously mentioned use of the term *rokkon shōjō* by the group of Shintō-oriented pilgrims on Gassan, mentioned above, to describe the intention of their arduous journey, is a further example of the way in which critical, transformatory religious patterns can be crystallised within the primal religious pattern. In complex societies, this primal pattern is constantly subject to pressure and stimulation from the various "critical" religions, i.e. from religious orientations which demand or seek for more than is normally available in life's natural routines. The precise status of such "Shintō" pilgrims is unclear, and this ambiguity, which is typologically speaking prior to the emergence of a full-blown new religion, is facilitated by the arrangement known in Japanese as a *kō*, a religious interest group. Such groups are often formed specifically to perform religious journeys, which are in turn thought to contribute to the spiritual development or transformation of the individual in mind and body.

The very idea of a religious development in the individual is much stronger in some kinds of religion than in others, so that it is necessary to coordinate that too with any consideration of the general typology of religions. If it is an individual process which involves both body and mind, then it will involve matters not only of a "spiritual" kind, as they are sometimes referred to in religious contexts, but also of a behavioural kind, ritual or otherwise. The phrases "mind and body" or "body and mind" are quite convenient expressions in English, but what do they hide? In other words, what exactly is the locus of religious or spiritual transformation in any one case? A well known Japanese expression is *sokushin jōbutsu* 即身成仏, "attaining buddhahood in this very body," which sounds clear enough, yet we have to remember that a state of buddhahood is at the same time a state of mind or consciousness, and is so presented in Buddhist contexts. So there is a close connection between mind and body. Indeed, if we think of the expression *shikishin funi* 色心不二 which is typical of Mahāyāna Buddhism, we are reminded that "form" (which includes body) and "consciousness" are non-dual.

Logocentricity and the body

We sometimes hear scornful references to "logocentricity", especially with respect to western Christianity. It may be that this is justified with respect to some variations of Protestantism, and in so far as it is so, then it may be argued that this arose because of the problem of authority in the church and the consequent emphasis on the Biblical writings as the preferred locus of authority, over against the papacy or even councils. This in turn led in Protestant sectarianism, to what may be called Biblicism, typical of the North American religious scene, a form of Christianity which fails to make the dialectical distinction between the New and the Old Testaments, and treats all biblical writings as being of equal status and even literal validity. However logocentricity is not typical of all Christianity. Indeed, in the major historic forms of Christianity there has usually been a very strong consciousness of the body as the essential locus of spiritual endeavour or spiritual growth. This can be seen in the long tradition of Christian asceticism, however imperfectly striven for. In so far as asceticism was rejected in the classical Protestantism of the historic Reformation, as an expression of the "works" through which nothing can be achieved except failure, there was in a sense a rejection of the relevance of the body for the spiritual life. On the other hand, the subsequent rejection of the body as such in the Puritan way of life, following some indications in the epistles of the New Testament, eventually gave way in favour of a new, apparently secularised centrality of the body in western culture, as seen in later modern times. How was this possible? The usual idea is that mediaeval concepts of the body as a suitable object of mortification were replaced, at least for some, by the revival of classical aesthetics during the Renaissance. At the same time however, we may see in the Protestant rejection of asceticism, because of its supposed contribution to a heretical reliance on "works", a freeing of the body from urgent theological and spiritual relevance. This freeing of the body, after the passing of the age of puritanism, ultimately led to its rediscovery as a new locus of spiritual value, as can be seen in the sustained interest in yogic meditation, mystical dance, neo-shamanic adventures, and so on, in the second half of the twentieth century and onwards till today. Room has even been made for this broad movement in various ways by the mainstream Christian churches. The result is that the idea of "religion" as being a purely cerebral or logocentric matter has long lost favour. Indeed, it has rarely if ever been specifically advanced as such, except in a certain way by the fundamentalist, Biblicist stream mentioned earlier. Even in such contexts, the so-called pentecostalist variations make considerable use of the body, although purely imitative and often strongly manipulative forms are usually dominant.

Spirituality as a contestable concept

The word "spiritual" and its cognates have now appeared several times. This term is of course contentious, just as the terms "religion" or "religious" have often been contentious. In the study of religions we are used to this. So what, especially in connection with the current theme, is the relationship between these leading terms? Recently there has been a strong trend to separate "religion" and "spirituality", sometimes by default, but sometimes by driving an intended wedge between them. According to this fashion, the area of "religion" is scorned, while something called "spirituality" is held in high esteem. This seems to be mainly because of a popular assumption that "religion" is something to do with "belief," or with "beliefs", and even more specifically with beliefs which cannot be entertained rationally. This assumption is even shared by clever people such as cognitive scientists who gleefully explain just how it is that "religious" people carry irrational beliefs in their heads about "supernatural agents". By contrast it is assumed (though not by cognitivists) that "spirituality" is a matter of the higher heart, somehow elevated and not conceptually limited, neither falsifiable nor verifiable, and therefore not really subject to any rational critique or even any intellectual systematisation. This loose usage has been taken up as a slogan-like catch-all for social scientists to claim major funding for new studies of "spirituality", thus cutting out those who would study such an out-of-date and discredited matter as "religion." From the point of the view of the study of religions, or Religionswissenschaft, such assumptions should of course be roundly rejected. There are two good reasons for thinking otherwise.

First, the area which is nowadays referred to as "spirituality" is of course not at all new, but has always been an aspect of religion. Even the term itself (in western languages) has a long pedigree. It is not for nothing that a Maurice F. Wiles' book about the interpretation of the Gospel of St. John in the early church was entitled *The Spiritual Gospel* (Wiles 1959), picking up the Greek term *pneumatikos* used by Christians and Gnostics alike. So there is nothing new about "spirituality."

Second, these matters are all best understood in terms of a correlation of the major aspects or dimensions of "religion," which can be defined and correlated most economically as four groupings: (i) the conceptual and symbolic, ii) the social and institutional, (iii) the behavioural and ritual, and (iv) the subjective and attitudinal. Sometimes one or other of these main aspects is emphasised, and this is quite natural when the study of religions is regarded as an interdisciplinary exercise. However it goes wrong when one of the four main aspects is highlighted to such an extent that another is lost from view. When people refer to "spirituality" they are usually highlighting the subjective and attitudinal aspect of religion, possibly with some reference to the conceptual and symbolic aspect as well. So when the term "spirituality" is used as a designation for a *pars pro totum*, distortion occurs, one aspect being picked out to stand for the whole. And the word used in this apparently fresh sounding sense is not in fact adding anything. It is like saying, "We aren't going to study fungi any more, and certainly not mycology; we're going to study mushrooms. So please fund us!" On the other hand, in so far as account might be taken of all four main aspects of religion, the study of "spirituality" would simply be a replacement for the study of religions, with no scientific advantage.

Insofar as there is an acceptable usage of the term "spirituality" in the study of religions, in the context of *Religionswissenschaft*, it would be a usage which intentionally focuses, quite strongly, on the subjective/attitudinal aspect of religion, even while taking account of the connecting threads to the other main aspects of religion: the conceptual/symbolic, the ritual/behavioural and the social/institutional aspects. In this case, spirituality could be a rival or a replacement for "religiosity," as often used by social scientists to refer to the subjective/attitudinal aspect of religion. Although we are not talking about systematic or pastoral theology here,[12] "spirituality" as a term highlights the positive intentionality of the religious persons whose experience is under study. There is no harm in that. It simply throws the emphasis on the initial tasks of recognition and characterization in the study of religions, work undertaken by those now regarded as having formed the "phenomenological school", rather than on the subsequent tasks of analysis and explanation, which are more characteristic of those who nowadays claim to represent the "empirical" social sciences. In fact, all of these tasks belong to the study of religion: recognition (of the phenomena), characterization, analysis and explanation. However, these matters concerning the methodology of the study of religions have been set out elsewhere.[13]

---

[12] This aside was necessary in the original context of the paper because of the range of participants present.

[13] Among the papers in Part One of the present work, see especially "Methodological integration in the study of religions" (1.2) and the diagram in "Getting

Purification and transformation

Returning to the overall title of this symposium therefore, it seems to me that by using these words, *Religious Transformations of Mind and Body*, we are establishing a certain focus. By referring to "transformations" we are pointing, by preference, to religious systems where purification is understood as a process which changes individuals as they go along through life. Such processes are typical of what I call "critical" religions. On the other hand we are not interested so much in demarcations between the profane and the taboo, however important these are in the primal religious systems for which such distinctions are typical. Moreover we are, on the other hand, conscious of the totality of the human person who is involved in transformatory processes, regarding mind and body as inseparable. The implication of this is that when religious teachers emphasise "the body" we will at the same time look for the patterns of interpretation which they bring with them. For example in Buddhist meditation we will take note of the underlying metaphysics which goes with it, even if it is "non-metaphysics". There is hardly any such thing as "just" doing meditation, supposedly without any conceptual presuppositions at all. In this regard the meditation suttas of the Theravāda Canon are of considerable relevance. And when religious teachers emphasise "mind" we will note carefully how they understand the relationship between consciousness and thought processes. This will link up with the way in which we explore the connecting threads between the subjective/attitudinal and the conceptual/symbolic aspects of religion. In this way we can follow through the patterns of spirituality found in various religious contexts, and understand how acts of conscious purification can lead to transformative processes, whether gradual or in discontinuous steps.

Bibliographical references

Cox, James L. 1977. From Primitive to Indigenous: The Academic Study of Indigenous Religions. Aldershot (Ashgate).
Dator, James Allan 1969. *Soka Gakkai.Builders of The Third Civilization. American and Japanese Members*, Seattle (University of Washington Press).

into trouble with the believers. Intimacy and distance in the study of religions" (1.6).

Pye, Michael 1989c. "Shintō and the typology of religion" in: *Method & Theory in the Study of Religion* 1(2): 186–95.
- 1995a "Religion and identity: clues and threads" in: de Gruchy, J. W. and Martin S. (eds.) *Religion and the Reconstruction of Civil Society (Papers from the founding congress of the South African Academy of Religion, January 1994)*. Pretoria (University of South Africa): 3–17. (Also at 7.2 below.)
- 1999b "Soteriological orientations in religion" in: Tenri Organizing Committee of Tenrikyo-Christian Dialogue (eds.), *Tenrikyo-Christian Dialogue*, Tenri City (Tenri University Press) : 99–113.
- 2004a. *The structure of religious systems in contemporary Japan: Shintō variations on Buddhist pilgrimage. (Occasional Papers 30)*. Marburg (Centre for Japanese Studies).
- 2009c. "Leading patterns in everyday Japanese religion" in: *Sphinx, Yearbook 2008–9* (Societas Scientiarum Fennica): 45–53.

Pye, Michael and Triplett, Katja 2007. *Streben nach Glück. Schicksalsdeutung und Lebensgestaltung in japanischen Religionen* (Mit Beiträgen von Monika Schrimpf) Berlin (LIT-Verlag).

Reader, Ian and Tanabe, George 1998. *Practically Religious. Worldly Benefits and the Common Religion of Japan*. Honolulu (University of Hawaii Press).

Towler, Robert 1974. *Homo Religiosus: Sociological Problems in the Study of Religion*. London (Constable).

Wiles, Maurice F. 1959. *The Spiritual Gospel. The Interpretation of the Fourth Gospel in the Early Church*. Cambridge (Cambridge University Press).

This paper is also due to appear in the relevant conference proceedings, planned for 2012.

Part Five
Tradition and Innovation

5.1 Introduction to Part Five

Readers who have taken note of the emphasis on the "dynamics" of religious systems in earlier parts of this collection will not be surprised to find that special attention is now being paid to both tradition and innovation. Innovation is obviously a dynamic matter. In the usage proposed here, so too is tradition, for it means not just something which is somehow stuck in the past, but a process of on-going transmission. This always involves adjustments and creative developments of various kinds, and so the process of tradition itself leads into innovation. Thus we do not have a question about innovation over against tradition, but a question of the coherence of tradition as a transmission process and the strains and stresses which lead to separations and to the emergence of new religious patterns, systems and institutions.

These matters, it is argued, especially in the short piece "Religious tradition and the student of religion" (5.2), need to be thought about with particular sensitivity by those engaged in the study of religions, for while not being committed to any transmission process themselves, as observers, they do need to be looking over the shoulder of those for whom these processes are important, or who are in any way caught up in them. In this sense, the article seeks to establish "tradition" as a workable category in the comparative study of religions today. A general affinity with the ideas set out in parts of "On comparing Buddhism and Christianity" (4.2 above) will be evident.

While the writer's own perceptions of these matters are largely drawn precisely from "looking over the shoulder" of those who forwardly convey religious systems, in the field, it is of course also instructive to see how earlier writers have dealt with these matters, with greater or less success. This is taken up in "Ernst Troeltsch and Gerardus van de Leeuw on tradition" (5.3). Here it can be seen how a phenomenological approach on the one hand (van der Leeuw) and a theologically oriented, but historical approach on the other hand (Troeltsch) have contributed to the highlighting of "tradition" in certain ways. Critical reflection on the approaches of these two writers is instructive for the understanding of the background to more recent work.

This category also has intimate links with the problematics of innovation in religion. With the term "innovation" we shift the parameters of attention beyond the popular subject of so-called "new religions" alone in order (a) to understand the latter in the wider context of religious shifts and developments among religions which are apparently already well established, and (b) to highlight the various innovations which are constantly being tested in processes of transmission, that is, tradition in the sense of handing forward. What is often lacking in research into "new religions", which are one feature of religious innovation, is any theoretical or well-grounded connection with the general processes of innovation which are characteristic of all processes of religious tradition or transmission. In "Elements of a general theory of innovation in religion" (5.4, first published here) a coordinating framework is therefore provided which links these things together. This is of necessity presented in a highly abstract manner, though with some examples. It is expected however that readers will be able to slot their own specialised knowledge on to this generic comparative matrix.

In order to overcome any impression of mere ungrounded abstraction, the remaining articles in this part provide illustrative case studies of "new religions," this term being used with some care. We continue therefore with a broadly conceived piece on "New religions in East Asia" (5.5). Here the interconnectedness of various aspects of religious innovation over a wide cultural area is brought out, with brief examples. It is well known that in Europe and America new religions or "new religious movements" have caused a certain amount of consternation, because of a perceived threat to established religions, and have therefore spawned a new research industry devoted to them, notably using the ill-advised abbreviation NRMs. It is important to realize that in other parts of the world, notably in East Asia, the emergence of new religions is not at all regarded as astonishing in itself, even if some movements are regarded by political and other authorities as undesirable.

Next we turn to two specific cases which have an unclear relation to what is otherwise thought of as "Buddhism." In "Won Buddhism as a Korean new religion" (5.6) an introductory account is given of this under-researched modern movement. It will be noticed that the terms "Buddhism" and "new religion" both occur in this title and, interestingly, this is in fact something which is entirely acceptable to representatives of the religion. Apart from its great intrinsic interest, therefore, this example throws us back into the delicate relations between tradition (i.e. the forward tradition or transmission of Buddhism) and innovation with institutional implications. This in turn requires us to reflect on whether a particular movement can really be counted as "Buddhist" or not, a question which researchers cannot simply dismiss as being not their business. Quite apart from a general responsibility on the part of scientists in any field to give public answers when occasion demands, the question of the relationship with preceding tradition arises when reflecting on the coherence or otherwise of transmission processes. Without such awareness and reflection, the history of religions would become completely impossible. To illustrate this same problem again from a more controversial angle, the case of the Japanese religion Aum Shinrikyō is adduced. While found to have been guilty of major criminal activities attracting a number of death penalties, the leaders of this group also claimed to be "Buddhist." Such a claim can hardly be left unremarked. Would we include a chapter on Aum Shinrikyō in a history of Japanese Buddhism? Probably not. The article, "Aum Shinrikyō. Can Religious Studies cope?" (5.7), also raises in a quite specific way some of the general questions of methodology and the researcher's relations to the field which were dealt with in Volume One, especially in connection with the "tension with believers factor" (1.6).

Although the writer's researches and teaching have also included various other Japanese new religions, in particular the Risshō Kōseikai and the Byakkō Shinkōkai, it is thought best to continue here by broadening the perspective in another way. The very process of transmission, which is what tradition amounts to, involves varied adaptive tactics and new combinations of relevant elements. We conclude Part Five therefore with some interesting examples of the way in which certain new religions from Japan have been relocated in Brazil among both long-standing immigrant communities and new Brazilian converts (5.8). Finally, it may be noted that many features of the underlying theoretical patterns of tradition and innovation advanced in the course of these papers are relevant to the discussion of transplantation and syncretism which will follow later in Part Six.

5.2 Religious Tradition and the Student of Religion

This paper arose in connection with an international conference of the Danish Association for the Study of Religions at the University of Aarhus in May 1987. It was written after the conference as an introductory statement for the proceedings edited by Armin W. Geertz and Jeppe Sinding Jensen. As it says in the preface to the proceedings, "One of the goals of the conference was to nurture a dialogue between historians of religion and social anthropologists from various European countries." For this, the concept of "tradition" is a crucial pivot. Light redactional changes have been made here.

In search of "tradition"

It is a remarkable fact that the nature of tradition, which in one way or another is crucial for the understanding of so many religious situations, has not been the subject of sustained analysis on the part of specialists in the study of religions. The word itself is frequently used, but all too often it is allowed to suggest something static, left over from the past and subject to the strains and stresses of a present which is thought to be different and new. At the same time aspects of religion which are evidently dynamic are considered under other headings such as interaction, renewal, or change. It is salutary however to recall the underlying meaning of the word "tradition," namely, "giving across," deriving ultimately from latin *trans* and *dare*. This is clearly brought out in the German term *Überlieferung,* which literally means "handing over." Admittedly, the term *Überlieferung* is also sometimes used unthinkingly, just as "tradition" is used in English (and indeed "Tradition" in German too), to refer to a cultural entity which has been handed down from the past but which in itself remains static and unchanged. The form of the Germanic word *Überlieferung,* however, does suggest the activity or process of handing on, and therefore the idea of tradition in the sense of transmission. It is desirable not to lose sight of this aspect when using the English term "tradition." Thus while people sometimes speak of "a tradition," by which they mean a more or less precisely fixed cultural element, the more interesting usage in the study of religion is "tradition" understood as the act of handing on, which implies process and movement. In fact, the specific cultural elements sometimes referred to as traditions can also be designated in other ways, e.g., as a ritual or a belief complex. Thus the word "tradition" is hardly required to specify such elements in themselves. For theoretical purposes, therefore, it is better to reserve the word tradition as far as possible for a whole stream of such elements regarded from the point of view of the process of handing on or transmission, with all the attendant features which this implies.

The movement spoken of here is movement from a time which the participants or actors in the process of tradition regard as the past (though for the observer it is only a past) into a time which for the participants or actors is a present bearing a presumed future (not yet available for the observer among the socio-cultural data at his disposal). Thus the participants or actors bear an existential responsibility which the observer does not directly share but which, if one seeks understanding, one dare not ignore.

While what has been said so far may be considered valid for tradition in general, we are concerned here, above all, with religious tradition. Religious tradition cannot be treated in isolation from the wider field of tradition in all its forms. Thus, a theory of religious tradition must be held wide open to the stimuli of various disciplines, especially, but not only, social anthropology. As a special case in the wider field, however, religious tradition displays some characteristics which cannot easily be reduced to or assimilated under a general theory of tradition. This is because the truth claims or value claims raised by at least some religious traditions pose, or at least imply questions of meaning, sometimes critically, for the cultures in which they are carried forward. In this respect, the appraisal which the observer might independently make of such truth or value claims is (for the discipline of the study of religions) not of any great significance. The existential questions to which such claims are ultimately addressed, even if only implicitly, persist within the human situation regardless whether any particular religion is deemed by the observer to be true or false, valuable or worthless. Moreover the articulate bearers of religious tradition, whether they are shamans, bishops, or Buddhist monks, are conscious of this existential and sometimes critical dimension to a greater or lesser extent.

Between anthropology and theologies

In view of the above, it is not surprising that an interest in tradition as an aspect of culture and especially of religion has arisen both among social anthropologists on the one hand and among the exponents of various traditions, that is, theologians and their equivalents in non-theistic religions, on the other hand. Social anthropologists are in principle not concerned with truth claims (unless it be in their spare time), whereas the theologians and other exponents of tradition are actively concerned with them, even if only implicitly, for their very task lies in the projection of meaning. The latter aspect further attracts its own type of scholarly literature which may have little to do with anthropology. This point may be illustrated by juxtaposing two well-known works, which deal in their different ways with the destiny of major religious traditions, Islam and Buddhism, in far-flung cultural contexts, namely: Clifford Geertz' *Religion in Java* (1960) and Alicia Matsunaga's *The Buddhist Philosophy of Assimilation* (1969). These two works are rather dissimilar in their approach while both are widely recognized to be excellent. The former is explicitly anthropological, and seeks to understand the relations between complementary aspects of a sociocultural system of which Islam forms a part. The latter assumes a more or less Buddhist standpoint while reflecting on the relations between Buddhist teaching and other religious beliefs in India, China, and Japan. The analysis is aided by concepts which themselves are Buddhist-derived.

An integrative theory of religious tradition is, therefore, required which is able to mediate between these different tendencies, and such a theory must be considered the responsibility of those who specialise in the historical and comparative study of religions. Why is this? How does such an intermediary role arise? On the one hand, the specialist in religious studies, like an anthropologist, aligns himself with the experience and the self-understanding of the people whose religious tradition is under study. His goal is the understanding of the tradition in question, an understanding which, in the first instance at least, should be phenomenological or, to use another terminology, emic. On the other hand, precisely because it is a religious tradition and not, for example, a question of pottery technology, this very activity leads him into that area of interpretation which under ordinary circumstances is the responsibility of the articulate exponent of the tradition.

It may be noted in passing that there is not any particular requirement, for the student of religion at least, to limit attention to non-literate or small-scale societies. Indeed, interesting questions arise precisely in the shift to literacy (which can ultimately lead to nostalgia for a non-literate time) and in the interaction between small-scale societies and relatively differentiated ones. The shift to literacy can be considered over a very long period in the case of the Japanese religion Shintō which may be regarded as an "adjusted primal religion" (cf. "Shintō and the typology of religion" 1989c and at 4.4 above) with a high nostalgia quotient in modern times. A more short-term example is the conscious cultivation of Maoriness (Maori-tanga) in recent New Zealand history, which means that Maori religion is accepting distance from a perceived past in the interests of self-conservation (cf. Schlang 1988[1]). The constant shift into complexity is important for the student of religion, for, within this shift, tradition is never static but always in some respects dynamic.

At any one time a religious tradition is never quite what it was before, or never bears quite the same meaning which it bore before, even if the changes which it undergoes or the development of its meaning are in a strong sense consistent with its past and possibly profoundly loyal to it. Thus the exponents of religious tradition bear a responsibility which is in part creative. This too must be understood by the observer, not just abstractly, but in terms of the specific case, and this means that to achieve the understanding mentioned above, he or she has to move so closely to the heart-beat of the tradition under study as to become aware of how its meaning is put into question in the given situation. By this is not meant, necessarily, an intellectual questioning. There may be such, but it may be admitted that on the whole religious tradition under observation more frequently appears to go unquestioned. Nevertheless, that the meaning is put into question is something which is sensed by the responsible exponents who are aware of the danger of non-tradition and the consequent loss of social and existential meaning. The very force of tradition is an indication of its fragility. Conversely, the fragility demands creative responsibility. If the very identification of the meaning of tradition in a particular situation demands a creative act on the part of the exponent, this, in turn, has to be followed through imaginatively by the observer. If this is not understood, the observer will always turn aside at the very point where the reception of the past becomes intense for the participant, that is to

---

1   Originally submitted as a doctoral dissertation at the University of Marburg.

say, wherever the meaning is subject to or threatened by change and thus takes on critical significance. If the observer is fully sensitive to the fragility of the situation and hence to the perceived need for the process of tradition to be carried through, he or she will realise that at one and the same time both the future and the past are at stake.

This principle may be summed up in what is probably the shortest sentence in the extensive works of Ernst Troeltsch, namely "Wesensbestimmung ist Wesensgestaltung" (Troeltsch, 1922: 421; cf. Morgan and Pye 1977: 162), the import of which may be paraphrased as: to define the tradition is to reshape it. The thrust of Troeltsch's argument at that point was to stress the inevitability of interpretative change with a view to the present situation and the presumed demands of the future. But the presupposition of such an interpretation is itself a view of the nature (or in his terms, essence, "Wesen") of the perceived tradition, of which, however, alternative views are possible. Thus, in the act of tradition, to put it provocatively, the past is subject to change. Notice that this point is not quite the same as the idea that traditions may be invented, semi-consciously, in retrospect, to fulfill a perceived need, which is worked out most interestingly in recent essays entitled *The Invention of Tradition* (Hobsbawm and Ranger 1983).

A polarity between anthropologists, on the one hand, and theologians, or those who look over the shoulders of theologians, on the other hand, was noted by Robert Redfield in his well-known lectures published as *Peasant Society and Culture* (Redfield 1956). Writing of the adjustments made between Islamic tradition and local tradition, he comments, "Here the Islamist comes to meet the anthropologist. Professor von Grunebaum, discussing the interaction between local saint and Islamic orthodoxy, sees from the top, so to speak, the same interaction that Westermarck, studying local saints in Morocco, saw from the bottom" (Redfield 1956, 85, cf. von Grunebaum 1955 and Westermarck 1926). However, in the light of what has already been said, this polarisation would seem to be not quite adequate. Redfield was concerned, as an anthropologist, with the relations between the cultural elements of a small-scale community, or peasant culture, and an incursive tradition with wider and socially different foundations. Hence arose his frequently cited and, indeed, illuminating distinction between "the great tradition" and "the little tradition," which is set out preeminently in a chapter bearing the significant title "The social organization of tradition" (Redfield 1956: 67–104). The social basis of this distinction is that a little tradition is carried unreflectively by a peasant or village society whereas a great tradition is cultivated by a class of professional exponents. It is important to note here that the two kinds of tradition fall within identifiable socio-cultural parameters, which are presumed to be distinct. It is by assuming these two distinct areas that reference could be made, painlessly, to the Islamist, on the one hand, (who deals with the great tradition) and the anthropologist, on the other hand (who deals with the little tradition).

While Redfield saw that the two should somehow be brought together, he tried to do so by defining each of the two sides more decisively. But is this the right approach? If an Islamist and an anthropologist in fact come together in the field at a point where the great and the little tradition meet, there is a third party in the conversation, who does not appear prominently in Redfield's account, except as a social object. This is none other than the carrier of tradition himself or herself, whose task it is to cope with the interaction of diverse cultural elements in a situation where the meaning for the time is still to be established. The carrier of tradition is responsible both to the past and to the future, and, as was argued above, the identity of tradition is therefore always at risk. To appreciate this critical openness at any one time, it is necessary to be something more than, or at least slightly other than, either an anthropologist or a philologically oriented cultural historian (i. e. in this case, an Islamist), at least in a restrictive sense of these terms. The student of religion has to be, under these circumstances, a kind of tradition carrier by proxy. To put it more provocatively, he or she is required to be, by imagination, or by almost participant observation, a theologian with interchangeable gods.

The delicate responsibility of the carriers of any tradition, which is to be entered into imaginatively by the student of religion (the *Religionswissenschaftlerin)*, leads on to the requirement of a special complexity in the overall theory of religious tradition, a complexity which is not always evident in limited case-studies, excellent and useful though they may be in themselves. A theory of tradition must include both an understanding of the dynamics of religious change as an observable socio-cultural process, which has taken place up to the present of the observer, and a hermeneutical openness in which the participant's responsibility for the handing on into the future is adequately reflected. On this basis some misunderstandings can be removed. As was said at the outset, "tradition" does not refer to what is old or left over from before. Hence it is not quite appropriate to speak of "tradition and renewal" as if these were opposites, for the act of tradition, in the sense of handing on, itself implies a renewal. A renewal is a recapitulation of what was, in a world which is no longer what it was. Similarly, it is not quite appropriate to speak of "tradition and interpretation" as if these were opposites, for there is no handing on without interpretation. The only way to avoid interpretation is to forget. Admittedly, forgetting has a healing power of its own, but it does not set tradition in motion. Tradition is always in motion.

Self-conscious tradition, participants and observers

Although it is quite beyond the range of this short statement to set out a detailed or fully systematic theory of religious tradition, a few words may be added about one more crucial feature, namely, the relation, sometimes tension-laden, between the unreflective and self-conscious forms of tradition. This feature is particularly important because the existence of both unreflective and self-conscious religious traditions demands a widely extended theoretical perspective, which is by no means easily achieved, especially if the main argument above is not to be allowed to lose its force.

Unreflective tradition, that is, tradition which takes place without the participants engaging in reflection on the process in which they are engaged, may be oral only, but may equally have a strong written component. This is not to deny that, as Vansina wrote, "Oral traditions are historical sources of a special nature" (Vansina 1965:1), but it does imply the need to look for the decisive features of an overall theory of religious tradition in a slightly different framework than that addressed in his important work *Oral Tradition,* which, as the sub-title says, is "A Study in Historical Methodology."

In so far as the student of religion reflects upon unreflective tradition, he will seek to develop a coherent image of the dynamics of religion, that is, of religion in terms of its movement. Thus, he will seek to understand the shifting correlations (syncretism, synthesis, assimilation, etc.) between religious and other cultural elements of diverse origin and to understand innovation, growth, decline, and disappearance. All of these are themes which have been treated with such a diversity of approach, and above all in the context of so many different cultural areas, that the provision of bibliographical details on a small scale here would be quite misleading. It is clear, however, that the distinction between oral and written tradition is a subordinate question in this perspective.

What is important for a theory of religious tradition is that all of the aspects of the dynamics of religion, which are frequently played out without self-conscious reflection, are marked with uncertainty. Thus, it is not surprising that the participants in the process of tradition themselves begin to indicate the landmarks of coherence. Above all, they create the symbols of authority, such as creeds; but they also permit deviation and ambiguity in varying degree. A ritual may be abbreviated without loss, for a while. When uncertainty sets in, continuity is called for, then reformulation, then innovation. Many a prophet is the final prophet. But the last prophet is continually set in context in accordance with later needs. Since the participants themselves notice this, and even debate it, the unreflective form of religious tradition is always giving way to the self-conscious form.

The observer is true to the participants and moves with them. He does not proudly restrict himself to a meta-language, invented by his profession, as if the world were inhabited by a combination of savages and scientists. He is aware that reflection on the process of tradition emerges both haltingly and controversially within religion itself. He is stimulated by the notions pertaining to consensus (only made necessary by the threat of divergent tradition, which could mean loss of tradition) developed in Judaism and Islam. He follows through the emergent theories about the status of previous prophets, and even of other revelations. He notes the rationalized adaptive tactics in the Buddhist books of discipline. Thus, upon a theory of the dynamics of religions, there has to be built a coordinated view of the self-conscious reflection on those same processes as developed by the participants themselves.

It is to be expected that there should be some relationship between these two levels. While pursuing these considerations together with the participants in religious tradition, the student of religion must refrain (in accordance with this discipline, though not necessarily in his or her spare time) from identifying himself finally with the normative requirements of the participants. Only in this way can he or she remain free to achieve that one further level of abstraction and coordination which will eventually be required to work out a comprehensive theory of religious tradition.

Bibliographical references

Geertz, Clifford 1960. *The Religion of Java*. Chicago (University of Chicago Press).

Hobsbawm, E. and Ranger T. 1983. *The Invention of Tradition*. Cambridge (Cambridge University Press).

Matsunaga, Alicia 1969. *The Buddhist Philosophy of Assimilation. The Historical Development of the Honji Suijaku Theory*. Tokyo and Rutland (Sophia University).

Morgan, Robert and Pye, Michael 1977. *Ernst Troeltsch: Writings on Theology and Religion*, London (Duckworth) and Louisville (Westminster/John Knox).

Pye, Michael 1989c. "Shintō and the typology of religion" in: *Method & Theory in the Study of Religion* 1/2: 186–95. (Summary version 1984 as "The place of Shintō in the typology of religion" in: Yamamoto, Y. (ed.) *Proceedings of the Thirty-first International Congress of Human Sciences in Asia and North Africa*. Tokyo) Institute of Eastern Culture): 1055–6.)

Redfield, Robert 1956. *Peasant Society and Culture. An Anthropological Approach to Civilisation*. Chicago (University of Chicago Press).

Schlang, Stefan 1988. *Religiöse Aspekte von Maoritanga*. Bonn (Holos-Verlag).

Troeltsch, Ernst 1913 (and 1922). *Gesammelte Schriften* II. Tübingen (Mohr and Siebeck).

Vansina, Jan 1965. *Oral Tradition. A Study in Historical Methodology*. London (Routledge ad Kegan Paul). (English translation of *De La Tradition Orale, Essai De Méthode Historique, 1961)*.

Von Grunebaum, G. (ed.) 1965. *Unity and Diversity in Muslim Civilization*. Chicago (University of Chicago Press).

Westermarck, Edward 1926. *Ritual and Belief in Morocco*. London (Macmillan).

This paper was first published in: Geertz, A. W. and Jensen, J. S., *Religion, Tradition and Renewal*, Aarhus (Aarhus University Press) 1991: 29–36.

5.3 Ernst Troeltsch and Gerardus van de Leeuw on Tradition

The paper was first presented at a joint conference of the Dutch and the German Associations for the Study of Religion in Groningen in May 1989 under the title "Reflections on the Treatment of Tradition in Comparative Perspective, with Special Reference to Ernst Troeltsch and Gerardus van der Leeuw" and later published in the proceedings. Light redactional changes have been made here.

On history, phenomenology and theology

If the names of Ernst Troeltsch (1865–1923) and Gerardus van der Leeuw (1890–1950) are linked in the title of this paper it is not because they were closely associated historically or in terms of intellectual dependence. When Troeltsch died, van der Leeuw was 33 years old, still relatively young. The first edition of the latter's *Phänomenologie der Religion* appeared ten years later (Van der Leeuw 1933), and contains hardly any references to Troeltsch. At one point van der Leeuw refers to Troeltsch's characterization of Baptists as a "sect," but signally fails 'to recognize the more general contribution made by Troeltsch to the typology of religious organisations through his distinctions between church, sect and mystical religion.[1] A second reference is also quite incidental, but as it has some significance for the subject of this paper it will be discussed separately below.[2] It is nevertheless worthwhile to bear the contribution of both these writers in mind when reflecting today on religious tradition from the point of view of historical, phenomenological or comparative research. Each had a characteristic standpoint which reflected major themes in the early twentieth century and

---

1   Van der Leeuw 1964: 263. That Troeltsch's approach was not more fully considered is all the more surprising in that his *The Social Teachings of the Christian Churches (Die Soziallehren der christlichen Kirchen und Gruppen,* (Troeltsch 1912, 1919) is mentioned in the bibliography.
2   Van der Leeuw 1964: 688. The reference is to Troeltsch's *Gesammelte Schriften*, Vol. II, 490, note 2.

continued to influence thought about religion in the later twentieth century. Although there was no detailed correlation at the time, and there has been little later, there are certain important affinities between the two writers. These will be considered here not simply out of antiquarian interest but because there is still a task to be performed in the development of a theory of religious tradition.

Firstly, while both van der Leeuw and Troeltsch were keenly aware of the relativities into which modern historical and sociological knowledge plunge us, both continued to see great value and elevated meaning in religion, especially Christian religion. Although Troeltsch has been criticised by some for betraying the uniqueness or superlativeness of Christianity's claim to truth, he has also been regarded as "the systematics spokesman" for the history of religions school centred on Göttingen.[3] As Robert Morgan puts it: "His restless attempts to do theology on this historical critical foundation constitute his claim to the attention of succeeding generations who have still not fully mastered his problems".[4] Thus, however his achievement may be assessed from later theological standpoints, which themselves continue to be diverse, it is clear that he regarded the delineation and presentation of the sense of Christianity on the basis of modern presuppositions as his central objective. Van der Leeuw, for his part, though he attended to religion in the main as a socio-cultural phenomenon in comparative perspective, has been criticised as a crypto-theologian among phenomenologists of religion.[5] Indeed he was sometimes less than cryptic! It is only necessary to recall that he concluded his massive phenomenological work with a chapter entitled "The mediator" in which Christianity assumes a normative position. Here the mediator "in the truest sense" is Christ. Van der Leeuw tells us at this point not only what the phenomenologist can perceive but also what he cannot perceive, thereby moving into the position of the theologian. Jesus, or Christ (he uses the designations indiscriminately), is compared favourably with mediators in Buddhism or in Hellenism. It is before the Christian faith that the "contemplative and comprehending servant of research reverently withdraws."[6]

The concluding sections of the earlier *Inleiding tot de Godsdienstgeschiedenis* (Van der Leeuw 1924) and of the important study on

---

3   So Robert Morgan in Morgan and Pye 1977: 4.
4   Morgan and Pye 1977: 5.
5   Cf. Pye 1972: 29.
6   Van der Leeuw 1964: 666–7.

the relation between religion and art *Wegen en Grenzen* (Van der Leeuw 1932) are no different! Thus:

> Aan deze beide gevaren ontsnappen dan ook telkens weer zij, die het onuitsprekelijke, het gansch andere en ééne noodige het veiligst ver af van menschelijke willekeur en het zaligst nabij aan menschelijken deemoed weten in de persoon van Jezus Christus, waarachtig mensch en een 'gestalte': 'geboren uit de Maagd Maria'; waarachtig God, heilig en gansch anders, dan al het geschapene: 'geworden en niet gemaakt'.[7]

And again:

> Zoo vinden wij als phaenomenologen, als mannen van de kunst- en godsdienstwetenschap, wegen en grenzen. Zoo beleven wij als religieuze menschen telkens het wonder van de samenvloeiing der beide stroomen van religie en kunst. Als theologen, die de openbaring in Christus en het schijnbaar andere, dat ons als openbaring is gegeven, noch kunstmatig kunnen scheiden, noch in de algemeenheid van een godsgedachte willen vervagen, vinden wij de eenheid van kunst en religie daar, waar wij alleen eenheid kennen, in de leer der Incarnatie. Als geloovigen vinden wij de mogelijkheid van volkomen Schoonheid in Hem, in wien wij alles vinden, in de goddelijke Gestalte, in den Zoon van Maria, Zoon van God, in den Schoonste. En wij zeggen het 't oude volkslied na:
>
> Alle die Schönheit
> Himmels und der Erden
> Ist verfasst in Dir allein.[8]

In spite of the careful differentiation between the phenomenologist, the theologian and the believer indicated here, this conclusion provides an uncompromising religious perspective for the whole. It is arguable that the force of such conclusions can be cancelled out by the more carefully stated methodological discussion in the "Epilegomena" of *Religion in Essence and Manifestation* (chapters 107–110). Those who see difficulties even with these chapters may be referred to the introduction to *Wegen en Grenzen,* where the statement about what he meant by phenomenology of religion is really quite clear.[9] The point being noted

---

7   Van der Leeuw Haarlem 1924: 214.
8   Van der Leeuw 1932: 217.
9   See in particular the paragraph entitled "Methode" (pages 4–5) which runs as follows:
    "Wij zullen zien hoe wegen zich in de geschiedenis hebben gebaand en grenzen afgeteekend. Toch stellen wij geen historisch onderzoek in. Wij zullen voor de vraag komen naar de laatste waarde van het Heilige, Schoone, Goede en Waare, elk op zichzelf en in hun onderlinge verhouding. Toch draagt ons onderzoek geen wijsgeerig of dogmatisch karakter. Het is veeleer van *phaenome-*

here however is simply that even on a cool reading of van der Leeuw's work, which is to some extent justified by the massive range of distanced observation, the norm of Christian faith as an ultimate reference point is as clearly present as it is with Troeltsch. Thus each of them lived with the tension between abstraction, in the sense of scientific enquiry into the nature of religion, and religious faith or mystical devotion.

Religious disclosure versus the evolution of religion

There are other similarities too, at the most general level. Both saw the essential disclosure (van der Leeuw's term) of religious meaning as being primarily personal and subjective. It is a remarkable fact that this is so, despite their extensive attention to the social forms and teachings of various churches and religions and in van der Leeuw's case to the iconographic and artistic aspects of religion, which imply an inter-personal field of meaning. The essentially protestant assumption that divine reality, salvation, or even revelation, is experienced above all by the individual has remained astonishingly effective in many variations deep into the present century. Its roots may be seen both in the "appeal to Jesus" of Jan Hus, implying a combination of biblical objectivity and subjective recognition of divine value beyond the reach of a conglomerate human council, and also in the stress on the communicative power of the Holy Spirit which took extreme form with George Fox and other Quakers. In the long run the downgrading of hierarchical decision-taking and of external forms has led to the individualised, post-Christian view that "I" can decide for myself what religion is going to be, either

---

nologischen aard. De phaenomenologische methode is in den laatsten tijd op allerlei terrein toegepast. Wij kunnen in dit verband/natuurlijk geen uitvoerige uiteenzetting van haar doeleinden' geven. Alleen dit: waar de geschiedenis vraagt: hoe was het? vraagt de phaenomenoloog: hoe begrijp ik het? waar de wijsbegeerte onderzoekt naar de waarheid of werkelijkbeid, stelt de phaenomenologie zich tevreden met de gegevenbeid als zoodanig zonder naar de waarheid of werkelijkbeid daarvan te vragen. Wij zoeken dus geen causale relaties na te speuren, maar begrijpelijke verbanden. Wij zoeken niet de waarheid achter de verschijnselen te doorgronden maar die verschijnselen zelf in hun eenvoudige gegevenbeid te verstaan.

Dat deze methode haar grenzen heeft, wij zijn er zelf algeheel van overtuigd. Dat zij evenwel voor alle historisch zoowel als systematisch onderzoek onmisbaar is, moge, in plaats van theoretische uiteenzetting, ons practisch onderzoek zelf aantoonen."

by selecting from the alternatives available or by reinventing it according to personal taste. Needless to say, a particularly important modulation of this principle, still in a clearly protestant frame of reference, was found in Schleiermacher's view of the essence of religion as lying in a sense of absolute dependence. It is in this tradition that both Troeltsch and van der Leeuw fall, speaking very broadly, and in which they are to be seen in the company of others such as Rudolf Otto, who departed from Troeltsch's position however in important respects,[10] and Joachim Wach, whom van der Leeuw cites frequently.

Oddly enough it is precisely this principle which led into van der Leeuw's (second) citation of Troeltsch, whom he was able to adduce as an ally in his stance *against evolutionism*. Because religious disclosure is regarded as personal, the phenomenological task involved in its elucidation is considered to be equally relevant to any point in history. There is thus no development in the experience of the divine. For this reason van der Leeuw regarded the idea of historical development as inimical to his undertaking. He wrote: "Thus phenomenology knows nothing of any historical 'development' of religion, still less of an 'origin' of religion."[11] A footnote refers to Troeltsch at this point, which will be pursued below. First let it be noted however that the passage is not an isolated one. The preface to the German edition, written in Groningen, stresses that theories "which attempt to reveal the 'primary origin' of Religion have from the outset been excluded" (the German term translated as "primary origin" is simply *Ursprung*).[12] Indeed the same point was thoroughly emphasised much earlier, in his *Inleiding tot de Godsdienstgeschiedenis*, published in 1924, which in various ways clearly set the pattern for the later phenomenology. See here especially the section "Het wezen der verschijnselen" (the essence, or nature of the phenomena) which begins as follows:

---

10 As is well known, Otto argued for the irrational a-priori character of the sense of the numinous *(Das Heilige. Über das Irrationale in der Idee des Göttlichen und sein Verhältnis zum Rationalen,* 1917, *The Idea of the Holy,* Harmondsworth 1923). Troeltsch had argued, in "Das Wesen der Religion und der Religionsgeschichte" *(Kultur der Gegenwart,* I, 4, 1906) that there is "an a-priori law of the formation of religious ideas existing in the nature of reason" (Engl. translation Morgan and Pye 1977, 116, and cf. discussion of this point on page 241.)
11 Van der Leeuw 1938, 1964: 688.
12 Quoted from English translation: *Ursprung* (or Dutch *oorsprong*) just means origin.

5.3 Ernst Troeltsch and Gerardus van de Leeuw on Tradition

> Het behoeft, na het reeds gezegde, niet uitvoerig betoogd te worden, dat wij het 'wezen' der verschijnselen niet zoeken in hun historischen oorsprong. Wij doen dit al dadelijk niet, omdat wij overtuigd zijn, dat die oorsprong niet te kennen is, noch langs historischen noch langs psychologischen weg. Wat als de 'oorspronkelijke' gestalte van een verschijnsel geldt, is dan ook gewoonlijk spoediger te vinden in de onmiddellijke nabijheid van den onderzoeker dan in een grijs verleden. Bovendien is het niet de juiste methode het wezen van een verschijnsel uitsluitend te zoeken in de vroegste vormen daarvan. Wanneer men wil weten, wat het gebed is, moet men zeker zien naar de gebedsvormen der primitieve en oudste volken; maar evengoed naar de gedaante, die het gebed in het zeer ontwikkeld Boeddhisme of in ons huidig Christendom heeft aangenomen.[13]

The passage in Troeltsch's essay "Wesen der Religion und der Religionsgeschichte" to which van der Leeuw refers runs as follows:

> Noch schlimmer steht es mit einer weiteren üblichen Fragestellung, die gern mit dem Begriff des Wesens [das heißt der Religion] verbunden oder gar als mit ihm identisch angesehen wird, mit dem Begriff 'der *Entstehung* der Religion'. Soll damit die 'Entstehung' im eigentlichen Sinne gemeint sein und nach Art und Weise wie nach Grund und Ursache der Entstehung gefragt sein, so kann es nur die Entstehung der Religion in jedem einzelnen heutigen oder früheren uns bekannten religiösen Individuum bedeuten.[14]

Here too we see the primacy of any one religious experience being regarded as normative, regardless of its moment in history. This stance may thus be regarded as a third point of similarity between the two. However Troeltsch continues:

> Allein eine völlige Neuentstehung haben wir hier nie vor uns: die individuelle Religion entsteht immer aus der Ueberlieferung religiöser Gedanken, die Ueberlieferung mag noch so schmal oder die Umbildung der Ueberlieferung mag noch so groß sein. Eine völlige Urzeugung zu beobachten, ist uns versagt, und als Ursache der Entstehung mag immer in erster Linie die Fortsetzung und Macht der Tradition angegeben werden.[15]

Here the emphasis is different, away from the individual and rather on the role of tradition, a tradition, the tradition in question. Troeltsch's thought is not pursued by van der Leeuw in this regard.

---

13 Van der Leeuw 1924: 7.
14 Troeltsch 1913 (1922): 490; cf. English translation, Morgan and Pye 1977: 113.
15 Troeltsch 1913 (1922): 490–491; Engl. Translation: 113.

Working out the dynamics of tradition

At the same time van der Leeuw in fact had a profound historical consciousness resulting in part from his wide-ranging knowledge in the history of culture (including the results of contemporary ethnological research) but also, more specifically, to the pervasive influence of the German history of religions school. Even if a comprehensive evolutionist or development scheme is eschewed, the fact of movement and alteration in religion, in any period whatever, remains apparent to the historically sensitive analyst. Thus it was that van der Leeuw, while rejecting the notion of development, concentrated his attention, however briefly, on what he called the dynamics of religion (see especially chapters 93 and 94 of *Religion in Essence and Manifestation*).[16] Under this heading he considered topics designated as syncretism, mission, transposition(s) (German: *Verschiebung*), revivals (German: *Erweckungen*) and reformations.

These brief sections seem to us today to be very sketchy and could be criticised in various respects. However the opening section contains some important words:

> In other terms, if we wish to discover the essence of the so-called 'great religions', which must now be discussed, it is imperative for us not merely to contemplate their static character, but also to consider their dynamics. A historic religion, then, is a form, an organized system. Nonetheless its characteristics are not fixed and rigid; rather they are in perpetual flux: not manufactured but growing, and in a state of incessant expansion.[17]

This passage occurs in the context of comments on "syncretism," in respect to which the further discussion remains in some regards less than satisfactory. We read, for example, with respect to Theosophy, Anthroposophy, Christian Science and Neo-Sufism, that these "pay homage to syncretism, to some extent in principle, because of their conviction that all religions, at bottom, are only one in different guise."[18] Thus there is a tendency to identify "syncretism" either with synthesis or, when van der Leeuw goes on to say "these medleys often produce a very peculiar and confused impression," in effect with eclecticism. However the definition of "syncretism" as a useful term in the study of religion is not the

---

16 Note that the chapter numeration was changed for the second German edition, in which see chapters 94 and 95. The second German edition contains various additional material.
17 Van der Leeuw 1938: 609.
18 Van der Leeuw 1938: 610.

subject of discussion at this point.[19] The main plea, for a recognition of the importance of the dynamics of religion, covers not only syncretism but also the other topics mentioned above.

It is perhaps remarkable that this aspect, "the dynamics of religion," compared with the massive typological exposition of different styles of religious feeling, should have remained relatively undeveloped in van der Leeuw's work. However, it was present. A greater imbalance has appeared later in Eliade's account of religion as a sequence of more or less timeless hierophanies. It was important that van der Leeuw located syncretism in the context of a more long-term sequence of changes which may be occurring at different places and at different times and that these are so widely conceived (though the matter is briefly stated) as to include, for example, "reformations." Here too he argues from particular cases, including the establishment of Mahāyāna Buddhism and of mediaeval Christianity, to the general, speaking of reformation, accommodation and relapse. "The sole certainly, then," he writes, "is that *living religion is in perpetual activity,* and reformation is therefore not some sort of arbitrary act, but one form of the very life of a religion."[20] The renewed stress on individual experience as the motor for reform may be regarded as a deviation from the main point, though for van der Leeuw it was an important deviation.[21]

In this context attention may be drawn again to the concept of transposition (or, in the German, *Verschiebung*). The importance of this lies in the recognition that if "living religion is in perpetual activity" then its constituent elements may change their meaning. They may gain meaning, and they may lose meaning. For example, "thus almost all Protestant religious communities retained the sacrament of communion, but 'transposed,' with a changed meaning, and this too after the Roman church itself had already accepted it from the ancient church and had transposed it."[22] Needless to say, this gives the study of religions in many fieldwork situations much of its subtlety and charm. At the

---

19 For more recent discussions of "syncretism" see Pye 1971a, Berner 1979 and Rudolph 1979. Even in the 1920's however, a much clearer use of the term syncretism was made by Raffaele Pettazzoni with respect to Shintō (where van der Leeuw is misleading) (Pettazzoni 1929, especially pages 8–11). Pettazzoni's view that syncretism was unknown in the religious history of the west after the triumph of Christianity does require qualification however.
20 Van der Leeuw 1938: 614.
21 Van der Leeuw 1938: 611.
22 Van der Leeuw 1938: 611.

same time, it may be noted, religions now presumed dead (as opposed to "living religions") were in their historical reality living religions. Hence they too were subject to a constant series of transpositions of meaning, which in turn gives the history of religions much of its interest. In principle we may observe here the beginnings of the idea, for van der Leeuw, that the typological analysis of religion may seek ideal patterns running through religions considered in terms of their dynamics, that is, their emergence, their socio-cultural coordination and adaptation, their flowering, expansion, experience of crisis, renewal, reformation, stagnation and decline.

The overall question is whether these starting points in van der Leeuw's account of religion are sufficient for the development of a full-scale theory of religion under its dynamic aspect, which might better be named a theory of religious tradition. This designation presupposes that "tradition" means first and foremost "handing on" and thus implies process and movement.[23] In effect van der Leeuw's ideas on this subject may be regarded as valuable hints but not yet as a fully coordinated analytical typology of religious tradition.

Ernst Troeltsch was equally sensitive to historical shifts in religious meaning and well aware of their significance for the interpretation of religion. Admittedly, the interpretation of religion meant for him, in the last analysis, a theological task. Even though his theological position reaped disapproval he certainly remained true in his own mind to his vision of the nature of theological activity, which he attempted to carry forward on the basis of what he regarded as unavoidable modern, critical presuppositions. Because of his fundamental orientation he failed to translate his most important reflections on the problem of interpreting religious tradition into a comparative perspective. There is also a certain Euro-centrism in all of Troeltsch's writing which is remarkable when one considers the valiant effort which Weber made, for methodological reasons, to escape this.[24] It may be noted however that church-sect-cult theories which owed their original impetus to Troeltsch remained Euro-American in conception decades later in spite of changed international circumstances. For this, others are responsible. However there seems to be no reason why Troeltsch's characteristic insight into what for van der Leeuw was the "dynamics" of religion may not be ap-

---

23 Cf. Pye 1991c.
24 Assessed and criticised in Pye 1976.

propriated in a comparative perspective for the benefit of a theory of religious tradition yet to be fully developed.

That the translation into comparative terms of Troeltsch's profound grasp of the meaning of historical depth for present-day tradition is quite feasible, is evident from the fact, for example, that in Buddhism as in Christianity there are competing views about the location, meaning and communication of its crucial import. That is, as van der Leeuw said, "Every historic religion, therefore, is not one, but several… "[25] Troeltsch's key writing in this respect is the long essay "Was heißt 'Wesen des Christentums'?"[26] Something of the challenge of Troeltsch's position is conveniently summarized in the following sentences. "At any one point the future destiny of a religious tradition is not known, but what is clear is that its character up till then has been continuously re-decided, even if the changes are almost imperceptible for long periods. In fact one may say that religious tradition is created retrospectively from out of each successive present, and with a view to the future. It is not really created authoritatively from the beginning of the religion, as most people naively conceive of it, and then simply unrolled towards them as the centuries pass. Rather it is continually recreated, so to say, backwards, and this is a process in which the believers share, more or less naively or purposefully."[27] Since the days of Troeltsch and of van der Leeuw the term "tradition" has been used and abused in many contexts. For example, with the massive development of social anthropology, an autonomous vocabulary has developed which is at first sight totally unrelated to the continued use of the word in the context of the major theistic religions. How many of those who occasionally quote Redfield's account of "the social organisation of tradition" (Redfield 1956), distinguishing between the peasants and the professional exponents of tradition, are aware that there are in fact deep underlying connections, and that these may be pursued in the context of Christian, Islamic or Buddhist culture without strain? At the same time there have been not a few studies on particular aspects of the dynamics of religion,

---

25 Van der Leeuw 1938: 610.
26 Troeltsch 1913 (from 1903), English translation Morgan and Pye 1977. For discussion of the relevance of Troeltsch's argument to Buddhism see also Pye and Morgan 1973.
27 Morgan and Pye, 1977: 250–1.

to recall van der Leeuw's phrase once again, e.g. on syncretism, on religions in their newness, or religions in process of disappearing.[28]

In sum there remains theoretical obscurity to a large extent. It is indeed difficult to take account of several or many relevant factors at once, as van der Leeuw in his brief notes on the subject tried to do. It is also difficult to sense the interpretational imperative as keenly as Troeltsch did, while yet leaving the next interpretation to the believing participant in a tradition, as the historian of religion is bound to do. It is easy enough to speak of tradition "and" interpretation. But what if tradition *is* interpretation? (This is reformulated from Troeltsch.) Or what if religion is *always* in motion? (This is reformulated from van der Leeuw.) How can the sensitive historian of religion, especially if he is dealing with currently existing examples of religion, give a satisfactory analytic account of two or more cases at once, in the interests of comparison, while refraining from participation in the expression of new meaning? Van der Leeuw was aware of the skill required here by the phenomenologist of religion (cf. chapter 109 of *Religion in Essence and Manifestation*). However his distinction between phenomenology (in which typological analysis in effect plays a major role) and history may have been misleadingly easy. Pettazzoni noticed this point when he called for a unified science of religion which would overcome this provisional distinction.[29] A distinction between phenomenology and history is too easy. A grand developmental view of history may not be sought after, but a typology of the diachronic structure of religion can only be sought within history, that is, as a theory of tradition. And in a theory of tradition the interpretative threshold can never be disregarded.

Bibliographical references

Berner, Ulrich 1979. "Der Begriff 'Synkretismus' – ein Instrument historischer Erkenntnis?" in: *Saeculum* 30 (1): 68–85.

---

28 The least worked aspect is the last mentioned, but note Hartmut Zinser 1986 (ed.) entitled *Der Untergang von Religionen*, being proceedings of the German Association for the History of Religions (Deutsche Vereinigung für Religionsgeschichte) with many representative essays. (Retrospective note: the name of this association has since been changed to Deutsche Vereinigung für Religionswissenschaft.)

29 Pettazzoni 1954 and 1959 (esp. pages 9ff and 14).

Morgan, Robert and Pye, Michael 1977. *Ernst Troeltsch: Writings on Theology and Religion,* London (Duckworth) and Louisville (Westminster/John Knox).
Otto, Rudolf 1917. *Das Heilige. Über das Irrationale in der Idee des Göttlichen und sein Verhältnis zum Rationalen.* Breslau (Trewendt & Granier).
– 1923. *The Idea of the Holy.* Harmondsworth (Penguin) (English translation of *Das Heilige.*)
Pettazzoni, Raffaele 1929. "La religione nazionale del Giappone e la politica religiosa dello Stato giapponese" in: *Nuova Antologia* (June issue): 3–19.
– 1954. "Manuali di Storia delle Religioni" in: *Numen* 1 (2): 137–140.
– 1959. "Il metodo comparativo" in: *Numen* 6 (1): 1–14.
Pye, Michael 1971a. "Syncretism and ambiguity" in: *Numen* 18 (2): 83–93.
– 1972a. *Comparative Religion. An Introduction Through Source Materials.* Newton Abbot (David and Charles) and New York (Harper and Row).
– 1976. "The end of the problem about 'other' religions" in: Clayton, John P. (ed.) *Ernst Troeltsch and the Future of Theology,* Cambridge (Cambridge University Press):172–195.
– 1991a. "Religious tradition and the student of religion" in: Geertz, A. W. and Jensen, J. S. (eds.) *Religion, Tradition and Renewal* .Aarhus (Aarhus University Press): 29–36. (Also at 5.2 above.)
Pye, Michael and Morgan, Robert (eds.) 1973. *The Cardinal Meaning. Essays in Comparative Hermeneutics: Buddhism and Christianity (Religion and Reason 6).* The Hague (Mouton).
Redfield, Robert 1956. *Peasant Society and Culture. An Anthropological Approach to Civilization.* Chicago (Chicago University Press).
Rudolph, Kurt 1979. "Synkretismus – vom theologischen Scheltwort zum religionswissenschaftlichen Begriff" in: L. Neulande (ed.). *Humanitas Religiosa. Festschrift für Harald Biezais zu seinem 70. Geburtstag..* Stockholm (Almqvist and Wiksell): 194–212.
Troeltsch, Ernst 1906 "Das Wesen der Religion und der Religionsgeschichte" in: *Kultur der Gegenwart,* I, 4. (English translation: Morgan and Pye 1977)
– 1912. *Die Soziallehren der christlichen Kirchen und Gruppen* (also 1919, *Gesammelte Schriften* I) Tübingen (Mohr and Siebeck). (English Translation: *The Social Teachings of the Christian Churches.*)
– 1913 (and 1922) *Gesammelte Schriften* II. Tübingen (Mohr and Siebeck): 386–451 (Engl. translation Morgan and Pye, 1977).
– 1913. "Was heißt 'Wesen des Christentums'?" in: Troeltsch 1913: 386–451. (Originally 1903 in: *Die Christliche Welt.*)
– 1977. "What does 'essence of Christianity' mean?" (English translation of "Was heißt 'Wesen des Christentums'?" 1913) in: Morgan and Pye 1977: 124–181.
Van der Leeuw, Gerardus 1924. *Inleiding tot de Godsdienstgeschiedenis.* Haarlem (De erven F. Bohn)
– 1932. *Wegen en Grenzen. Studie Over De Verhouding Van Religie En Kunst.* Amsterdam (H.J. Paris).
– 1933. *Phänomenologie der Religion.* Tübingen (Mohr/Siebeck).

– 1938 (1964). *Religion in Essence and Manifestation* (English translation of *Phänomenologie der Religion),* London (George Allen and Unwin).
Zinser, Hartmut (ed.) 1986. *Der Untergang von Religionen.* Berlin (Reimer).

Previously published as "Reflections on the Treatment of Tradition in Comparative Perspective, with Special Reference to Ernst Troeltsch and Gerardus van der Leeuw" in: Kippenberg, Hans G. and Luchesi, Brigitte (eds.) 1991. *Religionswissenschaft und Kulturkritik.* Marburg (Diagonal-Verlag): 101–111.

5.4 Elements of a General Theory of Innovation in Religion

This paper is based on various outlines which have been presented in Germany, Britain, Finland and Japan and which have been under regular revision for teaching purposes. It is divided into Prolegomena, A General Theory of Innovation in Religion, and Epilogomena.

1. Prolegomena

1.1 The need for a general theory of innovation in religion

Interest in so-called "new religions" or "new religious movements" has been extremely great in recent years, and yet it is remarkable that it is not possible to point to a general theoretical orientation which does full justice both to their variety and to their location in the general history of religions. This is partly because "new religions" are often treated as a special problem in a particular region, Europe, the Americas, Africa or Asia, and this quite often for social and political reasons which are not strictly relevant to scientific enquiry. As a result they are not seen in terms of *a general theory of innovation in religion*, which would provide a more balanced context for their study. A general theory of innovation in religion, on the other hand, ought to include but not be restricted to "new religions." While such a theory is long overdue, its general outlines are not unduly difficult to delineate. They will be set out here in abstract form with just a few examples.

Such a theory, however simple, does not of course just arise from nowhere. It is important to take account of a sufficiently wide range of phenomena, and this presentation is indeed based on a consideration of examples from all regions of the world. In addition, the positions advanced here have been presented and discussed in various academic contexts.[1] At the same time it is utterly impossible here to enter into de-

---

1 On the background of a long-term interest in new religions in various parts of the world, especially but not only in Japan, this general overview of "innovation in religion" in the context of a joint seminar on "new religions" carried out

tailed discussion with the wide range of academic work in this field of study, and therefore the references are fragmentary. The argument is not a guide to the literature of the subject but, being conceived abstractly, may be considered as a systematic guide to its main features.

1.2 Reasons for current lack of a satisfactory theory

Among the various reasons for the lack of such an overall theory hitherto, three interrelated ones may be highlighted: (a) interest in the study of "new" religions has arisen in the context of rather diverse academic disciplines, but not all of these have windows to the general history of religions; (b) the terminology for identifying the subject matter has frequently been misleading, being framed in interesting but well insulated cultural contexts, e. g. Japan or Africa, rather than in a general perspective; (c) the distinction between analytical and explanatory theory (see Volume One, 1.2 above) has often been obscured. These reasons for the present unsatisfactory state of affairs will now be explored in more detail.

First, the main disciplines from within which studies of "new" religions have emerged have been sociology (sociology of religion), social anthropology (ethnology) and the study of religions (*Religionswissenschaft*). There have also been accounts from within religiously oriented institutions with a strong ideological interest but without a strong theoretical orientation, and other accounts by journalists active in various media who are not even making a claim to serious theoretical analysis; however these will not be further considered here. Interaction between the main relevant disciplines, though sometimes actively pursued, is not always well structured or conceptually disciplined. While the academic study of religions (or *Religionswissenschaft*) is in general quite widely open to the influences of sociology and social anthropology, it must be said that the relations between sociology and social anthropology are themselves not always close, or clear. Moreover, there is a tendency for the representatives of these larger disciplines to concentrate on identifying themselves in ways which are internally acceptable, and thus to be socially and, ap-

---

with anthropologist Mark Münzel at the University of Marburg in 1997. Since then variations were presented at meetings of the British Association for the Study of Religions (at Lampeter, Wales, in 1999) and the Finnish Society for the Study of Religions (at Turku in November 2000). Most recently (2005–8) it has been discussed from time to time at Ōtani University in Kyōto. The present statement owes much to the helpfully critical reactions of those present on these various occasions.

parently, theoretically self-sufficient. *Religionswissenschaft* as a discipline does not get into such a situation because the number of persons involved is much smaller. Since specialists in the study of religions are few in number, they cite more studies and arguments from those who stand outside their own discipline, while by contrast social anthropologists and sociologists legitimate their arguments and positions mainly by reference to peers within their own academic world. So although the study of religions to a certain extent has its own methodological and theoretical discussions and perspectives, these go largely unnoticed among sociologists and anthropologists. The problems are increased by the patterning of scientific literature, for in spite of lip-service to interdisciplinarity, leading journals in the larger disciplines most commonly help to reinforce separate discipline identities. Commercial publishers are not usually interested in the finer points of these relationships. As will be evident to those familiar with the bibliographical journal *Science of Religion*[2] it is arguable that journals dedicated to the field of the study of religions are, in general, more interdisciplinary in outlook than the professional journals in sociology and anthropology. This can easily be explained by the relative size of these disciplines. Inevitably, this situation has an influence on the way in which theories are developed and debated with regard to particular topics such as "new" religions. However no claim is made to present the following outline in terms of some other discipline. It arises out of accumulated knowledge and perceptions in the historical and comparative study of religions or *Religionswissenschaft*.

The second reason for theoretical confusion over "new religions" lies in the terminology which from time to time has found fashion. The current strong interest in "new religions" or "new religious movements" in particular areas often creates one-sided or imbalanced perspectives, simply because the wide variety of relevant phenomena in the history and present situation of religions is not sufficiently known. Particular concerns lead to particular views of the field being developed by specialists with divergent disciplinary orientations. Thus some sociologists of religion in western societies are particularly concerned with religions which have been added to the traditionally dominantly Christian culture and which

---

2   This journal was edited for many years in the Netherlands by Remmelt Bakker, then by the present writer (being published by Roots and Branches) and is currently under the direction of Katja Triplett and published by Brill of Leiden. The point about a structured bibliography is that it compels a correspondingly structured conceptualization of the subject under consideration.

seem to threaten its security. It is symptomatic that such religions have been given nicknames such as "Jugendreligionen" in Germany (though the term is no longer fashionable) or "NRM"'s (i. e. new religious movements) in the Anglo-Saxon literature. These terms have not so often been applied, however, to the numerous new religions of sub-Saharan Africa, many of which are regarded by church historians as "independent" churches or referred to in general, somewhat mysteriously, as "independency." In Oceania, a particular group of new religions is designated with the collective terms "cargo cults," and such terms may well seem convenient and even justified in that they single out a leading characteristic of a group of religions with a common history. In the case of the "cargo cults" a significant and indeed distinctive feature was their appearance in response to a dominant incursive culture. However, some other innovatory religious movements may share the feature of cultural response without really expecting the delivery of marvelous riches as cargo from the sea. Vittorio Lanternari sought to make precisely such a generalization.[3] And the other hand, response to an incursive culture cannot be the sole or even the major explanation for many innovatory religious movements if wider history is considered. For this reason there is some justification for other terms such as "revitalization cults." However, "NRM"'s are by no means all "revitalization cults." The very use of such phrases reminds us of the problems which have been created by widespread inaccurate use of the terms "cult" and "sect" which, as is well known, have become terms of abuse in their own right in the media of some countries. All these are reasons for taking a step back and making use of the more general notion of "innovation in religion." This will help to clarify the perspectives in which particular phenomena such as new religions can be located.

Even the very term "new" has often been used quite uncritically. It comprises an unfortunate ambiguity in that it can mean "new" as opposed to "old" or "established" and at the same time it can mean "new" in the sense of "having come recently into being." However, this point, though occasionally mentioned, has not really been pushed through to its conclusion. Studies from whatever quarter have often simply adopted the phrase "new religions" without deciding whether "innovative" or "recent" is meant. The expression "new religious movements" (often abbreviated to "NRMs") is remarkably unhelpful because it includes this deep-seated ambiguity. In much writing it is

---

3   Lanternari 1963: *The Religions of the Oppressed.*

also unthinkingly restricted in reference to western societies. Some of the discussions of so-called "NRMs" would look very strange if transported to Ming China! Yet at the same time, as documented by Overmyer, the theory of relative deprivation was in effect, if not in precisely these terms, first pointed out by a local official during that dynasty.[4]

But this ambiguity is a matter of great theoretical moment. If by "new" we mean "recent," we will be referring to a particular phase in history, and thereby also to some particular regions of the world, e.g. post-nineteen-sixties Europe and America, or post-war Japan, or the period of European imperialist expansion in Asia and elsewhere. Consequently, the theoretical thrust will be directed towards the historical situation which is presumed to be the matrix of the then newly emerging religions. For examples of this we only have to look to well-known older studies by Peter Worsley (1957), Vittorio Lanternari (1964), or to works considering recently founded or recently imported religions in the European or American context (e.g. Clarke and Somers 1993). If however by "new" we mean "innovative," then a different set of theoretical questions is raised in the study of religions. Although the historical situation is always relevant to the understanding of particular cases, it is important to consider, in the construction of theory in the study of religions, what the frequently recurring features of "innovation" in religion are. This does not in itself depend on whether the cases in question are relatively recent, from our present point of view, or on the other hand not at all recent. Buddhism for example, when it first appeared, was a new religion. The Buddha himself had a new message, and he was criticised for leading young people astray. A theoretical perspective on innovation in religion must therefore be broader than limited analyses, whether sociological or other, of what is taking place in specific historical situations.

The third reason for confusion lies in the failure to distinguish between analytical and explanatory theory in the study of religions. In some disciplines, especially sociology and psychology, there is a tendency to advance general "explanations" before investigating the culturally specific character of the particular phenomena to be explained. Thus, unthinkingly, explanatory theory is often given priority over analytical theory. Four major steps are required in the study of religions, and these steps also fall into a natural logical sequence. The first two steps are the eluci-

---

4 Overmyer 1976: *Folk Buddhist Religion. Dissenting Sects in Late Traditional China* (see especially 28–29).

dation and the characterization (of the phenomena), and these steps are essentially *recognitional*. The third and fourth steps are, respectively, analysis (of the internal structures of the phenomena) and correlation (with other other cultural, social or psychological elements). Both of these are *explanatory* and thus *theoretical*. In the first case, parts of a given system or systems are explained in terms of their relation to other parts of the same system or systems. In the second case parts of a given system or systems, or whole systems, are explained in terms of their relation to external factors. In the first case we have to do with *analytical* theory and in the second case with *explanatory* theory. Analytical theory is the task, above all, of specialists in the study of religions. If "others" provide it, they are welcome! They are then in effect becoming specialists in the study of religions. Explanatory theory may be attempted by specialists in the study of religions, or of course also by others. Depending on the interaction between specialisms, the work of explanatory theory may be regarded as interdisciplinary. However, analytical theory is logically prior, simply because it is advisable to have a good theoretical understanding of the internal relations between the various parts of any system before seeking to explain it further in terms of something else.

One might think that the distinction between analytical theory and explanatory theory ought to be a common-place feature of the study of religions, as a discipline in its own right. Yet while both are easily found, here and there, it still seems necessary to point them out clearly not only in the context of teaching but even at the level of mature academic interaction. A more definite assertion of the need for both kinds of theory may encourage specialists in the study of religions to make sure that they positively develop their own contributions, in particular at the level of analytical theory. Some find it helpful to adduce ideas from the general philosophy of science in support of it. Without disagreement, I would assert at the same time that it is perfectly possible to set out the routine steps in the study of religions without calling on the testimony of scientists from elsewhere, who themselves may never have studied any religions. The basic steps in scientific procedure are common knowledge. Experience in the study of religions, as opposed to just talking theoretically about studying religions, is not so common.

The distinction between analytical and explanatory theory is particularly important in connection with the subject of innovation in religions, including the study of "new religions," meaning "religions when they are new." Moreover it is important to get the order of priority right. All too often theorists have stretched out for wide-ranging explanatory theories without first having an adequate analytical grasp of the phenomena. This may be a natural temptation for sociologists, social historians and others who are very interested in "the big picture." As a classic example we may adduce here once again the valuable work by Lanternari (1964). Instructive and stimulating as it is, the very title *The Religions of the Oppressed* poses an underlying problem with the idea that "new religions" have emerged as a response to the challenge of invasive, superior cultures, a matter which thereby explains their appearance. This explanatory theory, which informs Lanternari's whole work, is plausible in many of the cases adduced. However it does not hold good for all cases. It is not very convincing, for example, in the case of Tenrikyō (Japan), which is treated briefly there, nor is it convincing for very numerous other recently founded religions which do not appear in the book. As for many other religions which were "new" at other times, for example Buddhism, Manichaeism or Sikhism, these are not even treated. As a result, what has happened in this case is that the idea of "new religions", conceived in a temporally restricted perspective, has been linked to a particular historical context (the challenge of western colonialism and imperialism) and to one particular *explanatory* theory. A stable analytical theory of the "newness" of "new" religions or, more widely, of innovation in religions is evidently lacking.

It seems important therefore to take a step back and consider the very notion of "innovation in religion." This will help to clarify the general perspectives in which particular problems can be located.

2. A general theory of innovation in religion

We come now to the central features of a general theory of innovation in religion. The view is taken here that a general theory in the study of religion, as in other fields, should be as economical as possible. The further details will be complex enough when account is taken of all the particulars of history. Some of the points already discussed will reappear at appropriate points in the systematic treatment which now follows.

2.1 Religious innovation is related to religious tradition (transmission)

First, the forwarding of all religious culture, that is tradition, in the active sense of *Überlieferung,* involves some degree of innovation. Even in a case when a complex of religious phenomena appears to be completely unchanged, if such could ever be found, a change would nevertheless have occurred in that this same complex would take on a different symbolic force in the changing circumstances surrounding it. This is widely recognised by religious people themselves who appreciate that things have to change in order to remain in some sense the same! Thus tradition, in the sense of transmission, is the general matrix of innovation. This may be summed up in the statement by Ernst Troeltsch: "Wesensbestimmng ist Wesensgestaltung", i. e. "to define the essence is to shape it afresh." On the dynamics of tradition thus conceived, see the preceding articles 5.2 and 5.3 in this volume.

By positing that the theory of innovation in religion stands in broad relation to the theory of tradition (transmission) in religion, we *exclude* the idea that the social analysis of a particular historical period, or of any one region of the world can be determinative for the general theory of innovation in religion. On this basis it will not be theoretically appropriate to say, for example, that new religions occur as a response to the invasive challenge of a stronger external culture. This may be an important social trigger in many cases, as shown by Lanternari and others, but it does not in itself amount to a general theory of innovation in religion. Similarly it is not appropriate to draw a general theory of innovation in religion from observations of "new religious movements" in post-industrial western societies alone, however important these "NRM's" may seem to the politicians and sociological advisors of the day.

The theory of innovation in religion, in its most general form, should stand in relation to the theory of tradition. In this respect, too, the terminology has not always been accurately or clearly used, particularly across disciplinary borders. In the study of religion "tradition" means the passing onward, or forward, of elements of religion. This meaning is quite clear in the German word *Überlieferung*, which means handing over or transmitting. It may be helpful to think of "tradition" as understood in the context of *Religionswissenschaft*, as "transmission." In this sense, tradition (*Überlieferung*) is not at all contrary to innovation. Tradition is the very matrix of innovation. Note that this usage differs from some anthropological usage (c.f. 5.2 above in this volume).

Admittedly, in a secondary sense, strongly innovative movements may come to be perceived to be contrary to the main stream of tradition. However this main stream, in turn, is likely still to be moving forward in its own ways. Hence, within the debates of religious people themselves, tradition may be regarded by some as being backward and rigid. For example, a modern Catholic might regard someone who prefers to "hear the mass" in Latin rather than the vernacular as "a traditionalist." But such usage is either meant as a criticism or, from the other side, as a claim to authenticity. Such views or use of words do not in themselves contribute to the theory of innovation as required in the discipline of *Religionswissenschaft*, and proposed here.

Finally, can anything ever be completely new? Some account should be taken of the idea, currrent in not a few religions, that the teachings or experiences which they provide really are in some sense significantly new. If this idea is taken seriously, such religions, being new, might be thought to have nothing whatever to do with other recognisable tradition. However, in so far as the study of religions (*Religionswissenschaft*) is a historical, social and cultural science, it has great difficulty in identifying any elements in religion which have no antecedents of any kind. Naturally, history is always in some ways new. For this reason religions, too, are always new in that they are affected by change, even when they are considered by their believers to be immutable. But the religious claim that a new revelation has occurred which is qualitatively different from all previous ones, cannot itself in any one case become part of a theory of innovation in religion. The very fact that such claims are made from time to time, though not by any means with the same degree of absoluteness in the case of all new religions, indicates that use is being made of a concept of "revelation" which is already available in the tradition. The example shows only the more clearly how necessary it is to develop a theory of innovation in religion which is not itself dependent on the claims of the religions which might be studied with its help. Once this is understood, the way is clear to study the *sense* of newness which people experience in many cases, and to try to understand how this is related to other aspects of innovation, whether conceptual, social or behavioural.

2.2 Four kinds of innovation in religion

The innovative process may be broadly subdivided into four general forms:

2.2.1 Innovation within current norms
2.2.2 Innovative reform leading to clear distinctions within tradition
2.2.3 Innovation with difference but without clear consequences
2.2.4 Innovation with difference, giving separate forms

5.4 Elements of a General Theory of Innovation in Religion

These need to be related to each of the four aspects of religion. For example, as regards the social aspect of religion:

a) innovation within the norms of current organisations
b) innovative reform leading to organisational separation
c) innovation with difference, but without clear organisational consequences
d) innovation with difference, including new organisational forms

This differentiation should also find appropriate formulation, depending on any particular analysis, with respect to the other main aspects of religion: the conceptual/symbolic, the subjective/attitudinal, and the behavioural (including ritual) aspects. These four forms may seem to be more or less obvious to those familiar with a variety of religions around the world. Should that be the case, so much the better. It lends weight to the analysis. Yet sometimes, once stated, things seem to be very obvious which until that time were not. It is usually overlooked, for example, that innovation in the form of new religious movements or new religions is in most cultures not unrelated to innovation in the context of existing norms. As to the third form (c) it has only recently become really evident in the context of western cultures that it is as much worthy of attention as the others.

Further comments will now be made on these four forms of innovation with special attention to the social aspect of religion (a-d above). It must be kept in mind that this procedure could be essayed with respect to the other main aspects of religion, but to do so would break the limits of this article.

2.2.1 Innovation within current norms

Innovation within current norms refers to the process of up-dating or adapting a religion to new circumstances, while not questioning its overall rightness or appropriateness. It may involve conceptual change, that is, the adjustment of ideas, but it may also involve changes in any other aspect of the religion: social, behavioural or subjective.

As an example consider the use of guitars in place of organs and harmoniums in church services. An earlier example would be the use of harmoniums instead of organs. An even earlier example would be the introduction of the pipe organ into the context of Christian liturgy, where it was previously unknown. Looking to East Asia, an interesting, rather recent innovation is the provision of posting slots for visiting cards in some stone memorials in Buddhist cemeteries. An earlier innovation was the introduction of Buddhist cemeteries to start with, which as far as known was not specifically recommended by the Buddha himself! The process of innovation is sometimes specifically recognised within religious organisations, as for example when Roman Catholic leaders have spoken of *aggiornamento*. On the other hand it is often resisted by others in the same organisations, who fear that adaptations will betray the substance. An interesting recent example of a case where potential innovation is resisted may be seen in a discussion in Finland about the appropriateness or inappropriateness of making space for the use of "oriental" medicine in traditional church contexts.[5]

Such discussions frequently take place in the context of "missiology," and examples may be taken almost at random. Frans Wijsen, writing under the title "Popular Christianity in East Africa: inculturation or syncretism?" (Wijsen 2000) describes how, starting with translations and liturgical adaptions, especially musical ones, a process of radical inculturation of Catholic Christianity has been in process for some decades among the Sukuma people of Tanzania. This came to include all aspects of Sukuma culture, for example, herbal-medicinal and healing traditions, use of amulets, aspects of ancestor reverence and so on, so that in some eyes the process seemed to go too far. Wijsen himelf uses the case to explore reflectively, from a system-internal theological point of view, the range of options for Christian missions from adaptation, through inculturation to what has frequently been criticised as "syncretism." For the study of religions such cases provide interesting materials, and the reflection too is part of the materials. In this particular case the reflective process itself could be criticised for the uncritical use of the term "syncretism," though this is more or less usual in studies which fail to take the study of religions seriously. It is also evident from this example that there is no widely recognizable theory of innovation in religion on which the author might draw. Although a reflective level is reached here, the reflection is theological and internal to one religious tradition.

The process of innovative adaptation is also quite normal in the case of "primal" religions, that is, the religions of specific natural communities. Modern Shintō, within Japan, has therefore become an "adapted primal religion." It also occurs when populations emigrate into different

---

5   Attention was drawn to this by sociologist of religion Helena Helve, who commented on it from an observer's point of view in an article in the Finnish ecclesiastical newspaper *Kirkko ja Kaupunki*.

situations, as with Confucianist Chinese to America, or Hindus to Britain or Germany. Adaptive tactics are also quite normal when religions are consciously transplanted through missionary activity. Not a few religions have their own ways of reflecting on the forms of innovation which might seem to be necessary, or effective. As seen already, this reflectivity is known in the case of Christianity as "missiology." The forms of innovation referred to here could be further subdivided systematically, and the greater the detail, the more the secondary judgements might begin to diverge. For example, an adjustment could also be a moderate reform, that is, the attempt to reinstate elements in the religion which were thought to be neglected or lost.

What all such innovations have in common, however, is that they take place *within* the framework of norms current in the religion in question, which are not themselves put into question. If anything is put into question, it is the innovations. All the more striking is the fact that so many innovations themselves later come to be seen as very normal, and not at all new, like the use of organs in churches. Arguably this first category is the most frequent and the most influential form of innovation in religion, even while those participants in religious systems who find it acceptable are shocked by the other forms of innovation, to which attention will now be turned.

2.2.2 Innovative reform leading to organisational separation

Significantly innovative reforms take place when religious leaders consider that the religion to which they adhere is misleadingly or inadequately understood and presented. When a "reform" is widely accepted, its implications for the religious organisation do not go beyond the adaptations or updating already mentioned. However, many reforms are intrinsically challenging to current routines, and consequently they may easily become provocative, disruptive and separative.

There are many examples of this in the historical development of Protestantism, but also elsewhere in the history of Buddhism, Judaism and Islam. What such forms of innovation have in common is the religious will or drive to transmit what has been received *authentically*, and a strong preparedness to restate what is transmitted in order to achieve this. Thus care for the act of tradition (i.e. handing on) leads to its own forms of innovation, and eventually to separation. Such separation is commonly referred to by religious people themselves as schism or sectarianism. This does not preclude a grudging acceptance of the idea that such divisions have occurred "within" one and the same religion. A classic example of this is the argument over the addition of the word *filioque* in the Nicene creed. While on the one hand some modern secular parlance refers to different Christian churches as different "religions," few would go so far as to say that Protestant churches are "new religions." Here again we can see that general language conventions are not themselves adequate as theoretical definitions in the study of religions. There is also a certain tension with the self-understanding of "reformers," for they do not always themselves imagine that they are innovating, even when they are. (This is a good example of the TWB factor.) A classic example of the close correlation of reform and innovation in the religious consciousness itself is that of the Japanese Buddhist Nichiren who developed new symbols to represent what he took to be original, but meanwhile threatened truths. Though a marginal case, Nichiren's Buddhism may be regarded as a reform movement rather than as a new religion.

2.2.3 Innovation with difference, without clear organisational consequences

In the case of innovation with difference there is no dominant intention to remain within the current norms of an existing religion, whether by adaptation or reform. Rather we observe the emergence of newly conceived options which compete with currently existing religions. In the first place we note a range of phenomena which are not clearly organised, or at least not for the majority of the persons involved. These have recently been referred to as "informal spiritualities" (Helve and Pye 2003). Contemporary "New Age" religion is often understood to be a phenomenon of this kind, but there have been shifts in religious interest and style in past periods which did not at first issue in institutional changes. These are inevitably difficult to chart in retrospect.

2.2.4 Innovation with difference, including new organisational forms

In the fourth form of religious innovation there is no evident intention to remain within the current norms of any existing religion. Rather, the newly conceived options compete as organisations with currently existing religions. As with the last category, this may or may not be consciously so conceived at the time. With this variety of innovation we come to those cases where it is consistent with the self-understanding

5.4 Elements of a General Theory of Innovation in Religion 143

of the religious people themselves to speak of "new religions," whether or not this expression is directly used by them.

Since the term "religion" itself has only become widely current in modern times, one can hardly expect to find the phrase "new religion" being used by those who participate in one of them, except in recent cases. Lately however it has become a self-designation, as in Japan where there is an "Association of New Religions." Nevertheless it is usually quite clear when a religious development is intended to be more than an internal reform in the interests of rediscovering authenticity within an accepted perspective. This is not in itself a sufficient criterion for identifying a new religion, as will be seen later, but it is an excellent guide for positively identifying a large number of cases.

The relationship between new religions and existing traditions displays a spectrum of variations. In some cases the new religion is closely related to one parent tradition, as in the case of certain Indian or Japanese religions such as the teaching of Sri Aurobindo at the community of Auroville, or the Japanese religion Kurozumikyō, which began in a Shintō shrine. On the other hand a new religion may have a complex relationship to more than one existing religion or other cultural traditions. Organised Gnosticism (in the Hellenistic period) is a good example of this. So too are the Latin-American Umbanda and Candomblé cults. In the case of the Cargo Cults, elements are clearly drawn from two previously distinct cultural worlds. Elsewhere in the history of religions, intentional eclecticism and synthesis can be documented, as in Manichaeism or in the Cao Dai religion of Vietnam.

It was said that such innovative movements compete with existing religious organisations. This means for example, that they may seek comparable legal or political status. In particular they compete for adherents, even while in some cases asserting that new converts are not required to leave their current religious affiliation.

The question as to just how new a new religion really is, or can be, was already addressed in the prolegomena. Sometimes a new religion is remarkably like previously existing ones, and indeed a successor relationship is often claimed. Thus Mohammad is understood to be the final Prophet in a series of prophets. As the messenger (*rasul*) of God he is believed to have received a new, but final revelation. According to The Church of Jesus Christ of the Latter Day Saints (commonly referred to as the Mormon Church) Joseph Smith is the final prophet. He too "discovered" a new and final revelation. Sometimes the identification of newness is a matter of deep interest to the believers, even when prior tradition is in some sense recognised. In the case of the Korean "Won Buddhism" for example, it is asserted that this is a new religion, and at the same time it is claimed that its founder had an important precursor in the Indian Buddha, from whose life-work Buddhism began. "Won" means perfect and complete, but the teaching and practice of Won Buddhism is understood as offering a new beginning for humankind, and not as a mere reform of Buddhism. Only after conceiving the main outlines of the teaching did the founder inspect various existing religions and conclude that Buddhism was the closest precursor. On this basis the name of the religion was then formulated to include "Buddhism" within it. (Cf. "Won Buddhism as a Korean new religion" at 5.6 below.)

2.3 Correlatory explanations of religious innovation

Finally there is an important implication to be noted for *explanatory* theories of religious innovation, whether these are developed in a sociological, a socio-psychological or some other similar perspective. The purpose of such theories should be clearly stated, and it should be understood that they go beyond the analytical theory of religious innovation. This "going beyond" may seem urgently desirable and advantageous, especially within the discourse of the discipline involved. However, it is even more urgent for would-be proponents of explanatory theory to take into account the contours of the general theory of religious innovation. In particular the features of religious innovation exposed by an analytical theory such as the present one should be presupposed. An explanatory theory should include a specification of which of the four main types of innovation it is supposed to be related to.

Naturally, major determining factors such as colonialism, missionary activity, culture clash, economic development, modernisation processes, the emergence of post-industrial culture, etc. (to name just a few of the sociologically relevant ones) must be identified, as these will surely play a part in attempts at explanatory theory in particular cases. At the same it should be realised that, because all such factors are historically relative, completely generalised explanations in terms of such features are doomed to failure. In other words, we should expect explanatory theories of innovation in religion *to be diverse*. Not expected to be diverse, on the other hand, is the overall analytical theory of religious innovation, in the context of which particular explanatory theories can be formulated.

Note that all of the above commentary could be repeated with appropriate variations for the other main aspects of religions apart from the social aspect.

3. Epilogomena

In these epilogomena some implications and connections to various themes in the theory of religion will be considered. Connections to the general theory of religious tradition are particularly important here. This is also regarded as pertaining to the analytical rather than the explanatory theory of religion, as defined above.

3.1 Innovation and the theory of tradition

Clearly, the theory of innovation in religion should be consistent with other aspects of a theory of tradition in religion, in so far as these have been satisfactorily formulated.

One of the main features to be taken into account in analysing religious tradition or transmission is the diversity of possible interpretations and the dynamic openness of the *process* of tradition which is under consideration. The forms of innovation referred to above all include an element of uncertainty as regards their interpretation. The question of the "authenticity" of tradition, or of its coherence, is therefore thrown up again and again. Whether or not a recent religious movement is an "authentic," statement of the parent tradition, bearing a clear and close relationship to the centre of that tradition, whether it becomes a separate sect, or whether it is no less than a new religion in its own right, are questions which in many cases cannot be answered immediately. While proponents and other participants in the process offer their opinions with urgency, it may be necessary for specialist observers to wait, even for several decades, before a sound historical judgement can really be formed on such questions. To illustrate, it has become clear by now, for example, that Christian Science is a new religion, rather than a Christian sect. The same *might* be also said already for Unitarian Universalism, but the matter is probably still debatable.

3.2 Instinctive dynamics and self-conscious innovation

The relation between instinctive dynamics and self-conscious innovation may be understood as a spectrum in which different actors stand in different positions. The considerations arising over this question arise in relation to *all* kinds of innovation in religion and not only in the case of new religions.

The first point to be grasped in this connection is that the range of possible processes or options remains, broadly speaking, constant. For example it is possible for a teaching formulated in one culture to be either more, or less, radically adapted when the teaching is transmitted to another culture. The questions about which elements are crucial, which are dispensable, and which can be newly incorporated, will arise in every case. The answers fall somewhere within the range of possibilities, while the specifics depend on the particularities of the religion and of the originating and newly hosting cultures.

The second point is that the degree of reflection about these processes and the myriad decisions concerning them which are taken by participants and believers varies from religion to religion. In Mahāyāna Buddhism the concept of "skilfulness in means" or "skilful means" is a wonderfully clear example of the development of reflection on these matters occurring at the very heart of a dynamic development within the tradition itself. It was of constitutive importance at the time when Mahāyāna Buddhism was formulated over against earlier Buddhist ways of thinking, somehow incorporating these and at the same time claiming to articulate clearly and faithfully their inner workings. In the case of Christianity the obvious locus for such reflection is provided by studies known as "missiology," while particular terms such as "inculturation" or "syncretism" (used theologically and pejoratively, unlike in the study of religions) have played a clear role. In Catholicism more distinctive terms such as "accommodation" and "aggiornamento" (up-dating) may also be found. It is doubtful whether the appearance of such reflective terminology in any religion really makes much difference to the range of options open to its representatives. However it may make the legitimation or the condemnation of certain options easier in the context of the arguments internal to the traditions themselves.

As to the relationship between such internal reflection and the study of religions (*Religionswissenschaft*) it should be clearly understood that they are not the same. The correlation of "missiology" and "study of religions" (*Missionswissenschaft* versus *Religionswissenschaft*) is, at least for the latter, misleading. This should not be overlooked, although the reflective process within particular religions is not only part of the phenomenon to be studied, but may also provide valuable hints for theoretical development within the study of religions.

Of particular interest in connection with the relation between instinctive dynamics and self-consciousness is the mentality, and the intentionality of initiators in religion. The term *initiators* may be used as the most general term to include founders, reformers, prophets, etc. Not all initiators regard themselves as "founders" of a religion. Indeed, many would be rather surprised if they could learn, later, that they had "founded" a new religion. Thoughtful observers have often remarked that the main figure at the centre of the origins of a new religion was not really the founder, but rather it was his or her immediate followers who constructed the religion as a response or an addition to the initiator's activity. Thus, paradigmatically, Jesus did not "found" Christianity, but it is sometimes said that Paul did, though this is certainly an oversimplification. Similarly, reformers wish to reform their religious institutions, and it is only by default and with hindsight that they or their followers discover that they have formed a new religious association. On the other hand many initiators are well aware that they are innovating and in some cases founding. In some cultures, as in the countries of East Asia, this option is even taken for granted as the kind of thing which one might decide to do.

3.3 Innovation and syncretism

A specific aspect of the general theory of religious tradition may be addressed with the help of the term "syncretism." However, considerable care is needed here. The term "syncretism" has been widely used not only in the literature of *Religionswissenschaft* but also, less critically, in that of anthropology and oriental studies of various kinds. It has also been used by theologians as a term of opprobrium, and indeed frequently still occurs in this sense. For theologians it usually means an adaptive mixture which loses track of essentials and is therefore no longer admissable. Here, however, we are concerned with a quite different usage, thought to be an analytically helpful use of the term in the context of the (non-theological) study of religions. This is not the place to go into more detail on the theory of "syncretism," which is a leading theme in Part Six of this volume. Note however that the preferred use of the term "syncretism" has a close relationship to the wider theory of religious tradition, to the question of conscious intentionality in the construction of religion, and to theoretical reflection about innovation in religion including the creation of new religions. For some reason, writing about new religions often includes reference to their syncretic character. However, new religions are as syncretistic, or not, as older religions. The term "syncretism" should be used to refer to the dynamic, open interactions of elements of diverse origin in a particular religious situation. It is therefore *not* desirable to use "syncretistic" simply to mean the same as either "synthetic" or "eclectic." When syncretism is understood, dynamically, as "the temporary ambiguous coexistence of elements from diverse religious and other contexts within a coherent religious pattern," then it follows that a syncretistic situation can be resolved in three different ways:

> assimilation (the domination of one strand of meaning by another)
> dissolution (the drawing apart of the associated elements)
> synthesis (the coalesence of originally disparate elements in a new religion).

It is in this sense that there is an interesting relationship between syncretistic processes and the emergence of new religions.

3.4 What counts as a new religion?

This section of the theory states which aspects of religion must be innovative for a new religion to have come into being. In the general morphology of religion, there are four main aspects to be considered: the conceptual, the behavioural, the social and the subjective. For a new religion to come into being, innovation in all of these aspects would normally be present, and is necessary to a clear degree in two, namely the conceptual and the social.

There must be a socially identifiable religious group or community which is not identical with a previously existing one, for otherwise the innovation would have taken place, however noticeably, within the existing religion (type 1). On the other hand, there must be a significant cluster of new conceptual elements, that is, a new symbolic *Gestalt* must be available, for otherwise the new group would be, precisely, a sect within the dominant stream of tradition (type 2). Having regard to the other aspects, there will surely be some degree of innovation at the same time in the subjective and the behavioural aspects. However such innovation, in itself, can also be accommodated within existing religion (type 1) and is therefore not alone sufficient to produce a new religion or to count as one. In sum therefore, the emergence of a new re-

5.4 Elements of a General Theory of Innovation in Religion

ligion requires a sufficient degree of innovation in a combination of at least the social and conceptual aspects of religion. A good example for thinking this through in detail would be the case of early Buddhism as a new religion.

3.5 Innovation, consistency and authenticity

This in turn leads on to questions about the relation between innovation, consistency and authenticity. Some observers are impatient with these questions, simply declaring, for example, that anybody who claims to be a Buddhist is one. However this reaction is not adequate either for a serious history of religions or for a serious theory of religious innovation.

The Buddhist tradition is so widely established, in so many cultural regions and cultures, that the question frequently arises as to whether a particular movement of organisation is Buddhist or not. Sometimes a movement claims to be "Buddhist," but the claim is questioned by others. And in other, rather fewer cases a religion which claims to represent a new revelation may offer little but repackaged Buddhist ideas. Won Buddhism is a special case in that, as noted already, is representatives describe it as a "new religion" and "Buddhism" at one and the same time. The question must be addressed therefore as to whether Won Buddhism is "Buddhist" and if so, in what sense, a question which has been addressed in more detail elsewhere (cf. "Won Buddhism as a Korean new religion" at 5.6 in this volume). The concept of "orthodoxy" may play a role in such deliberations. The teaching of Won Buddhism has much in common with the ideas of Mahāyāna Buddhism, and yet we may still hear the question whether this in turn is "orthodox" from the point of view of other Buddhists. This is difficult not least because a rigorous attempt to apply the term "orthodox" to the history of Buddhism would probably leave hardly anything over. However the fundamental difficulty is that the term "orthodox" adds nothing (though often carelessly adduced) because it implies a normative decision, while the specialist in the study of religions, or the historian of religion is supposed to have no such standpoint. Nevertheless it is sometimes necessary to attempt to provide an answer to the question as to whether a particular movement may fairly be described as "Buddhist" or not. Sometimes claims are made which are evidently spurious, as in the case of the Japanese religion Aum Shinrikyō (see "Aum Shinrikyō: Can Religious Studies cope?" at 5.7 below in this volume). This question is really part of a much wider and older discussion about the question of consistency within historically extended religious traditions (cf. Pye and Morgan 1973). In disputed cases the question of relative authenticity has to be addressed by historians of religion, but this is a question of historical coherence and reasonableness of claims to identity, rather than a question of "orthodoxy" which can only be decided upon by a religious authority from its normative point of view. The term "orthodox" has no place in the study of religions except as a concept within the field under study.

3.6 Claims to universality and finality

It is notable that in the case of new religions, there is commonly found, in one form or another, a claim to universality and finality, or at least relative finality for our time. This arises for two reasons. First, new religions are by definition not primal religion, traces of which can be discerned even in pre-history. That is to say, new religions arise over against any primal religion which is current in their context and define themselves critically or transformatively in relation to it. Second, major critical religions, soteriological, gnostic and other, have also been in place for many centuries. For new religions, these are a fact of life. Consequently, new religions are faced with an apologetic need to present some kind of standpoint vis-à-vis the existing major religions with which they, in theory, compete (even if it is part of their religious stance that they claim not to compete). Because of the frequently observed cross-over effect from critical religions to primal religion, the theoretical distinctions made in the typology of religion are quite likely to be blurred in the apologetic statements of new religious leaders.

Various options are available to new religions here. First, it may be maintained that the existing religions are inadequate and should be abandoned. Second, it may be maintained that the existing religions were appropriate to past times, but have now found completion or fulfillment in the new religion, and may or should therefore be abandoned. Third, it may be argued that the existing religions are inadequate in profound matters of religion, but may or should be maintained for practical reasons, such as the provision of funeral arrangements. Fourth, it may be argued that all religions are essentially one and the same, so that older religions may be respected while the new religion which realises this is to be preferred. Fifth, rarely, it may be suggested that the new religion is both new and at the same time identical with an existing major religion. Any of these arguments may be found to be advanced by the representatives of new religions with respect to older, established religions. At the same time there is rarely a case where a new religion provides a legitimation of this kind in relation to another new religion. The contemporary competition is simply ignored.

This state of affairs arises because of the historically entrenched position of certain major religions which already make universal claims, especially Buddhism, Christianity and Islam. In more recent periods of history new religions mounting a claim to universal salvation or universal truth need to explain why it is that a new message in this regard is necessary. This explains why it is that quite a number of new religions specifically claim to solve the perceived problem that there is a plurality of religions. On this basis they include dialogues with major established religions in their programs, while usually showing little interest in carrying out dialogues with other new religions which are their rivals. Moreover there is a striking absence of discussion within new religions about the fact that there are also other new religions which complement, fulfill or supersede existing religions.

Bibliographical references

Clarke, Peter B. and Somers, Jeffrey (eds.) 1994. *Japanese New Religions in the West*. Sandgate Folkestone (Curzon Press).
Earhart, Byron H. 1970. *The New Religions of Japan: A Bibliography of Western-languae Materials*. Tokyo (Sophia University). (Second Edition 1983, Ann Arbor (Center for Japanese Studies, The University of Michigan.)
Helve, Helena and Pye Michael 2003. "Theoretical correlations between world- view, civil religion, institutional religion and informal spiritualities" in: *Temenos* 37–8 (2001–2): 87–106.
Lanternari, Vittorio 1963. *Religions of the Oppressed*. (Originally 1960 *Movimenti religiosi di libertà e di salvezza dei popoli oppressi*, Milano (Giangiacomo Feltrinelli Editore.)
Overmyer, Daniel L. 1976. *Folk Buddhist Religion. Dissenting Sects in Late Traditional China*, Cambridge Massachusetts (Harvard University Press).
Pye, Michael and Morgan, Robert (eds.) 1972. *The Cardinal Meaning. Essays in Comparative Hermeneutics: Buddhism and Christianity* (Religion and Reason 6), The Hague (Mouton).
Wijsen, Frans 2000. "Popular Christianity in East Africa: inculturation or syncretism?" in *Exchange* 29 (1–4): 37–60.
Worsley, Peter 1957. *The Trumpet Shall Sound: A study of "cargo cults in Melanesia*. London (MacGibbon and Kee).

This paper is published here for the first time.

5.5 New Religions in East Asia

This article is conceived as an overview of new religions in various countries of East Asia which brings out some of their common features. The present version contains small improvements over the original publication. However, the transliteration of Chinese could not be standardised in this paper because of the variety of secondary sources quoted.

Introduction

The social, political and cultural patterns of the countries of East Asia are quite varied and, since each is extremely complex in its own right, specialists usually concentrate on just one of the countries concerned. On the other hand, the common heritage deriving from China, albeit developed in strong new ways by the recipient countries, Korea, Japan and Vietnam, makes it interesting and valuable to consider particular subjects in a wider East Asian perspective. This applies not least to the emergence of new religious movements, which have rarely been considered in this way. Such movements, usually referred to here as *new religions*, have appeared at various times in all four countries mentioned and have been confronted, rejected or digested by the powers of the day in accordance with the varying exigencies of their historical situation. At the same time some common assumptions and perspectives can be discerned which, even if simply stated, help us to understand what is going on in particular cases. After a little more discussion of this background some introductory information will be given about specific new religions in China, Vietnam, Korea and Japan. In view of the large number of such new religions it will only be possible to present selected examples, and even then only very briefly.

The most significant common feature of the four countries of East Asia is that over many centuries they shared, and variously developed, the written culture derived from ancient China. In the transcriptions used here no diacritical marks are provided except for an indication of the long vowels in Japanese. Variations may also occur because of the sources used.

Even today, although Korean is mainly written with its own phonetic script (*hangul*) and Vietnamese is written with an accent-laden Roman script, it is possible to see within these languages a large common stock of vocabulary. This holds good also for Japanese, in which the Chinese characters are still widely used in combination with two Japanese phonetic syllabaries (*kana*). In the field of religion, one has only to think of the names of religions such as Tenrikyō (Japanese meaning "The Teaching of Heavenly Reason"), Won Bulgyo[1] (Korean meaning "Perfect Buddhism"), or Cao Dai (Vietnamese meaning "High Palace" or more literally, "High Platform"). Naturally such terminology carries different nuances in the different languages, just as the use of terms has shifted within Chinese itself and may vary as between the People's Republic of China, Taiwan and among widely dispersed overseas Chinese. Moreover there has been influence in more than one direction, for some terms, though based on Chinese characters, were introduced into modern Chinese and Korean from Japanese during the nineteenth century, at a time when there was a particularly rapid linguistic development in that country to take account of the political and cultural pressure of the western world. This applies notably to the nineteenth century usage of a common term for "religion" (Japanese: *shūkyō*, Chinese: *zōngjiào*), although this itself has a pre-history which is usually overlooked (Pye 1994, and Part Four of the present work, *passim*). In the internal discourse of the religions themselves, there are common themes such as "long life", "growth", "spiritual world", "obligation(s)", "gratitude", "parent(s)", which are all based on a widely recognisable religious vocabulary and can usually be expressed by means of Chinese characters.

In view of these cultural and linguistic relationships it is not surprising that typical responses to the appearance of new religions also display some recognisable similarities between the countries of East Asia. The days when China provided an immediate political model for its neighbours to adopt and follow are long past, and no attempt will be made here to summarise the historical developments of many centuries. Nowadays the political systems vary considerably. Yet even so there are certain assumptions concerning the management of religions which continue to be widely shared. The first of these is that it is regarded as quite normal that there should be more than one religion, and that religions are different from each other. In other words religious

---

1   Won Pulkyo is also found.

pluralism is recognized as a matter of fact, and hence as a political fact. Second is the assumption that certain dominant traditions have a kind of priority. Traditionally these were the "three teachings;" namely Confucianism, Buddhism and Daoism (Taoism in the older transcription). In modern times Christianity has moved into this general category of perception, especially in China, Korea and Vietnam, but also in Japan in spite of the fact that the numbers there have remained very small. The same is true for Islam in modern, mainland China, though on the other hand the Chinese People's Republic regards Confucianism not as a religion but as a rival ideology. In Japan, Shintō remains in this dominant category, even after its separation from the state after the Second World War. The same might be said for the reconstructed "Shamanism" which has been promoted recently as a significant feature of Korean culture. All of these dominant traditions have somehow achieved a position from which they cannot really be dislodged. Third, on the other hand, is the assumption that *innovation* in religion leading to a diversity of schools, sects or associations, is not surprising. Indeed it seems to be widely expected when particularly gifted teachers or charismatic leaders appear. Such innovations may be regarded either as variants of the dominant traditions or, alternatively, as standing in a position of tension with them. For the political powers of the day, that is a serious question. Fourth, consequently, is the assumption that such innovatory diversity should be considered from the point of view of the general welfare of the state and the public. Can the innovatory movements be contained within known patterns, or are they likely to cause confusion and trouble? Above all, it is thought, such new religious movements or groups should not be permitted to pose a danger to the state. If anything, just as the dominant traditions usually are, they should in some way be supportive of the state. Fifth is the assumption that the task of registering and regulating religions, like that of regulating currencies and calendars, is the duty of the state and its civil servants.

These assumptions all seem very evident in the countries of East Asia. Yet it should not be forgotten that while some of them may be found elsewhere, they are not universal. There are many countries in the world where there is no official register of "religions" or of "new religions". The particular mix of assumptions about the position of well-established religions and relatively new religions is different in the various countries of Europe, in India, in Indonesia, in the Americas (north and south) and in Russia, to name just a variety of interesting cases. While there are, nowadays, significant variations between the countries of East Asia, the underlying cluster of assumptions nevertheless continues to be widely shared in that region. The number of registered religious bodies in Japan is huge as compared with the five which are officially recognised in the People's Republic of China. These are: Buddhism, Daoism, Catholicism, Christianity and Islam. ("Christianity" means Protestant Christianity in this case.) Yet the idea that it is the state which decides which religions are to be recognised, and which are not, has a long history in all the countries of East Asia. So, too, does the perception that a new religion might present a threat to the established order, not only to the dominant religions but also to the political system. The matter was crystallised in a short treatise ascribed to the first ruler of the Ming dynasty (1368–1644) who decided, after having established overall military control, that it would be a good idea to regulate "the three teachings" (*sānjiào*) and associated matters such as the "network of gods and spirits" and thereby to exclude newly appearing minority religions which might upset the political order.[2]

The politicians of today, whether their perspective is socialist or capitalist, also wish to know whether any particular new religion is likely to disturb the political system which they favour, or perhaps succeed in upsetting one which they disfavour. New religions of East Asia which cannot be studied in detail without some reference to politics include Cao Dai (Vietnam), Tonghak and Tongilkyo (Korea), Taiping and Falungong (China), Sōka Gakkai and Aum Shinrikyō (Japan). These examples are only the tip of the iceberg. Even religions which may seem to be politically quiet represent a reliable voting mass which politicians in democracies need to take into account. Independent observers, for their part, should not be taken in by simple shouts for "religious freedom", when what is really implied by some well-publicised activities is a call for political change. The negative reaction to a call for political change by members of a new religion such as Falungong, is not simply an expression of current political power structures. It also has a historical background in the well-established East Asian idea that new religions might be a cloak for political unrest or even an attempt to topple the state. The Taiping rebellion in modern, pre-communist China was a clear example of this. The role of the Cao Dai in the sequence

---

2 For a translation and commentary on the Emperor's own short treatise on the subject see Taylor 1983. For further discussion see "Three teachings (*sānjiào*) theory and modern reflection on religion" (2.4 in Volume One above) and "Syncretism in Chinese temples of South-East Asia and China" (6.6 below).

of Vietnamese wars is also a case in point, since it even maintained its own army. In fact there are so many examples of political influence wielded by new religions that it is not surprising that governments react nervously.

A more theoretical question concerning the new religions of East Asia is whether they can properly be viewed as belonging to a particular historical period, such that a specific explanation for their emergence can be drawn from that period. Would it be right to explain the emergence of new religions in Japan, for example, by saying that in the context of the defeat of the Japanese Empire in 1945 there was a spiritual vacuum which new religions rushed to fill? While superficially attractive, such explanations cannot achieve a more general validity. This is simply because new religions have appeared at various times in history. They have arisen both in times of poverty and in times of prosperity, in times of relative peace and in times of relative instability or political insecurity, and so on. Observers of the Japanese scene used to speak of "newly arisen religions" (shinkōshūkyō), a term which has something of the nuance of *nouveaux riches*, only for this to be corrected by the response of the religions themselves who felt that the term was degrading.[3] They preferred simply to be called "new religions". After all, some of the "new religions" had not just "arisen" but were by then already quite well established, having their origins in the Tokugawa Period, before the onslaught of the western powers. The term "newly arisen" is therefore usually avoided by foreign writers, even though in its English form it is not necessarily pejorative and descriptively is not entirely inappropriate. Then again, in the nineteen-eighties, the existing club of new religions, some of which formed a "league" to protect their common interests, were shocked to see the emergence of yet more new religions, described by journalists and academics, without any good theoretical reason, as "new new religions" (shinshinshū-kyō). The difficulty with all such terms is that they are inherently journalistic, by which I mean that they overemphasize the importance of a particular, current situation. Of course the particular context is important. On the other hand it is important to understand that the religious culture of East Asia has long been capable of producing innovatory forms, which

---

3   The term was used, without polemical intent, by sociologist Takagi (Hiroo) in his work entitled *Nihon no shinkōshūkyō* (i.e. "The newly arisen religions of Japan") which was an important starting point in the post-war study of Japanese new religions (Takagi 1959).

in many cases turn into fully-fledged new religions, at more or less any time.

Chinese new religions

Against this overall background we can appreciate the report of a Ming dynasty official in 1597, as reported by Daniel Overmyer in his fascinating account of what (in 1976) he called "dissenting sects in late traditional China" (Overmyer 1976). This official argued that four kinds of people regard disorder as advantageous: the hopelessly poor, those who are by nature cruel and greedy, those who propound "heresies" such as the White Lotus Society, and political adventurers. With a heart-rending account of the poverty of the masses the mandarin then exhorted the emperor to see to it that consumption at the top was reduced and the needs of the people met. In effect, we find here that the theory of *relative deprivation*, advanced as an explanation of the rise of "dissenting sects", was first expounded in a memorial to the throne written by an unusually perceptive and compassionate Chinese civil servant. Admittedly, a precise reading of the texts adduced by Overmyer does not precisely document a *causal* argument from (a) relative deprivation to (b) the propounding of "heresies," Rather, both of these, along with lust for riches or power, were viewed as combining to produce disorder.

The White Lotus movement at the centre of Overmyer's study was focused on a mantra, of which the original Chinese characters (reproduced on the dust-jacket) mean "homeland of true voidness, unbegotten father and mother". From this we may deduce that, in terms of its own self-understanding, that is, from the emic point of view, this movement was neither seditious nor superstitious. The words "unbegotten father and mother," Overmyer suggests, may have had a mythical reference (Overmyer 1976: 238); but they should also be understood as being complementary to "homeland of true voidness." Thus apart from any mythical reference the characters making up this mantra point straight to the heart of Mahāyāna Buddhism. As a form of rhetoric such mantras are a little reminiscent of the political slogans current today in mainland China.

Much of the diversity in traditional Chinese religion would not in all eyes be regarded as being provided by "new religions". Should the cults focused on particular divinities such as Mazu, the popular protectress of sailors, or Guānyīn, the Buddhist bodhisattva who appears in many different forms to give assistance as required and at the same to promote the *Lotus Sūtra*, be regarded as "religions" in their own right, and hence at the point of their emergence as new religions? The alternative is to see them as elements within a wider pattern of religious culture, providing options for particular providers and particular consumers. However there was a time when these forms of devotion were new. The Mazu cult, now so popular in Taiwan, goes back to the Song Dynasty. The Guanyin cult has Indian origins, but developed markedly within China when Guanyin himself was identified with a local goddess, thereby taking on the female form so popular today in China and other countries of East Asia. These examples illustrate the general propensity towards religious innovation, even though by today, especially in Taiwan and among overseas Chinese, they have simply become established as a significant part of the overall religious repertoire. Even in mainland China, the Guanyin cult is not nowadays regarded as problematic. There are two simple reasons for this. First, it is regarded as a feature of the Buddhist tradition, which is permitted. Second, the devotees of Guanyin do not advance political claims.

A major feature of specialised lay movements in China has been vegetarianism, and this has often been coupled not only with the Buddhist ideal of asceticism but also with the cultivation of longevity, which is more typical of Daoism. In Buddhism longevity is regarded as something of a diversion, since it holds the individual even longer within the ordinary cycle of birth-and-death. Thus such movements have not infrequently been regarded, from a Buddhist point of view, as unorthodox or heretical. From within however, the argument has been rather that "the three teachings are one," the third teaching being Confucianism. In this way a claim to regularity and even orthodoxy could be made, even while an independent organisation was being set up. However it was precisely the existence of separate organisations which was usually regarded by the authorities as problematic and therefore often led to repression. Though new groups could be prohibited, prohibitions could also be lifted. An example is the religion known as Lijiao, which was first forbidden along with White Lotus sects at the beginning of the nineteenth century but in 1883 was declared to be harmless. Lijiao was even regarded quite positively because of its prohibition of alcohol and smoking, at a time when opium was a major threat to society. On the other hand, since meat-eating was permitted, the followers could take part in normal daily life without strain. In 1948 the religion is thought to have had about fifteen million followers, about half a million of them living in Tianjin. Following the Communist revolution Lijiao has continued in Taiwan, albeit with a greatly weakened following.[4]

It should not be concluded from this that "sects" have been suppressed under Communism but freely permitted in Taiwan. A group with a considerable following known as "The Way of Unity" (Yiguandao, also I-kuan Tao), is a case in point. "Unity" in this case means something like reliable consistency or integration. It was founded effectively in the 1880's by a certain Mr. Lu, who assumed the personal name of Zhongyi, meaning "central unity." The teaching includes the idea that Lu was the seventeenth recipient of a "celestial mandate" (*tianming*) in a complex succession including Confucius and others. Lu Zhongyi (1853–1925) was also regarded as the incarnation of the expected Maitreya Buddha (Chinese: Mi Le Fo) and at the same time the first patriarch of the "White Yang Epoch." In the twentieth century, under the successor leadership, The Way of Unity experienced political difficulties because it was suspected of collaborating with the Japanese invaders of China. From the communist point of view it was regarded as "a reactionary secret society which, under the cover of religious activities, served the Japanese invaders and Kuomintang reactionaries."[5] However it was also compelled to operate outside the law in Taiwan until 1983.[6]

The name Yiguandao has usually been translated as "The Unity Sect," but nowadays it seems more misleading than ever to use the word "sect" when Dao (Tao in the older Wade-Giles romanisation) can perfectly well be translated as "Way" in line with the self-understanding of the believers themselves. Unfortunately, sinologists have long been unable to shake off the terms "sect" and "sectarianism," which reflect on the one hand the dominant interest of the political powers in China and on the other hand the continuing influence of J. J. M. de Groot's two-volume work *Sectarianism and Religious Persecution in China, A Page in the History of Religions* (Amsterdam 1903). In the

---

4   The information on Lijiao is drawn from Hubert Seiwert's *Volksreligion und nationale Tradition in Taiwan* (1985), see especially 182–4.
5   *A Chinese-English Dictionary* (Beijing Institute of Foreign Languages 1978): 810.
6   This information is drawn from David K. Jordan's extremely interesting chapter on the subject in Jordan and Overmyer 1986. In line with the policy of that work the group is referred to there, using the Wade-Giles romanisation system, as I-kuan Tao. Jordan's account includes very much valuable information based on personal observations and encounters, and indeed the whole book is to be recommended for various reasons.

colonial period the underlying motivation for an interest in the fate of "sectarianism" was the wider question of freedom for religious activities in the interests of Christian missions. However the history of religions as conceived today is not required to be either colonial or neo-colonial; in fact it should be required to be neither.

A major Chinese new religion in modern times was the Taiping movement which began as a preaching organization in 1844 and ended with a military rebellion against the central government. The rebellion was put down in 1854. The meaning of the name Taiping is "great peace." This term has a long history, for the "heavenly kingdom of great peace" was the name given to an alternative government set up in north China by a rebellious movement which which was active from 184 until 207 C.E.. Taiping also occurs as an era name during the Song dynasty.

The nineteenth century Taiping movement was started by Hong Xiuquan, the son of a poor Hakka family in southern China. Hong was a keen student of the classics but failed several times in the public examinations used to select civil servants. After giving up he became ill, and during the illness he experienced a vision of an old man in heaven who told him that humanity was worshipping demons instead of the creator. In the vision, Hong received a sword in order to kill demons. In later visions he met with a middle-aged man who instructed him in the methods of killing demons and to whom he referred as his elder brother. Later, on the basis of a miscellany of protestant missionary writings provided by a cousin named Li, he identified these two figures with God the Father and with Jesus. Hong considered himself to be a further son of God with a mission to kill demons and establish the true form of worship. Hong and Li baptised each other, and Hong began a preaching career. On discovering that the "true teaching" was also being taught in Kanton (Guangdong) Hong sought to join the mission, led by an American missionary. However he was refused baptism, thus experiencing a second major rejection, and consequently returned to his own independent religious teaching.

The political turn came about as a result of an armed conflict between the Hakka, to whom Hong belonged, and another group in the region. Hong played a decisive role in the conflict and quickly found himself surrounded by his own local army. In 1851 he was proclaimed "Emperor of the Heavenly Kingdom of Great Peace" thereby becoming both the religious and the political head of the movement. In a period of weak central government, the local mandarins could do nothing. Further campaigns followed, intended to establish the new "heavenly kingdom" on a secure earthly footing. Not only considerable territory but even major cities such as Nanjing were taken over. In 1854 the threat to the central Manchu government was such that only foreign intervention was able to put a stop to it. While it lasted, the Taiping movement was a force for modernisation in Chinese society. Foot-binding and prostitution were forbidden, and women's organisations were formed in parallel to those of the men. The male members were known for their long unbraided hair, avoiding the traditional "pig-tail". Opium, tobacco and alcohol were forbidden.

Against this background a few remarks may be made on the meditation movement known as Falungong, which has attracted considerable media attention in recent years. The self-presentation of this movement, in widely available pamphlets, emphasises a meditational practice based on the symbol of the wheel (*lun*) of dharma (*fa*), which is expected not only to bring about a positive personal development but also to renew society in general, in particular current society in mainland China.[7] This is where the difficulties begin. The question for the Chinese government today is therefore none other than the traditional question which has always been posed regarding separatist, innovative religious movements, namely whether Falungong represents a social and ultimately a political threat. A relatively new feature in the situation is that this question clashes with a requirement for religious freedom (for all and any "religions"?) advanced by leading western powers.[8] However even this is not quite new, for the same demand was made of the countries of East Asia in the nineteenth century with a view to opening the various countries for missionary work from the west. It is not surprising that a religion which is organised from a base in New York and which encourages its members to choose the symbolically crucial Tiananmen Square as a place to meditate arouses a suspicious and heavy response.

---

7   For what was possibly the first detailed academic treatment, see Seiwert 2000.
8   This requirement is mainly pushed by the USA as a means of causing difficulties for the Communist government of mainland China, but it should be noted that by no means all "western" powers have the same arrangements for "religious freedom" and for the relations between religions and the state. There are major differences between Germany and the USA, for example, over the treatment of Scientology, which in Germany is widely regarded as a threat to the constitution.

Vietnam and Korea

It may seem strange at first sight to link Vietnam and Korea in a single section, for they are far apart and have few mutual contacts. Yet there are excellent reasons for so doing. Both Vietnam and Korea have been massively influenced over many centuries by the literary, political and ethical culture of China. Their governmental structure was dominated by Confucianism. The Buddhist traditions of both countries are also largely Chinese-derived. In this Vietnam differs from the other countries of South-East Asia, where Indian or Sri-Lankan derived Theravāda traditions are dominant. In Vietnam, as in Korea, the Mahāyāna Pure Land and Chan traditions have been historically dominant. In both countries Daoist elements and various divinatory techniques common to East Asia have been accompanied by indigenous shamanist or spiritist practices with ancient roots and considerable influence in modern times. Both countries underwent colonial domination during the period of Asian modernization, suffered as hot war zones during the so-called Cold War between the big powers, and are now seeking to build their own nations, independently, with a strong consciousness of cultural identity. The current division of Korea into two states may be regarded as temporary and by the time this account comes to be read, readers may already be hearing about further coordination and even integration between north and south, as in Vietnam.[9] Of course there are and will be political differences, however a certain convergence of economic culture is already apparent.

The most influential and fascinating case of religious innovation in modern Vietnam is without doubt the Caodai religion. The complex story of its development as an independent religion and its involvement in political events make it inseparable from the modern history of the country. Available accounts in French and English should therefore be read against this background.[10] The beginnings are to be seen in the French colonial period when, in the urban context of Saigon, the practical services of Vietnamese diviners and mediums were complemented by the western notion of medium-led "spiritism" then popular-

---

9 Retrospective note: unfortunately the creation of healthy relationships throughout the Korean peninsula is taking longer than one might wish.
10 The historical information provided here is derived from Gobron 1949, Pham Cong Tac 1953 and Oliver 1976.

ly current in France.[11] Divine messages and revelations were eagerly awaited in informally arranged séances. Thus developed a syncretic religious counter-culture which was neither traditionally Buddhist nor beholden to the new, powerful Catholic missions. It was in this context that the specific organisation known as Caodai originated. In 1919 a spiritist named Nguyen Van Chieu received a message from a divinity understood to be the absolute God whose name was revealed to be Caodai, meaning "High Palace". In 1921 he was instructed in another séance to become vegetarian, and not long afterwards the symbol of the single all-seeing divine eye was revealed, which later appeared over Caodai altars. Chieu himself was a respected spiritist and ascetic who impressed increasing numbers of participants in spiritist groups. The initiative to organize the new religion was taken by a different person, Le Van Trung, and under his leadership it developed dynamically. In 1926 an official opening ceremony took place at Tay Ninh, to the northwest of Saigon. A "hierarchy" wearing newly designed robes was presented, evidently after the model of the Catholic Church, and soon afterwards an impressive new centre was built for liturgical purposes. In 1927 the arbitrary influence of miscellaneous séances was shaken off, and only the séances at Tay Ninh itself were regarded as normative. New revelations, for example from the spirit of Victor Hugo, were recorded in writing. Eventually they petered out. Most occurred in the 1920's, twenty-two occurred in the 1930's and two more occurred in the 1950's. By 1928 the membership was claimed to have reached one million, though this number may have been an exaggeration for promotional purposes. Chieu's contribution continued to be honoured, being described as the esoteric way of non-action (*vo-vi*, equivalent to the well-known Chinese concept of *wu-wei*). Le Van Trung's alternative was the exoteric path of universal salvation (*pho-do*). This is equivalent to the Chinese Buddhist term *pu-du*, in which the *du* means to "bring across," as with a ferry over a stream.

Politically, Caodai was significant at first as a Vietnamese response to French colonial and cultural influence. Catholic missionaries were perturbed, while a number of non-Catholic French colonials were evidently intrigued and entertained by this flamboyant local alternative. In the end the sheer size of the religion caused it to be perceived as a threat. A number of Caodai personalities were banished to Madagascar in 1941,

---

11 For a fascinating detailed account of how ritualized possession is performed see Simon and Simon-Barouh 1973.

then also under French colonial control. The Caodai bishop of Phnom Penh, whose duty had been the pastoral care of the numerous Cambodian converts, returned to Vietnam and sided with the Japanese in ejecting the French from Vietnam. Following the end of the Second World War the French returned against the armed opposition of the Caodai and the Viet Minh. The French captured Tay Ninh, whereupon the Caodai forces were allowed to change sides and defend their own centre and the province of Tay Ninh against the Viet Minh. When the French were finally ejected from Vietnam, in 1956, the Caodai army was integrated into a common South-Vietnamese army under Ngo Dinh Diem. From these manoeuvres it can be seen that Caodai-ism was generally regarded as an independent force to be reckoned with. It was not beholden to any other political force and changed sides as convenient. The military strength of Caodai was finally broken with the victory of the Vietcong, and since that time much of the activity of the religion has taken place, with anti-communist overtones, in the diaspora.

Caodai was appraised by the German historian of religions Friedrich Heiler as a supra-confessional religious community, the kind of thing which he regarded as offering hope for the future development of religion and the happiness of mankind. Its characterization by Frits Vos as an "eclectic" movement is more pertinent. Both the architectural symbolism and textual presentations emphasise the adoption and incorporation of elements from various religions, especially from the "three teachings" of China plus Christianity. As an eclectic and well-integrated synthesis it is by no means a general forum for interreligious activities. Rather, it forms a new religion in its own right, selecting from others but by no means fully combining them.

Turning to Korea, the interaction with western pressures and the availability of underlying Chinese-derived models provided the context for the emergence of Tonghak. The name means "Eastern Learning", as opposed to the "western learning" (*sohak*) which was being heavily promoted at the time. The origins of Tonghak may be seen in the year 1860 when the thirty-seven years old founder, Choe Che-U, experienced a revelation of the "Way of Heaven" (*chondo*), a term which was later taken up in the name of the successor religion Chondogyo (The Teaching of the Way of Heaven). The Chinese characters used to write *chondo* 天道 would be read in Chinese *tiāndào*, so that the close affinity with Chinese-influenced culture can easily be recognised.

The founder had been exposed to a complex pattern of religious influences including Buddhism and Catholic Christianity (not permitted at the time). Impressed by the onward march of western culture and colonialist expansion, he concluded that while this success was presumably based on a "mandate of heaven" (*chonmyong*, equivalent to the Chinese *tiānmìng* 天命 already mentioned in connection with Yiguandao above), the same mandate could also be assigned, in response, to eastern peoples. Indeed Che-U said that his teaching was identical with that of the west, but now definitively revealed in the east. The determinative starting point for this was his belief that the heart of Chonju, the Lord of Heaven, was united with his own heart. The term Chonju was a challenge in two directions, for it corresponded to the term which had been selected for "God" by Catholic missionaries in East Asia.

The spread of the religion was controversial from the beginning. One of the practices was to provide sick people with paper amulets bearing calligraphic inscriptions. These were to be burned and the ash taken as medicine. This led to the accusation that Che-U was misleading the people, a classic Chinese reproof against minority religions. The teaching continued underground but eventually Che-U was imprisoned and executed in Taegu in 1864. A revolt to avenge his death occurred in 1871 and while this was suppressed another occurred in 1894, leading to intervention by Chinese troops, then by Japanese troops and to war between Japan and China. Japanese victory in 1895 led to further repression of the religion. Nevertheless the religion survived as, among other things, a focus of anti-Japanese dissent. The name was changed to Chondogyo in 1905. Today there are said to be some 700,000 followers, but many more belong to various splinter groups.[12]

In terms of sociological explanation Tonghak may be seen as an independence movement or a revitalization movement, asserting eastern values against powerful western pressure. However, to present it simply as a political rebellion as in some general histories such as Cordier's *Histoire Générale de la Chine et de ses Relations avec les Pays Etrangers* does not do it justice.[13] The followers of Tonghak themselves regarded their religion as a self-sufficient vehicle of revelation. In any case, Tonghak, and later Chondogyo, represented popular interests both against a Chinese oriented government in Korea and later against the Japanese colonial power. Even today there are not a few Koreans who, without being be-

---

12 For descriptions of these developments see Vos 1977 and Grayson 1989.
13 Cordier 1920, Vol. IV: 184.

lievers, are somehow a little bit proud of the role played by Tonghak in the modern history of a country caught between powerful neighbours.

The strong presence of Christianity in Korea, which may be explained at least partly by its function of providing an alternative to the hegemony of Japanese religious and political ideology, is the background for the emergence of Tongilkyo, literally "Unification Teaching", but widely known in English as the Unification Church. This "church" may be regarded as a Korean version of, or a Korean answer to the relatively strong churches established by Christian missions. Key factors are the claim to overcome denominational divisions perceived as the result of religiously irrelevant quarrels in western history, and an emphasis on family life which corresponds to what might be called a post-Confucian, but still Confucian mentality within Korea. The founder and leader, the Reverend Moon (after whom the media nickname "Moonies" was invented), is both charismatic and authoritarian. The charismatic aspect corresponds to an evangelical preaching style, while the authoritarian aspect derives both from his sense of religious authority and from the hierarchic concepts of Confucianism. A dramatic result of this combination is the celebration of multiple arranged marriages between believers, with much pomp and ceremony, which is believed to reinforce the values of family life. The strongest growth within Korea corresponds to the period of political polarisation, when the movement profited both from anti-communism and investments in the arms industry. Strident anti-communism brought in friends in various western countries, and the use of financial strength to support conference programmes, youth programmes, etc. is widely known. While the Unification Church has developed an international profile, attracting young members from many countries, its base has significant East Asian or Korean elements which are often ignored by western commentators.

Equally internationally minded, and equally Korean, is the new religion known as Won Bulgyo (also transcribed as Won Pulkyo), or in English Won Buddhism. This religion describes itself, with considerable justification, as Buddhism, and it also describes itself with similar justification as a "new religion". This is because the founder, Pak Chung-Bin (1891–1943), having launched the movement on the basis of a deep personal experience, investigated the major religions of the world in search of parallels and concluded that his teaching was a form of Buddhism. Pak's "awakening" occurred on 28th April 1916, and after this he founded an association known as the Buddhist Dharma Research Association and gathered disciples around him. Pak himself came to known as the "Great Master Sot'aesan," and after his death in 1943 the religion has been led by a series of "Prime Masters". It was Sot'aesan's successor Chŏngsan who introduced the name Won Buddhism (Won Pulgyo) in 1947. The movement has strong rationalising and modernising tendencies and attacts a professional and upwardly mobile membership. While theoretically a lay movement, a specialised leadership has developed which consists of married men on the one hand and a very effective order of celibate Dharma Sisters on the other hand. While there are "temples" spread throughout Korea, which in appearance are more like Presbyterian churches than like the traditional Buddhist temples of Korea, the main religious centre is in the city of Iksan where the current Prime Master resides. Here too a major university is maintained, which is widely respected in Korea. Won Buddhism is also known for its social work in various domains. On the other hand, not being politically controversial it has not attracted the attention of researchers until recently.[14]

In a sense, Won Buddhism may be regarded as an impressive and influential parallel to the Unification Church. However from the point of view of the history of religions, that is, making an assessment on the basis of perceived continuities in the constituent elements, Won Buddhism's claim to be Buddhist is probably stronger than the Unification Church's claim to be Christian. In any case, both may be regarded as extremely effectively organized Korean new religions which will continue to play a significant part in the years to come.

Japan

When it comes to new religions in Japan it is hard to know where to start and even harder to know where to stop. Dozens have been listed in various general overviews and guides, an early leading role in English having been played by the insightful bibliographical publications of Byron H. Earhart.[15] In Japanese, veritable guidebooks have been published, of

---

14 For a fuller introductory account, perhaps the first in English by a non-member, see Pye 2002c, also at 5.6 below.
15 Earhart's bibliography (Earhart 1970, 1983) had the merit not only of drawing attention to works which appeared before and after the second world war but also of providing an introduction to the subject in general. It will not be possible here to provide bibliographical details of the many monographs and shorter studies of particular religions.

which one has been translated into German by Johannes Laube.[16] Several of the new religions, such as Tenrikyō or Risshō Kōseikai, have become an established part of the religious scene in contemporary Japan. Politically visible religions such as Ōmotokyō and Sōka Gakkai have attracted particular attention, while more recently the sensational news stories surrounding Aum Shinrikyō have led to a flurry of academic activity, both within and outside Japan.[17] Following the sarin gas attack on an underground railway line in March 1995, in which twelve people died and many were seriously injured, criminal charges were brought against various individuals in leadership positions in Aum Shinrikyō, and in June 2002 Niimi Tsutomu was condemned to death for his part in this act of terrorism.[18] However it is important to pay attention also to less dramatic and less well-known cases of new religions, of which examples will be given below. Considerable leadership has been shown in the study of Japanese "new religions" by Japanese scholars. Takagi Hiroo, a sociologist at Tōyō University in Tokyo, has already been mentioned. Araki Michio[19] is an example of a scholar who takes a more historical and phenomenological approach, while others such as Shimazono Susumu[20] combine this with sociological considerations.

The term "new religions" is not only well established in the Japanese language but also accepted by most of the religions themselves, some of which are even associated in a "League of New Religions" (*Shinshūkyō Renmei*). The oldest Japanese religions which are today commonly designated as "new" derive from the nineteenth century, namely Kurozumikyō (founded 1814), Tenrikyō (founded 1838) and

---

16 This immense labour was a major service and the result appeared as *Neureligionen: Stand ihrer Forschung in Japan. Ein Handbuch* (Laube 1995). The Japanese original, compiled by eight editors, was entitled *Shinshūkyō kenkyūchōsa handobukku*, and first appeared (in Tokyo) in 1981.
17 Outside Japan, informative analyses and discussions of Aum Shinrikyō have been provided by Martin Repp (1997) and Ian Reader (2000). For a consideration of some implications of the Aum Shinrikyō case for the style and methodology of the study of religions see my article "Aum Shinrikyō. Can Religious Studies cope?" (Pye 1996b), reprinted as 5.7 below.
18 Retrospective note: in the meantime other death penalties have been assigned, but not yet carried out. The time is not yet ripe to provide a full history of all these sad matters.
19 Until his death, a specialist in the study of religions at the important, state-sponsored Tsukuba University.
20 Previously of Tsukuba University and later of the University of Tokyo, following the sociologist of religion Yanagawa Keiichi.

Konkōkyō (founded 1859). In other words these three religions all appeared *before* the beginning of the Meiji Period (from 1868) which ushered in so much frantic modernization in competition with the western world. Thus, in their present healthy and well-established condition, looking back over much more than a century of eventful history, these religions are no longer new.

If the term "new religions" is restricted in reference to religions in an early phase of their development, then it may fairly be asked whether there were not new religions in earlier centuries. Certainly there was much religious innovation. The question whether vital Buddhist movements such as Zen, Shin, and Nichirenite Buddhism in their own day (twelfth and thirteenth centuries of the western calendar) amounted to "new religions" would require detailed analysis for which space is not available here.[21] However the question is very relevant to the perspective in which we view the Nichirenite Lotus Sutra movements such as, preeminently, Reiyūkai, Risshō Kōseikai and Sōka Gakkai. Even if it is emphasized that these are lay Buddhist movements, in which the path of the bodhisattva is open to all without leaving "the household life," it has to be said that the ideal of monastic asceticism as the sole or even the major path to enlightenment was definitively abrogated in the context of thirteenth century Jōdo Shinshū. As taught by Hōnen and above all by Shinran, who renounced celibacy, the practice of the *nenbutsu* (calling on the name of Amida Buddha) opened to all who relied upon the other-power of this Buddha the possibility of being reborn in the Pure Land in the West. Nichiren, who focused his teaching on the *Lotus Sūtra*[22], did not himself abolish monkhood, but his emphasis on the buddha-nature of all beings meant that the distinctions between monk and lay were no longer important. While Nichiren's own teachings continue to command respect in the three movements mentioned, it is above all the *Lotus Sūtra* itself which provides doctrinal orientation. Common to all three, and to other Nichirenite denominations, some of which also count as "new religions" according to some authorities, is the practice of reciting the *daimoku*, that is, the title of the sūtra prefaced

---

21 This perspective was taken very seriously in a relatively early work on the new religions of Japan by Werner Kohler entitled *Die Lotus-Lehre und die modernen Religionen in Japan* (Kohler 1962).
22 The Lotus Sūtra derives from the formative period of Mahāyāna Buddhism in India, approximately at the beginning of the Christian era in the western calendar. As a religious text in Japan it is recited according to the Chinese translation of Kumārajīva, and provided with various explanations in Japanese.

by the honorific phrase *namu*. The resultant mantra, often recited many times over, runs: *Namu Myōhō Renge Kyō*.

The Reiyūkai is the oldest of these movements, having been founded in 1925, and numbers some three million adherents. The founders, Kubo Kakutarō (1892–1944) and Kotani Kimi (1901–1971), emphasised the care of ancestors who lacked personal descendants, in other words lost souls, or as the Buddhist phrase has it, "buddhas without affinity" (*muenbotoke*). Shortly after the Second World War the Reiyūkai experienced a brief spell of notoriety in the press because of alleged drug use and tax irregularities. Several groups split off and organised themselves independently, examples being Myōchikai and Busshogonenkai. In recent decades however Reiyūkai has been effectively led by Tokyo University educated Kubo Tsugunari and his wife, and has offered a picture of stability. Building on the earlier idea of caring for "buddhas without affinity" it emphasizes family values, combined with an outreach to young people through various stimulating activity programs such as "Inner Trip".

Also influenced by Reiyūkai were the founding figures of Risshō Kōseikai, Naganuma Myōkō (1889–1957) and Niwano Nikkyō (1906–1999). This movement has five or six million members, depending on the method of counting. Though it has no formal connection with any monastic group, the members make a point of visiting the mausoleum of Nichiren at Mount Minobu, where the headquarters of the leading Nichiren denomination (Nichirenshū) is located, and also the nearby Mount Shichimen which is a sacred to a goddess who protects the *Lotus Sūtra* and its devotees. A distinctive practice in the Risshō Kōseikai is known as *hōza*, which means approximately "dharma session." A number of believers assemble in a circle under the leadership of an experienced person and analyse various problems in their lives, for example why a small business is not doing so well, why a husband is drinking more than usual, or why children are experiencing difficulties at school or college. The analysis is based on the Buddhist model of cause and effect, the cause usually being identified as somehow lying in one's own behaviour. The headquarters consist of a considerable number of large and very impressive buildings in Wada-chō, Tokyo. The movement is now led by the son of the founder, Niwano Nichikō, who like his father makes a point of being visible in various international activities for the promotion of peace etc.

The Sōka Gakkai was founded in approximately its present form at the end of the second world war, when Toda Jōsei emerged from prison. He and his teacher Makiguchi Tsunesaburō had been incarcerated for not by maintaining an amulet from Ise Shrine and thus failing to honour the Emperor system. Makiguchi himself died in prison. He himself had founded an association called "Academic Society for Education in the Creation of Value" (Sōka Kyōiku Gakkai), but it was only gradually that the *Lotus Sūtra* came to play an important role, being emphasized especially at the time of the re-foundation in 1952. "Value" was not only a general good, but in particular came to be understood as benefits in the present world (*genzeriyaku*). This aspect proved to be most attractive and, together with an extremely effective organization with a concerted conversion program, led to a steady and massive increase in membership. As a result there are some sixteen million members at the time of writing. It may be assumed that the majority of them vote for the political party known as Kōmeitō ("public brightness party" or, less literally, "clean government party") which was initially founded within the Sōka Gakkai but became formally independent in 1970. For many years the Sōka Gakkai had an institutional relationship with one of the smaller denominations in the Nichiren tradition, the Nichiren Shōshū, but this relationship eventually broke down and all ties were severed. Overseas the Sōka Gakkai is widely active in the form of Soka Gakkai International (SGI).

Tenrikyō, the "Teaching of the Divine Reason" was already mentioned as one of the nineteenth century foundations which is now firmly established. The main temple is in the city of Tenri, near Nara, the city (and the railway station) being named after the religion itself. Tenrikyō is known in particular for its liturgical dance performances. The most central ritual (the *kagurazutome*) is only partly visible, taking place in a deepened recess in the main temple. This is the place, it is taught, where humankind was originally created, known in Japanese as the *jiba*. Here too a new day will dawn for humanity, when heavenly dew is collected on a specially built pillar which awaits it. This will open the way for a new "joyous life" (*yōkigurashi*). The pillar, which is open to the skies, is called the *kanrodai*, that is, the "stand for the heavenly dew." The number of Tenrikyō believers is reckoned to be about two million, a number of whom reside outside Japan. Both in the main temple and in the regional "churches" (Japanese: *kyōkai*) the ordinary believers also perform their own dance, the *te-odori* or "hand-dance," a slow, graceful movement in which various spiritual movements are enacted, for example the brushing away of "the eight dusts" of the mind. The teaching of Tenrikyō (which a Chinese person would simply read without any difficulty as *Tianlijiao!*)

goes back to the experience of the foundress Nakayama Miki (1798–1887) who felt herself unexpectedly seized by a divinity named as Tenri-ō-no-mikoto, i.e. "The August King of Heavenly Wisdom" and who is also known among other things as "God the Parent" (Oyagami). Notice that the term "God the Parent" is gender-neutral. Nowadays the city of Tenri is an important pilgrimage centre which attracts the faithful from all over Japan. It also boasts a hospital, schools, a university and a museum with a superb collection of artefacts illustrating the various phases of human culture. Perhaps not of central importance for the average Tenrikyō member, but of interest for academic readers, the central library includes what is probably one of the best balanced collections in the world for the study of religions, including the history of religions east and east, the historical development of the subject, etc.. Recently the leaders of Tenrikyō have shown an increasing interest in inter-religious dialogue, accompanying the internationalization of Japanese culture in general.

Though brief, mention must also be made of Ōmoto (also Oomoto), "Great Source," which has a pre-war history of rivalry with the nationalist ideology of the state, leading to its repression with tanks, and a post-war history of peace propaganda, Esperantism, and the integration of various religions. The founding figures were Deguchi Nao (1837–1918) and Deguchi Ōnisaburō (1871–1948), the first revelation being received by Deguchi Nao in 1892. Ōmotokyō ("the teaching of the great source") proved indeed to be a source for the emergence of other new religions of considerable importance such as: Ananaikyō (an early interfaith community), Seichō no Ie ("House of Growth") and Sekaikyūseikyō ("Teaching of the Salvation of the World").

As more and more "new religions" are mentioned, each with a considerable following, it is perhaps becoming clear that many are being left out of account altogether. It is with regret that more details cannot be given, for example, of the "dancing religion," Tenshō Kōtai Jingū Kyō, which began immediately at the end of the second world war and emphasises the dance of "non-self" (*muga*), an enthusiastic religion with superb headquarters by the architect Tange, an artist in concrete. Or think again of PL Kyōdan, the Religion of Perfect Liberty (PL), with its principle (just the first of ten) that "Life is Art," its golf courses and its artistic memorial stones for members. Or should we now turn to the so-called "new new religions" (*shinshinshūkyō*) which have attracted more attention recently? These include Agonkyō, which has nothing very much to do with the Agon (Āgama) sutras; and Aum Shinrikyō, already mentioned because of its terrorist attacks and subsequent notoriety. Another recently influential movement is Kōfuku no Kagaku (Science of Happiness), a business-like religion which sells huge numbers of very imaginative paperback publications by its founder. Whatever the precise derivations of these various organizations, it may be noted that the term "new new religions" is deeply flawed from a theoretical point of view. First, it consolidates the idea that "new" religions somehow belonged to a particular period in the recent past, whereas in fact there have been new religions in practically all known periods of human history. Second, what term will then be left for the decades immediately to be anticipated, during which innovation is unlikely to cease? Shall we perhaps be taught to say "new, new new religions"? Since the processes of innovation, invention, consolidation, and in some cases relative decay are evidently not bound to particular events such as the end of a world war, any designations which tie analysis to particular decades alone will be misleading.

While a number of monographs have provided very valuable studies of the more well-known new religions of Japan, other religions have never been described or discussed in detail at all. Indeed some of them are not even known to the general public in Japan by name. A good example of such a religion, as yet little known, which has between three and four hundred thousand members, is Ennōkyō, the "Perfectly Adapted Teaching". Based on the teaching of its almost illiterate foundress, Fukuda Chiyoko (1887–1925) who worked as a servant in a remote village in Hyōgo Prefecture, Ennōkyō draws on Buddhist and Shintō traditions to provide a focus on family life and care for the ancestors. Members are proud of their fine headquarters where the foundress, later leaders and they themselves are memorialised. Regular worship is carried out before a simple curtained focus (without images) in the branch churches located all over Japan. The religion is uncontroversial, and therefore goes largely unnoticed.[23]

Another religion which has received little attention is Byakkō Shinkōkai, the "White Light Fellowship Association." In brief, this is a peace movement, a religion which regularly carries out an impressive liturgy

---

23 Ennōkyō is sometimes mentioned very briefly in lists and guides (e.g. in the work translated by Laube mentioned above). I am currently preparing a more detailed account, having frequently introduced it as a typical example of a new Japanese religion in teaching programs. My attention was first drawn to it by my wife when we were going for a walk, trying to take a rest from the study of religions.

for world peace, celebrating all the countries of the world which at any one time are recognized by the Japanese Foreign Office. In the background it is more mysterious. The founder, Master Goi, was evidently a charismatic medium, and his follower Saionji Masami is no less so. Master Goi's excellent whistling can still be heard during the liturgy at the headquarters, Hijirigaoka in Chiba Prefecture. He still receives the petitions of his followers in envelopes which, since they are ceremonially burned, should not include money. Masami-sama, as his successor is respectfully called, has called new programs into being with far-reaching titles such as "I myself am God" or "Humanity is God." Somehow this is more than a peace movement. We should also give thanks to our "guardian spirits." If we are Japanese we will rejoice that there is a special place for Japan in the salvation of the world.[24]

To conclude, consider the as yet entirely undocumented, rather secretive religion named Bankeitaishisō Chiesonkyō, or Chiesonkyō for short, based in the city of Tochigi. This religion is esoteric in the correct sense of the term, for the printed materials are normally available only available to members. The founder, Katō Bungo, eclectically combined elements of Confucianism and Buddhism with references to the spirit world. These were codified in a short work entitled *Chiesongaku* (i. e. "The Study of Holy Wisdom") by his successor Katō Toshio, published in 1979. The declared intention is to give new vitality to rituals in everyday life. This is done by practising the "Art of Holy Wisdom" (*chiesonjutsu*).[25] Prayer is regarded as the foundation of happiness, and rituals of purification (*kiyome*) are particularly recommended. Instructions are given for example on the purification of one's wrist watch every morning and evening. It is quite common for the leadership of new religions in Japan to pass down through the family. However, even in 1980 Chiesonkyō seemed no longer to be thriving as it did during time of its founder. Some twenty years later, considerable irritation is shown when materials are known to have fallen into the hands of non-believers, even when simple enquiries are not in principle unsympathetic.

---

24 This religion in fact provides an identity structure for Japanese persons trying to come to grips with the fact that Japan is not alone in this world but shares a history with many other states, which are duly called up in the liturgy. The peace movement profile is only part of something which in fact is considerably more complex (see Pye 1986).
25 Art in the sense of "technique."

Conclusions and outlook

Even when the attitude of Chinese officialdom to minority religious movements was an understanding one, as in the unusual case of Lü K'un's memorial, or hostile, as it more often was, the attempts to interpret them were akin to not a little modern sociology in failing to recognize the central importance of religious concepts and motivations for founders and followers themselves. The mandarins of former centuries, some sociologists today, not to mention most politicians and most journalists, see alternative, "new" religions as deluded, misleading or downright malevolent. In other words they are regarded as a threat to the society which they know. It is inevitable that innovation may appear to be threatening to those in established positions, and this applies no less to religious innovation than in other spheres of life. Indeed in several of the cases considered above the alternatives to the prevailing political and religious culture have been rather clear. They have challenged the cultural and ideological assumptions of the more powerful. By so doing, the new religions of East Asia have frequently played a positive role in articulating the interests of particular sections of society. In some respects they have been disruptive of existing order, but in other respects they have contributed to modernisation processes and provided empowerment, success and stability for those who participate in them. Naturally the balance is varied from case to case, and the spectrum of possible effects is wide. Some religions promote greater rationality while others may seem, to the scientific mind, disconcertingly irrational. Some religions contribute to general emancipation and greater gender equality, while others reinforce traditional, hierarchic family structures. Some religions promote self-discipline and self-giving, while others promote self-interest and personal profit and enjoyment. Some religions promote internationalism and peace projects of various kinds, while others represent a haven for conservative nationalism. Indeed the pattern is in many cases baffling, for it seems that opposing tendencies may coexist within one and the same movement or organization. On closer examination a rationale for such complexities may sometimes be discovered.

In the academic study of religions, it is essential to maintain an elementary respect for the way in which believers understand themselves. It is misleading to presuppose simplistic, reductionist explanations. Rather, serious account should be taken of the self-understanding of the believers and participants themselves before attempting a full appraisal. If this is not done, misinterpretations are sure to arise.

For example, it is only by taking a careful look at the detail of new symbolic and ritual systems that the relationship to the major tradition or traditions upon which they draw can be adequately assessed. This is particularly important in the case of Buddhist-related movements which in some cases, such as Korea's Won Buddhism or Japan's Sōka Gakkai, may be regarded at one and the same time as "Buddhist" and as "new religions". Aum Shinrikyō, on the other hand, is not Buddhist, though it has claimed to be so (cf. 5.7 below).

Another very delicate area is the relationship between syncretism, eclecticism and synthesis. These theoretical, or at least reflective terms should not be confused with each other or just used as if they were vaguely synonymous, as is so often seen in writing on the religions of East Asia. Eclecticism refers to the selection of materials, symbolic elements, ritual practices etc. from a variety of previously current traditions. In this sense, some new religions are markedly eclectic (Caodai) and others less so (Won Buddhism). Syncretism is a feature of all religions in varying degree and at various stages of their history. It is not a specific characteristic of new religions alone. The term synthesis may be used to refer to the achievement of a newly integrated religious Gestalt, whether the route to such a conclusion, itself historically temporary, was more, less, or scarcely eclectic.[26]

Since the total number of new religions in East Asia is very large, especially if the full history is taken into account, it was only possible here to provide introductory information on a few selected examples, mainly well-known ones. In such a short survey, it is only possible to draw attention to the need for detailed studies to be continued in the future. However it is hoped that this will provide a springboard for further studies and further reading, bearing in mind the continuities and the parallels in the social and cultural experience of the countries concerned.

Bibliographical references

Beijing Institute of Foreign Languages 1978. *A Chinese-English Dictionary*. Beijing (Shāngwù Yìnshūguǎn).

---

26 On these questions, see Pye 1993 and other articles on syncretism in Part Six of the present work.

Cordier, Henri 1920. *Histoire générale de la Chine et de ses relations avec les pays étrangers* (4 vols.). Paris (Librairie Paul Geuthner).
De Groot, J. J. M. 1903–4. *Sectarianism and Religious Persecution in China.* (Two volumes). Amsterdam (Koninklijke Akademie van Wetenschappen)
Earhart, H. Byron 1970. *The New Religions of Japan. A Bibliography of Western-language Materials.* Tokyo (Sophia University). (Second Edition 1983, Ann Arbor (Center for Japanese Studies, The University of Michigan.)
Esherick, Joseph W. 1987. *The Origins of the Boxer Uprising* Berkeley/Los Angeles (University of California Press).
Franke, Otto 1956. *Geschichte des chinesischen Reichs* (5 vols.). Berlin (Walter de Gruyter and Co.).
Gobron, Gabriel 1949. *Histoire et Philosophie du Caodaïsme.* Paris (Éditions Dervy).
Grayson, James Huntley 1989. *Korea: A Religious History.* Oxford (Clarendon Press).
Hummel, Arthur W. 1943. *Eminent Chinese of the Ch'ing Period.* Washington (United States Government Printing Office).
Jordan, David K. and Overmyer, Daniel L. 1986. *The Flying Phoenix. Aspects of Chinese Sectarianism in Taiwan.* Princeton (Princeton University Press) 1986
Kohler, Werner 1962. *Die Lotus-Lehre und und die modernen Religionen in Japan* – Zürich (Atlantis Verlag).
Laube, Johannes (ed.) 1995. *Neureligionen in Japan: Stand ihrer Erforschung. Ein Handbuch.* Wiesbaden (Harrassowitz).
Murakami, Shigeyoshi 1980. *Japanese Religion in the Modern Century.* Tokyo (University of Tokyo Press).
Oliver, Victor 1976. *Caodai Spiritism. A Study of Religion in Vietnamese Society.* Leiden (E. J. Brill) 1976
Overmeyer, Daniel L. 1976. *Folk Buddhist Religion. Dissenting Sects in Late Traditional China.* Cambridge Massachusetts and London (Harvard University Press).
Pham Cong Tac (Ho-Phap) 1953. *Le Caodaïsme. 3e Amnistie de Dieu en Orient.* Paris (Éditions Dervy).
Pye, Michael 1986. "National and international identity in a Japanese religion: Byakkōshinkōkai" in: Hayes, V.C. (ed.) *Identity Issues and World Religions, Selected Proceedings of the International Association for the History of Religions*, Netley Australia (The Australian Association for the Study of Religions): 234–241.
– 1993. "Syncretism versus synthesis" in: *Occasional papers of the British Association for the Study of Religion.* Cardiff (BASR) Republished in: *Method & Theory in the Study of Religion*, 6 (3) 1994: 217–29.
– 1994a. "What is 'religion' in East Asia?" in: Bianchi, Ugo, Mora Fabio and Bianchi Lorenzo (eds.) *The Notion of "Religion" in Comparative Research: Selected Proceedings of the XVIth Congress of the International Association for the History of Religions, Rome, 3rd-8th September, 1990.* Rome ("L'Erma" di Bretschneider): 115–22.

- 1996b. "Aum Shinrikyo. Can Religious Studies cope?" in: *Religion,* 26 (3): 261–273.
- 2002c. "Won Buddhism as a Korean new religion" in: *Numen* 49 (2): 113–141.

Reader, Ian 2000. *Religious Violence in Contemporary Japan. The Case of Aum Shinrikyō.*
- London (Curzon).

Repp, Martin 1997. *Aum Shinrikyo. Ein Kapitel krimineller Religionsgeschichte.*
- Marburg (Diagonal Verlag).

Seiwert, Hubert 1985. *Volksreligion und nationale Tradition in Taiwan. Studien zur regionalen Religionsgeschichte einer chinesischen Provinz.* Stuttgart (Franz Steiner Verlag).
- 2000 "Falun Gong – Eine neue religiöse Bewegung als innenpolitischer Hauptfeind der chinesischen Regierung " in: *Religion – Staat – Gesellschaft. Zeitschrift für Glaubensformen und Weltanschauungen* 1(1): 119–144.

Simon, Pierre J. and Simon-Barouh, Ida 1973. *Hầu Bóng. Un culte viêtnamien de possession transplanté en France.* (École Pratique des Hautes Études, Cahiers de l'Homme, Nouvelle Série XIII). Paris and the Hague (Mouton).

Takagi, Hiroo 1959. *Nihon no Shinkōshūkyō.* Tokyo (Iwanami Shoten).

Taylor, Romeyn 1983. "An Imperial endorsement of syncretism.Ming T'ai Tsu's essay on the three teachings: translation and commentary" in: *Ming Studies* 16: 31–38.

Ter Haar, B. J. 1992. *The White Lotus Teachings in Chinese Religious History*
- Leiden (E. J. Brill).

Vos, Frits 1977. *Die Religionen Koreas.* Stuttgart (Kohlhammer).

Weller, Robert P. 1982 "Sectarian religion and political action in China" in: *Modern China* 8 (4): 463–83.

This article was first published as 'New Religions in East Asia' in James R. Lewis (ed.), *Oxford Handbook of New Religious Movements* (Oxford University Press, 2004). Reprinted here by permission of Oxford University Press, USA.

5.6 Won Buddhism as a Korean New Religion

This article provides a general introduction to Won Buddhism, based on primary sources and personal observations, with particular reference to selected aspects such as gender balance and the question of its categorization as a new religion and as Buddhism. The bibliographical details have been revised.

Introduction

Won Buddhism, in Korean Wŏn Pulgyo (or Wonbulgyo[1]), is one of the major new religions of modern Korea. It may be said to have originated in the year 1916 when, on 28th April, its founder Pak Chung-Bin (Park Chungbin) experienced an awakening to "the truth". Pak came to be known to his followers as the Venerable Sot'aesan, and the religion which developed under his leadership was later termed Won Buddhism, meaning Perfect Buddhism. The designation "Buddhism" arises because, while his awakening and message were regarded by himself and his followers as being independently authentic, he retrospectively identified them with those of the historical Buddha, dating from more than two thousand years earlier. This identification will be analysed further below. During the course of the 20th century, with all its political sufferings and changes, Won Buddhism has established itself firmly within Korean society, developing a wide range of interesting features. On general historical grounds alone, therefore, it deserves to receive more attention than it has hitherto enjoyed.

One looks in vain, however, for any general introduction to this religion in English written by an independent observer.[2] While various

---

1   Transliteration from Korean follows the McCune-Reischauer system; variants which may also be found in relevant sources, especially Won Buddhist writings, are added in brackets at the first occurrence. For convenience, the accent is omitted from "Won" when used in the anglicised proper noun Won Buddhism.
2   For what was possibly the first general academic account of Won Buddhism in a western language by a non-member, though very short, see Pye 1998b. The present article builds on the information given there, providing additional ma-

non-members have visited Won Buddhist institutions and engaged in discussions with representative persons, none seem to have felt called upon to write even a brief general account of the religion. Admittedly even a brief introduction, if it is to be fair, requires somewhat more knowledge than casual impressions alone can provide. The purpose of the present contribution is to fill this gap by giving a short, reliable, observer's account, which can serve as an orientation for more specialised studies in the future. At the same time a few matters of particular interest for the history of religions are raised, such as the role of Won Buddhism in the modernisation of Korea, the question of gender balance in Won Buddhism, and the appraisal of Won Buddhism as a "new religion" on the one hand and as "Buddhism" on the other hand.

Won Buddhism has not gone completely unnoticed in surveys of Korean religion. Frits Vos, for example, mentions it very briefly in his substantial history *Die Religionen Koreas* (1997). James Huntley Grayson, in his wide-ranging and generally excellent work *Korea, A Religious History*(1989) gives it a little more attention, in fact just enough to throw up one or two problems.[3] His view that Won Buddhism is "clearly an orthodox Buddhist movement"[4] is not shared here, as will be clear from the more detailed exploration of the relation between Won Buddhism and the general tradition of Buddhism undertaken below. Furthermore, Grayson's use of the term "syncretism" as, in effect, a synonym for synthesis, is not regarded as appropriate by the present writer. Such usage is quite widespread both in missiological and in anthropological writing, but it is an equation which makes the term "syncretism" itself redundant and obscures the interesting, dynamic features of syncretistic situations.[5] Finally his discussion of possible influence from Christianity on Won Buddhism is plausible, but this question seems to require more detailed historical study. It seems a little out of balance to have raised it in such a short account, especially when there are, quite obviously, innumerable other sources of influence on Won Buddhism from within East Asian religious culture.

---

terial and reflections and a few small corrections. The same volume contains a contribution by Woo Hai-Ran entitled "Die Dialogbewegung aus der Perspektive nicht-westlicher Religionen. Das Beispiel des Won-Buddhismus". On Woo Hai-Ran's recent dissertation and on publications from the believers' point of view, see note 7 below.

3   See especially pages 250–254.
4   Grayson 1989: 254.
5   See Pye 1971a, 1993 and on syncretistic dynamics particularly 1996c.

There are probably various reasons for the lack of rounded presentations of Won Buddhism by specialists in the study of religions. One reason is undoubtedly that it has not impacted controversially on western societies as has, for example, the Unification Church, in Korean T'ongil-kyo (Tongil-gyo). Another reason is that, in spite of its notable social significance and influence in Korea, it has not played a controversial political role as have, for example, the Sōka Gakkai or Aum Shinrikyō in Japan, the Cao Dai in Vietnam or more recently the Falungong in China. Not a few specialists in the study of religions understandably feel called upon to provide studies of these religious groups which are constantly referred to in the media for various reasons. This leads to a relative neglect of less controversial groups such as Won Buddhism, even though these are really just as important, if not more so. Such uncontroversial religions may be of interest for a wide variety of reasons, just a few of which are taken up below. In any case we should not overlook that Won Buddhism simply forms part of the overall field of the study of religions, and is therefore worthy of attention by those who specialise in this field.

Won Buddhism's self-presentation

A rather different reason for neglect of the subject may be, ironically, that Won Buddhism itself has a large number of highly educated representatives who are perfectly capable of presenting their own religion to the wider world. In this regard a particularly important role is played by Wonkwang University (Wonkwang Taehak), an impressive institution of higher learning situated at the religion's headquarters in Iksan City. A quantity of the resultant literature in Korean has been analysed in considerable detail by Woo Hai-Ran, a non-member, in a doctoral dissertation.[6]

---

6 This dissertation, entitled *Kritische Untersuchungen von Erklärungsmodellen zu Neuen Religionen unter besonderer Berücksichtigung des Won-Buddhismus*, was submitted successfully at the University of Marburg in February 2001 and is probably the first dissertation dealing with Won Buddhism by someone who is not a member. A significant proportion of the thesis is devoted to more general questions in the study of new religions. One extensive chapter is specifically related to Won Buddhism, its main purpose being to analyse Won Buddhist attitudes towards previously existing religious traditions in Korea and to other movements in modern Korean society. These particular themes are documented,

The publications promoted by Won Buddhist organisations, and published by its own publishing house, are of course indispensable sources for informing any first acquaintance with the religion. Of fundamental significance here is the *The Scripture of Won Buddhism (Won Pulkyo Kyojun)* (1988), which had appeared in an older English version as *The Canonical Textbook of Won Buddhism (Won Pulkyo Kyojun)* (1971).[7] The designation of this book as a "scripture," presumably by analogy with the Christian scriptures, is quite appropriate, partly because of the fact that its contents are presumed to be normative. This is why such care was taken to provide not only the first translation, but later also a revised version. It is also appropriate because of the physical appearance, for the work is presented as "scriptures" are widely imagined to appear. It has a formal dark cover, nicely rounded corners, gilded edges to the pages and an integral cloth bookmark. The scripture contains an overview of the doctrine, instructions for the daily practice of the religion, and "The Discourses of the Great Master," i.e. the founder Pak Chung-Bin, known to believers as the Venerable Sot'aesan. These discourses or sayings are set out, in many cases, in the context of brief narratives or dialogues indicating the occasion on which they were delivered.

It might be argued that there is hardly a better general introduction to Won Buddhism, from the insider's perspective, than the "scripture" itself. Nevertheless it is also interesting to read the less formal articles and chronicles, sometimes illustrated, which can be found in the English language journal entitled *Won Buddhism*, published for a general readership from 1962 onwards. Useful orientation may be found, too, in the booklet by Chung Bong-Kil entitled *An Introduction to Won Buddhism, Wonbulgyo* (1994), of which the copyright is held by the Overseas Missions Bureau of Won Buddhism. Here are to be found a brief account of the origins of Won Buddhism, the main outlines of its doctrine and practice, and some selected texts.

There are also significant historical materials which can be freely inspected in an exhibition room at the Won Buddhist headquarters at Iksan.

---

and analysed, with extensive bibliographical references to works in Korean by members of the religion, which will surely be of value to future researchers. See also Woo 2004, based on the dissertation. Other dissertations located by a general bibliographical search seem to derive from members of the religion.

7   The 1971 edition was published in Seoul, with 384 pages, by Kyohak-sa Publishing Co. The 1988 edition was published at Iri (now Iksan) by Won Kwang Publishing Co. with 394 pages. Retrospective note: a new standard official version has been published in the meantime: see CATWBS 2006.

This exhibition gives not only hagiographical presentations of the life of the founder but also extremely important documents such as posters and books from the early, foundational period. Such documents illustrate, among other things, the relationship between the innovatory, modernising thrust of the new religion and central themes of Mahāyāna Buddhism, a point which will receive further attention below.

In view of all this information it may not be immediately clear, especially to believers, what an outside observer can really add. However the information referred to in this section is all presented from within the shared perspective of the believers. The more popular presentations are quite pious and the missionary intention is usually more or less clear. Although there is no unusual problem about the presentations found within the literature of Won Buddhism, there does remain a question as to whether this alone is a satisfactory source of information about Won Buddhism for the wider world. There may be some value, even for believers, in a general account which is known *not* to be the presentation of a believer. On the other hand such an account may also give rise to reflections which may or not be of concern to the members but are appropriate for further enquiry in the general study of religions.

From a methodological point of view it is necessary to be conscious of what I have termed the "tension with believer factor" (TWB factor).[8] In this case there have not so far been any disturbing problems. However small difficulties may arise. How, for example, should the non member historian of religions refer to the founder of Won Buddhism and his successors in the highest office? One would not normally, in a historical writing, refer to "The Lord Buddha" or "The Blessed Virgin Mary" or "The Holy Father." Similarly it is doubtful whether titles like "The Venerable Sot'aesan" or "The Great Master" are really appropriate in scholarly writing when referring to the founder Pak Chung-Bin. In this article the religious titles and names have in fact been used in some places, in order to communicate the appropriate atmosphere. No disrespect is intended in other contexts where, for ease of reading, the religious names are used without the full titles, or where a historical name alone is used. This usage may seem to fall short of consistency both from a religious and from a non-religious point of view, thus providing a simple example of the TWB factor. Other examples of this delicate interface will occasionally be found below.

---

8   See 1.6 in Volume One above.

Personal impressions

It is of course important, when attempting to characterise a living religion, to complement these immensely significant documentary materials with direct personal impressions. I would therefore like to note quite explicitly the occasions which lie behind the present account. My first encounter with Won Buddhism occurred during a conference of the International Association for Buddhist Studies in Oxford, England, in 1983. During a lecture by Professor Ryu Byung-Duk of Wonkwang University, all the participants at the conference appeared to be learning something about Won Buddhism for the first time, and I myself had the privilege of serving as interpreter for Professor Ryu (via a common knowledge of Japanese) during a lengthy and enthusiastically received discussion period.[9] It was some years later, in 1991 and in 1997, that I had the opportunity of visiting Won Buddhist institutions in Korea. For me, as for most visitors, the starting points then were the Won Buddhist Centre in Seoul, the main religious centre of Won Buddhism in the city of Iri (later renamed as Iksan) and the already mentioned Wonkwang University, in Korean Wonkwang Taehak, the precise meaning of which is "University of Perfect Light."

The year 1991 saw the one hundredth anniversary of the birth of the founder, "Great Master" Sot'aesan, celebrated at Iri. These celebrations were presided over by the then "Prime Master" Taesan (Daesan), whose appearance at an open air rally was welcomed rapturously by thousands of believers. It was during this year that the commemorative hall with its statue of the founder Sot'aesan was inaugurated. Beneath it in the same building is the museum mentioned earlier. At the anniversary celebrations a number of foreign guests took part in a symposium of which the proceedings were published in substantial commemorative volumes by the Editorial Committee for Papers Presented at the One Hundredth Anniversary of the Birthday of the Great Master Sot'aesan (Editorial Committee 1991).

---

9 Professor Ryu has also published articles in Japanese (as well as much in Korean) on topics such as "Wonbukkyō no Kankoku shakai ni oyoboshita eikyō" (The influence of Won Buddhism on Korean society) 1984, and "Kankoku bukkyō shisō no tokuchō" (Special features of Korean Buddhist thought) 1998. Full details of the commemoration volumes in which these appeared, in Japan, could not be found.

In January 1997 I was permitted to visit the Won Buddhist Kangnam (Gangnam) Temple in Seoul, directed by "Dharma Sister" the Reverend Pak Chung-Soo (Park Chung-Soo), under whose guidance I was also introduced to other centres of Won Buddhist activity in the capital. During this visit I shared in the daily routine of the Kangnam Temple, including early morning meditation, and observed the course of the Sunday morning service. Reverend Pak and her assistants spared no effort in introducing me to various aspects of their daily work, which has a strong social component. Following this up with a visit to Iksan, I held conversations with leading members of Wonkwang University arranged by the kind efforts of Dr. Ryu Sung-Tae.[10] With his help I was also granted an interview with the Venerable Chwasan (Jwasan), who had been installed as Prime Master in 1995. Apart from answering my own general questions, he dwelt in some detail on the problems of environmental conservation and world peace, emphasising that all humanity "in the west, as in the east" should work together for the solution of these problems. Both of these visits were made possible by the kind support of Chon Pal-Khn, a Dharma Sister who over the long term has played a substantial role in the international presentation of Won Buddhism. She edited the English language magazine Won Buddhism, mentioned above, of which the collected issues of thirty years were published in a single volume (Chon 1993). She also played a leading role in preparing The Canonical Textbook of Won Buddhism (Won Pulkyo Kyojun) (Chon 1971) and the revised edition, The Scripture of Won Buddhism (Won Pulkyo Kyojun) (Chon 1988) of which details were given above.

The historical development of Won Buddhism

From the point of view of Won Buddhists themselves the history of the movement is seen as a more or less continuous, steady development, following "generations" of 36 years. This development is symbolised, in the religious understanding, by the formal religious names of the founder himself and his (so far) three followers in the topmost leadership position, all of which include the element *san* meaning "mountain." The honorific titles, names and dates of these leaders, starting with the founder himself, are as follows:

---

10 On the significance of his own academic activity see further below.

Great Master Sot'aesan (Pak Chung-Bin 1891–1943)
Prime Master Chŏngsan (Song Kyu 1900–1962, Prime Master 1943–1962)
Prime Master Taesan (Daesan) (Kim Tae-Gŏ 1910–1998, Prime Master 1962–1995)
Prime Master Chwasan (Jwasan) (Yi Kŏn-Huŏng 1936-, Prime Master from 1995 onwards).

"Great Master" is the standard Won Buddhist English rendering of *tae chong sa* while "Prime Master" stands for *chong sa*. These impressive titles could be more closely translated as "great religious teacher" and religious teacher" respectively, whereby "religious" (*chong*), as can be seen from the Chinese character used to write it, means something like "standing in the authoritative tradition." The related formal name Chusan (Jusan) was conferred on Song To-Sŏng (1907–1946), but he did not take up office as Prime Master because of illness which led to his early death.

The historian of religions, who writes as an observer, does not feel obliged to follow the formalistic idea of generations of 36 years when analysing historical developments. Nevertheless it so happens that there is a broad appropriateness in this presentation, even from a non-religious point of view. The reason is that the main leadership periods bear a striking relationship to three important phases in the political and social history of modern Korea. The main outlines of the development of the religion will therefore be set out in this way, in all brevity, not for religious reasons, but because such a view is historically compelling. The two most recent Prime Masters, Taesan and Chwasan, can be regarded, so far at least, as falling into the same general historical period.

Both formative and normative for Won Buddhism is the religious experience and teaching of the founder Pak Chung-Bin, whose spiritual awakening, as mentioned earlier, is dated to 28th April 1916. Shortly after this he founded an organisation known as the Buddhist Dharma Research Association, in Korean Pulpŏp Yŏnku Hoe (see further below). The designation Wŏn Pulgyo (Won Buddhism) was not introduced until 1947 and therefore can only be applied to this period retrospectively. As president of the Buddhist Dharma Research Association, of which an extremely interesting historical poster is on display in the museum, he also launched a very practical land reclamation project. Underlying this action was the idea that practical and spiritual life should go hand in hand, an idea which found expression in a saying of the founder which runs: "As material civilization develops, cultivate spiritual civilization accordingly." This saying has been treated thereafter as a key statement and accordingly is highlighted on page 2 of the *Scripture of Won Buddhism (Won Pulkyo Kyojun)*, directly after the symbolic circle, Il-Wŏn-Sang (Ir-Wŏn-Sang) (see also below). The land reclamation project was completed in August 1919 and following that the Venerable Sot'aesan withdrew with nine disciples to Pongnae (Pongrae, Bongrae) Temple at Pyŏngsan. Here the leading principles of the teaching and the organisation of the religion were drafted and his systematic teaching began. Not surprisingly, the teaching of the founder himself was subject to a later systematisation process, during which important elements were highlighted. Moreover the story of the founder's own life was integrated into the teaching and into the "canonical" scripture. The maturely developed teaching therefore displays both a systematic and a narrative aspect. Some of the features of the teaching of Won Buddhism will be referred to at various points in the sections which follow.

This first period in the development of Won Buddhism, during the life of Sot'aesan himself, was the time of Japanese colonial domination and the two world wars, ending with the liberation of Korea from Japanese rule at the end of the second world war, shortly after Sot'aesan's death. Under these conditions it is appropriate to regard Won Buddhism, like the Korean religions Tonghak (Donghak) and Ch'ŏntokyo (Chondogyo), as a kind of "revitalization" movement working in favour of an independent Korean culture. As we have seen, the "awakening" of Sot'aesan was regarded as autonomous. From this starting point the complete truth was to be proclaimed from Korea, and not for example from Japan or from the countries of the west. Thus Won Buddhism stands firmly within the trend for Korean self-determination, independent of the western powers, and yet also independent of China and Japan.

After Sot'aesan's death in 1943 the Supreme Council of the Buddhist Dharma Research Association elected the Venerable Chŏngsan as his successor in the main position of leadership, the "Great Master" (*tae chong sa*) now being followed by a "Prime Master" (*chong sa*).[11] It was Chŏngsan who, in 1947, introduced the name Wŏn Pulgyo (Won Buddhism), thus providing a compact designation which emphasised the central points of the teaching as being "Buddhist" and at the same time "perfect," somehow superseding other forms of Buddhism. Under his leadership the essential writings of Sot'aesan were collected, together with narratives about his life and teaching activity. These were

---

11 Unfortunately I have not yet been able to establish just when these terms were introduced.

published under the title *Kyochŏn* (or *Kyojun*, c.f. the English translations mentioned above). In addition a place of education was founded for the ever growing membership, known as Wonkwang College. This later developed into Wonkwang University, which is one of the most respected institutions of higher education in Korea today.

Although Chŏngsan assumed the role of Prime Master during the world war in 1943, the period of his leadership coincides significantly with the end of the world war, the end of Japanese domination and the construction of an independent Korea. This may be regarded as the second period in the development of Won Buddhism. The task of trying to rise out of the ruins of the second world war was immensely complicated by the terrible proxy war waged over the Korean peninsula and the consequently hesitant growth of modern democracy. Nevertheless substantial progress was made and it can be concluded that the systematic development of Won Buddhism as the organisation which it is today took place against the background of the emergence and stabilisation of an independent modern Korean state.

In 1962 the leadership passed to the Venerable Taesan. The Won Buddhist movement, or organisation, continued to gather strength, and it is from this time onwards that significant international contacts were sought. Dialogue and cooperation with other religions within Korea and elsewhere came to be a respected activity, while caritative, social and cultural programmes within Korea took on ever greater proportions. By 1995 the membership had grown to a million in Korea itself. The number of assembly halls had grown to 454. To these figures must be added 30 temples in various foreign countries.

The third phase in the history of Won Buddhism, the time of the Venerable Taesan and from 1995 of his successor the Venerable Chwasan, set its own accents which in their turn were in accord with the national situation. The continuing division of Korea has been a theme of discussion and concern among Won Buddhists during this period, and various attempts have been made to provide practical assistance to the population of North Korea, notably for example by Dharma Sister Pak Chung-Soo, mentioned above. In spite of the division of the country and in spite of political tensions in South Korea itself during much of the time, there has been relative peace and prosperity as a background against which Korean leaders in all walks of life have sought to take their place on the international scene. The activities of Won Buddhism have therefore reflected the needs, the interests and the possibilities of the country during this period.

General features of Won Buddhism as a religion

The attractiveness of Won Buddhism for its believers seems to lie above all in the simplicity and clarity of its teaching, in its emphasis on personal commitment and personal activity and in its generous, open and well-balanced ethos. Although the teaching in some respects has a mystical quality, value is also placed on rational clarity, on the rejection of "superstition," and on personal self-discipline, for example in the prohibition of tobacco and alcohol. This mixture seems to have attracted an upwardly mobile, professional population which helped to establish the religion in influential sectors of society. Such members respect religion and education as a key to the right use of scientific and material progress, in accordance with the previously quoted statement.

The rationalising trend does not exclude a certain tendency to develop a personality cult around the founder which is reinforced by the extremely high respect paid to his successors. Thus while the Venerable Sot'aesan has been described as "sage of sages" or as "the great sage of creation and grace," Prime Master Taesan has been described as "light of the universe."[12] During the one hundredth anniversary celebrations mentioned above, the kindly and slightly aging figure of Prime Master Taesan was applauded and celebrated like a Catholic pope in modern times. In this way the office of the leader itself becomes a focus of devotion and loyalty, and thus of an authority which transcends and to some extent suspends rationality.

Nevertheless the organisation is a little cautious about this aspect, as may be illustrated from an incident in 1991. During the centenary celebrations a statue of the founder was unveiled in a commemorative hall at Iri (now Iksan) showing him in the meditational position of a Buddha. This statue is housed in a raised, round hall, open invitingly to the front. The walls show depictions of motifs from the life of Sot'aesan. In 1991 the statue was surrounded by a sculpted lotus petal base enclosed by a firm, smooth edging. This naturally encouraged most visitors, without thinking, to place their right hand upon it as they went around the statue in a clockwise direction. In other words it guided people into performing a kind of circumambulation around the statue of the new Buddha, even though such a custom is by no means the kind of thing which Won Buddhism normally encourages. There is no doubt that the architecture, the free-standing statue itself, and traditionally respectful attitudes

---

12 E.g. in *Photos, Today's Won Buddhism* (Wonkwang Publishing Co. 1986).

conspired to lead to a religious action which is otherwise well known in Buddhist contexts. However it is not typical for Won Buddhism. On the contrary, practices of an individual kind which could lead to "superstition" are frowned upon. It appears that this effect of the statue and its presentation was not really intended. Indeed my impression is that in the meantime the arrangement around the statue has been altered.[13] The presentation is now quite similar to a smaller statue of Sot'aesan, which can be seen in the museum, on the floor below, along with other exhibits relating to his life. In the last analysis therefore these statues are intended to serve as a respectful memorial to the founder of the religion and not as the objects of worship which Buddha statues effectively have become in other forms of Buddhism.

The description given immediately above could hardly derive from a member, and care should be taken that we are not deflected by such secondary observations from the main practices of the members. For them, meditation before the symbol Il-Wŏn-Sang is of central importance. This may be carried out privately, but it is also the communal starting point for the daily life of the Dharma Sisters, in so far as they live in small groups. Every morning at five o'clock a seated meditation before the Il-Wŏn-Sang symbol is carried out, preceded and concluded with a short recitation. The complete procedure takes one hour. Of considerable importance, too, are the regular assemblies in the local temples or "teaching halls" (*kyotang*). These have something of the appearance of a plain Methodist or Presbyterian church. The congregation sit on benches like church pews, while to the front is a raised platform for preaching. Behind the place where the preacher stands is a large version of Il-Wŏn-Sang. The service consists mainly of silent meditation, preaching and hymn singing and is followed by refreshments and social interaction. These assemblies evidently strengthen the community spirit of the participants and encourage them to order their daily lives in accordance with the moral aspects of the teaching of Won Buddhism. Apart from the specific symbol and the references to the special tradition of Won Buddhism, the whole procedure of sermon and songs could al-

---

13 From 1991 I have a clear memory of visitors going round the statue, trailing their hands respectfully on a rim. In 1997 I had the impression that any such rim had been removed, but it is possible that this was due simply to the absence of a temporary floral display set up during the time of the celebrations. It would be interesting to compare photographic evidence from 1991 and later years, if available.

most be mistaken by an outsider for a Protestant Christian service. The contrast with the prostrations of visitors to traditional Buddhist temples, still normal today in the Chokye (Chogye) denomination, is striking. Moreover the otherwise widespread assumption that this-worldly benefits can be ensured by prostrations and by the acquisition of amulets is decidedly rejected in Won Buddhism as "superstition." According to members, the small symbols such as key-rings or mementos hanging in motor cars, which seem to be treated with some affection, are not protective amulets but simply reminders of one's own religious orientation. The same applies to the rosaries made of large light brown, roughly surfaced seeds, also used in and thus perhaps reminiscent of India, which include in this case a tiny glassed portrait of the founder Sot'aesan in a focal position.[14]

A major characteristic of the life of the Won Buddhist community is the social commitment of its members, which is seen most clearly in the charitable works of the Dharma Sisters. An exemplary case is the provided by the many-sided acitivities of Sister Pak Chung-Soo of Kangnam Temple, mentioned previously, who is to be seen regularly in a Catholic leprosy hospital and who helps other helpless people in all kinds of ways, both in Korea and abroad, for example in India. Her energy and leadership in these works is without doubt a great inspiration to younger recruits. Charitable works of this kind are supported financially by the lay members, not a few of whom are well situated and economically successful.

The educational institutions of Won Buddhism are highly regarded not only by believers but also quite widely in Korean society. In this connection Wonkwang University plays a crucial role, being attended not only by believers but also by many non-members. The basic idea that "religion" should not issue in some kind of superstitious dependence but on the contrary should help to bring out the independent achievements and contributions of free and rational people can be traced back to the influence of the founder. It is symbolised, for example, by the previously mentioned land reclamation programme which has found its way into the highly respected, corporate, narrative memory.

---

14 The seeds are probably of a variety of Elaeocarpus.

Gender parity in Won Buddhism

At this point it will be appropriate to draw attention to the relatively strong role played by women in Won Buddhism. Since Korean society was strongly influenced by Confucianism for centuries the traditional relationship between the sexes has usually been one of male predominance. However modernisation processes can involve a shift in the balance between the roles of the sexes and it is therefore interesting to note the extent to which a more equitable gender balance has been achieved in the context of Won Buddhism, which prides itself on its contribution to these processes.

Historically speaking, the first nine disciples of the founder, who together with him made up the round number of ten, were all men. As the necessity for structured organisation became apparent however, a "supreme council" was set up. This institution, established in 1931, consisted of nine men and nine women. Thus, if we leave the founder himself out of account at this point, some kind of equality of the sexes was institutionalised at an early stage in Won Buddhism. There seems little doubt that this move was intended to give a sense of parity between the sexes, and it is evident to the observer that this consciousness continues to prevail among the members of Won Buddhism today in daily life.

This equality is somewhat relativised when we take into account that the "Prime Masters," who ensure the religious continuity of Won Buddhism since the founder's time, have so far always been men. At the same time it should be noticed that the title "Prime Master" is an English version of the original term *chong sa* which in itself is gender-neutral.

A second inequality, or at least asymmetry between the sexes comes to the surface in the performance of professional roles in the religion. Male pastors usually wear ordinary clothes like lay persons, and may marry, while women pastors are supposed to belong to the order of Dharma Sisters, do not marry, and wear a simple uniform and hairstyle. There is no doubt that the Dharma Sisters are a major force in the organisation, and they may be more influential corporately than the male pastors. The question of discrimination through the differentiation of these roles could be worked out in either direction! Some Dharma Sisters express the view that they could fulfill their role as pastors even if they were mothers. Older Dharma Sisters take a more conservative line, emphasising that family life might disturb the meditation routine and the social work which arises out of it. It is of course understandable that, as in other religions, those who have spent most of their lives following one set of rules do not wish to see them set aside for the following generation. That would imply a downgrading of the discipline to which they originally submitted themselves. Informal reports suggest that the current Prime Master has excluded any change in these arrangements during his own period of office, which may well last for quite a long time. This guarantees stability. On the other hand he has reportedly said that the matter "should be thought over" during his period of office, so that some kind of change in these arrangements might conceivably be planned for the future.

While these two points might be regarded as problematic, it remains true that both the organisation and the membership of Won Buddhism are characterised by an attitude towards gender equality which is hard to match in the Buddhist world or in Korean society. In general there is no doubt that the success and respect ascribed to Won Buddhism in Korean society is due in no small part to the self-confident and effective activities of the Dharma Sisters, not least the leading personalities already mentioned. This is recognised by the male members, and the impression is nowhere given that men might for some other reasons be more important.

In what sense is Won Buddhism a "new religion"?

If Won Buddhism is "Buddhism," why, and in what sense, is it a "new religion"? Consider first the self-understanding of Won Buddhists themselves. The standard statement that the founder's "awakening" at the age of twenty-five took place "without the help of any teacher" emphasises his independence from any of the Buddhist traditions current in Korea at the time. In the tradition of Sŏn Buddhism by contrast. the equivalent of Chinese Chan or Japanese Zen Buddhism, the usual assumption is that the experience of enlightenment is normally achieved under the preliminary guidance of a teacher, even if, paradoxically, it cannot be directly taught. While "transmitted" enlightenment is retrospectively identified with the experience of the historical Buddha, and guaranteed by the spiritual lineage or genealogy, in this case it was Pak Chung-Bin himself who decided, on reflection, that among the religions of the world the experience and the teaching of the historical Buddha was the most similar to his own. For this reason, believers regard Won Buddhism as "Buddhism," and indeed as "perfect" (wŏn)

Buddhism, and at the same time as a "new religion," This may seem to be a paradox to those who like to distinguish sharply between established religions and new religions, but it is not a paradox for the members of Won Buddhism. Thus from the point of view of the comparative study of religions it provides an interesting, particular type within the overall range of religions. It can also be regarded as a paradigmatic case within a general theory of innovation in religion such as I have attempted to outline elsewhere.[15]

The relation between Won Buddhism and Mahāyāna Buddhism in general is therefore an extremely interesting question. Is Won Buddhism a Mahāyāna sect (in the best possible sense of that word) which familiarises modern people with the original ideas of Buddhism in a new and convenient way? Or is it a new religion in its own right, drawing important themes from Mahāyāna Buddhism but making its own contribution which leads in a different direction? In the second case Won Buddhism would fall into the category, speaking in terms of the history of religions, of those new religions in East Asia which in their various ways have contributed to the regeneration and modernisation of their countries. To illustrate, without asserting specific points of comparison, one might adduce a whole string of examples such as Cao-Dai in Vietnam, Tonghak and Chŏntokyo in Korea, Kurozumi-kyō, Ōmotokyō, Risshō Kōsei-kai and Sōka Gakkai in Japan. These religions display a varyingly close or distant relationship to the older traditions in their surroundings, Confucianism, Buddhism or Shintō.

The assertion that Won Buddhism is a new religion can easily be documented. The presentational work *Photos, Today's Won Buddhism*, for example, states firmly: "Won Buddhism is a new religion which goes back to the enlightenment of its founder, the Venerable So'taesan."[16] We have seen that, as far as the self-understanding is concerned, there is no reason to hesitate in referring to Won Buddhism as a new religion. On the other hand there have been many movements and organisations in the past which in their time seemed to be new and creative, and which yet later have been found a place in the complex history of the ever unfolding Buddhist tradition. Who would say today, for example, that Zen Buddhism is not Buddhism? There are reasons for

---

15 See "Elements of a general theory of innovation in religion" above in this volume (5.4).
16 Wonkwang Publishing Co. 1986: 8.

thinking that Won Buddhism may be so regarded retrospectively by others, that is, not only by members but also by observers or historians.

Given this self-understanding on the part Won Buddhists and, as may be presumed with confidence, on the part of the founder himself, it would not really be appropriate to regard Won Buddhism as a reform movement. There is an element of reform to be observed, in so far as it stands in a dialectical relationship to the more traditional kinds of Buddhism in Korea in which ritual action plays a more dominant role, in particular the Chokye School, organised under this name from 1941.[17] Although the founder Pak Chung-Bin did publish a work on the renovation of Korean Buddhism, which is displayed in the museum mentioned above, the reform motivation appears not to have been dominant in the foundational period. The impetus of the founder's own experience was too strong for the movement to present itself merely as the true or loyal form of an original tradition which had been overlaid or lost. Had it done so, it would have to be classified, in the context of a general theory of religious innovation, as a reforming "sect," in the precise, technical sense of that word. On the contrary, in the terms of the same theory, Won Buddhism may fairly be designated as a new religion. Moreover this theoretical assessment coincides with its own self-understanding. The fact that the new religion, Won Buddhism, also identifies itself retrospectively with "Buddhism," leads to other questions about its relation to that more general tradition which will be considered next.

Won Buddhism and the wider Buddhist tradition

So how does Won Buddhism relate itself to the Buddhist tradition in general, and to what extent are its statements in this connection plausible? The Buddhist tradition is so widely established in so many cultural regions and cultures that the question frequently arises as to whether a particular movement or organisation is Buddhist or not. Sometimes a movement claims to be "Buddhist," but the claim is questioned by others. And in other, rather fewer cases a religion which claims to represent a new revelation may offer little but repackaged Buddhist ideas. Won Buddhism is a special case in that, as we have already seen, it claims to be a "new religion" and "Buddhism" at one and the same time.

---

17 For the key points in the modern reorganisation of Korean Buddhism, see Grayson 1989, chapter 13.

The question must be addressed therefore as to whether Won Buddhism is "Buddhist" and if so, in what sense.

In attending to this question the term "orthodox," as already mentioned in the introductory section, is rather unhelpful. The difficulty is that the assertion of "orthodoxy" implies that a decision can be taken on the basis of a normative standpoint which is known to the person who makes the judgement. But this is the prerogative of those who, for religious reasons, adopt a position within the tradition. The historian of religion has no such ideal standpoint. A rigorous attempt to apply the term "orthodox" to the history of Buddhism in terms of an abstracted, normative ideal would probably leave hardly anything over. Yet this conclusion would shock many Buddhists who themselves claim orthodoxy. Nevertheless it is sometimes necessary, in the general study of religions, to attempt to answer the question as to whether a particular movement may fairly be described as "Buddhist" or not. Sometimes claims are made which may be spurious, as in the case of the Japanese religion Aum Shinrikyō which I recently discussed in some detail.[18] Such claims need to be assessed. This is really part of an older and wider discussion about the question of consistency within historically extended religious traditions.[19] In disputed cases the question of relative authenticity has to be addressed by historians of religion, but this is a question of historical coherence and reasonableness of claims to identity. Quite different is the claim to "orthodoxy" which can only be asserted by a religious authority from its own normative point of view.

Whether and in what sense Won Buddhism is "Buddhist" will now be considered in all brevity on the background of these considerations. Speaking generally, let it first be established that the teaching of Won Buddhism certainly has much in common with the widely current ideas of Mahāyāna Buddhism. The syllable *wŏn*, corresponding to a single Chinese character, means rounded, complete and perfect. In the teaching of Won Buddhism it refers to the final "truth" or reality of the cosmos, which is complete and integrated and can therefore be represented by a simple circle. This central symbol of the religion, called Il-Wŏn-Sang, has already been referred to because of its importance in the practice of Won Buddhism. Il-Wŏn-Sang means literally "the form of one circle", and the Chinese character for "form" used here is the same as that used in Buddhist tradition for the characteristics or qualities

---

18 See Pye 1996c, also at 5.7 below.
19 Systematically introduced in Pye and Morgan 1973.

of existence. So we may understand that the circle (which, incidentally, is not in itself a Chinese character) allows us to symbolise the ultimate character of existence in the best possible way. In his work *A Diagram for Practice of the Doctrine of Won Buddhism*, issued by Prime Master Taesan, we find that Il-Wŏn-Sang and the Dharmakāya Buddha are shown together (Kim Tae-Gŏ (Taesan) 1988:1). That means that Il-Wŏn-Sang is identical with the inexpressible, ultimate Buddha-nature, of which the various individual Buddhas in Mahayana Buddhism are but representations or appearances. Much more could be said in the interpretation of Il-Wŏn-Sang, of course, as we see in the second part of the *Scripture of Won Buddhism (Won Pulkyo Kyojun)*, but that would lead too far afield at this point.

On the other hand it is to be expected that the normative position ascribed to the founder, Venerable Sot'aesan, will not be simply accepted by other Buddhists. After all, he put himself on the same level as the historical Buddha, which must at least appear as something of a challenge for a traditional Buddhist, even taking account of the idea that there has been a sequence of Buddhas through time. The expectation of a future Buddha, Maitreya, is as well known in Korea as elsewhere. In fact one of the most substantial buildings at the temple Kŭmsan-sa near Iksan, is a hall with a large image of Maitreya, and Sot'aesan spent a month here while thinking over where the headquarters of the new religion should be located. In other words the future Buddha Maitreya was an available concept, and yet the newly enlightened Sot'aesan was not identified with him.

Apart from its clear relationship to Buddhist tradition, Won Buddhism has a decidedly universalist message for the whole of humanity. Not only does it teach that all human beings are equal regardless of race or gender, it also teaches that all religions are in principle one. It is on this basis that Chon Pal-Khn called for the establishment of a "United Religions" in order to spread these values, regarded as spiritual values, throughout the world.[20] Although it might be said that these ideas are at least implied by Mahāyāna Buddhism, they are not really Buddhist teachings as such, in a direct sense. Indeed, Buddhism in its

---

20 Chon 1989. This idea was also put forward during the centenary celebrations in 1991. Since then, apparently without due acknowledgement, the idea of a "United Religions" has been organisationally developed by a group based in the United States. It seems to me that more credit should be given to Chon Pal Khn in this regard.

older forms was far from announcing the equality, let alone the unity of all religions. On this background Won Buddhism's social and cultural call to "unity among humankind can be seen as a forward thrust which goes beyond the teachings of traditional Buddhism.

Won Buddhism illustrates in its own particular way the close relationship which can exist between religious innovation and reflection about the possible relations between religions in their plurality. It is a normal function of new religions, emerging in a world which is already occupied by various existing religions, to reflect on the way in which these various religions do or could relate to each other. Won Buddhism's founder Sot'aesan spent the first part of his life thinking deeply about the problems of human existence. He made a positive appraisal of Buddhism, or at least of the historical Buddha, but his thought as transmitted to us in the *Scripture of Won Buddhism (Won Pulkyo Kyojun)* is replete with observations on the other religions current in Korea during his time, especially Confucianism and Tonghak ("the eastern teaching"). This feature of his thought provided the starting point for the active interreligious dialogues which have been promoted by the later leadership.[21] In other words, we can see in this example a close relationship between the the push towards an innovative message, the recognition that religions exist in plurality and the attempt to think deeply over the inner meaning of religions. This combination permits the self-confident announcement of a new solution to what the historian might indeed view as a long perceived problem.

The tension between innovation and the appropriation of Buddhist ideas can also quite easily be documented by reference to exhibits in the museum mentioned earlier. Here we see displayed writings by the founder with titles (translated from the Korean) like "The Reform of Korean Buddhism," "The Correct Canon of Buddhism" or "Rules of the Buddhist Dharma Research Association."[22] These alone tell us that Sot'aesan thought carefully about the state of Buddhism in Korea at the time. Yet if we look closely at a poster for the "Buddhist Dharma Research Association," exhibited near a frequently reproduced photograph of Sot'aesan himself, it can be seen that even then quite original

---

21 Cf. Woo Hai-Ran 1998.
22 This name could alternatively be translated "Society for the Study of the Buddhadharma," for it was a religiously committed study group rather than an independent research institute, but "Buddhist Dharma Research Association" is literally correct and preferred in Won Buddhist circles.

elements played an equally important role for him. Without any precise connection being made to Buddhist sources, we see for example that "the essential way of humanity" (*insaeng ŭi yoto*) is presented schematically with various subordinate features.

This view of the relationship between Won Buddhism and Buddhism in general was confirmed for me by the present Prime Master Chwasan.[23] According to him, western Christianity arose from the root of Judaism, and Buddhism from the root of Brahmanism. However Won Buddhism does *not* stand in a similar relationship to Buddhism, he said. Rather, the teaching arose on the basis of the great enlightenment of Sot'aesan. The special character of Won Buddhism, according to Chwasan, lies in the fact that it emphasises not so much the past as the present and the future, and for this reason it is a new and independent religion. However, on account of the great similarity which the founder himself recognised between his own teaching and that of the Buddha, the teaching was later designated as Won Buddhism. Prime Master Chwasan thus reasserts the relationship between Won Buddhism and Buddhism which is generally current in the tradition.

The question of the relationship between Won Buddhism and Buddhist tradition in general could be investigated further at various points. The commentary on Il-Wŏn-Sang is rather distinctive, for example, while there is also a finely balanced relation between teaching and practice which is obviously influenced by the style of Buddhism. Many nuances in the texts need to be weighed up carefully, taking account of widely current East Asian and more specifically Korean assumptions and allusions. Naturally, these matters are also analysed in detail by Won Buddhist academics writing within the tradition such as Dr. Ryu Sung-Tae mentioned above (Ryu 1995, 1996).

In its teaching and its practice alike Won Buddhism displays an active ability both to select and to integrate. On the basis of this creative development it is not inappropriate therefore to categorise Won Buddhism as a "new religion," even while it explicitly includes the word Buddhism in its name. For the history of religions, the categorization preferred by the members at any one time may not be the most appropriate. In this case however it is difficult to come to any conclusion which is better than that of the members themselves, namely that Won Buddhism is at one and the same time a new religion and a

---

23 I am grateful to Choi Seong-Hee for translating handwritten notes in Korean made by Dr. Ryu Sung-Tae during the interview with Prime Master Chwasan.

form of Buddhism, however paradoxical this may seem to others. This double designation represents a challenge, at once critical and peaceful, to traditional forms of Buddhism, and in particular to those which continue to be current in Korea. In this sense it is a sign of the thoroughly modern character of Won Buddhism.

Bibliographical references

CATWBS 2006 (Committee for the Authorized Translation of *Won*-Buddhist Scriptures). *The Scriptures of Won-Buddhism (Wonbulgyo Kyojŏn)*.Iksan (Department of International Affairs of *Won*-Buddhist Headquarters).
Chon, Pal-Khn (trans.) 1971. *The Canonical Textbook of Won Buddhism (Won Pulkyo Kyojun)*.Seoul (Kyohak-sa Publishing Co.) (See also CATWBS 2006.)
– 1988. *The Canonical Textbook of Won Buddhism (Won Pulkyo Kyojun)* (revised edition). Iri (now Iksan) (Won Kwang Publishing Co). (See also CATWBS 2006.)
Chon, Pal-Khn 1989. "Toward organization of United Religions" in: *Won Buddhism* 6/6: 8–12.
Chon, Pal-Khn (ed.) 1993. *Won Buddhism. The Periodical 1962–1992 The Complete Set*. (now Iksan) (Research Institute for Overseas Missions, Wongkwang University).
Chung, Bong-Kil 1994 (2nd corrected edition). *An Introduction to Won Buddhism, Wonbulgyo*. Iri (now Iksan) (Overseas Missions Bureau of Won Buddhism).
Editorial Committee 1991 (Editorial Committee for Papers Presented at the One Hundredth Anniversary of the Birthday of the Great Master Sot'aesan) *Illyu munmyong kwa Won Pulgyo sasang* 人類文明□圓仏教思想 (i.e. "Human Culture and Won Buddhist Thought", original title not Romanized; in two volumes). Iri (now Iksan) (Won Buddhism Publishing Company).
Grayson, James Huntley 1989. *Korea, A Religious History*. Oxford (Clarendon Press).
Keil, S., Jetzkowitz, J. and König, M. (eds.) 1998. *Modernisierung und Religion in Südkorea*, Köln (Weltforum Verlag).
Kim Tae-Gŏ (Taesan) 1988. *A Diagram for Practice of the Doctrine of Won Buddhism*. Iri, (now Iksan) (Wonkwang Publishing Co.).
Pye Michael 1971a. "Syncretism and Ambiguity" in: *Numen* 18 (2): 83–93.
– 1993. "Syncretism versus synthesis" in: *Occasional papers of the British Association for the Study of Religion*. Cardiff (BASR) Republished in: *Method &Theory in the Study of Religion*, 6 (3)(1994): 217–29.
– 1996b. "Aum Shinrikyō. Can Religious Studies cope?" *Religion*, 26 (3): 261–273.
– 1996c. "Syncretism: Buddhism and Shintō on one island" in Doležalová, Iva, Horyna, Břetislav and Papoušek, Dalibor (eds.) *Religions in Contact. Se-*

lected Proceedings of the Special IAHR Conference held in Brno, August 23–26, 1994, Brno (Czech Society for the Study of Religions): 159–62.
- 1998b."Innovation und Modernität im Won-Buddhismus" in: Keil et al. 1998: 183–94.

Pye, Michael and Morgan, Robert (eds.) 1973. *The Cardinal Meaning. Essays in Comparative Hermeneutics: Buddhism and Christianity*. (Religion and Reason 6). The Hague (Mouton).

Ryu, Sung-Tae 1995. *Wŏnpulkyo wa tongyang sasang* ("Won Buddhism and Eastern Thought"). Iksan (Wonkwang Taehak).
- 1996. *Tongyang ŭi suyangron* ("Theory of Personality Formation in Eastern Thought"). Iksan (Wonkwang Taehak).

Taesan (Prime Master): see Kim Tae-Gŏ 1988.

Vos, Frits 1997. *Die Religionen Koreas*. Stuttgart (Kohlhammer).

Wonkwang Publishing Co. (ed.) 1986. *Photos, Today's Won Buddhism*. Iri (now Iksan) (Wonkwang Publishing Co.).

Woo, Hai-Ran 1998. "Die Dialogbewegung aus der Perspektive nicht-westlicher Religionen. Das Beispiel des Won-Buddhismus" in: Keil et al.1998: 251–270.
- 2001. *Kritische Untersuchungen von Erklärungsmodellen zu Neuen Religionen unter besonderer Berücksichtigung des Won-Buddhismus*. Marburg (Ph.D. Dissertation).
- 2004. Neue Religionen anders verstehen. Das Beispiel des Won-Buddhismus. München (Biblion).

This article was first published under the same title in *Numen*, 49 (2) (2002): 113–141. The original publication included four illustrations (two doctrinal diagrams by Prime Master Taesan, a portrait of Pak Chung-Bin and a poster for the "Buddhist Dharma Research Association"), which are not included here.

5.7 Aum Shinrikyō. Can Religious Studies Cope?

Aum Shinrikyō has become a textbook case for considering the relationship between a descriptivist approach to the study of religion and the need for critical awareness and evaluation. This article explores the issues on the basis of materials from the field in late 1995. An evaluatory stance is adopted on various issues which arise, illustrating how the specialist in the study of religions may proceed in a socially responsible manner without compromising the hard-won independence and integrity of the discipline.

Recovering the Bodies

In September 1995 the Japanese police spent several days at three different sites looking for the bodies of a lawyer, his wife, and their child, all murdered in 1989 by one or more members of the Aum Shinrikyō. Before his murder, the lawyer had been preparing a case against the religion for alleged drug abuse and fraud during ceremonies. The weather was most unhelpful. A series of typhoons brought heavy rain, and the painstaking digging was done to a large extent under tarpaulins while bulldozers moved the extracted mud from place to place. Eventually the remains were recovered. The recovery showed that information about their whereabouts given recently by members of Aum Shinrikyō was correct. This is turn demonstrated that one or more members were deeply implicated in the killings and probably directly responsible for them. In September some of the suspects had already been arrested and others were being sought. Posters at every Japanese railway station, with photographs of further suspects, sought the assistance of the public. Towards the end of the year in 1995 the court case with various charges is continuing. In the same month of September admissions were forthcoming that Aum Shinrikyō was also implicated in the sarin nerve gas attacks in Nagano Prefecture and on the Tokyo underground, in which several people were also killed. The circumstantial evidence was by then already overwhelming.

These sensational events are, fortunately, not typical data with which to begin an essay on a religious movement. One might say immediately that Aum Shinrikyō is *not* really a religious movement. This would safeguard 'religion' as a good thing. This is the line of argument taken by members of other religious groups in Japan who are fearful of negative appraisal of all religion in the media and among the public. Unfortunately the matter is not that simple. In the other direction it has been argued that the Aum case is the beginning of the end of 'religion' in Japan. Although there are some empirical grounds for drawing this conclusion (see further below), it will probably also prove to be mistaken in the long run.

Certainly the prominence given to the Aum case in the Japanese media has generated a bandwagon effect of its own. It has led to a general flurry of interest in what it means to be 'religious', mainly with negative overtones. It has led specialists to reconsider (through informal discussions in cyberspace) what it means to understand and to explain religious movements academically, and at what point the option of critical comment arises.[1] In this regard it may end up by becoming a textbook example.[2] It has also led to a political process within Japan in that the definition of the rights and obligations of 'religious juridical persons' became a matter for stock-taking, for dispute and for new decisions.

The sustained coverage of the recovery of the bodies, sustained because the process was physically very difficult and socially quite traumatic, may be regarded as a symbolic, defining moment in the emergence of these questions. Hence it is taken here as a starting point for providing some orientation in what may otherwise seem to be a mass of confusing and conflicting images. The lawyer whose work threatened, at a relatively early date, to blow the whistle on Aum Shinrikyō, was in fact killed. So too, savagely, were his wife and young child. These are inescapably real facts. Equally real were the arbitrary deaths of those who died in the gas attack and the injuries of those, many more, who suffered physically as a result of it. Any appraisal of Aum Shinrikyō will have to take account of these facts.

---

1   In cyberspace see in particular contributions in late 1995 by Clark Chilson and Ian Reader (Religious Studies UK list).
2   For a general account of Aum Shinrikyō, see also Shimazono 1995. However Professor Shimazono's article appeared shortly after the present article was written and is therefore not taken up in detail here.

Aum Shinrikyō Defined as a Religious Group

Aum Shinrikyō is a religion. It was generally regarded as such before the above mentioned events took place. From the point of view of the 'academic' study of religion (*Religionswissenschaft*) the fact that criminal acts have been committed is not a sufficient reason for changing this way of regarding it. Atrocities have also been committed in the names of other religions.

Aum Shinrikyō may be regarded as a religion not merely because it was legally registered as one in law but because of various characteristics which it has displayed. These include: a range of ideas about the cosmos and the place of the individual in it which seem to provide meaning for the adherents; regular, ritualized practice of various kinds including chanting and meditation; a community of believers defined by the identity of belonging to Aum Shinrikyō in which an important part is played by the largely unquestioned leadership of a charismatic leader; and a sense of personal realization and certainty felt by the followers. These points may seem fairly obvious, but they need to be recorded because, like the murders, they also do not go away. Such basic aspects or dimensions of religion can be documented here as in other cases.

More detailed description would build on one or the other point. Consider here the psycho-religious orientation of believers. This was evident precisely at the time of crisis, when the bodies were recovered by the police, from the fact that many of its members found ways of closing their eyes to the realities shown daily on television. Such members had a religious explanation, well known in its general outlines to students of religion, for the sharp criticisms directed towards their leaders. Of course the world rejects Aum Shinrikyō, their thoughts ran, because it does not understand it. The world reflects an order which is in process of being swept away. Clearly Asahara Shōkō (the leader) is misunderstood and falsely accused, they say. Thus covered, they continue to practise meditation and to sell promotional literature.

Defining and Criticizing

At this stage a warning about possible methodological confusion is necessary. It is important to bear in mind the distinction, well established in the discourse of religious studies, between operational and normative definitions of religion.³ An 'operational' definition is the starting point for a non-evaluative description, that is, it is a working definition for the purposes of study. A 'normative' definition, by contrast, establishes an evaluatory norm for the recognition of religion, and accordingly is the starting point for an evaluatory appraisal. In terms of studying religions 'academically' Aum Shinrikyō falls within the range of any broadly based operational definition. In terms of taking a normative decision about what religion 'really' is or should be, it might be legitimate to argue that Aum Shinrikyō is something like a religion, but that it is not a 'real' one. Such an argument, however, would be a philosophical or theological assessment or statement going beyond the historical and comparative study of religion as a shared science. As far as the historical and comparative study of religion is concerned, Aum Shinrikyō is certainly a real religion.

The distinction made immediately above is very well established and is not put in doubt here. It is essential for the maintenance of the independence and integrity of the scientific study of religion. The Aum 'shock', however, has made it equally clear that it is unavoidable for academic specialists in the study of religion, insofar as they are also people living in the world, to find themselves crossing the boundaries of their immediate discipline from time to time. This does not necessarily mean that they have adopted some specific, normative religious viewpoint. They *might* adopt some such normative religious viewpoint, or they might apply other criteria in their reflections and judgements about religion or about anything else. Crossing the above-mentioned boundaries, knowingly, does not necessarily damage the investigative and analytic research which they normally do, provided that the necessary distinctions are made. Nor is it necessary to deny that they are persons when they are doing their research into religions! Being persons, they are able to distinguish between various actions which they perform. It is important to be able to differentiate clearly between their work as such, in the narrow sense, and their further participation as persons in informed, public discussion. It is not inappropriate for academics to take part in such discussion.

The Aum case illustrates the point clearly, and radically. While the academic study of religion does not in itself involve condemning acts of

---

3   See Pye 1972a, especially references there to Kishimoto Hideo's espousal of this simple but helpful terminology (Kishimoto 1961).

murder, it can hardly be taken amiss if a person who is professionally engaged in the academic study of religion expresses horror or dismay at such acts, especially when they are committed within the range of phenomena or events covered by his or her research. At the risk of not ever getting any research cooperation, not to mention funding, from Aum Shinrikyō, I am bound to record that I find involvement of Aum Shinrikyō in acts of terrorism and murder quite deplorable. This involvement now seems to be beyond all reasonable doubt, whatever the outcome of legal proceedings against specific individuals may be.

What Kind of a Religion is Aum Shinrikyō?

There are various kinds of religion, and this is not the place to attempt a systematic survey of the very large number of religions throughout the world. Awareness of the sheer number and variety of different religions should make it clear, however, that it is not justified on the basis of one case to conclude that 'religion' is 'bad'. Nor can it be concluded that 'religion' is likely to disappear in Japan as a result of the Aum case. This question is discussed further below.

Restricting ourselves to the overall religious situation in Japan, there are certain general bearings which are widely known, and represent something of a consensus among observers (who may skip to the end of the next paragraph). The two largest religious forces are Buddhism and Shintō. Buddhism deals above all with the departed, while providing a general orientation of meaning in life and, for those interested, the option of meditation or other forms of ritual participation such as pilgrimage. Shintō attends much more to the assurance and the celebration of life in this present existence. While Shintō continues to have a certain national, and in some cases nationalist orientation, the extreme political role of Shintō during the late nineteenth and early twentieth centuries was brought to an abrupt halt in 1945. After this, the new laws on the separation of religion from the state and the registration of 'religious juridical persons' provided new rules for the status and activities of all organizationally distinct religions in Japan.

In this extended post-war situation a large number of religious groups have been competing for the attention of the public. Buddhism and Shintō continue to prosper and are very strongly established in their recognized spheres of influence. In addition there is a large number of 'new religions', some of which, having been initiated in the eighteenth and nineteenth centuries, are in fact quite old. Even religions founded in the aftermath of the war are by now very well established. Membership in these is a matter of personal choice, although by now, in many cases, family loyalty plays a significant role. These religions, often the result of revelations received by charismatic leaders, are influenced in some cases more by Shintō and in some cases more by Buddhism. Some movements claim to represent the full, clear teaching of Buddhism for the modern world. Others are simply themselves. Christianity, it may be added, continues a more or less tenuous existence with its Catholic, Orthodox and various Protestant forms. Among self-conscious followers of religions mentioned above, the Aum Shinrikyō case has been only slightly worrying. This is because non-members, i.e. non-members of Aum Shinrikyō, do not regard it as anything to do with them. This attitude is well understood by others and is easily summed up in the colloquial Japanese phrase *kankei nai* (nothing to do with me).

Apart from the institutionally registered, and thus publicly recognized organizations, there is in addition a wide, general pattern of religious activity with which all Japanese people are more or less familiar and in which the institutional religions themselves participate. I regard this, taken as an organically coherent web, as Japan's 'primal religion'. Since the end of the second world war, this primal religion has come to be the matrix of all religious activity in Japan. Shintō, after a long and complex development, has finally been displaced from this role. The last twist was its disestablishment at the end of the war, which led to its being much more precisely defined as one specific religion among others. The pervasive primal religion of Japan is in many respects more or less obligatory. Though publicly undefined, it also emerges again and again in many different contexts. It cannot be described fully here.[4]

One example of the pressure of this primal religion may suffice, taken from the traumatic days during which bodies of the Sakamoto family were discovered. Journalists and cameramen continually visited the sites, often with great difficulty because the roads were closed off and in some cases a cross-country hike was necessary under wet and muddy conditions. However, they were not the only visitors. Local people laid a few flowers at the spots. Not long after the discovery, journalists

---

4   I have advanced this concept briefly in various places (Pye 1994b, 1996e, and so on).

from Tokyo were somewhat bemused to see that a substantial 'stupa' had been erected at one of the sites. A 'stupa' in this case is a strong square post with an inscription on it 'for the Sakamoto family', a focal point for prayers to be said for their peaceful transfer into the common realm of ancestors (in which the concepts of gods and buddhas, which people become after death, tend to flow into each other). Interviewed for television, it was clear that the local people had mixed feelings. While being shocked like the rest of Japan, they were also evidently worried about the fact that the burial of the remains had taken place near them. One explanation for the erection of the stupa was that the tiny child would feel uncared for in 'such a lonely place'. Another response suggested, however, that the spirits of the murdered people should be enabled to rest. In other words the villagers were taking no chances. They did not want to have uncared-for spirits in their neighbourhood.

The primal religion of Japan has many other features which are, conversely, life-affirming. It includes assumptions about sacred space and about the calendrical sequences of life. It provides a matrix of well-worn patterns, including the acceptance of religious authority where relevant. This primal religion is, admittedly, hardly recognized as 'religion' by Japanese people themselves. Remember, however, that the vast majority of Japanese people are not themselves specialists in the study of religion. They just do it. At the same time they tend to reserve the term 'religion' (shūkyō) to institutions or organizations demanding a personal involvement or commitment based on a decision of faith.

Most of the new religions are very clear cases of 'religion' in this more limited sense, being precisely such a matter of felt personal need or interest. Since they compete with each other in a finite, though apparently large market, new ones are constantly being started. If they run, they run. If they show less success in attracting individuals they may also stagnate and fade away again. An example of a religion which has almost disappeared is Chiesonkyō, a religion which as far as I know has never been described, and which discourages investigations by outsiders. Highly successful, recently launched religions in this category are Agonshū (literally "Agama Religion") (cf. Reader 1988) and Kōfuku no Kagaku (literally 'Science of Happiness'[5]). Both of these religions arrange

---

5   Retrospective note: This religion has recently changed the English version of its name to "Happy Science" which is an inaccurate translation of the name, adopted according to members for its better marketability. The Japanese name remains unchanged.

huge public shows. Agonshū has public fire ceremonies (*goma*) in the Shingon Buddhist tradition. Thus one may doubt that it truly has a close relationship to the "Agamas", that is, the sutras of early Buddhism. Science of Happiness arranges huge events centred on its founder – Ōkawa Ryūhō, who appears in a dazzling light, for example in the massive Tokyo Dome, otherwise known popularly as Big Egg.

Aum Shinrikyō is a recently founded example of this type of religion, and accordingly it got itself registered, and describes itself, as a "religious juridical person." Its leader, Asahara Shōkō, now in custody, was previously a member of Agonshū. Aum Shinrikyō has been able to attract the interest of, mainly, younger people. They become members by choice and, to judge from the promotional literature and the way in which they themselves appear in television interviews, evidently regard it as a way of exploring their own inner consciousness and of finding their identity as individuals in a larger group. Apart from learning to meditate in various ways the members are in many cases happy to receive reassurance that they are making progress and that they are important within the group itself.

A telling example is that of Mr Tomomasa Nakagawa. Mr Nakagawa is a young doctor (since struck off the list at his own request) who graduated in 1988 and joined Aum Shinrikyō in 1989. According to newspaper reports he was instructed to use his medical knowledge to inject the kidnapped Sakamoto with a lethal dose of potassium chloride. Later, he suffocated the baby. Mr Nakagawa, who has admitted killing both the anti-Aum lawyer Sakamoto and his baby son, explained to police that while he had felt misgivings about murdering the 'helpless baby' he had also felt 'elation and pride' in being selected to join the hit squad. After only two months of membership he had been taken into a group of high-ranking members and trusted aides of 'the master'. In late October he also admitted in court that he had taken part in the production of sarin gas at the order of Asahara, but had not expected that it would be used. From this dramatic example (reported in *Asahi Evening News,* 13 September 1995) it may be seen quite clearly that as the commitment of members increases, along with their personal investment of time and money, their sense of responsibility is increasingly defined by the overall religious authority of the group, rather than by any values which they may previously have entertained.

Belief and Practice in Aum Shinrikyō

For at least two reasons there is no simple answer to the question "What does Aum Shinrikyō believe?" First, it is not clear to what extent Asahara Shōkō himself or his close associates themselves believed what he taught up to the time of his imprisonment. It is now unlikely that this can ever be ascertained. It must be said, however, that it is difficult to correlate some of the teachings propounded with what turns out to have been, over an extended period, organized crime. Thus the suspicion of cynicism or at least opportunism must be regarded as well-founded. Second, the teachings presented to believers or potential believers have been distinctly eclectic. Among the threads given prominence in recent literature of the cult the following four may be mentioned as particularly important.

First is the claim that Asahara himself has achieved special status among human beings as a result of his spiritual practice. In this he is one of a few who have appeared from time to time. One booklet in Japanese bears the title "Birth of a Saint," and explains that the truth (*shinri*) of an ancient tradition, said to be 2600 years old, has now re-emerged with Asahara's teaching. Publications usually show repeated pictures of Asahara himself in a spiritually serene state. He is portrayed as able to show the way to such attainment through a method of practice specially devised for people who are busy in the modern world. Asahara is referred to by believers as Sonshi, which means "revered teacher" and is translated as "Master" in Aum materials. On the one hand the believers are encouraged to feel that they can follow in his tracks. On the other hand his superiority and special status are constantly made clear, so that submissive discipleship is presented as the right way to make progress. This claim is reinforced by other publication titles such as "The absolute Truth" (*Zettai no shinri*), being part 5 of "Asahara Shōkō's world."

Second, Asahara claims that his teaching is the same as that of ancient yogis. Their authority is set alongside that of Buddhism. Because of this perspective, he made a point, when travelling to India, of including meetings with various modern yogis: Yogeshwaranand (described as an 'astral guru'), Swamis Cidananda and Krsnananda, Swami Akhandananda, Swami Vihar Maharaj, Swami Dayananda and Pilot Baba who told him "You can save Japan." The booklet setting out these meetings also gives prominence to Tibetan lamas including the Dalai Lama (see further below). The main point made is that Asahara's spiritual attainment and religious mission are recognized by authorities who practise asceticism, Asahara himself appears in various clothing which is apparently thought to be suitable for a holy man, sometimes white, sometimes red. His robes are usually simple, but occasionally more complex outfits are attempted. His long hair and beard (unusual for Japanese) also imply a special, and perhaps ascetic way of life. These features of his appearance are not imitated by his followers.

Third, regarding Buddhism, attention is paid both to Mahāyāna Buddhism in its tantric form, as being of special value for interesting meditational practice, and to Pāli Buddhism, as being early and authentic. In this way the claims of various schools of Buddhism in Japan are largely outflanked. For tantric Buddhism inspiration is drawn not from Japan's Shingon tradition but from Tibet, and this version of Buddhism is offered as one which assists the self-realization of the individual. Asahara has also studied the 'Āgamas,' that is the sutras of early Buddhism, though this in fact probably means the Chinese versions of texts corresponding to the Theravāda Pāli tradition. Part 14 of 'The World of Asahara Shōkō' implies as much, for it contains a list of standard Sino-Japanese expressions for which a 'corrected' version from the Āgamas is offered. Thus Buddhism also provides two threads of special authenticity, according to the published presentations of Aum Shinrikyō. Both of these ideas may indeed owe quite a lot to the Japanese religion Agonshū, as a result of Asahara's earlier membership. The large scale *goma* ceremonies of Agonshū were, however, not imitated by Asahara.

The fourth thread to be noted is the emphasis on practice, referred to with the established Japanese term *shugyō*. Followers are always encouraged to practise. The word appears on fans and T-shirts. When the first arrests were made and serious difficulties began to appear for the religion, believers were confronted with a challenge from journalists. Apart from the conceptual alibi mentioned earlier, their response was that they would practise harder. In Aum Shinrikyō this practice consists of various stages of meditation including elements drawn from a range of yogic and Buddhist traditions. To illustrate, one summary statement runs: 'The method consists of Kundalini Yoga, Jnana Yoga, the Six Extreme Disciplines, the Mind of Four Immeasurables, termination of one's subconscious, Six-step Tantric Initiation, and more'. The purpose is the attainment of 'supreme bliss and infinite freedom'. It may be noted that the Buddhist-related elements mentioned here are neither early nor central traditions from within Buddhism.

Is Aum Shinrikyō Buddhist?

Is Aum Shinrikyō Buddhist? No, Aum Shinrikyō is not Buddhist.[6] This may be seen from the fact that its literature is strikingly eclectic and contains the commendation of a large number of teachings which simply are not Buddhist. The picture is reminiscent, if older models are sought at all, of Theosophy. The 'master', Asahara himself, is presented as coming from a higher, 'astral' level from which he brings spiritual messages. He is a god. His followers do their best to ascend to this level, or at any rate to various levels higher than that of ordinary existence. One publication declares on its cover that his beloved disciples are reborn as gods (*kami*) from the world of humans. This is associated with the path to the attainment of 'supernatural powers', a term deriving from Buddhist tradition but usually treated there with more caution. In one lecture Asahara said that he would soon be having other matters to attend to (as indeed proved to be the case!), but that his followers need not worry about the loss of his teaching as he would by then have instructed other 'Buddhas' who could carry it on (*Supreme Emancipation,* page 92). Such statements are no more than an opportunist hijacking of the word Buddha.

The goal of Aum Shinrikyō's practice is ambivalent, and probably not really Buddhist for most participants. The emphasis in Aum Shinrikyō is placed on 'Enjoy Happiness', the English words being written out in cursive English script though the main text is in Japanese. Under the heading 'Voice of Buddha' Asahara tells his readers how to transcend light and enjoy happiness, this being a 'message of happiness' from a completely liberated being. Buddhism, it may be said, is certainly not intended to make people unhappy, but its goal, nirvana, is differently defined. It might be argued that Buddhism often works with proximate goals for the benefit of those who are not yet ready for nirvana, and indeed the concept of skilful means is used to justify this procedure. This concept, however, also has the important regulatory feature of leading back towards central Buddhist conceptions. There is no evidence that

---

6   The question of whether groups can be defined as Buddhist simply because they say they are is of course a subtle problem at the interface between phenomenology of religion and history of religion. This section has benefited from discussions at Bath College of Higher Education, England, and in particular with Helen Waterhouse who is pursuing research on various Buddhist groups in the United Kingdom.

this is the case in Aum Shinrikyō. On the contrary, it is apparent that other goals are espoused.

Asahara went to some trouble to try to establish world-wide Buddhist credentials. He was welcomed, and indeed feted in Myanmar and Sri Lanka. He met with the Dalai Lama, a meeting of which much is made in the promotional literature. In this connection serious doubt must be cast on the judgment of the Dalai Lama. It is part of his style to express himself warmly and in full confidence that his words are based on a strong spiritual perception. It appears that he acquiesced in the judgment that Japanese Buddhism in general is moribund and this-worldly. As a spiritual leader of great reputation he expressed his confidence in Asahara's ability to lead Japan into the way of true Buddhism. One can only conclude from this that the Dalai Lama is, as the saying goes, 'either a knave or a fool'. Either it suited him, or he was taken in. In other words, either he understood that Asahara was a skilled religious operator and cynically encouraged him in accordance with the principle that all publicity is good publicity, or he totally miscalculated Asahara's character, which says little for his spiritual perception. I regret that it is necessary to criticize the Dalai Lama, who is a genuine Buddhist at the same time as being a political leader. Such criticism is currently not at all fashionable in western countries because of the effects of the Cold War, in which the Dalai Lama allowed himself to become implicated. However, the criticism is unavoidable in a situation in which specialists in religion find themselves being criticized because they did not previously make clear statements about Aum Shinrikyō.

Although Aum Shinrikyō documents make some reference to Buddhist ideas, the overall pattern of these documents, as said above, is one of extreme eclecticism. For example, in one magazine Asahara's connections with the supposedly mysterious culture and religion of ancient Egypt are heavily emphasized. The impression is created that he is in tune with the inner teachings of all the major religions. In fact, the religious culture of ancient Egypt is not particularly mysterious, and Asahara's knowledge of it is probably minimal. In the same way, the Buddhist elements in Aum Shinrikyō may be regarded as a kind of opportunist scooping. Similar considerations would be appropriate in respect of the use of 'Buddhist' elements in the teachings of Agonshū and of Kōfuku no Kagaku. In all these cases the followers are often pitifully ignorant of real Buddhism. The well-known lay Buddhist movements of modern Japan, by contrast, all have a strong and genuine relationship to ancient Buddhism, even though it is pointed up in a particular way in each case. The range available for observation here makes it quite clear that without wishing to offer a normative definition about what authentic Buddhism must be like, the historian of religion can nevertheless provide some discerning differentiation.[7] Just because someone or some group claims to be Buddhist, the claim is not necessarily plausible. On the contrary, it is up to the specialist in the study of religion to point out the implausibility of particular claims when interpretation is strained beyond widely perceived coherence.

The End of 'Religion' in Japan?

The 'Aum incident' as it came to be called in Japanese, naturally set off numerous reactions in Japan's popular and semi-popular magazines, always on the look-out for sensational items. Of particular interest to the specialist in religion is an article by Yamaori Tetsuo in *Shokun* (June 1995), in which he argues that religion in Japan is on the way out as a consequence of the Kōbe earthquake and the Aum-related sarin nerve gas attack. The sensational recovery of the bodies might seem only to strengthen his argument. It is ironic that Yamaori seems to be matching, or countering, Aum Shinrikyō's end-of-civilization scenario with an end-of-religion scenario! However, the analysis is flawed, as explained later below.

Following this, also in connection with the Aum incident, an interesting quantitative enquiry was carried out for the Asahi Shinbun (a leading Japanese newspaper), and the results published on September 23rd 1995. According to this the older generation increasingly tends not to hold any 'religious faith' (*shinkō*). That is, more people over 50, and even more people over 60, now regard 'religion' as 'not important', when compared with a survey carried out in April 1981. This change of attitude, however, could not be correlated with the impact of the Aum case. On the contrary, those whose attitude towards 'religion' has changed most as a result of the Aum case are in their lower twenties

---

7   The related problems of coherence and authenticity in religious traditions are bound to exercise the minds of theologians or their equivalents within any specific tradition. The problem is tackled in comparative perspective by various authors in Pye and Morgan 1973. For more recent orientation see Pye 1991a and 1991b (also at 5.2 and 5.3 above).

(48 % admitting a change of attitude), and the proportion decreases in a smooth curve towards the over seventies (of whom 27 % admit to a change of attitude). Note, however, that in all these statistics the numbers of people in all generations who continue to regard 'religion' in some sense as relatively important still remains quite high overall.

There is no doubt that 'religion' suffered a public relations blow in Japan as a result of the Aum case. At the same time a great deal speaks against the view that the impact will be negative for religion in general over the long term. Such a view betrays a lack of understanding of the real centre of gravity of religious perspectives and activity in Japan. It arises mainly on the basis of the well-worn but erroneous idea that Japanese people are on the whole no longer very 'religious'. The error arises in part because of the definition of 'religion' as being specifically connected to 'faith', and thus being a matter of individual interest or choice. In fact the bedrock of Japanese religion consists of an extremely consistent pattern of ideas and practices which, as indicated earlier, may be regarded as the 'primal religion' of Japan. The major specific traditions of Shintō, and Buddhism are firmly set in this matrix with clear social functions and ideological perspectives of their own.

Strongly entrenched too are several large 'new' religions which over the decades have established a secure following through transmission from one generation to another. During the month of September 1995, when the bodies of the Sakamoto family were recovered, I had occasion to visit the headquarters of some of the older new religions in Japan. In all conversations which at some point turned towards the Aum incident, whether with religious representatives or with taxi drivers, coffee shop owners and the like, there seemed to be no difficulty at all in separating other 'religions' from the Aum case. In other words, guarded resilience was the dominating response to these events. The overall pattern of Japanese religion is therefore unlikely to change significantly as a result of the Aum crisis.

As to the so-called 'new new religions', i.e. those of the latest wave of new foundations, to which Aum Shinrikyō belongs, the situation is somewhat more volatile. Since by definition they have a first generation membership, they should be regarded for the time being as epiphenomenal growths which may or may not succeed in establishing themselves over a long period. Aum Shinrikyō has doubtless suffered a setback in 1995 and it remains to be seen how far it can recover credibility among relevant sections of society. Many members of other recently founded organizations, such as Agonshū or Science of Happiness, will be able to convince themselves that their own religion, being true, is not affected by the troubles of Aum Shinrikyō. In this respect too, therefore, the troubled waves may be expected to subside. The long term stability of the various groups will depend on various factors, and not only on the Aum shock.

Finally it should be noted that during the autumn and early winter of 1995 there was public discussion of a possible revision of the law on religious juridical persons. There is concern over this increased pressure in some religious quarters, a concern which may be regarded as legitimate in view of the difficult long-term history of relations between government and minority religions in Japan (and elsewhere). However, the general feeling so far has been that a tightening of the law is inevitable and desirable. This is likely to involve tighter obligations on religious organizations to report their activities. These obligations will make it harder for them to use their facilities for storing large quantities of poison gas.

Conclusions

The Aum shock illustrates clearly the need for clear, reliable observation and characterization of religious phenomena. Many of Japan's 'new religions' remain undescribed. Indeed there are numerous religions all over the world which cannot be studied in detail because of inadequate research funding. It is also clear that current social analysis alone is not sufficient for an adequate appraisal. A perspective in the wider history of religions is also important. Because of the dramatic criminal acts in which members of Aum Shinrikyō have been implicated, the case enables the distinction between the independent study of religions and the occasional need for the adoption of a critical stance to be clarified easily. Both are thereby enabled, while the independence and the integrity of the academic study of religions is not compromised.

Bibliographical references

Kishimoto, Hideo 1961. "An operational definition of religion" in: *Numen* 8 (3): 236–40.

Shimazono, Susumu 1995. "In the wake of Aum: the formation and transformation of a universe of belief" in: *Japanese Journal of Religious Studies* 22 (3/4): 381–415.

Pye, Michael 1972a. *Comparative Religion: An Introduction through Source Materials*. Newton Abbot (David and Charles) and New York (Harper and Row).
- 1991a. "Religious tradition and the student of religion" in: Geertz, A. W. and Jensen, J. S. (eds.) *Religion, Tradition and Renewal* .Aarhus (Aarhus University Press): 29–36.
- 1991c. "Reflections on the treatment of tradition in comparative perspective, with special reference to Ernst Troeltsch and Gerardus van der Leeuw" in: Kippenberg, Hans G. and Luchesi, Brigitte (eds.) *Religionswissenschaft und Kulturkritik*. Marburg (Diagonal-Verlag):101–111.
- 1994b. "Religion: shape and shadow" in: *Numen. International Review for the History of Religions* 41: 51–75.
- 1995a. "Religion and identity: clues and threads" in: de Gruchy, J. W. and Martin, S. (eds.), *Religion and the Reconstruction of Civil Society (Papers from the founding congress of the South African Academy of Religion, January 1994)*. Pretoria (University of South Africa): 3–17.
- 1996e. "Shintō, primal religion and international identity" in: *Marburg Journal of Religion* 1/1.: <http://www.uni-marburg.de/fb03/ivk/mjr/pdfs/1996/articles/shinto1996>.

Pye, Michael and Morgan, Robert (eds.) 1972. *The Cardinal Meaning. Essays in Comparative Hermeneutics: Buddhism and Christianity* (Religion and Reason 6), The Hague (Mouton).

Reader, Ian 1988. "The rise of a Japanese 'new new religion' –themes in the development of Agonshū" in: *Japanese Journal of Religious Studies* 15 (4): 235–61.

This paper was first published as "Aum Shinrikyo. Can Religious Studies cope?" in *Religion* 26 (3) (1996): 261–273.

5.8 Distant Cousins: Transmitting New Japanese Religions to Brazil

The original title of this paper was "Thinking about distant cousins: cultural distance in the transplantation of Japanese religions to far countries." It was devised for a conference marking the centenary of Japanese immigration to Brazil held in São Paulo in August 2008.

Introduction

This paper considers the question of "cultural distance" in the transplantation of Japanese religions to far countries, that is, to countries which are distant from Japan, both geographically and culturally. In particular, I refer to selected examples of what in Japan are regarded as "new religions," some of which such as Ōmotokyō, Sekai Kyūseikyō, Seichō no Ie, Shinnyoen, Tenrikyō and Tenshō Kōtai Jingū Kyō, are quite active in Brazil.[1] It is most significant that we now look back on a hundred years of Japanese immigration to Brazil. This provides a large pool of potential members for Japanese religions, even though many aspects of the imported culture may have been neglected or forgotten. It is also significant that Brazilian society, especially urban society, provides a context of vibrant religious pluralism, giving many possibilities of individual choice. There is in Brazil, quite evidently, as in most parts of the world, a keen interest in various kinds of meditation, self-development, healing, and other informal spiritualities. However, to understand what is going on in these Japanese religions in Brazil it is also important to know the situation from which they are derived. We need to have some understanding of the background in Japan in order to appraise

---

1 The Hepburn romanisation is used here, as recommended by the Japanese Ministry of Science and Education for international usage, except in quotations or references where different decisions have been taken by religious bodies (e.g. the form Oomotokyō) or by translators into Portuguese (where for example 'ss' may be preferred to 's').

what, in reality, is being transmitted, and what is being left behind.² This paper will therefore draw attention to some fundamental characteristics of Japanese religious life, locate the "new religions" in that context, and thus illuminate some aspects of their transmission to the world beyond Japan. I am very grateful for the opportunity to spend some time in Brazil on this occasion.³ It has provided me with a more differentiated view of some of the same religions, and there have been a few corrections or additions to this paper as a result.

My own first contact with a Japanese "new religion" was in 1961, when I paid a brief visit to the Tokyo headquarters of Seichō no Ie (House of Growth) under the guidance of Raymond Hammer, who had been working on the concepts of divinity in Japanese new religions.⁴ At that time there was still much very direct interest in the effects of the atomic bombs on Hiroshima and Nagasaki, and a leaflet advertised the "Conquest of Diseases – Cancers –Atomic Diseases –etc. Through Spiritual Teachings."⁵ The question of how to respond to and deal with foreigners, i. e. especially with the victorious US-Americans, was also a central one in Japan. Evidently, these matters are of no comparable signifi-

---

2 Retrospective note. This was also recognized in Clarke 1994 (to which my attention has been drawn in the meantime), but unfortunately the brief article is marred not only by numerous mistakes in Japanese transliteration (notably over long and short vowels) but also by a failure to distinguish between Pure Land Buddhism and True Pure Land Buddhism (or Shin Buddhism) which are major but distinct denominations. It is also remains unclear why the popular distinction between "old new" or "new" and "new new" religions (for Japan) makes any difference when it comes to their transference to other places such as Brazil. Much more interesting (see also below) is whether a particular religion was already in existence when immigrants arrived in Brazil or was only founded later and is therefore a secondary import with different features of attraction.
3 The conference, while academic in character, was sponsored by the Igreja Messiânica Mundial do Brasil. I am most grateful to Prof. Frank Usarski for his arrangements leading to an extended guest professorship at the Pontifical Catholic University of São Paulo, and participation in other academic gatherings. This enabled me to spend much more time in Brazil than would otherwise have been possible. I am also very grateful to Maria Otávia Freitas (Goiânia) for guidance to many places of interest for the study of religions in Brazil, thus providing contextual information.
4 Dr. Hammer worked in Japan as a missionary and was among one of the early writers on Japanese new religions, which during his time were regarded as strong rivals to the post-war Christian missions.
5 Flyer for a book entitled *You Can Heal Yourself*, by the founder Taniguchi Masaharu.

cance in Brazil. Since then the House of Growth has itself grown considerably. The headquarters have expanded such that the original building in Tokyo seems to be relatively small and is mainly of historical and symbolic interest. In the meantime there are important centres in other parts of Japan (e.g. at Uji near Kyōto) and abroad, for example in Brazil. Since 1961 my observations of the changing scene of Japanese new religions have continued. At various times through the years I have visited the centres of several others, such as Konkōkyō, Kurozumikyō, Tenrikyō, Reiyūkai, Sōka Gakkai, PL Kyōdan, Tenshō Kōtai Jingū Kyō, Ennōkyō and Bentenshū. In some cases I have called on very local "churches" (*kyōkai*) of new religions, while in other cases I have perused the religious literature which they publish in large quantities. In February 2008 I had an additional opportunity to visit the headquarters of several new religions in Japan in a concentrated sequence, being accompanied by the Swedish "new religions" specialist Liselotte Frisk.[6] The religious headquarters which we visited at that time included the following: Seichō no Ie (Tokyo and Uji), Kōfuku no Kagaku, Sekai Kyūseikyō, Shinnyoen, Agonshū, Konkōkyō Izuo Kyōkai (Ōsaka), Ittōen, Tenrikyō, Tenshō Kōtai Jingū Kyō and Ōmotokyō. In all of these, interviews were conducted and up-to-date materials were collected. The original Japanese names for these religions are used here because they represent a certain linguistic challenge to those whose native langue is Portuguese. Later we will consider this linguistic challenge with special reference to "Sekai Kyūseikyō", which is known in Brazil as "Igreja Messiânica Mundial" or just "Messiânica" for short. Hardly anybody in Japan knows what "Messiânica" is, and this illustrates the linguistic and cultural distance which has been covered.

Theoretical orientation

Theoretically, this subject may be said to fall into the general area of the "dynamics" of religion, including such topics as "transplantation," "syncretism," "acculturation or inculturation" or "innovation." These topics form part of the general theory of "tradition" and of "innovation" in the study of religions or the science of religions.[7] Without going into this

---

6   Dalarna University. Her work has hitherto been focused on new religions of Asian derivation in Sweden.
7   Cf. the papers included both in Part Five and Part Six of the present work.

theoretical background in the study of religions in detail, please allow me to draw attention quite briefly to three general points which are very relevant to our current theme. First, the dynamic processes of *tradition* in the sense of "handing on" (*Überlieferung*), transplantation and so on, are a complex stream of socio-cultural events forming the history of religions. Any discourse about new religions makes reference to a part, or an aspect, of this whole complex stream. It does not make sense to study new religions without reference to this wider history of religions and the processes which can be observed within it. Second, there has been widespread discussion of the term "syncretism"; however it is important not to confuse this with mere mixtures or syntheses, but to think of *syncretistic situations* dynamically, as dynamic correlations of ambiguous elements. This is of particular importance when considering general processes in religious change. Third, there is currently much interest among western sociologists of religion in "new religious movements" ("NRMs"), but for various reasons I prefer to speak of "religious innovation" within the above mentioned stream of tradition, and only in that context, when it is appropriate, of "new religions." In many cases, religious innovation does not in fact lead to the foundation of a new religion as a distinct socio-cultural entity, but it is still interesting as "innovation" within a dominant tradition. In other words a "movement" may just as well be outside or inside an existing stream of tradition. On these matters see further "Elements of a general theory of religious innovation" (5.4 above).

Indeed there are not a few Shintō shrines and Buddhist temples which in effect set themselves up as new religions, even though they are not listed as such in official statistics. A traditionally Buddhist temple at Kurama, for example, just north of Kyōto, is formally speaking in the tradition of Tendai Buddhism. But at the same time it has been promulgating a new teaching about celestial divinities, in particular a cosmic divinity referred to as Sonten, which has little to do with Buddhism. Though apparently not particularly successful in winning believers over to this, it is in effect setting out its stand as a new religion. Moreover, this is not denied at the temple itself. Similarly, an ancient Shintō shrine known as Tsubaki Grand Shrine, while emphasising that it is the specific location where Shintō divinities first came to earth, has recently been offering what it claims is a teaching of universal relevance to all humankind. Consequently it also promotes a mission in the USA, seeking to attract non-Japanese members. We can see therefore that the emergence of specific new teachings and symbolism, promulgated by enterprising religious leaders, is something which continues today just as it has taken place in previous decades and centuries. It was in exactly this way that one of the oldest so-called "new religions" in Japan began, in the late eighteenth century, when a Shintō priest by the name of Kurozumi (Munetada) set forth his own particular teaching. This is now known as Kurozumi-kyō, that is, Kurozumi-Teaching. The original Shintō-style shrine is still there, near Okayama, but Kurozumi-kyō has become a new religion in its own right and has an impressive modern headquarters which displays only just a little symbolism reminiscent of Shintō in the ordinary sense.

Nevertheless, there are many examples of "new religions" in Japan in a fuller sense, and not surprisingly there is an easy Japanese equivalent for the expression "new religion/s," namely *shinshūkyō*. Some of the so-called new religions were initiated in the eighteenth century or even earlier, and so they are thought of as "new" in distinction to those which were there before; and at the same time some are quite well established by now. We should realise that some of the so-called new religions of Japan are not so very new in time, having been founded *before* the immigration of Japanese people to Brazil began, while others were founded considerably later. Indeed, the process of religious innovation in Japan itself has continued up to the present. Not so long ago, therefore, observers coined the expression "new new religions," translating the Japanese term *shinshinshūkyō*, to refer to new religions which had not yet become old. Even more recently it has become fashionable to speak of "spirituality" (Japanese: *reisei*), as if this were something separate from "religion" and particularly characteristic of a post-modern age. In my view this is a category error due to the constant misinterpretation of the term "religion" in Japan along nineteenth century lines. Be that as it may, "spirituality" is used by some (with another category error) to refer to a new wave of religious innovation which in some cases leads to the establishment of "new religions" as organisations, and in other cases is dissipated in the broader field of cultural expression. It is not at all clear whether such "spirituality" or "spiritualities" are the expression of a globally consistent culture or are in important respects culture-specific. My own impression, currently, is that they are both. In the Japanese case, the perception of some kind of spiritual level of experience is deeply rooted. It has therefore been common for a long time for Japanese religious leaders to speak of "messages" or "stories" from the spirit world (*reikai*), as for example in Ōmotokyō.

The basic pattern of Japanese religious culture

We should now think briefly about the basic pattern of Japanese religious culture. Japanese religious activity is so varied as to be quite confusing to the casual observer. Indeed introductory books often cause *more* confusion because of their lack of analytical discipline. Obviously, there are well known religious traditions and organisations going under the headings of Buddhism and Shintō. Buddhism divides up into major denominations such as Tendai and Shingon, Zen and Pure Land, and the Buddhism of Nichiren which emphasizes the Lotus Sutra. The group of denominations known as "True Pure Land" (Jōdo Shinshū) are not only large but, because of a relatively disadvantaged demographic base, particularly important among Japanese emigrants to other countries including Brazil. The Christian churches in Japan are relatively small, but somewhat influential through education and hospitals. The Chinese traditions of Confucianism and Daoism (Taoism) are present in a minor form, and as widespread cultural remnants. Then, as we know, there are also the so-called new religions, several of which have attracted followers numbering up to hundreds of thousands or even millions. Running through the whole culture there is a wide field of religious symbols and practices which have largely escaped definition, including various kinds of fortune telling and healing. But how do all these elements correlate with each other? How can we get beyond a mere listing of various religious perspectives?

It seems appropriate, in the general morphology of religions, to make a major distinction between the "primal religion" of any society and those religions which in that society at some point were founded in dialectical relationship to it, becoming in some sense distinct entities. Please note that "primal religion" is *not* equal to "primitive religion." Primal religion is received from the ancestors, and is consequently assumed to be more or less obligatory for all members of the society in question (and not for members of other societies). Primal religion is calendrical and local. It provides life rites for individual members of society and corporate rites to assure social and economic welfare. Primal religion therefore provides *proximate salvation* but *not* other-worldly salvation. The general, primal religion of Japan is largely limited to Japan itself, except in so far as Japanese persons abroad take it with them. In principle it cannot be universalised because it is related to a specific ethnicity.

How does "primal religion" fit with Shintō and Buddhism in Japan? For some, the primal religion of Japan is Shintō, which is indeed hardly open to non-Japanese participation. In modern times, however, Shintō has become a highly organised religion, one among others, and the primal religion of the Japanese population may be characterised in more general terms. The celebration of New Year, for example, takes place partly at Shintō shrines, but also at Buddhist temples, at the headquarters of new religions, in the home, and in public life. This is an example of an important ritual complex at the level of primal religion. Many Japanese people will say that they are "not religious," but at the same time they will admit that they take part in New Year activities. Indeed, in a social sense, these are more or less obligatory. The same applies to ritual activities relating to the ancestors, taking place at the equinoxes and in midsummer, at the festival known as *o-bon*. These are partly related to "Buddhism," but millions of people participate in them who have no personal or spiritual interest in "Buddhism." It is simply necessary to care for and communicate with the ancestors.

Founded religions, on the other hand, especially recently founded or "new" religions are by contrast *voluntary*. They are able to separate themselves from society in general, and they have a message which is believed to be universal and hence transferable to people in other societies. They offer some kind of "salvation" for the whole world. New religions are typically founded by a charismatic religious personality. They offer a teaching and/or practice which sets itself apart from existing ones, even while drawing on them in various respects.

Of course this transplantation, or mission, of founded religions is not always successful. Very often there are too many elements from the original culture which make no sense in the new situation. For example, if emphasis is placed on "purification," this may not be easily understood everywhere. The ritual of having one's car "purified," to ensure safety, is widespread in Japan, but this can be taken much further. For example, one little known Japanese new religion, Chiesonkyō, has a number of purification rituals which include the purification of one's watch. This idea makes sense in Japanese culture, where a sense of time can be quite important in daily life, but perhaps not in all parts of the world. Without naming them, I think we know that there are some countries where such a precise sense of time is not so important. So the question is always to what extent the vocabulary and the modes of practice can be transferred from the Japanese conceptual system to a different one. Would there be any point in purifying one's watch in Brazil, I wonder?

At the same time the receiving communities in some other part of the world such as Brazil, are themselves part of a twofold and *contradictory social process*. Some people, of Japanese descent, are forgetting inherited Japanese conceptual systems, as the generations pass. Others, not of Japanese ancestry, are acquiring new concepts which attract them, but not in their original context! Thus the transmitted concepts may easily be ambiguous, leading to new variations and many fascinating syncretistic situations.

Ancestors and "Buddhism"

Let us consider more particularly the question of ancestors. In addition to the above distinction it should be noted that as "founded" religions become ever better established, they begin to contribute to the primal religion of the society in which they are to be found. Buddhism was originally a founded religion, which stood in some tension to the Indian society of its time. Ancient Indian society at the time had its own dominant primal religion, Brahmanism. The historical Buddha himself did not seek to contribute to this, and referred to it only to emphasise some aspect of the new teaching. His followers, in so far as they were ordained, as the first monks were, abandoned the household life and with it any responsibilities in the daily religious system. In particular, the Buddha apparently taught little or nothing about ancestors. However, during the further historical development, especially in East Asia, Buddhism adopted important functions in connection with funerals and hence with the ancestors. As is well known, this is of great importance in China, Korea and Japan. Many Japanese people know which Buddhist denomination they belong to simply in the sense that they know which temple is looking after their ancestors, in the cemetery and at their house altar. Serving the Japanese immigrant community of Hawaii are a number of Buddhist temples, as well as Shintō shrines and other religious centres. The Buddhist temples are partly involved in transmitting Buddhist teaching and teaching religious practice. Much more important however is the role of the cemeteries. One "temple" which I visited briefly, on "the big island," consisted of nothing but a cemetery and an office. It provided no facilities whatever for teaching or practice, and claimed to be "not denominational." There was simply no welcome for visitors who had no ancestors there. Thus the founded religions can "cross over" into providing services for the general pattern of primal religion. They can even do so to the extent of losing all recognizable connection with their original impetus.

What we see in Brazil in this connection is that Shin Buddhism and Zen Buddhism have a continuing pastoral role in the support of care for the ancestors, for those of Japanese ethnic descent, while at the same time they attract, and seek new members from among the population which is not of Japanese descent. The common denominator between Shin and Zen Buddhism is the fact that they address a wide-spread interest in meditation. This may seem obvious in Brazil, but from a Japanese point of view it is not at all obvious for the simple reason that Shin Buddhism in Japan does not encourage or provide meditation sessions. There are doctrinal reasons for this, namely that the practice of meditation is based on the assumption of "self-power" (*jiriki*) while Shin Buddhism highlights reliance on the "other-power" (*tariki*) of Amida Buddha. Nevertheless, a major Shin Buddhist temple in Brasilia, O Templo Budista de Brasilia, makes a major point of promoting "meditation," and of setting the recitation of the *nenbutsu* (the invocation of Amida Buddha) in the context of meditation. Thus the temple becomes "um oásis para meditar," "an oasis for meditation."[8] There are some reasons why this could be justified in terms of the development of Buddhist thought, in particular the argument that the *nenbutsu* itelf arose in the context of meditative practice. But Shin Buddhists in Japan do not normally see it in that way.

Generally speaking, new religions in Japan have not yet developed their attention to the ancestors so strongly as Buddhism did, although most of them make sure that the ancestors are cared for somehow. Some of them just leave it to the established Buddhist temples. However, both Seichō no Ie and Sekai Kyūsei Kyō have an important place for the veneration of ancestors, or the care of ancestors. In the transplantation of these religions to other cultures, the emphasis on the importance of ancestors meets with some resistance, in that this is not what potential converts are seeking. By contrast, the rather exclusive religion Tenshō Kōtai Jingū Kyō not only rejects the ancestor system with its Buddhist house altars and so on but also sees no particular place for the ancestors in its general understanding of the human condition. In this religion Buddhism, like Christianity, is regarded as belonging to "the old calen-

---

8 Information bulletin entitled *Pureza e Serenidade*, July 2008.

dar." In their place, it is believed, came a completely new revelation, in 1945. It may be noted incidentally that in Tenshō Kōtai Jingū Kyō the chanting of the Buddhist-derived expression *Namu Myōhōrengekyō* does not imply any recognition of the authority of the Buddhist Lotus Sutra, but is simply understood as a way of addressing the spirit world.

As a result of these complexities there is often considerable confusion when religious traditions are transplanted to new cultural and social situations. A traditional Japanese Buddhist denomination may provide much needed reassurance of social continuity for emigrant Japanese people (e.g. in Hawaii or Brazil) who are still concerned about their ancestors. On the other hand a non-Japanese Brazilian convert may be seeking some fundamental form of Buddhist teaching in the context of a Japanese denomination such as Jōdo Shinshū. Unknown to him or her, or disregarded, this tradition was itself an extremely innovatory form of Buddhism when it arose in the thirteenth century. Its relation to other forms of Buddhism and in particular to early Buddhism remains controversial. Buddhism is often associated with meditation. Yet meditation is easily replaced by chanting, as in Pure Land Buddhism or True Pure Land Buddhism (Jōdo Shinshū). At the same time "meditation" is offered by some Japanese new religions which haved nothing to do with Buddhism, e.g. Seichō no Ie (House of Growth). It seems that, for Brazilians, the "Japaneseness" of this religion might lend some kind of exotic authenticity to the teaching of "meditation," referred to in Seichō no Ie as "Shinsokan" (*shinsōkan*) and glossed as "meditacão para contemplar a Deus." Seichō no Ie itself, the "House of Growth" is a distinct "new religion." About that there is no question. It does not claim to be Buddhist, though it does care about the ancestors.

On the other hand, we should note that some of the "new new" religions make wild claims to represent Buddhism in a new and authentic way. Three such religions are Agonshū, Aum Shinrikyō (now known as Aleph) and Kōfuku no Kagaku (Science of Happiness).[9] From a prudent standpoint in the history of religions their claim to represent "Buddhism"should be treated with great caution. Indeed it should probably be rejected. This does not mean that no "new reli-

---

9   The English name Science of Happiness (for Kōfuku no Kagaku) has recently been changed to Happy Science. This new designation is said to have been adopted because foreign members might like it better. However it has a different meaning in English and bears no precise relationship to the Japanese name which literally means science of happiness.

gions" claiming to represent Buddhism have a valid claim. Three well-known modern movements, the Reiyūkai, the Risshō Kōseikai and the Sōka Gakkai (corresponding to Soka Gakkai International), can all be referred to quite reasonably as "lay Buddhist movements," even while they also fall into the category of "new religions." A similar case is the Korean religion known as Won Buddhism, which itself claims to be *both* a new religion and Buddhist (Pye 2002c, and 5.6 above). In my judgment Aum Shinrikyō (cf. Pye 1996b and 5.7 above) and Science of Happiness (Kōfuku no Kagaku) cannot really be counted as "Buddhism," even though this has been claimed.

The Japanese believers or members of Science of Happiness have a special booklet (which is not for general distribution) called *The Dharma of the Right Mind* or in Japanese *Bussetsu Shōshinhōgo* (Ōkawa 1994). The term *bussetsu* usually refers to a sūtra supposedly pronounced by the Buddha, but in fact this work was written by the founder of Science of Happiness, Ōkawa Ryūhō. If we study this book we can see that it picks up various Buddhist ideas, about which the believers have very confused knowledge in any case, but in many ways its teaching clearly departs from Buddhism in emphasising "souls" or "spirit"" as "children of Buddha." Promising a wonderful, better life in future, it fits in with the general programme of Science of Happiness, which contains many other non-Buddhist teachings, outweighing the Buddhist elements. At the end of this "Buddha's teaching," there is a long section about overcoming the enemies of the Dharma, entitled "The Devil-Quelling Sutra." We must recall that this book is intended only for believers, but it should be publicly known that these believers are called upon, for example, to "drive back the devils living on earth" (p.119). This seems to be a potentially dangerous message, and, against a certain background of religiously motivated violence in Japan, should be noted. The other very prominent "new new religion" mentioned above, Agonshū, also seems to have a very marginal claim to be "Buddhist" if we consider its main practices and teachings. A claim is certainly made to Buddhist identity for public relations purposes, and connections with Sri Lankan Buddhism and with the Dalai Lama are cultivated prominently. However the main attraction for huge numbers of participants is undoubtedly the hope for this-worldly benefits, for which huge *goma* ceremonies are performed in the "sacred enclosure" (Portuguese: Área Sagrada). There is also a very strong emphasis on astrology, fortune-telling and the sale of amulets.

Of course, the question of what "counts" as Buddhism is a complex subject. We have to remember that what was once very innovatory has in the meantime become quite well established. Many forms of Mahāyāna Buddhism such as the "esoteric" Buddhism of Tibet or the widespread devotional Buddhism addressed to Amida Buddha or bodhisattvas such as Avalokiteśvara (Japanese: Kannon), were quite unknown to the historical Buddha. On the other hand, these forms of Mahāyāna Buddhism do have a reasonable claim to Buddhist identity for various reasons which cannot be discussed here. My point is that not everything which presents itself as "Buddhist" can be regarded as having a strong claim for this validation.

The transmission of new Japanese religions with a universal claim

If a Japanese "new religion" is to be successful in its own country, Japan, it has to fit somehow into the basic pattern of the Japanese religious culture from which it springs, even if at the same time some special characteristics are emphasised. Without doing so the new religions cannot succeed there. The question then arises about what happens to their discourse and their practice when they are transplanted elsewhere. Let us consider three major characteristics.

First, the new religions, being voluntary, appeal to individuals and their families, and they therefore address the concerns and problems of individuals. This may be disconnected from any relationship to the local Shintō shrine or to the family Buddhist temple and cemetery. Typically, the new religions offer solutions to questions of personal identity, the resolution of family problems, the healing of sickness, and paths to success in work and business. The concept of "this-worldly benefits" (*genzeriyaku*) is widespread among most Japanese religions (though not universally accepted), but the new religions in general seek to lead people into a personal path to which they are invited to be committed. Simple practices illustrate this. In Sekai Kyūseikyō for example there is the practice of *jōrei* (expressed in the Portuguese literature with the non-standard romanisation Johrei), a kind of mutual, meditative blessing expressed by a raised hand. In Konkōkyō there is the practice of *toritsugi*, a brief session of guidance provided by the religious leaders of local churches. In Tenrikyō, blessings are received in a form known as *sazuke*, which suggests the promise of healing where necessary. Sōka Gakkai members are taught that by reciting the holy name of the *Lotus Sūtra* in the formula Namu Myōhōrengekyō they will personally receive this-worldly benefits and be successful in their endeavours. In the Byakkō Shinkōkai there is not only a publicly prominent liturgy for world peace, but also a more private practice of prayer and purification which is believed to alleviate problems (cf. Pye 1986 etc.) In Shinnyoen there is the practice of *sesshin*, a term which usually means intensive meditation but in this case means a face-to-face interview about personal problems accompanied by an intense hand symbolism deriving from the "esoteric" tradition of Shingon Buddhism. The Risshō Kōsei-kai is known for its practice of *hōza*, providing a small group context in which the problems of individual members are analysed in terms of a simply stated Buddhist teaching. All such practices help to draw members into a personal commitment to the group. Moreover, this factor presumably provides the main point of attraction for individual members in a distant culture, especially an urban one. We have already seen that Seichō no Ie (House of Growth) emphasises a kind of meditational practice, and it is interesting to see how easily the Portuguese language materials can make use of the term *meditacão* for this. Nevertheless there remains the question about how this is envisioned in Brazil, as it seems to suggest a widely based culture of meditation in Buddhist or more general Indian yogic terms.

Second, most of the new religions emphasise very graphically the relations between human beings and the spirit world. The general idea of powerful spirits is easily acceptable in Brazil with its own variety of religions predicated on a spirit world (including the Catholic saints and Pentecostalism). Quite frequently we come across the names of divinities in the new religions of Japan which are variations on exisiting ones. But how translatable, or relevant, are the names of spirits or divinities, e.g. those of Tenrikyō, which draw on the ancient Japanese myths? This factor could lead to differences of perception at the symbolic or "theological" level. For example, in the teaching of Tenshōkōtai-jingūkyō, mentioned above, the term *kami* is used both for the chief divinity of the universe and for the foundress herself. In the religious literature of this religion, *kami* is translated into Portuguese as DEUS, using capital letters. However the term *kami* has different associations because in Japan there are widely thought to be many *kami*, even though the religion in question of course puts its own particular interpretation on the term. We will look at some further examples of this problem below. It is well known that the term "Deus" can have a very general meaning in Brazil, so in one sense it might be thought to be an excellent translation of *kami*. However the major saints in Brazil such as Santo Antônio, Padre Cicero, São Jorge, Nossa Senhora Aparecida, could easily be referred to in Japanese as *kami-sama*. They are, in effect, divinities (*kami*).

Third, consider the prominent emphasis on the ancestors and our loyalty to them. This is something which one can learn, but for most people in Japan it is more self-evident than it may be in other parts of the world. It is well known that Buddhist-oriented movements such as Reiyūkai and Risshō Kōseikai place great emphasis on the veneration of ancestors. The very meaning of Reiyūkai is "spirit friendly society," by which is meant in particular care for spirits who are descendants without ancestors or "buddhas without affinity" (*muenbotoke*). In this case "buddhas" (*hotoke*) refers to persons who have died, and without descendants to care for them, there is some concern about their welfare. It is doubtful whether this concept really applies in societies with significantly different religious culture. Interestingly, the ancestors play a significant role in most of the new religions of Japan, and very often the main focus of worship is accompanied by an altar for the veneration of the ancestors not only of the founder but also for the ancestors of the believers. We see this in various cases such as Ennōkyō and Sekai Kyūseikyō. In the latter case it is recognised by representatives that this factor creates a disjunction between different kinds of members, i. e. between those with a Japanese social memory and those without it, who join for more individual reasons.

To some extent the strains of acculturation vary in accordance with the extent to which the teaching is spritualized. Thus a Brazilian writer, Kátia Metran Saita, gives a personal account of how the teachings of Seichō no Ie can be followed by people who otherwise continue to observe Catholic religious rites such as marriage and baptisms (Saita 2005). This is regarded as equivalent to the way in which members use the double hand-clap characteristic of Shintō when praying, said to be natural for persons of Japanese descent but strange for other Brazilians (Saita 2005: 31). It must be said that the members are evidently *all* expected to pray in this way, but the relativisation of external ritual is subordinated to the emphasis on the central way of thinking which sees religious values and orientations as essentially invisible and hence unitary. In the case of the author's practice of the Catholic rites "the ceremonies were carried out according to the rituals of the religion taught by my ancestors with elements dictated by Brazilian culture," which itself is presumed to be "Catholic." The purpose of this kind of observance is apparently "in order to recognize the religious tradition of the ancestors," so that we have in this very decision a method for incorporating the Japanese emphasis on the ancestors. As a result the actual practice of Catholic rites becomes ambiguous, in what may be regarded analytically as a syncretistic situation. An experienced representative of Seichō no Ie informed me that the religion has little difficulty in being transmitted to other cultures because it is based on the recognition that all human beings are children of God, so that the true teaching is equally accessible for them.[10] However this religiously optimistic view does not take account of the real processes of transmission, as described in the above example. It means that the individual believers are left to themselves to strike some kind of balance between their inherited tradition, regarded as defective in some respects, and the newly adopted religious orientation with its differing theology.

It may be noted that the Shintō-derived handclap is also continued in Sekai Kyūsei Kyō, but in this case there are three claps. Among overseas members this aspect of ritual behaviour is not well understood or highly valued. Rather, the missionary strategy is said to have three strands: (a) the practice of *jōrei,* understood as having meditational and healing functions rather than a purificatory one, (b) programmes of natural or biological farming, and (c) an emphasis on art and museums, especially at the main centres.

Transmission and translation

In these cases we have been thinking about the transmission of religious orientations, but of course this is intimately connected with the transposition from one language to another. There are two points of interest here. On the one hand translations can lead to a shift of emphasis, while on the other hand the decision *not* to translate key terms can give rise to a certain mysteriousness which is not necessarily there in Japanese.

Equally prominent terms in other Japanese religions are often left untranslated. Perhaps the most well-known is the term *nenbutsu* (also written

---

10 Rev. May (an Americanized name), interviewed in Tokyo, February 2008. The explanation corresponds in general to Seichō no Ie teaching.

nembutsu) in the context of Shin Buddhism. This refers to the expression *Namu Amida Bu(tsu)* with which the believers call upon Amida Buddha. But the element *nen* means to call to mind, or to hold in one's mind, i.e. to call (the mythical) Amida Buddha to mind. This is important because it shows that the ritual is not merely an external one. Indeed there is such a strong emphasis in Shin Buddhism on the right attitude of mind, the "mind of faith" (*shinjin*), that this term is often left untranslated in western languages. Shin Buddhism has a structure of "faith" which is very comparable to that of Protestant Christianity, and at the same time, as these terms indicate, the inward meaning of faith is almost meditational in its implication. This means that Shin Buddhism and Zen Buddhism can be associated rather easily, even though the conceptual traditions are different.[11] Of course, these forms of Buddhism are mainly present among the Japanese population in Brazil because of their role in the ancestor system. Thus the Japanese Buddhism (so-called "yellow Buddhism") which is apparently losing its strength in Brazil (Usarski 2008) does not have the same function as the kinds of Buddhism which may seem attractive to modern Brazilians who are not of Japanese descent. Of course it can be more complicated still. Brazilians of Japanese descent who might make a renewed claim to some form of Buddhism will not be reappropriating the primal religion of Japan, because of their ancestors. Rather they will be behaving as new Brazilians with an interest in meditational and spiritual matters. Their knowledge and understanding of non-ancestor-related Buddhism is probably only partial and not related to the fact of their Japanese descent.

Some fascinating terminological questions arise in connection with the well established "new religion" Tenrikyō. This is of interest because the leaders of this religion have put considerable thought into the world-wide mission. In particular, the well-known and truly excellent museum of Tenri University, the Sankōkan, has a valuable section on the transmission of Tenrikyō, via immigration, to Brazil.[12] One of its important texts is called the Mikagura-uta, translated into Portuguese

---

11 This is a wide subject in its own right, relevant here partly because Shin Buddhism was a kind of "new religious movement" way back in the thirteenth century, and partly because there is a significant presence of Shin Buddhism in Brazil. Unfortunately, Portuguese translations of works such as the *Tannishō*, though in existence, were not immediately available when this paper was being prepared.

12 For information see Tenri Sankōkan Museum Permanent Exhibition Catalogue (Tenri Sankōkan 2001).

as Hinos Sagrados. Now *uta* means songs, and here they are special songs or *hinos*. But apart from that, the expression *hinos sagrados* is a very general expression indeed. The word *kagura* refers to the dance of the gods (*kami*), while the prefix *mi-* is honorific, so the *Mikagura-uta* are the songs of the divine dance. This is significant because the central ritual of Tenrikyō is the performance of *mikagura* at its main temple in Tenri, these dances (which are hidden from normal view) being based on the actions of the gods as transmitted in the ancient Japanese myths. Connected with this is the fact that Tenrikyō also has a special term for this focus of its central location, namely *jiba* 地場. We can find this in the ninth stanza of the fifth song:

> Koko wa kono yo no Moto no Jiba,
> Mezurashi tokoro ga arawareta. (*Mikagura-uta. Hinos Sagrados* 14–15)

In the word *jiba* is incorporated the character for land 地 (*chi, or ji*) combined with another meaning "place" 場 (*ba*). This special term can be quickly understood by Japanese people, even though it is not otherwise used. It has the implication of referring to the place where this world was created and where the process of salvation will ultimately reach its consummation. If *jiba* is left untranslated, this is because, though easily understandable, it is a very special word. If we do translate it, for example as "the very place", representatives of the religion will tell us that this is not an expression which they use. Left untranslated however, in English or in Portuguese, it will always sound more mysterious than it does in ordinary Japanese. In Tenrikyō ("The Teaching of Heavenly Reason" – or "The Teaching of Heavenly Wisdom") there is a well established office of mission, where experienced translators carefully guard the terminology which has been selected. At the same time, the objectively ascertainable degree of success in transmission and in mission is another question.

Some special terms in "Messiânica"

I wonder how many of those present [at the conference] know the name Sekai Kyūsei Kyō? It was mentioned about that in Brazil this religion is known as the Igreja Messiânica Mundial do Brasil. Here we immediately see the problem of linguistic and conceptual distance. The Brazilian, or Portuguese name reflects the English designation "Church of World Messianity," which however is currently little used in publications by the group. For example, the booklet *Daily Inspirations. Teachings of Meishu-sama*, published in Japan in 1990 (revised in 2000) and in the USA in 2002 uses the Japanese name.[13] In a similar Portuguese work entitled *Meishu-sama e o Johrei* (published in São Paulo in 2007), however, we do find reference to the Igreja Messiânica Mundial. Why is this of interest? The Japanese word *kyūsei* 救世 means "salvation," or more literally "saving the world," and is reminiscent of the term 救済, meaning "salvation." The word "messianity," with Judaeo-Christian associations, tends to suggest specifically the coming of a particular "messiah." However, the founder of Sekai Kyūsei Kyō, Okada Mokichi (1882–1955),[14] is usually referred to as Meishu-Sama (Senhor da Luz), as in the expression *Ensinamentos de Meishu-sama*, rather than as a personalised "messiah." Admittedly, in the Portuguese name the expression *Messiânica* is an adjectival form referring to the whole church. But then again, the Japanese name Sekai Kyūsei Kyō does not in fact refer to a "church," but to a "teaching." It means literally "The Teaching of World Salvation." The expression "teaching" often occurs in the names of new religious groups in Japan, simply because the new leader is expected to propound a "teaching." The reason why this religious movement or group is referred to in English as a "church" or in Portuguese as *igreja*, is to make it sound comparable to the Christian churches. Indeed, with the name alone, some people might even think at first that it is a very up-to-date and inclusive Christian denomination, with an interesting oriental practice known as *jōrei*. At the same time, ordinary Japanese people do not get this impression from the name Sekai Kyūsei kyō. The general problem which arises with all such designations can be seen in the main part of the title which I already quoted, namely *Meishu-Sama e o Johrei*. To understand this title in Portuguese (as a non-Brazilian), I only need to know two little words: *e* and *o!* This shows that the publishers are quite aware of the language gap which needs to be crossed, and in this title they hardly tried to do it.

There is another interesting aspect to the Japanese words used here, namely the ending *-sama* in the name Meishu-sama. As is well known, *-san* is the ending commonly used after Japanese names (in Japan) which

---

13 In the US edition we even have the specific designation "Sekai Kyusei Kyo Izunome Kyodan", referring to the main denomination of the Sekai Kyusei Kyō, based in Atami, Japan.
14 Usually occurring as Okada Mokiti in Sekai Kyūseikyō sources, using a different transliteration system.

corresponds to Senhor or Senhora, and is even used with personal names, not only with family names. *Sama* is a more elevated version of the same thing, being used for extreme politeness towards guests or customers, but also for extremely elevated figures such as religious leaders and also for the names of heavenly beings in Buddhism, Shintō and other religions. So the expression *kami-sama* means God, whether in a general or a specific sense. However this association is presumably not present in the minds of Brazilian members of Sekai Kyūsei Kyō.

First, and most simply, there are evidently some cases where the translation from Japanese is not direct and not really accurate. I would like to return here once again to the Sekai Kyūseikyō, the Igreja Messiânica Mundial. Quite well known in São Paulo is the Solo Sagrado, which was the destination of an excursion by conference members. The original Solo Sagrado is at Atami in Japan, and there is a secondary one in Kyōto. The one in São Paulo is modelled, generally speaking, on the one at Atami. Now the expression "Solo Sagrado" sounds like a proper name, but in fact it translates the straightforward Japanese word *seichi* 聖地, which is freely used by Japanese non-members commenting on the Sekai Kyūseikyō. At least two other major new religions in Japan have their own *seichi*, these being Seichō no Ie (House of Growth) and PL Kyōdan (Perfect Liberty Fellowship). What is a *seichi*? In effect, a *seichi* is a spiritual headquarters covering a rather large area which serves as a magnet for pilgrimage by the believers and other visitors. In other words it is a *terra sagrada*, a kind of paradise focused here on earth. It is more than simply the earth, ground or soil. So how did it come to be translated as *solo* rather than as *terra*? Probably we can no longer find this out. However, it is reasonable to speculate that the original process of translation was based on an inadequate explanation of the element *chi* in the sense of "earth" (*tsuchi*). While the character for *tsuchi* ("earth" or "solo") is 土, the character for *chi* in *seichi* is in fact 地. This has the more complex meaning of something which arises out of the element of "earth" (one of the five elements in ancient East Asian thought), namely an area of land. A *seichi* is an area of sacred land. Of course, the expression *solo sagrado* has now become established as a proper noun or name for this special area, here in Brazil. But the choice seems to represent a shift from the meaning which the expression has in Japanese.[15]

---

15 For another brief account of the Solo Sagrado, with an intra-Brazilian comparison, see the writer's "Nossa Senhora Aparecida and Solo Sagrado: creating sa-

Second, we have many examples where missionaries have consciously decided not to translate important terms because any translation would be misleading. Thus in the same religion we have the previously mentioned term *jōrei* 浄霊. Significantly, this term does not appear in itself in an ordinary word-processor. When typing Japanese, the two characters have to be selected separately and added together. What do they mean? The first means "purification" and the second means "spirit." The first element therefore picks up the broad tradition of purification conveyed in Shintō, but also to some extent in Japanese Buddhism, especially esoteric Buddhism, as in the expression *rokkon shōjō* 六根清浄. This latter term is used in Shintō-oriented mountain pilgrimages (e. g. to Dewa Sanzan). It also occurs in a deviant form in the standard prayer of Tenshō Kōtai Jingū Kyō, with the same pronunciation but using the characters 六魂清浄, thus implying the purification of six evil spirits. Returning to Sekai Kyūseikyō, the second character of *jōrei* 浄霊 means "spirit" as in terms such as "spirit world" but referring here to the spirits of individual persons. Thus *jōrei* 浄霊, as a central practice in the Igreja Messiânica Mundial (Church of World Messianity), emphasises the spiritual purification of the individual. It could be translated without too much difficulty with an expression such as "purification of the spirit," but by keeping the Japanese expression it is presented as something distinctive, which it is. In Japanese it is also a distinctive term, but one which is immediately comprehensible to Japanese people when seen written down in characters. On the other hand, the very distinctiveness of the term when used in Brazil may lead to a loss of meaning, exotic, but esoteric and obscure. It is interesting therefore, but not surprising, that my first informant in Brazil who was familiar with the term told me that it meant "blessing," clearly a post-Catholic interpretation which assumed that the raised hand was used to confer a blessing.

Conclusions

It is time to draw some general conclusions. Whether in research, teaching or personal communications, language is full of mysteries and misunderstandings. But these are not only superficial matters. Language

---

cred space in Brazil" (Pye 2009a). in Jürgen Court and Michael Klöcker (eds.) *Wege und Welten der Religionen. Forschungen und Vermittlungen. Festschrift für Udo Tworuschka*, Frankfurt am Main (Lembeck), 457–62.

variations often illustrate, betray, or conceal, deep assumptions. Vocabulary choices are made, sometimes expertly and sometimes clumsily, to position claims in the wider culture, in this case religious culture. Thus it is important to be sensitive to selected terminology if we wish to understand the processes of transmission and change in religious matters. This applies to processes of innovation and successful transmission and also to processes of decay. At the same time, if we are specialists in the study of religions, we need to be familiar with the wider characteristics of religious systems, and in particular with questions of typology. This has implications for our understanding of the phenomena. For example, if a Japanese religious movement or teaching is really a new one, with its universal message of salvation, then it does not necessarily matter if some Japanese terms get "lost in translation," or are misunderstood. This only seems strange to persons who happen to know the other language. On the hand, if religious practices such as care for the ancestors in a Buddhist manner begin to lose their force for demographic and cultural reasons, then this is not necessarily a loss for "Buddhism" in a more carefully considered sense. It simply means that the elements in the primal religious system of the population in question have shifted, and this too is a natural process in the context of emigration and settlement.

Bibliographical references

Clarke, Peter B. 1994. "Japanese 'old', 'new' and 'new new' religious movements in Brazil" in: Clarke, Peter B. and Somers, Jeffrey (eds.) *Japanese New Religions in the West.* Sandgate Folkestone (Curzon): 149–161.

Itoo, Eizo 1987. *Oomoto. A Vida de Nao e Onisaburo Deguchi.* Jandira /São Paulo (Verso).

Ōkawa, Ryūhō 1994. *The Dharma of the Right Mind / Bussetsu Shōshinhōgo.* Tokyo (Kōfuku no Kagaku).

Pye, Michael 1986. "National and international identity in a Japanese religion: Byakkōshinkōkai" in: Hayes, Victor. C. (ed.) *Identity Issues and World Religions, Selected Proceedings of the International Association for the History of Religions,* Netley Australia (The Australian Association for the Study of Religions): 234–241.

– 1988. "Nationale und internationale Identität in einer japanischen Religion" (Byakkō Shinkōkai) " in: Zinser, Hartmut (ed.) *Religionswissenschaft. Eine Einführung.* Berlin (Dietrich Reimer): 239–251. (German translation of Pye 1986.)

– 1996b. "Aum Shinrikyo. Can Religious Studies cope?" in: *Religion* 26 (3): 261–73.

- 2002c. "Won Buddhism as a Korean new religion" in: *Numen* 49 (2): 113–141.
- 2009a. "Nossa Senhora Aparecida and Solo Sagrado: creating sacred space in Brazil" in: Court, Jürgen and Klöcker, Michael (eds.) *Wege und Welten der Religionen. Forschungen und Vermittlungen. Festschrift für Udo Tworuschka.* Frankfurt am Main (Lembeck):457–62.

Saita, Kátia Metran 2005. "*How can a religion born in Japan coexist in Brazil, a Catholic country?*" in: Seicho-No-Ie International Headquarters (ed.) *Religious Pluralism and International Peace by Faith Movement. The Case of Seicho-No-Ie* .Tokyo (Seichō no Ie): 27–36.

Sekai Kyusei Kyo Izunome Kyodan 1990. *Daily Inspirations. Teachings of Meishu-sama.* Atami 1990 (revised 2000) and New York (Izunome Association) 2002.

Sekai Kyussei Kyo 2007. *Ensinamentos de Meishu-sama. Meishu-sama e o Johrei.* São Paulo (Fundação Mokiti Okada). (N.B. Kyussei is the correct Portuguese transcription for Kyūsei.)

Tenrikyō Department of Overseas Missions 2000. *Ofudesaki (Ofudessaki)*, Tenri/São Paulo (Tenrikyō Overseas Department).

Tenrikyō Department of Overseas Missions 1975 (3rd edition 2002). *Mikagura-uta. Hinos Sagrados*, Tenri/São Paulo (Tenrikyō Overseas Department)

Tenri Sankōkan (ed.) 2001. *Tenri Sankōkan Museum Permanent Exhibition Catalogue*.Tenri City (Tenri Sankōkan).

Usarski, Frank 2008. "'The last missionary to leave the emple should turn off the light.' Sociological remarks on the decline of Japanese 'immigrant' Buddhism in Brazil" in: *Japanese Journal of Religious Studies* 35 (1) : 39–59.

This paper was first published in Portuguese translation (from an earlier version) as "Refletindo sobre Primos Distantes. Distância cultural na transplantação de religiões japonesas em países distantes," *Rever* 11/2 July/December 2011, 11–31. A few adjustments have been made.

Part Six
Transplantation and Syncretism

6.1 Introduction to Part Six

The early article on "the transplantation of religions" which begins this section arose largely on the basis of observations of situations and processes in Japanese religious culture, observed between 1961 and 1966. It is included here not for nostalgic reasons, but because conceptually it meshes with the approach taken to syncretism which follows in more detail thereafter. Transplantation leads into syncretism in that it involves ambiguity, a term which I have consistently highlighted in such contexts, that is, the ambiguity of the various elements involved. Transplantation also involves a sequence of varied positioning by the actors in the process. In those days, the post-modernist style of analysis had not yet become fashionable, and had it been, the points being made might have been couched in such terms. But then already, as now, it was presupposed that the systems which are being "transplanted" are not reified objects. Rather they are the constructs, and in due course the baggage of particular "actors," that is in this case, the people who make use of, promote, and transmit religious concepts and practices.

Of course, these processes can be seen from within any given tradition, and this has been consciously the case both in Buddhism and in Christianity. In a short review article entitled "Assimilation and skilful means" (Pye 1971b, not included here) particular attention was drawn to a Buddhist concept which is remarkably relevant in this regard. The details and implications of this concept were being researched by the writer at the time, and so the article was pointing the way to a full-length study entitled *Skilful Means. A Concept in Mahāyāna Buddhism* (Pye 1978a, 2003). The concept of "skilful means" has been understood within the Mahāyāna Buddhist tradition to account for the presentation of the Buddhist "Dharma" under many guises. The idea has now passed into the general vocabulary of religious studies and even more of western theology, being widely referred to as *upāya*. In fact this is something of an abbreviation, for the Sanskrit word *upāya* in fact just signifies "a means." The aspect of skilfulness (in means) is brought in when there is talk of *upāyakauśalya*. At least in the early Mahāyāna texts, the diversity of possible expressions of Buddhist teaching was supposed to lead back to the central understanding of Dharma, for otherwise any device adopted for its expression would be a mere waste of time.

The process of the transplantation of Buddhism to Japan had been explored in a large and fascinating work by Josef Kamstra entitled *Encounter or Syncretism* (1967).[1] It was partly in response to his understanding of syncretism that "Syncretism and ambiguity," again a very short article, was conceived. The purpose now was to clarify further the way in which the term "syncretism" could be used to analyse religious dynamics without bringing theological judgements to bear, and thereby be used as a heuristic notion in the general study of religions.

The key term which links the above mentioned articles is in fact "ambiguity," the point being that any one element, such as a concept, a symbol or a particular rite, can bear different values or meanings in accordance with its position in a given religious system at any one time. The elements may be ambiguous, while even the systems themselves are numerous and shifting, following each other both in geographical spread and generational succession.

If there was silence on this subject for some time after the above articles appeared, it was because of the work involved in writing *Skilful Means* and in translating the writings of Tominaga Nakamoto. Tominaga's ideas (which figure prominently in Volume One, Part Two) are themselves remarkably relevant to this area of analysis in that he brought in his own explanation for the variations in Buddhist schools, shadowing the internal Buddhist discourse from a decidedly etic standpoint —as early as the 1740s, as we should remember. In the meantime however the term "syncretism" was being further discussed in the contemporary western literature. It has continued to be even more widely misused, especially by social scientists and orientalists, as a mere synonym for mixture or synthesis. Substantial studies by Ulrich Berner (1982) on the other hand turned out to be broadly speaking in line with the usage espoused here, though they were evidently independently conceived. While Kamstra's discussion of the entanglements of the term in theological discourse was pursued further by Kurt Rudolph (1979), the latter seems to have somewhat misunderstood my own position. My review of Kamstra's position was intended to be sympathetic and respectful, and yet the term "syncretism" for me, as for Rudolph, lies precisely in its use as an external observer's term with potential analytical value. Of course this can only be so if

---

1   Full details of this and other literature mentioned here will be found in the relevant papers below.

the term is used in a sensible and accurate manner, and not as a mere equivalent to mixture or even muddle. The accusation that I was myself somehow engaging in a normative discourse was therefore quite misplaced. To clear up these relationships, the further article "Syncretism versus synthesis" was conceived (6.4). This article included an illustrative case study from the famous Shintō shrine at Kumano in Japan. By first examining the academic, theoretical discourse that takes up the concept of syncretism, and then looking at its application in a Japanese case study, the argument put forward in this paper looks at a) how the usage of the term syncretism in cultural studies has become disconnected from any theoretical framework, b) how syncretism is not synthesis and c) how, within the process of acculturation, syncretism is a necessary theoretical concept that demands academic attention. The case study explicating characteristics of syncretistic patterns is included in order to demonstrate clearly the viability of the concept of syncretism in actual research. The concept of syncretism, when properly conceived, emerges as a powerful analytic tool in the study of religions.

The section is completed with two further articles which show how the term "syncretism" can be operationalized in particular cases. The first, "Buddhism and Shintō on one island" (6.5) is also set in Japan, while the second seeks a wider perspective by providing materials from Chinese contexts (6.6). Both benefit from very recent additional field observations. It should be clear from these analyses that, for those engaged in the study of religions, "syncretism" is not an essentialist concept but one which helps us to understand the dynamics of a particular situation in terms of ambiguous positioning.

It should by no means be overlooked that the complicated relationships between diverse religious traditions had not exactly escaped the notice of thinkers in East Asia. Indeed they attended to them considerably before they came across the western concept of syncretism. Of particular interest here is the Chinese idea of "three teachings" (*sānjiào* 三教), which came to be known in the other countries of East Asia which adopted the Chinese writing system and much Chinese thought. This idea was already presented in Part Two (2.4), but further reference will be found to it below in the detail of contemporary contexts. In brief, the term has a long history, and the usage is sometimes apologetic and normative, asserting the superiority of one of the three over the others, sometimes eirenic, asserting an essential hidden unity of all the three, and sometimes analytical, looking at all three and considering what part they do or could play in the general scheme of Chinese society and culture. What becomes clear in "Syncretism in Chinese temples of South-East Asia and Taiwan" (6.6) is that the "three teachings" idea cannot just be applied directly, for the component elements are far too varied and the relationships between them, syncretistic ones, assume different patterns from case to case.

In general, the materials and arguments in this section illustrate important features of the fascinating research challenge posed by the multifaceted dynamics of religious shifts and interactions. For worthwhile studies to be carried out, great care must be taken over the ways in which analytical terminology used. The refinement of such terminology, taking case studies into account, is one of the continuous tasks of the scientific study of religions. The academic discourse about syncretistic situations, processes and positions is an example of this.

Bibliographical references

Berner, Ulrich 1982. *Untersuchungen zur Verwendung des Synkretismus-Begriffs.*
– Wiesbaden (Harrassowitz).
Kamstra, Josef H. 1967. *Encounter or Syncretism; the Initial Growth of Japanese Buddhism.* Leiden (Brill).
Pye, Michael 1971b. "Assimilation and skilful means" in: *Religion* 1 (2): 152–8.
– 1978a. *Skilful Means. A Concept in Mahayana Buddhism.* London (Duckworth) and (Routledge – 2nd edition 2003).
Rudolph, Kurt 1979. "Synkretismus – vom theologischen Scheltwort zum religionswissenschaftlichen Begriff" in: L. Neulande (ed.). *Humanitas Religiosa. Festschrift für Harald Biezais zu seinem 70. Geburtstag..* Stockholm (Almqvist and Wiksell): 194–212.

6.2 The Transplantation of Religions

The following paper was conceived shortly after a period of extended residence in Japan (1961–66), where cultural transplantations of many kinds, and the transplantation of religions in particular, are matters of great interest for any alert observer and hence call for reflection. Geared in general terms to "the phenomenology of religion," influential at the time, the text has been left unchanged from 1969. Sub-headings have been added.

The dynamics of religion

This article offers some ideas about the transplantation of religions which are thought to be sufficiently widely illuminating to be considered as a phenomenological theory.

What Van Der Leeuw called "the dynamic of religions" (Van Der Leeuw 1964: 609) has always been the most neglected aspect of the phenomenology of religion. This neglect may have been at least partly due in recent times to the necessity of distinguishing clearly between the history of religions and the phenomenology of religion, which naturally led to the focusing of the latter on static structures rather than on anything which smacked of chronological development. R. Pettazzoni's *"Aperçu Introductif"* in the first volume of *Numen* (Pettazzoni 1954) illustrates this clearly. He explains the purpose of phenomenology as being to explain "le sens" of religion (Pettazzoni 1954: 3) and quotes Van Der Leeuw's dicta: "Die Religionsphänomenologie ist nicht Religionsgeschichte" and "von einer historischen Entwicklung der Religion weiß die Phänomenologie nichts" (Pettazzoni 1954: 4). The distinction between the two disciplines could not be more emphatically stated, and it is significant that it is the notion of development which betrays itself as an important distinguishing factor.

Conversely, Pettazzoni himself attempted to draw the two together precisely by emphasising "la fenomenologia dinamica". In the phenomenology of the dynamics of religion he saw the point of identification between phenomenology and history (Pettazzoni 1954b and 1959: 9ff and 14). He was, it seems to me, partly right. On the one hand it is important to hold history and phenomenology firmly apart, as their relationship is one of interplay. A "dualism" of mental categories such as Pettazzoni feared does not necessarily affect the unity and coherence of that which is studied. However on the other hand Pettazzoni's instinctive demand for a phenomenology of the dynamics of religion was completely justified. Such a phenomenology is just as important as a phenomenology of the static structure of religion, though it may be more difficult to develop.

Perhaps the main difficulty in elaborating a theory of the "dynamic" aspects of religion is indeed that it can easily be mistaken for history. A phenomenological theory draws on histories of religions and relates again to further historical research as a heuristic principle, but it is itself an abstraction (or set of abstractions) and as such quite different from those wide generalised sweeps of history which are sometimes illuminating but which more often simply obscure the actual complexities of things. The integrity of the historical method as such, which must be defended from the idolatry, so to speak, of specific phenomenological theories, may be safeguarded if one assumes, at any rate for a few centuries or so, that no phenomenological theory can claim to be *exhaustively* illuminating, especially if the field of religion is defined, for operative purposes, at its widest. Nevertheless a theory is valuable if it illuminates some similarities between some religions which are dissimilar in other respects, or if it sets up a framework in terms of which varying degrees of some characteristics may be considered in the case of a series of religions. It is in this spirit that the following ideas about the transplantation of religion, in expressly formal and non-historical terms, are offered.

Van Der Leeuw himself devoted only nine pages (Van Der Leeuw 1964: 609ff) out of several hundred to "the dynamics of religion", in the course of which he dealt with syncretism, transposition, mission, revival and reformation. Of the five terms mentioned "mission" stands out as carrying with it heavy associations of one specific religion, Christianity, and I therefore suggest that it should be dropped for phenomenological purposes in favour of *transplantation*. Similarly I prefer the word *ambiguity* (for which see later) to *accommodation* as the latter has specifically Buddhist overtones for those who are aware of them.

In the above cases the preferred terms also have the advantage over the rejected ones that they do not necessarily imply conscious activity. Van Der Leeuw admitted that "mission" may be completely unconscious (Van Der Leeuw 1964: 611) but it must be said that it can scarcely be so in the specifically Christian context from which the word was drawn. Transplantation allows us to include conscious and unconscious activity without strain. I admit that even transplantation, if taken too literally, suggests some kind of gardener rearranging his flowers and vegetables, but *propagation,* which is unconscious enough in botany, has already been snapped up by the Vatican. So we shall have to make do with *transplantation,* forgetting the gardener and allowing that seeds are sometimes blown about by the wind or carried unwittingly by animals and birds. The use of the word *transplantation* will also allow us to detail a rather more comprehensive theoretical pattern which will link "mission" not only with "syncretism" as in Van der Leeuw's chapter 93 but also with "revival" and "reform" as in his chapter 94.

Patterns of transplantation

The transplantation of a religion involves a complex relationship between tradition and interpretation, or in other words an interplay between what is taken to be the content of the religion and the key factors in the situation which it is entering. This relationship may be considered in terms of three principal aspects (designated below as 1.1; 1.2; 1.3) and five sets of differentia (designated 2.1; 2.2; etc.). In order to explain the theory in consecutive prose it will be convenient to detail briefly two pairs of differentia as an introduction, then the three principal aspects as the hinge of the theory, then the three further sets of differentia by way of elucidation.

2.1. Transplantation may be geographical or chronological. It may be geographical as in the case of the spread of oriental cults in the Roman Empire, or the spread of Buddhism, Christianity, Islam, Manichaeism, etc. into the areas concerned (c.f. "syncretism" and "mission" (Van Der Leeuw 1964: 609 ff.). It may also be chronological, not in the trivial sense that geographical transplantation takes time, but in the sense that a religion may find itself running on the spot to reassert itself in changing cultural circumstances (cf. "revivals" and "reformations" (Van der Leeuw 1964: 613 ff.) with which should also be considered "transpositions" (Van der Leeuw 1964: 610) and also restatements and "aggiornamento").

2.2. The factors in the situation into which a religion is transplanted may be themselves specifically religious or not, or both. If a religion already present in the situation under consideration is itself undergoing a chronological transplantation, then religious struggle may ensue. Sometimes however political or economic or other non-religious factors may be more important than the claims of rival religions.

1.1. Contact (the first principal aspect of transplantation). This is a very simple matter involving the setting up or presentation of means of communication, styles of activity, etc. e.g. writings, ideas, buildings, rituals. These means bear some relation to the factors of the situation into which the religion is being transplanted, i.e. writings are translated or retranslated etc.

I.2. Ambiguity (the second principal aspect of transplantation). This involves a degree of acceptance of factors prevailing in the situation into which the religion is entering, such that the question of heresy and orthodoxy, rightness or wrongness, is thereby raised, i.e. the question as to the identity or otherwise of that which is expressed in the new situation and that which gave the initial impulse to the transplantation, or in other words the question as to the persistence or dissipation of the tradition. Ambiguity may appear as one symbol with two sets of associations (e.g. Māra, cf. Ling 1962) or simply in the unresolved coexistence of elements belonging to the transplanting tradition and to the situation which is being entered (e.g. Christian and pagan elements in Beowulf).

1.3. Recoupment[1] (the third principal aspect of transplantation). This involves the reassertion or reclarification of that which was being transplanted in some adequate way. On the one hand the new expression of the religion will have a reasonable claim to identity with that which

---

1 Since working out the above ideas I have come across the use of the word "recoupment" by I. R. Faruqi in his "History of Religions: its Nature and Significance for Christian Education and the Muslim-Christian Dialogue" Faruqi 1965: 83) where he says: "Therefore, there can be no doubt that Semitic Christianity had itself developed into Islam, and that the latter's contention with Orthodox Christianity is only a backward look within the same stream from a point further down its course – in short a domestic recoupment within the one and same Semitic consciousness itself." Clearly the usage is not yet technical in the sense in which I am trying to establish it, but at the same time it is a clear attempt to delineate a chronological transplantation (for more details of which see Faruqi 1965: 81 ff.) which coincides with Islam's account of itself, and to claim the Quranic revelation as an adequate reassertion of the essential meaning of the tradition. Faruqi insists that the historical truth involved must be discovered and established. But the extreme complexity of analysis should be recognised, especially in the case of the aspect of recoupment, complicated as it is by problems of religious self-interpretation on the part of the religions involved.

gave the impulse to the transplantation; but on the other hand it will not be simply identical with older forms since it has expressed itself in terms of the factors of the situation which it has entered. The recoupment aspect is the most difficult to evaluate because it involves some sorting out of heresy and orthodoxy (or similar), that is, some attempt to elucidate the essential characteristics or content of the religion concerned, which is frequently a theological problem (or similar) for the adherents of the religion themselves.

2.3. The three aspects may appear chronologically in the order given and are perhaps thus most easy to recognize, as e.g. in the ease of the hellenisation of Christianity. However they may also be relevant in some other order. For example, the work of Nichiren, considered as a case of chronological transplantation ("reform"), began with the extremely fluid and ambiguous state of Buddhism in Japan at the time, developed into a conscious attempt at recoupment by the seeking out and setting forth of what he took to be orthodox essence of Buddhism, and finally flowered into new symbols (new *gohonzon, daimoku,* and new *kaidan*) which in turn made contact with that and subsequent generations. Indeed the three aspects may be relevant in a quite un-chronological way. For example, the *gohonzon* in Nichirenite Buddhism might be considered simultaneously under all three aspects.

2.4. The three aspects may be more or less tightly linked one with another. E.g. in the case of Christianity the prevailing instinct seems to be to insist on recoupment following closely on the ambiguities caused by contact, although this judgement depends partly on how one delineates Christianity as a historical phenomenon. Buddhism allows for a greater degree of ambiguity, as does Shintō (so that relationships between the two are very difficult to chart), while Manichaeism allowed so much ambiguity that it was never able to recoup properly and died out altogether.

2.5. The adherents of religions may themselves be conscious in varying degrees of the transplantation process. They may react quite unconsciously to situations which arise and thereby ensure the automatic chronological transplantation of their religion (cf. Van der Leeuw's comments on "syncretism" and "transposition" *op cit.* pp. 609 ff). Conscious furtherance of a transplantation process may be variously motivated, e.g. politically, economically (Diana of the Ephesians!) or religiously (mission or apostolate, etc.) or by some subtle combination of these. The lowest degree of sophistication in the conscious furtherance of transplantation is reliance on contact; second in order of sophistication comes the recognition that in a resultant ambiguous situation orthodoxy is at risk and that recoupment is demanded; and thirdly comes the conscious acceptance of a tolerable amount of ambiguity as the price of successful transplantation.

Concluding remarks

The theory I have outlined, I should insist, is not an invitation to vast frescoes of the history of religion. In practice, under the umbrellas of the big names, Buddhism, Christianity, Hinduism, Islam, many transplantation processes are taking place at once, just as the situations in which a religion is potentially influential are innumerable and various. When a particular case is under consideration the eight points which have been detailed might be thought of as questions to be raised. Some of the questions may not prove easy to answer, especially those concerning ambiguity and recoupment, and especially if those two aspects are almost simultaneous and very tightly linked. However, it is essential, in my view, to raise such questions in the study of religions, since transplantation is an ever-present aspect of that which is under study.

Bibliographical references

Ling, Trevor O. 1962. *Buddhism and the Mythology of Evil*. London (Allen and Unwin).
Pettazzoni, Raffaele 1954a. "Aperçu Introductif" in: *Numen* 1 (1): 1–7.
– 1954b "Manuali di storia delle religioni" in *Numen* 1 (2): 137–140.
– 1959. "Il metodo comparativo" in: *Numen* 6 (1): 1–14.
Faruqi, Ismail Raji al- 1965 "*History of Religions: its Nature and Significance for Christian Education and the Muslim-Christian Dialogue*" in: *Numen* 12 (1 and 2): 35–65 and 81–86.
Van der Leeuw, Gerardus 1933. *Phänomenologie der Religion*. Tübingen (Mohr/Siebeck).
– 1938 (1964). *Religion in Essence and Manifestation* (English translation of *Phänomenologie der Religion),* London (George Allen and Unwin).

This article was first published in *Numen. International Review for the History of Religions* 16 (3) (December 1969): 234–9 (published under the name E. M. Pye).

6.3 Syncretism and Ambiguity

This article is republished here without alterations except for the addition of subheadings and bibliographical streamlining. Attention is drawn in particular to the definition of syncretism with which it concludes.

Syncretism among the phenomenologists of religion

Dr. J. H. Kamstra has recently published a lecture about the significance of syncretism for the phenomenology of religion, and its connection with theology.[1] His interest in this topic arose out of his experience of the mutual resistance set up between the syncretistic Japanese and Christianity, and out of his detailed study of the oldest case of syncretism in Japan, namely that brought about through the arrival of Buddhism in that country (Kamstra 1967). He complains that since the work of Hendrik Kraemer (Kraemer 1963), little has been done in the analysis of syncretism, and that it has been neglected in the general study of religion. No reference to it is made at all, for example, in the 634 pages of Geo. Widengren's recent *Religionsphänomenologie (Widengren 1969)*. Moreover most practitioners of the study of religion are strongly influenced by Christianity and tend to see syncretism as an illicit contamination, as a threat or a danger, as taboo, or as a sign of religious decadence.

Kamstra notes that the word *synkretizein* was first used by Plutarch to mean "to come to concord, just as the Cretans do when threatened by a common enemy" and that Erasmus used it in the sense of reconciliation. Theologians in the seventeenth century began to use it also pejoratively. Kamstra himself proposes to use the word to mean: "the coexistence of elements foreign to each other within a specific religion, whether or not the so elements originate in other religions or for example in social structures" (Kamstra 1970: 10). He elaborates the various ways in

---

1   Kamstra 1970 (*Synkretisme op de Grens tussen Theologie en Godsdienstfenomenologie*). Cf. a short review of this work by the present writer in *Religion: A Journal of Religion and Religions* 1 (1), 1971.

which these elements can be related, and then divides his attention between (1) "the theological approach to syncretism: the real roots of syncretism" and (2) "the phenomenological approach to syncretism: the dynamics of syncretism".

In the context of theological approaches to syncretism Kamstra pays special attention to the analysis of Hendrik Kraemer. Kamstra considers it important to move away from analyses which are theologically loaded and to move instead to a phenomenological base. His criticism of Kraemer, with this in view, is particularly illuminating because, sensing that Kraemer's analysis was theologically conditioned, he turned his attention precisely to that religion which Kraemer had claimed was not in principle syncretistic, namely Kraemer's own religion, and found the roots of syncretism there. Or rather, as he further explains, the roots of syncretism lie neither in the "naturalism", whether primitive or monistic, of which Kraemer had spoken in distinction to the "prophetic" religions, but rather in the very structure of human existence. "To be human is to be a syncretist", he writes (Kamstra 1970: 23). And by this he means: "Even a prophet – however filled he may be with the divine – simply needs the speech and the situation of his audience in order to be comprehensible at all (Kamstra 1970: 23ff).

In the text of his lecture Kamstra appeals to the authority of Paul to illustrate this point, while in a note thereto he suggests that Buddhism can provide a helpful nuance in its distinction between *saṃvṛti* and *paramārtha satya*, i.e. between conventional and absolute truth. It seems that it would be possible to elaborate Kamstra's thesis at this point on a stronger comparative base. Perhaps this should strictly speaking be done, if what he says is to be allowed to stand as a generalisation in the study of religion. On the other hand there is little point in tediously going over what will almost certainly not be seriously challenged. However I would emphasise briefly that there may be a slight problem here in that Kamstra's position could be taken as representing an alternative *theological* standpoint to that of Kraemer with regard to the interpretation of the nature of prophetic religion in general and the Christian religion in particular. After all, one remembers that the very title of his fascinating book *Encounter or Syncretism* (Kamstra 1967) involved the use of a word fashionable in twentieth century Christian theology, even though the book itself dealt with a completely different area of the history of religion. I do not myself consider that Kamstra's analysis of the roots of syncretism does suffer from this defect, but it might have been better to free his analysis from the strains set up by the fact that it was conceived in reaction to Kraemer's theologically conditioned view.

In support of Kamstra at this point, one might add a complementary voice from a different quarter, namely that of Professor G. Maeda, who has argued that Christianity is a Mahāyānistic (*daijōteki*) religion (Maeda 1962: 93 ff). By this he meant that it takes in elements foreign to itself and in this way extends its influence. That Maeda should make this point and should illustrate it also in the context of Israelite religion in Canaan (in spite of the prophetic reaction to which I referred above, which is really part of the total process) independently strengthens Kamstra's contention that syncretisms may be generally discerned also in those "prophetic" religions thought by Kraemer to be in principle not syncretistic.

Having freed himself from theology Kamstra goes on to approach the question of syncretism from a phenomenological point of view. As a matter of fact, by doing this he opens up a field for a better understanding of theology and eventually returns to it. While agreeing that this can be done, my own argument will find it necessary to return to theology *and its equivalents* rather sooner, and in this way, I believe, will reduce the no-man's-land which Kamstra has left between theology and phenomenology. As will be seen, the frontier between the two is perhaps as tight as anywhere when one is considering the nature of syncretism.

Kamstra finds, as I have found (Pye 1969: 234) that only one author, namely Gerardus van der Leeuw, has dealt to any extent with the question of what he calls the "dynamics" of religion (Van der Leeuw 1938, chapters 93 and 94). He singles out especially Van der Leeuw's conception of "transposition" (*Verschiebung*) as a clue on which to build further. This simply means that religions are changing all the time, and that therefore the meanings of different elements within different religions, many of which they borrow from each other, are also likely to change according to the context. Kamstra is particularly impressed by the fact that very frequently elements continue to exist within a religion even though they have really lost their original meanings, and intriguingly calls this "syncretism from within". This syncretism from within is a kind of alienation (*vervreemding*) within a religion with regard to items in its structure which continue to exist there simply because of their familiarity. I believe Kamstra has touched here on a kind of religious or spiritual experience which many have known in modern times, especially in the West with regard to Christianity but perhaps also in the East with regard to various traditions, notably Buddhism in Japan. As

Kamstra himself says (with an unfortunate unguarded theological allusion), "Examples of this syncretism from within are in our time legion" (Kamstra 1970: 27).

However, it seems to me that it is also at this point that there is a major error in Kamstra's argument. He writes, "After all that we have said, syncretism is therefore also the result of alienation in an existing religion. This alienation can arise as a result of all kinds of structural changes. The *criterion* for syncretism is therefore alienation: something which either comes in as alien from without or which is alienated from within-whichever it is" (Kamstra 1970: 27). I would challenge the view that alienation is "the criterion" for syncretism of all kinds. Kamstra found he needed to use the word "alienation" to characterise syncretism from within, but he has by no means shown that it is an appropriate word to characterise syncretism from without, which he has now simply slipped in along with the former. Indeed, fascinating though I find the idea of syncretism from within, it seems to distort our general vision of syncretism for two other reasons. Firstly the word "alienation" is itself unsatisfactory because it is too reminiscent of prophetic religions. It tends to suggest that we are estranged from that to which we should turn, we have wandered from our true home, we are cast out from the Garden of Eden, etc. Secondly, Kamstra is at this point too fascinated by the idea of "the within" of a religion, too introvert, feeling too much that religions are declining things being dissolved from within and attacked from without, no longer sensing the urge which many religions have to move out and to move on. Hence he sees syncretism "from without" as indeed a threat to an existing constellation. Why speak, one may ask, of syncretism "from without"? Why not "*towards* without"? If we speak of syncretism as something which can be "towards without" it cannot be said that alienation is the chief category for understanding it. It is perhaps not too much to say that Kamstra's analysis here, if not theologically conditioned as he had shown Kraemer's analysis to be, is at least spiritually conditioned, and that while this leads to some valuable insights, it also leads to a distortion of the true nature of syncretism.

Before attempting to grasp the nature of syncretism by another route, one of the byproducts of Kamstra's approach is worth noting. This is that as a result of his emphasis on syncretism "from within" he is able to recognise a parallel hermeneutical activity in quite diverse traditions. In any religion considered dynamically syncretisims may be seen to be in the process of being unmasked and broken off while at the same time new ones are being built up again. Kamstra says that in this sense every theologian and every theological faculty moves in a frontier territory. More significant methodologically however is perhaps the frontier to which the comparative basis for these remarks leads, not the frontier of theology with the world, but the frontier between phenomenology and theology. It would seem that if theology, buddhology and other equivalents, considered as ongoing activities contributing to the dynamics of their respective religions, can in fact be studied in parallel or comparative terms, then this opens the way for a much more precise attempt to indicate the ways in which they operate. This in turn would lead to the possibility of experts acquiring a grasp of the principles and variables involved, so that theologians (and their equivalents) would no longer work on the basis of an intuitive sensitivity to the strains and stresses and possibilities of their own tradition, sometimes throwing up an effective new syncretism and more often not. Rather they would proceed on the basis of a scientific grasp of the nature of the dynamics of religion, so that while their activity would still be an imaginative one compared with some activities it could also be considered as a technological one. Building sacred bridges, or helping people to recognise them when they appear on the initiative of divinities (for in phenomenology we dare not beg the question about the divine initiative), would become analogous to building ordinary bridges (except with regard to leaving open the matter of divine initiatives). A comparative and phenomenological study of the dynamics of religion, with special reference to the hermeneutical activities of individuals acting with varying degrees of self-consciousness, would therefore become part of the fundamental equipment of any would-be theologian or buddhologian. Indeed insofar as technological know-how indicates the viability of various options open to the engineer, the phenomenology of religion would begin to put pressure on its frontiers with theology, by no means necessarily with a deleterious effect. However this is not the place to begin to develop such a comparative science of hermeneutics.[2] It is necessary for the time being to return to the specific problem of syncretism.

---

2   Such a comparative approach to hermeneutics really needs a much wider basis than that offered by an examination of syncretism alone. It would also have to consider at least the manner in which religious traditions reassert themselves in intolerably ambiguous situations (cf. Pye 1969), and further the nature of the criteria applied in various religions in the definition or redefinition of the "essence" (*hṛdaya*) of their respective traditions. This of course raises hosts of theological problems, -and their equivalents!

As I said above, it is necessary to return to theology and its equivalents rather sooner than Kamstra does, in order even to understand the nature of syncretism. Note however that we do not turn to theology in a concealed way. Nor should we be swayed by sensitivity to one religious situation. It is necessary to turn to theology *and its equivalents* comparatively and hence phenomenologically (since one cannot be a committed exponent of all the equivalents at once), in order to approach the *meanings* of syncretism. The meaning, if there is a meaning, can only be found through the meanings. Here therefore theology and its equivalents put pressure on phenomenology. Indeed if some few of the equivalents are thought to be particularly helpful in elucidating the meaning of syncretism, the pressure of those equivalents will be particularly strong, and care should be taken to see that the presuppositions of no one religious tradition distorts our view even when it is not our own religious tradition. Although Kamstra is very interested in the meanings of syncretistic situations, his definition of syncretism quoted above contains no reference, direct or indirect, to meanings. This can be rectified, but it should be done in such a way that no one religion is called upon to supply the meaning. I hope to indicate that meanings can be referred to in an indirect and neutral way, such that the general theory of syncretism points back again for its specific meaning to specific cases.

A further curiosity of Kamstra's definition of syncretism is that it also contains no reference at all to one of his other main concerns. Again and again he emphasises the importance of the dynamics of religion, but this does not appear to have influenced his formulation in any noticeable way. This is a second point to which attention will be paid below.

Syncretistic ambiguity between Buddhism and Shintō

It is on the notion of the coexistence of elements foreign to each other that we must build. As a clear case of syncretism I should like to refer to the relations between Buddhism and Shintō, especially as developed under the influence of the theory of *honji–suijaku*. These relationships have been referred to in various publications and have been examined in detail recently by Alicia Matsunaga in *The Buddhist Philosophy of Assimilation* (Matsunaga 1969). It is interesting that this writer traces the Buddhist ideas underlying this theory back to the Chinese Buddhist distinction between *pen* and *chi* and thence to the Indian Buddhist distinction between *saṃvṛti* and *paramārtha satya*, referred to earlier. I think it would be generally agreed that the relations in question are a clear case of syncretism in that they obviously involve the coexistence of elements foreign to each other in a single religious context.

We must now approach the matter of the meanings. For the Buddhist the meaning was that in the form of a local divinity (*kami*) there was latently present the being of a Bodhisattva or a Buddha. Thus the *kami* Ōmiya was considered to be a manifestation of Śākyamuni, the *kami* Hachiman was sometimes considered a manifestation of Amida, etc. In this way existing focal points of religious devotion were drawn into a syncretistic field and interpreted in terms of Buddhist meaning. It appears from the Shintō side that the movement into syncretism may at first have been one of self-defence, in that the alternative to accommodation would have been the extinction of Shintō meanings altogether (Eliot 1959). However that may be, there is no doubt that in this way Shintō meanings were able to persist, and in due course there came the Shintō reaction known as *han-honji-suijaku*, i.e. *honji–suijaku* in reverse, in terms of which the Buddhist meanings were treated as but superficial manifestations of the profounder Shintō *kami*. The point about all this is that the elements under consideration became *ambiguous*. They were able to bear two distinct meanings depending on the different points of view of the people involved with them. These meanings were tussled over again and again, and it is a mark of the resilience of the Shintō religion that its *kami* were not after all completely assimilated. Syncretistic tension continued to be felt until there was a remarkable attempt at recoupment from the Shintō side. It is important not to allow either one of the two possible meanings of a symbol being used in *honji-suijaku* terms to overwhelm the phenomenological approach to syncretism. Of course it is the meanings which matter, but we can neutrally seize the importance of the various meanings here by recognizing the *ambiguity* of the situation.

It should not be thought that this type of relationship between Buddhism and Shintō can be observed only in cases where the theory of *honji-suijaku* can be applied. Consider for example the story of the visit of the monk Gedatsu to the Grand Shrine of Ise, as told in the *Taiheiki*:

> "Once this holy man went to the Grand Shrine of Ise to worship at the Outer and Inner Shrines and speak secretly of the delights of complete response to the teachings of Buddhism. These shrines are not as other shrines, for their bargeboards are not curved, nor do their pointed boards bend backward. Wherefore it seemed to Gedatsu that they were as 'the straight

way that rejects what is roundabout!. And beholding the ancient pines lowering their branches and the old trees spreading out their leaves, he likened them to bodhisattvas descending from heaven to save living things here below. Although the names of the Three Treasures of Buddhism may not be spoken here, he thought weeping, yet in this way too men may reach salvation." (McCullough 1959: 368)

Or consider the following spell used by *yamabushi* to exorcise the malevolent influence of the god Konjin over certain quarters of the compass.

"Because of ignorance the three worlds are a prison / Because of enlightenment the ten directions are free. In truth there is neither East nor West / Where then are South and North?"[3]

This spell clearly operates on two quite distinct levels or in two quite distinct spheres of meaning. Moreover the two spheres of meaning are mutually exclusive. If one really believes that the exorcism is desirable or necessary one clearly has not yet reached the point of insight into the nature of phenomena to which Buddhist philosophy tends. Yet the spell makes use of Buddhism to allay fear. Conversely if one takes the Buddhist analysis to heart the spell becomes redundant. Yet the two are coexisting in a single religious pattern even while the ambiguity shows signs of being intolerable.

Ambiguity as the pivot of syncretism

Nor is the relevance of this analysis restricted to the Buddhist-Shintō situation. The transpositions referred to by van der Leeuw and by Kamstra all display this character of ambiguity. They all refer to elements within a coherent religious pattern around which pivot two or more sets of meanings. Again, the notion of ambiguity does not restrict us either to what Kamstra would call "syncretism from without", which is what the cases we have examined are. It is equally crucial, and is equally neutral with regard to particular meanings (unlike the loaded word "alienation"), in the context of "syncretism from within", where the circles of meaning turning around particular elements in a tradition sometimes seen to move and slide like shifting sand, so that the specific elements themselves are ambiguous.

---

3   Cf. Renondeau 1964: 140.

To take ambiguity as the main characterization of syncretism is consistent also with Kamstra's view that it stems from man's very nature in the sense that each man is a limited being unable to grasp the revelation of the divine or the ultimate truth except in so far as this or these are refracted in terms of his own situation. Every constitutive element in a given religious pattern is ambiguous, one might say, in that it has a meaning at one and the same time both in the general situation of the man to whom it is meaningful and in the symbolic context which bears the revelation of the religion in question. However, while the nature of syncretism is clearly to be found in the nature of religion in general and the nature of religion in the nature of man, I would prefer to continue to speak more specifically about ambiguity as the keynote of syncretism, that is, in connection with the relationship between elements originally foreign to each other and (to accept Kamstra's theory of syncretism from within) elements becoming foreign to each other, in religious situations.

If ambiguity may be taken as the keynote of syncretism of all kinds, it is necessary now to emphasise that this is to be understood dynamically. Syncretism, as the coexistence of elements of diverse origin interacting ambiguously, is a natural *moving* aspect of major religious traditions such as Buddhism, Shintō, Christianity, and indeed, I would venture to suggest, of all religious traditions. It is part of the dynamics of religion which works its way along in the ongoing transplantation of these religious traditions from one cultural context to another whether geographically or in time, while their more or less sophisticated adherents are more or less aware of what is going on. But since the traditions are moving all the time, and since the meanings are continually being refashioned, any particular case of syncretism is necessarily *temporary*. The ambiguous clash of meanings demands some resolution and even if this is not forthcoming immediately the demand is still there inherent in the relationship. Three resolutions seem to be possible in practice as in logic, apart from a postponement of any resolution. The first is the extension of one meaning to the point of the effective elimination of the other, in which case we may speak of *assimilation*. The second is the fusion of the diverse elements such that while a single coherent pattern of meaning has been attained that pattern is so different from any of the patterns hitherto available that *a new religion* may be deemed to have emerged. The third is the drifting apart of the two meanings, in which case we may speak of *dissolution*. These three forms of resolution are all possible whether we consider syncretism from (or towards) without or syncretism from within; although usually syncretism from without will probably make us think more often of the assimilation of an existing religious pattern while syncretism from within will make us think more often of the dissolution of an existing religious pattern. It would be interesting to analyse the emergence of a new religion in terms of its dependence on syncretism from without and from within preceding religious traditions respectively. (Kamstra refers briefly to some new religions in the context of the latter.) It should be noted further that there is a certain amount of tension between individuals and groups over all this. An ambiguous syncretistic situation may resolved in terms of one meaning or other for an individual or even a series of individuals, even though the syncretism persists long after as a wider cultural phenomenon offering its various possibilities to further individuals. This is why syncretistic situations may persist for a long time and even indefinitely, even though they are as explained above, intrinsically temporary. It would be quite wrong to call them permanent. To describe them as temporary is to indicate that they are situations of tension (whatever the various protagonists may say about harmony, toleration, etc!) and that they are to be understood entirely in terms of the dynamics of religion.

To emphasise tension as I have done should not be taken as an invitation to conclude that syncretism is altogether incoherent. A syncretistic situation is coherent even while demanding resolution in that there are variously coherent meanings for the various people involved, and also, for the phenomenologist of religion, in the sense that it is a collection of events in the history of religion which have a recognisably coherent structure. Finally I would agree with Kamstra that the elements involved in a syncretistic religious situation need not necessarily be themselves all of religious origin but may include political, philosophical and other secular elements of all kinds.

For the above reasons I would define syncretism as *the temporary ambiguous coexistence of elements from diverse religions and other contexts within a coherent religious pattern.*

Bibliographical references

Eliot, Sir Charles 1959. *Japanese Buddhism.* London (Routledge and Kegan Paul).

Kamstra, Josef H. 1967. *Encounter or Syncretism; the Initial Growth of Japanese Buddhism.* Leiden (E. J. Brill).
– 1970. *Synkretisme op de Grens tussen Theologie en Godsdienstfenomenologie.* Leiden (E. J. Brill).
Kraemer, Hendrik 1937. *De Wortelen van het Syncretisme.* 's-Gravenhage (Boekencentrum).
Maeda, Gorō 1962. "Nihon no Kirisutokyō" in: *Shisō* April 1962: 93 ff.
Matsunaga, Alicia 1969. *The Buddhist Philosophy of Assimilation The Historical Development of the Honji-Suijaku Theory.* Tokyo (Sophia University) and Rutland Vermont (Tuttle).
McCullough, Helen (trans.) 1959. *The Taiheiki, A Chronicle of Medieval Japan.* New York (Columbia University Press).
Pye, Michael 1969. "The Transplantation of Religions" in: *Numen. International Review for the History of Religions* 16 (3): 234–9 (published under the name E. M. Pye).
Renondeau, G. 1964. *Le Shugendô: Histoire, Doctrine et Rites des Anachorètes dits Yamabushi* (Cahiers de la Société Asiatique 8). Paris (Imprimerie Nationale).
Van Der Leeuw, Gerardus 1933. *Phänomenologie der Religion.* Tübingen (Mohr/Siebeck).
– 1938 (1964). *Religion in Essence and Manifestation* (English translation of *Phänomenologie der Religion),* London (George Allen and Unwin).
Widengren, Geo. 1969. *Religionsphänomenologie.* Berlin (De Gruyter).

"Syncretism and ambiguity" was first published in *Numen. International Review for the History of Religions* 18 (2) (1971): 83–93.

6.4 Syncretism versus Synthesis

This paper was first presented as the annual guest lecture of the British Association for the Study of Religion (BASR) at its annual conference at Winchester in 1992. It consists of two parts, a theoretical discussion and a briefly presented case study of a festival at Kumano Shrine in Japan.

1. Theoretical discussion

1.1 Introduction

In recent years the concept of syncretism, itself much older, has attracted a certain amount of theoretical attention in studies of religion. Several attempts have been made to clarity and refine it, for example, in Europe, by Helmer Ringgren (1969), Josef Kamstra (1970), the present writer (1971), Karsten Colpe (1977), Kurt Rudolph (1979), and Ulrich Berner (1976; 1979; 1982). Other studies have investigated particular phenomena presumed to be amenable to analysis under the concept of syncretism. Good examples are those by Judith Berling for China (1980) and Luther Martin (with theoretical force) for the ancient Mediterranean (1983). A notable multi-authored work of this class, entitled *Syncretism*, was edited by Sven Hartman (1969), to which Ringgren provided introductory reflections as mentioned above.However the term also continues to be used widely in an incidental manner by social anthropologists on the one hand and by theologians on the other, often without any reference to the theoretical discussion. Moreover the theoretical discussion itself has not been notably coherent, probably due to language or cultural barriers.

Berner's major work on the subject for example, *Untersuchungen zur Verwendung des Synkretismus-Begriffes* (1982), ignored the discussion arising out of Kamstra's *Synkretisme op de Grens tussen Theologie en Godsdienstfenomenologie* (1970), although Rudolph had taken note of it (1979). The same is true for Berling's lengthy introductory discussion to her work *The Syncretic Religion of Lin Chao-en* (1980), in which she took issue most effectively with Robert Baird's attempt (1971) to remove the term from scientific vocabulary altogether. In Berling's work we find however no reference to the *positive* discussion elsewhere, which, had it been taken into account, could have made her terminological orientation much easier. More detailed discussion of these two last-named authors will be found below.

The relative inefficiency of academic cooperation becomes even more clear when it is noticed that none of the above-mentioned publications paid any attention to Latin American questions. A computer-based bibliographical search carried out even in 1982 (then still a relative novelty in the humanities), using "syncretism" as a key-word, produced an emphasis on subjects relating to Latin America or the Caribbean (especially among anthropologists in the Herskowits tradition). Indeed the term has been freely used by Latin American specialists in religion, though without much reference to the mainly European publications mentioned above. The bibliographical search further produced articles relating to Africa, which also do not feature strongly in the above-mentioned publications. This imbalance arises partly because of a lack of interaction between the social sciences and the humanities. The historical surveys provided by Rudolph and Berner concentrate on the use of the term in the context of European intellectual history and historical research into periods and areas connected with the history of Christianity and its earlier context. It may be admitted that Berner (1982) brings in a wide range of other examples, including not a few from India and central Asia, but these are based on the secondary literature current in Germany at the time and are treated quite cursorily. Berling, in the work already mentioned relating to a theme in China, did not even consider it necessary to take account of Kamstra's *Encounter or Syncretism: The Initial Growth of Japanese Buddhism* (1967), much less the syncretistic situations characteristic of the Hellenist and Roman worlds, viewed by writers such as Luther Martin (1983) as a natural starting point because of the history of the term.

The apparent inadequacy of academic interaction on this subject may be taken as a clue for further reflection. It seems to me that the very diversity of starting points in the historical studies of quite different civilisations, or in geographically distant fieldwork may help to continue the process of balancing out the concept of syncretism so that it becomes more useful both in the analysis of particular cases and in comparative research. In China and Japan, notably, but also in some other East Asian countries, the context in which syncretistic situations require to be assessed is marked by a more or less continuous religious pluralism (often involving considerable tension between particular religious organisations) with an accompanying commonality of features occurring in the context of religions which are otherwise different. Thus the initial agenda of investigation has not been the same as in those regions and periods where a single religion such as Christianity or Islam has been dominant for long periods. Increasingly however it has become evident that the process of acculturation even of apparently exclusive religious teachings, such as Islam as well as Christianity, is extremely complex and includes syncretistic relationships which may be only partly evident to the participants in the process, if at all. At the same time the distinctive characteristics of mobile, transplantable traditions, especially of religions with a universalist claim such as Buddhism, Christianity and Islam, result in differentiated responses to the pressures of actual situations on the part of the self-conscious representatives of these traditions. The same is true in principle for many religions with only a few adherents, but the major religions offer a more reliable base for reflection in this respect because of the additional possibilities of internal comparison.

Thus in order to make satisfactory use of a concept such as syncretism in the study of religion it is necessary to gain as wide a perspective as possible. This wide perspective will itself contribute to a further freeing of the term from some of the less desirable connotations which it had in prescientitic usage. In principle this development has already taken place and has been thus documented by Rudolph, the title of whose writing mentioned above (1979) may be translated as "Syncretism: from a theological term of reproach to a coneept in the science of religion". In the same sense Ulrich Berner's extensively differentiated concept may be seen as a successor to a process already set in motion by Raffaele Pettazzoni and Gerardus van der Leeuw and held up, or usurped, by the theologian Hendrik Kraemer. In this sequence (to which the present writer [Pye 1971a] considers himself to belong) the term "syncretism" is operationalized in order to facilitate the analysis of dynamic religious processes which in fact take place. It is no longer used to imply a reprehensiblc diminution or jumbling up of religion: in other words, description and analysis replace theological judgment.

1.2 Syncretism is not synthesis

This principal shift of usage has two deep-seated and very helpful implications for a more precise use of the term. First, a syncretistic situation in the history or current state of affairs in religion is not a mere mixture. This would hark back to one-sided theological usage, for a "mere" mixture is what is despised by many theologians, anxious to emphasize the purity of a specific tradition. But for the specialist in the study of religion there is no such thing as a *mere* mixture. A mixture is *interesting*. What sort of a mixture might it be? A syncretistic situation is interesting in that it contains multiple possibilities in coherent tension. Synthesis implies that, out of multiple possibilities, a new conclusion has been reached. In a syncretistic situation however the potential claims of the constitutive elements are still alive. Syncretism should therefore be differentiated both from mere mixture and from synthesis. This point was made briefly by Åke Hultkrantz (1969) in the context of a specific study of North American Indian religion, and pursued by Edward Ch'en (1986) in a work available to the present writer too late to be considered in detail.

Second, if coherent mixture, or synthesis, represents the conclusion to a process which is thereby completed, syncretism by contrast is to be understood as dynamically open and indeed patent of resolutions *other* than synthesis. These might be, in particular, the outright dominance of one strand of meaning by another (assimilation), or the avoidance of synthesis through the drawing apart of distinct elements and the consequent collapse of the syncretism (dissolution). The precise discernment of possible alternative outcomes is naturally a matter for detailed study, and varied interpretation is to be expected. The central point is however that alternative outcomes are to be expected and, at least in broad outline, agreement ought to be achievable about what the main alternatives are.

The language which has been used above implies that no major modification is necessary to the argument advanced by the present writer in *Numen* (1971a) under the title "Syncretism and ambiguity." This study concluded with the definition of syncretism as "the temporary ambiguous coexistence of elements from diverse religious and other contexts within a coherent religious pattern." But what is the point of such a definition, it may be asked! The purpose lies in its heuristic application as a model in the analysis (description and explication) of particular religious situations. With this in mind a few further comments may be made on the theoretical literature which has arisen in the meantime: however, in the interests of clarity these will be extremely brief. These comments will be followed by presentation of a particular case study, recently observed in the field, in order to show how the model can be applied.

1.3 Critical perspective

One of the arguments advanced by Baird against using the term syncretism at all is that, if all religions are syncretistic, nothing is gained by describing any one of them as such. This argument contains a logical error, for while it is true that all religions are syncretistic it is not the only thing that can be said about them. The value of the term syncretism lies in drawing attention and focusing clearly on a particular aspect, one among others, of all religions. Thus Baird's argument, contrary to his intention, actually draws attention to the importance of syncretism as a widely significant aspect of religious processes. While Baird's position has been justifiably criticised in this and other respects by Berling, it is noteworthy that she for her part tends to emphasize the integrative features of religious borrowing. Thus for her (1980: 10), while syncretism is not eclecticism, it seems to end up as a positive synthesis or "incorporation of various elements into a home tradition," defined above as assimilation. This view arises because of the particular achievement of the person whose life-work is under consideration in her book, Lin Chao-en (sixteenth-century China), and thus, in spite of the value of the work as a whole it represents a misappropriation of the term syncretism. If Baird has various reasons for not advancing a model at all, Berling fails to differentiate clearly between different models, being mainly concerned with one case.

Ulrich Berner's work is instructive for a quite different reason. It is clear to him that a theoretical model is required for this aspect of religious processes, and he attempts (1982: 92) to clarify it in great detail (distinguishing clearly for example between syncretism and synthesis). As a result he correctly emphasises process as a crucial feature of syncretism. Difficulties arise in another respect. The model is differentiated to such a degree that it is swamped by complex additional terminology such as "vertical systematisation" or "perfectionizing rationalization". It therefore lacks clear contours as a theoretical model and begins to lose its otherwise promising heuristic value.

The instinct of most specialists in the study of religion, especially if they are regularly engaged in case studies, will be to make use of models with sufficient, but less differentiation; otherwise it is scarcely possible to analyze particular cases in an illuminating manner. This instinct is evident in the conclusion to Rudolph's survey when he emphasises five "types" of syncretism largely following Colpe, namely symbiosis, amalgamation, identification, metamorphosis, and isolation. These cannot

6.4 Syncretism versus Synthesis

readily be further evaluated since hardly any examples are given. More convincing is his emphasis, following van der Leeuw, on the dynamic and thus the diachronic nature of syncretism as an aspect of religious change. However some confusion appears when he emphasises (1979: 210) a "functioning synthesis" *both* as a presupposition for a viable syncretism *and* as a result of the syncretistic process, in the same sentence. Would the latter not in effect be an amalgamation?

1.4 Summary: Theoretical standpoint

After these extensive complaints it is surely desirable to summarize briefly the theoretical position as understood here. This may be done in three steps.

1.4.1. Basic theoretical standpoint defined within the tradition of usage. The term "syncretism" has often been used to mean a mere conflation of different religions, in effect a synthesis. However the close association of elements of diverse origin is commonly more complex than that and is not neccessarily stable or permanent. It is noteworthy that closely associated traditions may rediverge after some time, with a reassertion of distinct strands of meaning. Buddhism and Shintō provide an example. Syncretistic situations must therefore be understood dynamically. Syncretism is not the same as synthesis.

1.4.2. Characteristics of a syncretistic pattern. A syncretistic pattern has three main characteristics. It is *coherent* for the believers or participants at the time. It is *ambiguous* in that divergent meanings are latent within it. It is *temporary* in that the inherent ambiguity tends towards some kind of resolution, whether after a long period of cultural history or repeatedly in the experience of individuals.

1.4.3. The resolution of a syncretistic pattern. The resolution of a syncretistic pattern, dynamically perceived, may take any of the following three courses. It ·may lead to the *assimilation* of weaker elements by a dominant tradition, the controlling significance being drawn in a particular direction. It may be resolved by *dissolution,* that is, the reassertion of the separate identity or divergent meaning of disparate elements which are consequently drawn apart. Or it may produce a *new religion* (which *would* be a synthesis), that is, the irreversible formation of a new pattern of religious elements with its own distinctive identity, in which none of the contributing traditions is dominant, and which is able to function as a system and as a tradition in its own right.

2. Kumano: A case study

2.1 Introduction

A specific case will now be adduced in order to illustrate the theoretical standpoint adopted in this paper, namely a festival held at Kumano, Japan, in which Shintō and Buddhist elements are syncretistically present. For the sake of brevity, the presentation of this example, which was observed by the writer in April 1990, will be structured under four headings: the participants, the sequence of events, the spatial disposition, and the meanings. Observation took place over the full length of the three day festival during which I resided with two companions, Japanese Shintō specialists, in the shrine lodge.

A full study would of course be more complex, not least because hundreds of years of tradition are involved, in the course of which the relations between Shintō, Japanese shamanism, Shugendō, and Buddhism, have seen shifting emphases of considerable import. Suffice it to say here that Kumano was for a long period a major point of interaction between Shingon Buddhism, Shugendō, and Shintō, but that this tradition was radically broken during the government-induced separation of Shintō and Buddhism in the nineteenth century. When I first visited the shrine in 1973 there was only one visible sign of Buddhist influence, namely a Buddhist silk painting on a side wall in the *haiden* ['public prayer hall']. Unusual in itself, this was inconsequential compared with the position during the Japanese middle ages, during which the *kami* revered at Kumano was clearly identified with a Buddhist bodhisattva. In 1990 the painting was not visible because of renovation work, though the chief priest when interviewed did, unsolicited and surprisingly, refer to the *kami* as a *gongen* (i.e., a Buddhist *avatar*). This was interesting because there are no publicly displayed clues which would induce the ordinary shrine visitor to think of the *kami* in this way. In brief it would be correct to understand Kumano Shrine, as it is today, as a purely Shintō shrine, administered and used like many other historic Shintō shrines across the country. The sister shrine at Nachi, not far away, is striking for the close juxtaposition of the Shintō shrine and a Buddhist temple which serves as the starting point for one of the two most illustrious Buddhist pilgrimages in Japan. But at Kumano there is no Buddhist temple. All the more interesting is the complexity of the festival held annually in April.

2.2 The participants

The participants in any Japanese festival (*matsuri*, a hroad and freely used concept) are extremely diverse- Naturally there are the specialised persons, priests and others, the memhers of the procession, and others who have a particular role in one or other of the rites included in the festival. There are also many others: tourists, photographers, police, restaurant owners and stall-holders, even occasional foreigners. Thus I myself was a participant, not merely by being present, but because I was expected (as a result of the contacts which led to satisfactory access to the proceedings) to offer a branch of the evergreen *sakaki* to the divinities, which I did. Amid all the complexity of participation, which is not itself under study here, I draw attention mainly to the activities of the religious specialists for the sake of the subsequent analysis. In this respect two groups are important: a) the Shintō priests of Kumano Shrine, who have no particular relationship to Buddhism, and b) the Yamabushi, lay practitioners of Shugendō, a form of esoteric Buddhism close to the Shingon tradition, who are at the same time considered to represent a shamanist tradition.

2.3 The sequence of events

The festival extends over a period of three days, its principal elements being as follows:

First day (13.4.1990)
a) corporate visit to a hot spring, with Shintō ceremonies held indoors
b) ascent of a mountain ("abbreviated", i.e. cancelled on this occasion because of torrential rain)

Second day (14.4.1990)
a) offerings at the central shrine by Shintō priests and a small number of participants

Third day (15.4.1990)
a) offerings at the central shrine by Shintō priests, representatives of the community, and by the Yamabushi in full costume
b) procession with 41 *mikoshi* ['mobile shrine'] through the village area, first: to a natural shrine (known as the *manisha*, being a spring which is identified as a shrine by a shimenawa ['demarcation rope'], and second: to the former site of the main shrine (where it was located before it had to be moved because of flooding)

c) offerings by Shintō priests at the original site of the shrine, using a temporary enclosure and altar, and an outdoor fire ceremony by the Yamabushi (on which more below).

2.4 The spatial disposition

The festival itself is focused on five sites: a) the main shrine; b) the hot spring; c) the mountain; d) the spring at the edge of the village; e) *kyūshachi* ['the former shrine site']. A full geography of the Kumano festival would have to look further afield for various reasons. First, Kumano Shrine is one of a group of three linked shrines consisting of Kumano Taisha (Kumano Grand Shrine), Nachi (named after the famous waterfall) and Shingu (i.e., New Shrine). Second, the historical association between Shintō and Buddhism at these shrines is complicated by the fact that they were of great importance in the activities of the *yamabushi*, i.e. the ascetic mountain *(yama-)* practitioners of Shugendō.[1] The *yamabushi* begin their training in Yoshino, traverse the mountains in stages, and conclude their journey at Kumano. Third, the participants reflect not only these historic connections but also regional and even pan-Japanese threads of affiliation and patronage.

For the current discussion the spatial layout of the former shrine site is of particular interest. Four features are important for the present analysis: a) a temporary shrine area (without a building) containing the *mikoshi* ['portable shrine' I in which the *kami* has been escorted to the former shrine site: b) a temporary mandala marked out on the ground far the performance of the fire ceremony; c) a memorial stone for the Pure Land Buddhist saint Ippen Shōnin: d) a temporary raised stand from which luck-bringing *o-mochi* ['rice-cakes'] are thrown out to the crowd. The whole area is further enlivened by rows of stalls selling snacks and mementos. The open space is surrounded by trees, thus accentuating the feeling that it is a single site. It is approached by a single broad pathway which is first entered onto from the main road of the village through a symbolic Shintō-style *torii* ['gate'].

---

1   For the earlier history of the *yamabushi* see especially Renondeau 1964.

2.5 The meanings

Without attempting to recreate this many-layered event in full, a few salient points will now be noted about the various significances discernable in this festival, and their relations one to another. This analysis focuses particularly on the events of the third afternoon at the former shrine site.

The first leading thread is to be seen in the activities of the Shintō priests and their assistants. It is generally understood that they are performing a springtime fertility festival which has several successive elements. These rites also have a community integration function which is seen both in the participation of community representatives in making offerings and in the procession of the *mikoshi* through the village.

A second thread is evident in the actions of the *yamabushi*. They take part in the rituals mentioned so far, making offerings at the shrine with the general public, attending the ritual at the hot spring, and joining in the procession with the *mikoshi*. However they are prominent on account of their distinctive dress, deerskins still representing a shamanic closeness to the animal world. Occasionally they blow their conches, giving off a throaty blast: this represents the proclamation of Buddhist Dharma (blowing the conch of the Dharma), though this may not be generally realised. Their distinctive presence is tolerated courteously by the Shintō priests.

Thus for some while the Shintō strand and the Shugendō strand run side by side, the latter being subordinate to the former, but not fully subsumed under it or synthesized with it. They may be said to form part of a single syncretistic field.

On the third day, in the afternoon, the syncretic structure is dramatised radically. Shintō offerings are given at the temporary shrine at the old site, as they had been at the main shrine. However when the *yamabushi* have given their offerings in their turn, with slightly extravagant bearing and a little haste, they move quickly across the open space to the Ippen Shōnin memorial stone and recite the Buddhist *Heart Sūtra* (*Hannya Shingyō*). Following this they perform the *goma* ['fire ceremony'] at the pre-arranged site. This involves lighting a large fire which burns up sticks of wood on which prayers have been written, as in a usual *goma* ceremony in a Shingon or Tendai Buddhist temple. However in this case the officiants are *yamabushi*, not priests of a Shingon or Buddhist temple. The very numerous bundles of sticks have been sent or brought from various parts of the country, thus compounding the geographical complexity of this festival (see above).

The Shintō priests have nothing to do with the fire ceremony. For their part they are completing their own ritual of offerings and getting ready to escort the mobile shrine back to the main shrine. It has been noted already that the old shrine site is a single field with a wooded perimeter. At the same time there is no further spatial coordination between the Shintō ritual area and the position of the fire ceremony. The *yamabushi* introduce the fire ceremony by reciting mantras (as in Shingon Buddhism) and by firing an arrow in each of the four directions. This cosmic symbolism is not further related with any of the Shintō sites or activities. Thus at the close of the festival two distinct ritual foci are established.

The meaning of the burning of the sticks of wood bearing the prayers of the people is that the passions of humankind are thereby consumed. It is a paradoxical action which invites people to give expression to their this-worldly desires, which are then symbolically destroyed. Even while the fire is burning, assistants on the Shintō side are distributing rice-cakes representing happiness. Thus the desires of the people are being destroyed and fulfilled at the same time. However this is not the Mahāyāna Buddhist paradox already contained in the fire ceremony. Rather, there are two significances running in divergent directions, one Shintō and one Buddhist.

For the many participants involved the festival is a coherent if complex unity. Yet it has various meanings. In particular, the meanings enacted by the Shintō priests and by the *yamabushi* though running concurrently, are ultimately diverse. That this is so is not necessarily a matter for conscious reflection for the participants. Yet it is so. In general, not all the meanings of a festival will be equally obvious to all who participate in it. A meaning which is less obvious in articulate terms is not necessarily less important; for example, the ritual assertion of social cohesion or integration may be quite important for people to whom it is not superficially evident. In sum, the festival is both coherent and ambiguous.

Since the relations between Buddhism and Shintō have undergone various changes, not to mention the other diachronic variations, the form of the festival at any one time, or what might be called the syncretistic field, must also be regarded as in principle temporary. This is clearly illustrated by the fact that the current form of the festival is based on a) the existence of Kumano Shrine as an almost entirely "pure" Shintō institution (because of the separation of Buddhism and Shintō) and b) the use of the "old shrine site" for the climax of the festival in which the *yamabushi* are able to purvey a meaning independent of Shintō.

3. Conclusion

It may be freely admitted that this analysis is rather streamlined. It is meant to illustrate the approximate balance which is required between description and reflection in order to help bring stability to analytic models in the study of religion. Whether the cases are drawn from history or from fieldwork is not significant in this regard, except that in some historical cases the kind of information which a particular theoretical model calls for may no longer be available.

It may be felt that this kind of analysis is an oversimplification. Its purpose here was to indicate the strong outlines. To illustrate further complexity it will suffice to point out that this fascinating case may in fact be regarded as a double syncretism. There is, as already indicated, the syncretism between Shintō and the *yamabushi* who, in their own special way, represent esoteric Buddhism. However there is a more subtle syncretism within the activities of the *yamabushi* themselves. The *yamabushi* represent a form of shamanism, which has been, broadly speaking, assimilated by Buddhism many centuries ago. Or has it? There has been a strong revival of esoteric Buddhism in Japan in recent years which has been called the *"mikkyō* boom". But is it Buddhist? In some cases it surely is. Yet one sometimes senses a different mood. The reassertion of a cosmic vision combined with a claim to special spiritual powers is not essential to Buddhism and may even conflict with some understandings of Buddhism. It is unclear where this ambiguity will lead. In this respect therefore we may speak of a secondary syncretism which is additionally discernible within this one festival.

This auxiliary analysis illustrates a further aspect of the development of theory in the study of religion. More complexity in the real world does not necessarily demand extensive ramifications of theory, which in the end become quite unwieldy. Theory, while of course requiring adequate reflection, should remain as economical in scope as possible. Only so can it mediate comparatively between the great diversity of real situations. What is important in the face of complexity is careful attention to more of the living data.

The term "syncretism" has by now undergone considerable refinement both in debate and in case studies. It is emerging as a relatively stable theoretical concept for the study of religion in certain respects. Its usage for this purpose should be distinguished from carelessly uninformed judgments made by those who do not even seek to contribute to the study of religion. In particular, its use as a mere synonym for synthesis would appear to be redundant and misleading. When it comes to the detailed application in case studies there will of course continue to be individual preferences. Judgments may differ, for example, about the degree of ramificatory analysis which is heuristically productive. However there would appear to be a tendency towards agreement that, by contrast with an already achieved synthesis, the fascination of a syncretistic situation lies in its still unresolved dynamics.

Bibliographical references

Baird, Robert 1971. *Category Formation and the History of Religions.* The Hague (Mouton).
Berling, Judith A. 1980. *The Syncretic Religion of Lin Chao-En.* New York (Columbia University Press).
Berner, Ulrich 1982. *Untersuchungen zur Verwendung des Synkretismus-Begriffs.* Wiesbaden (Harrassowitz).
– 1979. "Der Begriff 'Synkretismus' – ein Instrument historischer Erkennntis?" in: S*aeculum* 30: 68–85.
– 1976. "Entwurf eines heuristischen Modells der Synkretismus-Forschung" in: *Göttinger Miszellen. Beiträge zur ägyptologischen Diskussion* 19: 59–72.
Ch'en, Edward T. 1986. *Chiao Hung and the Restructuring of neo-Confucianism in the Late Ming.* New York (Columbia University Press).
Colpe, Karsten 1977. "Syncretism and secularization: complementary and antithetical trends in new religious movements?" *History of Religions* 17: 158–176.
Hartman, Sven (ed.) 1969. *Syncretism: Based on papers read at the symposium on cultural contact, meeting of religions, syncretism.* Scripta Instituti Donneriam Aboensis III. Stockholm (Almqvist and Wiksell).
Hultkrantz, Åke (1969). "Pagan and Christian elements in the religious syncretism among the Shoshoni Indians of Wyoming" in: Hartman 1969: 15–40.
Kamstra, Josef 1967. *Encounter or Syncretism: The Initial Growth of Japanese Buddhism.* Leiden (E. J. Brill). 1970. *Synkretisme op de Grens tussen Theologie en Godsdienstfenomenologie.* Leiden (E. J. Brill).
Martin, Luther 1983. "Why Cecropian Minerva? Hellenistic religious syncretism as System" in: *Numen. International Review for the History of Religions* 30: 131–145.

Pye, Michael 1971a. "Syncretism and ambiguity" in: *Numen. International Review for the History of Religions* 18 (2): 83–93.

Renondeau, G. 1964. *Le Shugendô: Histoire, Doctrine et Rites des Anachorètes dits Yamabushi* (Cahiers de la Société Asiatique 8). Paris (Imprimerie Nationale).

Ringgren, Helmer 1969. "The problem of syncretism" in: Hartman 1969: 7–14.

Rudolph, Kurt 1979. "Synkretismus – vom theologischen Scheltwort zum religionswissenschaftlichen Begriff" in: L. Neulande (ed.). *Humanitas Religiosa. Festschrift für Harald Biezais zu seinem 70. Geburtstag.*. Stockholm (Almqvist and Wiksell): 194–212.

As an annual guest lecture (1992) for the British Association for the Study of Religions (BASR), this paper first received circulation as No. 8 of the BASR Occasional Papers series, Cardiff 1993; it was then republished in the journal: *Method & Theory in the Study of Religion*, 6 (3) (1994): 217–29.

6.5 Buddhism and Shintō on One Island

A first draft of this paper was presented at a special IAHR conference at Brno, Czech Republic, on the subject of "Religions in Contact" in August 1994. The present paper is a revised and expanded version which also takes account of the passage of time.

Introduction: dramatis personae

This paper introduces the situation of contemporary religious arrangements on one small island in Japan as a brief case study in syncretistic processes between Buddhism and Shintō. The tiny island of Chikubushima in Lake Biwa, Japan,[1] is entirely devoted to religious activities. These activities are related diversely to the Buddhist and Shintō traditions, but at the same time they are linked by a common reverence for the divinity Benzaiten 弁才天 (or 辯才天), an Indian-derived goddess of music and eloquence with the original name of Sarasvatī. As to Buddhism, the island is also an important pilgrimage site for the bodhisattva Kannon-sama (equivalent to Chinese Guānyīn and Sanskrit Avalokiteśvara) who is also worshipped here.

The present analysis is based largely on observations which were first made in August 1993 and reported soon afterwards (Pye 1996c),[2] but in March 2012 it was possible to make another visit to the island. At that time the number of visitors was much smaller, and indeed, high winds threatened the viability of the ferry crossing. Yet it was business almost as usual. In spite of various cultural and social changes over the last twenty years, the syncretistic complexities in question appear to continue in more or less the same mode now as then.

By way of introduction, the story of the relationships may be told briefly as follows. Historically, Buddhism and Shintō have been very closely associated on this island, and for many centuries the pilgrim scarcely needed to distinguish them. The politically motivated separa-

---

1 Lake Biwa is a major freshwater lake not far from Kyōto.
2 I.e. in the original version of this article.

tion of Shintō and Buddhism in the nineteenth century, however, led to changes on the island. The image of Benzaiten was transferred from the Shintō shrine to the Shingon Buddhist temple, Hōgonji, as early as 1874. Eventually, in 1942, Benzaiten was set up in a grand new worship hall away from the historic Shintō shrine. Kannon, usually referred to with a kind of familiar politeness as Kannon-sama, was never totally separated however, because a covered walkway led from her hall to the Shintō shrine and vice versa. Apparently this differentiation was considered to be sufficient at the time.

Benzaiten must now also be briefly introduced. The suffix –*ten* means heavenly being or, in effect, divinity. Known popularly as Ben-ten-sama, Benzaiten is a transposition of the Indian goddess Sarasvatī introduced to East Asia in the context of Buddhism. In India she is the goddess of the wonderful sounds of the river Sarasvatī, and therefore a goddess of music and eloquence.[3] In Japan too she may be referred to as Myōonten ("goddess of wonderful sounds"), as at her very own shrine at Demachi in Kyōto. Carried along in the context of Buddhism, she also stands for wisdom. There is a chapter on Benzaiten in the *Sutra of Brilliant Golden Light*, showing her as a great supporter of the Buddhist Dharma, but while this sutra was important when Buddhism was originally imported into Japan it now plays no particular role in popular devotions. More significant today is the fact that Benzaiten was incorporated into the group of divinities known as the Seven Gods of Good Fortune (*Shichifukujin*) and that she is thought to bring wealth as well as eloquence. This arose because of a play on the characters used to write her name, in that *zai* can be written with a character which means wealth as well as one which means ability (弁財天 in place of 弁才天). She is the only female divinity among the Seven Gods of Good Fortune (except when Kishijōten is included as a supernumerary). Benzaiten is particularly celebrated at three famous sites in Japan: the small island of Enoshima near Kamakura, the famous scenic spot known as Itsukushima, the island in the Inland Sea well-known for the red symbolic gates of the Shintō shrine standing in the water, and Chikubushima in Lake Biwa which is the subject of this paper. Note that the word *shima* in the names of these place-names means island. Indeed Benzaiten is frequently identified with islands, even very small ones. A well known artificial lake with an island for Benzaiten is to be found in Ueno Park in Tokyo, not far from Ueno Station, a popular

---

3   For a substantial study on the Indian goddess Sarasvatī see Ludvik 2007.

place for people going out for a stroll. This was originally designed as an Edo Period replication of Chikubushima itself. But such small islands, artificial or otherwise, may be found in many places and it is remarkable that Zen temples, perhaps thought of as severe, do not lag behind in their provision.

Because of the connection with water, Benzaiten has a complex mythological relationship with a water spirit named Ugajin, represented either as a dragon (i.e. Ryūjin the "Dragon God") or as a white snake.[4] At her shrines there are therefore quite frequently votive tablets depicting the snake who, admittedly at least nowadays, is not always white. At the Rinzai Zen temple Shōkokuji in Kyōto there is a small Benzaiten shrine, without water, but with some old votive tablets of this kind, one showing a white snake coiled around her lute. The main point is that the snake, or the dragon, is tamed by Benzaiten. When we realize that in the grounds of Ryōanji,[5] the Rinzai Zen temple in Kyōto which boasts what is probably the most famous stone garden of all, there is also a large artificial lake with an island on which there is a small Shintō-style shrine to Benzaiten, we can understand why the name of this temple means the place where the dragon comes to rest.

---

[4] These endless ramifications cannot be pursued here because they would lead far away from our subject. One of them is the legend of Matsura Sayohime. The key elements in this legend, studied in detail by Katja Triplett (2004), are as follows. On the one hand there is the filial piety of a girl who sells herself to an unknown man in order to finance the rites which will enable her deceased father to attain the peace of Buddha-hood. The purchaser, on the other hand, is acting in order to fulfill his own duty in providing a sacrifice to a huge water-snake in a distant part of the country, where this responsibility is presumed to fall to various families in turn. The girl is placed on a sacrificial stand in the middle of a lake, in order to be eaten, but when she reads from a copy of the *Lotus Sūtra* which was given to her by her mother as a protective memento, the dragon-like water-snake is deeply moved and attains Buddha-hood. The sacrifice is thereupon abandoned, the water-snake is revealed to be the bodhisattva Kannon-sama, waiting to reward the pious, and the girl herself to be the goddess Benzaiten of Chikubushima. Quite apart from the theme of human sacrifice, the legend is interesting for the way in which a dramatic, and apparently tragic story highlighting filial piety turns out to lead into a Buddhist revelation. At the same time the cult of Benzaiten is given a strong legitimation through these identifications. In quite another direction the snake god Ugajin has also been identified with the harvest deity of the Inari shrines.

[5] Note the unusual reading *ryō-* in place of the *ryū* of Ryūjin.

Alternative stories

With this necessary orientation, the arrangements on Chikubushima can be better understood. In fact, the story of the island can be presented from two points of view, Shintō and Buddhist, which are put about in popular pamphlets for visitors. The Shintō version emphasizes that the oldest institution on the island is the Shintō shrine itself, which was supposedly first set up in the third year of the Emperor Yūryaku, i.e. 458 CE. This assertion reaches back into the legendary period of Japanese tradition, since seriously documentable history does not begin until the sixth century (reign of Kinmei, 539–571). However, even if the foundation date of the shrine cannot be exactly ascertained in a historical sense, there seems no reason to doubt that at some point the shrine was originally established to revere the goddess who created the island, named as Asaihime-no-mikoto. This name is connected with the dominant Asai family which historically at least played a key role in the island's fortunes. At the same time, in the Shintō understanding, every natural phenomenon can in principle have its own *kami* (divinity), and in the case of prominent natural features such as mountains or islands these were given names which are quite likely to predate their retrospective historical documentation.[6] Thus some three hundred years later, either some time during the reign of Tenji (668–671) or in 724 (the first year of the Jinki Period under Emperor Shōmu), the goddess Ichikishi-mahime-no-mikoto, daughter of the sun-goddess Amaterasu-ō-mikami, was installed at the same shrine as "guardian goddess of the court." This installation can be understood as a statement of political influence by the ruling clan over what was previously a local shrine. It was Ichikishi-mahime-no-mikoto who was later identified with the goddess from India, Sarasvatī or Benzai. In addition the Shintō shrine reveres Ugano-mitama-no-mikoto, a god of agriculture and commerce. Since Ugano-mitama-no-mikoto is alternatively identified with Inari-ō-kami (or Inari-sama), a connection is made here with his cult, which is widely popular because of its assumed benefit for commerce. However it is not certain when this divinity was first installed at the shrine, and the connection with Inari-sama is probably relatively late. The snake divinity itself, otherwise known as Ugajin, and as Ugafukujin, has often been identified with Benzaiten. Indeed the god-

---

6   This does not apply to many of the supposedly ancient *kami* who were installed in shrines during the Meiji Period in a rush to create additional tradition.

dess is often sculpted with an effigy of Ugajin upon her head, a coiled snake with a man's head.[7] Since Ugajin loves water, the Shintō shrine at Chikubushima has a secondary shrine facing the lake, and this is in fact the one which attracts most religious activity by visitors in the Shintō-oriented part of the island.

The Buddhist version of how things came to be tells the story of the founding of the temple Hōgonji. This took place, so it is recorded, on the basis of an Imperial Edict isued in 724, the first year of the Jinki Period, following "a divine message" received by the Emperor Shōmu from none other than the sun goddess Amaterasu-ō-mikami. According to this divine message, it was the heavenly Benzaiten who had come down to earth on the island of Chikubushima and who should therefore be revered there. Accordingly the monk Gyōki (668–749), also known as Gyōki Bosatsu – the Bodhisattva Gyōki, sailed over to the island and installed an image of Benzaiten carved by himself in the shrine, which we may therefore presume to have already existed, and in addition installed a many-armed image of Kannon-sama in a neighbouring hall specially built for the purpose. This Kannon Hall (Kannondō) is Number 30 of Japan's most famous pilgrimage route devoted to the bodhisattva, the Saikoku Thirty-three. This aspect also attracts many visitors to the island and is therefore also given considerable prominence in the Buddhist presentation. The currently standing Shintō shrine with its covered walkway to the Kannon Hall is of considerable significance from an aesthetic point of view. Yet it is overshadowed by Benzaiten. According to the Buddhist story the actual spot where Benzaiten came down to earth in Japan is a little higher up on the island, in fact precisely where the grand new Benzaiten Hall, which was erected in 1942, now stands. As such, this hall, which is termed the *honden* (main hall), is the leading focus of Benzaiten worship in Japan, being senior, it is emphasised, to the two other famous Benzaiten sites mentioned above: Itsukushima in southern Honshū and Enoshima near Kamakura. The original image housed in the partly invisible depths of the hall is only 25 centimetres tall, so it is said. This can hardly be checked, for it is treated as a "hidden Buddha" (*hibutsu*). It is only revealed once every sixty years, and the next occasion will be in 2039. Fortunately for visitors, there are two other impressive figures standing in the entrance area, which is also well stocked with amulets and other mementos.

---

7   For a substantial historical account of the iconography as well as the historical political machinations surrounding the island see Watsky 2004.

The island as a religious theme-park

It is important to realize that the visitors to the island, whose motivation ranges over a well-known spectrum of religion and tourism, treat the whole island as a single religious and architectural complex with a variety of optional activities. For them it is in effect a "theme park" with a range of attractions which they enjoy in sequence. This coherence can easily be seen in the popular guide maps of the island which give a proposed route and show all the various buildings in the same way, without reference to distinct religions. The discerning visitor will of course be oriented in part by the associations conveyed in the designations of the buildings, but such discernment is neither demanded nor brought to bear at a popular level. Moreover, the first walk-way up to the Benzaiten Hall, managed by Shingon Buddhists, is provided with the symbolic gateways *(torii)* normally associated with Shintō shrines, thus compounding the sense of cohesion for the visitor.

Since the disestablishment of Shintō at the end of the Pacific War, the Shintō shrine has undoubtedly been in a weaker position on the island. The main pathways from the landing stage lead most of the visitors first of all up to the hall of Benzaiten, which belongs to the Buddhist temple. On the way, before getting that far, there is a small office where they are able to get their shirts, scrolls or pilgrimage books stamped and inscribed in memory of their visit to Kannon-sama. Thus, if this is their main purpose, as for many "pilgrims" it surely is, they need never even go on to the Kannon Hall itself, not to mention going beyond that to the Shintō shrine. Observation suggests that some do not visit the Shintō shrine at all, although the majority of visitors follow the pathways round the island and hence walk through its grounds, apparently with a gradual diminution of interest. What they have to decide is whether to pay yet another fee of 500 Yen to look at the famous shrine carvings, after already spending 3280 Yen in order to get to the island (boat fare plus a "landing fee" of 300 Yen), to have their pilgrim book stamped (300 Yen) and to visit the treasure museum of the Temple (300 Yen).[8] By this time they will probably already have spent considerably more because of a need for amulets and other mementos for their families back home, which are prominently on sale in both the Bentendō (Benten Hall) and the Kannondō (Kannon Hall). It is there-

---

8 These prices from 1993 have been increased here and there. The ferry costs vary depending on the route taken.

fore a relatively expensive religious excursion, and the Shintō shrine is at the end of the line.

Reclaiming Benzaiten

Shortly before the end of the Shōwa period however, i.e. prior to 1989, in a position ancillary to the Shintō shrine itself, and not actually in the main shrine, a new cult of Benzaiten has been tentatively initiated. This is based on a white painted figure of the goddess (evidently antiquarian but not further identified) which was donated by a well known *biwa* player named Tanaka Hōsui who specialized in Chikuzen Biwa music. The figure is located in a low, open-fronted shelter which is easily accessible to visitors and Benzaiten is presented here mainly as a goddess who invites happiness. In fact a large signpost calls her Shōfuku Benzaiten, i.e. Happiness Inviting Benzaiten. Another refers specifically to the flourishing of commerce which she facilitates. She has no connection at all with Buddhism in this arrangement. There is evidently a wish, or at least a readiness, on the part of the tenders of the Shintō shrine not to leave the cult of Benzaiten, which apart from anything else is very lucrative, entirely in the hands of the Buzan-ha sect of Shingon Buddhism. Asked in 2012 what the administrators of the Buddhist Bentendō think about this, the chief priest (*gūji*) of the shrine, Rev. Ikushima Itsuo 生島厳雄, could only shrug his shoulders and say that he did not know. It appears that there is remarkably little communication between those who tend the various facilities on the island. The person in charge of the Kannondō, a stone's throw from the new Benzaiten shelter just below, was completely unaware of its existence, or at least claimed to be. In any, case, he pointed out with some irritation, the "real" Benzaiten is further up the hill in the Buddhist Benten Hall. In that hall an otherwise most informative attendant also disclaimed any knowledge of the recently installed figure near the main Shintō shrine. It appears that the initiative with the recently installed image has not yet succeeded in establishing a strong secondary focus for the worship of Benzaiten, pulling her back into the Shintō realm. At the same time it does reinforce the claim that the Shintō shrine was her original home, which is what the chief priest was at pains to emphasize. After all, it is at the shrine that she was originally worshipped, and even today she figures significantly at the annual festival on June 10th in which about two hundred people are said to participate. Moreover the Benzaiten of Enoshima and Itsukushima are also regarded as visiting at that time (in Japan it is quite commonly thought that divinities are able to go on journeys) and they also have a small joint shrine for themselves just at the foot of the main shrine. In addition, a signboard in the shelter for the recently installed image directs attention to the "Five Benzaiten of Japan", that is, to five sites where Benzaiten is revered as a "great divinity" (ō-kami) in five different provinces (kuni) of old Japan. These are:

>   Aki no kuni: Itsukushima Ō-kami
>   Yamato no kuni: Tenkawa Ō-kami
>   Ōmi no kuni: Chikubushima Ō-kami
>   Sagami no kuni: Enoshima Ō-kami
>   Rikuzen no kuni: Koganeyama Ō-kami

Thus a claim is made for this particular Benzaiten, worshipped at this particular shrine, to be a part of a national chain of key sites where she is revered.

A syncretistic tug-of-war

In conclusion, the situation on Chikubushima today Ōkami is an extremely interesting example of the way in which a tug-of-war can operate between religions which are usually, and indeed correctly, regarded as relatively tolerant of each other. It illustrates the power of the primal religious mentality, which does not easily distinguish between the two leading traditions, as well as the effects of changing political and economic circumstances. The shifting relations between the participating elements are affected both by general or secular factors and by the relative strength of particular strands of religious signification at any one time. To understand syncretistic processes we need to observe the dynamic aspects of apparently slow-moving situations, taking particular note of their intrinsically temporary and ambiguous character. In tune with this, a syncretistic pattern such as that conveniently circumscribed on this one island, and unwittingly documented in maps for visitors, displays on the one hand a real coherence for many of those who participate in it, but on the other hand a dynamic tension between divergent strands of interpretation.

Bibliographical references

Ludvik, Catherine 2007. *Sarasvatī. Riverine Goddess of Knowledge.* Leiden/Boston (Brill).
Triplett, Katja 2004. *Menschenopfer und Selbstopfer in den japanischen Legenden. Das Frankfurter Manuskript der Matsura Sayohime-Legende. (Religiöse Gegenwart Asiens / Studies in Modern Asian Religions 2).* Münster (Lit-Verlag).
Watsky, Andrew M. 2004. *Chikubushima: Deploying the Sacred Arts in Momoyama Japan.* Seattle (University of Washington Press).

A precursor to this paper was published as "Syncretism: Buddhism and Shintō on one island" in: Doležalová, Iva, Horyna, Břetislav and Papoušek, Dalibor (eds.) 1996. *Religions in Contact. Selected Proceedings of the Special IAHR Conference held in Brno, August 23–26, 1994*, Brno (Czech Society for the Study of Religions): 159–62.

6.6 Syncretism in Chinese Temples of South-East Asia and Taiwan

This article is an integrated successor to three shorter accounts which have been prepared over the last few years. The materials on Taiwan are new and provide significant extra orientation. For details and acknowledgements see further below.

Introduction

Recent field observations of Chinese temples among the overseas Chinese of South-East Asia and in Taiwan provide fascinating examples of syncretistic situations and selected cases are introduced here. The article builds on previous accounts and could only be completed in its final form with the assistance of others.[1] The theoretical perspective adopted is that "syncretism" is neither an ideological program in itself, nor to be confused with a conclusive synthesis. Rather, in a manner consistent with the other papers on syncretism in this volume,[2] the term is used to refer to dynamic processes of interaction, however long-term, between religious systems and elements which continue to be distinguishable in analysis.[3] Hence we refer to syncretistic "situations" and syncretistic "positions" within those situations. The "Chinese temples" of South-East Asia and Taiwan are supported and visited by local com-

---

1 The section on a temple in Singapore draws on an earlier account embedded in discussions on religion and rationality (Pye 2003). For more details of the South-East Asian cases, partly based on joint observations in Indonesia with Edith Franke, see Pye 2006b. Some points have been corrected here. Since then, new material from Taiwanese cases has provided a much needed wider balance. The Taiwanese material is drawn from joint observations carried out with Peiying Lin in 2011, and I am very grateful indeed for her efficient guidance and linguistic assistance. The observations in Taiwan were also highlighted in a related but shorter article entitled "Syncretistic positions in Chinese temples" which awaits publication elsewhere.
2 I.e. (Pye 1971a and 1993, also at 6.3, 6.4, above).
3 This is also broadly consistent with the use of the term developed by Ulrich Berner, e. g. in Berner 1982.

munities for various reasons. They house divinities of local and regional significance in a variable hierarchy, with Buddhist figures often being found just next door to other gods, or upstairs on a higher floor. While the syncretistic "positions" have arisen for various historical and social reasons, they can nowadays be read spatially, so to speak, in iconographic and architectural terms. Systemic coherence is seen in the ritual behaviour which is taken for granted by visitors to the temples, whichever divinities they are primarily dedicated to. At the same time the spatial location of the various divinities, of which there are usually more than one, give clear indications of symbolic positionings which at the very least make alternatives available.

In Indonesia and elsewhere such temples may be referred to as "Chinese temples" (in Bahasa Indonesia, *kelenteng*) because they are differentiated in this way from other places of religious recourse, especially mosques but also non-Chinese Buddhist temples (sometimes called *vihara*, see below) and Christian churches. The term *kelenteng* was probably originally derived from Chinese words meaning "Chinese people's hall"[4] though naturally this etymology is no longer present in people's minds. When reference is made to "Chinese temples" or *kelenteng* today the implication is that there is a differentiation from the surrounding, predominantly non-Chinese culture, and also that the *kelenteng* are all more or less similar in character. In fact the variety of arrangements within such "Chinese temples" is quite marked and requires careful observation and analysis. Needless to say, in Taiwan there is no need to refer to temples of this kind as "Chinese" at all. They are just temples or "halls" (*táng*, *miào*). Nevertheless, and not surprisingly, they still display significant similarities and significant variations, just as do those of overseas Chinese in the wider region.

There is a certain tendency to refer to the arrangements in these temples as representing a "synthesis" of the various traditions of Chinese religion. However, the variety of devotional foci and of reasons for founding and supporting the temples belies any easy assertion of this kind. As an internal, emic concept which is occasionally used for explaining the integrational aspect, the term *sānjiào* 三教, literally "three teachings" must at least be considered. In all brevity, the use of this term can be explained as having developed in three phases.[5] In the first instance, in view of the de facto existence of the three traditions

---

4 In standard modern Chinese *huáréntáng* 華人堂, but of course via dialects.
5 For a more complex presentation see Gentz 2006.

Confucianism, Buddhism and Daoism in China, there was an *apologetic* usage, in which the superiority of either one over the other two was asserted. Second came a harmonizing or *synthesizing* approach which proclaimed the inner unity of the three. Third the concept was drawn upon *analytically*, apparently in the first instance by the founder of the Ming Dynasty (1368–1644), or his amanuensis. His short treatise on the subject, the *Sānjiàolùn* 三教論, sought to work out a simple theoretical pattern for the existent religious phenomena which would be acceptable in statecraft.[6] An early modern discussion of the three teachings as a purely analytical or theoretical exercise is found in the writings of the Japanese writer Tominaga Nakamoto (1715–46). It is the second of these types of usage, the synthesizing approach, which is sometimes drawn upon to make sense of complicated arrangements in Chinese temples. However, such an explanation does not really work for independent observers today. This is because, first, there are often more than three strands to be observed, and second because insofar as there is a plurality of devotional foci, these are at least to some extent alternative options for the attention of those who patronize the temples.

Since the following analysis refers to Chinese religious institutions in five different countries, a word is needed on the linguistic aspect of presentation. Names which are on display in any specific case are shown in the form taken at the site in question. Variations may occur both because of the diversity of dialects and because of inefficient transliteration methods. Thus for Guānyīn we may in fact find Kuan Im or Kwan Im. When names or terms are provided from the observer's viewpoint in this article, the *pīnyīn* system is used and can be recognized by the fact that tonal accents are also provided. This system is standard in mainland China but is also used to some extent in Taiwan, with variations. In the field, the names of temples and divinities are usually also shown in characters, only rarely with non-standard forms, so the written language is in a sense the *lingua franca*. In the countries other than Taiwan, however, knowledge of both written Chinese and of standard spoken "Mandarin," is uneven.

---

[6] See Taylor 1983. Note however that the term "syncretism" as used there apparently implies a synthesis and is therefore not in accord with our usage. In fact, in the case of the Ming Emperor's conceptualization there were further fissiparous elements not covered by the big three.

Sānjiào and Guānyīn in Melaka and Singapore

It is possible that the "three teachings" concept is met with in temples of South-East Asia for the simple reason that much migration and colonization took place during the Ming Dynasty, when it seems to have been more or less officially promoted. We will look at this briefly in connection with a well-known Chinese temple in the Malaysian harbor town Melaka (also Malakka or Malacca) and an even more well-known temple in Singapore.[7] Both give prominence to a Buddhist divinity, the bodhisattva Guānyīn, and yet both display elements which are typical of other Chinese religious activity.

The temple in Melaka, known as the Cheng Hoon Teng 青雲堂 (as in other cases, we retain the spelling used on the spot for proper names) or Blue Cloud Temple, is basically *the* temple of the local Chinese community. Among other things it celebrates the first director of the community, Tay Kie Ki (also known as Tay Hong Yong), installed by the Portuguese colonists of the time. It was his successor Wei King from Amoy who established the temple in 1646. This makes it the oldest Chinese temple on the Malayan peninsula including Singapore, then not yet in existence. The importance of the community ancestors may also be seen in the prominence of the impressive, indeed beautiful Chinese cemetery on Bukit China (China Hill) which is said to be the oldest Chinese cemetery outside China itself. As is usual in Chinese cemeteries, each of the substantial tombs, keyhole shaped and set into the slope of the hill, is accompanied by a small side shrine for the earth god Tǔdìgōng 土地公. Here, as at other Chinese cemeteries including those in Java, it is so easy to see why the classic work by J. J. M. de Groot was on the one hand entitled *The Religious System of China* (de Groot 1892) and on the other hand was devoted to an overwhelming large degree to the burial arrangements and ancestor veneration. It is not surprising that he so referred to "the" religious system of China, although a modern systematic "study of religions" treatment should probably balance the analysis much more carefully. Nevertheless it is of course a major feature of the primal religion of China, as of Japan and indeed elsewhere, that past generations are understood to co-determine subsequent ones very significantly.[8]

---

7   Visited in 2002 and 2004.
8   Cf. Pye 2004a.

Let us now return to the Blue Cloud Temple. Here a signboard put up by the municipality bears among other things the following statement:

> Truly a masterpiece of its time, Cheng Hoon Teng is a proud testament to the three teachings observed by the Chinese people – Buddhism, Taoism and Confucianism, collectively called San Y Chiao.[9]

So we do we find on entering the temple? There is a central hall which houses Guānyīn and a surrounding corridor in which we find an altar for Tay Kie Ki and a large number of ancestral tablets. These were referred to by an informant as the Confucian aspect. However there is no figure of Confucius himself as may be found in other temples. Worshippers usually begin by paying reverence to Heaven (tiān 天), in an outdoors direction to the front of the temple complex, by waving incense sticks up and down in the usual way. It cannot really be said that this amounts to "Confucianism" in a conceptual sense. Similarly there is no explicit reference to Daoism, although one informant simply asserted that this too was to be seen in the various sections of the outer corridor. To the right and left of the main figure of Guānyīn two other divinities are installed. To the right is Guāndì (also Kwan Ti), a warrior god who is here responsible, as were the administrative Kapitans under the Portuguese, for justice in the Chinese community. To the left is Mah Choe Poh, i.e. Lady Māzǔ, otherwise known as Lín Mònián 林默娘, the goddess of seafarers and fishermen who is widely celebrated in the ports and settlements of the southern Chinese seas. Whether these two should be classified as "Daoism" is a matter of classificatory decision, notably difficult in the case of Daoism. So do we have the "three teachings" here? In a sense yes, and yet for the observer there must a certain unease about the application of this concept. In the last analysis the temple is certainly dominated by the central figure of Guānyīn (who will be known to some readers by the Indian name of Avalokiteśvara). In front of her, ordained nuns recite Buddhist texts. An ordained and head-shaven male is also in evidence. In sum we find here a complex situation in which various elements typical of Chinese religion can be distinguished, while the main significations hover between establishing the security of the community tradition and entering the world of Buddhist spirituality through the gate of Guānyīn. This is precisely what we understand by a syncretistic situation.

---

9   2003. San Y Chiao: i.e. 三一教 (in standard pīnyīn: sānyījiào).

By contrast, there is a more recently established "Chinese temple" opposite the city library named Kim Sa Kiong. The style of the library (Perpustam) and the stream of school-age visitors, remind us that we are here largely in Malay territory. The Kim Sa Kiong however is most evidently Chinese. The main function of this temple, dedicated to a divinity named Teoh Kon Seng Koon who was "brought" from China, is to preserve the identity of a specific group of Chinese immigrants whose story is documented on the walls. It could be treated as evidence for the rightness of de Groot's emphasis on the burial/ancestor/descent in his "system" of Chinese religion. In this case there are no very evident signs of the "three teachings" and no sign at all of Buddhist themes. Cheng Hoon Teng by contrast does include at least in some sense the variety of elements which the expression "three teachings" might lead us to expect. On the other side of the same road, Jalan To Kong, there is, interestingly enough, a clearly Buddhist temple of the Malaysian Buddhist Association (Malacca Branch). Although the iconography is Chinese in style it is exclusively Buddhist. In the case of Cheng Hoon Teng, this is not so, but at the same time the Buddhist element is central. This dominant focus may be an accentuation which has been developed over the course of time, in tune with increasing emphasis on Guānyīn in general.

Turning now to Singapore, visitors there are likely to be familiar with the old Guānyīn Temple in Waterloo Street, parallel to Bencoolen Street. The low, swinging roofs of this highly decorated temple, known on the spot as Kwan Im Thong (観音堂, but written right to left over the entrance), are almost lost among the modern blocks of flats and businesses. Indeed the huge skyscrapers of contemporary Singapore are cathedrals to the success of investor capitalism supported by the ancient Confucian virtues of diligence and thrift. But these virtues do not just run by themselves. Diligence today partly takes the form of technological dedication, itself backed by modern science. Thrift, which enables investment, is accompanied by consumerism, which in turn is necessary to reward investment. Moreover diligence alone is not enough. It is widely presumed that good fortune is also needed. Hence the numerous visitors to the Guānyīn temple are not tourists, though these are also seen, but practitioners. On a Sunday the place is so crowded that it is hardly possible for mere tourists to get in at all. The ritual has two main features. First a bundle of burning incense sticks is offered, held upwards from the forehead, away from the temple itself towards "heaven" (tiān). In fact the people might appear to be praying towards tall blocks of shops and flats. But fortunately there is a small patch of sky in between, and that counts as "heaven". Then they turn inwards towards the temple and make the same gesture towards Guānyīn, often referred to in English (not inappropriately) as the Buddhist goddess of mercy. The second stage of ritual, for those who proceed into the centre of the temple building, is the identification of one's destiny and the offering of prayers accordingly. There is room for about thirty people at any one time to take up position on a central carpet for this purpose. A box of divination rods is collected from the attendant, the shoes are removed, and a kneeling position is adopted. The box is shaken about vigorously until one of the sticks protrudes. The number on the stick then indicates to the attendant which fortune slip is the correct one for that particular person. In addition, two bean shaped divining beads are dropped to the floor, the position in which they fall also indicating current fortune. Since a considerable number of persons are performing these actions at the same time, the hall is characterised by an intense bustle of coming in, kneeling down, getting up, and above all the rattling of the divination sticks. The visitors just have time to say their prayers, with eyes closed and bowing their foreheads to the ground several times, but beyond that they are in a hurry to re-join the activities of the great commercial city outside. To illustrate their concern, one divination slip reads: "Jades are found in rocks. A fool would seek elsewhere. A fool too would borrow a light when he is in possession of matches yet he knew not that fire is obtain [sic] from their usage." Then comes the instruction: "Make hay while the sun shines. Be alert to take advantage of the right situation and be selective lest you make mistakes." Such advice can evidently be transferred to commerce and investment, although any mistakes would still be the responsibility of the investor.

A little further down the street may be found Fortune House, a large, tall block of shops where all kinds of astrological and quasi-medicinal services are on offer. The lower floors have shops with a vast array of religious accessories, in which Guānyīn and Mílèfó[10] are prominent. The upper floors continue this provision and add such benefits as palmistry, foot massage, vegetarian food, and beauty treatment, in short everything needed to improve one's destiny and lengthen one's life. All these services are clearly a cultural extension to the more specific activities carried out in the temple.

Almost next door to the Kwan Im Thong is an Indian temple sacred to Sri Krishna, and in general Chinese persons do not normally go inside

---

10 Miroku in Japanese, the Buddha of the future who in his smiling corpulent form, above all to be seen in China, has become a god of good fortune.

there, while Singaporeans of Indian descent are not usually to be seen inside the Guānyīn temple. However in front of Sri Krishna's temple is a stand where Chinese persons also burn incense. Since they apparently have otherwise nothing to do with Indian traditions, this suggests that anybody who could buy a plot of land in Singapore and set up something like a temple would be able to sell incense to Chinese people passing by, businessmen and businesswomen, students, housewives and tradespeople! The desire to burn a few sticks of incense in front of anything suitable is also evidenced at the large Chinese cemetery in Singapore, at which the several buildings for memorial services look like sanitized protestant chapels (though without a pulpit) while the columbaria, where the very numerous urns are housed with their inscriptions, photographs and flowers, are provided with incense burning basins.

How can the orientation of Kwan Im Thong be characterized? While the main figure is unambiguously Guānyīn herself (here Kwan Im), we see to her left the figure of "the doctor Hua Toh" (i.e. Huá Túo 華佗/华陀). A temple attendant explained that he represents the Daoist tradition (a contestable assertion, given his lifetime in the Hàn Dynasty) and is therefore an expression of the principle of the "three teachings." To the right of Guānyīn however is the Chán patriarch Bodhidharma, representing Buddhism. Thus overall Buddhist elements may be said to predominate. If the reverencing of Heaven is regarded as Confucian, then the "three teachings" are all somehow present. However it seems better to regard both the reverencing of heaven and the use of divination practices as part of the common language of Chinese religion. It is towards this level of primal religious practice that the Buddhist element is oriented. Therefore, this is an unevenly balanced syncretistic situation rather than a neat example of the "three teachings." The Buddhist perspective is set into a cradle of more general religious activity.

While still in the region of South-east Asia, a few words may be added on Chinese temples in Phnom Penh, Kampuchea. Here the concept of the "three teachings" is not always relevant. In one side-street for example we find a small, evidently "Chinese" temple where there is little sign of anything but Buddhism. The prominent divinities are Guānyīn and Mílèfó, while in a side hall Āmítuófó (the Buddha of the western Pure Land) is also installed. However attention may also be drawn here to a fairly large mixed temple named Xié Tiān Gōng 協天宮, built in 1886. Documentation indicates that this was erected by immigrants from Fújiàn in mainland China. The central iconographic figure is Guāndi, while the only evident Buddhist element consists of two tall modern revolving containers for illuminated, miniature votive figures of the Buddha. Thus the ancestral framework of this temple allows of a certain incursion by Buddhist elements, and it may be that further shifts of emphasis will occur here in future. A simple conversation with the temple guardian showed that the term *sānjiào* was known to him, but curiously he defined them as dàojiào, *fójiào* und *shénjiào*, or in other words, Daoism, Buddhism and "the teaching of the gods." This formulation, omitting Confucianism, which as far as the standard traditional usage goes is inaccurate, shows that the concept of the "three teachings" has a very tenuous hold on contemporary consciousness, even among those who are themselves involved in the temple institutions. In the last analysis the modern observer needs to find his or her own way through the various portals and altars, and is likely to find an endless diversity of specific arrangements.

Chinese temples in Indonesia

Broadly speaking we find similar syncretistic situations at the Chinese temples of Indonesia, with the added feature of cautious interaction with the dominant ideological principles of the state, the *pancasila*, and even with the dominant religion of Islam. As explained above, the "Chinese temples" (*kelenteng*) are generically so named because of their perceived common character when compared with other places of religious activity. The Chinese of Indonesia present themselves cautiously because of the persecution which they suffered not long after independence, resulting paradoxically from a mixture of suspicion of their presumed communist leanings and envy at their commercial success.[11] This caution finds expression even today in some of the ways in which their "halls" or temples are presented.

Typically, the *kelenteng* are recognizable on account of the swinging roofs and the use of bright red and yellow paints. Not really counting as *kelenteng* are establishments such as the Vihara Bodhicitta Maitreya in Yogyakarta, which is a vegetarian Buddhist cult imported from Taiwan focusing on the future Buddha Mílèfó (Maitreya). Since the term *vihara* in the name, drawn from Sanskrit and/or Pāli, referred originally to a

---

11 For a general description of the historical events see Ricklefs 2001.

residence for Buddhist monks, it makes it clear that a Buddhist orientation is intended.

Quite frequently however, the more usual type of Chinese temple or *kelenteng*, with roots in the community, is also referred to as a *vihara*. Examples are the Vihara Lokesvara (otherwise known as Vihara Avalokitesvara) near Ungaran; the Vihara Buddha Prabha (also named in English as Buddha Prabha Temple) on Jalan Brigjend Katamso in Yogyakarta; the Vihara Tribhakti at Magelang, and the *kelenteng* at the harbour town of Cirebon named Cháo Júe Sì 潮覺寺 but also as Vihara Dewiwelasasih.[12]

In all of these, the diversity of devotional foci is quite varied. The Vihara Lokesvara, near Ungaran, is a case in point. Lokesvara is an alternative name for Avalokiteśvara (the Sanskrit designation of Guānyīn) and the temple is therefore also known in an Indonesian form (without any diacritical mark) as Vihara Avalokitesvara. From this name alone we might not suspect a "Chinese" temple, and yet that is what it is. The main divinities are indeed Buddhist: Guānyīn, referred to as Dewi Kwan Im, and the Buddha of medicine Yao Shi Fo (Yàoshīfó). But there is also a splendid Chinese-style tiger god, named as Houw Tjiang Kong, though the goddess of the earth has the Indian-derived designation Dewi Bhumi. On entering the complex there is a platform with a view outwards, and here it is usual first to pay reverence to Heaven (*tiān*), then inwards towards the buddhas. Overall it may be said that a popularly conceived form of Buddhism is dominant here. At Cirebon, on the other hand, the main divinity appears at first sight to be the Buddhist Guānyīn, but this bodhisattva is accompanied by the sailors' goddess Māzǔ, referred to as the "Holy Mother of Heaven" (天上聖母 Tiānshàng Shèngmǔ) and also Guāndì. It appears in this case that Buddhism is concentrated in the form of the Guānyīn cult and is well balanced by the Māzǔ cult.

At Magelang we find the bright red Chinese temple known as the Vihara Tribhakti, standing at one corner of the central square of this "Town of Hope" (Kota Harapa). The very name proposes a constellation of three kinds of devotion (*tribhakti*),[13] an idea which evidently owes something to the Chinese term *sānjiào*, though emphasizing worship rather than teaching. On one of the pillars supporting the temple we even find precisely the term *sānjiào* written in Chinese characters. This is therefore a clear ex-

---

12 Though of Indian derivation such names have been Indonesianized and hence are shown without diacritical marks.
13 The spelling *bakti* is also found in Bahasa Indonesia.

ample of an attempt to indigenize the concept for the Indonesian situation. It is significant that a later attempt to enquire about this temple under the name of Vihara Tribhakti was quite fruitless. It is only really known as "the" Chinese temple in Magelang or by the name Liong Hok Bio. This is a clear indication that its designation as a *vihara* is a relatively recent development which meant little to the temple's traditional supporters. Given the ideological perspective, it is not surprising that the ideological slogan *ketuhanan yang maha esa* is also prominently displayed. Inside the temple there is a series of altars for paying reverence. Although not all are clearly defined, one of them bears a large swastika symbolizing Buddhism and another bears a *yīn-yáng* symbol for Daoism. For Confucianism stands a statue of the sage himself, labeled in Latin script as "Nabi Khong Hu Cu" to show that he is "a prophet" (Khong Hu Cu being equivalent to Confucius). So the "three teachings" or "three cults" (*tribakti*) are represented. However in the main hall this balance is not so clear. There are three main figures: to the right is Guānyīn. However, less so than in other cases, Buddhism has not achieved a dominant position here, not even in terms of the Guānyīn cult. To the left is an unidentified figure, and in the centre stands a statue of "Hok Tek Ceng Sin" who was further explained to be "a male divinity." In fact, this divinity, in standard Chinese Fúdé zhèngshén 福德正神, is an equivalent to the earth god. In spite the signposting, there seem to be unresolved, un-synthesized arrangements here.

At the Vihara Buddha Prabha, probably the most well-known *kelenteng* in Yogyakarta, we find that the temple is named in Chinese as the "Temple of Blessed Spirits", in standard Chinese Fúlíng miào 福靈廟 (but with a non-standard variation for the term for "spirits"). The entrance and exit points to right and left are named for the Dragon and the Tiger respectively, as is usual. The central entrance is supposed to be reserved for the spirits themselves. The main temple is termed in Chinese the *miào* 廟, a word commonly used for ancestral or Confucian halls, while Buddhist temples may also be called *sì* 寺. In a substantial side hall there is indeed a statue of Confucius himself, standing ready to be revered. Behind the statue is a poster with a further portrait of the sage, an here he is further designated as a "prophet" (Nabi Khong Hoe). On the cover of a large book on display we find the name of the Indonesian Confucianist Association: Majelis Tinggi Agama Khonghucu Indonesia (MATAKIN). So in this partly Buddhist *vihara* a sage becomes a prophet. Yet there is a significant presence of Buddhism in further rooms. An important Indonesian Buddhist personality named Mahabiksu Ashin Jinarakkhita is celebrated with photographs. There is a place for GuanYin and for Mi Le Fo, and also for A Mi Tuo Fo (Amitābha Buddha), the names being displayed as shown here. Then follows a place for divination by fortune telling sticks, with their numbers in Bahasa Indonesia, or alternatively by throwing the beans. Finally, there is a stairway to a second floor, and here we find a presentation of the Buddha, or rather the abstract principle of supreme Buddhahood, Adibuddha. A signboard shows the formula "Namo Sanghyang Adi Buddha" accompanied with the *pancasila* phrase *ketuhanan yang maha esa*. Informants explained that in the difficult times under Soeharto this presentation had been made at the entrance to the temple as a whole, but that thereafter (by 2003) this had become less necessary and the complex had reverted to its more usual form as a Chinese temple. Although there is a certain amount of Buddhist activity such as meditation, this seems to be a more personal, and at any rate subordinate interest. Thus a cupboard marked "Sekolah Minggu Buddha" or "Buddhist Sunday School" stands directly next to the above mentioned image of Confucius. In general the situation in this temple raises most interestingly the question as to the relative spatial importance of front and rear in religious buildings, and indeed of downstairs and upstairs. We may ask which elements really have priority, which are leading towards others, and so on. This question will not however be simply answered, for it is possible to lead in more than one direction in a syncretistic situation. It will be noted that people are not unaware of which elements carry which significations.

A different but equally ambiguous orientation is found in a small Chinese temple in Jakarta, in the jungled streets of the old city centre (Kota), which is introduced by a signboard showing "Vihara Dharma Karya Angsapura." Behind this signboard, now less easy to see, is the title of the main figure housed here, in Chinese, which reads "The great administrator of the state of Lu" and thus indicates the importance of Confucius. This is repeated inside. However the temple offers a variety of altars for historical and legendary personages, not to mention the "earth god" who is located under the altar for the main figure. There is actually not much evidence of "Buddhism" except for an apparently growing collection of porcelain figures of Guānyīn such as are popular in Singapore and elsewhere and suitable as meritorious presents.

In general the emphasis on a Buddhist orientation during the Soeharto period served to position Chinese temples among the five religions (*agama*) which were legally recognized at that time. Unlike Hinduism and Buddhism, neither Confucianism nor Daoism were among them.[14] The first of the five ideological principles (*pancasila*) of the state required acceptance of "a single great deity" (*ketuhanan yang maha esa*). Over against this Daoism was played down because of the multiplicity of divinities, while Confucianism could be regarded as altogether god-less. While there are various buddhas and bodhisattvas in Buddhism, the argument was not infrequently advanced that one single buddha-principle underlies them all, and that this is consistent with the rule that a single god-head should be held in view as government policy requires.

Such variegated orientations in one temple are not always covered by the term *vihara* and yet are adapted in other ways to their Indonesian location. The Chinese temple in the port city of Semarang named Sam Po Kong is identified above all with the sea-hero Cheng Ho (Zhèng Hé 鄭和) whose exploits are claimed in a work by Kong Yuanzhi to be comparable to those of Columbus, da Gama and Magellan.[15] He is also claimed as a Muslim. Inside the long low temple, to the left and perhaps easily missed, there is a small room for Muslim prayers. Confucius, in the main temple, is explicitly designated as a *nabi* or prophet. Thus in this temple we find the foundation story and cult of the Chinese community of Semarang, who claim Cheng Ho as theirs, Confucianism and some elements of Daoism, and even a place for Muslim prayers. But of Buddhism there is no sign at all. Such is the tug-of-war of the traditions in the *kelenteng* of Indonesia.

In sum, quite apart from the variable emphasis on each of the three great "teachings," the Chinese temples also mark the points of entry of Chinese migrants, re-tell their foundational stories and provide homes for other divinities such as Māzǔ and Guāndì who take care of this-worldly needs of the people. But the emphasis varies considerably from temple to temple and is adjusted to the needs and political pressures of the times.

So just how "Buddhist" are these *vihara* in Indonesia? The term no longer refers to a residence for monks or nuns. Rather it has become just another formal word for "temple" even while *kelenteng* is the one used

---

14　See H. Muh Nahar Nahrawi: *Memahami Khonghucu Sebagai Agama* Jakarta (Gramedia) 2003; and Heriyanto Yang: "The history and legal position of Confucianism in post-independence Indonesia" in the internet journal *Marburg Journal of Religion* 10/1 (August 2005) which was originally a contribution to the international conference of the IAHR held in Yogyakarta and Semarang in 2004.

15　Kong Yuanzhi, *Muslim Tionghoa CHENG HO. Misteri Perjalanan Muhibah di Nusantara*, Jakarta 2000.

in speech, and *miào* hovers in the background for Chinese speakers (who are however by no means all Chinese-literate). On the other hand, in spite of the ancestral and this-worldly orientations which are usually evident, the popularity of Guānyīn should not be underestimated. This bodhisattva, while being an expression of compassion to the world, is also a window on the deeper significations of Buddhism as these are understood in the Mahāyāna tradition.

We cannot here go into the complex question "What counts as Buddhist?" (also thrown up in Part Five of the present volume in connection with innovation). Be it noted however that no "essentialist" answer is here presupposed or expected, since the "Chinese temples" (*kelenteng*) are not in the hands of any particular Buddhist orthodoxy. On the other hand this does not mean that the question simply drops away, or can be left altogether to the intentionally or unintentionally simplified accounts of participants. The realities on the ground escape capture not only in the terms like "three teachings" but also are not easily captured with terms such as "Confucianism," "Buddhism" and "Daoism."

As to Buddhism however, the importance of the Mahāyāna concept of skilful means (Chinese 方便 *fāngbiàn*) should certainly not be overlooked, for this term (albeit a system-internal or emic one) moderates the relations between provisional presentations and final meanings. In this sense it is in tune both with the possible variations of "Buddhism" and with the way in which we understand syncretistic ambiguities.

Syncretistic positions in Taiwanese temples

Although Taiwan does not count geographically as being a part of South-East Asia, the first major influx of immigrants from the Chinese mainland took place during the Ming Dynasty, bringing communities in particular from Fújiàn. This means that there are similarities in the general characteristics of temples in Taiwan and those in other areas to which the Chinese sea-borne expansion extended. Not surprisingly, Māzǔ is perhaps the most prominent single divinity who is celebrated on the island. At the same time the temples in Taiwan are of quite varied origin and have diverse dedications. The concept of *sānjiào* mentioned above does not usually play any particular role on the spot, no doubt because the need for explanation is much lower than in those countries where there is both a different surrounding culture and a western colonial past. On the other hand the Japanese colonial period had its own impact on temple arrangements, as will be seen in the case of the Temple of the City God at Xīnzhú below. During a journey in Taiwan in 2011 a number of rather different temples were visited in the company of various informants.[16] The temples visited, distributed over five different towns or cities, were as follows:

01 Xīnzhú Chénghuáng miào 新竹城隍廟
02 Táiběi Xiáhǎi Chénghuáng miào 台北霞海城隍廟 (Táiběi = Taipei)
03 Táiwān Shěng Chénghuáng miào 台灣省城隍廟 (in Taipei)
04 Fǎgǔshān 法鼓山 (Dharma Drum Mountain)
05 Jīnshān Jīnbāolǐ Māzǔ miào 金山金包里媽祖廟
06 Cǎotún Lín Jiāmiào 草屯林家廟 (Lin Family Ancestor Hall)
07 Cǎotún Bǎoshēng Dàdì 草屯保生大帝
08 Táinán Lù'ěrmén Tiānhòu gong 台南鹿耳門天后宮 (Māzǔ)
09 Táinán Lù'ěrmén Shèngmǔ miào 台南鹿耳門聖母廟 (Māzǔ)
10 Jiālǐ Zhào Zǐlóng miào 佳里趙子龍廟
11 Jiālǐ Jiāfú sì Guānyīn tíng 佳里佳福寺觀音亭
12 Táinán Wǔfǔ Qiānsùi Dàitiān fǔ 台南五府千歲代天府
13 Jiālǐ Chéng Míng Sùijūn miào 佳里陳明歲君廟

It is not possible to discuss all of these here, but we will focus on a few of them which are particularly illustrative for the present discussion. First, informed readers will immediately notice that the Buddhist foundation known as Dharma Drum Mountain (法鼓山 Fǎgǔshān) is included in this list. The reason for this is simply to recall that a substantial Buddhist institution will surely have its own hall for worship, focusing for example on Guānyīn, but without any reference to the other traditions of Chinese religion. Such places are hardly involved in the kind of syncretistic processes being discussed here, except perhaps in terms of it involvement with quite different cultural elements such as the possibilities of modern architecture. The same is true for the religious halls in other Buddhist educational institutions, for example educational ones such as the Buddhist College Fójiào Hóngshì Xúeyuàn 佛教弘誓學院. This situation is parallel to that of the "purely" Buddhist *vihara* in Indonesia, whether attuned towards Theravāda or to Mahāyāna Buddhism, although as we have seen, not every Chinese establishment which is called a *vihara* in Indonesia is only or even mainly Buddhist.

Second, conversely, there is a particular type of temple, the family ancestral hall (*jiāmiào*), which has no particular Buddhist elements at all. The Ancestor Hall of the Lin family at Cǎotún (06 above), when seen from

---

16 These visits were all carried out jointly with Peiying Lin, without whose guidance most of them would not have been possible.

the road, has the general appearance of "a Chinese temple" in terms of the colourful swung roof, tripartite entrance area, and so on, but it is without any really public entrance which would invite non-related people in from the street for general religious activities. It is simply visited on particular occasions by members of the relevant branch of the Lin family or clan. The main feature is the collection of ancestral tablets, places for burning incense, and a large wall plaque giving the historic legend of the Lins, of which the branch associated with this particular hall is only one among many. A small image of Māzǔ may be seen, but although the Lin family is connected with the original legend of Māzǔ this goddess is by no means the central point in the ancestral hall.

In between these two distinct cases, there is a wide variety of "temples" or miào, to use the most common designation, in which the interactive relations between the various traditions of traditional Chinese religious culture, with its particular Taiwanese accents, may readily be observed. Some are really large establishments which provide a wide range of opportunities for prayerful requests to the divinities, especially for this-worldly benefits such as success in commerce, good marriage arrangements, protection from ill-health or disaster, success in education, or whatever else may be uppermost in the mind.

Traditionally of course, Māzǔ, as the goddess of sailors, has been believed to be responsible for safety at sea and success in fishing, but her functions are now broadened to include any concerns of urban life. This can easily be observed in the Jīnshān Jīnbǎolǐ Māzǔ miào (05), the Táinán Lù'ěrmén Tiānhòu gōng (08) and the Táinán Lù'ěrmén Shèngmǔ miào (09). However Māzǔ's presence is not limited to the miào which bear her name. She may also be found as a secondary divinity in other temples.

This brings us to the halls of the Chénghúang or "City Gods", i. e. the gods of the walls and moats,[17] where Māzǔ is sure to be seen in addition to the main divinities. In the early intention, the various "city gods" have the main function of protection for a particular area, as the very idea of walls and moats suggests. But their temples usually offer other functions as well, particular in relation to this-worldly needs of individuals as mentioned above. Thus the Xiáhǎi Chénghuáng miào in Taipei (02), while offering special festival activities for a general if more or less local public, also has a thriving activity in attending to the needs of individuals, especially of women in search of partners. At this

---

17 For the significance of this concept from Míng times see Taylor 1977.

miào the ritual services of a brightly dressed Daoist priest are available and take place in full view of the throng of other visitors. At first sight oddly, there are two "city god" halls in Taipei. The reason for this, not immediately evident either to casual visitors or to residents who take them for granted, is that the just mentioned Xiáhǎi Chénghuáng miào was set up to serve a specific community of immigrants from Xiáhǎi 霞海. In fact, the original place in mainland China was called Xiáchéng 霞城 in Fújiàn Province (present day Tóng'ān 同安). The Taiwan Shěng Chénghuáng miào (03) on the other hand, was a later foundation set up following a Chinese governmental directive that all Chinese provinces (*shěng* 省) should have a hall for the God of Walls and Moats in their respective capitals. Hence this was set up in the capital Taipei. The latter is more substantial and has less popular functions. There is no particularly Daoist presence. The main focus is the City God himself, installed with his wife and his guardians, and conveying an appropriate impression of protective severity. To one side of the entrance however, just inside, we see a large statue of Guānyīn which is evidently more recent than the original foundation. Other Buddhist images can be found in subordinate positions inside, with a special hall upstairs. Thus not only Māzǔ but also "Buddhism" can be drawn into the ambit of the "City God" – if this simplificatory term may be used for convenience. It may be noted that Guānyīn, though a Buddhist bodhisattva, is also functioning largely as a benevolent goddess, sometimes and not inappropriately spoken of as a goddess of compassion, and the redirection of people's thoughts from personal benefits towards the deeper insights of Buddhist teaching may not always be immediate or automatic. But that is precisely how the ambiguous processes of "syncretism" are found to work.

Of particular interest is the *miào* of the City God of Xīnzhú, situated on the coast some distance from Taipei.[18] In this case the visitors to the temple enter first through a narrow gate and shopping street to the temple itself, but then it is necessary to keep slightly left in order to enter. The reason for this is that immediately to the right of it there is another temple which has some of the same architectural features but is set up for Buddhist figures inside. In between is a narrow covered corridor, named "Gate of Compassion," which leads to rooms at the rear. The reason for this arrangement is that during the period of Japanese colonial rule,

---

18 Thanks are due to Dr. Cheng Wei-yi and her very knowledgeable students for additional guidance at this temple.

the attempt was made to "separate" Buddhism and other divinities, in order to somehow apply the concept of *shinbutsu bunri*, the separation of gods and buddhas, in order to assert the ideologically driven purity of Shintō, to the situation in Taiwan. It seems that this administrative effort was met with partial understanding on the spot in Taiwan, for the buddhas were taken out of the residence of the City God, who was presumed to be an approximate local equivalent to Shintō deities. Paradoxically, this entrenched the further presence of "Buddhism" in the same complex, for there was nowhere else for it to go except immediately next door. The resulting arrangement is that there are four halls in all: to the left is the hall of the City God himself, behind which is the hall for the City God's wife. To the right is the first Buddhist hall, for Guānyīn, and behind that is a hall housing the future Buddha Mílèfó (Maitreya). Thus the overall site plan consists of four square halls forming a larger square, of which the two front squares are separated by a corridor leading to the rear. It is particularly interesting that a person can enter either hall at the front, then go to the hall behind it, and then proceed through a side entrance from the City God side to the Buddhist side, or vice versa. Thus a fusion or a synthesis was administratively broken up, and yet a syncretistic process continues all the more.

Given this fascinating clue, it is rewarding to look out for any signposting within the temple buildings of Taiwan. There are interesting cases where the visitor is directed "upstairs" for the Buddha hall, which can be very substantial. This arrangement will be found in the institutions numbered 03, 05 and 09 above. In 08 there is an additional hall is to the rear which also has its own upstairs. By contrast, the idea of going "upstairs" for the buddhas, Guānyīn, Mílèfó, Yàoshī and others, is one which could never occur in a Shintō shrine in Japan. Admittedly, one might see a parallel in Japan in some of the great Buddhist temple gates, which amount to buildings in their own right. These often house a selection of Buddhist images in an upper floor, reached by a very steep staircase, but in such cases there are no alternative divinities underneath. In the case of the "Chinese temples" discussed here the visitor is led easily from the one to the other, if the signs are read. Thus there are alternative significations and alternative religious orientations in one integrated complex.

Conclusion

In conclusion it may be reasserted that "synthesis" is not the right term for any of the situations described briefly above. Nor should the term "syncretism" be adopted as a mere synonym for fusion. Observation in the field shows that a variety of architectural and iconographic arrangements are correlated in a situation which can be adjusted or repositioned from time to time. The situation of the various positions taken, symbolized by the divinities but constructed by those responsible for them, includes not only collusion at the level of popular religious culture but also a variety of alternative significations which are not necessarily identical with each other and may even be in some sense contradictory. The range of phenomena exhibited by "Chinese temples" thus exhibits the processes of syncretism in the best sense of the word.

Bibliographical references

Berner, Ulrich 1982. *Untersuchungen zur Verwendung des Synkretismus-Begriffs.* Wiesbaden (Harrassowitz).

De Groot, J. J. M. 1892. *The Religious System of China.* Leiden (Brill).

Franke, Edith and Pye, Michael (eds.) 2006. *Religionen Nebeneinander. Modelle religiöser Vielfalt in Ost- und Südostasien.* Berlin (LIT-Verlag).

Gentz, Joachim 2006. "Die Drei Lehren (*sanjiao*) Chinas in Konflikt und Harmonie. Figuren und Strategien einer Debatte" in: Franke and Pye 2006:17–40.

Kong, Yuanzhi 2000. *Muslim Tionghoa CHENG HO. Misteri Perjalanan Muhibah di Nusantara.* Jakarta 2000.

Pye, Michael 1971a. "Syncretism and ambiguity" in: *Numen. International Review for the History of Religions* 18 (2): 83–93.

- 1993. *Syncretism versus Synthesis.* (*Occasional papers of the British Association for the Study of Religion No. 8).* Cardiff (BASR). Republished in: *Method &Theory in the Study of Religion*, 6 (3) (1994): 217–29.

- 2003. *Rationality, ritual and life-shaping decisions in modern Japan.* Occasional Papers 29. Marburg (University of Marburg, Centre for Japanese Studies). Republished in Raud, Rein (ed.) 2007. *Japan and Asian Modernities*, London (Kegan Paul): 1–27.

- 2004a. *The structure of religious systems in contemporary Japan: Shintō variations on Buddhist pilgrimage.* (*Occasional Papers 30).* Marburg (Centre for Japanese Studies).

- 2006b. "Die 'Drei Lehren' und das Tauziehen der Religionen in chinesischen Tempeln Südostasiens" in: Franke, Edith and Pye, Michael (eds.) *Religionen Nebeneinander. Modelle religiöser Vielfalt in Ost- und Südostasien.* Münster (Lit-Verlag): 41–60.

Ricklefs, M. C. 2001. *A History of Modern Indonesia since c. 1200* (third edition). Stanford (Stanford University Press).
Taylor, Romeyn 1977. "Ming T'ai-tsu and the Gods of the Walls and Moats" in: *Ming Studies* 3: 31–49.
– 1983. "An Imperial Endorsement of Syncretism. Ming T'ai-tsu's Essay on the Three Teachings: Translation and Commentary" in: Ming Studies 16: 31–38.

This paper is published here in its present form for the first time. However, see Note 1 above for related versions.

Part Seven
Some Contextual Questions: Identity, Plurality, Education, Dialogue, Peace

7.1 Introduction to Part Seven

This collection of essays began with some strict requirements about the integrity and, as some might see it, the purity of an academic discipline termed "the study of religions." From the very beginning however, there was a recognition that this discipline had to be cultivated in specific contexts, and that these are culturally diverse. This diversity needs to be taken into account when seeking to maintain constructive institutional and networking arrangements, it was argued (especially in Part Three). However, in later sections the emphasis has been placed on a more or less purist delineation of certain patterns of analysis and explanation relevant to both historical and contemporary contexts.

At the same time, academic work does not take place in a social, cultural or political vacuum. Various events take place all around us, some dramatic, and draw our interest and concern in many ways. The key words at the head of this section: identity, plurality, education, dialogue and peace, indicate themes which have been of particular interest to the present writer over many years. In this last part therefore a selection of papers is assembled which, though not really systematic, gives some idea of these wider interests. They may help to dispel any idea that to work at the study of religions condemns one to unremitting positivism. The famous "ivory tower" is an illusion. The distinction between observation/analysis/explanation on the one hand and contention and debate on the other hand should of course continue to be made. A the same time, while care should be taken that general debate does not distort regular studies, the results and insights gained through research may, in the other direction, provide something of a perspective for the development of sound judgments in wider fields. These relationships were set out briefly in the form of a number of "theses" co-authored with Edith Franke and published in the freely accessible internet journal *Marburg Journal of Religion* (Franke and Pye 2004). It is notable that these "theses" arose out of some joint presentations to institutions of higher education in Indonesia (in 2003) and were initially very strictly conceived as a statement about the study of religions (consistent with the positions advanced in Part One above), but the audiences, their thoughtfulness sharpened by the beginnings of the Iraq war, required a more robust presentation of the relationship between such study and the issues of the day.[1] This initiative is described in more detail in 7.7 below.

The first two articles below are both, in a very general sense, about religion and identity. This theme was of great importance during the emergence of the new democratic South Africa in the early 1990s and so it was taken up in "Religion and identity: clues and threads" (7.2) at Pretoria. The location was not far from the Voortrekker Monument, which had been symbolic of the Apartheid regime. The "clues and threads" relating to the role of identity in religious terms are drawn from the distinction between primal and critical religions in the general typology of religions, which was already thematised in Section Four above with reference to Japanese religions. We see from this that theoretical positions in the analysis of religions, though not necessarily clearly understood by believers and participants on the spot, can be quite relevant in shifting political situations.

The question of identity recurs in "Christian churches and political change in eastern Europe" (7.3) in which will be found reports and reflections based on personal experience of the Cold War and its ending, formulated in retrospect (1992–3) on the basis of notes and documents. The writer's experience during various journeys in the period before 1989/90 was that religious orientations had been rather more important in the countries of Eastern Europe than was widely assumed in the western world at the time. Related material may also be found in Part One, in "Political Correctness in the Study of Religions: Is the Cold War Really Over?" (above at 3.5) especially in the section on the Buryatian Buddhist figure Dandaron. In that case a problem arose less because of his Buddhist orientation than because this orientation was linked to a minority identity question, namely that of the Buriats in the Baikal region bordering Mongolia. Needless to say, such matters were and are usually contentious. In the case of Poland, as reported below, a particularly interesting matter was the ambiguous positioning of the Polish lay Catholic organization Pax. While Pax invested heavily in Polish identity, it was evidently syncretistic in that it constantly repositioned Polishness, Communism and Catholicism with apparently studied ambiguity. The analysis is consistent with the studies of syncretist situations in Part Six, and is at the same time of political interest.

---

1 Heartfelt thanks are due to our hosts in various institutions of higher education in Java, and for overall facilitaton on the part of the Departemen Agama (Ministry of Religion) in Jakarta. For further details see Franke and Pye 2004.

It is remarkable that while a most significant presupposition of the modern study of religions is the recognition that religions are to be found in their plurality, this has in the meantime become a matter of wide public and political interest, simply as a matter of fact in most countries of the world. This is taken up in "Reflecting on the plurality of religions" (7.4).[2] The question is how the theoretical perception of plurality can be made useful for the wider discussions which have to take place in non-academic, public arenas. It should be noted that the term "pluralism" is *not* used here, because it has long since been hijacked by theologians for use in a programmatic sense, that is, with the meaning of a normative theological assertion about the desirability of plurality. In the study of religions there is no programme for the promotion of "pluralism" as a desired objective, but there is a steady perception of *the fact* that religions are there in their plurality. This, in itself, regardless of the negative or positive stance of various theologies towards it, has implications for public debate. Moreover, religions often exist, in their plurality, in close proximity to each other. More recently therefore I have conceptualized this as "religious adjacency," a phenomenon which in turn gives rise to questions about the nature of inter-religious and political responses.[3]

Of related interest is "The study of religions and the dialogue of religions" (7.5). Again, the shared presupposition is the perception of the plurality of religions. Here, too, it is important that the study of religions as an academic discipline should not be confused with the dialogue of religions, either in terms of its methodology or its goals. Nevertheless it has become evident that specialists in the study of religions, insofar as the participants in religious dialogue want this, can perform significant functions of communication and mediation. As always, the necessary distinctions should be maintained. Some of the writer's own experience of participation in religious dialogues as a neutral facilitator is documented in the paper.

---

[2] A shorter version of this text appeared in the journal *World Faiths Encounter*, published by the World Congress of Faiths (Pye 1996d); at the same time it may be noted that the writer has not been a regular member of specific "interfaith" groups.

[3] Cf. Franke and Pye 2006: *Religionen Nebeneinander. Modelle religiöser Vielfalt in Ost- und Südostasien* (with further contributions by Joachim Gentz, Manfred Hutter, Katja Triplett and Woo Hairan). The literal meaning of "*Religionen nebeneinander*" is "religions next to each other," and such a state of affairs is expressed more abstractly by "religious adjacency."

The article "Presuppositions of an integrative religious education" (7.6) arises out of a concern which dates back to 1966–68, when the writer was involved in teacher education with special reference to religion at York, England. A central point of interest is just how the discipline of the study of religions, rather than the doctrinal tradition of a particular church, can be correlated with religious education in the classrooms of pluralist societies. To some extent the argument presupposes the twists and turns in the development of religious education in England, but it is argued here that the basic positions are of potential relevance for many societies around the world. In Japan there is currently no public religious education, and if there were to be it might easily become ideologised. By contrast, an open and at the same time integrative approach is desirable. Interestingly, a Japanese lay Buddhist movement, the Risshō Kōseikai, took up this challenge many years ago and published its own textbooks for religious education in which religions other than Buddhism were also included (see Pye 1972b).

We conclude with a matter which is surely of concern to many, namely world peace. It is often simply stated that the religions of the world have something to do with this, or ought to have. But what, if anything, does it have to do with the study of religions, which claims to offer reliable facts and analyses? Some guidelines on this were worked out in "Peace and the dialogue of religions" (7.7), drafted in response to a request by representatives of the Korean movement, Won Buddhism (cf. 5.6 above). As ever, we have to be clear about what serious study can achieve in its own right, but then also about how the experience and knowledge gained by it can be brought to bear on matters of wider concern. In short, researchers and teachers in the study of religions have to do their jobs properly, and strictly; but at the same time we need to understand and explain how knowledge, judicious analysis and considered reflection about religions can also contribute to the resolution of problems which are of wide concern for a struggling humanity.

Bibliographical references

Franke, Edith and Pye, Michael 2004. "Ilmu agama dan kontribusinya terhadap penyelesaian masalah dalam dunia yang plural / The study of religions and its contribution to problem solving in a plural world" in: *Marburg Journal of Religion* in 2004:<http://www.uni-marburg.de/fb03/ivk/mjr/pdfs/2004/articles/franke-2004.pdf>

Franke, Edith and Pye, Michael (eds.) 2006. *Religionen Nebeneinander. Modelle religiöser Vielfalt in Ost- und Südostasien*. Berlin and Münster (Lit-Verlag).
Pye, Michael 1972b. "A Buddhist approach to comparative religion in schools" in: *British Journal of Educational Studies* 20/3: 270–81.
– 1996d. "Reflecting on the plurality of religions" in: *World Faiths Encounter* 14: 3–11.

7.2 Religion and Identity: Clues and Threads

This paper was given as a plenary address to the first conference of the newly formed South African Academy of Religion on the theme "Religion and Civil Society," on January 17th 1994. The present text is a substantially edited and reduced version, which however maintains the original argument at all points. Original footnotes have been left, but some cross-references have been added to other papers published above.

Religious forces, academic structures, religious identities

This paper is given on a very special occasion, namely the founding conference of the South African Academy of Religion. Since this new Academy is an organized institution, we begin with some reflections on the relation between religious forces and academic structures. We then move on to wider questions about religion and identity which are of particular importance to South Africa at this time of highly significant political change.[1]

Religious forces and academic structures have long stood in a complex relationship with each other. Many universities began as religious foundations, not only in the western world but also in Asia. At the same time, major critiques of religion have also been purveyed in universities, often to the consternation of religious leaders, and above all of

---

1 The writer was privileged and extremely happy to attend the opening conference of the new South African Academy of Religion, to meet colleagues from various universities in South Africa and to make brief visits not only to Pretoria, where the conference was held, but also to Cape Town, Stellenbosch and Bloemfontein. I am very grateful for the support of the South African Human Sciences Research Council. It is widely hoped that the New South Africa will be able to go beyond the current electoral process (with all its attendant difficulties and concerns) to build stable institutions and become a model of world-wide repute for multi-ethnic democracies elsewhere. The first conference of the South African Academy of Religion, with its theme "Religion and Civil Society," demonstrated that finely tuned minds of varied provenance are profoundly engaged with a wide range of relevant questions. The same is true for those university departments which I was privileged to visit. This holds great promise for the future of the country.

religious followers. This complexity is reflected in our other kinds of academic association, our societies and academies. It may also be seen in the vague labeling of subjects such as "religious studies." There is sometimes a danger of heavily incursive religious motivation or sponsorship, which in turn may turn out to be a threat to free-wheeling academic reflection.

Looking at this situation positively, people come to religious studies from various contributory backgrounds, and it is therefore quite natural and necessary that there should be an on-going process of "discipline identification."[2] The establishment of The South African Academy of Religion, which will have several differentiated constituent associations, will help greatly in clarifying the relations between the study of religions, Biblical studies and theology, and in permitting appropriate interactions between them. This will assist an incoming generation of scholars in the clarification of their objectives and methods without strife.[3] It will also help to stabilise the relationship between the intellectual, reflective study of religion and the hopes and fears of believing, and often disagreeing communities.

The power of religions in the world today is really quite surprising for those who have felt, in one way or another, the force of critical philosophy or even just the vague attraction of liberal humanism. Sociologists who have spent much effort in the discussion of secularization processes, whether in the context of godless western materialism or of communist atheism, are now having to redirect their efforts. Recently

---

2 Cf. "Religious studies in Europe: structures and desiderata" at 3.2 above.
3 This holds particular interest for one who writes as Secretary-General of the International Association for the History of Religions, to which the Southern African Association for the Study of Religion has been affiliated for some time. Some readers will be aware that there has been considerable controversy in some quarters about the ways in which the "history of religions" (a phrase with more meaning than is sometimes realised) or the "study of religions" may be associated, if at all, with church-related, theological or other religiously motivated studies. There are indeed real difficulties here. However it is of great importance, particularly at times of political stress and creativity, that people in fact talk to each other, both in specific countries and also internationally, and contribute to the wider formation of ideas. The answer lies in genuine mutual respect, a realistic understanding of different kinds of motivation which may be brought to bear on reflection about religion, and in a fair and open structuring of the relevant associations and institutions so that the dangers of manipulation and majorisation are avoided. The South African Academy of Religion looks set to avoid these dangers which, it must be said, have not always been avoided elsewhere.

they must concentrate more attentively on a lively resurgence of religion almost all over the globe, either in neo-traditional or complicatedly novel forms. The data-handling, communications and media revolution is also relevant. It means that some forms of religion have become much more immediately available globally and that individual choice, or manipulation directed at individuals, has been multiplied. The New Age is everywhere at once, and the tele-evangelism of America can be matched by the huge healing shows in Russia, which have just been banned by presidential decree.

However, the effects of such trends are partial. We must take care not to be blinded by buzz-words such as globalism and post-modernism, often used by those without much involvement in real communities or in long-term field work. Much of the reality of religion is in fact not global but parochial, not effervescent but persistent, not a matter of light individual choice but of inescapable communal realities and identities. In many countries there is a heavy investment in religious symbol systems for the negotiation of community strife, and, alas less often, for the negotiation of peace. For this we need look no further than the United Kingdom or the Republic of South Africa. The media in the UK currently have about four scenes in view where questions of religion and identity have particular prominence: Northern Ireland, Bosnia, Sudan, and Palestine/Israel.

It is evident that the end of the Cold War has left many religions in an unexpectedly strong position. This at least is the way things are widely perceived. Yet care is needed over this perception. Historians in future may well conclude that religion was already much stronger than dominant political and journalistic powers in the western world wanted us to believe. The situation in Poland, for example, is quite subtle. It is arguable that the national identity value of Catholicism in Poland was greater before 1989 than it has been since. After the formation of the non-communist government, at least some sectors of the population began to be wary of Catholic triumphalism, and enthusiasm for religion seemed to wane more than it had ever done under communist government pressure. There is no longer an Association for the Promotion of Lay Culture in Poland, and yet we may be seeing the hesitant beginnings of a new phase of secular culture in that country. At the same time, it must be admitted that the very perception of a resurgence of religions has a fly-wheel effect on their political influence, as for example in the case of Orthodoxy in Russia or Islam in the central Asian states.

All these changes in today's world mean that the study of religions, or if the looser term be preferred, "religious studies," is of greater relevance than ever before. It is quite essential for some of us to study religions, and today this inevitably means religions in the plural, whether we are positively disposed to the truth claims of any specific religion or not. It would be worthwhile to study religions simply because they are interesting. Let us not fear to point out, however, that it is necessary to study religion because of its actual importance. "Religion" refers here, of course, not merely to the formal theologies of particular churches. Rather, the scope of the study of religion extends to a wide range of movements and worldview orientations, to the ways in which meaning is projected through a great variety of symbolic systems, to patterns of behaviour and belief which are perhaps more disturbing, even violent, than those which are positively sanctioned in formal teaching or in gentle interfaith dialogues. Consider the recent storming and destruction of the mosque at Ayodhya in Uttar Pradesh, India. Consider insistent claims to land in the Near East made today, but based on biblical stories and allusions of long distant times, often simplistically presented. Such matters can only be set properly in perspective if there is a well-articulated domain of academic discourse in the study of religions. Mere journalism often fails to get it right. Politicians sometimes do not even want to get it quite right, though some do. What is "right" is a matter of evaluation and not of research. But are we not permitted to hope that study may inform good judgment and play its part in preserving humankind from further follies?

The foundation of this new South African Academy of Religion is indeed, I believe, a most auspicious occasion. It comes at a time of hope and trembling for the new South Africa, as the world awaits the first run-through of elections on the basis of universal suffrage. The creation of new institutions within such a political context sets marks for a long time to come. May this particular institution set the right marks in its chosen field, and may the fruits of its endeavours be harvested by later generations. I would like to make three further comments on this development.

First, let it be noted that the ground has been prepared by the academic labours of many over the years. Speaking for one of the sectors represented in the Academy (as Secretary-General of the International Association for the History of Religions – IAHR), it may be said that South African scholarship in this field has been internationally known and respected for a very long time. It is a matter of historical record that the South African Association for the Study of Religion has remained affiliated to the IAHR for many years throughout the period of sanctions. In spite of sanctions-related decisions taken by individual scholars in other countries, respect-worthy in themselves, it seems that the decision of our association to attempt political non-alignment, and by implication to maintain contacts through the years, has been broadly vindicated. To put it in wider context, the IAHR held two regional conferences in 1992. The first was in Beijing, China, and the second was in Harare, Zimbabwe. The conference in Harare was attended by several colleagues from South Africa. I think this perspective speaks for itself. If the IAHR has sought to be non-partisan in political terms, just as it is religiously neutral, this strategy has nevertheless been in a pro-active mode in the interests of the development of international discourse. The next major congress will be in Mexico City in 1995, and it is to be hoped that a number of scholars from South Africa will be able to attend.[4] Second, the coming into being of the South African Academy of Religion as an academic institution implies a widespread intellectual readiness to observe religion reflectively, and not merely to be swayed by it, or to use it. If the study of religion takes place in a context of rapid change, high aspirations, political tension, conflict, and in some cases tragedy, then it is quite essential to be clear-headed about the objectives and possible functions of this kind of study. A common solution is simply to adopt a severe historico-philological stance in the attempt to secure the integrity of academic study. This could be little more than a self-preserving alibi for refusing to look at the real world. However, if academics think about their own role in culture and society, then the matter has to be more complex. It would be wrong to think that just anything goes in "religious studies," yet the key lies in being able to distinguish complementary levels of discourse or steps of argument. We must differentiate between the elucidation of sources (oral, written or material), the phenomenological characterization of specific religious systems, the development of comparisons and typology, the search for theories and explanation, and the readiness to enter into debate. If such steps are adequately differentiated, then a wide range of academic discourse can be harnessed for reflective and humane understanding.

Third, the very foundation of this Academy implies a profound recognition of the plurality of religions. Studies of religion in South Africa

---

4 Retrospective note. Strikingly, the subsequent quinquennial IAHR congress in 2000 was very successfully held in Durban, in the new South Africa.

have in fact been fed over the years by a strong awareness that this plurality has a social importance. Religions arise, flourish and decline in close association with the path of specific communities, and even whole peoples, in their multiplicity. This is true for South Africa and, in an intertwined history it is true for (my own country) the United Kingdom. Without reference to religion it is hardly possible to understand national or community-based identities in either of these countries. On account of the extreme topicality of these matters therefore, but without pretending to special knowledge of South Africa, I would like to continue now by presenting some clues and threads which are relevant to the understanding of the theme of identity and religion.

The theme of "identity" has long attracted tremendous interest. This was reflected at the 1985 Congress of the IAHR, entitled "Identity Issues and World Religions" (Hayes 1986). Here, however, I leave aside the many-faceted questions about the meaning of the term, the psychological role of religion in the formation of individual personality, and the diachronic and synchronic coherence and identity of religious systems, and so on (cf. Seiwert 1986, in the proceedings). Nor will attention to be paid to the relative importance of, for example, language, ethnicity and religion for perceptions of identity.[5] The emphasis is placed here on religions as a focus of social and political identity. Among other things, religions are understood to be traditions or systems of substantial symbolic power which have their own characteristic dynamics. While languages share a common function of communication, at least within particular groups, the identity forming functions of religions are more diverse. Religions are not all of the same type, and hence they also have variable functions with respect to identity. Unfortunately the complexities of religion are often misunderstood and manipulated, sometimes wilfully, by politicians.

Primal religion and critical religion: a key distinction

Much of the confusion over questions of identity and religion arises because of a misunderstanding about the relationship between what is here called primal religion on the one hand and critical (i.e. in principle so-

---

5 In the original lecture situation this was expanded by considering the relationship of these various factors in identity perceptions of Bosnian, Serbo-Croat speaking Muslims.

teriological) religion on the other hand. The history of this distinction has not been carefully traced, but a systematic typology of religion can hardly avoid attending to it even if the proposed definitions have varied and are not all acceptable.[6] In brief, these two terms refer to (a) primal religions which are coterminous with a specific, natural society and (b) critical religions which stand in some tension to natural society and provide a differentiated perspective upon it. In the first case a specific, primal religion can be consciously identified with a natural society whose borders are believed to be known. In the second case a world-related identity comes to the fore in that soteriological or critical religions usually advance universal claims for the attention of the whole of humankind. Complications arise when this initially plausible distinction requires modification. Complexities arise out of the interactions between these two kinds of religion and even more so out of complete crossovers. A clear crossover occurs when a religion which has been thought by many to be the salvation of all humankind is pressed into service as the primal religion of one specific group which seeks to protect or promote itself alone.

For these reasons both main types of religion display ambivalent tendencies over identity. This leads to questions about change in specific religious traditions, but the specialist in religion will be interested in these not merely as circumstantial historical alteration but as questions of dynamics to be understood in terms of the overall typology.

It will be expedient to provide a brief explanation of the terms "primal religion" and "critical religion" here, before discussing the complexities which lie beyond this initial typology.[7] Some dissatisfaction has been expressed with the term "primal religion," mainly because it sounds a bit like "primitive," which has often been used as an insulting term; yet "primal" is not the same word as "primitive," and it should be permissible to use it in its own right (cf. Pye 2004a). The reference of "primal religion" has also hitherto been mainly limited to the context of small-scale and often pre-literate societies. However this limitation

---

6   Any attempt at a typology of religion must, surely, begin with selected major distinctions which help to bring out important characteristics. Going beyond a well-worn distinction between prophetic and mystical religion associated with Nathan Söderblom, Ninian Smart was engaging in this in his work *Reasons and Faiths*, when he wrote of the mystical, the numinous and the incarnational "strands" (Smart 1958).

7   The original text has been abbreviated here. For more details cf. 4.1, 4.2, 4.4 and 4.5 above.

is not obligatory. By contrast, the term is extremely useful in the analysis of contemporary Japanese religion, in a society which is highly literate and not exactly small-scale. The main value of the word "primal" is that it suggests some kind of fundamental priority, though this does not necessarily have to be a chronological one.

Primal religion notably gives recognition to the ancestral lineage of a specific family, clan or nation, and to the myths and legends which articulate it. It secures social continuity by means of rites of transition, and it secures the economic base of society, so perceived, by calendrical rites. In emergency, occasional rites are also available, for example to avert drought or epidemics, or in Britain to avert undue rainfall. Such rites may be summed up as proximate soteriology, for there is no further soteriology which goes beyond ordinary life in this finite world. The conceptual perspective is characterized by cosmological symbolism suggesting repetition and stability, in spite of known dangers. Divine power is understood to be focused or located in a particularistic and therefore polytheistic mode. Thus meaning is geographically delimited and distant, exogenous groups are of little interest except as a potential threat.

The Japanese religion Shintō is an example of a primal religion in this sense, but it has also adapted to complex developments over many centuries, and is therefore now viewed as "adjusted primal religion."[8] While Shintō in modern times has lost its comprehensive relationship to natural Japanese society, the place of primal religion in Japan has been occupied by a new amalgam from various sources, in which almost the whole population does participate. This shows that the term "primal religion" is relevant in the context of one of the world's most advanced societies, and so there is no question of any inappropriate correlation with "primitive."

The problem in social and political development is to extend the mixture and the range of any given primal religion to cater for the newly emerging parameters of the group or nation. Thus there was discourse in ancient times about the way in which the gods of different parts of Japan were related as members of a far-flung family. In fact such stories may still be heard today in country shrines. The interwovenness of the myths in all their diversity betrays a hard-won political unity which undoubtedly was paid for with much suffering. Japanese today often make a point of their ethnic homogeneity, for which they are very thankful. The reality is that in distant times they were al-

---

8   See "Shintō and the typology of religion" at 4.4 in this volume.

most certainly ethnically diverse or at least diffuse. Probably they were not so varied, objectively speaking, as the races of modern South Africa. Yet at a time of political stress the difference does not need to be great; it only needs to be perceived for it to be troublesome. Thinking along these lines, could South Africa find new, coherent symbols which take in more of its complex lineage in one single interwoven story? Or is this too simple? Does the modern equivalent to such processes lie in multiple access to a variety of symbols, which would have to be held latently available by a benevolently secular state?[9]

By contrast with primal religion a "critical" religion is one which implies that natural life as normally lived is not satisfactory and that therefore some kind of salvation or release from it is necessary. This is reflected in its typical rites: rites of initiation or incorporation and rites of reinforcement.[10] The first (e.g. Buddhist ordination and Christian baptism) incorporate the newly convinced into a community which may be both less than and more than the natural society to which they so far belonged. The second type of ritual (e.g. Buddhist *uposatha* and Christian Eucharist) maintains the critically separated individual in the new community. These two types of ritual are typical for critical religions and pertain to their fundamental nature. They can be observed especially clearly in new religious movements with a strong soteriological consciousness, which have not yet adapted heavily to the surrounding society.

Although such religions are commonly regarded as being "soteriological" or "universal" in their purport, there are some difficulties with these terms. For one thing, "soteriological" may suggest rather too firmly the function of a saviour figure (*soter*). When it comes to meditational systems such as Jainism or Buddhism, or indeed to various modern programs of self-realisation, a saviour figure may be less important, in spite of the important role of spiritual teachers. so that the term "soteriological" becomes misleading. The common point in critical religion is not "salvation" but that particular individuals, or sometimes family groups, are separated out of the natural society which is presupposed by primal religion. Thus, "leaving the household life" is not an

---

9   This would be akin to what David Chidester has called for in the conclusion to his book *Shots in the Streets, Violence and Religion in South Africa* (Chidester 1991). For a perspicacious and detailed survey of the overall situation see the same author's *Religions of South Africa* (Chidester 1992).

10 This point was stated earlier in "On comparing Buddhism and Christianity" (see 4.2 above).

idle phrase in Buddhism; rather it reflects a structuring feature based on the model of the "great renunciation" of the Buddha himself.

The term "universal religion" is also open to misunderstanding for various reasons. The universal claim of "religions of salvation or release" (cf. 4.2 in this volume) arises out of conviction that the initial critical awareness or even renunciation of daily life, and the consequently elaborated path of the believer or follower, are of value for other people as well as oneself. This is a very natural conclusion to draw. However the initial movement in which critical conviction is conceived is logically prior, and in the formative period it is usually chronologically prior. Buddhism is a clear example, for the "great renunciation" of the Buddha and his "going forth into homelessness" naturally preceded his attainment of Enlightenment, which is in turn the condition for the first proclamation of the Dhamma or teaching to his first disciples. This is illustrated in the legend about how the Buddha had to be persuaded to teach at all. He had to be beseeched three times by the god Brahmā, the story goes, who also gave him cogent arguments to consider. This demonstrates that the universal claim (i.e. the proclamation of Dhamma to others) emerges secondarily, if naturally enough, from the critical consciousness (i.e. the Awakening itself).

Another complication arises in that primal religion may also seem to advance universal claims. First, it is sometimes argued, for example in Shintō contexts, that primal religion is universal because it can be found in all societies.[11] This apologetic position seeks to maintain the position of a primal religion while coming to terms with the evident existence and impact of external societies. Second, primal religions sometimes produce their own universalizing forms; the emergence of various forms of modernized and internationalized "Hinduism" illustrates this. Although this gives rise to a host of definitional questions, such movements are best categorized as new religions. For these reasons, the concept of universalism is best avoided at this level of typological differentiation.

Crossovers and identity questions

This might all seem to be very straightforward if the picture would only remain simple in the actual history of religions. However it does not.

---

11 Cf. the discussion of the adaptive options open to Shintō in an age of internationalism in Pye 1996e.

Primal religions colour quite deeply the critical religions which arise in their midst. Critical religions, having a universal message, tend to expand their claims and pervade natural societies. Some are more "tolerant" than others, leaving things to some extent as they are (seasonal rites, sacred spots such as springs or mountains, and so on), while others take over more and more functions for themselves. In fact, even Buddhism is not as "tolerant" as is sometimes thought. In several cultures it has taken over the funeral rites, a typical feature of primal religion which has little to do with the teaching of the Buddha as such. Similarly, in South-east Asia and Sri Lanka Buddhist ordination has taken on characteristics of an adolescent rite of transition for males. Christianity has largely allowed baptism to become a rite of transition for infants, and confirmation (separated from baptism) a rite of transition for adolescents. Birth, marriage and death are times for going to church, it is often said, in societies where Christianity has become the primal norm and is no longer the critical difference.

Even more complicatedly, primal religions have not only been the matrix of critical religions which have distanced themselves dialectically (Buddhism from Brahmanism, Christianity from Judaism) but they have also given rise to secondary forms which seem to provide a universal message while claiming to represent the authentic meaning of the primal matrix. Examples are the universalising forms of "Hinduism" or some movements derived from Shintō shrines such as Kurozumikyō or Taishakyō.

The reason for these complexities is that the two main types do not exist in a socio-cultural vacuum. They interact with each other, as of course with various other social factors, and in the course of their development either type may take on significant features of the other. This leads to crossovers of intention and function between the two most fundamental types of religion. Hence there arise complications, and often confusion, in our picture of the relations between religion and identity.

Consider two examples of great worldwide importance. Christianity, as its representatives would often agree and indeed claim, is a soteriological, and therefore by extension a universal religion. Yet in its specific forms it has often been used to demonstrate the identity of apparently natural communities. Obvious examples are Catholicism in Poland during the Cold War period ("To be Polish is to be Catholic" was a current explanation), Catholicism and Protestantism in opposition in Northern Ireland, Orthodoxy and Catholicism in opposition in the Serbia and Croatia of what was Yugoslavia, and Protestantism for significant groups of whites in South Africa. Much the same may be said of

Buddhism. The teaching of Buddhism, being about release from the ills of this life, is in principle a teaching for all human beings, or sentient beings, everywhere. For this profound reason it has been recognized in modern India as able to lift people out of the discriminatory caste system. Ironically this same Buddhist movement in India, which began under the leadership of the Buddhist modernist Dr. Ambedkar, now seems to have settled down into being a mark of community identity. It is well known that Buddhism has been important in the creation of national identity in other countries such as Sri Lanka (anti-colonialist and anti-Tamil), Thailand ("to be Thai is to be Buddhist", as the saying has run), Tibet (anti-foreign and anti-Chinese), Mongolia and Buryatia (anti-Soviet, and in Mongolia recently anti-foreign), Korea and Japan (partial responses to invasive foreign culture).

When considering such matters the specialist in religion will have the usual questions about the diachronic and synchronic coherence of religious traditions in mind. He or she will also rise to the phenomenological challenge of taking the consciousness of the believer or tradition-bearer with great seriousness, whatever the apparent plausibility or implausibility of any truth-claims which may be asserted. No such sensitivities however are the concern of politicians. They understand things only too well at an instinctive level, and are able to manipulate the dynamics of religious tradition in their own interests. For example, politicians have shown themselves able to use religions whose teaching apparently transcends discrimination by caste or race to set such discriminations in place and defend them, as in the *apartheid* system. Hence great care is needed over the analysis of religious identities.

The phenomena I have mentioned are in general well known, and I have purposely chosen very obvious examples. The point here however lies in the crossover of functions which becomes of particular importance when questions of identity are considered. Primal religious systems promote and defend identity by delimitation, each reinforcing its own natural society, whereas communities such as the Christian Church or the Buddhist Saṅgha, conscious of being critically extracted from the natural situation, promote a transcultural identity. However, as soon as the critical religions pervade natural societies and take on some of the roles of primal religion in a new environment, a primal identity formation takes over and a religion which theoretically has universal implications can come to be the badge of a particular people. This in turn may lead to conflicts which seem to stand in contradiction to the original impulses of the faith in question. Religious people themselves vary in their sensitivities in this regard, and it is this which enables switches to be made between the two poles of identity. It also enables political leaders to play on religious identities in a manner which might at first be unexpected.

In conclusion, it might be thought that, academically speaking, the matter could be left to rest there. However, the needs of society are sufficiently great, and urgent, for theoretical impulses of this kind to be fed through into educational and media-led consciousness. If there is a wider understanding of such matters, then there might be more chances of dealing with them constructively in our modern pluralist societies. It is to be hoped that the understanding of theoretical matters such as these, and others mooted at this conference, will contribute to stable understandings for the benefit of all and, I may add, particularly for the benefit of the New South Africa.

Bibliographical references

Chidester, David 1991. *Shots in the Streets, Violence and Religion in South Africa.* Boston (Beacon Press).
– 1992. *Religions of South Africa.* London (Routledge).
Hayes, Victor C. (ed.) 1986. *Identity Issues and World Religions.* Netley Australia (Australian Association for the Study of Religions).
Pye, Michael 1996e. "Shintō, primal religion and international identity" in: *Marburg Journal of Religion* 1/1. : <http://www.uni-marburg.de/fb03/ivk/mjr/pdfs/1996/articles/shinto1996>.
– 2004a. *The structure of religious systems in contemporary Japan: Shintō variations on Buddhist pilgrimage. (Occasional Papers 30).* Marburg (Centre for Japanese Studies).
Smart, Ninian 1958. *Reasons and Faiths.* London (Routledge and Kegan Paul).
Seiwert, Hubert 1986. "What constitutes the identity of a religion?" in: Hayes 1986: 1–7.

The first edition of this paper was published in: 1995. "Religion and identity: clues and threads" in: de Gruchy, J. W. and Martin, S. (eds.), *Religion and the Reconstruction of Civil Society (Papers from the founding congress of the South African Academy of Religion, January 1994).* Pretoria (University of South Africa): 3–17.

7.3 Christian Churches and Political Change in Eastern Europe

This paper is based on information gathered over a period of about thirty years running to the end of the Cold War, and was first presented at the University of Bristol, England, in the winter of 1992–3 when reflection about the changing situation in wider Europe was in increased demand. Now, some twenty years later, many can no longer recall the situations reported here, and so there is all the more reason to recall this history, which in some respects remains contestable.(Apologies are tendered for the omission of accents in Czech and Polish names and terms.)

Introduction

The impressions and reflections presented here are based on a number of journeys and meetings in eastern European countries from 1961 through to the end of the Cold War. These journeys, about a dozen in all, came about for various reasons, including overland transit from western Europe to Japan and to Finland. They were undertaken, as opportunity allowed, to gauge the political and social situation with special regard to religion. My information is not based on quantitative fieldwork but rather on personal observations and in-depth conversations. Nor is the documentation at my disposal comprehensive, though it is qualitatively interesting. Similarly my reflections here are not systematically anchored in any particular academic discipline. Rather, they freely mix sociological, political and theological matters. The reportage is focused above all on the following times and places: Prague 1961, Warsaw 1974, Leipzig 1989. But these are only selected symbols of a wider pattern of associations and interests covering a huge triangle from Irkutsk in Siberia, where there is a Polish Catholic church, to Helsinki and Istanbul in the west, with their minority Russian and Greek Orthodox churches. As a matter of fact there is also a Polish Catholic church in Istanbul. For me, even Britain plays a part, for in the seventies I became conscious of the Polish, the Ukrainian and the German churches of

Leeds and Bradford, with all their special questions of ecclesiastical allegiance and cultural and ethnic identity.[1]

Prague 1961, Warsaw 1974 and Leipzig 1989 all stand for meetings of people with religious motivation and a high degree of political awareness. Prague 1961 saw the "First All-Christian Peace Assembly", and Warsaw 1974 an international assembly convened by the Polish Pax Association (not to be confused with Pax, or with Pax Christi).[2] Leipzig 1989 saw the autumn meetings in the Nikolai-Kirche, and then outside it in the form of political demonstrations which enabled East Germany to turn the corner of political change.[3] I shall be looking briefly at each of these in turn, and then offering some reflective perspectives in conclusion. If I say that I hope this may at least provoke further discussion, this is no mere polite wish; for since the end of the Cold War history has been badly abused, both with respect to Germany and to the whole of central and eastern Europe. Many people are writing it busily from a triumphalist point of view, but when they have finished it will have to be done all over again.

Czechoslovakia 1961

The "First All-Christian Peace Assembly" held in Prague (13th – 18th June 1961) was indeed a remarkable ecumenical gathering with participants from almost all of the communist countries, strong if ecclesiastically less senior participation from western Europe, and a further admixture from every continent.[4] It was arranged by an on-going organization known as the "Christian peace Conference" (Krestanska Mirova Konference) which had already held smaller meetings in Prague and which has continued, under changing conditions, up to the present day. Leadership at that time was given by the Czech theologians Josef Hromadka and Jaroslav Ondra, while notable external contributions were made by Russian Archbishop Nikodim, Rumanian Metropolitan

---

1   This interest was focused in the activities of the Community Religions Project of the Leeds University Department of Theology and Religious Studies, at that time in an early stage of development.
2   I was fortunate enough to attend these two meetings.
3   I followed these events daily in the German media from Marburg, Germany, where I was resident continuously between 1982 and 1990, and was able to discuss them later in Leipzig with residents.
4   For details and documents see Schneeberger 1961.

Justinian, Episcopalian Bishop Ting from the People's Republic of China, and Martin Niemöller from the Federal Republic of Germany. The immediate political background was the summit meeting between Kruschchev and Kennedy in Vienna, which dramatised the urgent need to manage and defuse the Cold War. Still very present in people's minds were the images of war-ravaged Europe. Reconciliation after the last calamity was still an urgent subject (as seen in a contribution by Renate Riemeck), even while many in the world seemed to be preparing the next. Caught in this trap, Martin Niemöller found himself almost apologising for repeating what he was known to have said before. The demands of the new political situation were in direct succession to those of the old. Further afield the post-war process of de-colonialisation was still taking place. In the case of Chinese participation the Cold War emerged as the successor to pre-war American involvement on that continent. Given the wide diversity of nationalities and the range of ecclesiastical traditions, it is not surprising that this meeting also saw a variety of theological standpoints and methods, which cannot all be reviewed here. Attention will have to be restricted to a few issues arising out of the perspective of the Czechoslovak hosts themselves, for they shared in the further story of events as they unfolded in their country.

It is important to realise that Josef Hromadka was an extremely accomplished theologian. Born in 1889 he had studied theology in Vienna, Basel, Heidelberg and Aberdeen. Having also studied philosophy at Prague, he became the first professor of systematic theology (in 1920) at the protestant faculty of theology named after Jan Hus. He was fortunate to spend the war years in the United States as a visiting professor at Princeton Theological Seminary, but he returned to Czechoslovakia and became Dean of the Comenius Theological Faculty in Prague. His method of correlating theology and politics was essentially dialectical and dialogical. In general terms he supported socialist policies, but considered that Christian witness concerning world issues should remain independent of political world-views. This independence means that, in the situation of Cold War, Christians were called upon not to be imprisoned by the concepts of one side, even if they approved the political judgments which their leaders made from time to time. His understanding of the necessary mode for Christian thinking may be summed up in his own words to the conference as follows:

> "It is above all important today that we come together as witnesses of the Gospel, that we work together, struggle for the right insight together and

help one another. We are divided by diverse ideological, political, sociological and racial conditions and opinions, we live in an era of tensions that can result in disastrous consequences but on the other hand may involve great promise. In such an era it is up to us with God's aid to transform this time of dangers into a time of promises. This also means that we have to understand the situation in which we find ourselves and to find the right place for our encounter."[5]

We see in this quotation an absolutely fair approach to the fact that Christians found themselves, following on the traumas of the world war, on both sides of the Cold War divide, partly through choice, but also through chance or historical circumstance. Given that Hromadka himself had *chosen* to return to post-war Czechoslovakia, it is understandable that he saw a historical function in the development of socialism, particularly over against the fascism which had invaded his country and the colonialism by major powers which had led to conflict all over the world. With this general orientation, Hromadka and many other Czechoslovak protestants were able to enjoy relative freedom of association and thought in the days leading up to the Prague Spring in 1968. At the same time, having personal knowledge of the more liberal pre-war and pre-Stalinist history of Czech socialism, Hromadka and others undoubtedly contributed to the general currency of the idea that socialism with a human face might be possible and desirable. The much larger Catholic Church in Czechoslovakia on the other hand preferred to maintain aloofness or critical distance from the state.

In 1968 Archbishop Nikodim was again in Prague for a continuation meeting of the Christian Peace Conference, but relations were strained by the political tension. After the Soviet invasion, the much tougher political line within Czechoslovakia gradually took its toll on church activities. The activities of the Christian Peace Conference were curtailed. Although the formal structures continued, there were changes in the personal position of individuals. Its general secretary Jaroslav Ondra was forced out of office, and Hromadka refused to stay as president without him. Without this leadership, and under the more difficult conditions, the dialogical relationship between Christianity and political forces naturally ossified.[6] The Christian Peace Conference continued to receive the support of Czechoslovak churches as an ecumenical

---

5   Short statement printed on conference brochure, 1961.
6   I heard an account of this phase, and about the extremely limited options which remained open, in a long talk which I was privileged to have with Jaroslav Ondra in summer 1992, just over thirty years after the first All-Christian Peace Assembly.

organization, but this was withdrawn in 1990 leaving membership up to individuals and local churches on a one-by-one basis. This change was linked to the perception that the association had been too close to the government in the intervening years. An office continues to be maintained even today on a minimal financial basis, publishing a newsletter on Christian social and political responsibility, with a special interest, now that the Cold War is over, on third world issues. The result is that although the churches now enjoy a totally different freedom to run religious affairs *per se*, their critical appraisal of political questions is currently of negligable interest. Moreover, the state of Czechoslovakia no longer exists.

A Polish perspective

Anyone who is familiar with Polish affairs will be aware that the Catholic "Pax Association," to which I will now briefly turn, was relatively close to the communist government. It is for this very reason that its activities and ideas were interesting and instructive, at least in the early 1970's, before the stage came to be dominated by Solidarnosc and the election of a Polish Pope. In 1974 Pax organized an international meeting in Warsaw to consider questions of Christian responsibility in politics, one of the main themes being the possibility of maintaining divergent world-views, i. e. Catholic and Marxist, within shared political arrangements. This particular meeting took place against the recent background of foreign minister Stefan Olszowski's visit to the Vatican (November 1973), and a sharp struggle on the part of Cardinal Wyszynski against the introduction of changes in the educational system, which he criticised in a public Christmas sermon.

Pax Association (Stowarzyszenie Pax) was a lay catholic movement which in 1972 claimed a total of 12,624 members and "candidates" (provisional, non-voting members). It described itself as "laity organized for action in public life," and was consciously distinct in its political role from the church hierarchy. Clergy could not be members, though it was of course open to them to be ideologically associated. Pax drew its funds from commercial operations, particularly in publishing. Its daily newspaper *Slowo Powsechne* (The Universal Word) had an average edition of 70,000 which more than doubled on Sundays. This was accompanied by a variety of journals, notably *Kierunki* (Trends), directed towards various sections of the population. Apart from its newspaper and weeklies books were also published, including many translations from modern western literature. Other business interests (employing over 8000 people in 1970) included factories in the chemical and engineering sectors, and a lucrative line in religious accessories. Politically Pax was securely esconced in national councils, holding five permanent seats in the Sejm under the designation PAX Parliamentary Circle.[7] The rather well known figure Boleslaw Piasecki, president of Pax, was a member of the Council of State, the country's supreme constitutional organ. Across the country the association was well organized in national groups, and correspondingly it also had representatives in local government.

Pax Association was a non-marxist organisation distinct from the Catholic church organization as such, but apparently friendly to, and clearly tolerated by, successive communist leaders in Poland. What was the explanation and the significance of its succesful existence? The simple answer, namely that it was a "fellow-travelling" arrangement which sailed particularly closely to the political powers (more closely for example than another, in some respects comparable association named Znak) is undoubtedly misleading. Its strength lay in the fact that as a political organisation it was both near to the government and far from it, indeed very far from it, except in so far as one can say that Polish governments have themselves shared in this complexity! This needs further analysis.

Pax identified three quite distinct strands of thought or allegiance which were held in a remarkable balance, or rather a syncretistic tension[8]: socialism, Catholicism and nationalism. Now these three strands need slight elucidation. By socialism was meant the acceptance of socialist political arrangements, not however the adoption of a Marxist worldview or membership of the Communist Party. The purpose of training courses, according to a Pax statement, was "to improve the manifold qualifications needed in public life." It continued: "The stress is especially on more depth in the Catholic knowledge of world view essential to anyone active in public life, eminently in a socialist state, where at every step he must meet the requirements both of the internal Christian dialogue and that with his Marxian partners."[9] In 1974 Pax members made a distinction between ideology and world-view. Ideology

---

7   Kolo Poselskie PAX.
8   For the differentiation of terms see "Syncretism versus synthesis" at 6.4 above.
9   Typescript document: "Pax Association, What it is and what it stands for", available in 1973.

meant systematic political judgments and plans, concerning which in broad terms agreement with the government could be reached. World-view (*Weltanschauung*, or in Polish, *swiat topoglad*) meant a philosophical basis which might, in particular, be atheist or not. Thus socialism, for Pax Association, was an ideology but not a world-view. Their world-view was provided by Catholicism. By Catholicism was meant a straightforward acceptance of the teachings of the hierarchy and of its pastoral role in spiritual matters, but not necessarily of the political positions adopted by leading ecclesiastical figures vis-à-vis the state. Nationalism was understood to lie in the holding high of Polish national and cultural identity over against Germans to the west and Russians to the east. This was symbolised in the feelings of affection vested in the rebuilding of the old city of Warsaw brick by brick according to original plans, as contrasted with the standard joke about the massive, Russian-donated Palace of Culture and Science being the best place *from* which to view the city. Nationalism, during the communist period, was also rooted in a profound sense that Poland, whose borders after all had been shoved significantly to the west at the end of the war, had to find a secure identity between the two powerful neighbours of its recent history.

When active members were asked (in 1973, 1974 and again in 1979), which of these three, socialism, Catholicism or nationalism, might be the most important, the answer was always quite steady, namely that they were of *equal* importance. This is of interest because in Cold War terms the position of religion in eastern Europe was commonly presented, not only from outside, simply as a question of survival under communism. But the holding of all three strands in at least temporary equilibrium suggests (and continuously suggested then) another level of complexity. There are two points to note. Firstly, it would have been possible, as seen in Czechoslovakia and elsewhere, to have debate and dialogue, conflict or cooperation, between Christianity on the one hand and Marxism or communism on the other hand, without any notable intervening reference to patriotism or nationalism. Second, while Catholicism in any case bears an intrinsic allegiance towards Rome as a focus of authority outside one's own country, it is significant that neither the Catholicism *nor* the nationalism strands in the pattern espoused by Pax pointed towards a further allegiance in Moscow.

In the Pax package therefore *two* of the three strands were not identified with Moscow-led communism, which gives these strands a kind of majority in consciousness. On this basis its leaders could afford to be quite close to the government in Warsaw, knowing that their rank and file membership were, in the main, Catholic patriots. Thus even while being politically correct to the point of being scorned as sinister by such western cold warriors who had heard of them, Pax latently symbolised the independence of Poland from Moscow. It might seem that we are left with a conundrum about which ideological element was serving which. No doubt for different people the answer was ultimately different (including the possibility of agent activity), so that a definitive answer cannot be given. Yet Pax was adept at articulating distance from Moscow, while being acceptable to the Polish government. At a level deeper than vague agreement on a socialist approach to health and transport services, is it not this very feature which made it acceptable to powerful members of the government? Further from the government was Znak, and further still the Catholic hierarchy itself. Yet Pax, by its relative closeness to the communist government, paradoxically symbolised the management of Polish affairs by Poles, who "under the circumstances" of political pressure from the east were understood naturally to be Catholics. Observing the complexities of the Pax organisation, in the early seventies, led the writer compellingly to the conclusion, that "the Russians" (as people say), except in a very general and overall military sense could not really organize or control "the Poles". Moreover, if Poland could not be controlled, however could countries such as France, Italy, the larger part of Germany or Britain, with all their irreducible special characteristics, be controlled by the Soviet system? Of course there was Soviet hegemony in eastern Europe. But the realities were far more complex than was often realised. In fact "the Soviet threat" was largely an invention with political functions of its own in the west.

In the Polish equation religion was a key factor. It compounded natural ethnic insubordination. Was religion then merely a function of a political need? It certainly was this, and today, as the Church finds itself triumphant in Poland, the basis of a new and more insidious secularisation has been laid by the disappearance of this need. Yet it was also more than this.

The subsequent developments are well known: the appearance of Catholic trade-unionism, making itself both irreproachable and attractive with the ideologically, wonderfully ambiguous name Solidarnosc; the election of a Polish Pope, surprising a majority elsewhere who had naively swallowed the Cold War propaganda that religion had been disallowed and abolished under communism; the Jaruzelski government which prudently postponed change while leaving Catholic organizations almost entirely intact. With Polish subtlety the same Jaruzelski played an important role in facilitating the change when it came after all. It seemed appropriate that the first non-communist government in the eastern bloc should be formed here, the avowed Catholic (and ZNAK member) Mazowiecki taking what seemed like endless days over this in the early autumn of 1989. But by then everybody was on the move.

Swords into ploughshares

Just as Mazowiecki was forming his government I happened to be in a train, returning from Warsaw to Berlin, and as a result of inefficiency or corruption (double sale of seat tickets) I ended up in two Polish carriages which seemed to get stuck at the station Berlin Ost, in the capital of the German Democratic Republic, while the rest of the train was routed on westwards to Hannover. The mainly Polish travellers were quite patient since they were after all only waiting to pop over into West Berlin to sell small items for relatively much money. After an hour or so, with no signs of any railway activity affecting our decoupled carriages, I called out to a couple of officials walking casually down the otherwise deserted platform asking them who was responsible for the train. "Die Deutsche Reichsbahn" came the answer immediately, but with remarkable nonchalance. I had the feeling that even though the names of the structures were still known (and the East German guards still stood adequately armed at Friedrichstraße station) the people were simply getting ready to pack up. Was our train simply going to be left there indefinitely? The officials seemed aware of the absurdity of Poles passing right through their country for a day trip on the other side of a wall which they themselves could not pass. So they took their time.

I tell this impressionistic story to indicate that by then, before the wall actually came down, it was evident that the whole of eastern and central Europe had entered an unstoppable process of change. It was partly just a generation question in the leadership, and therefore it is natural that political shifts occurred in the Soviet Union and in Hungary before they occurred in Czechoslovakia and the German Democratic Republic. By this time religious perspectives on politics were no longer so crucial. Freedom of thought had become a relatively commonplace excitement in most of the communist world. What then is the significance of Leipzig 1989 for understanding the relationships between religion and politics in this context?

The slogan "Swords into ploughshares!" (Schwerter zu Pflugscharen!) can still be seen in the Nikolaikirche in Leipzig on a poster which has taken on a historic meaning. In August 1992 it was still there, bearing a little sticker saying that the next prayers for peace would take place on the 31st, after the summer holidays (!). People in Leipzig still pray for peace, and they pray and work for the unemployed, for tolerance towards foreigners, for repentance over the conquest of the Americas by whites. The Nikolaikirche will not so easily stop being a centre of political responsibility. It should be remembered however that "Swords into ploughshares" was the slogan of the *East* German peace movement at the time of the great demonstrations in many countries (in the West) against the setting up of cruise missiles. Now it is likely that Gorbachev was influenced by the massive popular demonstration of anti-weaponry opinion in the west, as well as by the implications of the Chernobyl disaster in his own country; influenced, that is, in the direction of making peace moves at a rate faster than suited many western politicians. It is notable however that western politicians and, largely, the western media, regarded as totally insignificant the entirely visible and steadily growing peace movement in the German Democratic Republic. This movement was significant for three reasons.

Firstly it was an authentic expression of Christian conscience in a world in which the main course of political events was still determined by the Cold War. As in the case of the Prague-based Christian Peace Conference, and associated activities which there have also been in the German Democratic Republic and in Poland,[10] the possibility of Christian statements in this regard was partly dependent on the formal political positions of the respective governments, in which peace policy had played an important role. The governmental position was usually that war is caused by capitalism, imperialism and colonialism (which is indeed hard to deny). Christian calls for peace, even when sailing with this wind, had their distinctive styles and ingredients. They suggested, by their very existence, an interesting complexity of thinking and a community of responsibility with other Christians who were not the subjects of socialist states.

---

10 For example, the "Warsaw Christians peace Forum" which held a PAX-supported conference on the theme "Christians and Responsibility for Peace" on the 1st and 2nd September 1979, being the fortieth anniversary of the German attack on Poland. This meeting also enjoyed ZNAK participation.

Second, it was a reminder that there was a community of Christian existence correlating the two Germanys which was not just a tool of political expediency from either side, though it had been partly this. It is interesting that during the Cold War there was heavy financial support from western Germany for the protestant church in the east. For example the clergy training college (Predigerseminar) in Erfurt was supported from the west, and is *now* being closed since it is "no longer needed"! A community of biblical and theological scholarship had continued throughout the whole period, suffering from restrictions of access in both directions but benefiting from a common language and theological tradition. The Luther anniversary in 1983 was taken up as a major cultural event in the German Democratic Republic (with state support) because important towns in his life such as Eisleben, Erfurt, Wittenberg and Eisenach lay in its territory. But Luther was a symbol of the German language and of the Christian culture of all Germany. Interesting that East German Christians should begin quoting the prophet Micah!

Third, the peace movement in east Germany was part of that increasingly important function of the church in providing a legal, non-state area for the exchange and development of ideas relevant to contemporary questions. The general assumption in the western world, as also in some parts of eastern Europe such as Poland, was that in the German Democratic Republic thought, as such, simply did not take place. This was quite false. The mental tug-of-war of course took place in specific cultural areas, especially in that marked out by religion. Note also that music and musical education gave both a strong reminder of religious tradition and of pan-German ethnic identity. It also contributed to the imaginative extension of the peace movement, as for example in Karl Ottomar Treibmann's choral symphony "Der Frieden", first performed in Leipzig in 1984.[11] Eventually the space was created for criticism and complaints of an increasingly general kind to be aired, the prime example of this being the Monday prayers in Leipzig which ended up as mass demonstrations.

Christian responsibility however did not simply issue in the demand to be able to drive to the rich Federal Republic by the shortest possible route, instead of having to go all the way around through Hungary. As the stream of one-way travellers gathered force, it was church leaders who presented the view that Christians would not necessarily wish to join it. Christian responsibility, it was held (as by the Czech protestants

---

11 Text by Volker Braun.

referred to earlier), should be exercised in the place where one *is*. In this they had grass roots support, for at the Nikolai-Kirche demonstrations, the placards saying "wir wollen raus" (we want out) were matched by others saying "Wir bleiben" (we're staying). There were, moreover, several churchmen who attempted to play a constructive political role in the unity process while it was still understood as a process of growing together. In other words, the concept of social responsibility as developed in the German Democratic Republic was one which they did not regard as simply dispensable. In the end, however, the idealistic, positive aspects of the revolution as seen from within eastern Germany, were hijacked in favour of rapid currency union and annexation.

Some concluding reflections

The "Christian Peace Conference" in Czechoslovakia at its best strongly confronted the spectre of war; and it sought ways of overcoming both nationalism and rigid ideological confrontation which were rightly discerned as major causes of war. Leading figures such as Hromadka and Ondra (partly through association with Niemöller) demonstrated the ability of theology to establish its own dialectical freedom while not abdicating political responsibility. The Pax Association in Poland was instructive especially for the Polish situation itself. The very fact that it was the form of Catholicism which operated most closely to Communism showed in the early 1970's that Communism could never exclusively rule minds, and moreover that the Soviet Union could not successfully dominate its client states. The Leipzig story is a wonderful story of shifting human consciousness, leading to the opening of the borders and the fall of the wall. It is also a revolution which was hijacked and betrayed.

The revolution in Eastern Europe has had three catastrophic results which were not expected except by a few critics. These are: (1) large-scale economic misery, for no simple transition to entrepreneurial "capitalism" was ever possible on such a scale; (2) widespread deterioration in human behaviour, for ethics have become optional and "me-first" values have largely replaced social values; and (3) warfare based on nationalism. The relation of religion to these three areas of concern is of course varied and will be interesting to observe and analyse in coming years. Here are a few perspectives.

With regard to the first it is unlikely that some astonishing new protestant work-ethic will emerge which is able to drive forward an economic miracle for half a billion people. Rather, religion will provide a comfort and an escape, especially in Poland, the Baltic states, Ukraine, Byelorus and Russia; in other words it will indeed be one of the drugs of which the masses will make use. There is nothing wrong with taking comfort in religion, for those who wish to, but cynical connivance with this function of religion by others who themselves despise it is surely deplorable.

With regard to the second, personal morality will struggle with self-interest, and in Poland for example this will lead to some secularisation now that the question of national identity and independence is resolved. Catholic influence on legislation is enjoying totally new possibilities in that country at least, as seen in the recently passed anti-abortion law. However the various newly independent states as such, priding themselves on being less repressive than the communist system, have little control over the commercialisation of vice. In such a climate religious leaders alone will be, and indeed already are relatively helpless in the face of massive increases in drug-peddling, prostitution and violent crime. The contribution of non-traditional religions or meditation cults of Asian derivation, which have attracted surreptitious interest for many years but now flourish openly, will also be extremely marginal when it comes to patterns of private and public morality. In general different societies tend to permit different kinds of immorality and crime, and the relation between privilege and corruption is partly a matter of tradition and definition. As yet there are few grounds to assert that there has been a real improvement since the end of communism, or even to hope that there will be.

As to the third consequence, the picture is extremely bleak. The Baltic states have lived (survived) and not died by nationalism, at least so far. Estonians and other east Europeans appeared shocked and disbelieving when I publicly warned against this danger at a conference in Helsinki in early 1990. However, as is well known, but increasingly little reported, there has been fighting on ethnic and religious lines in several parts of the former Soviet Union. It did not even wait for the Communist Party to be formally disestablished. The Armenian-Azerbhaijani conflict was already raging in summer 1990, and described to me by an Azerbhaijani as "war". Similarly scorn for a perfectly acceptable form of secular multi-nationalism and multi-culturalism has destroyed Yugoslavia. For this, all who in the last few years (like German foreign minister Dietrich Genscher) have urged the rapid recognition of new independent nations (such as Croatia and the rest), bear some responsibility. It is not so long ago that the Helsinki accords were hailed as progressive in that future boundary changes were to be eschewed! In the absence of other social ideals these nationalist "solutions" demand an ethnic and religious coherence which in most cases simply cannot be brought about without bloodshed and destruction. There is always some kind of minority to repress and destroy. The Neo-Nazis in Germany are simply the most sensationalised version of this trend. Christians should be the first, and not the last, to realise that religion has already been catastrophically misused all over Europe in this regard. Yet once again, and not least in Russia itself (where the churches have admittedly suffered much), religion is being harnessed for petty, or not so petty, nationalist ends. Thus in central Siberia, July 1990, I was treated to a two-hour harangue in favour of the triumphalist renascence of the Russian Orthodox Church in tandem with Czarism. This trend has only been stiffened in the meantime by intensive Protestant and Catholic proselytization in the Orthodox sphere of influence. Is all this a successful conclusion to the Cold War? Not at all. At the time of writing (December 1992) the conclusion has not yet even been played through; there are tragedies still waiting to occur.

These may seem rather pessimistic conclusions to draw. It is, however, easy for religiously oriented people to delude themselves. Religions, mainly well-known forms of Christianity but also Islam and some others, have survived far more effectively in communist countries than many propagandists wanted us to believe could be possible. Admittedly there have been restrictions, sufferings, even persecutions. Such things have been known under other political systems too. But religion has assisted, both in the examples considered and in various other cases too, in the creation of social and ultimately political space. This has partly been due to its function in defining ethnicity, as, very clearly, in Poland. Yet it has also been partly due to the ideologically critical or evaluatory dimension of Christian faith, which is by no means ethnically determined.

Judgments about this have differed and will differ; this dimension of religious consciousness has sometimes been exercised in conflict and sometimes in dialogue with communism or socialism. But those who sought the continuation of religious thought in difficult, and sometimes extremely difficult, political circumstances should be honoured. What does this mean? It means that we should not lightly disregard the critically conscious religious call to social and political responsibilities. In the aftermath of the euphoria felt by many at the end of the Cold War, social and international construction has to be started all over again. It also means that we should not accept simplistic accounts of the past, and merely swallow undifferentiated versions of all these events without further enquiry. The categories of the Cold War itself do *not* provide the means for understanding either the communist period or the lives of those who lived during it.

Bibliographical references

Schneeberger, V.D. 1961. *And on Earth Peace. Documents of the First All-Christian Peace Assembly.* Prague (The Christian Peace Conference).

This article was first published in: Gill, Sean, D'Costa, Gavin and King, Ursula (eds.) *Religion in Europe, Contemporary Perspectives*, Kampen, Netherlands 1994: 188–200.

7.4 Reflecting on the Plurality of Religions

The first draft of this paper goes back to a conference of the International Interfaith Centre at Westminster College, Oxford in April 1995. It then appeared in the journal of the UK based World Congress of Faiths, "World Faiths Encounter." The main purpose is to explore the significance of a shared presupposition of the academic study of religions and the active development of interfaith relations, namely the fact of the plurality of religions.

Tensions

The academic study of religions and the activity of cultivating good relations and dialogue between religions, or faiths, share one profoundly important presupposition, namely the recognition that human culture in fact knows a plurality of religions. Hence the title of this paper "Reflecting on the plurality of religions," originally written for a conference of the International Interfaith Centre at Oxford in the UK.[1] This deep-seated recognition underlies the recent establishment of the International Interfaith Centre, which seeks to correlate interfaith activity with an appropriate program of academic research and exchange. The question posed for the conference was whether these two activities can really be fitted together. Does or can the study of religions, pursued in an academic manner, really promote good interfaith relations? Or does it just upset religious people by disturbing the basis of their faith, and thereby have a negative effect on the positive dialogue they might otherwise achieve if left to their own devices?

Even when the *de facto* plurality of religions is recognised, there are markedly divergent ways of dealing with it which all have their own intellectual and motivational strengths and weaknesses. The arguments and the psychology are often mixed. Negatively appraised, they range, for example, from an exclusivism which is sharp-witted but essentially self-protective, to an inclusivism which is undiscerning, patronising and in the last analysis self-advancing.

---

1 Opening lecture, April 19th 1995.

Positively appraised, we may note philosophically sophisticated accounts of an underlying coherence between religious traditions. Even those espousing such positions in their capacity as "academics" have usually arrived at them as a result of important personal experience and observation, as in the interesting case of John Hick.[2] Also in positive vein, we may note the generous spirit emanating from a good number of religious groups which, among their other activities, make a point of promoting positive relations between religions in their plurality. This generous spirit in many cases derives from the freely ranging far-sightedness of religious leaders and founders such as Guru Nanak, Sot'aesan or Niwano Nikkyō, or from the indirect influence of particular individuals such as Thomas Merton or Abe Masao. In both cases long lists could be adduced here. There are indeed many praiseworthy things done by human beings, especially when they are open to the perspectives offered by their religious experience; and it is good to find ways of celebrating this in ways appropriate to the radically interdependent, one world of today. Those active in interreligious activities have played an important role here.

It seems natural to expect the reflective study of religion, carried on "academically," to contribute on the positive side to this extremely important intercultural development. Yet there may be a slight hesitation on the part of many, simply because of the inconvenient questions which sometimes arise and which might be thought to hold up the progress of interfaith relations. After all there has been a long history, at least since the time of the European Enlightenment, of reflective and more or less critical studies creating a religious disturbance.

Most simply, this disturbance occurs at the level of historical fact. Many statements made by religious people contain assertions about matters of historical fact which, on independent enquiry, turn out not to be the case. Some of the epistles of the Apostle Paul were not written by the Apostle Paul. The Gospel According to Saint Matthew was not written before the Gospel According to Saint Mark, but after it. The texts "discovered" by the Mormon founder Joseph Smith were not written in Egyptian. The Shroud of Turin does not bear the imprint of the face of the historical Jesus. The sūtras of Mahāyāna Buddhism were not uttered by the historical Buddha but came into being at earliest some five hundred years later. Indeed it is hard to find a religion in which there are no statements about some favoured text or an object

---

2   This is set out in his own words in *Disputed Questions* Hick 1993: 139 ff.

of reverence which turn out not to be true. This even applies to Zen Buddhism, which sometimes claims not to depend on statements at all but whose promoters constantly peddle tales about Bodhidharma and Hui Neng which are historically worthless.

It might be argued that it does not matter if religious people like to cherish favoured beliefs which dull historians know not to be factual. However, difficulties may arise when specialists in religion are drawn into religious activities and enterprises, especially those with an interfaith dimension.

It is a commonplace that history is not just a collection of facts. More importantly, it is a way, or competing ways, of viewing and interpreting the past. But it is still possible to be wrong about the facts. It may be regarded as most impolite to refer to such matters in the context of interfaith dialogue. But can the world of religious dialogue afford to take all religious statements from all quarters at their face value? Is the polite acceptance of self-delusion, or the delusion of others, the best basis for a joint enterprise in search of the truth?

The academic study of religions is not only historical. It is also comparative and analytical. In this sense it includes morphological and typological studies which arise out of phenomenological investigations. It also includes explanatory analyses of a sociological or psychological kind. All of these studies, not just those which are sociological or psychological, are likely at some point to run into conflict with the self-understanding of the believers themselves.

In today's world there is, further, a wide range of extremely important ethical questions which affect us all. Indeed this is probably the most urgent area in which religious leaders and indeed whole religious communities need to share their underlying beliefs and current appraisals. In this context, issue-related academic enquiry may also have a significant role to play. It is possible and probably desirable for academics with a professional knowledge of religions to mediate in high-level dialogues between religious parties. Such mediation consists in part in being cultural interpreters. Should it also consist in making a contribution to the setting of the agenda itself, and in proposing new ethical directions in our rapidly changing global situation? Here too the academics are likely to cut across the received positions of particular religious authorities, particularly where these are relatively clear-cut as in the case of the main Islamic authorities, the Roman Catholic Church and Evangelical Protestantism.

In spite of all the opportunities for tension, I would like to return to the point that the academic study of religions and interfaith dialogue do share one important presupposition, namely the sheer recognition of the fact that religions are more than one in number. Naturally enough, there then occurs a divergence. In the academic sphere the recognition of this plurality has led to the reflective and critically alert study of religions. In the case of interfaith relations, the recognition of plurality leads to the launching of programs to cope with it religiously. These two trends have often overlapped each other, providing mutual stimulation, assistance and it must be said, in some cases, confusion. But where does the presupposition come from? After all, this simple recognition was not, and indeed still is not always present in all minds.

I believe it is possible to discern long-term threads in the general history of religions which help to clarify the matrix both of the academic study of religions, world-wide, and of the various attempts to spur good relations between religions which, at least superficially, are different. In particular, there seems to be an organic relationship between religious innovation, religious pluralism, and considered reflection on religion. To use other terminology, there is a relationship between religious change (which involves innovation as well as decay), religious encounter and religious studies! These are very long-term matters, and their history can be viewed and told in various ways. If time permitted it would be interesting to draw a detailed comparison between the emergence of reflection on the plurality of religion in Europe on the one hand and in the leading cultures of Asia on the other hand. Here, only the briefest of suggestions can be offered.

Asian angles

Contemporary scholarship in the study of religions is currently quite active in most Asian countries, but I am not seeking to review it here. Rather I wish to point out a few aspects in the development of thought about religious pluralism which predate extensive intellectual interaction with the western world. The autonomous intellectual development in this regard is frequently underestimated in Europe and America.

One way of reading the history of Jainism and Buddhism is to see these religions as an innovatory challenge to the Brahmanism which existed at the time of their emergence. Because of the state of the sources it is easier to pursue the details with respect to early Buddhism. One of the important features of the impact of Jainism and Buddhism was their renunciation of the normal patterns of everyday life, as regulated by the religion of the day. This created, irreversibly for India, the possibility of intellectual distance in matters of religion. As to pluralism, it is clear from the early Buddhist texts that a more or less polemical relationship existed between Brahmanism on the one hand and Jainism and Buddhism on the other hand. The recognition of this diversity was the direct result of the innovations in religious life which had occurred.

What then of China?[3] The concept of "three teachings" indicates a frame of reference which has characterised Chinese views of religion for centuries and which has greatly influenced neighbouring countries such as Korea and Japan. In the last century or two we have got used to religions in East Asia being counted differently, and not necessarily as "three." On the other hand it is difficult to go back to a time in Chinese history when it was not consciously recognized that there were at least two religions. Moreover the *relationship* between the various teachings has been a matter of discussion ever since Buddhism was introduced into China, and it is in this context that the concept of "three teachings" arose. While *jiào*, unlike *dào*, admittedly suggests "teaching," rather than "way" or "practice," it should be remembered that it is after all a Chinese term and not a foreign one. Moreover a particular *jiào* can easily be understood to have a behavioural, a self-disciplinary or a mystical dimension.

It is important to notice that giving prominence to the concept of "three teachings" does not necessarily imply a particular standpoint or decision about *how* these teachings are, or were, related. "Three teachings" is an interesting frame of reference precisely because it has been interpreted in various ways. Often it has been used to support a synthesist view of religion. This leads to statements such as "the three teachings are one." However it may also imply a critical recognition of the plurality of religions. The direction in which it is taken depends on which author one reads, and how one reads. The suggestion made here is that the concept of "three teachings" be regarded as summing up a frame of reference which, at its best, gives rise to critical reflection on religions in their plurality. If so, may it not be seen as one of the starting points for the modern study of religion in a Chinese perspective? It appears that the very short "Treatise on the three teachings" (*Sānjiào lùn*) by

---

3 . For more details on the following, see "Three teachings (*sānjiào*) theory and modern reflection on religion" at 2.4 above.

the first Ming Emperor (reigned 1368–1398) was particularly influential in setting this frame of reference.[4]

The "three teachings" concept had a later development in the critical works of the Japanese writer Tominaga Nakamoto (Tominaga being the family name). Since Tominaga lived during the first half of the eighteenth century he was a contemporary of European "Enlightenment" figures such as Lessing, although he (and the Europeans) were quite unaware of each other. Tominaga argued against a synthesist view of the three teachings, and questioned the restriction of a positive interpretation of religious meaning to three religions only. Why should one not consider more than three, he argued. It is important to note that when he used the term "three teachings" as a chapter heading to indicate his subject matter, what he meant was something like "religions in their plurality and in their interrelationships." Thus we see in his writings the beginnings of what is referred to in some European languages as a "science of religions." In this case it is framed by the long-established concept of "three teachings," but it is *not* determined by a religious point of view.[5]

In some descriptions of Chinese religion there is a tendency to emphasize the practical harmony which has often existed between the various religions in their plurality in China. However the main point being made here is a little different. I do not necessarily seek to emphasise the practical harmony of "three teachings." Rather I am suggesting that recognition of religions in their plurality is a fundamental frame of reference in terms of which the study of religions can be carried out. This is different from, for example, a frame of reference which conceives of the study of "other" religions (i.e. "other" than the dominant one) or of the study of "popular" religion (rather than the official one). These latter frames of reference are common in Europe and in Latin America respectively.

European angles

The history of how and why "comparative religion" arose in Europe cannot be pursued in detail here. However a few comments upon it are needed to complement the Asian angles referred to already. The

---

4   See in particular Taylor 1983 as well as 2.4 above.
5   See translations and introduction in Pye 1990a. The point made here was addressed in detail in Pye 1984.

question is part of a wider question as to how the study of religion in general, or the "science of religion (*Religionswissenschaft*) has arisen and developed. In the western world this may be regarded, very broadly, as arising from a combination of (a) the historical and philosophical critiques of Christianity, which have partly taken place within theology itself, (b) the extensive additional knowledge made available by the growth of oriental studies, and (c) the impact of the social sciences: social anthropology, sociology, psychology and social psychology.

It is important to note that there are alternative views of intellectual history as affecting the development of comparative studies of religion. In his *Comparative Religion, A History* Eric Sharpe regards the advent of Darwinism or evolutionism as the major trigger for the development of comparative religion, and Max Müller as the "father" of this subject.[6] Peter Harrison however, I think rightly, sees the emergence of the "science of religion" as occurring substantially in the late seventeenth and early eighteenth centuries, i.e. with Deism and the Enlightenment (Harrison 1990). While there is something to be said for both of these views, for much turns on definitions, it is notable that *both* are entirely eurocentric. The truth is, as has been seen above, that comparative religion also appeared in a certain way in East Asia. This took place with particular clarity in eighteenth century Japan, where it continued to develop, if fitfully, through to present times. Currently the academic study of religions is well established, with variations relating to the current situation, in China, Korea and Japan.

It should also be noted that the development of comparative religion (or more generally, the study of religions) in Europe and America has not only been an aspect of the history of ideas. The subject has been and still is determined by the socio-political environment. This aspect really requires further thorough review under the following headings: 1) discovery and colonialism; 2) missionary activity; 3) exoticism and orientalism; 4) the cold war and the end of the cold war; 5) oil; 6) social needs in pluralist societies.

Within the European field the emergence of the "history of religions" (including comparative religion) in Germany is of particular interest. It may be seen as the result of a dual thrust coming (a) from philological and oriental studies *towards* theology and (b) from theology *towards* the study of various religions. The first thrust (a) led to the "history of religions" school (*religionsgeschichtliche Schule*), which emphasised

---

6   Sharpe 1975: Chapter 2, esp. Page 35.

the religiously complex origins of both Israelite and Christian religion (from Wrede to Bultmann), and studied these on the basis of uncompromisingly historical presuppositions. In this group Ernst Troeltsch is of particular importance in providing connections with wider questions in theology and the philosophy of history. A second tradition (b) which I propose to call "the German religion and religions" school, runs from Schleiermacher through Otto to Heiler, possibly including others such as Söderblom (who, though Swedish, spent part of his life in Berlin), Wach and Ratschow, diverse though these various figures are. The linkage between these occurs because of a network of assumptions, namely: that an inward experience is the determining feature of religion, that this experience is known positively in many religions, and that the details, when investigated, show that Christianity is the clearest and ultimately the most valuable form of religion.

The first of these schools, i.e. the "history of religions" school, tended to disrupt the sense of security of protestant Christianity, especially as the implications were drawn out by Troeltsch and by Bultmann. The second on the other hand tended to establish it, for the diversity of religions was embraced positively, but at the same time drawn into the controlling orbit of Christian dogmatics.

To some extent these two trends are found again in French studies of religion, themselves contextualised by the Catholic religion and its critique. Important early figures here are Chateaubriand, Alfred Loisy (a Catholic modernist sparring partner for Harnack) and Ernest Renan, after whom is named the French association for the history of religions. These figures have been regarded as threats to Christianity. Ugo Bianchi has pointedly argued (Bianchi 1989) that studies of religion by specialists remaining loyal to Catholic theology benefit (as compared with much protestantism) from the assumption that truths of reason and hence natural theology may be present in non-Christian religions. These are thought by such researchers to be worthy of exploration if only as a clarification of the ground for evangelism. At the same time the Catholic faith itself is preserved from unwelcome attention, he suggests, since it is fenced around with the category of revelation.

Returning to the two Protestant schools mentioned above, it is ironic that the representatives of the "religion and religions" school such as Otto, Heiler and Ratschow, in spite of the generous perspective which they display, tend in the last analysis to be less useful for the interfaith dialogue of today. This is because, in the end, they draw everything back into their own religious perspective. The "history of religions school," on the other hand, though in the eyes of many Christians more threatening to the religious faith of their own tradition, goes further in providing a secure basis for interfaith explorations of religion. While those who set store by the "religion and religions" school still continue even today to pose their questions about "other religions," the line of thought emanating from the "history of religions" school sees all religious traditions as equally available in human cultural history from the start. Incidentally, although the challenge of this line of thought was first addressed to Christian theology, it is just as relevant to representatives of other religions who continue to approach questions about the relations between religions on the basis of the prior, or final superiority of their own religion.

Conclusions

As has been seen, any attempts to view religions in their plurality, in a conspectual frame of reference, involves the intellectual act of comparison. The academic study of religions, or more loosely, Religious Studies, cannot avoid the question of comparison. Even if not approached consciously, it will creep back in somehow. Comparison, or comparisons, depend partly on the detail of specific studies; but as we have also seen, the frame of reference can be culturally varied and is of great importance. Unfortunately the work of refining an interculturally based frame of reference is still in progress. Indeed, it is still in its infancy. A relevant perspective from the Chinese cultural area was adduced above, but there are contributory perspectives to be derived from other important parts of the world, for example from Latin America and from Africa. Correlating these perspectives is not the same as simply imposing one of them. There is a complex, shared endeavour to be undertaken here.

Those who engage in the academic study of religions, that is, the historical and comparative study of religions and all that flows from it, can make common cause with those who, in the interest of developing interfaith relations, are prepared to accept the critically open analysis of religious traditions as these have in fact developed. If this is the basis of our work, there is no inherent reason why one of these two lines of endeavour should be thought to threaten the other. On the other hand, admittedly, they may jointly threaten some of the entrenched religious positions which prefer to remain intellectually closed. In other words, there will be questions; but at their best, the academic study of religions and interfaith activities may be viewed as non-contradictory and complementary. I therefore conclude by asserting the importance of (i) the multi-focal and multi-cultural derivation of the comparative study of religions, and (ii) clarity in the relations between study or research on the one hand and encounter or dialogue on the other hand. If these are kept in mind, our common attention to religions in their plurality can be both critically aware and constructive in effect.

Bibliographical references

Bianchi, Ugo 1989. "The study of religion in the context of Catholic culture" in: Pye, Michael (ed.) *Marburg Revisited, Institutions and Strategies in the Study of Religion*. Marburg (Diagonal-Verlag): 49–53.
Harrison, Peter 1990. *Religion and Religions in the English Enlightenment*. Cambridge (Cambridge University Press).
Hick, John 1993. *Disputed Questions*. London (Macmillan).
Pye, Michael 1984. "Tominaga Nakamoto (1715–1746) and religious pluralism" in Daniels, G. (ed.) *Europe Interprets Japan*, Tenterden (Paul Norbury):191–7.
– 1990a. (trans.) *Emerging from Meditation (Tominaga Nakamoto)*. London (Duckworth) and Honolulu (University of Hawaii Press).
Sharpe, Eric 1975. *Comparative Religion, A History*. London (Duckworth).
Taylor, Romeyn 1983. "An imperial endorsement of syncretism, Ming T'ai Tsu's essay on the three teachings, translation and commentary" in: *Ming Studies* 16: 31–49.

Earlier versions of this paper were published in: *World Faiths Encounter* 14 (July 1996), 3–11 (shorter version); and *Marburg Journal of Religion*, Volume 2, No. 1 (May 1997) at http://www.uni-marburg.de/fb03/ivk/mjr/pdfs/1997/articles/pye1997.pdf (a longer version with some additional examples).

7.5 The Study of Religions and the Dialogue of Religions

The article draws in particular on two lectures given at universities with a Buddhist orientation, Ōtani University in Kyōto, Japan, and Wongkwang University at Iksan, Korea. The resultant text has been correlated with "Peace in the Dialogue of Religions" at 7.7 below. Various themes which have been treated more extensively in other articles above are only briefly adduced here as necessary for the sequence of the argument.

Distinguishing between science of religions and dialogue of religions

The purpose of this article is to consider some of the ways in which the academic study of religions may be able to assist in the continuing process of dialogue between religions. To do this, it is necessary first to distinguish clearly between the two. The academic, scientific study of religions (science of religions, or *Religionswissenschaft*)[1] is itself a non-religious activity. It is agreed in many quarters, and here, that it should not be confused with theological and dialogical activities which have their own *rationale*. The dialogue between religions, for its part, certainly is in some sense a religious activity. It involves the presentation and exchange of religious experiences and religious positions. It is possible for such dialogues to take place without reference to the academic, scientific study of religions. Indeed this often happens. Yet it is conceivable that those involved in such dialogues might benefit from the perspectives which this discipline opens up. The present article, based on earlier presentations, makes some suggestions in this direction.[2]

---

1 The regular German term *Religionswissenschaft* is more compact, and a comparable term in Japanese is *shūkyōgaku*.
2 The article draws in particular on two lectures given at universities with a Buddhist orientation, Ōtani University in Kyōto, Japan, and Wongkwang University at Iksan, Korea. The lecture for Wonkwang University (2006) is the basis for "Peace in the Dialogue of Religions" at 7.7 below, but a section entitled

Since the study of religions is in principle a *non*-religious, scientific undertaking, it does not, as a secular enterprise, promote or contribute to religious programmes. This may seem to suggest that there is not and should not be any relationship between the study of religions and dialogue between religions. From one point of view this is correct. How can "the study of religions" have an involvement with any dialogues between religions at all, apart from simply observing them? Indeed, it would be easy for specialists in the study of religions simply to withdraw from the arena of public discussion. This would be legitimate in itself, and some specialists may prefer to adopt such a course, perhaps claiming purism. However, if we are not oblivious to the human situation as a whole, and if we take the totality of society and culture seriously, perhaps something more may be expected, even from careful specialists. Nor do the necessary distinctions need to be obscured.

The strict view of the "science of religions" is not just a contemporary fashion, nor a western invention. It was anticipated in a statement by the eighteenth century Japanese thinker Tominaga Nakamoto, at the end of chapter 24 of his *Shutsujōkōgo*, where he says "I am not a follower of Confucianism, nor of Daoism, nor of Buddhism. I watch their words and deeds from the side and then privately debate them." (Pye 1990a: 168). In principle, agreement with this view is presupposed here. Only a science of religion which is independent of particular religious viewpoints can be expected to carry out steady, systematic observation and provide a worthwhile analysis of religious systems.[3]

"Observation" in this context does not merely mean looking. Rather it implies looking *at* with a view to understanding, analysing and explaining. In other words it implies the full range of "scientific" reflection in relation to the particular field of religious systems. While this is not the place to provide a general introduction to the methods and

---

"How can religious dialogues be structured?" has been used here. Thanks are also due to the organisers of a lecture and seminar programme at Ōtani University in October 2000, which was conceived as a continuation of the 3rd Rudolf Otto Symposium held in Marburg 1999 (see further below). For a formalised version of this lecture (first delivered in Japanese) see Pye 2001b. Two sections of that lecture, entitled "Dominant models of religion dependent on cultural difference" and "On taking account of all four main aspects of religion" are omitted here because the themes have already been treated in other papers above.

3 Cf. for example, Pye 1994b, 1999a (and at 1.2 above), 2000a (and in part at 1.3 above), 2000b (and at 1.5 above).

theory of the study of religions (cf. 1.1 and 1.2 in Volume One above), it may be helpful to recall the four main steps in such research. They can be set out as follows:

(preliminary theory)
    (1) elucidation
    (2) characterization
    (3) analysis
    (4) correlation
      ...(subsequent theory)

Of these the first two steps are "recognitional" in that they are concerned with perceiving and understanding religious phenomena. The second two are "explanatory" in that they *explain* both by means of an analysis of internal structures (step 3) and by establishing correlations with other social and cultural factors (step 4). While moving through these four steps, both the relevance of comparison and the possibility of tension with the believers increases. This may be referred to as the "tension with believers factor" or TWB factor (cf. 1.6 above). It is important for those who study religions to be aware of the varying level of this "tension with believers factor." If it is high during the recognitional steps, there is something wrong with the method of enquiry! If it is untypically low during the explanatory steps, this may suggest that the explanations are weak, or it may suggest something interesting about the nature of the religion under study.

    It is important therefore clearly to distinguish between the activity of carrying out religious dialogues and the activity of studying religions as systems. Religious dialogues may be part of the field of study. Because of the complexity of the field of study, which is not only a historical field but also a living, active part of contemporary culture, it is natural for the specialist to be drawn close to the events of the day, and in a certain sense to participate in them. This is an opportunity for participant observation, and sometimes even of observant participation. In addition to this normal feature of a research process, it is also possible, and indeed probable, that some of the theoretical perspectives of the study of religions could be relevant to the future progress of dialogues between religions. In the next section therefore a few reasons will be adduced for encouraging a close proximity between the study of religions and the various activities of religious dialogue.

Why is the study of religions relevant to the dialogue of religions?

The representatives of various religious organisations who engage in dialogues with each other are usually most sincere and respectful in their approach. However, even with the best of intentions it is possible for misunderstandings to occur. How can a real dialogue between religions come about unless accurate information and instructive analysis is available? It may be helpful therefore if specialists in the study of religions are permitted in some way to share in dialogue events when they take place. Even though they do not *represent* a particular religion, they may nevertheless be able to assist in the work of elucidation and analysis. Thus their participation may help to stabilise and facilitate the process of dialogue in particular situations.

What sometimes happens is that the more sensitive participants in a dialogue between religions, after making their first contact, in effect leave their committed positions to one side and begin to take up the study of religions for themselves. They realise and understand that accurate and reliable knowledge is required, not only about their own religion, but about the other religion also. They may also press forward to a comparative analysis. Dietrich Korsch, for example, a systematic theologian participating in the 1999 Symposium in Marburg between Shin Buddhism and Protestant Theology, noticed that it would be interesting to analyse comparatively the formal structures of different religions. (Barth et al. 2000: 163–164) Since such an analysis would be independent of the specific details of the belief contents of any particular religion, it amounts to a reinvention of the science of religion, or at least of part of it. It would be similar to what has earlier been called "comparative hermeneutics" (Pye and Morgan 1973), and more generally it would be related to the analysis of the dynamics of religious tradition, that is to questions about transmission, adjustment, correlation, and so on.

Of course, this process of analysis does not *always* take place. In some cases, after an initial exploration, a concluding solution is found by some of the dialogue partners which simply favours the "home" religion. In that case no further information is really perceived to be necessary. In other words the *religious* position becomes dominant again, and "the study of religions" is left to one side. If a person has faith in "the name of Jesus" for example, why should he or she be interested in studying various religions and analysing their similarities? It will probably seem to such a person to be more valuable to emphasise difference. The same thought may occur to a person who has faith in Amida's fundamental vow (*hongan*). However, while such simple faith may be necessary, and even sufficient, for living and dying, the questions of reason remain, even if they are secondary questions. Thus, as soon as we begin to *think* about it all, the study of religions in a comparative perspective inevitably arises once again.

Finally, and not least important, social and political discussions about the legal position of various religions are being carried out today as never before, although these discussions also have a considerable history. Should historically strong religions like Christianity, Islam, Buddhism or Shintō have a privileged position in society, or not? If so, what about newer, smaller religious groups and movements, of which there are very many? Should these even be permitted to exist? Religions which have come under criticism recently from this point of view are Aum Shinrikyō (in Japan), Scientology (in Germany) and Falungong (in China). These have all been regarded, with greater or less evidence being adduced, as threatening to undermine established society. At the time of their origins, the same was said with regard to Buddhism and Christianity. Of course, all of these religions are not just the same as each other. Moreover some cause more social disruption and suffering than others. But how will social commentators, journalists and politicians be able to discuss these matters properly unless they have clear and reliable information about the various religions in question? For this, the study of religions is necessary.

With all this in mind, it appears that it would be valuable for those engaged in religious dialogues to take "the study of religions" seriously and to assist in its development. This is not because specialists in the study of religions necessarily have more knowledge at their disposal. In fact, when a specialised dialogue is taking place the representatives on each side are almost certain to have more specialised knowledge, at least about their own side. In wider discussions, however, the study of religions as a discipline may be able to provide a theoretical and comparative reference point or perspective which can be shared by those who otherwise have different religious or other convictions.

A shared presupposition

A most important underlying presupposition which is shared by the scientific study of religions and all forms of religious dialogue, different though these are, is the perception of the plurality of religions as a state of affairs (cf. 7.4 above). Significantly, it was one of the starting points for the European Enlightenment's reflection about religion, and at the same time for the eighteenth century Japanese thinker Tominaga Nakamoto who was quoted above. It is significant that the quotation was drawn from his chapter on the "three teachings" (sankyō 三教), a well-known Chinese expression (sānjiào) which sums up the *plurality* of religions in one simple phrase. In the study of religions itself, therefore, the perception of the plurality of religions is not problematic. It is a natural state of affairs.

This presupposition can be seen in a discussion paper by sociologist of religion Peter Berger, published in the first issue of the journal *Buddhist-Christian Studies* in which he discussed "the pluralistic situation" and "the coming dialogue" between the world religions, as he referred to them. (Berger 1981: 31–41) His concluding question was how two religions, such as Buddhism and Christianity, can be "true *together*"? This question replaces the older western questions about *which* religion is true, and why. However we should not get carried away here by the idea that there might be an easy solution to the new questions. Even if some Buddhists and some Christians agree on a selected "something" there are so many religions in the world as a whole that it is difficult to see how they can all be true "together" unless the statements which they make, or which arise by implication, are relatively meaningless. So there remains an open philosophical question about the nature of truth claims in religion and the criteria by which it might be meaningful to assess them. While the scientific study of religions is not directly concerned with the philosophical assessment of truth claims advanced by religions, it may be able to assist in their identification and clarification.

Although the same presupposition underlies many well-meaning approaches to religious dialogue or "inter-faith" programmes, the perception of the plurality of religions *may* seem to be problematic from the point of view of religious conviction or commitment. This is because the very existence of diverse religious orientations may seem to relativise the truth or value of the "home" religion, thereby creating danger. In other religious understandings, however, the plurality of religions is not regarded as a problem because the final truth is simply regarded as going beyond them all. Thus historically, the emergence of the comparative study of religions (in their plurality) has often been associated with the view that there is a common principle or essence underlying them all. Nowadays however, in scientific terms, this idea is widely regarded as a blind alley. As a result, thinking about the plurality of religions separates into two directions. In connection with the scientific study of religions, the unity of religions is not even necessarily regarded as a reality, and certainly not as an objective. The study of religions simply concentrates on the analysis of religions, in the plural, as they happen to be. The activity of dialogue between religions on the other hand has as its objective such values as mutual understanding, coexistence and cooperation. These relations can be shown by means of a simple flow-chart, as in Diagram 1.

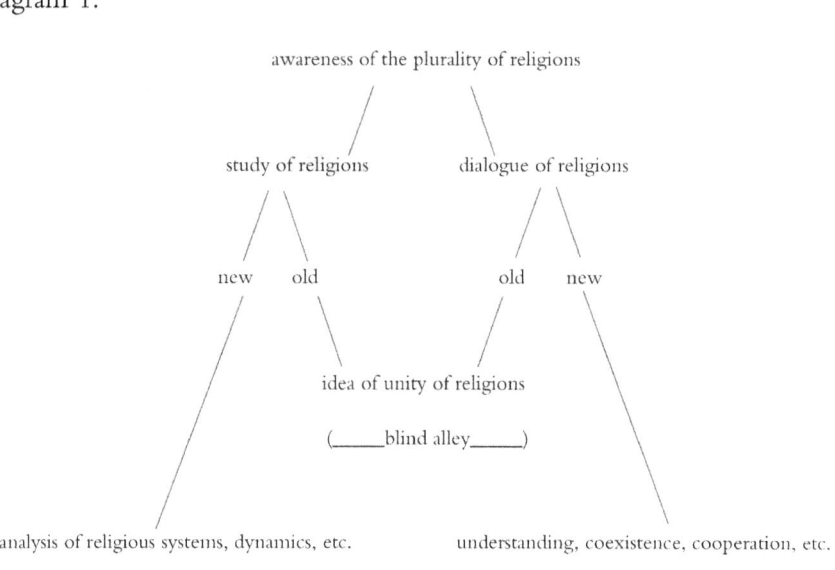

Diagram 1: Flow-chart illustrating the section entitled "a shared presupposition."

Religious solutions to the perception of plurality

At this point, looking at it from an observer's point of view, it will be helpful to note that there are various ways in which dialogue between religions has been approached by religiously oriented people. Some of these are highly organised and some are rather informal. While in general the sincerity of the participants need not be questioned there may be a multiple motivation. Sometimes an important function is to achieve a public relations effect within the home religious community. This often plays a role in Japanese religions, reflecting the more general use of elements of foreign culture to provide legitimacy or added value to Japanese cultural activities or commercial products. In religion, it makes a good impression for leaders to be seen having an audience with the Pope or the Dalai Lama and for the photographs to appear in magazines circulating among the believers at home. Among the various ways in which religious dialogue is taken up by religious people, let us note the following four.

First, well established religious organisations discover, on the margins of their institutions, that there is a problem of correlation with so-called "other" religions. This problem is sometimes addressed negatively and polemically, and sometimes constructively and cooperatively. As a result there is a tradition of writing, especially in Christian theology, about the relationship between Christianity and "other faiths", this relationship being variously conceived. Often, the question of how to think about the "other" religions is left to a secondary, relatively unimportant position in the theological system. This habit of thinking has occasionally been criticised by those who study the general history of religions. (Smart 1962, Pye 1976, 1979b) Usually there is a clear conception of the religion which forms the starting point, and a less clear understanding of the "other" religions which have to be taken into account. This holds good both for those with a negative view of the religions (e. g. the protestant theologian Karl Barth) and in some cases for those who take a more positive view (e. g. the liberal catholic theologian Hans Küng). In any case the attempt is made, perhaps understandably enough, somehow to fit the various "other" religions into the worldview of the starting point. It is of course not only the Christian tradition which has produced reflection upon its own procedures in this regard. Consider for example the instructive title *The Buddhist Philosophy of Assimilation. The Historical Development of the Honji Suijaku Theory* (Matsunaga 1969), in which the thought processes leading up to that particular solution are studied in detail. Various attempts have been made to chart systematically the options which are available in the correlation of an "own" tradition with an "other" tradition, a recent substantial study being that by Andreas Grünschloss in *Der eigene und der fremde Glaube* (1999). While this work addresses a theological audience in some parts (and indeed the author describes himself as a *Grenzgänger*, that is, a frontier-crosser) the main intention is to analyse possible positions and procedures on the basis of the observation of several religions.

Second, there are more recently founded religions which, from their very inception, have a point of view about the integration or mutual harmony of existing religions. The Japanese religion Ananaikyō may be mentioned as an example. Other examples which are globally active are the Unification Church which originated in Korea and the Baha'i religion, which originated in Iran. Such religions start out with a view about the relationship between various religions for the simple reason that at the time of their conception it was already evident that there were other well organised religions in existence (cf. "Elements of a general theory of innovation in religion" at 5.4 above). In such cases it is therefore a natural, almost a necessary requirement to say what part these play in the new message. Interestingly, although there are quite a lot of religions which somehow assert "the unity" of all religions, these do not usually cooperate very much with each other, if at all. On the contrary they continue to offer their own distinctive, superior message. Little thought seems to have been given about how this endemic problem could be overcome.

Third, there are an increasing number of interreligious or "interfaith" organisations which operate independently of the institutionalised religions, e.g. the World Congress of Faiths, the World's Parliament of Religions, and the recently founded United Religions. In general these organisations are supported by individuals who themselves have an extremely positive attitude towards the various religions of the world. The history of such "interfaith" organisations is in fact quite long, and in view of the rapid development of global consciousness in the twentieth century it is perhaps surprising that they are not even stronger than they are. There are various possible reasons for this. For one thing, the activists who support them either come from small religious groups themselves, like the Brahma Kumaris active in the International Interfaith Centre at Oxford, England, or they are *non-typical* members of larger religions, e.g. Anglican or Catholic priests acting with at best very tenuous hierarchical legitimation for their interfaith work. Moreover the various interfaith movements to some extent compete with each other as organisations, each with their own leaders and characteristic interests. Any suggestion that they might consider integration usually falls on deaf ears. This is presumably because each organisation has its own social dynamics, leadership aspirations, legitimational needs for funding, and so on.

Fourth, there have been a small number of clearly organised dialogues between genuinely representative groups from established religions. Such dialogues are very demanding, for the simple reason that there is a very strong sense of responsibility to the specific religious traditions concerned, together with a real need for new knowledge and new awareness of the partner tradition. This pattern may turn out to be more significant, in the long run, than has hitherto been recognised. Examples and recommendations will be found further below.

Different kinds of religions: primal and critical

Though "religions" or religious systems, religious orientations or religious traditions, are plural, this does not mean that they are all the same. There are different kinds of religions. Though this is a huge field of study, let us briefly consider at least one fundamental distinction in the typology of religions which appears to command a certain assent. This has implications for dialogues between religions. Though the same general distinction may be current under varied terminology, the the terms "primal" and "critical" are preferred by the present writer. The term "critical religions" is used to include sub-categories such as soteriological religions, "awareness" or "gnostic" religions, and "guidance" (*michibiki*) religions, while avoiding an undue emphasis on any one of these sub-categories. The point is simply that a "critical" religion distances itself in some way from the more or less unthinkingly accepted, primal religious culture of the time, creating a difference. To illustrate with straightforward examples, Buddhism is a critical form of religion over against Brahmanism (i.e. the "Hinduism" of the period in which Buddhism arose), Christianity is a critical form of religion over against Judaism, Islam is a critical form of religion over against pre-Muslim polytheism, and Konkōkyō or Tenrikyō are critical forms of religion over against Shintō. This does not mean, as far as the study of religions is concerned, that either the critical or the primal types of religion are to be preferred. They are simply different types of religions which can be noted in the general history of religions. However, it will be evident that it does not make sense to speak loosely of "dialogue between world religions" as if all religions were simply the same kind of thing. There really are different *kinds* of religions. Following this relatively uncontroversial typology, the question arises whether there is a particular relation between the main types of religions and the kinds of dialogue which take place or which might be expected. There seems to be! Let us look at the possible relations in a simplified way. At this point borderline cases and cases where religions switch from one type to the other will be disregarded. The three standard relations are

(1) primal-to-primal (parallels and selected contemporary themes)
(2) primal-to-critical (critical points and selected contemporary themes)
(3) critical-to-critical (parallels and selected contemporary themes)

First, then, there might be a dialogue between "primal religions." This could involve two or more of, for example, the religions of North American Indians, of the Sami of Lapland, Yakutian shamanism and Japanese Shintō. Of course there are many differences here because Shintō, in particular, has undergone an immensely complicated development in connection with modernisation processes. The general point however is that there is not really any question of alternative truth claims here. Rather, such religious systems are the primal religions, or the adapted primal religions of different peoples. So their representatives and even their researchers are able to enjoy having conversations and making comparative studies of, for example, the North American "sweat lodge," the Finnish "sauna" and the Japanese "o-furo" (Jetsonen and Pentikäinen 2000), or they might have a conference on the theme of their relation to the environment, forest use, etc.

The second typical dialogue relation would be between primal religion(s) and critical religion(s). Such relations can be either cooperative or competitive. In the history of religions a sharing of functions can often be seen, the classic case for this being the history of Buddhism in various lands. The development of an intellectually reflective process about this, which is the beginning of "dialogue," may be somewhat onesided. For example, more thought has been put into these questions from the Buddhist side of things than by those engaging in the worship of local spirits in South East Asia. Moreover the relationship, or dialogue, between critical and primal religions can be quite competitive, especially if the particularist aspect of primal religions is strongly criticised from the universalist standpoint of a salvationist religion. An example of this is the relationship between Christianity and Shintō in Japan, in which Shintō is usually criticised from the Christian side. However there may be new possibilities for positive dialogue here, especially if thematic subjects such as environmental questions and problems in medical ethics are considered.

The third typical relation would be between two "critical" religions. This can of course be very competitive but it can also lead to a dialogue between similar partners, even if they are not equal in all respects. Examples which will be discussed further below are the dialogues between (a) Tenrikyō and Catholicism and between (b) Shin Buddhism and German Protestant theology. In these dialogues significant analytical parallels have been noted while there has also been a wide range of common interests and common themes, such as ethical questions, the challenge of secularisation and so on. The competitive aspect might be expected to be high when the organisational interest is high (cf. below on different kinds of organisation), and yet this must not always be the case. A clear organisation can also lead to an effective dialogue, effective at least in the sense that a significant learning process can take place.

Dynamics, innovation – and dialogues

Religious systems, or religious traditions, are not just fixed entities but are of course subject to change for various reasons. Quite apart from the influence of external factors there is an innovative dimension to religion which takes various forms. This means that reinterpretations are unavoidable, and to some extent this may itself be part of the process of religious dialogue. It is therefore important for participants in religious dialogues to be aware of the processes of change, reinterpretation and adaptation. This raises the whole subject of the dynamics of religion, in which there are many sub-problems (for the academic study of religions) which cannot detain us here.

In brief, it seems that it might be of interest, even of importance, for participants in religious dialogues to reflect on their own position in the religious dynamics which are current at any one time. Not all religious systems move at the same speed with respect to adaptive changes, and different parties within the same religion also move at different speeds. While it is obvious to the observer that every religious group includes both conservatives and reformers or liberals, it is possible that this is not merely because people tend to disagree about the speed of change, but because the system as a whole simply requires all of these parties in order to keep going. This needs to be understood in the situation of religious dialogues.

In an attempt to provide a general theory of religious innovation (which is only part of a wider theory of religious dynamics) four main modes of innovation in religion may be delineated as follows:

a) innovation within the norms of current organisations
b) innovative reform leading to organisational separation
c) innovation with difference, but without clear organisational consequences
d) innovation with difference, including new organisational forms.

This somewhat clinical classification is probably not controversial, and similar ones are not uncommon.[4] The second mode leads to schismatic religious bodies or sects, in the classical or proper sense of the term, while the fourth leads to new religions. However, the implication for religious dialogues is that the third mode of religious innovation might be regarded, from an institutional point of view, as relatively irresponsible. This is because it is precisely *not* institutional. An example would be much of the innovative religious culture which goes under the name of "New Age" or new "spirituality", a term used with little discipline. A significant proportion of the population of industrial or post-industrial societies participates in such activities. This represents a considerable challenge for the understanding of religious dialogues or for the analysis of the various options available.

It seems that in considering the relevance of innovation to religious dialogues a typology of relative institutionalisation is required. At one end might be clear-cut ecclesiastical institutions such as the Vatican, while at the other end there might be rather unclearly organised contributions to religious culture in the New Age style, as referred to above. More structured dialogue may be expected to be carried out by the representatives of institutions, while less structured dialogue is carried out between individuals as the bearers of non-institutional elements of religious culture. Can religious dialogues be carried on by more or less independent or even isolated individuals? Perhaps in some ways they can. On the other hand, dialogue may seem to be more serious, and more

---

4   The detailed argument will be found in "Elements of a general theory of innovation in religion" (at 5.4 above). The term *innovation* is the most neutral and general term for these divergent modes, of which the appearance of "new religions" or so-called "new religious movements" (NRMs) is but one. Naturally, other scholars thinking about these processes with particular interests in mind provide similar summaries of the options, but with some variations. A close parallel may be found in Repp 2005a: 524.

binding, when there is some kind of institutional social structure to the dialogue, as in some of the organised dialogues to be mentioned below. In short, the question is who has the right to carry out a dialogue, and on the part of whom? Unfortunately the answers to this are not simple. Perhaps they are inevitably endless.

A further distinction may be made between "hard" dialogue and "soft" dialogue. In this usage, hard dialogue would be self-presentational, uncompromising and in the end unproductive. On the other hand, soft dialogue might be understood to be gentle, patient, imaginative and creative, leaving many questions open for future consideration. In general people are not prepared to be identified with hard dialogue. Rather, even while standing firmly in a specific religious tradition, they prefer to think of themselves as taking part in soft dialogue. Consequently, even though there may be quite clear and strong institutions in the background, such as the Higashi Honganji for Shin Buddhism, or the German Protestant Church (Evangelische Kirche Deutschlands), it seems best to preserve the terms hard and soft for *attitudes* rather than for relative institutionalisation. It is quite possible for those representing institutions to be gentle and creative, or in other words to engage in soft dialogue. At the same time we need to have some sensitivity to the relative pace of hard and soft dialogue, for these can be related to the internal dynamics of the religious traditions involved, to reforms, innovations, conservative reactions, and so on.

How can religious dialogues be structured?

At this point we will consider two clear models for dialogues between members of different religious communities or representatives of different religious traditions, whether the meeting has a particular theme such as peace, education, family ethics, or some other matter of mutual interest. Both of these models include a mediatory function on the part of specialists in the study of religions. Of course, it is quite possible for religious representatives simply to meet each other without the involvement of any other parties. There is no objection to that. However, dialogues whose social structure also involves specialists in religion – who are not themselves representing a religious viewpoint – may bring more results. The first model is that of meetings between representatives of two specific religious communities, with specialists in the study of religions in attendance. It has already been recommended within the context of the examples given below. (Pye 2004b) The second model is provided by those meetings where the representation is less clearly defined and the various functions are assumed by individuals rather than by designated groups.

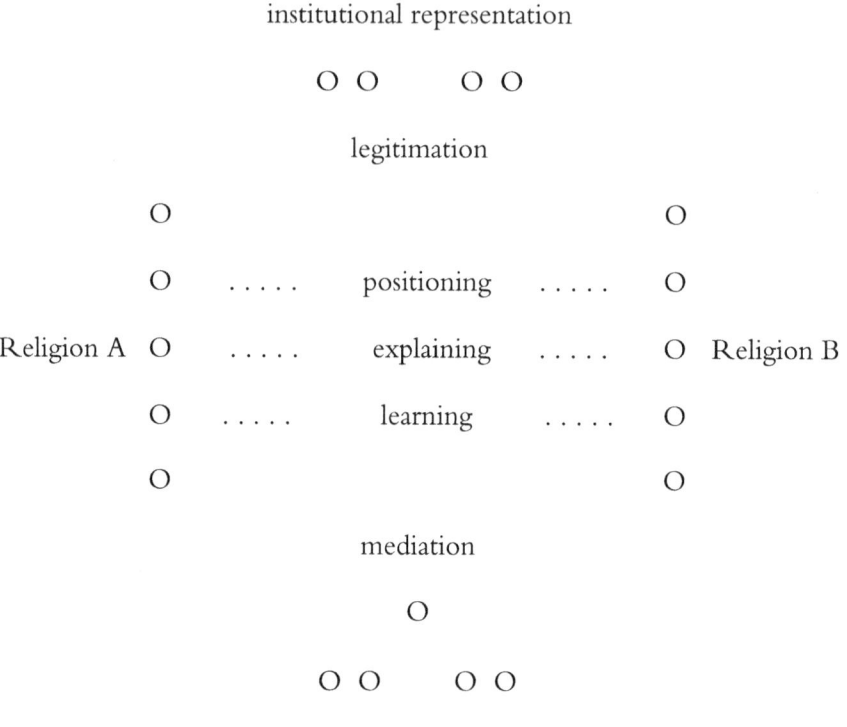

Diagram 2: Dialogue with structured institutional participation

In the first model (see Diagram 2), the ideal is in fact a fourfold structure consisting of (a and b) academic representatives of each of the two religions plus (c) specialists in the study of religions with relevant expertise plus (d) representatives of central institutions of each of the two religious groups (e.g. from a head temple or a coordinating committee). The last mentioned provide support and *legitimation* for the academic representatives of the religious institutions, while the specialists in the study of religions for their part have the task of mediation perhaps linguistically, but above all in the exchange of ideas. The specialists should have expertise in one or both of the religious systems in question, and be able to represent their ideas fairly. This involves careful listening, with a view to assisting in the removal of misunderstandings which might otherwise go unnoticed. Here *mediation* is the key function (c.f. Franke 2005).

This model has already been illustrated very well in two quite different contexts. First, meetings have taken place between academic representatives of Tenrikyō, from Tenri University, and the Catholic Church, mainly from the Gregorian University in Rome. Again some leading representatives of central institutions were present, as well as specialists in the study of religions with relevant knowledge. The latter were able to assist in the shaping of some of the selected themes, which included both patterns of salvation and questions of family ethics, and to spot some misunderstandings which would otherwise have been left in the air.[5] These meetings took place first in Rome and then in Tenri City, Japan, and the proceedings were published both in Japanese and in English.[6] The first of these meetings, held at the Gregorian University, was accompanied by an informative exhibition about the Tenrikyō religion. While the contents of the discussions were serious, it cannot be disputed that the relative organisational strength of the two religions is very different. Yet the dialogue itself, not least because of the gracious attitude adopted on both sides, did not seem one-sided at the time. Because of the imbalance of size between these two dialogue partners, the significance of the dialogue for the Tenrikyō side was considerably greater than it was for the Catholic side. The vast majority of Catholics, even of clergy and teachers, will probably never even hear that this dialogue took place, whereas on the Tenrikyō side it is much better known though publications for the members.

In a quite different context dialogues with a similar structure have been conducted between academic representatives of the Japanese Buddhist denomination Jōdo Shinshū, mainly but not exclusively from Ōtani University, Kyōto, and representatives of the Faculty of Protestant Theology of the University of Marburg, Germany. In the case of Shin Buddhism representatives of the Higashi Honganji (the head temple and administrative centre of one of the major denominations of Shin

---

5   The four were: Martin Kraatz (Marburg), Johannes Laube (München), Michael Pye (Marburg) and Ninian Smart (Santa Barbara). They were asked both to produce their own papers and to moderate sessions.
6   See The Organizing Committee of Tenrikyō-Christian Dialogue (ed.) 1999, and The Organizing Committee of Tenrikyō-Christian Dialogue II (ed.) 2005.

Buddhism) were also present, and on the Protestant side there were also persons with regional church functions. A full symposium took place twice, with particular themes such as the challenge of secularisation being pursued, while additional meetings followed which built on the basic pattern. Proceedings were published in German and in Japanese (Barth et al. 2000a, Pye et al. 2003, Barth et al. 2004), a major editorial role being played by Japanese colleagues Kadowaki Ken, Minoura Eryō and Miyashita Seishi. The special feature of this dialogue is that it was already well known, academically, that there are most interesting similarities in the structures of faith, belief and practice between these two religions. If only for this reason, the intellectual level of the contributions from both sides was very demanding. This meant that great efforts had to be made as far as linguistic translation and interpretation are concerned. It also meant that a serious process of getting to know the other tradition was set in motion, which would not otherwise have occurred for most of the participants. The initial event was accompanied not only by an exhibition of books and hanging scrolls pertaining to Shin Buddhism, but also by a *gongyō* service carried out by representatives of the Higashi Honganji in the festive lecture hall of Marburg University. Needless to say, this dialogue is itself part of a much wider and complex interaction between Buddhism and Christianity which has been documented and discussed in great detail by writers such as John D'Arcy May (1984), Michael von Brück and Whalen Lai (1997) and Perry Schmidt-Leukel (1992). However a special feature of this particular case is that the dialogue took place between representative *groups*, probably for the first time between these two well balanced dialogue partners. It may also be noted that in this case, too, a mediatory function was carried out by specialists in the study of religions.

The second model is less formally structured in that it does not consist precisely of a meeting between two sides. There is no institutional intention to mount a dialogue between the representatives of two religious traditions, even though this might be a significant by-product of the meeting. The meeting, held around a specific theme, is *academically* conceived, while at the same time the religious affiliation of many participants is undeniable and usually undenied. Specialists in the study of religions with relevant knowledge are present among the group, sometimes to offer a particular contribution of their own but above all to provide mediation. The difference from the first model is not very great, but in general the representation is less clearly defined and the various functions are assumed by individuals rather than by designated groups. It is noteworthy that some participants whose main responsibility is to represent a religion as "theologians" (or the equivalent thereof) are quite likely to begin to function also as specialists in "the study of religions," and indeed this process has sometimes been called for from within a theological perspective.[7] This doubling of functions may sometimes be confusing for others, but on the other hand the increased interest shown in the factuality of diverse religions can be welcomed. Apart from specialists in the study of religions, other academics may be involved who provide yet other interdisciplinary perspectives, e. g. sociology or psychology, but who are also not representing any religious community as such. Meetings following this second model are academically conceived from the start, and accordingly have rather less symbolic significance for the institutions of the two religious traditions, which are not formally represented. They are quite common, but here mention will be made here of one example only in in which the present writer found himself involved. A second example is described in "The study of religions and the dialogue of peace" at 7.7 below. For the present we may adduce a recent symposium on "prayer" held at Marburg, Germany, in 2006 and attended by various academics from Tenri University and from Marburg University. It included a majority of Christian (in this case Protestant) and Tenri theologians, two specialists in psychology and sociology, and four persons specialising in the study of religions with knowledge of Tenrikyō and Christianity respectively. Although not a few of the participants in this symposium themselves had a religious orientation as well as an academic one, the roles were much less clearly articulated than in the previously mentioned joint conferences between representatives of Tenrikyō and of the Catholic Church. This was a case where individuals not infrequently switched roles from time to time. In particular one could observe how participants with a religious orientation perceived a need to develop a "study of re-

---

7   As for example by Martin Repp, who writes at the conclusion of his article "Religionsgespräche zwischen Jesuiten und Buddhisten im Japan des 16/17 Jahrhunderts": "In gleicher Weise verlangt auch das Engagement im interreligiösen Dialog das gründliche Studium der betreffenden Religion, inklusive deren Sprache und Primärquellen...Hier hat die Theologie wieder neu die Religionswissenschaft zu entdecken, die sie so lange sträflich vernachlässigt hatte. Das Studium der anderen Religionen hat um ihrer selbst willen zu geschehen...Dies wiederum hat zum Ziel, in konstruktiv-kritischer Auseinandersetzung sich für die Verwirklichung des Religionsfriedens einzusetzen." (Repp 2005b:53).

ligions" framework for the exchange of perceptions concerning the phenomenon of prayer.[8]

Just two models of dialogue have been briefly illustrated here, with examples. This does not exclude the possibility that a wide range of variations could be conceived. The general point being made here however is that, whichever of these two models is espoused, it is possible, and indeed desirable, for "the study of religions" to maintain its independent character. At the same time, this does not mean that specialists in the study of religions cannot take part, in an appropriate way, in the complex dialogues currently taking place between various religious traditions. Indeed, their participation is desirable, for they may be able to contribute both useful knowledge and communicatory mediation.

Dialogue can be more than the exchange of ideas

It is rather common to assume that in a dialogue people meet to exchange their ideas, but in reality religious systems include much more than ideas. Looking at the morphology of religion from the standpoint of the academic or scientific study of religions, it is rather straightforward to delineate four main aspects which need to be considered in every case, namely: the conceptual or symbolic, the subjective or affective, the behavioural, and the social. Each of these stands in some relationship to the others, as I have explained in more detail elsewhere (Pye 1972a, 1994b). The point to note here is that these four main aspects, in so far as they provide a stable and comprehensive morphological starting point for specialists in the study of religions, also should be taken seriously by participants in religious dialogues. To put it briefly, dialogue is not only in the head. There is also, secondly, an affective aspect. Thirdly, it is possible to carry out dialogue "by doing" something, for example by taking part in joint meditation exercises or shared social welfare activity. Finally, the dialogue will be carried out by persons who stand in a social relationship of some kind to each other, whether it is highly official or relatively tenuous. It is not possible to go into examples of all these aspects here. Let the point be illustrated however, most briefly, with reference to the dialogue between Shin Buddhism and Protestant Christianity.

---

8 Retrospective note. For proceedings see Hashimoto 2007.

Most frequently, interest has been shown in the various ways in which the conceptual apparatus of these two traditions can be understood. In particular the idea is current that modes of thinking might be transferred from one tradition to the other in a fruitful way. It has been argued, for example, that the concept of demythologisation can be transferred from debates in Christian theology to the interpretation of the figure of Amida Buddha and the Pure Land. What do "mythological" concepts mean existentially? In the other direction the suggestion has been entertained that the idea of skilful means might be transferred from Buddhism to Christianity. (Pye 1990c, 1998a, Sharma 1990, Hick 1993) It was also suggested during the Marburg symposium that a "deontologisation" of leading concepts might be undertaken, such as is familiar in Mahāyāna Buddhism, but which has hitherto been viewed with more caution in Christianity. These are matters for discussion by experts in the two traditions. However it would appear that an active development of ideas in these two directions would lead to a much closer mutual appreciation developing between the intellectual representatives of the two traditions. What should be noticed however is that such exchange tends also to lead to a shift, on both sides, in the *affective* aspect. That is to say, people can begin to *feel* differently about the symbolic systems with which they are familiar. The participants are then somehow involved with their own "religiosity" as the psychologists like to call it.

But what about the other aspects? What about entering into a dialogue of behaviour or behaviours, or a dialogue of socio-institutional relationships? This of course is not easy, though the history of religious dialogues is full of examples. Some things have often seemed to be possible, like joint meditation between Zen Buddhists and Catholics, but others not, like joint recitation of the *nenbutsu* or joint participation in a Eucharistic service. One of the regular practices carried out at the Higashi Honganji by the believers (*monto*) is a cleaning program, understood to be a religious activity expressing gratitude. As an example of dialogue "by doing" it might be conceivable for a group of believers from the German Protestant church to visit Japan and assist in this activity! That would represent, in dialogue, the aspect of religious behaviour.

These of course are only illustrations. The main, underlying point is that in so far as the scientific study of religion seeks a balanced view of the phenomena under study by taking account of each of the four main aspects, then the same stable view may be used as a resource and as a corrective in the planning of religious dialogues. Of course, such a complex pattern of dialogue would involve many more uncertainties for the participants, who may prefer to shelter behind the more traditional exchange of conceptual systems alone.

Conclusion

The subject of religious dialogues has been approached above from the perspective of the study of religions, and the opportunity has been taken to make various suggestions. While there is a need to distinguish clearly between the study of religions and the actual carrying out of religious dialogues, there seem to be many ways in which the former can be of assistance for the latter. Those who represent religious traditions in dialogue situations should therefore take account of the theoretical perspectives and normal tasks of the study of religions. They may even wish to contribute to its further development. Specialists in the study of religions, for their part, should feel free to participate in contemporary discussions, provided that they maintain a clear view of the academic discipline for which they are responsible.

The common point of all the examples mentioned above is that specialists in the study of religions play an assistive or mediatory role, the value of which has also been recognised by the other, religiously oriented participants. The structures described have been tested, and they can be recommended. Of course the specific subject matter or behavioural focus of any encounters may be quite varied. For example, such dialogues could also focus on questions relating to peace, and indeed this can only be repeatedly recommended in our troubled times.

Bibliographical references

Barth, Hans-Martin, Minoura Eryō, and Pye, Michael (eds.) 2000a. *Buddhismus und Christentum. Jodo Shinshu und Evangelische Theologie. III. Internationales Rudolf-Otto Symposion am Fachbereich Evangelische Theologie der Philipps-Universität Marburg in Zusammenarbeit mit der Otani-Universität Kyoto.* Hamburg (EB-Verlag).
– 2000b: *Bukkyō to kirisutokyō no taiwa. Jōdo Shinshū to fukuinshugishingaku.* Kyōto (Hōzōkan). (Japanese edition of Barth et al. 2000.)
Barth, Hans-Martin, Kadowaki Ken, Minoura Eryō and Michael Pye (eds.) 2004a. *Buddhismus und Christentum vor der Herausforderung der Säkularisierung.* Hamburg (EB-Verlag).

- 2004b: *Bukkyō to kirisutokyō no taiwa III: Sezokuka kara no chōsen ni shokumen suru bukkyō to kirisutokyō.* Kyōto (Hōzōkan). Japanese edition of Barth et al. 2004.)
Berger, Peter 1981. "The Pluralistic Situation and the Coming Dialogue between the World Religions" in: *Buddhist-Christian Studies* 1: 31–41.
Brück, Michael von and Lai, Whalen 1997. *Buddhismus und Christentum. Geschichte, Konfrontation, Dialog.* München (Beck).
Franke, Edith 2005. "The task and function of the academic study of religions in the face of religious diversity" in: Franke et al. 2005: 47–56.
Franke, Edith and Pye, Michael 2004. "The study of religions and its contribution to problem-solving in a plural world" / "Ilmu agama dan kontribusinya terhadap penyelesaian masalah dalam dunia yang plural" in: *Marburg Journal of Religion* 9 (2): <http://web.uni-marburg.de/religionswissenschaft/journal/mjr.>
Franke, Edith, Mas'ud, Abdurrahman, Pye, Michael and Wasim, Alef Theria 2005. *Religious Harmony: Problems, Practice and Education. Proceedings of the Regional Conference of the International Association for the History of Religions, Yogyakarta and Semarang, Indonesia, September 27th – October 3rd, 2004.* Yogyakarta (Oasis Publisher).
- 2005b: *Harmoni Kehidupan Beragama: Problem, Praktik dan Pendidikan. Proceeding Konferensi Regional International Association for the History of Religions, Yogyakarta dan Semarang, Indonesia, 27 September – 03 October, 2004.* Yogyakarta (Oasis Publisher). (Indonesian version of Franke et al. 2005a.)
- 2006. Revised English edition of Franke et al. 2005. (*Religion and Reason* 45). Berlin (de Gruyter).
Grünschloss, Andreas 1999. *Der eigene und der fremde Glaube.* Tübingen (Mohr Siebeck).
Hashimoto, Taketo (ed.) 2007. *Prayer as Interaction. (Tenri University and Marburg University Joint Research Project September 2006).* Tenri (Tenri University Press).
Hick, John 1993. *Disputed Questions in Theology and the Philosophy of Religion.* Basingstoke (Macmillan).
Jetsonen, Jari and Pentikäinen, Juha 2000. *Löylyn Henki. Kolmen Mantereen Kylvyt.* Helsinki (Rakennustieto Oy).
Lys, Candice 2006. "Demonizing the 'Other': Fundamentalist Pakistani Madrasahs and the Construction of Religious Violence" in: *Marburg Journal of Religion* 11(1): http://web.uni-marburg.de/religionswissenschaft/journal/mjr.
Matsunaga, Alicia 1969. *The Buddhist Philosophy of Assimilation The Historical Development of the Honji-Suijaku Theory.* Tokyo (Sophia University) and Rutland Vermont (Tuttle).
May, John D'Arcy 1984. *Meaning, Consensus and Dialogue in Buddhist-Christian Communication.* Bern (Peter Lang).
Pye, Michael 1972a. *Comparative Religion. An Introduction through Source Materials.* Newton Abbot (David and Charles) and New York (Harper and Row).

- 1976. "The end of the problem about 'other' religions" in: Clayton, John P. (ed.) *Ernst Troeltsch and the Future of* Theology. Cambridge (Cambridge University Press): 172–195.
- 1979b. "Theologie im Kontext des religiösen Pluralismus" in: Kremkau, Klaus (ed.), *Christus allein – allein das Christentum? (Vorträge der vierten theologischen Konferenz zwischen Vertretern der Evangelischen Kirche in Deutschland und der Kirche von England)*. Frankfurt am Main (Verlag Otto Lembeck): 11–25.
- 1990a. (trans.) *Emerging from Meditation (Tominaga Nakamoto)*. London (Duckworth) and Honolulu (University of Hawaii Press).
- 1990c. "Skilful means and the interpretation of Christianity" in: *Buddhist-Christian Studies* 10: 17–22.
- 1994b. "Religion: shape and shadow" in: *Numen.International Review for the History of Religions* 41(1): 51–75.
- 1998a. "Die 'geschickten Mittel'. Zur Dialektik der Ausdrucksformen in Buddhismus und Christentum" in: Viertel, Matthias (ed.) *Buddhismus und Christentum*. Hofgeismar (Evangelische Akademie Hofgeismar): 41–64.
- 1999a. "Methodological integration in the study of religions" in: Tore Ahlbäck (ed.) *Approaching Religion, Scripta Instituti Donneriani Aboensis XVII (1)*, Åbo/Turku, Finland (Donner Institute for Research in Religious and Cultural History): 188–205.
- 2000a. "Westernism unmasked" in: Jensen, Tim and Rothstein, Mikael (eds.) *Secular Theories of Religion. Current Perspectives*. Copenhagen (Museum Tusculanum Press): 211–230.
- 2000b "Participation, observation and reflection: an endless method" in: Nils. G. Holm et al. eds. *Ethnography is a Heavy Rite. Studies of Comparative Religion in Honor of Juha Pentikäinen* (Religionsvetenskapliga skrifter 47). Åbo (Åbo Akademis Tryckeri) 2000: 64–79.
- 2001b. "The study of religions and the dialogue of religions (Shūkyōgaku to shūkyōtaiwa)" in: *Marburg Journal of Religion* 6 (2): < http://web.uni-marburg.de/religionswissenschaft/journal/mjr>
- 2002. "Won Buddhism as a Korean new religion" in: *Numen* 49 (2): 113–141.
- 2004b. "Zur Legitimation, Struktur und Durchführung von interreligiösem Dialog" in: Barth et al. 2004a: 13–20.

Pye, Michael and Morgan, Robert (eds.) 1973. *The Cardinal Meaning. Essays in Comparative Hermeneutics: Buddhism and Christianity*. (Religion and Reason 6). The Hague (Mouton).

Pye, Michael, Miyashita, Seishi and Minoura, Eryō 2003. *Bukkyō to kirisutokyō no taiwa II: Jōdo shinshū to fukuinshugi no shinkō. Hans-Martin Barth kyōju Gerhard Marcel Martin kyōju wo mukaete (Dialog zwischen Buddhismus und Christentum II, Jōdo Shinshū und Evangelischer Glaube: Mit Hans-Martin Barth und Gerhard Marcel Martin im Gespräch)*. Kyōto (Hōzōkan).

Repp, Martin 2005a. *Hōnens religiöses Denken. Eine Untersuchung zu Strukturen religiöser Erneuerung*. Wiesbaden (Harrassowitz Verlag)
- 2005b. "Religionsgespräche zwischen Jesuiten und Buddhisten im Japan des 16./17. Jahrhunderts" in: Benjamin, Simon und Wrogemann, Henning

(eds.) *Konviviale Theologie. Festgabe für Theo Sundermeier zum 70. Geburtstag.* Frankfurt am Main (Otto Lembeck): 41–53.

Schmidt-Leukel, Perry 1992. *"Den Löwen brüllen hören." Zur Hermeneutik eines christlichen Verständnisses der buddhistischen Heilsbotschaft.* Paderborn (Schöningh).

Sharma, Arvind 1990. "'Skill in means' in early Buddhism and Christianity" in: *Buddhist-Christian Studies* 10: 23–33.

Smart, Ninian 1962. "The relation between Christianity and the other great religions" in: Vidler, A. R. (ed.) *Soundings, Essays Concerning Christian Understanding.* Cambridge (Cambridge University Press): 103–121.

The Organizing Committee of "Tenri-Christian Dialogue" (ed.) 1999. *Tenrikyo-Christian Dialogue.* Tenri City (Tenri University Press). (Japanese version: Tenrikyōdōyūsha 1998. *Tenrikyō to Kirisutokyō no taiwa.* Tenri City (Tenri Jihōsha).)

The Organizing Committee of "Tenrikyo-Christian Dialogue II" (ed.) 2005. *Tenrikyo-Christian Dialogue II: Religion, Education, and the Family.* Tenri City (Tenri University Press). (Japanese version: Tenrikyōdōyūsha 2002. *Tenrikyō to kirisutokyō no taiwa II. Tenri kokusai simposiumu 2002. Kyōiku, kazoku, shūkyō.* Tenri City (Tenri Jihōsha).)

An earlier version of this paper was published in *Marburg Journal of Religion* 6/2 (June 2001) and a revised and a shortened version in *Japanese Religions* 32 1/2 (2007): 89–109.

7.6 Presuppositions of an Integrative Religious Education

This paper was first prepared in 2002 for the "Tenri International Symposium 2002 – Tenrikyo-Christian Dialogue II", on the subject of "Religion, Education and the Family," jointly sponsored by Tenri University, Tenri (Japan) and the Pontifical Gregorian University in Rome (proceedings published in 2005). Related arguments were later advanced in a contribution to the World Congress of the International Association for the History of Religions in Tokyo, 2005. This explains the prominence of Japan-related references.

1. A common basis for religious education?

There is an urgent need in modern societies for a responsible form of religious education, not only in private schools run by religious institutions but also in the public sector. There are various reasons for this, not least the potential of religious commitments and identities for the stimulation of social and political conflicts and in some cases, one may hope, for the resolution of such conflicts. Schooling in one religion alone, at least in most cases, is unlikely to lead to the resolution of conflicts. An integrative religious education is required.[1] The purpose of such educa-

---

1   Retrospective note. Having been involved in teacher training in the United Kingdom in the late nineteen-sixties, with special reference to Religious Education (RE) and an appointed member of the Church of England General Synod's Board of Education for about ten years, the writer has been very conscious of subsequent RE developments and in particular of the "multi-faith" context and of differing conditions in various countries. It was therefore of particular interest, in Marburg, to supervise research by Wanda Alberts for a detailed study of "integrative religious education" in three countries: England, Sweden and Germany. Her dissertation (examined September 2006) has since been published as *Integrative Religious Education in Europe, A Study-of-Religions Approach* (Religion and Reason 47) Berlin (de Gruyter) 2007, and an account of contributions by leading figures (Ninian Smart, Robert Jackson and others) in the British context will be found there. It may be underlined that, while the origins of the English phrase "integrative religious education" remain obscure, it was

tion is, so far as it already exists, to assist children in the development of an understanding both of the religion of their own family and community, and of the religions of others. Since this concept is not widely understood it is important to consider what the basis of such a religious education could or should be.

In recent decades various attempts have been made to answer this question, mainly in the countries of northern Europe: Germany, the Netherlands, the United Kingdom, the Scandinavian countries and Finland. In most other countries of the world the matter has not really been addressed. At the same time, in a few countries such as Japan, there is an increasing recognition that some such element in education, some kind of "religious education," is necessary not only in the private but also in the public sectors. I will not attempt here to review the answers developed in particular countries. Rather I will try to give a summary formulation of the guiding principles which should be taken into account anywhere. I will also show that the academic discipline known as the study of religions is a significant element in the development of an integrative religious education. The term "integrative religious education" is itself relatively recent, but attempts to develop religious education which could be so designated go back at least as far as the nineteen-sixties, when the first "Agreed Syllabuses" including reference to non-Christian religions were developed in Britain, in particular in Wiltshire and in the West Riding of Yorkshire (as it then was).

The first point to notice is that the general basis of modern religious education cannot itself be the "faith commitment" of any one, single religious community. This would defeat its object from the beginning. Rather, the religious education programme must recognize and respect the varied commitments of religious communities or traditions, as far as these are compatible with wider aspects of ethics, human rights and law. In other words, a most important basis for religious education, in modern times, is that it should take account of the plurality and diversity of religious traditions and commitments.

---

publicly used by the present writer for this paper in 2002 (and not first taken up in 2004 as mistakenly stated in Wanda Alberts' Introduction, Note 3). It will be no surprise that her dissertation contains arguments which are in general consistent with those advanced here. In particular, it is most important to see that worthwhile programs of religious education should have a *dual* anchorage in the study of religions and in educational studies. These are the two home academic disciplines which guarantee the integrity of RE in the sense espoused.

This in turn means that the character of an integrative religious education cannot simply be deduced from the doctrines of any one religion, be it great or small, influential or less well known. It is inappropriate to attempt to base religious education on "theology" or its equivalents in any one specific religion such as Hinduism, Shintō, Catholicism, Tenrikyō, Baha'i, Zen Buddhism, etc. A religious training programme based on the particular teaching of one religion should be, rather, a matter for the religious community itself and for the parents in the families which it supports. In some contexts, the distinction has been made between religious education, which is general, and religious *nurture*, which is specific to one community of faith.[2] From the point of view of the secular state, in which no one religion is established, there is no need to deny the value of religious nurture within religious communities and in schools maintained by religious organisations within the private sector. Nevertheless some coordination is desirable to ensure consistency.

As far as a general programme of religious education is concerned however, open to persons of different religious traditions or none, the main reference point is not one particular religion, however worthy or profound that religion might be. The academic reference points for the development of an integrative religious education should be on the one hand the academic study of religions (German: *Religionswissenschaft* or Japanese: *shūkyōgaku*) and on the other hand educational science. Religious education involves getting the right correlation between (a) a broad, insightful and factually correct understanding of religions and (b) the educational needs of children at the various stages of their development. For the first of these, the academic study of religions should normally be regarded as the relevant discipline in higher education and research while, for the second, educational science should be regarded as responsible. Naturally the methodologies and results of these two academic disciplines should be coordinated for best results.

This religiously neutral conception makes it possible to devise curricula for religious education which are compatible with the legal neutrality required in various secular constitutions, such as that of Japan or France, in which no particular religions are privileged. Some people regard it as a problem that, with constitutions such as these, while they are

---

2   This quite useful distinction was commonly made in the deliberations of the Board of Education of the Church of England, of which I was an appointed member from 1972 to 1982.

excellent in guaranteeing fair opportunities for various religions and preventing the ideological domination of the state by any one of them, it seems difficult to make any provision for religious education at all, except in the private sector. Thus it is very important to have a clear idea about what "religious education" might be, and how it can be related to the secular state. In the last analysis there is no reason why a properly conceived programme of religious education should not be found to be compatible with a secular constitution, provided that no one religion is privileged over against the rest.

In the case of Japan it has become clear recently that simply not having any religious education at all leads to confusion and abuse in religious matters. A turning point came with the Aum Shinrikyō incident, which showed that it is desirable for young people, as they grow up, to develop the ability to make mature judgments about the religious commitments which might fascinate them for this or that reason.[3] Not all religions are benign. Thus the possibility of a general form of religious education in Japanese schools should be considered.[4] On the other hand this should not be confused with a return to the indoctrination of ideology and nationalistic "values" as in the pre-war *shūshin* system.

On this background it is time for Japanese educationists and religionists to join the international discussion on the appropriate profile and methods of religious education. It is notable that the "mix" of religions in Japan is rather different from that of Britain. In Britain for example the Sikh faith is quite well established and is often brought into religious education programmes. In Japan, apart from the dominant forms of Buddhism and Shintō, the scene is enriched by well-established religious groups such as Kurozumikyō, Tenrikyō and others. Since there is quite a large number of religious groups in Japan, and since these also have some experience of talking with each other, it seems that Japanese colleagues might have quite a lot to contribute to the international discussion on religious education.

---

3   This point was made in my short article on the Aum incident: "Aum Shinrikyō. Can Religious Studies cope?" (1996b and at 5.7 above).
4   I have been calling for this for some time, e.g. at a public symposium in Tokyo organized by the International Shinto Foundation, and in a public lecture entitled "Religion and conflict in Japan, with special reference to Shinto and Yasukuni Shrine" (Pye 2003a). The latter first appeared in the CIPHS journal *Diogène* as "Religion et conflit au Japon. Concernant surtout le Shinto et le Sanctuaire de Yasukuni" (Pye 2002d).

2. Faith commitment and religious education

It was stated above that religious education should correlate (a) a broad, insightful and factually correct understanding of religions with (b) the educational needs of children at the various stages of their development. This might seem to suggest that the religious development of the individual person is not a proper objective for religious education. Now this is a most delicate matter.

On the one hand this view is correct, for it is above all a matter for religious teachers, pastors, priests and parents to be take responsibility for the religious development of children and young people in their various "faith" communities. A secular school cannot intervene here. A teacher specialising in, or providing religious education in a general, open situation, must realise that he or she should not take the opportunity to advance the interests of one religion over against others. This would be proselytism. It would involve taking advantage of the educational situation, in which trust and responsibility should be paramount, to push forward a particular religious view.

On the other hand, the criticism of dry "positivism" might be advanced. How can religious education be meaningful or worthwhile if there is no opportunity to somehow enter into the "spirit" of being "religious"? This is an important point. Religion is not simply a conceptual matter. As is widely recognised, it is also a matter of personal attitudes and feelings, of religiously informed behaviour including ritual activities, and of social participation. Each of these in its own way complements the conceptual aspect.[5] Religious education should take account of each of these four main aspects in an appropriate manner, not forgetting to consider their relations to each other. Some kind of imaginative "entering in" to the overall experience of religion is called for, which at the same time does not involve advancing the claims of any one particular religion. It might seem impossible for teachers to develop such an educational activity, and it is especially difficult when teaching younger children from whom a mature "academic" detachment cannot be ex-

---

5 As I have explained in various places, these are the four major aspects of religion. Some authors leave one or another of these out altogether, thereby having an imbalanced view of religion. Other authors differentiate in more detail, speaking of six or seven "dimensions", but only by making subdivisions of the four main aspects named here.

pected. And indeed it is not easy. On the other hand it is essential that this should be attempted, if religious education is to be in any sense a shared enterprise which can be maintained in the context of a secular educational system. So how can it be done?

A helpful way of thinking about the question of participation is to think of the comparison with some other imaginative subjects such as music, art and literature. In all of these subjects, it is important that the imagination be aroused and developed, partly by "doing." On the other hand, nobody imagines that every school child is himself or herself expected to "be" a Rembrandt, a Bach, or a Murasaki Shikibu. In other words, while some singing, painting and writing is involved in the educational process, there is also much to learn about others who have already contributed great things. At the same time, religion is not exactly the same as these other fields. An important difference lies in the belief element, which for many believers seems to be crucial. So it may be. With this in mind, the element of participation "by doing" may be rather less easy to put into operation. On the other hand it is possible to learn a great deal about religious beliefs and practices, not just by reading, but by participating in various educational activities, without necessarily commanding or requiring a commitment of belief to a particular system. This leads to the question about what kinds of activity or "practice" are acceptable in an educational context in connection with religious education.

3. Can or should religious education include religious practice?

First let us consider some kinds of religious activity which may be important in religious "nurture" but are *not* appropriate for an integrative religious education. Key examples are prayer, worship and meditation. All of these are important in religious nurture and in spiritual development. However they are problematic in the context of public religious education because they involve assumptions which go beyond the activities themselves. People would rightly ask the following questions. To whom are we praying? Whom are we worshipping? Since there are various differing beliefs involved here it is simply not possible to encourage such activities in schools in the public sector.

It is often thought that while prayer involves commitment, meditation does not. This is a mistake which often goes unnoticed. The mistake arises not least because it is quite often asserted, misleadingly, by meditation teachers themselves. Such teachers, who are religious teachers rather than educationists, say this in order to make it easy for people to begin to take part in the practice which they promote. They suggest that there is no need to give up traditional beliefs, and that no "dogma" will be required, which sounds very convenient. However the meditation which they teach almost always brings a sequence of ideas along with it in some way or other. Most of the meditational practices of Indian origin, commonly marketed as "yoga," include some kind of cosmological vision which may or may not be shared by others. Even the Japanese Sōtō Buddhist practice of *zazen* has conceptual implications relating to the "Buddha-nature" of all beings, even though the presence of conceptual implications may be denied by Zen Buddhist teachers. The point can most easily be documented with the meditation sutras of early Buddhism, whether based on the process of breathing or on the parts of the body. The latter in particular are based on the idea that the ordinary experience of the body is transitory, one of the fundamental ideas of Buddhism. The idea may in itself be true, in all its simplicity, but that is not the point. The point is that the transiency of all normal human experience is a strand of some importance in the pattern of Buddhist teaching. Because of doctrinal implications of this nature, which always come to surface in some way or another, "meditation" is no more suitable than "prayer" for active participation by schoolchildren in a neutrally based religious education.

At the same time it is valuable for children to observe and understand that adult persons, or at least some of them, are from time to time deeply involved in prayer, or worship, or meditation. This will enable them to recognize the seriousness of such activity. Such learning may take place if it is possible for children to pay a group visit to a place of worship for observation purposes. With this in mind, visits to mosques, temples, synagogues and churches, are quite frequent in religious education programs in the United Kingdom.

By contrast with the above mentioned practices of prayer, worship and meditation, an imaginative participation in the celebration of festivals which are important in particular cultures may be very productive. In fact, this is one of the most important points of entry, educationally speaking, into an understanding of what various religious communities do. For this reason the Shap Working Party on World Religions in Education (in the United Kingdom) has published guides to religious festivals for teachers.[6] Obvious examples are Christmas, Easter, Ramadan and its conclusion, Diwali, New Year and O-bon. In such matters it will certainly be possible for local participants or representatives to offer information and illustration of what takes place, and for children to engage in some educational activities which are relevant to the festival in question. It is easy to see that imaginative teaching about the religious festivals of those religious communities which are prominent in the local community may be of great importance. To take but one example, thinking about how the birthdays of religious founders are commemorated might be accompanied by drawings and story-telling, or in the case of older children by the appreciation of selected religious art. This can eventually lead into learning about the important narratives in the major religions and coming to understand what is important in these narratives for the religious believers, and what is less important. Children will also come to learn that in different religious communities different stories are told, or in some cases the same stories are told in different ways.

In general, however, because of the far-reaching significance of participation in many if not most religious activities, extreme caution must be exercised in the educational context. The conclusion must be that religious "practice" or "practices" in a full sense cannot really be part of an integrative religious education. The reason is that, to a greater extent than music or art, a commitment to experience may be implied which could contradict either the self-understanding of the religion from which the practice is drawn, or the self-understanding of religions to which the families of the children belong. It is all right for children to sing songs and to paint pictures, but it would scarcely be correct for them to "do" a baptism, to engage in *zazen*, or to perform a religious dance which has a ritual function in a particular religion (such as the *o-tsutome* in Tenrikyō.

On the other hand, the importance of participatory experiences in religious "nurture" should not be underestimated. This is a matter for families, for parents and grandparents, and for the religious communities

---

6   This organization, founded in 1969, has played a major role in the development of broadly based programmes of religious education in Britain. The book is entitled *Festivals in World Religions*. It appeared first in 1986 under the editorship of Alan Brown and published in revised form under the editorship of Peter Woodward in 1998. In addition, because of the changing dates of festivals, the organization has regularly published *The Shap Calendar of Religious Festivals*.

themselves in their internal education programmes. In the secular educational context it will often be possible to allow or encourage children to talk about their own experience and practices in the context of the religious community to which they or their families belong.

4. Which religions should be considered?

One of the most difficult problems in the development of integrative religious education programmes, outside the religions themselves, is that the number of religions in the world is very large. Sometimes indeed it seems surprisingly large. Moreover, different religions are important in different countries. Yet the need is felt to maintain some kind of overall view. As a result the concept of "world religions" has been rather popular during recent decades. This term, however, has never been satisfactorily defined. In Germany the idea of the five "Weltreligionen" has become popular in the public mind, referring to Hinduism, Buddhism, Judaism, Christianity and Islam. In Britain, in recent decades at least, Sikhism has sometimes been counted in as one of the "world religions."

There are three main problems with this concept. First, not all the religions referred to have a universal message. Judaism and Hinduism are, in the main, religions of particular peoples. In this case, why not include the religions of other peoples, such as Shintō? Admittedly there are some versions of "Hinduism" which offer a universal message, such as the Ramakrishna movement, the message of Sri Aurobindo or the Hare Krishna movement, but are they still Hinduism? It would be more appropriate to regard these as new religions in their own right, and not as forms of Hinduism. They are analogous to some of the new religions in Japan which have roots in the Shintō tradition, such Kurozumikyō, or more widely viewed, Tenrikyō.[7] These religions are not forms of Shintō. On the contrary, they have their own justification to be regarded as offering a universal message and, if that is the criterion, to be "world religions."

Second, if the criterion for inclusion in the concept of "world religions" is that a religion should have a major influence in the history of the world, then Confucianism should also be included. Another candidate for inclusion would be Daoism, which is influential even beyond

---

7   Note that it is not appropriate to regard Tenrikyō as a "Shintō sect," a term which should be rejected on other grounds in any case.

7.6 Presuppositions of an Integrative Religious Education 385

Chinese cultural areas. On the other hand, it would be appropriate to regard Catholicism, the Orthodox churches and protestant forms of Christianity as distinct religions. Their influence in the world, and also their own self-understanding has often been very different. The same might be said for widely differing forms of Buddhism: Theravāda Buddhism, Tibetan Buddhism, and the various schools of Sino-Japanese Buddhism. Moreover there is a case for taking account of at least some religions which are now institutionally extinct (even if they have some continuing influence) such as the religions of ancient Egypt, of ancient Greece and Rome and of pre-conquest Central and South America. The word "religions" should really be read in inverted commas, because there is also a serious question about whether there really are such entities as "religions." What about all those activities and interests which come under the general area of "New Age" religiosity? What about the interest in "shamanism" which is quite wide-spread but only has a loose relationship to the historic forms of shamanism which were located in North Asia? There is no question but that religions which have had a major influence in the history of the world, and which continue to be important for people in many ways, should be considered somehow in programmes of religious education. However, the difficulty of getting agreement on a limited list of "religions" to be considered should be squarely regarded. Indeed, it would probably be better to abandon the idea that such agreement could be reached.

Third, an important reason for paying attention to a particular religion in religious education programmes in schools and calling it a "world religion" is that the religion plays a significant role in local or regional communities. For this reason, a certain amount of attention is paid to Sikhism in British schools, even though it is almost completely neglected in German schools. Sikhism is treated, for example, in the above mentioned *Festivals in World Religions*. But Sikhism would not normally be regarded in Germany as a *Weltreligion* (world religion).- Treating religions of local significance is certainly a positive principle in educational terms, for children should become acquainted with the religious traditions of those who might be their neighbours in the great multi-cultural cities of modern Europe. On the other hand this should not lead to the neglect of major traditions, such as Buddhism, which sometimes get left out simply because there are no Buddhists living nearby. In a certain sense, nowadays, the whole world is nearby. Moreover there are some really major and complex religious traditions, such as Buddhism, which have a broadly established claim to attention, whether there are any Buddhists living in the same street or not. Thus local or regional significance is relevant, but cannot alone determine the full range of the curriculum.

In sum therefore, the idea of "world religions" is best avoided. Because of its imprecision it plays no role in the academic study of religions. Specialists in education are therefore requested to abandon it.

5. Child development and religious maturity

This is not the place to go into the detail of various stages of child development, which is in any case a matter for on-going specialist attention by educational psychologists. However it is presupposed, and explicitly asserted here that there are significant differences in the ways in which children can be expected to respond to religious education programmes depending on their age and their individual developmental stage. For example, at an early age children are able to respond to storytelling and to community participation, while it would be unrealistic to expect advanced intellectual detachment. Religious symbolism is likely to be taken literally. The idea that there might be various kinds of religious language and even various kinds of religious "truth," that is religiously valid statements, presupposes a considerable intellectual advance which may be achieved, at least implicitly, by early adolescence, or not. In adolescence children are confronted with important new aspects of their own being, and consequently with various new "tasks."[8] New kinds of identification, new searches for meaning, and new enthusiasms play a tremendously important role. This coincides with a time in which received values and ideas are questioned, so that the possibility of making a shift from literalist to symbolic interpretations of familiar stories, traditions and rituals is very important. Religious education itself must move forward with the children, taking more account of the plurality of religions, and of their complexity. Religious education cannot provide children with "religion," but it can assist them, in an intellectually valid manner, in the search for their own religious maturity. In such ways, religious education programmes should take account of the various stages in child development, both in general terms and in connec-

---

8   The suggestive term "adolescent tasks" was used, I believe, by Harold Loukes, a pioneer in the development of non-confessional religious education in the United Kingdom, but possibly by other educationists as well.

tion with their relation to the possibilities of religious development. This task should be undertaken without recourse to proselytism, which would destroy the educational process.

It will be clear by now that "belief" as such cannot be a basis for the development of religious education programmes, while at the same time the beliefs or belief systems of religious people should be taken seriously in religious education. As children become older, they should be permitted, and even encouraged, to develop the habit of critical reflection upon belief systems and upon the implications of religious behaviour. Educationists have on the one hand a positive responsibility towards validly constituted religious communities within society, towards their rights and their contributions. On the other hand they have a responsibility to assist in the development of free and responsible citizens who will not be led astray by socially irresponsible and even destructive movements and organizations. Children should be enabled to develop their own mature judgments about the difference between the positive and the negative aspects of religion.

6. Some institutional options

What has been said so far, apart from occasional examples, has been intended to have a potential general validity. In practice the situations in different countries are quite varied, and it is not possible to review them in one short paper. Nevertheless the institutional options must be considered.

First, if the educational programme is right, and if the teachers are correctly taught, it does not matter too much if the teachers, individually, are believers in one religion or another. The main point is that they should avoid proselytism and that they should have a responsibility to the educational process itself.

Second, if the educational system is a unified, secular public system, there will be no difficulty in having a coherent public system of religious education, provided that it is desired. This should take particular account of the religious traditions current in the country concerned, Buddhism in Thailand, Christianity in Britain, Islam in Iran. However it should also take account of religious minorities within the country and the variety of religions in the world as a whole.

If the educational system is partly public and partly private, then there will probably be schools with a religious foundation as in Britain and in Japan. Such schools used to be called "church schools" in Britain, but more recently they have been called "faith schools" because of the introduction of Jewish and Muslim schools.[9] Now faith schools do not only offer religious education, they offer a total educational process which is informed by a specific religious ethos, Anglican, Catholic, Jewish, Muslim, or in Japan Buddhist, Tenrikyō etc. The question in these cases is whether such schools are prepared to provide a religious education programme which is consistent with a secular programme of religious education, thereby removing the joint dangers of proselytization and ghettoisation. This question must be addressed by those responsible for confessional schools or "faith schools." If this question is left unanswered, the fear must be that isolated identities will be reinforced, as for example in Northern Ireland, where Catholics and Protestants continue to fight in the streets, or as has more recently been seen in racial riots in the towns of northern England, where the Muslim and Hindu communities have been isolated. In Japan this might seem to be less of a danger. However there is another danger, namely that some closely protected communities are religiously "safe" while much of society is exposed to arbitrary and irresponsible religious activity and exploitation. Thus an opening to the variety of religions is very valuable in Japan in the programmes of "faith schools," that is, private schools with a religious foundation. Just as an example I would like to note here some textbooks published for use in the Risshō Kōseikai, which include information about various religions other than Buddhism.[10]

Finally, as far as "faith schools" are concerned, a most interesting initiative has just been started in England, whereby a "multi-faith" school has been established jointly by four religious communities namely Muslims, Jews, Christians (Anglican) and Hindus.[11] It appears that the religious education programme in particular will partly be shared and partly split between the faith orientations. Similarly the children will participate in morning prayers according to their specific religion, but they will also come together for a "school assembly" (traditional in British schools) with a common ethical focus. It will be interesting to see how this initiative will develop. Is a comparable initiative conceivable in other countries? Or could there be such a co-operation between re-

---

9 In fact, Jewish schools have quite a long history in Britain.
10 I reviewed this commendable initiative many years ago: Pye 1972b.
11 I follow a report in *The Guardian*, Monday July 8th 2002, page 6.

ligions other than the four mentioned in this case? It ought to be conceivable, for they are not all particularly closely related to each other.

7. Conclusion

I would like to return to the main subject of this paper and conclude by reaffirming the desirability of an "integrative religious education" in all sectors. First, if correctly conceived and carried out, it may be provided within the public sector. This does not necessarily contradict a secular constitution which separates religion and the state, which does not privilege any one religion above others, and which thereby recognizes religious plurality and guarantees religious freedom. However, second, the same program, or a closely related program, can also be carried out within the private sector, in schools in which a particular religion is privileged as a focus. The recognition and celebration of particular traditions in a private school does not mean that such a school cannot also take part in, and contribute to, an integrative religious education which recognises and respects plurality.

Bibliographical references

Alberts, Wanda 2007. *Integrative Religious Education in Europe, A Study-of-Religions Approach* (Religion and Reason 47). Berlin (de Gruyter).
Brown, Alan (ed.) 1986. *Festivals in World Religions.* London and New York (Longman). (Edited on behalf of the Shap Working Party.)
Pye, Michael 1972b. "A Buddhist approach to comparative religion in schools" *British Journal of Educational Studies* 20 (3): 270–281.
– 1996b. "Aum Shinrikyō. Can Religious Studies cope?" in: *Religion* 26 (3): 261–273.
– 2002d. "Religion et conflit au Japon. Concernant surtout le Shinto et le Sanctuaire de Yasukuni" in: *Diogène* 199: 52–70.
– 2003a. "Religion and conflict in Japan, with special reference to Shinto and Yasukuni Shrine" in: Diogenes 50 (3): 45–59. (English version of Pye 2002.)
Woodward, Peter (ed.) 1998. *Festivals in World Religions.* Norwich (Canterbury Press). (Revised version of Brown 1986.)

This article was first published in: The Organizing Committee of "Tenrikyo-Christian Dialogue II" (eds.) 2005. *Tenrikyo-Christian Dialogue II:*

Religion, Education, and the Family. Tenri (Tenri University Press): 267–286.

7.7 Peace in the Dialogue of Religions

This paper is based on a lecture for Wonkwang University, Iksan, Republic of Korea, October 2006, at a conference to mark the 60th anniversary of its foundation. Wonkwang University is associated with Won Buddhism (introduced in 5.6 above.) The original title, taking account of the conference theme, was "Peace and Religious Dialogue. Facts, Structures, Perspectives."

Non-partisan studies and social relevance

This short paper is presented from the perspective of a person whose main professional work has been to study religions in an academic and non-partisan way. In other words, it is not based on a religious point of view as such (even though I do have my own religious affiliation).[1] On the other hand, such studies of religion are considered to have a wider relevance for education and society. At the very least, "the study of religions" as a discipline (cf. German *Religionswissenschaft*), when undertaken in a careful historical and comparative manner, may provide much information of relevance to current social and political problems. Not only that, those who are experienced in the study of religions are sometimes able to assist in the structuring of dialogues between quite varied religious traditions and communities. Such dialogues in turn may be useful in creating new understandings on the part of their participants which are relevant to education and to social and political exchange. Ultimately, this may further the cause of peace in the world –which is urgently necessary.

This may sound rather optimistic. However it all involves very careful work. It is not good enough simply to say that we are in favour of peace in the world. We need to work out how to structure the necessary exchanges between societies and especially religious communities, so that they will be as fruitful as possible. Of course there are many specialists interested in such work nowadays. We find university courses with names such as "peace studies," "conflict research," or a combination

---

1   Anglican Communion (Church of England).

such as "peace and conflict research."[2] There are also university programmes on "war studies," but we may suppose that these have a very different emphasis, even being linked to "strategic studies" and thus contributing to the deplorable idea that it is quite normal to have wars! Most courses of this kind are provided by political scientists or sociologists and, unwisely, they usually fail to ask specialists in religion to make any contribution. However I believe that specialists in the study of religions have a special contribution to make.

If the study of religions is not to be based on a particular religious viewpoint, how can it be socially relevant or socially engaged? An attempt to chart this relationship was set out in in a series of "theses" composed by myself and a colleague, Edith Franke (then of Hanover), which we first developed in order to present to university audiences in Indonesia in 2003. This was just at the time when the Iraq war was started by the United States and other countries which were "willing" or pressurised to take part in it. Being privileged to visit various educational institutions in Indonesia, we found that the colleagues and students wanted very much to know how the studies about religions which we were recommending could be connected to questions of peace, including the relations between religious traditions. The question was also posed several times, politely but insistently, by mainly Muslim hearers, as to how the study of religions, if it is non-theological and is not be based on a particular religious viewpoint, can be in any way socially relevant or socially engaged? As a result, the theses presented for discussion, which had begun by taking a very severe line over the nature of the study of religions, were progressively clarified and extended.[3] Consequent on these discussions we were able to assist in the arrangement of a conference in Java in 2004 (a dual site conference in Yogyakarta and Semarang) on the subject of "Religious Harmony: Problems, Practice and Education," which was attended by scholars from many countries and also by leading Muslim scholars of Indonesia.[4] It was classified as a regional conference of the International Association for the History

---

2   German: Friedens- und Konfliktforschung.
3   These theses were later tested before other audiences in Indonesia and in Germany, and published in English and in Bahasa Indonesia (Franke and Pye 2004).
4   The proceedings of this conference have since been published both in English and in Bahasa Indonesia, under the editorship of Edith Franke, Abdurrahman Mas'ud, Michael Pye and Alef Theria Wasim (Franke et al. 2005 and 2006).

of Religions[5] and at the same time supported by the Indonesian Ministry of Religion (Departemen Agama). One of the key themes of this conference was "education," in particular religious education, and the programme included some visits to Muslim boarding schools, known in Bahasa Indonesia as *pesantren*. The impressions from these visits were considered in some detail at the conference, and the participants came to understand that these schools are *not* a training ground for the political radicalism which encourages violence. Rather, based on a strong consciousness of Muslim identity, young people are being educated into a constructive attitude to "religious harmony,"[6] as it usually called in this context. This is an example of how a most interesting meeting can really lead to new knowledge and new perceptions for the participants and also encourage those who are maintaining liberal and socially responsible positions in their own social context. The conference mentioned here was not formally structured as a "dialogue" and its dialogical character was rather accidental. It was intended to be a meeting of specialists in the study of religions from various countries including Indonesia itself. In fact however, since a large number of the participants were Islamic educationists, it was widely perceived by them as a many-facetted opportunity not only for dialogue with non-Indonesians, but also between Muslims and Indonesian non-Muslims. Thus it did not simply become a dialogue between two clear-cut parties. Moreover serious attention was given to methods and perspectives in the study of religions, as well as to various case studies of religious interaction, by various Indonesian and foreign participants. However it must be added that such meetings only take place with the help of a lot of imagination and hard work.

---

5 It may be noted that this was the first time that a conference sponsored by the International Association for the History of Religions (IAHR) was ever held in a predominantly Muslim country.

6 The discussion of this subject may be found in the published proceedings (see above). Apart from a range of wider papers, it was valuable that some really expert knowledge was available on the subject of the *pesantren*, both on the part of insiders and outsiders. A very special feature of the conference was the arrangement of visits to *pesantren*, and the concluding discussion about this is summarised by Ronald Lukens-Bull, himself an expert on the topic (Franke et al. 2006: 315–321, and cf. also Lukens-Bull 2005). Of course it is possible that other kinds of Muslim schools, for example in Pakistan, are not similar in this respect (cf. Lys 2006). We simply have to bear in mind that the major religious traditions are not monolithically consistent.

Religious adjacency as a matter of fact

In spite of this "hands-on" approach, and indeed because of it, the standpoint is maintained here that an important contribution by the discipline of the study of religions is simply no less than the provision of factual information. Such factual information need not be merely miscellaneous, for certain factual features can be gathered up in orientational concepts. An example of this is the fact of *religious adjacency*. This is a *fact* which in recent times has become increasingly apparent. However exclusive the teachings and claims of particular religions may be, it is impossible to overlook that different religions exist in the most varied manner side by side. This is true at a local level, where particular religions find themselves next to each other, and it is also true at a global level. No country is really isolated any more from all the others, even though some may seem to be so, or try to be so. For most of us, the religious communities of distant countries are our neighbours. Religious adjacency may have a long history, as in some Asian countries (cf. Franke and Pye 2006),[7] or for example in mediaeval Spain. In some countries it is perceived as a new "problem," as for example when it becomes necessary to coordinate the existence of Islam and Christianity as neighbours within a particular country such as Britain, Denmark, or Indonesia.

It is of interest here that religious adjacency is a matter about which particular religious traditions have developed their own theories. For example, Islamic teaching tolerantly regards the "people of the Book," by which is meant the Jewish and the Christian Bibles which preceded the Qur'an. Dialogue between religions need to take such theories into account. But we also need to recognise that the mutual adjacency of religions really is simply a matter of fact. This may attract particular religious theories or doctrines, but what is being emphasised here is that in the perspective of the study of religions it really is a *fact* to be reckoned with, whether the various theologies currently have resources to deal with it, or not.

While religious systems or communities may exist in adjacency to each other, this does not mean that they are all similar. Of particular importance

---

7   This work introduces the concept of the *Nebeneinander* (i. e. the "adjacency") of religions. It includes case studies by various authors concerning Indonesia, Malaysia, Singapore, China, Japan and Korea (with special reference to Won Buddhism).

in relation to the theme of peace and conflict is the fact that not all religious traditions or communities in fact encourage peace. On the contrary, religious representatives and leaders have very often taken the path of conflict, violence and war, justifying it on religious grounds, or allowing politicians to legitimise war by means of religion. Unfortunately these are facts. Any dialogues between religious groups "for peace" have to take these facts into account –and think about them. Dialogues which only look at the nice aspects of religions will not get us very far. For example, there may be meetings in Israel/Palestine between Jews, Muslims and Christians which seem to be quite enjoyable for the participants, but which do not comment on the political problems and military activities surrounding them. A report was issued about one such meeting which ended in an agreeable dinner, just as the war between Israel and Hizbollah was taking place, with the loss of many civilian lives and the massive destruction of parts of the Lebanon. There is no doubt that Israeli actions are influenced by the assumption found in many parts of the Hebrew Bible that the land of Palestine was given to them by God. Many Christian fundamentalists, who regard all parts of the Bible as equally "inspired," agree with this. It is not surprising that the Arab inhabitants of the country do *not* agree, and as most of them are Muslims (though some are Christians), they naturally adduce the teaching of Islam about the protection of Islamic areas. Conflict will inevitably continue until such beliefs are revised. Of course, any friendly meetings may be valuable, but it is useless to disregard these facts.

Religions may or may not be peaceful

It is quite significant that not every religious organisation or teaching supports the idea of "peace." This may be difficult to imagine in a setting like Wonkwang University, which is influenced in the background by Won Buddhism. My understanding of Won Buddhism is that it is a religion which emphasises rational and humane relations between people of all kinds, and therefore has an inbuilt bias in favour of peace.[8] But this is not at all true for all religions, whether old ones or new ones. We have all heard of "cults" or "new religions" which regard themselves as in some sense representing the final, select group of those who will be

---

8   For a brief introduction to Won Buddhism in English, perhaps the first by a non-member, see Pye 2002c (also at 5.6 above).

saved, and whose members are ready to commit violence in the name of their religion, whether against their own members or against the rest of the world. Examples are the Waco cult in the United States, Solar Temple in Europe and Aum Shinrikyō in Japan. On the other hand, some other religious groups are completely pacifist: examples are the Quakers (Friends), Jehova's Witnesses and the Baha'i. As a result they have also suffered persecution.

Most major religious traditions are, in fact, not pacifist, even though their representatives often argue that they are peaceful. The simple reason for this is that they become involved in the political structures of the countries in which they are strong and therefore, even if they have a peace message, they are also used to support political claims which in turn are based on military force. We know that this applies to Christianity and Islam. Believers in these two religions have fought each other over centuries in the name of God, and tragically there are still far too many believers in each of these religions who feel called upon to do this. Of course, the teachings of these religions are usually interpreted differently. Islamic teachers emphasise that military force is to be used in self-defence, and particularly in the defence of the Islamic community. Christian teachers also point out that Christianity is mainly a religion of peace, even though self-defence was justified in later theory. There is a serious contradiction here in the Christian world. There is no doubt that Jesus Christ rejected the option of armed rebellion against the Romans, which many of his Jewish compatriots wanted at the time. In fact, it can be seriously asserted as a matter of historical fact that Jesus himself was a pacifist. This all changed in the Christian world at the latest with the espousal of Christianity by the Emperor Constantine, whose famous vision was that of a cross in the sky together with the words "In hoc signo vinces" (with this sign you will conquer). Pacifists in Christianity are now a small minority, and no major churches officially preach pacifism, even though they often call for peace.

However there is another interesting fact which should not be forgotten here, namely that this problem can also be found in the Buddhist world. The Buddha's teaching was not really about peace or war as such. Nevertheless the implications of his teaching suggest non-violence, if only because violence is not at all conducive to the attainment of enlightenment or nirvana. However, many wars have been fought since then between Buddhists, for example in South-East Asia, and sometimes they even stole each others' Buddhist images violently! Military activity has not only been a matter for laymen in Japanese Buddhism. It is well known that in earlier periods of Japanese history there were large groups of armed monks who tried to influence the course of political events by aggressive military action in and around the capital city of the time, Kyōto. More recently, Japanese military power, which caused so much suffering in Korea, China and elsewhere, was supported by Buddhist organisations, while of course most military personnel were in some sense Buddhists. Indeed, in spite of a significant peace movement among Japanese Buddhists in recent years (see below) there are Buddhist temples in Japan which continue to have places which encourage commemorating "the fallen" (*shinbotsusha*), while omitting reference to those whom they may have killed. As one example among many we may refer to the large-scale Ryōzen Kannon at the Rinzai Zen Buddhist temple Kōdaiji, in Kyōto, where people also go to pray for various other things. Here "the fallen" are referred to as *eirei* meaning "heroic spirits" (a term also used at Yasukuni Shrine). The subject is very complicated however. At a well-known temple in Shikoku, Ishiteji (temple no. 51 of the well-known pilgrimage round 88 temples on that island) there is a substantial monument to "the fallen" in Burma, while at the same time there have recently been various activities protesting against the war in Iraq, and arguing for the implementation of Buddhist values against war, e.g. by making use of the concept of mutual interdependence.

Primal religion, critical religions and peace orientations

In my own studies of religions I distinguish between two major types, "primal" religion which is related to a particular ethnic group, and "critical" religions which are somehow able to distance themselves from ordinary life and are understood to offer a message of universal validity.[9] This distinction leads to a particular problem when we consider the relation between religion and peace. Primal religions presuppose a simple group loyalty, are mainly not pacifist, and assume the necessity of self-defence and even of armed expansionism. Such expansionism is a simple accompaniment to the natural process of extension of any ethnic group within the possibilities of its geographical and political environment. Very obvious examples of such religions, whatever else they may teach, are Shintō and Judaism.

---

9   The term "world religions" is not used here because it is intrinsically confusing. Cf. the discussion on religious education in 7.6 above.

The current situation in Japan is quite interesting in these matters. On the one hand we have the well-known problem about Yasukuni Shrine. This shrine is supported by a strong right-wing trend which cherishes Japanese nationalism and is not in any sense concerned with peace. Rather, the military actions of Japan in past times are celebrated, even glorified. This tendency is quite strong in the presentation of the recently redeveloped museum which belongs to the shrine, the Yūshūkan. Of course, the visits by prime minister Koizumi (and others) to Yasukuni Shrine were given another interpretation, namely that it is "natural" for Japanese people to show gratitude to those who gave their lives for their country. At the same time he asserted that he prayed for peace in the future (though there could have been other ways of doing this). The subsequent prime-minister, Abe Shinsō, also supported this line of interpretation. The matter might seem to be quite harmless to some observers, especially in countries such as the USA or the UK which have their own significant war memorials for "the fallen," that is, their *own* fallen. According to one presentation for children at Yasukuni Shrine there is a place where people of other countries who died are also commemorated. However when I found this little place at the side of the shrine (in 2005) there was nothing to see except for a small boarded up area, and no way to commemorate them. Moreover, there is another fundamental problem with the apparently benign interpretations usually heard. Since enshrinement is restricted to those under military orders, innumerable people who died in the wars are *not* commemorated at Yasukuni Shrine. In particular there is no reference to the victims of military activity. Apart from "the fallen" or "soldiers," we should remember that many civilians died in the wars. This includes, just to give one significant example, many Koreans who died as slave labourers in Hiroshima. Not only are are they not commemorated in Yasukuni Shrine (and probably would not want to be), but their survivors and their descendants have also received no pensions or other compensation, for the simple reason that they are not Japanese.[10]

The reason why all this is a problem is that the Shintō religion is mainly an *ethnically* conceived tradition. It is the traditional primal religion of Japan which has been adapted in many ways to follow the course of social and cultural developments. Thus it is not a religion which has an intrinsic teaching about peace, or indeed very much teach-

---

10 I understand that a small commemorative site has recently been set up for this Korean community in Hiroshima itself.

ing at all, but one which structures the ritual life of a particular group of people, namely the Japanese. This is what a primal religion is, or what a primal religion does. This seems quite natural to many Japanese people, especially to busy politicians. However it is also important to know, again as a matter of fact, that by no means all Japanese people agree with this perspective.

Currently the Shintō world has been adapting itself to the post-war situation in Japan. This process has been rather slow, considering that the Pacific or East Asian War ended some sixty years ago. Nevertheless it should be reported that there are certain movements towards regarding Shintō as a force for peace. These tendencies are based on two ideas. The first is the idea that different peoples have their own life areas and appropriate divinities, and that these can all coexist in a peaceful way next to each other, also outside Japan. Not only that, they can cooperate in the consideration of important problems such as the protection of the environment or in the field of medical ethics. This idea is supported by what may be called the moderate party within Shintō, and it should be respected. The second tendency is for religious groups within the wider cultural context of Shintō to develop a universal message and an international outreach. Two examples of this are the teaching and activities of Tsubaki Grand Shrine and of the Konkōkyō Izuo Church in Ōsaka. The Konkōkyō Church mentioned here is an independent variation of the older religion of Konkōkyō.[11] These are also very respectworthy approaches, although it must be said that they somehow depart from the normal pattern of Shintō, understood to have an ethnic range, and can be regarded as more or less independent new religions.

Now this is not to say that "primal" religious systems tend to support conflict, latently, while others do not. We have already see that the wider history of both Buddhism and Christianity are marked by much participation in conflict, even though this might seem to run contrary to the initial impetus of these traditions. The "critical" religions however, do seem to harbour greater resources for self-reflection. For example, a significant feature of the situation of contempory Japanese religion is that some major Buddhist denominations have been thinking very seriously in recent years about the question of war responsibility. The most striking cases are the two leading denominations of Shin Buddhism, the Ōtani-ha and the Honganji-ha. Not only have these denominations issued statements of responsibility and repentance (*zange*)

---

11 The original form of Konkōkyō was itself a "new religion," founded in 1859.

for having been involved in warlike attitudes in the past. They have also embarked on an educational programme among their followers to instruct them concerning matters of war and peace, and of course to encourage the latter. This is a very positive development. There has also been a similar process in Sōtō Zen Buddhism.

From these examples we can see that the basic typological dfferentiation between "primal" and "critical" religions has relevant implications, at least tendentially, for the way in which religious traditions should be assessed as far as questions of peace are concerned.

Factual knowledge and inter-religious dialogues for peace

How can inter-religious dialogues assist the development of peace? Unfortunately wars frequently take place, and we should remember that they all occur on the basis of human responsibility. They are not like earthquakes, *tsunami* or typhoons. It is therefore very desirable that dialogues between religious communities or the representatives of various religious traditions should, again and again, include the question of peace on their agenda. As suggested above in "The study of religions and the dialogue of religions" (7.5), structured dialogues should include, but of course by no means be limited to specialists in the study of religions. Religious dialogues with serious themes of social and political importance require reliable introductions into various relevant facts – facts about religion as well as other relevant historical and political facts. They also require a responsible searching of traditional teachings, and self-critical reflection on the part of the religious representatives. If this is all carried out in a spirit of mutual exchange, with effective mediation, then valuable results can be achieved. Much patient work lies ahead for all who care about such matters.

Bibliographical references

Franke, Edith, Mas'ud, Abdurrahman, Pye, Michael and Wasim, Alef Theria 2005a. *Religious Harmony: Problems, Practice and Education. Proceedings of the Regional Conference of the International Association for the History of Religions, Yogyakarta and Semarang, Indonesia, September 27th – October 3rd, 2004.* Yogyakarta (Oasis Publisher).
– 2005b: *Harmoni Kehidupan Beragama: Problem, Praktik dan Pendidikan. Proceeding Konferensi Regional International Association for the History of Religions, Yo-*

gyakarta dan Semarang, Indonesia, 27 September – 03 October, 2004. Yogyakarta (Oasis Publisher). (Indonesian version of Franke et al. 2005a.)
- 2006. Revised English edition of Franke et al. 2005. (*Religion and Reason* 45). Berlin (de Gruyter).

Franke, Edith and Pye, Michael 2004. "Ilmu agama dan kontribusinya terhadap penyelesaian masalah dalam dunia yang plural / The study of religions and its contribution to problem solving in a plural world" in: *Marburg Journal of Religion* in 2004:<http://www.uni-marburg.de/fb03/ivk/mjr/pdfs/2004/articles/franke-2004.pdf>

Franke, Edith and Pye, Michael (eds.) 2006. *Religionen Nebeneinander. Modelle religiöser Vielfalt in Ost- und Südostasien*. Berlin and Münster (Lit-Verlag).

Lukens-Bull, Ronald 2005. *A Peaceful Jihad. Negotiating Identity and Modernity in Muslim Java*. New York (Palgrave Macmillan).

Lys, Candice 2006. "Demonizing the 'Other': Fundamentalist Pakistani Madrasahs and the Construction of Religious Violence" in: *Marburg Journal of Religion* 11/1: <http://web.uni-marburg.de/religionswissenschaft/journal/mjr>

Pye, Michael 2002. "Won Buddhism as a Korean new religion" in: *Numen. International Review for the History of Religions* 49:113–141.

An early draft of this text, under the title "Peace and religious dialogue: facts, structures and perspectives," was made available in a conference booklet of Wonkwang University (2006). However, to avoid overlap with 7.5 above, a longer section on the structuring of religious dialogues has been removed and some other revisions have been made.

Author's Publications Cited in the Present Work

This integrated overview lists publications by the author which are cited in one or both volumes of the present work. The lettered sequences found here (a, b, c, etc.) are adopted within the bibliographies of particular articles. A more detailed list including writings not cited in these volumes, going up as far as 2003, was kindly compiled by Renate Stegerhoff-Raab and included in Kleine, Christoph, Schrimpf, Monika and Triplett, Katja (eds.) 2003: *Unterwegs. Neue Pfade in der Religionswissenschaft (Festschrift…)*, München (Biblion Verlag):17–28. Multi-authored or multi-edited works which include the present writer are listed in a separate section below, following the alphabetical sequence of the first person to be named.

1969
"The transplantation of religions" in: *Numen, International Review for the History of Religions* 16 (3): 234–9. (N.B. published under the name E.M.Pye.)

1971a
"Syncretism and Ambiguity" in: *Numen. International Review for the History of Religions* 18 (2): 83–93.

1971b
"Assimilation and skilful means" in: *Religion* 1 (2): 152–8.

1972a
Comparative Religion: An Introduction through Source Materials. Newton Abbot (David and Charles) and New York (Harper and Row).

1972b
"A Buddhist approach to comparative religion in schools" in: *British Journal of Educational Studies* 20 (3): 270–81.

1973a
"Aufklärung and religion in Europe and Japan" in: *Religious Studies* 9: 201–217.

1973b
"Comparative hermeneutics in religion" in: Pye and Morgan 1973: 1–58.

1974
"Problems of method in the interpretation of religion" in: *Japanese Journal of Religious Studies* 1 (2–3): 107–123.
1975
"Japanese studies of religion" in: *Religion* (Special Congress Issue): 55–72.
1976
"The end of the problem about 'other' religions" in: Clayton, John P. (ed.), *Ernst Troeltsch and the Future of Theology*. Cambridge (Cambridge University Press): 172–95.
1977
"Troeltsch and the science of religion" in: Morgan and Pye 1977: 234–252.
1978a
Skilful Means. A Concept in Mahāyāna Buddhism. London (Duckworth) and (Routledge – 2nd edition 2003).
1978b
"Diversions in the interpretation of Shintō" in: Anthony, D.W. (ed.), *Proceedings of the British Association for Japanese Studies 1977 (Volume Two, Part Two: Social Sciences)*, Sheffield (University of Sheffield: Centre of Japanese Studies): 77–92. (Republished Pye 1981.)
1979a
The Buddha. London and Dallas (Duckworth).
1979b
Theologie im Kontext des religiösen Pluralismus, in: Kremkau, Klaus (ed.), *Christus allein – allein das Christentum? (Vorträge der vierten theologischen Konferenz zwischen Vertretern der Evangelischen Kirche in Deutschland und der Kirche von England)*. Frankfurt am Main (Verlag Otto Lembeck): 11–25.
1980a
"On comparing Buddhism and Christianity" in: *Studies (Tsukuba Daigaku Tetsugakushisōgakkei Ronshū)* 5 (1979 issue): 1–20.
1980b
"Comparative hermeneutics: a brief statement" in: *Japanese Journal of Religious Studies* 7/1 (1980) 25–33.
1981
"Diversions in the interpretation of Shintō" in: *Religion*. 11: 61–74. (Republication of 1978b).

1982a
"The study of religion as an autonomous discipline" in: *Religion* 12: 67–76.
1982b
"Diversions in the interpretation of Shintō" in: *Religion*. 11: 61–74. (Republication of Pye 1978).
1982c
"Religion and reason in the Japanese experience" in: *King's Theological Review* 5 (1): 14–17.
1983
"The significance of the Japanese intellectual tradition for the history of religions" in: Slater, Peter and Wiebe, Donald (eds.) *Traditions in Contact and Change, Selected Proceedings of the Fourteenth Congress of the International Association for the History of Religions*. Waterloo Ontario (Wilfrid Laurier): 565–77.
1984
"Tominaga Nakamoto (1715–1746) and Religious Pluralism" in: Daniels, Gordon (ed.) *Europe Interprets Japan* (select proceedings of the den Haag conference of the European Association for Japanese Studies 1982). Tenterden (Paul Norbury): 191–7.
1986
"National and international identity in a Japanese religion: Byakkōshinkōkai" in: Hayes, Victor. C. (ed.) *Identity Issues and World Religions, Selected Proceedings of the International Association for the History of Religions*, Netley Australia (The Australian Association for the Study of Religions): 234–241.
1987a
O-meguri, Pilgerfahrt in Japan. Katalog einer Ausstellung. Marburg (Universitätsbibliothek der Philipps-Universität Marburg).
1987b
"A common language of minimal religiosity" in: *The Journal of Oriental Studies* 26 (1): 21–7.
1988.
"Nationale und internationale Identität in einer japanischen Religion" (Byakkō Shinkōkai) " in: Zinser, Hartmut (ed.) *Religionswissenschaft. Eine Einführung*. Berlin (Dietrich Reimer): 239–251. (German translation of Pye 1986.)
1989a
(ed.) *Marburg Revisited. Institutions and Strategies in the Study of Religion*. Marburg (Diagonal-Verlag).

1989b
"Cultural and organizational perspectives in the study of religion" in: Pye, Michael (ed.) *Marburg Revisited. Institutions and Strategies in the Study of Religion.* Marburg (Diagonal-Verlag): 11–17.

1989c
"Shintō and the typology of religion" in: *Method & Theory in the Study of Religion* 1/2: 186–95. (Summary version 1984 as "The place of Shintō in the typology of religion" in: Yamamoto, Y. (ed.) *Proceedings of the Thirty-first International Congress of Human Sciences in Asia and North Africa.* Tokyo) Institute of Eastern Culture): 1055–6.)

1990a
(trans.) *Emerging from Meditation (Tominaga Nakamoto).* London (Duckworth) and Honolulu (University of Hawaii Press).

1990b
"Philology and fieldwork in the study of Japanese religion" in: Tyloch, W. (ed.) *Studies on Religions in the Context of Social Sciences. Methodological and Theoretical Relations,* Warsaw (Polish Society for the Study of Religions/Polskie Towarzystwo Religioznawcze): 146–59.

1990c
"Skilful means and the interpretation of Christianity" in: *Buddhist-Christian Studies* 10: 17–22.

1991a
"Religious tradition and the student of religion" in: Geertz, A. W. and Jensen, J. S. (eds.) *Religion, Tradition and Renewal* .Aarhus (Aarhus University Press): 29–36.

1991b
"Religious studies in Europe: structures and desiderata" in: Klaus K. Klostermaier and Larry W. Hurtado (eds.), *Religious Studies: Issues, Prospects, and Proposals* (University of Manitoba Studies in Religion, 2). Atlanta (Scholars Press): 39–55.

1991c
"Reflections on the treatment of tradition in comparative perspective, with special reference to Ernst Troeltsch and Gerardus van der Leeuw" in Kippenberg, Hans G. and Luchesi, Brigitte (eds.) *Religionswissenschaft und Kulturkritik.* Marburg (Diagonal-Verlag):101–111.

1992a
"An Asian starting point for the study of religion" in: Nowaczyk M.

and Stachowski, Z. (eds.) *Language, Religion, Culture: In Memory of Professor Witold Tyloch.* Warsaw (Polish Society for the Study of Religion) 27–35.

1992b

"An Asian starting point for the study of religion" in: Despland, Michel and Vallée Gérard 1992. *Religion in History. The Word, the Idea, the Reality / La religion dans l'histoire. Le mot, l'idée, la réalité:* 101–9.

1993

Syncretism versus Synthesis. (Occasional papers of the British Association for the Study of Religion No. 8). Cardiff (BASR). Republished in: *Method &Theory in the Study of Religion,* 6 (3) (1994): 217–29.

1994a

"What is 'religion' in East Asia?" in: Bianchi, Ugo, Mora Fabio and Bianchi Lorenzo (eds.) *The Notion of "Religion" in Comparative Research: Selected Proceedings of the XVIth Congress of the International Association for the History of Religions, Rome, 3rd-8th September, 1990.* Rome ("L'Erma" di Bretschneider): 115–22.

1994b

"Religion: shape and shadow" in: *Numen. International Review for the History of Religions* 41 (1): 51–75.

1994c

"Syncretism versus synthesis" in: *Method & Theory in the Study of Religion,* 6 (3): 217–29. (Previously published in *Occasional papers of the British Association for the Study of Religion,* Cardiff 1993.)

1994d

Christian churches and political change in Eastern Europe" in: Gill, Sean, D'Costa Gavin and King, Ursula (eds.) *Religion in Europe, Contemporary Pespectives.* Kampen (Pharaos): 188–200.

1994e

(ed.) *The Macmillan Dictionary of Religion.* London (Macmillan) and as *The Continuum Dictionary of Religion,* New York (Continuum).

1995a

"Religion and identity: clues and threads" in: de Gruchy, J. W. and Martin, S. (eds.), *Religion and the Reconstruction of Civil Society (Papers from the founding congress of the South African Academy of Religion, January 1994).* Pretoria (University of South Africa): 3–17.

1995b

"Three teachings (*sanjiao*) theory and modern reflection on religion" in: Dai Kangsheng, Zhang Xinying and Pye, Michael (eds.) 1995. *Religion and Modernisation in China, Proceedings of the Regional*

Conference of the International Association for the History of Religions held in Beijing, China, April 1992. Cambridge (Roots and Branches): 111–16. (Chinese translation as "Sanjiaolilun yu duizongjiaode xiandai fansi" in *Shijie Zongjiao Ziliao* (ISSN 1000–4505) (1992/4): 1–3.)

1996a
"Intercultural strategies and the International Association for the History of Religions" in: Platvoet, J. Cox, J. and Olupona, J. (eds.) *The Study of Religions in Africa. Past, Present and Prospects, Proceedings of the IAHR Regional Conference at Harare, Zimbabwe 1992.* Cambridge (Roots and Branches): 37–45.

1996b
"Aum Shinrikyō. Can Religious Studies cope?" in: *Religion* 26 (3): 261–73.

1996c
"Syncretism: Buddhism and Shintō on one island" in: Doležalová, Iva, Horyna, Břetislav and Papoušek, Dalibor (eds.) *Religions in Contact. Selected Proceedings of the Special IAHR Conference held in Brno, August 23–26, 1994,* Brno (Czech Society for the Study of Religions): 159–62.

1996d
"Reflecting on the plurality of religions" in: *World Faiths Encounter* 14: 3–11.

1996e
"Shintō, primal religion and international identity" in: *Marburg Journal of Religion* 1/1. : <http://www.uni-marburg.de/fb03/ivk/mjr/pdfs/1996/articles/shinto1996>.

1997a
"Reflecting on the plurality of religions (full text)" in: *Marburg Journal of Religion* 2: (virtual pages). (Also published in abbreviated form in *World Faiths Encounter* 14 (1996): 3–11.

1997b
"East Asian rationality in the exploration of religion" in: Martin, Luther J. and Jensen, Jeppe Sinding (eds.) *Rationality and the Study of Religion.* Aarhus (Aarhus University): 65–77.

1997c
"Perceptions of the body in Japanese religion" in: Coakley, Sarah (ed.) *Religion and the Body.* Cambridge (Cambridge University Press): 248–261.

1997d
"Friedrich Heiler (1892–1967)" in: Michaels, A. (ed.) *Klassiker der Religionswissenschaft. Von Friedrich Schleiermacher bis Mircea Eliade.* München (Beck): 277–289 and (footnotes) 399–400.

1998a
"Die 'geschickten Mittel'. Zur Dialektik der Ausdrucksformen in Buddhismus und Christentum" in: Viertel, Matthias (ed.) *Buddhismus und Christentum.* Hofgeismar (Evangelische Akademie Hofgeismar): 41–64.

1998b
"Innovation und Modernität im Won-Buddhismus" in: Keil, S., Jetzkowitz, J. and König, M. (eds.) 1998. *Modernisierung und Religion in Südkorea*, Köln (Weltforum Verlag):183–94.

1999a
"Methodological Integration in the Study of Religions" in: Tore Ahlbäck (ed.) *Approaching Religion, Scripta Instituti Donneriani Aboensis XVII (1)*, Åbo/Turku, Finland (Donner Institute for Research in Religious and Cultural History): 188–205.

1999b
"Soteriological orientations in religion" in: Tenri Organizing Committee of Tenrikyo- Christian Dialogue (eds), *Tenrikyo-Christian Dialogue*, Tenri City (Tenri University Press): 99–113.

2000a
"Westernism unmasked" in: Jensen,Tim and Rothstein, Mikael (eds.) *Secular Theories on Religion. Current Perspectives.* Copenhagen (Museum Tusculanum Press), 211–230.

2000b
"Participation, observation and reflection: an endless method" in: Holm, Nils G. et al. eds. *Ethnography is a Heavy Rite. Studies of Comparative Religion in Honor of Juha Pentikäinen* (Religionsvetenskapliga skrifter 47). Åbo (Åbo Akademis Tryckeri) 2000: 64–79.

2001a
"Religion und Recht in Japan: Pluralismus, Toleranz und Konkurrenz" in: *Marburg Journal of Religion Vol. 6 No.1* (2001): <http://www.uni-marburg.de/religionswissenschaft/journal/mjr/pye.html>

2001b
"The study of religions and the dialogue of religions (Shūkyōgaku to shūkyōtaiwa)" in: *Marburg Journal of Religion* 6 (2): < http://web.uni-marburg.de/religionswissenschaft/journal/mjr>

2001c
"Political correctness in the study of religions: Is the Cold War really over?" in: Doležalová, Iva, Martin, Luther H. and Papoušek, Dalibor (eds.) 2001. *The Academic Study of Religion during the Cold War: East and West.* Frankfurt and New York (Peter Lang): 313–33.

2002a
"Memes and models in the study of religions" in: Giulia Sfameni Gasparro (ed.) *Themes and Problems in the History of Religions in Contemporary Europe. Proceedings of the International Seminar, Messina, March 30–3, 2001.* Cosenza (Edizioni Lionello Giordano), 245–59.

2002b
"Traces of Shinran Shōnin" in: Thierfelder, Constanze and Eibach, Dietrich Hannes (eds.), *Resonanzen. Schwingungsräume Praktischer Theologie (Gerhard Marcel Martin zum 60. Geburtstag)*, Stuttgart (Kohlhammer): 215–24.

2002c
"Won Buddhism as a Korean new religion" in: *Numen. International Review for the History of Religions* 49 (2): 113–41.

2002d
"Religion et conflit au Japon. Concernant surtout le Shinto et le Sanctuaire de Yasukuni" in: *Diogène* 199: 52–70.

2002e
" Modern Japan and the science of religions" in: Wiegers, Gerard A. and Platvoet, Jan G. (eds.) *Modern Societies and the Study of Religions. Studies in Honour of Lammert Leertouwer.* Leiden (Brill): 350–376.

2003a
"Religion and conflict in Japan, with special reference to Shinto and Yasukuni Shrine" in: Diogenes 50 (3): 45–59. (English version of Pye 2002.)

2003b
"Overcoming westernism: the end of orientalism and occidentalism" in: Schalk, Peter et al. (eds.) *Religion im Spiegelkabinett. Asiatische Religionsgeschichte im Spannungsfeld zwischen Orientalismus und Okzidentalismus (Acta Universitatis Upsaliensis. Historia Religionum 22).* Uppsala (Uppsala Universitet): 91–114.

2003c
Rationality, ritual and life-shaping decisions in modern Japan (Occasional Papers 29). Marburg (Centre for Japanese Studies). Republished in Raud, Rein (ed.) 2007. *Japan and Asian Modernities*, London (Kegan Paul): 1–27.

2003d
"Modern Japan and the science of religions" in: *Method and Theory in the Study of Religions* 15/1 (2003): 1–27. (Previously agreed publication of 2002e.)

2004a
The structure of religious systems in contemporary Japan: Shintō variations on Buddhist pilgrimage. (Occasional Papers 30). Marburg (Centre for Japanese Studies).

2004b
"Zur Legitimation, Struktur und Durchführung von interreligiösem Dialog" in: Barth et al. 2004: 13–20.

2004c
"Shinran als mystischer religiöser Denker" in: Schönemann, Friederike and Maaßen, Thorsten (eds) *Prüft Alles, und das Gute behaltet! Zum Wechselspiel von Kirchen, Religionen und säkularer Welt. Festschrift für Hans-Martin Barth zum 65. Geburtstag.* Frankfurt am Main (Otto Lembeck): 309–35. (Translated from the English of 2001 by Gerhard Marcel Martin.)

2006a
"Models of religious diversity: simplicities and complexities" in: Franke, Edith, Mas'ud, Abdurrahman, Pye, Michael and Wasim, Alef Theria (eds.) *Religious Harmony: Problems, Practice and Education. Proceedings of the Regional Conference of the International Association for the History of Religions, Yogyakarta and Semarang, Indonesia, September 27th – October 3rd, 2004.* Berlin (de Gruyter): 23–33.

2006b
"Die 'Drei Lehren' und das Tauziehen der Religionen in chinesischen Tempeln Südostasiens" in: Franke, Edith and Pye, Michael (eds.) *Religionen Nebeneinander. Modelle religiöser Vielfalt in Ost- und Südostasien.* Münster (Lit-Verlag): 41–60.

2006c
"Difference and coherence in the worldwide study of religions" in: Jakelic, Slavica and Pearson, Lori (eds), *The Future of the Study of Religion*, Boston and Leiden (Brill) 2006: 77–95.

2007
"Research on prayer in the contemporary study of religions" in: Hashimoto, Taketo (ed.) *Prayer as Interaction. (Tenri University and Marburg University Joint Research Project September 2006).* Tenri (Tenri University Press) 2007, 3–28.

2009a
"Nossa Senhora Aparecida and Solo Sagrado: creating sacred space in Brazil" in: Court, Jürgen and Klöcker, Michael (eds.) *Wege und Welten der Religionen. Forschungen und Vermittlungen. Festschrift für Udo Tworuschka* .Frankfurt am Main (Lembeck): 457–62.

2009b
"Ephemera in Japanese religion with special reference to Buddhist pilgrimage" in: Baskind, James (ed.) *Scholars of Buddhism in Japan: Buddhist Studies in the 21st Century. The Ninth Annual Symposium for Scholars Resident in Japan*, Kyōto (International Research Center for Japanese Studies) 2009: 67–78.

2009c
"Leading patterns in everyday Japanese religion" in: *Sphinx, Yearbook 2008–9* (Societas Scientiarum Fennica): 45–53.

2010
"'Polytheism' and 'monotheism' as a problem in the typology of religions" in: Charles Guittard (ed), *Le Monothéisme: Diversité, Exclusivisme ou Dialogue. (Actes de l'Association Européenne pur l'Étude des Religions (EASR) Congrès de Paris, 11–14 Septembre 2002)* Paris (Editions Non Lieu): 25–32.

2011a
"O Estudo das Religiões: novos tempos, tarefas e opções" in: da Cruz, Eduardo and De Mori, Geraldo (eds.) 2011. Teologia e Ciências da Religião. A Caminho da Maioridade Acadêmica. São Paulo (Ed. Paulinas): 15–24.

2011b (ed.)
Beyond Meditation. Expressions of Shin Buddhist Spirituality (Eastern Buddhist Voices 1). London (Equinox Publications).

2011c
"Refletindo sobre Primos Distantes. Distância cultural na transplantação de religiões japonesas em países distantes," *Rever* 11/2 July/December : 11–31.

2012 (ed.)
Listening to Shin Buddhism. Starting Points of Modern Dialogue (Eastern Buddhist Voices 2). London (Equinox Publications).

Jointly Authored or Edited Writings
(Alphabetical Order of the First Name Recorded)

Barth, Minoura and Pye 2000a:
Barth, Hans-Martin, Minoura, Eryō, and Pye, Michael (eds.) *Buddhismus und Christentum. Jōdo Shinshū und Evangelische Theologie. III. Internationales Rudolf-Otto Symposion am Fachbereich Evangelische Theologie der Philipps-Universität Marburg in Zusammenarbeit mit der Ōtani-Universität Kyōto.* Hamburg (EB-Verlag).

Barth, Minoura and Pye 2000b:
Bukkyō to kirisutokyō no taiwa. Jōdo Shinshū to fukuinshugishingaku. Kyōto (Hōzōkan). (Japanese edition of 2000a, Barth et al.)

Barth, Kadowaki, Minoura and Pye 2004a:
Barth, Hans-Martin, Kadowaki Ken, Minoura Eryō and Michael Pye (eds.). *Buddhismus und Christentum vor der Herausforderung der Säkularisierung.* Hamburg (EB-Verlag).

Barth, Kadowaki, Minoura and Pye 2004b:
Barth, Hans-Martin, Kadowaki Ken, Minoura Eryō and Michael Pye (eds.). *Bukkyō to kirisutokyō no taiwa III: Sezokuka kara no chōsen ni shokumen suru bukkyō to kirisutokyō.* Kyōto (Hōzōkan). Japanese edition of Barth et al. 2004a.)

Dai, Zhang and Pye 1995:
Dai, Kangsheng, Zhang,Xinying and Pye, Michael (eds.) *Religion and Modernization in China. Proceedings of the International Association for the History of Religions held in Beijing, China, April 1992.* Cambridge (Roots and Branches). A number of contributions appeared in Chinese translation in the journal *Shijie Zongjiao Ziliao* 世界宗教资料 (1992).

Franke, Mas'ud, Pye and Wasim 2005a:
Franke, Edith, Mas'ud, Abdurrahman, Pye, Michael and Wasim, Alef Theria. *Religious Harmony: Problems, Practice and Education. Proceedings of the Regional Conference of the International Association for the History of Religions, Yogyakarta and Semarang, Indonesia, September 27th – October 3rd, 2004.* Yogyakarta (Oasis Publisher).

Franke, Mas'ud, Pye and Wasim 2005b:
Franke, Edith, Mas'ud, Abdurrahman, Pye, Michael and Wasim, Alef Theria. *Harmoni Kehidupan Beragama: Problem, Praktik dan Pendidikan. Proceeding Konferensi Regional International Association for the History of Religions, Yogyakarta dan Semarang, Indonesia, 27 September*

– *03 October, 2004*. Yogyakarta (Oasis Publisher). (Indonesian version of Franke et al. 2005a.)

Franke, Mas'ud, Pye and Wasim 2006:
Franke, Edith, Mas'ud, Abdurrahman, Pye, Michael and Wasim, Alef Theria (eds.) *Religious Harmony: Problems, Practice and Education. Proceedings of the Regional Conference of the International Association for the History of Religions, Yogyakarta and Semarang, Indonesia, September 27th – October 3rd, 2004*. (Religion and Reason 45). Berlin (de Gruyter). (Revised English edition of Franke et al. 2005.)

Franke and Pye 2004:
Franke, Edith and Pye, Michael. "Ilmu agama dan kontribusinya terhadap penyelesaian masalah dalam dunia yang plural / The study of religions and its contribution to problem solving in a plural world" in: *Marburg Journal of Religion* in 2004:http://www.uni-marburg.de/fb03/ivk/mjr/pdfs/2004/articles/franke-2004.pdf

Franke and Pye 2006:
Franke, Edith and Pye, Michael (eds.). *Religionen Nebeneinander. Modelle religiöser Vielfalt in Ost- und Südostasien*. Berlin and Münster (Lit-Verlag).

Hackett and Pye 2010:
Hackett, Rosalind and Pye, Michael (eds.) 2010. *IAHR Congress Proceedings (Durban 2000). The History of Religions: Origins and Visions*, Cambridge (Roots and Branches): 284–297. Note that this was a limited print-run distributed to major libraries across the world and is not commercially available: enquiries may be made to the serving Publications Officer of the IAHR.

Helve and Pye 2003:
Helve, Helena and Pye Michael 2003. "Theoretical correlations between world- view, civil religion, institutional religion and informal spiritualities" in: *Temenos* 37–8 (2001–2): 87–106.

Morgan and Pye 1977:
Morgan, Robert and Pye, Michael (eds. trans.) *Ernst Troeltsch: Writings on Theology and Religion* London (Duckworth) and Louisville Kentucky (Westminster/John Knox).

Pye, Miyashita and Minoura 2003:
Pye, Michael, Miyashita, Seishi and Minoura, Eryō 2003. *Bukkyō to kirisutokyō no taiwa II: Jōdo shinshū to fukuinshugi no shinkō. Hans-Martin Barth kyōju Gerhard Marcel Martin kyōju wo mukaete* (Dialog zwischen Buddhismus und Christentum II, Jōdo Shinshū und Evangelischer

Glaube: Mit Hans-Martin Barth und Gerhard Marcel Martin im Gespräch). Kyōto (Hōzōkan).

Pye and Morgan 1973:
Pye, Michael and Morgan, Robert (eds.) 1973. *The Cardinal Meaning. Essays in Comparative Hermeneutics: Buddhism and Christianity* (Religion and Reason 6). The Hague (Mouton).

Pye and Triplett 2007:
Pye, Michael and Triplett, Katja. *Streben nach Glück. Schicksalsdeutung und Lebensgesaltung in japanischen Religionen* (Mit Beiträgen von Monika Schrimpf) Berlin (LIT-Verlag).

Pye and Triplett 2011:
Pye, Michael and Triplett, Katja. *Pilgerfahrt visuell. Hängerollen in der religiösen Alltagspraxis Japans* (Veröffentlichungen der Religionskundlichen Sammlung 5), Marburg (Diagonal Verlag) 2011.

Wasim, Mas'ud, Franke and Pye 2005:
Wasim, Alef Theria, Mas'ud, Abdurrahman, Franke Edith and Pye, Michael (eds.) *Harmoni Kehidupan Beragama: Problem, Praktik dan Pendidikan. Proceeding Konferensi Regional International Association for the History of Religions, Yogyakarta dan Semarang, Indonesia, September 27th – Oktober 3rd, 2004.* Yogyakarta (Oasis Publishers). (Indonesian version of Franke et al. 2005.)

Consolidated Index to Volumes I and II

To reduce the scale of this index the following are not included: contents pages and other pre-pages, items in the list of author's publications cited, names of editors of composite works, publishers and places of publication, elements of duplicated bibliographical references, and so on. All such references will be found at the relevant bibliographical positions. Also omitted are a number of terms or names appearing incidentally, e.g. in quotations, but not in themselves germane to the wider argument; and on the other hand general words which occur very frequently indeed such as: culture, history, society, sociology, tradition and some of their cognates. Some general entries point to compact sections of text where specific cases will be found. Foreign words with obvious English equivalents are often indexed under the latter, e.g. fenomenologia under phenomenology, Modernität under modernity. Diacritical marks are not used in this index if, for any reason, they do not occur in the main text; the index should therefore *not* be regarded as a conclusive guide to diacritical marks.

Abe, Masao *Vol. II*: 343
Abe, Shinsō *Vol. II*: 398
Abe, Yashiya *Vol. I*: 163
Aberdeen *Vol. I*: 239 // *Vol. II*: 329
Abrahamic religions *Vol. II*: 62
absoluteness *Vol. II*: 11, 31, 138
access, problem of *Vol. I*: 51, 54, 64 // *Vol. II*: 45, 271, 284, 322, 377
accommodation *Vol. II*: 21, 40, 64, 124, 146, 148, 248
acculturation *Vol. I*: 214 // *Vol. II*: 29, 220, 231, 245, 266
actors *Vol. II*: 64, 109, 146, 243
adaptation *Vol. I*: 141, 155 // *Vol. II*: 5-6, 20-21, 89, 107, 115, 125, 139-42, 146-7, 173, 299, 321-3, 362-3, 398-9
adherents *Vol. II*: 170, 204, 251, 261, 266
Adibuddha *Vol. II*: 298
adjacency *Vol. II*: 311, 394
adjusted *Vol. II*: 5-6, 44-9, 105, 111-2 139, 141, 299, 305, 321, 355
adolescence *Vol. I*: 73, 213 // *Vol. II*: 20, 70, 324, 386

adumbration (definitional) *Vol. I*: 12, 20, 22, 33-5, 39, 186 // *Vol. II*: 43, 73, 81
aesthetics *Vol. II*: 97
affective aspect *Vol. II*: 370-1
Afghanistan *Vol. I*: 229
Africa/n *Vol. I*: 137, 150, 153, 169-70, 174, 196-7, 206-7, 210-12, 214, 221, 248-9, 256, 261 // *Vol. II*: 40, 44, 60, 91, 130-1, 133, 140, 252, 265, 350
– Academy of Religion *Vol. I*: 267 // *Vol. II*: 60, 314-8
– African Assoc. for the Study of Religions (ASSR) *Vol. I*: 175, 211-2, 220
– assumptions *Vol. I*: 202,
– independent churches *Vol. I*: 256
– traditional religion/s *Vol. I*: 192, 256
– South Africa *Vol. I*: 74-6, 79, 150, 175, 208, 210-1, 244, 249, 256 // *Vol. II*: 6, 310, 314-9, 322, 324, 326
– Southern Africa *Vol. I*: 168, 219

Africanists *Vol. I*: 256
Afrikaaner *Vol. I*: 75
Afrikaans *Vol. I*: 87, 247, 256
agama (in Indonesian) *Vol. I*: 248, 274 // *Vol. II*: 297-9, 310, 312, 373, 39, 401, 413
Āgama/s *Vol. I*: 119 // *Vol. II*: 208-9, 211
agency *Vol. II*: 64-6
agent/s (supernatural) *Vol. II*: 64-66, 69-70, 80, 83, 98
aggiornamento *Vol. II*: 140, 146, 249
agnostic *Vol. II*: 16
Agonkyō *Vol. II*: 172
Agonshū *Vol. II*: 208-9, 211, 213, 215, 217, 220, 227-8
Ahlbäck, Tore *Vol. I*: 16, 31-2, 49, 68, 106, 261, 269 // *Vol. II*: 374, 408
Ahmadiyya *Vol. I*: 209-10
Akhandananda, Swami *Vol. II*: 210
Alberts, Wanda *Vol. II*: 376-7, 389
Alekseev, N A. *Vol. I*: 188, 193
Aleph (formerly Aum Shinrikyō) *Vol. II*: 227
Alexander "the Great" *Vol. I*: 210
alienation *Vol. II*: 255-6
Alinesitoué *Vol. I*: 138
Alles, Gregory *Vol. I*: 217
Almond, Philip C. *Vol. I*: 41, 47
altar/s
– Buddhist *Vol. I*: 100 // *Vol. II*: 225-6, 231
– Cao Dai *Vol. II*: 163
– Chinese *Vol. II*: 291, 295, 297-8
– Shintō *Vol. II*: 272
Amaterasu-ō-mikami *Vol. II*: 281-282
Ambedkar, Dr. *Vol. II*: 325
ambiguity *Vol. I*: 263 // *Vol. II*: 29, 39, 91, 96, 115, 128, 200, 243-4, 248, 250-63, 267, 269, 275, 310, 402
ambiguous *Vol. II*: 21, 148, 221, 225, 232, 244-5, 251-2, 257, 259-62, 267, 269, 285, 298, 303, 310, 334

America/s *Vol. I*: 112, 202, 217 // *Vol. II*: 106, 130, 134, 141, 154, 316, 336, 345, 348,
– Empress of the Americas *Vol. I*: 71-83, 88
– Latin *Vol. I*: 36, 137-8, 142, 153, 189-90, 197, 202, 204-6, 248-9, 253-6 // *Vol. II*: 265, 347, 350, 385
– North *Vol. I*: 9, 47, 147, 182, 232, 237, 245, 254-6
– South *Vol. I*: 175 // *Vol. II*: 385
– United States of *Vol. II*: 63 See also United States.
– American Association (NAASR) *Vol. I*: 223, 249
– Asociación Latinoamericana *Vol. I*: 220, 254
– assumptions about religion *Vol. I*: 202, 224 // *Vol. II*: 62, 97,
– Latin *Vol. I*: 164, 175, 202-6, 220 // *Vol. II*: 143, 265
– indigenous religion *Vol. I*: 192, 256 // *Vol. II*: 77, 267, 362
– missionary *Vol. II*: 160,
– North *Vol. I*: 174, 181, 210, 223, 260
– Sōka Gakkai *Vol. II*: 100,
– US *Vol. II*: 219, 329
Amida *Vol. I*: 7, 61, 97-9 // *Vol. II*: 82-3, 169, 226, 229, 233, 259, 356, 371
Amitābha *Vol. II*: 24, 298
– Amitayus (Amitāyus) *Vol. I*: 159
– Āmítuófó *Vol. II*: 294
– See also Amida
Amoy *Vol. II*: 290
Amstutz, Galen *Vol. I*: 41, 47
amuletism *Vol. I*: 83, 259
amulet/s *Vol. I*: 60-61 // *Vol. II*: 140, 165, 171, 191, 228, 282-83
Ananaikyō *Vol. II*: 172, 360
Ānanda *Vol. I*: 119
anātman *Vol. II*: 12
ancestor/s *Vol. I*: 101, 104, 209 // *Vol. II*: 140, 170, 173, 208, 223-7, 232-3, 238, 292, 301

– veneration of *Vol. I*: 96, 100 // *Vol. II*: 226, 231, 290
ancestral *Vol. II*: 291, 295, 297, 300, 302, 321
ancient (various religious cultures) *Vol. I*: 35, 44, 52, 61, 68, 98-9, 127, 132, 164, 184, 209 // *Vol. II*: 17, 89, 124, 152, 162, 210, 213-4, 221, 225, 230, 234, 236, 264, 281, 292, 321, 385
Andean religion *Vol. I*: 205
Anesaki, Masaharu *Vol. I*: 145, 155, 162-3, 168 // *Vol. II*: 29-30, 77
angels *Vol. I*: 95
Anglican *Vol. II*: 89, 360, 388, 391
animism *Vol. I*: 161 // *Vol. II*: 44
Anisimov, Arkadiy Fedorovich *Vol. I*: 230, 241
Antes, Peter *Vol. I*: 185, 193, 246, 260 // *Vol. II*: 87
An Thiên *Vol. I*: 141
Anthony, D.W. *Vol. I*: 48, // *Vol. II*: 403
anthropologist/s *Vol. I*: 1, 19, 48, 90-92, 138, 150, 178, 183-4, 205, 209 // *Vol. II*: 40, 77, 108, 110, 112-3, 131-2, 264-5
anthropology *Vol. I*: 3, 10, 17-18, 28-9, 41, 106, 182-3, 189, 204-5, 209, 217, 230, 250-3 // *Vol. II*: 43, 109-11, 113, 116, 123, 126, 128, 131-2, 137, 147, 180, 348
Anthropologie (of Eckhart) *Vol. I*: 146, 170
anthropomorphism *Vol. II*: 80
Anttonen, Veikko *Vol. II*: 79, 86
Aparecida *Vol. I*: 272 // *Vol. II*: 231, 236, 239, 411
apartheid *Vol. I*: 75, 79 // *Vol. II*: 310, 325
apologetic *Vol. II*: 150, 245, 289, 323
apologist/s *Vol. I*: 18, 130, 157, 165
Arab/s *Vol. II*: 62, 395
Araki, Micho *Vol. I*: 163 // *Vol. I*: 168
archaeology *Vol. I*: 17, 28, 74, 188, 228-9, 250, 255

Archbishop Nikodim *Vol. II*: 328, 330
architecture *Vol. I*:52, 77, 83, 259 // *Vol. II*: 164, 172, 189, 283, 288, 301, 303, 305
Área Sagrada *Vol. II*: 228
arhat Vol. II: 52
Arisaka, Takamichi *Vol. I*: 135
Armenia *Vol. II*: 339
artefact/s *Vol. I*: 27, 53, 63, 80, 82, 228 // *Vol. II*: artefacts 172
Asahara, Shōkō *Vol. II*: 204, 209-213
Asaihime *Vol. II*: 281
Asakusa *Vol. II*: 21
ascension *Vol. I*: 93-5
ascetic/ism *Vol. I*: 120 // *Vol. II*: 74-5, 87, 93, 97, 158, 163,169, 211, 272
Ashin Jinarakkhita *Vol. II*: 297-8
Asia/n *Vol. I*: 2, 5, 11, 109-70, 185, 192, 197, 203, 224, 230, 246, 254-5, 257 // *Vol. II*: 22, 36, 40, 49, 130, 134, 220, 314, 339, 345-7, 385, 394,
– Central Asia/n *Vol. I*: 188, 213, 229 // *Vol. II*: 265, 316,
– East Asia/n *Vol. I*: 4, 36, 41, 47, 71, 107-70, 182, 184, 189-90, 246-7, 257-9, // *Vol. II*: 70, 84, 106, 139, 147, 152-78, 180, 194, 199, 225, 236, 245, 265, 279, 300-4, 346-8, 399
– South-East Asia/n: *Vol. I*: 85, 140, 220 // *Vol. II*: 246, 287-300, 324, 362, 396
Aśoka/n *Vol. I*: 139-40, 257 // *Vol. II*: 17
aspects (of religion) *Vol. I*: 22-6, 29-30, 34, 39, 77, 91, 96, 205-6, 211, // *Vol. II*: 3-4, 14, 18, 21, 34, 52, 64, 68-9, 78, 98-100, 106, 108, 110, 114, 120, 126, 138-9, 148-9, 204, 248-52, 285, 370-1, 380
assimilation *Vol. I*: 83, 259, 263 // *Vol. II*: 110, 114, 116, 148, 243, 246, 259, 261-3, 267-9, 275, 373, 402

associations (for the study of religions) 173, 196-8, 220, 249 // *Vol. II*: 349
– African *Vol. I*: 211-2, 220
– Latinoamericana (ALER) *Vol. I*: 190, 220, 254
– Australian *Vol. I*: 265 // *Vol. II* 49
– British (BASR) *Vol. I*: 267 // *Vol. II*: 131, 264, 277
– Danish *Vol. II*: 108
– Dutch *Vol. II*: 117
– European (EASR) *Vol. I*: 245, 253 // *Vol. II*: 62, 71
– Finnish *Vol. II*: 131
– French (Ernest Renan) *Vol. I*: 184, 186, 217
– German (DVRW) *Vol. II*: 117, 127
– International Association for the History of Religions: see IAHR
– Japanese *Vol. I*: 145-6, 155-6, 162-3, 169
– North American (NAASR) *Vol. I*: 249
– Polish *Vol. I*: 50-51, 68, 179-80, 193-4, 224
– South African *Vol. II*: 317
– SSEASSR *Vol. I*: 220
– various national/regional *Vol. I*: 4, 175-7, 181, 212, 220, 245, 249
associations (Japanological)
– BAJS *Vol. I*: 264
– EAJS *Vol. I*: 114, 125-6, 135 143, 265
associations (various religious) *Vol. II*: 43, 48, 93, 154, 166, 171, 173, 186-7, 198, 201, 239, 292, 316, 328, 331-3, 338
– Association for the Promotion of Lay Culture in Poland *Vol. II*: 316
– Association of New Religions *Vol. II*: 143
– Association of Shintō Shrines *Vol. II*: 48, 93
assumption (ascension) *Vol. I*: 93
Aston, William G. *Vol. I*: 158, 168
astrology *Vol. II*: 228, 293
Atami *Vol. II*: 235-236

atheism/ist *Vol. I*: 79, 137, 188, 218, 227-228, 232 // *Vol. II*: 315, 333
Athens *Vol. I*: 179, 215
atomic *Vol. II*: 219
attainment (of enlightenment etc) *Vol. II*: 34, 210-212, 323, 396
attitudinal *Vol. II*: 3, 14, 22, 62, 68, 70, 98-100, 139
Auffarth, Christoph *Vol. II*: 74, 86
Aufklärung *Vol. I*: 110-111, 113, 125, 157, 169, 194, 236, 263 // *Vol. II*: 402
Aum Shinrikyō *Vol. I*: 102, 106, 258-9, 268 // *Vol. II*: 107, 149, 155, 168, 172, 176, 178, 181, 196, 200, 202-17, 227-8, 238, 356, 379, 389, 396
Aurobindo, Sri *Vol. II*: 143, 384
Auroville *Vol. II*: 143
Australian Association for the Study of Religions *Vol. I*: 265 // *Vol. II*: 49
authentic/ally *Vol. I*: 81, 201 // *Vol. II*: 141, 143, 145, 179, 214, 324, 336
authenticity *Vol. II*: 46, 138, 145, 149-50, 196, 211, 214, 227
authoritarian *Vol. II*: 21, 166
authoritative/ly *Vol. I*: 118, 127, 209, 233 // *Vol. II*: 11, 56, 126, 186
authorities *Vol. I*: 62, 90, 132, 200, 258-9 // *Vol. II*: 95, 106, 158, 169, 210, 344
authority *Vol. I*: 57, 118, 127 // *Vol. II*: 25, 59, 97, 115, 166, 189, 196, 208-10, 227, 254, 333
autonomous/ly *Vol. I*: 11-12, 14, 17, 32, 48, 115-6, 182-3, 185-9, 194, 226, 248-9 // *Vol. II*: 30, 126, 187, 345,
autonomy *Vol. II*: 59
Avalokiteśvara *Vol. II*: 229, 278, 291, 296
avatar *Vol. II*: 270
awakening *Vol. II*: 166, 179, 186-7, 193, 323
Ayodhya *Vol. II*: 317
Azerbhaijan *Vol. II*: 339

Babinski, Gregorz *Vol. I*: 254, 261
Babylonian *Vol. II*: 77
Bahasa Indonesia *Vol. II*: 288, 296, 298, 392-3
BAHR *Vol. I*: 181
Baillie, J. *Vol. I*: 217
Baird, Robert *Vol. I*: 35, 47 // *Vol. II*: 264, 268, 276
Bakker, Remmelt *Vol. II*: 132
bakti (= *bhakti*) *Vol. II*: 296. See also Tribhakti.
Baltic states *Vol. II*: 339
Bangalore *Vol. II*: 60
baptism *Vol. II*: 20, 60, 70, 92, 160, 231, 322, 324, 383
Baptists *Vol. II*: 117
Barrett, Justin L. *Vol. II*: 79-80, 86
Barth, Karl *Vol. I*: 12, 359
Barth, Hans-Martin *Vol. I*: 71, 266, 271, 273-5 // *Vol. II*: 10, 355, 368, 372-4
Basel *Vol. II*: 329
Basilica (of Guadalupe) *Vol. I*: 82, 88, 261
Baskind, James *Vol. I*: 68, 272
BASR *Vol. II*: 181, 267 // *Vol. II*: 177, 200, 264, 277, 305, 406
Bastow, David *Vol. II*: 38
Batchelor, John *Vol. I*: 158
Bath College *Vol. II*: 212
Batunsky, Mark *Vol. I*: 227-9, 241
Becker, Howard *Vol. I*: 203
behaviour *Vol. II*: 170, 338,
- (religious) *Vol. I*: 17, 23, 34, 57, 64, 72, 76, 93, 138 // *Vol. II*: 4, 19-22, 55, 68-70, 80, 96, 98-9, 138-9, 148, 232, 288, 317, 380, 387
- (ritual/religious) *Vol. II*: 4, 70, 80, 99, 232, 288
behavioural *Vol. I*: 17, 24
- aspect/dimension (of religion) *Vol. I*: 22-4, 138-9 // *Vol. II*: 3, 4, 14, 19, 346, 370-2
- sciences *Vol. I*: 4 // *Vol. II*: 80
Beijing *Vol. I*: 136, 143, 168, 197, 241 // *Vol. II*: 159, 176, 318, 407
beings

- living/sentient (Buddhism) *Vol. II*: 83, 169, 325, 382
- metaphysical/spiritual *Vol. I*: 95, 97, 99 // *Vol. II*: 53, 64, 73, 80, 83-6, 236
belief *Vol. I*: 57, 86, 92-94,138, 190, 257 // *Vol. II*: 13-14, 16, 27, 62, 78, 84, 98, 109, 116, 165, 216, 317, 355, 368, 381, 387
beliefs *Vol. I*: 25, 34, 91-2, 94, 137, 140, 205 228, 242 // *Vol. II*: 10, 38, 98, 344, 381-2, 387, 395
believer/s *Vol. I*: 4, 24-6, 30, 39, 46, 54, 57-9, 61, 72, 86-96, 98-106, 191, 201, 238 // *Vol. II*: 7, 9, 13-15, 19, 21-3, 25, 27, 29, 53, 57-58, 72, 76, 81, 85, 100, 107, 119, 126, 138, 143, 146, 159, 166, 170-1, 175-6, 180, 182-4, 189, 191, 193, 204, 210-11, 221, 228, 231-3, 236, 269, 310, 323, 325, 344, 354, 359, 371, 381, 383, 387, 396
Bělka, Luboš *Vol. I*: 231, 234, 241
Bellah, Robert N. *Vol. I*: 80, 255, 260
benefits (this-worldly) *Vol. II*: 83, 94-5, 101, 171, 191, 228-30, 293, 302-3
benevolence *Vol. I*: 132
Benten (-sama) *Vol. II*: 279, 283-4 See also Benzaiten
Bentendō *Vol. II*: 283-4
Bentenshū *Vol. II*: 220
Benzai/ten *Vol. II*: 70, 278-85
Beowulf *Vol. II*: 250
Berger, Peter *Vol. II*: 357, 373
Berlin *Vol. I*: 179, 210, 225, 228 // *Vol. II*: 335, 349
- Wall *Vol. I*: 225 // *Vol. II*: 335, 338
Berling, Judith *Vol. I*: 141-3 // *Vol. II*: 264-5, 268, 276
Berner, Ulrich *Vol. II*: 124, 127, 244, 246, 264-6, 268, 276, 287, 305
Besant, Annie *Vol. I*: 150
Bhumi (Dewi) *Vol. II*: 296

Bianchi, Ugo *Vol. I*: 21, 114, 184, 187, 193, 250 // *Vol. II*: 177, 349, 351
Bianchi, Lorenzo *Vol. I*: 114
Bible *Vol. I*: 48, 209, 323 // *Vol. II*: 394-5
Biblical *Vol. I*: 94 // *Vol. II*: 97, 120, 315, 317, 337
Biblicism *Vol. II*: 97
Biezais, Harald *Vol. II*: 128
bishop/s *Vol. I*: 78, 94 / *Vol. II*: 109, 328-30
– Cao Dai *Vol. II*: 164
Biwa, Lake *Vol. II*: 278-9, 284
biwa Vol. II: 284
Bleeker, C. J. *Vol. I*: 92, 250
Blessed Spirits *Vol. II*: 297
Blessed Virgin Mary *Vol. II*: 183
blessing/s *Vol. II*: 229, 237
Bloch, Ernst *Vol. I*: 251
Bloemfontein *Vol. I*: 79, 210 // *Vol. II*: 314
Blue Cloud Temple *Vol. II*: 290-91
Bocking, Brian *Vol. I*: 63, 68 // *Vol. II*: 83, 86
bodhi tree *Vol. I*: 117
Bodhidharma *Vol. II*: 294, 344
bodhisattva/s *Vol. I*: 62 *Vol. II*: 26, 53, 70, 158, 169, 229, 259-60, 270, 278, 280, 282, 290, 296, 299, 300, 303
bodies (corpses) *Vol. II*: 202-4, 207, 214-5
body *Vol. I*: 94, 120, 220, 268 // *Vol. II*: 25, 53, 60, 87-8, 90, 94-7, 100, 382
border/s *Vol. I*: 167, 175, 229, 24, // *Vol. II*: 137, 310, 320, 333, 338, 362
See also boundaries
Borowik, Irena *Vol. I*: 254, 261
Bosnian (identity) *Vol. II*: 319
Boston *Vol. I*: 175, 244
boundary/ies *Vol. II*: 59, 69, 89, 205, 340
See also borders
Boyce, Mary *Vol. I*: 184
bracketing *Vol. I*: 24, 190

Bradford *Vol. II*: 328
Brahmā *Vol. II*: 323
Brahma Kumaris *Vol. II*: 360
Brahmanism *Vol. I*: 132 // *Vol. II*: 54, 68, 199, 225, 324, 345-6, 361
brahmans *Vol. I*: 123
Brandon, S.G.F. *Vol. I*: 217
Brasilia *Vol. II*: 223, 226
Brazil (Brasil) *Vol. I*: 70, 137, 175, 257, 272 // *Vol. II*: 107, 218-39
Brazilian/s *Vol. I*: 253 // *Vol. II*: 107, 218, 227, 231-7
Brear, Douglas *Vol. I*: 47
Bristol *Vol. I*: 94 // *Vol. II*: 75
Britain *Vol. I*: 9, 71, 180-2, 184, 186, 189, 209, 245, 255 // *Vol. II*: 130, 321, 327, 334, 377, 379, 383-4, 387-8, 394
British *Vol. I*: 47-8, 71, 149-50, 182, 187, 210, 213, 229, 263-4, 267 // *Vol. II*: 80, 313, 376, 385
– BAHR *Vol. I*: 181
– BASR *Vol. I*: 181// *Vol. II*: 131, 177, 200, 264, 277, 305
– East India Company *Vol. I*: 218
– Empire *Vol. I*: 149
– schools *Vol. II*: 388-9
Brno *Vol. I*: 42, 152, 174, 212, 223, 230-31 // *Vol. II*: 201, 278, 286
Brown, Alan *Vol. II*: 383, 389
Buddha/buddhas *Vol. I*: 62 // *Vol. II*: 18, 26, 53, 82-3, 183, 189-90, 197, 208, 212, 228, 259, 295-6, 299, 304
– Adibuddha *Vol. II*: 298
– Amitāyus/Amitābha/Amida/Āmítuófó *Vol. I*: 97-9 // *Vol. II*: 24, 82-5, 169, 226, 229, 233, 293, 298, 371
– hidden Buddha *Vol. II*: 282
– historical Buddha *Vol. I*: 99, 101, 106, 117-124, 129-32, 157, 159-160, 165, 218 // *Vol. II*: 17, 25, 28, 52-53, 56, 134, 140, 144, 179, 193, 197-9, 225, 229, 323-4, 343, 396
– Maitreya/Miroku/Mílèfó *Vol. II*: 159, 197, 282, 295, 304

- without affinity *Vol. II*: 170, 231
- Yàoshīfó *Vol. II*: 296, 304
  See also under names of various buddhas
buddhahood *Vol. I*: 123 // *Vol. II*: 17, 96, 280, 298
Buddhadharma *Vol. II*: 198
buddha-nature *Vol. I*: 133 // *Vol. II*: 25-6, 83, 160, 169, 197, 382
Buddhism/Buddhist *Vol. I*: 87, 159, 254-5, 259 // *Vol. II*: 4-57, 62, 384-5, 387
- and Christianity *Vol. I*: 35, 161 // *Vol. II*: 4-6, 11-39, 41, 51-7, 105, 118, 124, 126, 164, 243, 356-9, 362, 367-71, 399
- and Confucianism/Daoism *Vol. I*: 109, 126-34, 136-42, 157, 163, 198, 202, 257 // *Vol. II*: 154, 174, 289-304, 346, 353
- and Shintō *Vol. II*: 93-4, 223-4, 236-8, 245, 258-60, 269-75, 278-86, 379
- critical history *Vol. I*: 116-24 // *Vol. II*: 343
- cosmology *Vol. I*: 127 // *Vol. II*: 276
- house altars *Vol. I*: 100
- identifying "Buddhism/ Buddhist" *Vol. I*: 102-4 // *Vol. II*: 106-7, 149, 158, 166-7, 180, 187, 193-201, 208-14, 209-15, 221, 227-9, 275, 295, 299, 310
- innovation *Vol. II*: 134-49, 154-8, 176, 233, 179-200, 345
- institutions (temples, social presence) *Vol. I*: 18, 100, 104, 140, 149 // *Vol. II*: 17-18, 21, 167, 169, 180, 182, 184-7, 229, 288-304, 325, 352, 356, 385-6, 388
- lay movements *Vol. I*: 58, // *Vol. II*: 169, 176, 227, 230-1, 312, 325
- magic *Vol. I*: 128-33
- pilgrimage *Vol. I*: 61-3, 99 // *Vol. II*: 74, 270
- reception history *Vol. I*: 40-41, 68

- ritual (incl. meditation) *Vol. I*: 61, 100, 104 // *Vol. II*: 18, 21, 73, 75, 77-9, 139-40, 190-1, 224-6, 230, 238, 272-5, 291, 322, 324
- studies *Vol. I*: 47, 51, 68, 96, 116-26, 157, 159-61, 163, 165, 183, 188, 199, 299-34, 241, 251, 256 // *Vol. II*: 8, 12, 184
- Sunday School *Vol. II*: 298
- texts/canon *Vol. I*: 61, 119-26, 150, 159-60, 165, 218, 231 // *Vol. II*: 35, 182, 343
- this-worldly *Vol. I*: 40
- thought/ideas *Vol. I*: 18, 38, 44-5, 97, 119-26, 133, 141, 146, 161, 229-30 // *Vol. II*: 12-15, 17, 22, 24-6, 51-7, 65, 67-8, 70, 93-4, 96, 100, 158, 163, 169, 193, 206-7, 212, 226-31, 233, 243, 248, 254, 258-60, 322-5, 345-6, 382,
- tradition *Vol. I*: 124-7, 134, 148, 157 / *Vol. II*: 14-15, 32-8, 94, 109-10, 115, 126, 142, 146, 158, 162-3, 181, 185, 193-201, 243-4, 249-51, 255, 261, 265-6
- war *Vol. II*: 396-9
  See also country names and denominational names, Pure Land Buddhism, Theravāda, etc.
Buddhist Dharma Research Association *Vol. II*: 166, 186-7, 198, 201
Buddhology *Vol. I*: 241 // *Vol. II*: 38 257
Bukit China *Vol. II*: 290
bukkyō/gaku Vol. I: 73, 161, 273-274 // *Vol. II*: 39, 184, 372-4
Bultmann, Rudolf *Vol. II*: 15, 349
burial *Vol. II*: 208, 290, 292
Burma *Vol. II*: 397 See also Myanmar
Buriat/Buryat *Vol. I*: 231-34, 241 // *Vol. II*: 310
Buryatia *Vol. I*: 229-31, 232-234 // *Vol. II*: 325
bussetsu Vol. II: 228
Busshogonenkai *Vol. II*: 170
Butsumyōkyō Vol. II: 83
Buzan-ha *Vol. II*: 284

Byakkō Shinkōkai *Vol. I*: 35, 265 // *Vol. II*: 107, 173, 177, 230 238
Byelorus *Vol. II*: 339

calendar/s *Vol. I*: 60, 230 // *Vol. II*: 154
– of Religious Festivals *Vol. II*: 383
calendrical *Vol. II*: 208, 321
calendricity *Vol. II*: 20
calligraphy/ic *Vol. I*: 62, 87, 98 // *Vol. II*: 165
Calvin/ism *Vol. I*: 40 // *Vol. II*: 16
Cambodia *Vol. II*: 164
Cambridge *Vol. I*: 10, 12
Canaan *Vol. II*: 255
Canada *Vol. I*: 115, 178, 236, 255
Candide *Vol. I*: 245
Candler, Edmund *Vol. I*: 149, 168
Candomblé *Vol. I*: 253 // *Vol. II*: 143
Canon/canonical (Buddhist) *Vol. II*: 28
– Chinese Buddhist *Vol. I*: 159, 168
– Theravāda Buddhist: *Vol. II*: 100
– Won Buddhist *Vol. II*: 182, 185, 187, 198, 200
Cantwell-Smith, W. *Vol. I*: 91, 93, 95, 106, 115-6
Caodai (Cao Dai) *Vol. I*: 5, 35, 259 // *Vol. II*: 143, 153, 155, 162-4, 176-7, 181, 194
Caŏtún Bǎoshēng Dàdì *Vol. II*: 301
capitalism *Vol. I*: 154, 240 // *Vol. II*: 155, 292, 336
Caquot, André *Vol. I*: 184
cardinal meaning *Vol. II*: 10, 34, 35, 38-9
cargo cults *Vol. II*: 133, 143, 151
Caribbean *Vol. II*: 265
Casadio, Giovanni *Vol. I*: 216
caste *Vol. II*: 325
catechisms *Vol. I*: 185
category/ies *Vol. I*: 23, 25, 30, 47, 49, 109, 138, 190, 205, 241, 256 // *Vol. II*: 4-5, 8, 19-20, 22, 28, 32, 40-42, 46, 48-9, 54-5, 57, 59, 62, 65-6, 68, 74, 90, 105-6, 141-2, 154, 94, 208, 222, 228, 248, 256, 276, 341, 349, 361

categorization *Vol. II*: 62, 79, 179, 199, 323
cathedral *Vol. I*: 14, 76, 78
Catholic/s *Vol. I*: 82-4, 88, 94-5, 137, 181, 184, 187-8, 203-5, 226, 253-4, 256, 259 // *Vol. II*: 7, 57, 60, 82, 138, 140, 163-5, 189, 191, 207, 219, 230-2, 237, 239, 310, 316, 324, 327, 330-2, 334-5, 339-40, 344, 349, 351, 359-60, 367, 369, 371, 388
Catholicism *Vol. I*: 75, 77, 82-3, 95, 204-5, 239, 253-4, 259 // *Vol. II*: 14, 28, 60, 67, 146, 155, 310, 316, 324, 332-3, 338, 363, 378, 385
causality *Vol. II*: 83
cause and effect *Vol. II*: 106
celibacy *Vol. II*: 167, 169
cemeteries
– Buddhist: *Vol. II*: 139-40, 225, 225, 229
– Chinese *Vol. II*: 290, 294
ceremony/ies *Vol. II*: 163, 202, 208, 228, 231, 271-4
Ceylon *Vol. II*: 17, 30
Chadwick, Owen *Vol. I*: 232, 241
Chamberlain, Basil Hall *Vol. I*: 158
Chan (Chán) *Vol. II*: 162, 193, 294
chantry *Vol. I*: 78
Chiao Hung *Vol. II*: 276
Cháo Júe Sì *Vol. II*: 296
characterization *Vol. I*: 24-6, 30-1, 36-7, 39, 86, 104-5, 247, 249
charismatic *Vol. II*: 166, 174, 204, 207, 224
Chateaubriand, François-René *Vol. II*: 349
Ch'en, Edward T. *Vol. II*: 267, 276
Chen, Zemin *Vol. I*: 203-4, 207
Chéng brothers *Vol. I*: 133
Cheng Hoon Teng *Vol. II*: 290-2
Cheng Ho *Vol. II*: 299, 305
Chénghuáng (Miào) *Vol. II*: 301-3
Cheng, Wei-yi *Vol. II*: 303
chi (earth, land) *Vol. II*: 234, 236
Chiao Hung *Vol. II*: 276,
Chichibu

- pilgrimage *Vol. I*: 67
- Shrine *Vol. I*: 161
Chidester, David *Vol. I*: 150, 168 // *Vol. II*: 217, 322, 326
Chiesonkyō (etc) *Vol. II*: 174, 208, 224
Chikubushima *Vol. II*: 278-82, 285-286
Chilson, Clark *Vol. II*: 203
China *Vol. I*: 74, 111, 120, 122, 129-30, 132, 134, 136-8, 140-3, 153, 164, 190, 192, 197, 202-4, 206, 209, 212, 224, 233, 240, 246, 249, 257-9 // *Vol. II*: 86, 110, 134, 152-5, 157-65, 181, 187, 225, 264-5, 268, 289-90, 292-4, 303, 318, 329, 346-8, 356, 394, 397
Chinese
- administration *Vol. II*: 303
- Buddhism *Vol. I*: 159-60 // *Vol. II*: 35, 211, 258, 278, 287-304
- Christianity *Vol. I*: 203-4
- culture *Vol. I*: 129, 204 *Vol. II*: 46
- foreign politics *Vol. II*: 165, 329
- language and characters *Vol. I*: 55, 117, 129, 138-9 // *Vol. II*: 152-3, 157, 164-5, 169, 186, 196-7, 245, 288-9, 296-7, 299-300, 347, 357
- new religions *Vol. II*: 157-65, 171
- overseas *Vol. I*: 54 // *Vol. II*: 15, 141, 153, 287-306
- People's Republic *Vol. I*: 259 // *Vol. II*: 154-5, 161
- religion/s *Vol. I*: 5, 111, 117, 129, 133, 136-41, 166-7 // *Vol. II*: 157, 223, 245, 301, 346, 287-306, 346-7
- scholars of religion *Vol. I*: 197
- views of religion *Vol. I*: 202-3, 204, 257 See also "three teachings"
Chinese temples *Vol. II*: 287-306
- Indonesia *Vol. II*: 295-300
- Kampuchea *Vol. II*: 294-5
- Malaysia *Vol. II*: 290-2
- Singapore *Vol. II*: 292-4

- Taiwan *Vol. II*: 300-4
chirashi *Vol. I*: 60
Choe Che-U *Vol. II*: 164-165
Choi, Seong-Hee *Vol. II*: 199
Chokye (Chogye) *Vol. II*: 191, 195
Chon, Pal-Khn *Vol. II*: 185, 197, 200
Chondogyo (Chŏntokyo) *Vol. II*: 164-5, 187, 194
chong sa *Vol. II*: 186-187, 192
Chŏngsan *Vol. II*: 167, 186-188
Chonju *Vol. II*: 165
chonmyong *Vol. II*: 165
Christ, Jesus *Vol. I*: 94-95, 102 // *Vol. II*: 25, 56, 60, 118, 143, 396
Christentum *Vol. I*: 94, 106, 109, 185, 193-4, 264, 269, 273-4 // *Vol. II*: 11, 31, 33, 39, 126, 128, 372-4
Christian/ity/ *Vol. I*: 35, 87, 137, 140, 142, 158, 161, 163, 185, 192, 199, 203, 207, 215, 246, 251, 254, 256-7, 259-60 // *Vol. II*: 68, 140-2, 147, 151, 154-5, 166, 180, 199, 207, 223, 226, 248-54, 261, 265-6, 324, 330, 333, 340, 384-5, 387, 394, 396
- and Buddhism *Vol. I*: 35, 161 // *Vol. II*: 4-6, 11-39, 41, 51-7, 105, 118, 122-8, 164, 191, 233, 243, 255, 356-9, 362, 367-71, 399
- and skilful means *Vol. II*: 36-7
- and Tenrikyō *Vol. II*: 59-60, 369
- behaviour *Vol. II*: 19-22, 97,
- essence/identity *Vol. I*: 12, 102, 109-11 // *Vol. II*: 12, 22-5, 33-4, 97, 147, 357
- feeling/sensitivity *Vol. II*: 23-4, 98, 120
- logocentricity *Vol. II*: 96-7
- politics *Vol. II*: 16, 62, 155, 160, 166-7, 310, 325, 327-41, 394-6 See also Cold War, colonialism
- prayer *Vol. II*: 75-77, 81-2,
- rites *Vol. II*: 19-22, 60, 70, 92, 139-40, 322, 324
- theology/thought *Vol. I*: 5, 9, 25, 87, 92-5, 180, 218, 256 // *Vol. II*: 12-13, 32-3 49, 62, 67,

118, 120, 146, 254, 348-50, 369, 371
  See also church/es, christlich
Christianization *Vol. I*: 205 // *Vol. II*: 16
Christian, Joachim *Vol. I*: 138
Christian Science *Vol. II*: 123, 145
christlich/en/er *Vol. I*: 109, 194 // *Vol. II*: 33, 117, 128, 375
Christmas *Vol. II*: 20, 331, 383
christocentric *Vol. II*: 25
Christus *Vol. II*: 119
Chū-agon Vol. I: 121
Chung, Bong-Kil *Vol. II*: 182, 200
church/es *Vol. I*: 34, 92, 95, 188, 203-4, 226-7, 232, 241, 243, 255-6, 267 // *Vol. II*: 16, 25, 27, 60, 67, 117, 120, 139-142, 223, 288, 310, 312, 315, 317, 324-5, 327-40, 382, 388, 396
– Anglican *Vol. II*: 89, 97-8, 376, 391
– Catholic *Vol. I*: 78, 82, 94, 204-5, 256 // *Vol. II*: 124, 163, 327, 330-2, 334, 344, 367, 369, 385
– Chinese Episcopalian *Vol. II*: 329
– history *Vol. I*: 180, 185
– Orthodox *Vol. I*: 77, 185, 215, 227, 232-3 // *Vol. II*: 327, 340, 385
– Protestant *Vol. I*: 203-4, 207, 255, // *Vol. II*: 60, 133, 142, 167, 190, 327, 337, 344, 365, 368, 371
– of England *Vol. II*: 376, 391
– of various other religions *Vol. I*: 59, 102, 201 // *Vol. II*: 67, 143, 166-7, 171, 173, 181, 190, 220, 229, 234-5, 237, 360, 399
Chusan *Vol. II*: 186
Chwasan *Vol. II*: 185-6, 188, 199
Cicero *Vol. I*: 42
Cidananda, Swami *Vol. II*: 210
CIPSH *Vol. I*: 196-7, 200 / *Vol. II*: 379
circulatory pilgrimage *Vol. II*: 74
circumambulation *Vol. II*: 189
Cirebon *Vol. II*: 296
CISR *Vol. I*: 184, 265

civil religion *Vol. I*: 13, 35, 69, 75-84, 209, 211, 255, 259, 260 // *Vol. II*: 55, 60, 63, 68, 71, 94, 151, 314
Clarke, Peter B. *Vol. II*: 134, 151, 219, 238
Clayton, John Powell *Vol. I*: 48, 257, 261, 264 // *Vol. II*: 39, 128, 374
clustering (of methods) *Vol. I*: 13, 15-18, 22, 29-31, 36-37, 51, 74, 86, 249
cognitive dissonance *Vol. I*: 90
cognitive science/tists *Vol. I*: 3, 20, 89, 217 // *Vol. II*: 64, 66, 79-80, 86-7, 98
Cold War *Vol. I*: 42, 151-2, 168, 170, 174, 179, 212-3, 221, 223-4, 226, 237-43, 270 // *Vol. II*: 164, 213, 310, 316, 324, 327-31, 333-4, 336-7, 340-1, 348
colonial/ism *Vol. I*: 42, 150-1, 165-6, 168, 183, 209, 213-4, 233, 256 // *Vol. II*: 136, 144, 160, 162-5, 187, 290, 300, 303, 325, 327, 330, 336, 348
Colpe, Karsten *Vol. II*: 29-30, 264, 268, 276
columbaria *Vol. II*: 294
Columbia *Vol. I*: 169, 254 // *Vol. II*: 39, 263, 276
Columbus *Vol. II*: 299
Communion *Vol. II*: 77
– Anglican *Vol. II*: 391
– first *Vol. II*: 60
– sacrament *Vol. II*: 124
communism/ist *Vol. I*: 51, 75, 138, 152, 180, 213, 223-30, 234-42, 254, 259 // *Vol. II*: 155, 159, 161, 164, 166, 295, 315-6, 310, 327-41
comparing/comparison (theory and acts of) *Vol. I*: 4-5, 9, 11, 21, 23, 26, 29-32, 36-8, 50, 60, 69-70, 75-6, 83-5, 93-5, 101-4, 110, 116, 128, 131, 139, 146, 148-9, 157, 167, 181, 184, 186, 207, 236, 246, 260-1 // *Vol. II*: throughout Vol. II

- comparisons *Vol. I*: 74, 93-5, 103 // *Vol. II*: 3, 6, 24, 38, 350
- comparative hermeneutics *Vol. I*: 242-3 // *Vol. II*: 6, 10, 32-9, 355
- with contrasting *Vol. I*: 4-5 // *Vol. II*: 1

comparative religion *Vol. I*: 4, 11, 13, 18-9, 29, 49, 85, 106, 148, 161-2, 168, 199, 217, 25 // *Vol. II*: 3-4, 9-10, 32, 51, 73, 87, 313

- comparative study of religions *Vol. I*: 41, 50, 69, 186, 190, 201, 250 // *Vol. II*: 6-7, 13, 29-30, 33, 35, 38, 49, 51, 72, 105, 110, 132, 194, 205, 348, 350-1, 358, 362

comparativism/ist *Vol. I*: 70, 148
compassion *Vol. I*: 97, 99 // *Vol. II*: 300, 303
conch (of Dharma) *Vol. II*: 273
Confucianism/ists *Vol. I*: 109, 111, 116, 117-9, 126, 127-34, 140, 142, 148, 157, 163, 198, 202, 257 // *Vol. II*: 35, 67, 141, 154, 158, 162, 166, 174, 192, 194, 198, 223, 276, 227, 289, 291-2, 294-5, 297, 299-300, 353, 384
Confucius *Vol. I*: 129, 131, // *Vol. II*: 159, 291, 297-9
congress/es
- of IAHR *Vol. I*: 112-4, 145-6, 155, 173, 175, 176, 181, 187, 197, 208-11, 215-6, 219-22, 236, 244, 246, 250 // *Vol. II*: 318, 319, 376
- other *Vol. I*: 244 // *Vol. II*: 40, 49, 60, 62, 71
Constantine *Vol. I*: 139-40, 257 // *Vol. II*: 396
constitution *Vol. I*: 225 // *Vol. II*: 161, 332, 378-9
- of IAHR *Vol. I*: 50,
- of Japan *Vol. I*: 152, 173, 181, 216 // *Vol. II*: 18, 43
Contra Deum *Vol. II*: 12
conversion/s *Vol. I*: 139 , 233 // *Vol. II*:16, 95, 171
convert/s *Vol. I*: 101 // *Vol. II*: 12, 107, 143, 164, 226-7

Conze, Edward *Vol. II*: 26
Cordier, Henri *Vol. II*: 165, 177
correlation/s
- methodological *Vol. I*: 3, 19-24, 27, 30-31, 238, 250-1, 274 // *Vol. II*: 146, 151, 378
- explanatory *Vol. I*: 26, 38, 42, 44, 75, 83, 86, 104, 237, 247 // *Vol. II*: 64, 70, 84, 98, 114, 118, 135, 142, 221, 321, 354-5
- intra-religious *Vol. II*: 359
cosmos/-ology/-ical *Vol. I*: 35, 43-4 123-4, 127, 193 // *Vol. II*: 46, 56, 60, 221, 274-5,196, 204, 321
council/s *Vol. II*: 332
- of Won Buddhism *Vol. II*: 187, 192
- of church *Vol. II*: 97, 120,
counter-intuitive *Vol. II*: 73, 80,
Cox, James *Vol. I*: 153, 169, 196, 207 // *Vol. II*: 91, 100
creation (religious) *Vol. II*: 24-5, 64, 189, 171
creed/s *Vol. I*: 95 // *Vol. II*: 115, 142
Cretans *Vol. II*: 253
Criollos *Vol. I*: 83, 259
Croatia *Vol. II*: 324, 339
crossover/s *Vol. II*: 6, 68, 320, 323-5
Culianu, Ioan Petru *Vol. I*: 94
cult/s *Vol. I*: 81-82, 137, 203, 253 // *Vol. II*: 70, 133, 143, 151, 157, 249, 295-7, 299, 339, 395
Czarism *Vol. I*: 233 // *Vol. II*: 340
Czech *Vol. I*: 231, 268 // *Vol. II*: 286, 327-8, 330, 337
- Republic *Vol. I*: 42, 152, 174, 212, 223 // *Vol. II*: 201, 278
Czechoslovakia *Vol. I*: 235, 237, 240 // *Vol. II*: 328-31, 333, 335, 338

Daesan *Vol. II*: 184, 186
Dai, Kangsheng *Vol. I*: 143, 273
daijōbussetsu *Vol. I*: 119
daijōteki *Vol. II*: 255
daimoku *Vol. II*: 82-3, 169, 251
Dainichi Sūtra *Vol. I*: 120
daisan bunmei *Vol. II*: 18

Daizōkyō Vol. I: 160, 168 // Vol. II: 35
Dalai Lama Vol. II: 210, 213, 228, 359
Dandaron, Bidiya Vol. I: 230-4, 241 // Vol. II: 310
Danish Association for the Study of Religions Vol. II: 108
Dao Vol. II: 67, 159
Dao giao Vol. I: 141
dàojiào Vol. II: 295
Daoism/ist Vol. I: 111, 117, 128-30, 140, 202, 257, 259 // Vol. II: 56-7, 154-5, 158, 162, 223, 289, 291, 294-5, 297, 299-300, 303, 353, 384
D'Arcy, C.F. Vol. II: 77,
Darjeeling Vol. I: 149-50, 213
Darwinism Vol. II: 348
Dator, James Allan Vol. II: 91, 100
Dawkins, Richard Vol. I: 253, 261
Dayananda, Swami Vol. II: 210
dà-yì Vol. II: 34
de Bary, W. Th. Vol. I: 109, 114 // Vol. II: 39
DDR Vol. I: 235-236
deconstructivist Vol. II: 63
definition/s Vol. I: 12, 22, 26, 35-6, 58, 145-146 // Vol. II: 8-9, 35, 42, 86, 142, 150, 203, 205, 214-6, 253, 257-8, 267, 320, 323, 339, 348
de Groot, J. J. M. Vol. II: 159, 177, 290, 292, 305
Deguchi, Nao Vol. II: 172, 238
Deguchi, Ōnisaburō Vol. II: 172, 238
deism Vol. I: 117, 217 // Vol. II: 65-6, 348
deity/ies Vol. II: 65-6, 280, 299, 304
deitism Vol. II: 70
de la Maza, Francisco Vol. I: 81, 85
demon/s Vol. II: 160, 245
de Montclos, Xavier Vol. I: 185, 194
demythologisation Vol. II: 37, 371
denomination/s/al
– Buddhist Vol. I: 61, 98-100, 148, 160, // Vol. II: 93, 169-71, 191, 219, 223, 225, 227, 367, 399
– Christian Vol. I: 9-10, 203, 207, 255 // Vol. II: 60, 166
– various Vol. I: 59, 102 // Vol. II: 235
deontologisation Vol. II: 371
Departemen Agama Vol. II: 310, 393
Despland, Michel Vol. I: 48, 115, 125
Deus Vol. I: 117 // Vol. II: 30, 65, 227, 230-1 See also *Ha Daiusu*
deus otiosus Vol. II: 65
Deutschland Vol. I: 179
devil/s Vol. II: 228
devotees Vol. II: 158, 170
devotional Vol. II: 229, 288, 296
de Vries, Jan Vol. I: 41, 48
Dewa Sanzan Vol. II: 94, 237
Dhamma Vol. II: 323
Dhāraṇī Sūtra Vol. I: 64
Dharma Vol. I: 99, 121, 132, 246, 248, 260 // Vol. II: 53, 83, 161, 166-7, 170, 185-8, 190-3, 198, 201, 228, 238, 243-4, 273, 279, 298, 301
Dharmakāya Vol. II: 197
Dharma Sisters Vol. II: 167, 185, 188, 190-3
dhikr Vol. II: 84
Dhyāna Vol. I: 133
dialectical Vol. I: 100, 121, 123-4, 269 // Vol. II: 36, 63, 97, 195, 223, 324, 329, 338, 374
dialogical Vol. I: 215 // Vol. II: 329-330, 352, 393
– dialogue Vol. I: 5, 81, 103, 187, 192, 201, 251 // Vol. II: 7, 10, 25, 51,61, 71, 90, 108, 151, 172, 180, 182, 188,198, 250, 252, 307, 309, 311-2, 317, 332-3, 340, 342, 344-5, 349, 352-75, 389, 391-401
Diem, Ngo Dinh Vol. II: 164
Diesel, Alleyn Vol. I: 256, 261
dimension/s Vol. I: 23, 32, 205, 207 138-9, 190, 234 // Vol. II: 4, 10, 14-19, 21-25, 27, 29-30, 43, 69, 78, 98, 109, 204, 340, 344, 346, 363, 380
Diószegi, Vilmos Vol. I: 228, 242

disciples *Vol. II*: 17, 25, 166, 187, 192, 212, 323
discipleship *Vol. II*: 210
discipline/s (various) *Vol. I*: 41, 45, 51, 228 // *Vol. II*: 9, 13, 41, 72, 76, 109, 131-4, 223, 247, 327, 364, 377-8
– study of religions *Vol. I*: 1-21, 26-32, 36-7, 46-7, 50-51, 73-4, 112, 116, 114, 148, 153, 156, 162, 173-6, 182, 186-93, 208-9, 215-8, 220-1, 224, 236, 246-52 // *Vol. II*: 4, 7, 13, 63, 73, 76, 109, 131-2, 135, 138, 144, 202, 205, 247, 309, 311-2, 352, 356, 372, 377-378, 391, 394
– discipline identification *Vol. I*: 9-10, 19, 182-5, 215 // *Vol. II*: 315
– religious *Vol. II*: 20, 28, 93, 115, 175, 189, 193, 211
dissenting sects *Vol. I*: 240 // *Vol. II*: 134, 151, 157, 165, 177
divination *Vol. II*: 162, 293-4, 298
divine *Vol. I*: 131 // *Vol. II*: 21, 25, 42, 51-2, 64-5, 86, 120-1, 163, 234, 254, 257, 261, 282, 321
Divine Reason, Teaching of *Vol. II*: 171
divinity/ies *Vol. II*: 7, 44, 65-6, 69, 80, 93, 157, 163, 172, 219, 221, 230-31, 257, 259, 271, 278-9, 281, 285, 288-92, 294, 296-7, 299, 300, 302, 304-5, 399
Diwali *Vol. II*: 383
Dobbins, James C. *Vol. II*: 9
doctrine/s *Vol. I*: 94-5, 132, 138, 141, 243, 259 // *Vol. II*: 4, 12, 24-5, 27, 36-7, 78, 182, 197, 200, 263, 277, 378, 394
dogma *Vol. I*: 247
dogmatic/s *Vol. I*: 17, 118, 121 *Vol. II*: 34, 349
Doležalová, Iva *Vol. I*: 152, 230 // *Vol. II*: 200
Dolmen *Vol. I*: 245
Donghak (Tonghak) *Vol. II*: 187
Donner Institute *Vol. I*: 15, 31-2, 49, 68, 183, 225 // *Vol. II*: 374

Dorje Ling *Vol. I*: 149
Dumoulin, Heinrich *Vol. I*: 146, 168
Durban (Congress) *Vol. I*: 175, 208, 214, 221-2, 244, 250, 274 // *Vol. II*: 318, 413
Durkheim/ian *Vol. I*: 92, 136, 217 // *Vol. II*: 44
Durt, Hubert *Vol. I*: 159, 168
Dutch *Vol. I*: 110, 151, 181, 183, 218, 247, 252 // *Vol. II*: 117, 121
dynamic/s *Vol. I*: 5, 75, 86, 123, 127, 179, 211 // *Vol. II*: 4-6, 15, 28-30, 91, 105, 108, 111, 113-5, 123-6, 137, 145-8, 180, 220-1, 244-8, 254-8, 261-2, 266, 269, 276, 285, 287, 319-20, 355, 360, 363-5

Earhart, Byron H. *Vol. I*: 68 // *Vol. II*: 151, 167, 177
EASR *Vol. I*: 220, 245 249 272 // *Vol. II*: 62, 71, 411
Easter *Vol. II*: 20, 383
ecclesia *Vol. I*: 203
Echigo/Echizen *Vol. I*: 98
Eckhardt, Hans von *Vol. I*: 185, 194
Eckhart, Meister *Vol. I*: 146, 170
eclectic/ism *Vol. II*: 123, 143, 148, 164, 174, 176, 210, 212-3, 268
ecumenical *Vol. I*: 92, 215 / *Vol. II*: 328, 330
Edo Period *Vol. I*: 156 // *Vol. II*: 280
education/al *Vol. I*: 5, 54, 57, 80, 100, 159, 161, 179, 189, 192, 227, 255 // *Vol. II*: 307-10, 326, 331, 337, 365, 378, 381, 385-8, 391-2, 400
– done by religions *Vol. II*: 171, 188-9, 191, 223, 250, 252, 301-2, 381, 383-4, 387-8, 393
– Japanese Ministry of *Vol. I*: 165-166, 210, 241, 248, 257 // *Vol. II*: 218
– religious *Vol. I*: 176-7, 251, 256 // *Vol. II*: 85, 393
– religious (integrative) *Vol. II*: 312, 376-90,

Egypt/ian *Vol. I*: 184, 255 // *Vol. II*: 213, 343, 385
eighteenth century *Vol. I*: 115, 119, 126, 141, 151, 156, 167, 190, 217-8, 246
Eisenach *Vol. II*: 337
Eisleben *Vol. II*: 337
Ekō *Vol. I*: 131
El Señor de la Viaje *Vol. I*: 77
Eliade, Mircea *Vol. I*: 32, 94, 106, 158, 221, 269 // *Vol. II*: 9, 15, 45-6, 77-9, 86-7, 124
Elijah *Vol. I*: 93
Eliot, Sir Charles *Vol. I*: 158, 168 // *Vol. II*: 259, 262
Elison, George *Vol. II*: 12, 30
Elsas, Christoph *Vol. I*: 178, 194
elucidation *Vol. I*: 24-6, 30-1, 36-7, 39, 104, 191, 246-7, 249 // *Vol. II*: 90, 249, 318, 332, 354-5
ema Vol. I: 60
Emerging from Meditation Vol. I: 110-12, 114, 117-26, 135, 141, 143, 157
emic *Vol. I*: 10, 103 // *Vol. II*: 110, 157, 288, 300
emigration *Vol. II*: 140, 238
empathy *Vol. I*: 10, 185, 189
Emperor/s
− Asoka *Vol. I*: 257 // *Vol. II*: 17
− Constantine *Vol. I*: 140 // *Vol. II*: 396
− Ming *Vol. I*: 111, 139-40, 257 // *Vol. II*: 155, 157, 289, 347
− Japanese *Vol. I*: 154, 156 // *Vol. II*: 171, 281-2
− Taiping *Vol. II*: 160
empire/s *Vol. I*: 139-40, 149 // *Vol. II*: 156, 249
empirical/ly *Vol. I*: 33, 37, 39, 146, 154, 188-9, 242 // *Vol. II*: 24, 64, 99, 203
Empress (of the Americas) *Vol. I*: 77, 79, 81, 83, 88
emptiness *Vol. I*: 87
encyclopaedia/s *Vol. I*: 94-95, 106 // *Vol. II*: 77-9, 86-7
Engels, Friedrich *Vol. I*: 236

Enlightenment
− Buddhist *Vol. I*: 96, 99, 117 // *Vol. II*: 17-18, 22, 55-7, 169, 193-4, 197, 199, 260, 323, 396
− European (reason) *Vol. I*: 11, 41-2, 109-11, 148, 154, 217, 236, 241 // *Vol. II*: 343, 347-8, 351, 357
− Japanese (reason) *Vol. I*: 117, 157
Ennōkyō *Vol. II*: 173, 220, 231
Enoshima *Vol. II*: 279, 282, 285
ephemera *Vol. I*: 13, 29, 50, 52-4, 56, 58, 60-66, 68, 272
Ephesians, Diana of *Vol. II*: 251
epistemology *Vol. I*: 25, 45
epistles *Vol. II*: 16, 97, 343
equinox/es *Vol. I*: 100 // *Vol. II*: 224
Erasmus *Vol. II*: 253
Erfurt *Vol. II*: 337
Esherick, Joseph W. *Vol. II*: 177
esoteric *Vol. I*: 97 // *Vol. II*: 93, 163, 174, 229-30, 237, 271, 275
Esperantism *Vol. II*: 172
essence (various) *Vol. I*: 204 // *Vol. II*: 33-6, 39, 41, 49, 112, 137, 251, 257, 199, 245, 250-1
− of religion *Vol. I*: 11-12, 17, 92, 132 // *Vol. II*: 3, 39, 69, 120-1, 123, 150, 231, 358
− of Buddhism *Vol. II*: 232 // *Vol. II*: 21-2, 36, 275
− of Christianity *Vol. I*: 109 // *Vol. II*: 12, 22-5, 33-4, 97, 147
essentialism/ist *Vol. I*: 11, 17, 87, 91 // *Vol. II*: 67, 73, 75, 79, 86, 245, 300
Estonia/n *Vol. I*: 230, 234-5, 238 // *Vol. II*: 339
ethical/ly *Vol. I*: 90, 140, 159, 205 // *Vol. II*: 21-2, 69, 162, 344, 363, 388
ethic/s *Vol. I*: 47, 180, 251 // *Vol. II*: 77, 87
ethnic/ity *Vol. I*: 78-9, 82-4, 233-4, 253-5, 261 // *Vol. II*: 44, 60, 226, 321-2, 328, 334, 337, 339-40, 397, 398-9
ethnocentrism *Vol. I*: 189, 247

ethnography *Vol. I*: 70, 85, 169, 235, 261, 269 // *Vol. II*: 374
ethnology *Vol. I*: 19, 31, 72, 183, 188, 190, 228 // *Vol. II*: 72, 80, 123, 131
etic *Vol. I*: 103 // *Vol. II*: 244
Eucharist *Vol. II*: 20, 25, 60, 70, 322, 371
Euhemer *Vol. I*: 51, 187, 224, 242-3
Euhemeros *Vol. I*: 42
Euro-American *Vol. I*: 202-3, 217-8 // *Vol. II*: 125
Eurocentrism *Vol. I*: 112, 189, 218, 246, 262
European Association for the Study of Religions (EASR) *Vol. I*: 220, 245, 249, 253 // *Vol. II*: 62
evangelical *Vol. I*: 255 // *Vol. II*: 72, 166, 344
Evangelische Kirche in Deutschland *Vol. I*: 264, 273-4 // *Vol. II*: 365
evangelism *Vol. II*: 316, 349
evangelizing *Vol. I*: 83, 259
Evans-Pritchard, E. E. *Vol. I*: 38, 41, 48
Evenks *Vol. I*: 230, 241
evidence/s *Vol. I*: 22, 33, 60, 64, 82, 159, 231
evil *Vol. I*: 99, 132 // *Vol. II*: 8, 22, 62, 237, 252
evolutionism/ist *Vol. I*: 41-2, 148, 217 // *Vol. II*: 121, 123, 348
exhibitions *Vol. I*: 63-4, 79, 80, 82, 89 // *Vol. II*: 182-3, 190, 198, 233, 239, 367-8
existence/s *Vol. II*: 23-6, 46, 52, 54, 56-7, 66, 80, 84, 86, 197-8, 206, 212, 254
existential/ly *Vol. II*: 13, 40, 109, 111, 371
exorcism *Vol. II*: 260
exoteric path *Vol. II*: 163
exoticism *Vol. I*: 42-3, 150, 169, 206, 234 // *Vol. II*: 227, 237, 348
experience/s (religious) *Vol. I*: 25, 40, 46, 88-9, 95, 191, 228 // *Vol. II*: 4, 8, 11, 13-15, 18-19, 23, 25, 27, 30, 45, 55, 69, 75, 80, 90, 95, 99, 121-2, 124-5, 138, 160, 164, 166, 172, 186, 193, 195, 222, 255, 343, 349, 352, 382-4
explanation *Vol. I*: 9, 20, 24, 26, 30-40, 53, 90-2, 127, 131, 136, 142, 182, 191, 247 // *Vol. II*: 14, 22, 80-1, 84, 99, 131,133-6, 144-5, 156-7, 165, 175, 204, 208, 232, 244, 289, 300, 309, 318, 324, 332, 344, 354

factionalism *Vol. I*: 57-9
factuality *Vol. I*: 101, 201, 210
Făgŭshān *Vol. II*: 301
faith/s *Vol. I*: 49, 116, 170 // *Vol. II*: 11, 15-16, 20, 23, 25, 28, 55, 60, 66, 85, 118, 120, 214-5, 311, 325, 340, 342, 349-50, 357, 359, 376-80, 388
– and reason *Vol. I*: 38 // *Vol. II*: 320
– individual *Vol. I*: 198, 247 // *Vol. II*: 83, 120, 208, 233, 239, 355-6, 368
– faith-schools *Vol. II*: 388
Fallaize, E. N. *Vol. II*: 77
Falungong *Vol. I*: 240, 258-9 // *Vol. II*: 155, 161, 178, 181, 356
family resemblances *Vol. II*: 56, 67
fāngbiàn *Vol. II*: 300 See also skilful means
Farquhar, J. N. *Vol. I*: 217
Faruqi, Ismail Raji *Vol. II*: 250, 252
Făxiăn *Vol. I*: 120
Federal Republic of Germany *Vol. I*: 179, 235 // *Vol. II*: 329, 337
feeling/s *Vol. II*: 14, 23-4, 43, 47, 94, 124, 380
Feil, Ernst *Vol. I*: 115
Fenollosa, Ernest *Vol. I*: 158
festival/s *Vol. I*: 52-3, 60, 65, 78, 88, 161, 163 // *Vol. II*: 19-20, 42, 47, 224, 264, 270-5, 284, 302, 383, 385
field *Vol. I*: 1-4, 6, 10, 12-13, 15-17, 19-20, 22, 27-8, 30, 31, 33-5, 36, 38, 39-40, 42, 44, 46, 48, 47, 50-1, 53, 60, 63-4, 69-71, 73-4, 76, 84-6, 90, 103, 145, 147, 150,

154-7, 160, 184, 188-90, 198-9, 202, 204-5, 210, 214, 221, 226, 229, 238, 240, 245-6, 249-51, 253-6, 258, 260, 264 // *Vol. II*: 14, 37, 42, 64, 73, 76-81, 83, 86, 95, 105, 107, 109, 113, 120, 131-2, 136, 150, 153, 181, 202, 222-3, 245, 248, 255, 259, 267, 273-4, 287, 289, 305, 309,316-7, 327, 348, 353-4, 361, 381, 399
fieldwork *Vol. I*: 13, 16, 20, 22, 30, 50-70, 74-8, 182, 191, 235 // *Vol. II*: 3, 124, 265, 275
filioque *Vol. II*: 142
Finland/Finnish *Vol. I*: 69, 76, 183-4, 186-7, 237-8, 242, 245, 247 // *Vol. II*: 131, 140, 327, 362
Firth, Raymond *Vol. I*: 209
Flasche, Rainer *Vol. II*: 74, 76, 78, 86
Florenz, Karl *Vol. I*: 158
Fójiào Hóngshì Xúeyuàn *Vol. II*: 301
folklore *Vol. I*: 157, 163, 165, 168, 183, 189, 228, 232, 234-5, 237 // *Vol. II*: 93
folk religion *Vol. I*: 13, 158 // *Vol. II*: 43, 90, 151
Folk Shintō *Vol. II*: 42,
foreign/ness *Vol. I*: 54-8, 88, 151
fortune/-telling *Vol. II*: 223, 228, 292-3, 298
  See also Seven Gods of Good Fortune
Foucault, Michel *Vol. I*: 20
founder/s (of religions) *Vol. I*: 93, 98,101, 131, 217 // *Vol. II*: 8, 144, 147, 164, 166, 170, 172-5, 179, 182-7, 189-95, 197-9, 209, 219, 228, 230-1, 235, 343, 383
Fox, George *Vol. II*: 120
France/French *Vol. I*: 181, 184-7, 194, 196, 217, 226, 245, 248 // *Vol. II*: 62, 162-4, 178, 334, 349, 378
Franco-Belgian school *Vol. I*: 232
francophone *Vol. I*: 42, 245
Franke, Edith *Vol. I*: 176-7, 271, 273-5 *Vol. II*: 177, 287, 305, 309-13, 367, 373, 392-4, 400-1

Franke, Otto *Vol. II*: 177
Freitas, Maria Otávia *Vol. II*: 219
Fremdreligionen *Vol. I*: 73
Freud, Sigmund *Vol. I*: 48, 92, 217, 251
Frisk, Liselotte *Vol. II*: 57, 60, 220
Fucan, Fabian *Vol. II*: 12
fuda *Vol. I*: 60-61
Fúdé zhèngshén *Vol. II*: 297
Fújiàn *Vol. II*: 294, 300, 303
Fukko Shintō *Vol. II*: 43
Fukuda, Chiyoko *Vol. II*: 173
Fúlíng Miào *Vol. II*: 297
function/s (of religion) *Vol. I*: 89, 96, 104, 140, 188, 202 // *Vol. II*: 18-21, 38, 40, 47, 51, 54, 60, 70, 79, 81-2, 89, 166, 198, 215, 225, 232-3, 273, 292, 302-3, 311, 319, 324-5, 334, 337, 339-40, 359, 362
functional *Vol. II*: 8
– definition *Vol. I*: 35
– explanation *Vol. I*: 40, 91 // *Vol. II*: 14, 22
functionalism/ist *Vol. I*: 20, 35
fundamentalism/ist *Vol. I*: 43, 46, 229 // *Vol. II*: 60, 62, 70, 97, 373, 395
funeral/s *Vol. I*: 96, 100 // *Vol. II*: 18, 20, 60, 70, 150, 225, 324
Furuno, Kiyohito *Vol. I*: 166, 168

Gangnam Temple *Vol. II*: 185
Gasparro, Giulia Sfameni *Vol. I*: 177, 253, 261-262, 270
Gassan *Vol. II*: 94, 96
Gauntlett, J. O. *Vol. I*: 166, 168
Gaus, Günter *Vol. I*: 179, 194
GDR (DDR) *Vol. I*: 235-6
Gedatsu *Vol. II*: 259
Gedatsu-kai *Vol. I*: 57, 68
Geertz, Armin W. *Vol. I*: 249, 261, 266 // *Vol. II*: 79-81, 86-7, 108, 116, 128, 217
Geertz, Clifford *Vol. I*: 91-2, 106 // *Vol. II*: 110, 115
Gemuyev, I. N. *Vol. I*: 242

gender *Vol. I*: 22, 54, 192 // *Vol. II*: 8, 64, 172, 175, 179-80, 192-3, 197
genealogy *Vol. II*: 193
General Assembly (of IAHR) *Vol. I*: 173, 197, 220, 250
Geneva *Vol. II*: 16
Genscher, Dietrich *Vol. II*: 339
Gentz, Joachim *Vol. II*: 288, 305, 311
genzeriyaku Vol. I: 97 // *Vol. II*: 83, 171, 229
Georgia *Vol. I*: 195
Gerasimova, Kseniya Maksimovna *Vol. I*: 229, 231
Germany *Vol. I*: 179, 181-8, 210, 215-6, 228, 235, 245 // *Vol. II*: 133, 141, 161, 328, 333-40, 348, 356, 365-8, 371, 376-8, 384-5
- West / Federal Republic of Germany *Vol. I*: 235 // *Vol. II*: 329
- East / German Democratic Republic *Vol. I*: 225, 228, 235-6 // *Vol. II*: 328, 337-9
- German Protestant Church (EKD) *Vol. II*: 327, 365, 371
- terminology *Vol. I*: 2, 9, 15, 40, 73, 109, 181, 183 257 // *Vol. II*: 74-6, 108, 121, 123-4, 133, 137, 391-2
- theology *Vol. II*: 349, 352, 363
Ghazāli *Vol. II*: 84, 87
Gill, Sam D. *Vol. II*: 78
Girardot, N. J. *Vol. I*: 41, 48
Giuriati, Paolo *Vol. I*: 253, 261
Gladigow, B. *Vol. II*: 86
globalization *Vol. I*: 218-9, 244, 247 // *Vol. II*: 222, 316, 360, 344, 394
Gnoli, Gherardo *Vol. I*: 95, 184
gnosis *Vol. II*: 5, 56-7, 59
gnostic religions *Vol. II*: 68, 150, 361
Gnosticism *Vol. I*: 235 // *Vol. II*; 56, 98, 143
Gobron, Gabriel *Vol. II*: 162, 177
God *Vol. I*: 81, 87-8, 199, 201 // *Vol. II*: 16, 25-6, 28, 63-5, 75-7, 81-2, 84-5, 119, 143, 160, 163, 165, 174, 232, 236, 330, 395-6

- God the Parent *Vol. II*: 51, 85, 172,
god/s *Vol. I*: 64, 210, 257 // *Vol. II*: 64, 69-70, 80, 86, 113, 155, 208, 212, 280-1, 284, 288, 323
- Chinese *Vol. I*: 139-40, 143 *Vol. II*: 290-306
- Japanese *Vol. I*: 88, 168 // *Vol. II*: 42, 46-7, 234, 260, 321 See also *kami*
- Seven Gods of Good Fortune *Vol. II*: 279
goddess *Vol. I*: 81-2 // *Vol. II*: 70, 158, 170, 278-82, 284, 286, 291, 293, 296, 302-3
godless *Vol. I*: 223 // *Vol. II*: 299, 315
godsdiens (Afrikaans) *Vol. I*: 247
godsdienst (Dutch) *Vol. I*: 247 // *Vol. II*: 263, 276
godsdienstfenomenologie Vol. II: 253, 264
godsdienstgeschiedenis Vol. I: 48 // *Vol. II*: 118, 121, 128
godsdiensthistorie Vol. I: 181
godsdienstwetenschap Vol. I: 181 // *Vol. II*: 119
gohei Vol. II: 89
gohonzon Vol. II: 251
Goldammer, Kurt *Vol. II*: 74, 87
goma Vol. II: 208, 211, 228, 273
gongen Vol. II: 270
gongyō Vol. II: 368
González Torres, Yolotl *Vol. I*: 261
Goodenough, E.R. *Vol. I*: 217
Gorbachev, Mihael *Vol. II*: 336
Gospel/s *Vol. II*: 16, 21, 98, 101, 329, 343
Gothóni, René *Vol. I*: 183
Gotō, Kōichirō *Vol. I*: 145
grace *Vol. II*: 16, 189
Grayson, James Huntley *Vol. II*: 165, 177, 180, 195, 200
Great Vehicle *Vol. II*: 53
Greece/Greek *Vol. I*: 70, 238 // *Vol. II*: 12, 98, 327 385
Gregorian University *Vol. II*: 51, 90, 367, 376
Greschat, Hans-Jürgen *Vol. I*: 250

Groningen, University of *Vol. I*: 183, 186 // *Vol. II*: 117, 121
Grünschloss, Andreas *Vol. II*: 359, 373
Grzymała-Moszczyńska, Halina *Vol. I*: 225, 242
Guadalupe *Vol. I*: 81-2, 88, 253, 259, 261
Guadalupenism/o *Vol. I*: 81-2, 83, 85, 259
Guāndì *Vol. II*: 291, 295-6, 299
Guānyīn *Vol. I*: 97 // *Vol. II*: 158, 278, 289-94, 296-8, 300-1, 303-4
guidance religions *Vol. I*: 35, 96 // *Vol. II*: 5, 22, 52, 56-7, 68, 193, 229, 361
Guittard, Charles *Vol. I*: 272 // *Vol. II*: 71
guru *Vol. I*: 234, 259 // *Vol. II*: 210
Guru Nanak *Vol. II*: 343
Gyōki Bosatsu *Vol. II*: 282

Habermas, Jürgen *Vol. I*: 251
Hachiman *Vol. II*: 259
Hackett, Rosalind *Vol. I*: 196, 214, 222, 274
Ha Daiusu Vol. II: 12
Haguro, Mount *Vol. I*: 68 // *Vol. II*: 94
haiden Vol. II: 47, 93, 270
Hajj *Vol. I*: 90
Hamilton, Ontario *Vol. I*: 115
Hammanskraal *Vol. I*: 219
Hammer, Raymond *Vol. II*: 219
Hampp, Irmgard *Vol. II*: 74, 87
hanging scrolls *Vol. I*: 60, 62-3, 68 // *Vol. II*: 283, 368
Hannya Shingyō Vol. I: 62 // *Vol. II*: 273
Happy Science, see Science of Happiness
harae Vol. II: 42, 46, 89, 92, 94
Harare *Vol. I*: 174-5, 196, 211, 268 // *Vol. II*: 318
Hardacre, Helen *Vol. I*: 68
Hare Krishna *Vol. I*: 88 // *Vol. II*: 384

harmony/harmoni *Vol. I*: 142, 176-7, 202, 273-5 // *Vol. II*: 262, 305, 347, 360, 373, 392-3, 400
Harnack, Alfred *Vol. II*: 33-4, 349
Harrison, Peter *Vol. II*: 348, 351
Hartman, Sven *Vol. II*: 264, 276
Harton, E. P. *Vol. II*: 75-7, 87
Hashimoto, Taketo *Vol. II*: 87, 370
Hastings, James *Vol. II*: 77-9, 87
hatsumōde Vol. II: 21
Hawaii *Vol. II*: 225, 227
Hayes, Victor C. *Vol. I*: 265 // *Vol. II*: 49, 319, 326
healing *Vol. I*: 34 97 // *Vol. II*: 5, 57, 59-60, 70, 114, 140, 218, 223, 229-30, 232, 316
Heart Sūtra Vol. I: 61-2 // *Vol. II*: 73-4, 273
heaven/s/ly *Vol. I*: 93-4, 123, 128, 164 // *Vol. II*: 81, 160-1, 171
– heavenly being/s *Vol. II*: 236, 260, 279, 282, 296
– Heavenly Reason/Wisdom *Vol. I*: 164 // *Vol. II*: 6, 153, 172, 234
– Lord of *Vol. I*: 137 // *Vol. II*: 165,
– Tiān *Vol. II*: 291-2, 294, 296
– Way of *Vol. I*: 140 // *Vol. II*: 164-5
Hebrew Bible *Vol. I*: 209 / *Vol. II*: 395
Hedin, Sven *Vol. I*: 150
Heiler, Friedrich *Vol. I*: 25, 32, 215, 250, 269 // *Vol. II*: 9, 41, 49, 74-7, 79, 86-7, 164, 349
Heilige, Das Vol. I: 45
Heisei Period *Vol. I*: 154
Hellenism *Vol. II*: 118, 143, 251, 265, 276
Helsinki *Vol. I*: 184, 238 // *Vol. II*: 327
Helve, Helena *Vol. I*: 237, 242, 274 // *Vol. II*: 140, 142, 151
henotheism *Vol. II*: 63-4, 66
heretic/s/al *Vol. I*: 120, 122, 132
heresy/ies *Vol. II*: 157, 250-1
hermeneutics *Vol. I*: 21, 24, 27, 191 // *Vol. II*: 113,

- comparative *Vol. II*: 6, 10, 28-39, 256-7, 355
Herskowits, Melville J. *Vol. II*: 265
heterodoxy/ies *Vol. I*: 119-22
heuristic *Vol. I*: 5, 35, 167
hibussetsu Vol. I: 119
hibutsu Vol. II: 282
Hick, John *Vol. II*: 343, 351, 371, 373
Hiei, Mount *Vol. I*: 98
hierarchic/al/y *Vol. II*: 47, 120, 163, 166, 175, 288, 331, 333-4, 380
hierophany *Vol. II*: 124
higan Vol. I: 100
High Platform (Cao Dai) *Vol. II*: 153
Hijirigaoka *Vol. II*: 174
hikaku shūkyō Vol. I: 162
Hiko, Mount *Vol. I*: 61
Hildesheim *Vol. I*: 220
Hīnayāna *Vol. I*: 120
Hinduism *Vol. I*: 35, 38, 198, 254, 256, 261 // *Vol. II*: 54, 56, 62, 64, 67, 70, 141, 252, 298, 323-4, 361, 378, 384, 388
Hinnells, John *Vol. I*: 184
Hiroshima *Vol. II*: 219, 398
historicism *Vol. I*:126-7,134
History of Religions School *Vol. II*: 118, 123, 348-50
Hizbollah *Vol. II*: 395
hōben Vol. II: 36 See also skilful means
Hōbōgirin *Vol. I*: 159
Hobsbawm, E. *Vol. II*: 112, 115
Hoffmann, Henryk *Vol. I*: 225, 242
Hōgonji *Vol. II*: 279, 282
Hok Tek Ceng Sin *Vol. II*: 297
holistic *Vol. I*: 23, 44, 211
Holm, Nils G. *Vol. I*: 183-4, 194, 237
Holocaust *Vol. I*: 210
Holtom, D. C. *Vol. II*: 43
holy (various) *Vol. II*: 128, 174, 183, 211, 230, 259, 296
- idea of *Vol. I*: 45 // *Vol. II*: 121
- places *Vol. I*: 62
- Spirit *Vol. II*: 81, 120
- Trinity *Vol. I*: 95
honden Vol. II: 93, 282
Hōnen *Vol. II*: 169, 374
Hong, Xiuquan *Vol. II*: 160
hongan Vol. II: 356
Honganji *Vol. I*: 98
- Higashi Honganji *Vol. I*: 159-60 // *Vol. II*: 365, 367-8, 371
- Honganji-ha *Vol. II*: 399
honji-suijaku Vol. II: 116, 258-9, 263, 359
Honko, Lauri *Vol. I*: 16, 32, 183, 237, 250
Hoppál, Mihály *Vol. I*: 228, 235, 238, 242
Hori, Ichiro *Vol. I*: 158, 168
Horyna, Břetislav *Vol. I*: 268 // *Vol. II*: 200, 286
Hosokawa, Gyōshin *Vol. I*: 98, 106
hotoke Vol. II: 231
hōza Vol. II: 170, 230
hozonkai Vol. II: 48
hṛdaya Vol. II: 257
Hromadka, Josef *Vol. II*: 328-30, 338
Huá Túo (Hua Toh) *Vol. II*: 294
Hugo, Victor *Vol. II*: 163
Hùihóng *Vol. I*: 131
Hui Neng *Vol. II*: 34, 344
Hultkrantz, Åke *Vol. II*: 267, 276
humanities *Vol. I*: 179, 181, 196, 244
Hummel, Arthur *Vol. II*: 177
Hungary *Vol. I*: 228, 235, 238 // *Vol. II*: 335, 337
Hus, Jan *Vol. II*: 120, 329
Hutter, Manfred *Vol. II*: 311
hymn/s *Vol. I*: 76, 87, 215

IAHR *Vol. I*: 4, 16, 21, 32, 42, 50-1, 112-3, 125, 136-7, 143, 145-6, 152-3, 155-6, 168-70, 173-7, 179-81, 183-4, 186-7, 193-4, 196-204, 206-25, 230, 236, 238, 241-6, 249-50, 254, 261, 265, 267-8, 271-5 // *Vol. II*: 201, 278, 286, 299, 315, 317-9, 376, 392-3, 400
See also congresses/IAHR
iconographic/y *Vol. I*: 28, 82, 87 // *Vol. II*: 72, 120, 282, 288, 292, 294, 305
icons *Vol. I*: 227
identity/identification

- individual/self *Vol. II*: 83, 209, 229, 386
- ethnic/social/political *Vol. I*: 5, 75, 78-9, 82-4, 234, 244-7, 259, 265, 267-8, 234// *Vol. II*: 6, 10, 16, 43, 47, 54, 57, 70, 92, 148, 162, 174, 292, 309-10, 314-26, 328, 332-3, 337, 339, 376, 388
- of discipline (study of religions) *Vol. I*: 5, 9-10, 18-19, 27, 33, 42, 92, 142, 146-9, 176, 182-5, 188-9, 192-3, 214-6, 244-7, 252 // *Vol. II*: 72, 113, 115, 131-2, 138, 247, 309, 315
- of religious traditions *Vol. I*: 101-2, 134, 203, 232 // *Vol. II*: 111, 113, 150, 179, 193, 195-7, 204, 228-9, 250, 269-71, 280-1, 393, 401

ideology/ical *Vol. I*: 84, 111, 151-2, 161, 166, 173, 188-9, 211-2, 223, 227, 235-41, 243, 251 // *Vol. II*: 26, 37, 63, 131, 154, 166, 172, 175, 215, 287, 295, 297, 299, 312, 330-4 338, 340, 379

idolatry *Vol. I*: 205 // *Vol. II*: 248
Ienaga, Saburō *Vol. I*: 135
Igreja (Messiânica Mundial do Brasil) *Vol. II*: 219-20, 234-7
Iksan City *Vol. II*: 167, 181-2, 184-5, 189, 197, 352, 391
Ikushima, Itsuo *Vol. II*: 284
Il Wŏn Sang *Vol. II*: 187, 190, 196-7, 199
Immeasurables (Four) *Vol. II*: 211
immigration *Vol. I*: 71, 137, 192, 255 // *Vol. II*: 107, 218-9, 222, 225, 233, 239, 292, 294, 300, 303
immortalism *Vol. I*: 139
imperialism *Vol. I*: 149-151, 155-6, 165-6 // *Vol. II*: 134, 136, 336
Imperial Household Shintō *Vol. II*: 42
Imperial Rescript on Education *Vol. I*: 161
Inari *Vol. II*: 280-1
incarnation *Vol. II*: 25, 119, 159, 320
incense *Vol. II*: 291-2, 294, 302

inculturation *Vol. II*: 140, 146, 151, 220
India/n *Vol. I*: 101, 117, 128-9, 131, 139, 149-50, 153, 164-6, 206, 215, 218, 248, 255 // *Vol. II*: 143, 210, 225, 230, 265, 278-9, 281, 291, 293-4, 296, 317, 325, 346
- Buddhist *Vol. I*: 99, 122-3, 129, 159-61, // *Vol. II*: 83, 110, 144, 158, 162, 169, 191, 258
- cosmologies *Vol. I*: 44
- logic *Vol. I*: 38
Indians *Vol. I*: 101, 122, 137
- Green *Vol. I*: 77-81
- Latin American *Vol. I*: 81-3, 137 // *Vol. II*: 77
- North American *Vol. II*: 267, 362
indigenisation *Vol. II*: 21, 29, 93, 297
indigenous religion *Vol. I*: 194, 202-5, 256 // *Vol. II*: 21, 88, 91, 100, 162
Indios Verdes *Vol. I*: 77-81
Indology/Indogaku *Vol. I*: 51, 161
Indonesia/n *Vol. I*: 95, 176-7, 183, 206, 248-9, 271, 273-5 // *Vol. II*: 21, 154, 301, 306, 309, 373, 392-4, 400-1
- Chinese temples *Vol. II*: 287-8, 295-9
- Indonesian Confucianist Association *Vol. II*: 292
inexpressibility *Vol. I*: 45
informant/s *Vol. I*: 55-7, 79, 191, 240 // *Vol. II*: 95, 237, 291, 298, 301 See also insider/outsider; intimacy (and distance)
initiation *Vol. II*: 20, 85
- rites of *Vol. II*: 19-20, 60, 92, 211, 322
Inner Trip *Vol. II*: 170
innovation *Vol. I*: 37, 46, 101, 121, 138, 157, 207, 214, 255-9 // *Vol. II*: 9, 103-7, 114-5, 130-50, 154, 156, 158, 161-2, 169, 173, 175, 183, 194-5, 198, 201, 220-2, 227, 229, 238, 300, 345-6, 360, 363-5 See also new religions

Inoue, Enryō *Vol. I*: 159-62, 168
Inoue Tetsujirō *Vol. I*: 160-2
inscriptions *Vol. I*: 29, 80 // *Vol. II*: 165, 294
insider/outsider *Vol. I*: 3, 13, 69, 71-3, 76, 84, 86-106, 207 // *Vol. II*: 182, 393
See also informant/s; intimacy (and distance)
instinctive dynamics *Vol. II*: 146-7
institutions/al
− academic *Vol. I*: 2, 4, 9, 46, 51, 55, 147, 156, 167, 173-4, 178-9, 181, 186-9, 199, 219-20, 224, 227, 249, 252 // *Vol. II*: 131, 309-10, 314-7, 392
− religious etc *Vol. I*: 60-1, 79, 100, 140, 239 // *Vol. II*: 48, 54, 57, 93, 98-9, 105, 142, 147, 151, 171, 180, 184, 188, 191-2, 198, 207-8, 281, 289, 295, 301, 304, 359-60, 364-71, 376, 385-9
Insurgentes *Vol. I*: 78-79
integrated study of religions *Vol. I*: 2-3, 13, 15-32, 36-7, 51, 86, 175, 186-8, 193, 204, 211 // *Vol. II*: 110
integrative religious education *Vol. II*: 312, 376-90
intentionality (of believers) *Vol. I*: 25, 29, 80, 91, 93, 96, 99, 100, 102, 104, 121, 123-4, 146, 229 // *Vol. II*: 80- 81, 89, 94, 96, 99, 142-3, 147-8, 174, 183, 300
intercultural *Vol. I*: 42, 125, 137, 152-3, 170, 182, 186, 196-200, 201-7, 252 // *Vol. II*: 41-2, 343, 350
interdisciplinary *Vol. I*: 31, 51, 183, 249, 252 // *Vol. II*: 99, 132, 135-7
interfaith *Vol. II*: 172, 311, 317, 342-5, 350-1, 357, 360
international *Vol. I*: 4, 50, 68, 112-4, 125, 136-7, 143, 145-7, 152-3, 155, 173-4, 176-7, 188, 196-207, 208-222, 228, 235, 248 // *Vol. II*: 6, 40, 108, 125, 166, 170-2, 185, 188, 315-8, 323, 328, 331, 340, 376, 379, 399
International Association for Buddhist Studies (IABS) *Vol. II*: 184
International Association for the History of Religions *Vol. I*: 4, 21, 32, 136-7, 146, 152, 155, 173-4, 179-81, 193-4, 196-207, 208-22, 223-5, 236, 238, 244, 249 // *Vol. II*: 299, 315, 317, 376, 392-3
See also IAHR
International Association of Shin Buddhist Studies (IASBS) *Vol. II*: 8
International Interfaith Centre *Vol. II*: 342, 360
internationalism *Vol. I*: 161, 163 // *Vol. II*: 175
internet *Vol. I*: 106, 219 // *Vol. II*: 6, 299, 309
interpretation *Vol. I*: 1-12, 14, 48, 52, 95, 116, 121, 136, 141, 169, 264-6 // *Vol. II*: 6, 11-13, 29, 32-3, 35, 37-9, 43, 48-9, 84, 98, 100-1, 110, 112, 114, 125, 127, 145, 197, 214, 249-50, 254, 267, 285, 347, 368, 371, 374, 398
interreligious *Vol. I*: 201, 271 // *Vol. II*: 7, 164, 343, 360, 374
interview/s *Vol. I*: 55-6, 60 / *Vol. II*: 209, 220
intimacy (and distance) *Vol. I*: 13, 86-104
intuitive *Vol. II*: 257
invocation *Vol. II*: 84, 226
Ippen *Vol. II*: 272-273
Ir-Wŏn-Sang *Vol. II*: 187, 190, 196-7, 199
Iran *Vol. II*: 360, 387
Iraq *Vol. II*: 309, 392, 397
Ireland (Northern) *Vol. I*: 227 // *Vol. II*: 316, 324, 388
Iri (=Iksan) *Vol. II*: 182, 184, 189, 200-1
Irkutsk *Vol. I*: 227, 233 // *Vol. II*: 327
irrationality *Vol. I*: 45-6

Ise Shrine (Ise Jingū) *Vol. II*: 43, 46, 95, 171, 259
Ishiteji *Vol. II*: 397
Islam *Vol. I*: 5, 35, 43, 87, 94, 111, 116, 137, 142, 152, 163-4, 180, 192, 199, 207, 228-9, 254-7, 259 // *Vol. II*: 77, 84, 110, 113, 115, 141, 151, 154-155, 249-250, 252, 266, 295, 316, 340, 356, 361, 384, 387, 394-396
– Islamic *Vol. I*: 116, 198-200, 210, 229 // *Vol. II*: 16, 64, 66, 112, 344, 393-394, 396
– Islamist/s *Vol. II*: 62, 112-3
– Islamology *Vol. I*: 241
Israel *Vol. II*: 16, 316, 395
– Israeli/s *Vol. II*: 62, 395
– Israelite *Vol. II*: 16, 255, 349
Istanbul *Vol. I*: 179 // *Vol. II*: 327
Italy *Vol. I*: 181, 184, 186-7, 238, 245 // *Vol. II*: Italy 334
– Italian *Vol. I*: 187, 245
Itō, Jinsai *Vol. I*: 134 // *Vol. II*: 35
Itō, Tōgai *Vol. II*: 35
Itoo, Eizo *Vol. II*: 238
Itsukushima *Vol. II*: 279, 282, 285
Ittōen *Vol. II*: 220
Iyanaga, Nobumi *Vol. I*: 151, 168
Izanagi *Vol. II*: 64
Izanami *Vol. II*: 64
Izunome Association *Vol. II*: 235, 239

Jablonna *Vol. I*: 193
Jackson, Robert *Vol. II*: 376
Jagellonian University (Jagiellońska) *Vol. I*: 225, 242 // *Vol. II*: 65
Jainism *Vol. II*: 56, 322, 345-6
Jakarta *Vol. II*: 298-9, 305, 310
jaken Vol. I: 121
James, William *Vol. I*: 217 // *Vol. II*: 14, 23
Japan/ese (cultural, intellectual, national, etc. abbrev.) *Vol. I*: 71,109-35, 144-70, 176, 210, 257 // *Vol. II*: 11, 35, 42-9, 152-4, 159, 164-6, 184, 187-8, 289, 300, 303-4, 312, 321, 347-8, 352-3, 359, 362, 376-89, 394-9

Japan/ese religion/s *Vol. I*: 1-5, 13, 28, 32, 40, 50-68, 88, 93, 96-100, 109-35, 137-8, 141, 144-70, 183, 190, 247, 258, 262 // *Vol. II*: 5-7, 9-10, 12, 18, 20, 25, 29-30, 42-9, 54, 56, 69-70, 72-4, 82-3, 87-96, 107, 111, 130-151, 154-6, 167-78, 194, 202-17, 218-39, 243-6, 251, 253, 255, 264-5, 270-5, 278-86, 321, 356, 360, 362, 367-9 See also Shintō, *shūkyō*, *yamabushi*, etc.
Japaneseness *Vol. II*: 42, 46, 227
Japanologist/s *Vol. I*: 183 // *Vol. II*: 47
Jaruzelski, Wojciech *Vol. II*: 334-5
Java *Vol. I*: 176 // *Vol. II*: 110, 115, 290, 310, 392
Jehova's Witnesses *Vol. II*: 396
Jensen, Jeppe Sinding *Vol. I*: 114, 268 // *Vol. II*: 108, 116
Jensen, Tim *Vol. I*: 49, 114
Jesuit/s *Vol. I*: 110 // *Vol. II*: 369
Jesus (Christ) *Vol. I*: 93-4, 101-2 // *Vol. II*: Jesus 16, 21, 25, 118-9, 120, 143, 147, 160, 343, 355, 396
Jewish/ness *Vol. I*: 251 // *Vol. II*: 16, 21, 63-4, 388, 394-6 See also Judaism
jiāmiào Vol. II: 301
jiba Vol. II: 171, 234
jinja Vol. II: 93
Jinja Honchō *Vol. II*: 93
Jinki Period *Vol. II*: 281-2
jiriki Vol. I: 99 // *Vol. II*: 24, 226
jissen Vol. II: 13
Jōdo (Pure Land) *Vol. I*: 57, 97, 159-60 // *Vol. II*: 8-9, 169, 223, 227, 367, 372, 374
John, Gospel of *Vol. II*: 28, 98
John-Paul II (Pope) *Vol. I*: 8, 82
John the Baptist *Vol. II*: 92
Johrei, see *jōrei*
Jordan, David K. *Vol. II*: 159, 177
jōrei (Johrei) *Vol. II*: 95, 229, 232, 235, 237, 239
joya no kane Vol. II: 20
joyous life (yōkigurashi) *Vol. II*: 171

Juan Diego *Vol. I*: 81
Judaeo-Christian *Vol. II*: 76, 235
Judaism *Vol. I*: 35, 88, 93, 111, 199, 255, 361 // *Vol. II*: 16, 54-5, 62, 68, 77, 89, 115, 141, 199, 324, 384, 397
Jugendreligionen Vol. II: 133
jukai Vol. II: 20
Julius Caesar *Vol. I*: 210
Jung, C. G. *Vol. I*: 217
Jusan (= Chusan) *Vol. II*: 186
Justinian (Metropolitan) *Vol. II*: 329
Juynboll, Th. W. *Vol. II*: 77
Jwasan (= Chwasan) *Vol. II*: 185-6

Kadowaki, Ken *Vol. I*: 273 // *Vol. II*: 368, 372
kagura Vol. II: 234
kagurazutome Vol. II: 171
kaidan Vol. II: 251
kajō Vol. I: 119, 124, 127
kakejiku Vol. I: 63
Kamakura *Vol. II*: 279, 282
kami Vol. I: 88 // *Vol. II*: 44, 69, 93, 212, 230-1, 234, 236, 259, 270, 272, 281, 285
Kampuchea *Vol. II*: 294
Kamstra, Josef H. *Vol. II*: 244, 246, 253-6, 258, 260-5, 276
Kan, Elio Masferrer *Vol. I*: 253, 261
kanbun Vol. I: 117, 126
Kangnam Temple *Vol. II*: 185, 191
Kannon *Vol. I*: 97 // *Vol. II*: 229, 278-80, 282-3, 397
Kannondō (Hall) *Vol. II*: 282-4
kanrodai Vol. II: 171
Kant/ian *Vol. I*: 45, 159
Kanton *Vol. II*: 160
Karelia *Vol. I*: 238
Karl Marx University *Vol. I*: 235
karma/karmic *Vol. I*: 122, 132 // *Vol. II*: 18, 22, 28, 52, 92
Katō, Bungo *Vol. II*: 174
Katō, Genchi *Vol. I*: 161, 169
Katō, Toshio *Vol. II*: 174
Katz, Stephen T. *Vol. I*: 24, 32
Kaulem, David *Vol. I*: 196
Kawaguchi, Ekai *Vol. I*: 150, 169

Kawasaki, Daishi *Vol. I*: 61
Keene, Donald *Vol. I*: 151, 169
kegare Vol. II: 42, 46
Keith, Berriedale *Vol. I*: 232
kelenteng Vol. II: 288, 295-7, 299
Kennedy, J.F. *Vol. II*: 329
ketuhanan Vol. II: 297-9
Khabarovsk *Vol. I*: 227
Khanti *Vol. I*: 238
Khong Hu Cu (Khonghucu) *Vol. II*: 297, 299
Kierunki Vol. II: 331
Kim Sa Kiong *Vol. II*: 292
Kim, Tae-Gŏ *Vol. II*: 186, 197, 200-1
Kimbangu, Simon *Vol. I*: 138
kindai Vol. I: 111, 154
King, Ursula *Vol. I*: 249, 267 // *Vol. II*: 341
kinship *Vol. II*: 46-7, 63
Kippenberg, Hans *Vol. I*: 183, 194, 216, 266 // *Vol. II*: 9, 129, 217
Kishijōten *Vol. II*: 279
Kishimoto, Hideo *Vol. I*: 161-2, 169 // *Vol. II*: 205, 216
Kishimoto, Nobuto *Vol. I*: 162
Kitagawa, Joseph *Vol. I*: 106, 158, 169
kiyome Vol. II: 92, 94, 174
Kleine, Christoph *Vol. I*: 263 // *Vol. II*: 402
Klimkeit, Hans Joachim *Vol. I*: 184
Klostermaier, Klaus, K. *Vol. I*: 32, 194
kō Vol. II: 96
Kōdaiji *Vol. II*: 397
Kōfuku no Kagaku *Vol. II*: 173, 208, 213, 220, 227-8, 238 See also Science of Happiness
Kohl, Karl-Heinz *Vol. I*: 150, 169
Kohler, Werner *Vol. II*: 169, 177
Kokugaku school *Vol. I*: 157 // *Vol. II*: 43-45
Kokugakuin University *Vol. I*: 161
Kokutai no hongi Vol. I: 166, 168
Kōmeitō *Vol. II*: 171
Komi *Vol. I*: 230, 238
Konakov, Nikolay Dmitriyevich *Vol. I*: 230
Kong, Yuanzhi *Vol. II*: 299, 305

Konjin *Vol. II*: 260
Konkōkyō *Vol. I*: 58 // *Vol. II*: 56, 91, 169, 229, 361
Konkōkyō Izuo Kyōkai (Church) *Vol. II*: 220, 399
Koran *Vol. I*: 88 See also Qur'an
Korea/n Korea *Vol. I*: 138, 153, 165, 246, 249 // *Vol. II*: 106, 144, 149, 152-5, 162-7, 176-7, 179-82, 184, 186-8, 190-200, 225, 239, 312, 325, 346, 348, 352, 360, 374, 391, 394, 397-8, 401
Koreans *Vol. I*: 54 // *Vol. II*: 165, 398
Korsch, Dietrich *Vol. II*: 355
Kota *Vol. II*: 296, 298
Kotani, Kimi *Vol. II*: 170
Kraatz, Martin *Vol. I*: 250 // *Vol. II*: 367
Kraemer, Hendrik *Vol. II*: 253-6, 263, 266
Kraków *Vol. I*: 225 // *Vol. II*: 65
Kremkau, Klaus *Vol. I*: 264 // *Vol. II*: 374
Krestanska Mirova Conference *Vol. II*: 328
Krishna *Vol. I*: 88 // *Vol. II*: 54-5, 293-4, 384
Kristensen, W. Brede *Vol. I*: 26, 32, 91-2, 95, 106
Krüger, Jacob/us *Vol. I*: 256, 261
Kruschchev, Nikita *Vol. II*: 329
I-Kuan-Tao (Yiguandao) *Vol. II*: 159, 165
Kuan Im *Vol. II*: 389 See also Guā-nyīn
Kubo, Kakutarō *Vol. II*: 170
Kubo, Tsugunari *Vol. II*: 170
Kumano Shrine *Vol. II*: 245, 264, 270-5
Kumārajīva *Vol. II*: 169
Kŭmsan-sa *Vol. II*: 197
Kundalini Yoga *Vol. II*: 211
Küng, Hans *Vol. II*: 359
kuni (Japanese provinces) *Vol. II*: 285
Kuomintang *Vol. II*: 159
Kuper, Adam *Vol. I*: 41, 48
Kurama (Temple) *Vol. II*: 221

Kurozumi, Munetada *Vol. II*: 54, 194, 222
Kurozumikyō *Vol. I*: 68 // *Vol. II*: 54, 68, 91, 143, 168, 194, 220, 324, 379, 384
Kwan Im Thong *Vol. II*: 289, 291-4, 296
Kwazulu-Natal *Vol. I*: 211, 256
Kyochŏn Vol. II: 188
Kyojŏn Vol. II: 200
kyojun Vol. II: 182, 185, 187-8, 197-8, 200
kyōkai Vol. II: 171, 220
kyotang Vol. II: 190
Kyōto *Vol. I*: 50, 97-9, 156, 159, 161 // *Vol. II*: 131, 220-1, 236, 278-80, 352, 367, 397
Kyōto School *Vol. I*: 146
kyūsaironteki Vol. II: 61
Kyussei (Kyūsei) *Vol. II*: 235, 239
kyūshachi Vol. II: 272

Labour Party *Vol. I*: 209
Lai, Whalen *Vol. II*: 368, 373
laity, see lay/laity
Baikal, Lake *Vol. I*: 233 // *Vol. II*: 310
Lake Biwa *Vol. II*: 278-82
Lamaism *Vol. I*: 149, 170, 229, 233 // *Vol. II*: 210
Lamotte, Étienne *Vol. II*: 34
Lancaster (University) *Vol. I*: 10, 180, 197 // *Vol. II*: 32
Landon, Perceval *Vol. I*: 149, 169
Lankāvatāra Sūtra Vol. I: 120
Lanternari, Vittorio *Vol. II*: 133-4, 136-7, 151
Lǎozǐ (Lǎo zǐ) *Vol. I*: 101, 132
Laperrousaz, Ernest-Marie *Vol. I*: 184
Latin America *Vol. I*: 36, 137-8, 142, 153, 164, 175, 189-90, 197, 202, 204-6, 220, 248-9, 253-6 // *Vol. II*: 143, 265, 297, 347, 350
Laube, Johannes *Vol. II*: 168, 173, 177, 367
Lausanne *Vol. I*: 86, 184
lay/laity *Vol. I*: 134 // *Vol. II*: 17, 53, 169, 271, 396

- Catholic (PAX) *Vol. I*: 75 // *Vol. II*: 310, 316, 331-2
- Buddhist movements *Vol. I*: 58, 102 // *Vol. II*: 83, 167, 169, 191-2, 213, 228
- vegetarian movements *Vol. II*: 158

Lebanon *Vol. II*: 395
Leclant, Jean *Vol. I*: 184
Leeds *Vol. I*: 80-1, 180 // *Vol. II*: 328
legend/s *Vol. I*: 209 // *Vol. II*: 4, 17, 28, 280, 286, 302, 321, 323
legitimation *Vol. I*: 209, 214, 229, // *Vol. II*: 146, 151, 280, 360, 366, 374, 395
Leipzig *Vol. I*: 235-6 // *Vol. II*: 327-8, 335-8
Lenin/ism *Vol. I*: 211, 223, 236-7, 239
Leningrad *Vol. I*: 179, 227-8, 230-2, 243
Lessing, Gotthold Ephraim *Vol. I*: 110-1, 157 // *Vol. II*: 347
Leuba, J. H. *Vol. I*: 217
Le Van Trung *Vol. II*: 163
Leviticus *Vol. II*: 89
Lévy-Bruhl, L. *Vol. I*: 217
Lévi-Strauss, Claude *Vol. I*: 20 // *Vol. II*: 45-6
Lhasa *Vol. I*: 149, 168-70, 213
Li/Hong *Vol. II*: 160
liberation theology *Vol. I*: 204
life rites *Vol. II*: 59, 69-70, 223
Lijiao *Vol. II*: 158-9
Lin Ancestral Hall *Vol. II*: 301-2
Lin Chao-En *Vol. I*: 141, 143 // *Vol. II*: 264, 268, 276
Lin Mònián *Vol. II*: 291
Lin Peiying *Vol. II*: 287, 301
lineage *Vol. II*: 193, 321-2
Ling, Trevor *Vol. II*: 17, 30, 250, 252
linguistic
- data features *Vol. I*: 27-8, 56, 93
- diversity *Vol. I*: 182, 244-5, 248

literalism *Vol. II*: 25, 85, 386
liturgy *Vol. I*: 70, 87 // *Vol. II*: 81-2, 89, 139-40, 163, 171, 173-4, 230
Lloret de Mar *Vol. I*: 184

local *Vol. I*: 34, 55, 59, 61, 77, 79, 100, 179, 232 // *Vol. II*: 3, 47, 112, 134, 158, 160, 163, 190, 207-8, 220, 223, 229, 259, 281, 287-8, 290, 302, 304, 331, 362, 383, 385-6, 394
logocentricity *Vol. I*: 92 // *Vol. II*: 96-7
Loisy, Alfred *Vol. II*: 33, 349
Lokesvara (Vihara) *Vol. II*: 296
longevity *Vol. II*: 158
Lord of Heaven *Vol. I*: 137 // *Vol. II*: 165
Lord's Supper *Vol. II*: 20
Lotus Sūtra *Vol. I*: 101 // *Vol. II*: 28, 36, 82-3, 158, 169-71, 177, 223, 227, 280
Lotus Sutra movements *Vol. II*: 169-71, 230
- White Lotus movement *Vol. II*: 157-8, 178
Loukes, Harold *Vol. II*: 386
Lourdes *Vol. I*: 219 // *Vol. II*: 57
Lü K'un *Vol. II*: 175
Lubbock, J. *Vol. I*: 217
Ludvik, Catherine *Vol. II*: 279, 286
Lukens-Bull, Ronald *Vol. II*: 393, 401
Lutheran/ism *Vol. I*: 40 // *Vol. II*: 7, 72, 337
Lys, Candice *Vol. II*: 373, 393, 401

maailmankuva *Vol. I*: 237
MacKinnon, Donald *Vol. I*: 12
Mādhyamika *Vol. II*: 37
Maeda, Eun *Vol. I*: 160
Maeda, Gorō *Vol. II*: 255, 263
Magelang *Vol. II*: 296-7
magic/al *Vol. I*: 38, 103, 122, 128-33
Mah Choe Poh *Vol. II*: 291
maha esa *Vol. II*: 297-299
Mahabiksu Ashin Jinarakkhita *Vol. II*: 297-8
Mahāparinirvāṇa Sūtra *Vol. II*: 25
Mahāvagga *Vol. II*: 28
Mahāyāna (Buddhism) *Vol. I*: 1, 61, 70, 117, 119, 127, 157, 160, 165, 218, 230 // *Vol. II*: 18, 28-9, 36-

7, 53, 82-3, 96, 124, 146, 149, 157, 162, 169, 183, 194, 196-7, 211, 229, 243, 255, 274, 300-1, 343, 371
mairi (o-mairi) Vol. II: 93-4
Maitreya Vol. II: 195, 197, 295, 304
Majelis Tingi Agama Khongfucu Indonesia Vol. II: 297
Makiguchi, Tsunesaburō Vol. II: 171
Malacca (Melaka, Malakka) Vol. II: 290-1, 293
Malay/an Vol. II: 290-2
Malaysia Vol. I: 166 // Vol. II: 290, 394
Malaysian Buddhist Association Vol. II: 292
Malinowski, B. K. Vol. I: 92
Mäll, Linnart Vol. I: 230, 242
Mandaean Vol. I: 235 // Vol. II: 92
mandala Vol. II: 272
mandarin/s Vol. II: 157, 160, 175
mandate of heaven (*tiānmíng*) Vol. II: 159, 165
Mandivenga Vol. I: 196
Manichaeism Vol. II: 136, 143, 249, 251
manisha Vol. II: 271
Mansi Vol. I: 238
mantra/s Vol. II: 87, 157, 170, 274
Mao, Tse T'ung Vol. I: 136
Maori/tanga Vol. II: 111, 166
Māra Vol. II: 250
Marburg University
– Conferences Vol. I: 173, 197, 215, 220, 249-50 // Vol. II: 72, 88, 353, 355, 367-9, 371
– Museum of Religion Vol. I: 63, 89, 228 // Vol. II: 6,
– personalia Vol. II: 76, 111, 131, 181, 309, 328, 376
Margul, Tadeusz Vol. I: 225, 242
Maria (Santa) Vol. I: 82, 253, 261 // Vol. II: 119 See also Mary
Mark, Saint Vol. II: 343
Martin, Gerhard Marcel Vol. I: 106, 270-1, 274-5 // Vol. II: 10, 374, 410

Martin, Luther Vol. I: 243 // Vol. II: 264-5
Marx, Karl Vol. I: 203, 235-6
Marxism Vol. I: 136, 187-8, 226-7 // Vol. II: 63, 331-3
Marxim-Leninism Vol. I: 223, 237, 239
Mary Vol. I: 81-2, 88, 93-5, 219, 253, 261 // Vol. II: 46, 183 See also Maria, Virgin Mary
Marzal, Manuel Vol. I: 205-7, 253, 261
Masami-sama Vol. II: 174
Masferrer Kan, Elio Vol. I: 253, 261
Mass Vol. II: 60, 138,
Master (in Won Buddhism) Vol. II: 167, 174, 182-89, 192-3, 197-201
Master Goi Vol. II: 174
Mas'ud, Abdurrahman Vol. I: 176-7, 271, 273-5 // Vol. II: 373, 392, 400
MATAKIN Vol. II: 297
Mathé, Roger Vol. I: 150, 169
materialism Vol. I: 137 // Vol. II: 315
Matsunaga, Alicia Vol. I: 110, 116, 258, 263, 359, 373
Matsura, Sayohime Vol. II: 280, 286
matsuri Vol. I: 88, 161, 170 // Vol. II: 42, 46-7, 271
Matthew, Saint Vol. I: 28, 343
mausoleum
– of Nichiren Vol. II: 170
– of Shinran Vol. I: 99
Mauss, Marcel Vol. I: 217
Maxwell, Patrick Vol. I: 256, 261
May, John D'Arcy Vol. II: 368, 373
Maya/n Vol. I: 80
Mazowiecki, Tadeusz Vol. I: 180, 225 // Vol. II: 335
Mazu/Māzŭ Vol. II: 157-8, 291, 296, 299-303
McCullough, Helen Vol. II: 260, 263
McCutcheon, Russell T. Vol. I: 41, 48, 261, 249, 261
Mcleod, Hew Vol. I: 101
meaning/s (religious) Vol. I: 24-5, 62, 76, 89, 92, 106, 123, 126, 128,

132-3, 180, 191, 202, 210, 243 // Vol. II: 11, 13, 15-16, 21-2, 26, 33-6, 38, 51, 73, 83, 85, 90, 93-4, 109-11, 113, 118, 120, 124-7, 135, 148, 153, 198, 204, 206, 233, 244, 250, 255, 258-62, 267-70, 273-5, 300, 317, 321, 324, 347, 386

meaning-in-life *Vol. II*: 22, 26, 206
Mecca *Vol. I*: 90
mediation *Vol. I*: 82, 131 // *Vol. II*: 311, 344, 365-8, 370, 372, 400
meditation *Vol. I*: 70, 259 // *Vol. II*: 7, 12, 72-86, 97, 161, 209, 204, 218, 227, 229-30, 232-3, 322, 339, 370-1, 381-2
– Buddhist *Vol. I*: 87, 96, 159, 261, 266, 272 // *Vol. II*: 13, 72-86, 100, 185, 189-90, 192, 206, 211, 226-7, 233, 298
– Christian *Vol. II*: 72-86, 371,
– *Emerging from Meditation Vol. I*: 110-2, 114, 117-26, 135, 141, 143, 157
medium/s *Vol. II*: 162, 174
meguri Vol. I: 63, 67-8, 98 // *Vol. II*: 74
Meiji Period/Restoration *Vol. I*: 146, 154-8, 162 // *Vol. II*: 169, 281
Meiji Shrine (Jingū) *Vol. I*: 61 // *Vol. II*: 43
Meishu-sama *Vol. II*: 235-6, 239
Melaka *Vol. II*: 290-1, 293
member/s *Vol. I*: 18, 146, 184, 187, 211, 220, 259 // *Vol. II*: 14, 17, 20, 47, 72, 95, 100, 155, 161, 166-7, 170-4, 179-83, 185, 189-95, 199, 202-4, 207-9, 215-6, 218, 221, 223, 226-8, 230-2, 236, 302, 311, 321, 331-3, 335, 360, 365, 367, 376, 378, 395-6 See also believers
membership *Vol. I*: 58, 90, 146, 184, 250 // *Vol. II*: 60, 163, 167, 171, 188, 193, 207, 209, 211, 215, 331-2, 334
meme/tic *Vol. I*: 175, 253
merit *Vol. I*: 97-100 // *Vol. II*: 84

Merton, Thomas *Vol. II*: 343
messiah *Vol. II*: 235
Messiânica *Vol. II*: 219-20, 234-7
Messianity *Vol. II*: 95, 234-7
Messina *Vol. I*: 175, 177, 253
metamorphosis *Vol. II*: 268
metaphor/ical *Vol. I*: 203-4, 209 // *Vol. II*: 64-70
metaphysics/al *Vol. I*: 95, 249 // *Vol. II*: 36-7, 100
Methodist *Vol. II*: 190
method/s *Vol. I*: 1, 3, 11-31, 33, 36-7, 39, 47, 49, 51, 53, 59, 64, 69-70, 72-86, 160, 162, 170, 183-4, 187, 236, 242, 249-50, 259, 261-9, 271 // *Vol. II*: 26, 39, 49, 67, 73, 101, 116, 128, 160, 168, 170, 177, 200, 210-1, 232, 248, 252, 277, 289, 305, 315, 329, 353-4, 374, 379, 393
methodology/ical *Vol. I*: 1, 3-5, 7, 9-10, 13, 15-32, 37, 49-51, 54, 68-70, 73-4, 76, 84-5, 86, 89, 99, 104, 106, 147, 175, 180, 186-7, 189-90, 193, 194, 198-9, 225, 29, 238, 242-3, 247, 249, 261, 266, 269 // *Vol. II*: 14, 86, 99, 107, 114, 116, 119-22, 125, 132, 183, 204, 257, 311, 374, 378
Mexico/an *Vol. I*: 210, 249, 261
– City *Vol. I*: 78, 88,
– civil religion *Vol. I*: 77-83, 210
– conferences *Vol. I*: 175, 190, 197, 250 // *Vol. II*: 318
– religion *Vol. I*: 69, 77-84, 88, 253, 259
miào Vol. II: 297, 301-303
Micah *Vol. II*: 337
Michaels, Axel *Vol. I*: 25, 216-7, 221, 269 // *Vol. II*: 87, 408
michibiki Vol. II: 56, 361
Middle East/ern *Vol. I*: 164, 176
Middle Way *Vol. I*: 120
Middle Treatise Vol. II: 83, 86
miei Vol. I: 62
migration *Vol. II*: 290
Mikagura/uta Vol. II: 233-4, 239
mikkyō Vol. II: 275

Mikoś, Kazimiera *Vol. II*: 65
mikoshi Vol. II: 271, 273
mikuji Vol. I: 60
Mílèfó (Mi Le Fo) *Vol. II*: 159, 293-5, 298
Ming (Míng Tàizǔ) *Vol. I*: 111, 136, 139-40, 143, 202, 257-8, 262 // *Vol. II*: 134, 155, 157, 178, 276, 289-90, 300-2, 306, 347, 351
Míngjiào *Vol. I*: 130-131
Minh Chi *Vol. I*: 141, 143
miniature temples *Vol. I*: 97
minimal religiosity *Vol. I*: 137, 143
Ministry of:
– Religion (Indonesia) *Vol. II*: 310, 393
– (Science and) Education (Japan) *Vol. I*: 165-6, 210, 257 // *Vol. II*: 218
Minobu, Mount *Vol. I*: 170
minority (religions) *Vol. I*: 164, 203, 205, 255 // *Vol. II*: 155, 165, 175, 216, 310, 327, 387, 396
Minoura, Eryō *Vol. I*: 273-274 // *Vol. II*: 368, 372, 374, 412-3
miracle/s *Vol. II*: 59, 77
miraculous *Vol. I*: 122 // *Vol. II*: 34
Miroku *Vol. II*: 293
Misogi-kyō *Vol. II*: 95
missiology *Vol. I*: 204, 213-5 // *Vol. II*: 140-1, 146, 180
mission/aries *Vol. I*: 42, 140, 149-50, 158, 214, 254, 256 // *Vol. II*: 16, 27-9, 54, 63, 123, 140-1, 144, 160-1, 163, 165-6, 183, 200, 210, 219, 221, 224, 232-4, 237, 239, 248-9, 251, 348
Miyake, Hitoshi *Vol. I*:163, 169
Miyashita, Seishi *Vol. I*: 274 // *Vol. II*: 368, 374
Mizuta, Norihisa *Vol. I*: 126, 135
M'Lennan, J. F. *Vol. I*: 217
model/s
– in method and theory *Vol. I*: 29, 51, 70, 73, 116, 130, 131-3, 136-7, 144, 153, 167, 175, 177, 191-3, 206-7, 237, 244, 248, 252-60 // *Vol. II*: 49, 181, 267-8, 275-6, 353
– for dialogue *Vol. II*: 365-70
modern *Vol. I*: 9-11, 38, 40-42, 44, 50-51, 77, 83, 99-100, 102, 110-2, 114-6, 136, 138-40, 141-4, 146-8, 150, 152-60, 162, 164-6, 168, 170, 174, 179, 203, 209-10, 242-3, 248, 259, 267, 270-2 // *Vol. II*: 10-11, 15-16, 34-6, 42-3, 45-9, 54, 59, 63, 77-8, 86, 89, 97, 106, 118, 125, 138, 140, 142-3, 153-5, 160, 162, 166, 175, 177-9, 181, 186, 188-9, 194-5, 200, 207, 210, 213, 222, 224, 228, 233, 255, 286, 288-90, 292, 295, 301, 305-6, 311, 321-2, 325-6, 332, 346, 376-7, 385
– modernism/ist/s *Vol. I*: 39, 41, 215, 217 // *Vol. II*: 64, 72, 243, 316, 325, 349
– modernity *Vol. I*: 45, 109, 147, 153-4, 164, 269, 270 // *Vol. II*: 15,167, 201, 305, 401
– modernization *Vol. I*: 112, 156, 161, 168, 176, 203, 207, 221, 241, 243, 267, 269, 273 // *Vol. II*: 144, 161-2, 169, 175, 180, 183, 192, 194, 200, 362
Mohammed *Vol. I*: 87, 93 // *Vol. II*: 143
Mongolia/n *Vol. I*: 230, 233-4 // *Vol. II*: 310, 325
monism *Vol. II*: 63-4, 67-8
monk/s (Buddhist) *Vol. I*: 118, 130-2, 141, 150 // *Vol. II*: 17, 33, 38, 53, 109, 169, 225, 259, 282, 296, 299, 397
monkhood *Vol. II*: 20, 169
monodaoism *Vol. II*: 67-70
monodeism *Vol. II*: 65, 67
monodeitism *Vol. II*: 66-70
monodivinism *Vol. II*: 65-66
monotheism *Vol. I*: 95, 161, 272 // *Vol. II*: 7-8, 62-8, 70-71
monto Vol. II: 371
monument/s *Vol. I*: 75-6, 210-1 // *Vol. II*: 310, 397

Moon, Revd. *Vol. II*: 166
moral/ity *Vol. I*: 127, 132, 134, 162, 168, 198, 231, 255 / *Vol. II*: 12, 14, 16, 22, 53, 190, 339
Morgan, Robert *Vol. I*: 46, 48, 109 // *Vol. II*: 6, 10, 29, 32-3, 35, 38-9, 112, 118, 121-2, 126, 150, 196, 214, 355
Mormonism *Vol. I*: 102 // *Vol. II*: 143, 343
Morocco *Vol. II*: 112, 116
morphology *Vol. I*: 22-3, 27, 37, 92 // *Vol. II*: 3, 6, 8, 53, 64, 68, 78, 223, 344, 370
Moscow *Vol. I*: 188, 228, 230, 233-234 // *Vol. II*: 333-4
Moses (assumption of) *Vol. I*: 93
mosque *Vol. I*: 88 // *Vol. II*: 288, 317, 382
motivation
 – intellectual *Vol. I*: 11 166, 240, 251, 255 // *Vol. II*: 160, 315, 342
 – religious *Vol. I*: 87, 146, 157, 181, 214 // *Vol. II*: 28, 94, 175, 195, 283, 315, 328, 359
Motoori, Norinaga *Vol. I*: 157, 165 // *Vol. II*: 45-6
Mount Haguro *Vol. I*: 68
Mount Hiei *Vol. I*: 98
Mount Hiko *Vol. I*: 61,
Mount Minobu *Vol. II*: 170
Mount Ontake *Vol. I*: 88
Mount Shichimen *Vol. II*: 170
Mount Sumeru *Vol. I*: 123
mountain/s *Vol. I*: 62, 68, 88, 163 // *Vol. II*: 93-4, 185, 237, 271-2, 281, 301, 324
muenbotoke *Vol. II*: 170, 231
muga *Vol. II*: 12, 172
Müller, Max *Vol. I*: 112, 159 // *Vol. II*: 348
Münzel, Mark *Vol. II*: 131
Murakami, Senshō *Vol. I*: 160
Murakami, Shigeyoshi *Vol. II*: 177
Murasaki, Shikibu *Vol. II*: 381
museum/s *Vol. I*: 52, 77, 79, 82, 22, 230 // *Vol. II*: 172, 184, 186, 190, 195, 198, 283,

 – Museum of Religions *Vol. I*: 63, 89,114
 – Museum of Religion and Atheism *Vol. I*: 227
 – Tenri Sankōkan *Vol. II*: 233, 239
 – Yūshūkan (Shintō) *Vol. II*: 398
music (in field) *Vol. I*: 76, 78, 82, 87
Muslim/s *Vol. I*: 90, 95, 102, 166, 176, 199, 210, 251, 229 // *Vol. II*: 16, 33, 84, 116, 250, 252, 299, 305, 319, 361, 388, 392-3, 395
Myanmar *Vol. II*: 213 See also Burma
Myōchikai *Vol. II*: 170
Myōhōrengekyō *Vol. II*: 83, 170, 227, 230
Myōkyō *Vol. I*: 130-134
Myōonten (Benzaiten) *Vol. II*: 279
mystic/al/ism *Vol. I*: 24, 30, 32, 46, 89, 139, 146, 170, 178, 184, 194, 234, 271 // *Vol. II*: 8-10, 40, 73-7, 84, 117, 120, 189, 320, 346
myth/ology *Vol. I*: 82, 161, 164-5, 205, 211 // *Vol. II*: 4, 14, 24-5, 27, 40, 46, 69, 72, 157, 230, 233-4, 252, 280, 321, 371

nabi *Vol. II*: 297, 299
Nachi Shrine *Vol. II*: 270, 272
Naganuma, Myōkō *Vol. II*: 170
Nāgārjuna *Vol. II*: 42, 83, 86
Nagasaki *Vol. II*: 219
Nahrawi, H. N. M. *Vol. II*: 299
Nairobi *Vol. I*: 212
Nakagawa, Tomomasa *Vol. II*: 209
Nakamura, Kōjirō *Vol. II*: 84, 87
Nakayama, Miki *Vol. I*: 93 // *Vol. II*: 172
Namas *Vol. II*: 83
Namo/Namu *Vol. II*: 83, 298
Namu Amida Butsu *Vol. I*: 61 // *Vol. II*: 82, 233
Namu Myōhōrengekyō *Vol. II*: 83, 170, 227, 230
Nanjing *Vol. I*: 203 // *Vol. II*: 161
Nanjio, see Nanjō
Nanjō, Bunyū *Vol. I*: 159-60, 169

narrative/s *Vol. I*: 93-4, 101 // *Vol. II*: 25, 182, 187, 191, 383
Natal *Vol. I*: 211, 256
Nathan the Wise *Vol. I*: 111
national/nations *Vol. I*: 71, 208
- affiliates of IAHR *Vol. I*: 4, 173, 196, 220, 249
- cult/identity *Vol. I*: 80-81, 157, 161-2, 168-9 // *Vol. II*: 42-3, 48, 285, 315-6, 319, 321-3, 325, 339,379
- traditions *Vol. I*: 42, 179, 186, 208, 226, 248 // *Vol. II*: 162, 177-8, 329
nationalism/ist *Vol. I*: 75, 161, 163, 255 // *Vol. II*: 172, 175, 206, 332-3, 338-40, 379, 398
National Women's Monument *Vol. I*: 210
nativistic religion *Vol. II*: 40
nativity (of Buddha) *Vol. I*: 101
NATO *Vol. I*: 237
natural community/life/society *Vol. II*: 4, 17, 19-21, 52, 54, 59-60, 96, 140, 320-4, 398-9
- farming etc *Vol. II*: 232
- religious foci *Vol. II*: 271, 281
- theology *Vol. II*: 349
naturalism *Vol. II*: 254
nature divinity *Vol. II*: 46,
Nebel, Richard *Vol. I*: 261
Nebeneinander Vol. I: 274
nenbutsu (nembutsu) Vol. I: 98 // *Vol. II*: 82-4, 168-9, 226, 232-3, 371
neo-Buddhist *Vol. I*: 218, 234
neo-colonialism *Vol. I*: 42, 151, 214 / *Vol. II*: 160
Neo-Confucanism *Vol. I*: 116-7, 134, 148 // *Vol. II*: 35
Neo-Nazis *Vol. II*: 340
neo-shamanism *Vol. I*: 18 // *Vol. II*: 97
neo-Sufism *Vol. II*: 123
Netherlands *Vol. I*: 92, 183-4, 186, 189, 228, 232, 245 // *Vol. II*: 132, 377

neutrality *Vol. I*: 117, 146, 199-200, 236-7
New Age *Vol. I*: 43, 83, 137, 203, 254, 259 // *Vol. II*: 57, 60, 142, 147, 316, 364, 385
new/ness *Vol. I*: 28, 82, 121, 127-8, 133, 206-7, 259-60 // *Vol. II*: 15, 24, 27, 29, 35, 37, 97-8, 105, 108, 113, 127, 136, 138, 143, 250-1, 256-7, 284, 321-2 344, 391, See also innovation, new religion/s
new religion/s (movements) *Vol. I*: 46, 58, 61, 79, 102, 137-8, 163, 204, 253-4, 259 // *Vol. II*: 4-5, 7, 29, 51, 55-7, 91, 95, 105-7, 130-151, 152-177, 179-200, 202-16, 218-39, 261-2, 267-9, 322-3, 356, 360-1, 364, 384, 395, 399
- newly arisen *Vol. II*: 156
- new new *Vol. II*: 156, 172-3, 215, 219, 222, 227-8
New Spain *Vol. I*: 82
New Testament *Vol. I*: 94, 101, 180 // *Vol. II*: 16, 21, 24-5, 27-8, 97
New Year *Vol. II*: 19-21, 224, 383
New York *Vol. II*: 161
New Zealand *Vol. II*: 111
Ngo Dinh Diem *Vol. II*: 164
Nguyen Van Chieu *Vol. II*: 163
Nicene Creed *Vol. II*: 142
Nichibunken *Vol. I*: 50
Nichiren/ite *Vol. I*: 163, 168 // *Vol. II*: 29-30, 142, 169-171, 223, 251
Nichiren Shōshū *Vol. I*: 59 // *Vol. II*: 18, 171
Nichiren-shū *Vol. II*: 170
Niebuhr, Richard *Vol. I*: 203
Niemöller, Martin *Vol. II*: 329, 338
Nietzsche, Friedrich *Vol. I*: 251
Nihon Shūkyō Gakkai *Vol. I*: 145-6, 155-6, 162-3, 169
Niimi, Tsutomu *Vol. II*: 168
Nikodim, Archbishop *Vol. II*: 328, 330
Nikolai-Kirche (Leipzig) *Vol. II*: 328, 336, 338

Ninnaji *Vol. I*: 97
Niños Heroes *Vol. I*: 78-9, 210
Nirvāṇa Sūtra Vol. I: 120
nirvana *Vol. I*: 99, 120, 231, 243 // *Vol. II*: 18, 22, 25-6, 28, 52, 83, 212, 396
Nishi Honganji *Vol. I*: 160
Nishida, Kitarō *Vol. I*: 146
Niwano, Nikkyō *Vol. II*: 170, 343
Niwano, Nichikō *Vol. II*: 170
nōkyōchō Vol. I: 62
Nordic scholars *Vol. I*: 237, 245
norito Vol. I: 52-3, 66, 68 // *Vol. II*: 47
normative/non-normative *Vol. I*: 1, 9-12, 34-6, 82, 115, 124, 127, 145, 165-6, 175, 180, 185, 198, 247 // *Vol. II*: 4, 6, 73, 115, 118, 122, 149-50, 163, 182, 186, 196-7, 204-5, 214, 245, 311
northern (various) *Vol. I*: 80, 165, 186-7, 238 // *Vol. II*: 94, 377, 388
Northern Ireland *Vol. I*: 227 // *Vol. II*: 316, 324, 388
Nossa Senhora Aparecida *Vol. I*: 272 // *Vol. II*: 231, 236, 239
nothingness *Vol. II*: 83
Novosibirsk *Vol. I*: 77, 193, 228, 230, 238
NRMs *Vol. II*: 106, 133-4, 137, 221, 364 See also new religions
Numen Vol. I: 181, 219, 250 // *Vol. II*: 247, 267
numinous *Vol. I*: 36 // *Vol. II*: 121, 320
nun/s (Buddhist) *Vol. II*: 53, 291, 299
nurture (religious) *Vol. II*: 376, 378, 381, 383

Oberlies, Thomas *Vol. II*: 74
objectivity *Vol. I*: 25, 190
observation/s *Vol. I*: 5, 9-10,13, 35, 38-40, 51-4, 58-61, 69-80, 76, 82, 84-5, 88-90, 92-100, 103-4, 142, 149-50, 167, 191, 204, 214, 219, 227, 239, 232, 259 // *Vol. II*: 14-15, 17, 22, 25, 28-30, 38 48, 68, 85, 94, 109, 111, 113-5, 120, 140, 145, 147, 149-50, 156, 159, 179-80, 183-6, 190, 192, 195, 206, 214, 216, 222-3, 243-5, 247, 267. 270, 278, 283, 285, 287-9, 289, 291, 295, 302, 305, 309, 318, 322, 327, 334, 338, 343, 353-4, 358, 360, 363, 369
– observant participation *Vol. I*: 72-3, 84, 89-90 // *Vol. II*: 105, 113-5, 354, 382
– participant observation *Vol. I*: 60, 72-3, 84, 89-90 // *Vol. II*: 354
– observer rationality *Vol. I*: 38-40
ōbutsu myōgō Vol. II: 18
Occidentalism/ist *Vol. I*: 113-4, 151, 166, 270
Oceania *Vol. II*: 133
Ofudesaki Vol. II: 239
Ogyū, Sorai *Vol. II*: 35
Okada, Mokichi (Mokiti) *Vol. II*: 235, 239
Ō-kami (various) *Vol. II*: 285
Ōkawa, Ryūhō *Vol. II*: 209, 228, 238
Okina no fumi Vol. I: 117, 126-130, 132-134
Old Testament *Vol. I*: 180 // *Vol. II*: 16, 97
Oliver, Victor *Vol. II*: 162, 177
Olszowski, Stefan *Vol. I*: 331
Olupona Jacob *Vol. I*: 153, 169-70, 207, 212, 221, 268
o-mairi Vol. II: 93-4
Ōmiya (*kami*) *Vol. II*: 259
Ōmoto (Oomoto)-kyō *Vol. I*: 57-8 // *Vol. II*: 168, 172, 194, 218, 220, 222, 238
Omuro *Vol. I*: 97
Ondra, Jaroslav *Vol. II*: 328, 330, 338
Ono, Sokyō *Vol. II*: 42, 49
Ontake, Mount *Vol. I*: 88
Ontario *Vol. I*: 115, 125, 194
Oomotokyō, see Ōmotokyō
operational definition *Vol. I*: 35-6
oracles *Vol. I*: 63, 68
oral sources *Vol. I*: 22, 27-8, 31, 36, 53, 60, 86 // *Vol. II*: 318

oral tradition *Vol. I*: 101, 191 // *Vol. II*: 114, 116
ordination *Vol. I*: 30 // *Vol. II*: 20, 52-3, 225, 291, 322, 324
orientalism *Vol. I*: 41-2, 47, 150-1, 168, 182-4, 187, 213, 217, 270 // *Vol. II*: 140, 244, 348
– reverse *Vol. I*: 96, 109, 112-5, 151, 247 See also westernism
– Orthodox Churches *Vol. I*: 87, 140, 215, 227, 232-3, 254 // *Vol. II*: 82, 92, 250, 207, 316, 324, 327, 340, 385
orthodox/y (various religions) *Vol. I*: 121 // *Vol. II*: 112, 149-50, 158, 180, 196, 250-2, 300
Ōsaka *Vol. II*: 220, 399
Ōtani University *Vol. I*: 160 // *Vol. II*: 8, 131, 352-3, 367
Ōtani-ha *Vol. II*: 399
otherness
– religious sense of *Vol. I*: 34
– of cultures *Vol. I*: 115, 125
Other power *Vol. I*: 97, 99 // *Vol. II*: 23-4, 169, 226
Otto, Rudolf *Vol. I*: 36, 45-6, 89, 217, 228, 248, 273 // *Vol. II*: 14, 121, 128, 349, 353, 372
outsider/s *Vol. I*: 3, 13, 58, 69, 71-6, 84, 103, 149, 213, 259 // *Vol. II*: 91,191, 208, 393
See also insider/outsider
Overmyer, Daniel L. *Vol. II*: 134, 151, 157, 159, 177
Oxford *Vol. I*: 32 // *Vol. II*: 184, 342, 360
Oyagami *Vol. II*: 172
Oyasato *Vol. II*: 57, 60

Pacific War *Vol. I*: 152, 161, 165 // *Vol. II*: 283, 399
pacifism *Vol. II*: 396-7
Warsaw Pact *Vol. I*: 237-8
Padre Cicero *Vol. II*: 231
pagan *Vol. II*: 44, 250, 276
Pailin, David *Vol. II*: 38
Pak, Chung-Soo *Vol. II*: 183, 185, 188, 191

Pak, Chung-Bin *Vol. II*: 166, 179, 182, 185-6, 193, 195, 201
Pakistan *Vol. II*: 373, 393, 401
palaces (in Warsaw) *Vol. I*: 75-6
Palestine *Vol. II*: 316, 395
Pāli *Vol. I*: 261 // *Vol. II*: 28, 211, 295
pancasila *Vol. II*: 295, 298-9
panentheism *Vol. II*: 63
pantheism *Vol. II*: 63
pantheon *Vol. I*: 82, 205
Papoušek, Dalibor *Vol. I*: 152, 221, 230 // *Vol. II*: 286
paradigm *Vol. I*: 84-5, 260 // *Vol. II*: 76
paramārtha satya *Vol. II*: 254, 259
Paris *Vol. I*: 155, 216, 220, 272 // *Vol. II*: 62, 71
Park: see Pak Chung-soo, Pak Chung-Bin
participant/s (religious) *Vol. I*: 24-6, 30, 35, 39, 64, 72-3, 75, 90, 92 // *Vol. II*: 38, 47, 74, 80, 85, 92, 109, 111, 113-5, 127, 141, 145-6, 163, 176, 190, 212, 228, 266, 269-72, 274, 300, 310-1, 328, 355, 358, 363, 368-372, 383, 391, 393, 395
participation (not conferences)
– by observer *Vol. I*: 13, 54, 69-85, 89-90, 104, 188 // *Vol. II*: 127, 205, 271, 311, 355, 370, 381-2
– by believers *Vol. I*: 61, 81, 84-86, 88-90, 97, 100 // *Vol. II*: 47, 54, 60, 85, 206, 224, 271, 273, 285, 371, 380-3, 386 See also observant participation/participant observation
particularism/istic *Vol. II*: 45, 48, 321, 362
Pascal, Blaise *Vol. I*: 46
pastoral care/theology *Vol. II*: 99, 164, 226, 333
pastor/s *Vol. II*: 192, 380
patriotism *Vol. I*: 75, 81 // *Vol. II*: 333-4
Paul (Saint) *Vol. II*: 16, 81, 147, 254, 343

Pax Association (PAX) *Vol. I*: 75 // *Vol. II*: 310, 328, 331-4, 336, 338
peace *Vol. I*: 5, 87, 192 // *Vol. II*: 280, 307-9, 336-7, 352, 365, 369, 372
– conference *Vol. II*: 328-330, 336, 338, 341
– great peace *Vol. II*: 160
– movement/work *Vol. II*: 170, 172-175, 185, 316, 330, 336-7, 391-401
– world *Vol. II*: 13, 62, 174, 230, 312, 391
peasant/s *Vol. II*: 112, 116, 126
pen-chi Vol. II: 258
Pentecostalism *Vol. I*: 253 // *Vol. II*: 60, 97, 230
– pingströrelsen *Vol. I*: 183, 194
Pentikäinen, Juha *Vol. I*: 69, 77, 85,183, 237-8, 269 // *Vol. II*: 362, 373-4
perestroika *Vol. I*: 180
Perfect Liberty *Vol. II*: 172, 236
performance/s *Vol. II*: 19, 47, 74, 78, 81, 89, 92, 163, 171, 189, 192, 228, 234, 272-3
periodization *Vol. I*: 153, 164, 226
Perles, Felix *Vol. II*: 77
persecution *Vol. II*: 159, 177, 295, 340, 396
Peruvian religion *Vol. I*: 205, 207, 253, 261
pesantren Vol. II: 393
petition/ary *Vol. II*: 74-7, 81-4, 86, 93, 174
Pettazzoni, Raffaele *Vol. I*: 187, 217 // *Vol. II*: 124, 127-8, 247-8, 252, 266
Pham Cong Tak *Vol. II*: 162, 177
phenomenon/a *Vol. I*: 2, 12, 17, 33, 39-40, 52, 89, 92, 97, 136, 142, 151, 173, 185-7, 192-3, 204-6, 236, 261 // *Vol. II*: 14, 43-6, 51, 53-6, 60, 66-7, 70, 73, 77-9, 81-2, 84, 99, 118, 121, 130, 132-6, 142, 147, 206, 216, 238, 251, 264, 289, 305, 311, 325, 354, 371

phenomenology of religion/s *Vol. I*: 18, 21, 161, 163 // *Vol. II*: 6, 17, 79, 81, 118-21, 127, 212, 252-3, 264, 247-8, 253, 257-8, 264
phenomenological method *Vol. I*: 12, 25-6, 103-4, 185, 190, 229, 253 // *Vol. II*: 13-14, 26, 38, 110, 117, 119-20, 168, 254-5, 257-9, 318, 325, 344
phenomenologists/school *Vol. I*: 10-11, 20, 24, 72, 91-2, 116, 183, 185 // *Vol. II*: 9, 72, 86, 99, 105, 118-21, 127, 253-62
Philippi, Donald L. *Vol. I*: 53, 68
philological/ly *Vol. I*: 9, 50-51, 53, 60, 86, 157, 159, 161, 184-9, 191, 234, 236, 250 // *Vol. II*: 3, 113, 318, 348
– historico-philological *Vol. I*: 20-22, 29, 59, 159 // *Vol. II*: 318
philology/ist *Vol. I*: 13, 36, 50-52, 54, 56, 58, 60, 62, 64, 66, 68, 182, 191, 194, 266
philosopher/s *Vol. I*: 12, 45, 178, 251
philosophical
– phenomenology *Vol. I*: 10, 92
– tests *Vol. II*: 26, 357, 373
philosophy *Vol. I*: 9, 45, 47, 188-9, 193, 196, 198 // *Vol. II*: 315, 329, 333
– culture-based *Vol. I*: 2, 160 // *Vol. II*: 46
– of history *Vol. I*: 109 // *Vol. II*: 36, 349
– of religion *Vol. I*: 38, 45, 182, 189, 191-2, // *Vol. II*: 205, 258, 260, 343, 348, 357
– of science *Vol. II*: 135
– religious (various) *Vol. I*: 146, 159-6, 182, 189 // *Vol. II*: 27, 63-5, 78, 110, 359
Phnom Penh *Vol. II*: 164, 294
Piaget, Jean *Vol. II*: 85
Piasecki, Boleslaw *Vol. II*: 332
Piatigorsky, Alexsandr Moiseyevich *Vol. I*: 230
Picken, S.D.B. *Vol. II*: 32, 38

pilgrimage/pilgrims *Vol. I*; 30, 62-4, 67-8, 97-9, 265, 271-2, 275 // *Vol. II*: 8, 10, 72, 74, 89, 93-4, 96, 101, 172, 206, 236-7, 270, 278, 282-3, 305, 326, 397
pīnyīn *Vol. II*: 289, 291
Pius XII, Pope *Vol. I*: 94
Platform Sutra Vol. II: 34-35, 39
Platvoet, Jan *Vol. I*: 153, 169-70, 196-7, 207, 212, 221
PL Kyōdan *Vol. I*: 59, 68 // *Vol. II*: 172, 220, 236
ploughshares *Vol. II*: 335-7
plurality of religions *Vol. I*: 5, 10-11, 48, 110-1, 126, 139-42, 157, 167, 170, 246, 248, 260 // *Vol. II*: 32, 151, 198, 289, 307-13, 317-9, 342-8, 350-1, 357-9, 361, 377, 386, 389
– of cultures *Vol. I*: 71 // *Vol. II*: 401
pluralism (religious) *Vol. I*: 81, 111, 117, 125-6, 128, 130-4, 141-2, 148, 152-3, 167, 202, 206-7, 254-5, 262, 264-5, 269 // *Vol. II*: 154, 218, 239, 265, 311-2, 345-346
– cultural *Vol. I*: 179, 234, 251 // *Vol. II*: 54, 312, 326, 346, 348, 357
Plutarch *Vol. II*: 253
pneumatikos Vol. II: 98
Poland/Polish *Vol. I*: 42, 74-6, 125, 187, 212, 224-7, 229, 234, 236-7, 240, 242, 245 // *Vol. II*: 310, 316, 324, 327-8, 331-5, 336-40
– Polish Society for Study of Religions *Vol. I*: 50-51, 68, 179-80, 193-4, 224
polemic/s *Vol. I*: 133, 204
polemical/ly *Vol. I*: 124, 130-131, 134, 157, 199 // *Vol. II*: 12, 34, 156, 346, 359
politics/al *Vol. I*: 22, 31, 34-5, 42, 47-8, 57, 80, 83, 111-2, 112, 136, 139, 149, 152-6, 158, 163, 165, 167, 170, 174, 179, 189, 204, 209, 212-3, 215, 219, 221, 223-44, 232-6, 238-41, 243-4, 247, 249, 251, 253-4, 257, 259-260, 267, 270 // *Vol. II*: 16-18, 26, 37, 42, 43, 48, 55, 93, 106, 128, 130, 137, 143, 152-68, 171, 175, 178-9, 181, 186, 188, 203, 206, 213, 250-1, 262, 278, 281-2, 285, 289, 309-11, 314-9, 321-2, 325-9, 330-40, 348, 356, 376, 391-3, 395-7, 399-400
poly-aspectual *Vol. I*: 24
poly-linguistic *Vol. I*: 248
polydeism *Vol. II*: 65
polydeitism *Vol. II*: 66-70
polydivinism *Vol. II*: 65-66
polymethodism *Vol. I*: 31
polytheism/ist *Vol. I*: 82-3, 95, 161, 259, 272 // *Vol. II*: 7-8, 62-4, 66, 68, 70, 321, 361, 411
Pongnae (Pongrae) *Vol. II*: 187
Poniatowski, Zygmunt *Vol. I*: 226, 236, 242
Pope *Vol. II*: 181, 331, 334, 359
– John Paul II *Vol. I*: 8, 82
– Pius XII *Vol. I*: 94
Pope, Liston *Vol. I*: 203
popular (religion) *Vol. I*: 60-1, 97-8, 137-138, 140, 142, 190, 228 // *Vol. II*: 18, 20, 27, 83, 90-91, 98, 140, 157-8, 162, 281, 283, 296, 298, 300, 303, 305, 347
popularisation *Vol. I*: 132
Portuguese *Vol. I*: 175, 248 // *Vol. II*: 218, 220, 228-30, 233-5, 239, 290-1
positivism/istic *Vol. I*: 93, 103
post-colonial/ist *Vol. I*: 41, 150, 213-4 // *Vol. II*: 72
postmodern *Vol. I*: 41
postwar *Vol. I*: 162, 166
Potsdam Declaration *Vol. I*: 154
Powell, Enoch *Vol. I*: 71
power/s
– socio-political *Vol. I*: 3, 150, 155-6 158, 165-6, 183 // *Vol. II*: 152, 154-7, 159, 161-3, 165-6, 175, 187, 315-6, 330, 332-4, 397
– spiritual *Vol. I*: 34, 87, 97, 99, 122, 206 // *Vol. II*: 52-3, 66, 76-7,

114, 120, 212, 230, 275, 285, 319, 321 See also Other power
practice/s
- of academic discipline *Vol. I*: 2, 13, 17-8, 70, 77, 104
- religious/ritual *Vol. I*: 34, 39, 63-4, 70, 93, 95-9, 120-1, 137-8, 149, 176, 210, 231 // *Vol. II*: 12-14, 21, 29, 34, 53, 57, 59-60, 67, 73, 82-3, 92-3, 95, 144, 161-2, 165, 169-70, 174, 176, 182, 190, 196-7, 199, 200, 204, 210-21, 223-6, 228-32, 235, 238, 243, 294,316, 346, 368, 371, 373, 381-4, 392
practitioner/s *Vol. I*: 86, 88-9, 91-3, 102-4 // *Vol. II*: 14-15, 72, 85, 95, 253, 271-2, 292
Prague *Vol. II*: 327-30, 336, 341
Pratt, J. B. *Vol. I*: 217
prayer/s *Vol. I*: 52, 60, 62, 68, 87-8, 95, 97, 271 // *Vol. II*: 7, 40, 47, 72-82, 84-7, 89, 93, 174, 208, 230-1, 237, 270, 273-4, 292-3, 299, 302, 336-7, 369-370, 373, 381-382, 388, 397-398
preaching *Vol. I*: 99, 118 // *Vol. II*: 27, 160, 166, 190, 396
precepts *Vol. I*: 132 // *Vol. II*: 20
Predigerseminar (Erfurt) *Vol. II*: 337
premodern *Vol. I*: 41
Presbyterian *Vol. II*: 167, 190
Pretoria *Vol. I*: 75, 210, 219 // *Vol. II*: 310, 314
Preus, Samuel *Vol. I*: 41, 48, 216
priest/s *Vol. II*: 40, 380
- Buddhist *Vol. I*: 100, 104, 159-60
- Christian *Vol. I*: 78, 95 // *Vol. II*: 89, 360
- Daoist *Vol. II*: 303
- Shintō *Vol. I*: 52-53, 161 // *Vol. II*: 47, 54, 89, 92, 222, 270-4, 284
primal religion *Vol. I*: 13, 83, 205, 230, 268 // *Vol. II*: 4-6, 19-21, 29, 40, 44-9, 51, 53-5, 57-60, 68-70, 81, 84-6, 88-92, 95-6, 100, 140, 150, 207-8, 215, 217, 223-6, 233, 238, 285, 290, 294, 310, 319-26, 361-2, 397-400
- adapted/adjusted (Shintō) *Vol. II*: 5, 44-9, 111, 321, 362
primary sources *Vol. I*: 22 // *Vol. II*: 13, 46, 179
Prime Master/s *Vol. II*: 167, 184-9, 192-3, 197, 199
primitive *Vol. I*: 48, 110 // *Vol. II*: 44-5, 77, 91, 100, 223, 254, 320-1
primordial *Vol. II*: 44
prophet/s *Vol. I*: 138, 163, 168, 210 // *Vol. II*: 29-30, 40, 115, 143, 147, 254, 297, 299, 337
proselytism *Vol. I*: 204 // *Vol. II*: 340, 380, 386-7
Protestant/ism *Vol. I*: 76, 94, 137, 181, 203, 254 // *Vol. II*: 14, 23, 28, 60, 75, 96-7, 120-1, 124, 141-2, 155, 160, 191, 207, 233, 294, 324, 329-30, 337, 340, 344, 349, 355, 359, 363, 365, 367-71, 385, 388
provisional (truth etc) *Vol. II*: 37, 59, 89, 300
proximate salvation/soteriology *Vol. II*: 5, 54, 57-60, 85, 92, 212, 223, 321
Psalms *Vol. I*: 81
psychologists *Vol. I*: 92, 178 // *Vol. II*: 79, 85, 386
psychology *Vol. I*: 20, 21, 26, 127, 166, 182, 188-9 // *Vol. II*: 13, 80, 122, 134, 144, 344, 348, 369
- of religion *Vol. I*: 19, 30, 40, 157, 183, 184, 194, 248 // *Vol. II*: 14, 22-3, 68, 85, 87, 95, 135, 204, 319, 342, 344
Puebla *Vol. I*: 77-8
Pulgyo/Pulkyo (Won) see Wonbulgyo
Pulpŏp Yŏnku Hoe *Vol. II*: 186
purgatory *Vol. I*: 123
Pure Land Buddhism *Vol. I*: 40, 57, 159 // *Vol. II*: 9, 23, 82-3, 162, 169, 219, 223, 227, 272, 294, 371

purity (religious/ritual) *Vol. II*: 89, 226
purification *Vol. I*: 87 // *Vol. II*: 7, 40, 42, 47, 88-100, 174, 224-5, 230, 232, 237
purism (academic) *Vol. I*: 199-201 // *Vol. II*: 309
Puritan/ism *Vol. II*: 97
purity
– of tradition *Vol. II*: 34, 267, 304
– ritual *Vol. II*: 88-89, 92, 94
Pyatigorskiy, Alexsandr Moiseyevich *Vol. I*: 230
Pyŏngsan *Vol. II*: 187
Pyysiäinen, Illka *Vol. II*:79, 86

Quakers *Vol. II*: 67, 82, 120, 396
qualitative research *Vol. I*: 64, 70, 74 // *Vol. II*: 327
quantitative research *Vol. I*: 64, 70 74 // *Vol. II*: 214, 327
Québec *Vol. I*: 48, 245
Queen of Mexico *Vol. I*: 81, 88
Qur'an *Vol. II*: 16, 394
Quranic *Vol. II*: 250

Radhakrishnan, Sarvepalli *Vol. II*: 217
Ramadan *Vol. II*: 383
Ramakrishna *Vol. II*: 54, 384
rangakusha *Vol. I*: 151
Ranger, Terence *Vol. II*: 112, 115
rasul *Vol. I*: 87 // *Vol. II*: 143
rationalism/ist *Vol. I*: 218 // *Vol. II*: 26
rationality *Vol. I*: 38-9, 46, 110, 112-4, 117, 218, 268, 270 // *Vol. II*: 63, 84, 98, 121, 175, 189, 268, 287
rational *Vol. I*: 33, 37-9, 46, 112, 117 // *Vol. II*: 64, 98, 191, 305,
rationalization *Vol. II*: 115, 167, 268
Ratschow, Carl Heinz *Vol. II*: 349
Raud, Rein *Vol. I*: 270 // *Vol. II*: 305, 409
Raveri, Massimo *Vol. I*: 183, 194
Reader, Ian *Vol. II*: 90-91, 101, 168, 178, 203, 208, 217

reason *Vol. I*: 109 // *Vol. II*: 24, 26, 121
– and faith etc *Vol. I*: 38, 46, 112 // *Vol. II*: 349-50, 356
– divine/heavenly *Vol. II*: 153, 171, 234
– religious reasons *Vol. I*: 104 // *Vol. II*: 89, 186, 193, 196, 226, 235, 288, 325
rebirth *Vol. I*: 40 // *Vol. II*: 83, 169, 212
recitation *Vol. I*: 52-3, 62, 98 // *Vol. II*: 47, 82-84, 94, 169-70, 190, 226, 230, 273-4, 291, 371
recognitional *Vol. I*: 24-6, 30-31, 36-7, 39
reconciliation *Vol. II*: 253, 329
recoupment *Vol. II*: 250-2, 259
Redfield, Robert *Vol. II*: 112-3, 116, 126, 128
reductionism *Vol. I*: 31, 91, 182-3, 185 // *Vol. II*: 13, 79, 175
reform/s *Vol. II*: 27-9, 124, 138-9, 141-4, 147, 195, 198, 249, 251, 364-5
reformation/s *Vol. II*: 123-5, 248-9
– Protestant *Vol. I*: 148 // *Vol. II*: 28, 97
reformer/s *Vol. II*: 29,142, 147, 363
Regamey, Constantin *Vol. I*: 232, 243
reification *Vol. II*: 243
reikai *Vol. II*: 222
Reina de Mexico *Vol. I*: 88
reisei *Vol. II*: 222
Reiyūkai *Vol. I*: 58, 68 // *Vol. II*: 169-70, 220, 228, 231
relative deprivation *Vol. II*: 134, 157
relativization *Vol. I*: 121
Religii Mira *Vol. I*: 188, 226
religie *Vol. I*: 247 / *Vol. II*: 119, 128
religion/s *Vol. I*: 1-284 // *Vol. II*:1-420
    See also definitions, adumbration (definitional); *agama, godsdienst, religie, shūkyō, zōngjiào*; comparative religion, comparative study of religions, religious studies, sci-

ence of religions; study of religions, morphology, typology
Religionsbegründung Vol. I: 178, 194
Religionsgeschichte Vol. I: 114, 181-2, 188, 270 // Vol. II: 31, 74-5, 87, 121-2, 127-8, 178, 247, 348 See also *godsdienstgechiedenis, storia delle religione*
Religionsgeschichtliche Schule Vol. II: 348-50 See also History of Religions School
Religionsgespräche Vol. II: 369, 374
Religionskritik Vol. I: 178, 194
Religionskundliche Sammlung Vol. I: 63, 68, 89, 228
Religionsphänomenologie Vol. II: 247, 253, 263 See also *godsdienstfenomenologie*
Religionspsychologie Vol. II: 75, 87
religionsvetenskap/elig Vol. I: 183
religionswidenskap Vol. I: 85, 181, 183, 194, 261, 269 // Vol. II: 374
Religionswissenschaft Vol. I: 2, 9, 11, 15, 18, 24-5, 29, 32, 45, 74, 173, 178, 181-2, 188, 194, 216-7, 236, 243, 247, 262-3, 265, 269 // Vol. II: 9, 13, 72-5, 77, 98-9, 127-9, 131-2, 137-8, 146-7, 204, 238, 246, 252, 277, 369, 373-4, 378, 391
Religionswissenschaften (plural) Vol. I: 15, 181
religiosity Vol. I: 35, 69, 78, 82-4, 137, 143, 163, 185, 265 // Vol. II: 8, 47, 99, 371, 385
religious Vol. I: 48, 63, 68, 181, 183, 185, 194, 205, 207, 253, 261, 264, 271, 274-5 // Vol. II: 10, 74, 87, 116, 119, 122, 128, 151, 178, 286, 305, 311, 313, 369, 374, 401
religious studies Vol. I: 5, 9, 14, 23, 32, 106, 115, 125, 137, 147, 163, 174, 178, 180-95, 218, 251 // Vol. II: 107, 110, 203-17, 243, 315, 317-8, 328, 345, 350 See also study of religions
religiovedeni(y)a Vol. I: 181, 188

religioznawstwa/o Vol. I: 181, 242
religiya Vol. I: 230, 241
Renaissance Vol. I: 148 // Vol. II: 97
Renan, Ernest Vol. II: 349
– Société Ernest Renan Vol. I: 184, 186, 217
renewal Vol. II: 108, 113, 116, 125, 233
Renondeau, Gustave Vol. II: 260, 263, 272
repentance Vol. II: 336, 399
Repp, Martin Vol. II: 168, 178, 364, 369, 374
resurrection Vol. II: 23-26
returners (as tech. term) Vol. II: 47
revelation/s Vol. I: 38, 82, 102, 178, 259 // Vol. II: 16, 34, 51, 55, 57, 115, 120, 138, 143, 149, 163-5, 172, 195, 207, 227, 250, 261, 280, 349
revitalization Vol. I: 161 // Vol. II: 187
revolution (various) Vol. I: 78-80, 154-5, 218, 231
Rhys Davids, T. W. Vol. II: 34
Richardson, Alan Vol. I: 106
Ricklefs, M. C. Vol. II: 295, 306
Riemeck, Renate Vol. II: 329
Ringgren, Helmer Vol. II: 264, 277
Rinzai Zen Vol. II: 280, 397
Risshō Kōseikai Vol. I: 57-8 // Vol. II: 107, 168-70, 194, 228, 230-1, 312, 388
rite/s Vol. I: 70, 77-8, 100, 142, 187, 193, 205, 257 // Vol. II: 4, 19-21, 29, 31, 40, 54, 59-60, 69-70, 74, 76, 92, 223, 231-2, 244, 263, 271, 273, 277, 280, 321-2, 324
ritual Vol. I: 28, 34, 38, 54, 61-63, 68, 87-89, 92, 112, 114, 191, 198, 270 // Vol. II: 4-5, 14, 19, 21, 40, 45-7, 55, 68-70, 72-3, 78-82, 84-90, 92, 94, 96, 98-99, 109, 115-6, 139, 163, 171, 174, 176, 195, 204, 206, 224, 231-4, 250, 273-5, 288, 292-3, 303, 305, 322, 380, 383, 386, 399 See also behaviour (religious)

Robinson, Richard H. *Vol. I*: 35, 45, 49
Rogation *Vol. II*: 20
rokkon shōjō *Vol. II*: 92-4, 96, 237
Roman Catholic Church *Vol. I*: 82, 94, 256 // *Vol. II*: 124, 140, 333, 344
Roman Empire *Vol. I*: 140 // *Vol. II*: 249, 265, 385
romanized script *Vol. II*: 153, 159, 200, 218, 229
Romanticism *Vol. I*: 42, 148 154, 157, 165, 218 // *Vol. II*: 45
Rome (congresses) *Vol. I*: 113-4, 187, 197 // *Vol. II*: 51, 90, 177, 367, 376
rosaries *Vol. II*: 191
Rudolph, Kurt *Vol. I*: 27, 32, 124, 184, 216, 235-6, 243, 246, 250, 262 // *Vol. II*: 128, 244, 246, 264
Russia/n *Vol. I*: 150, 174, 185, 187, 213, 219, 226, 228-34, 233, 238 // *Vol. II*: 154, 316, 327-8, 333-4, 339-40
Ryōanji *Vol. II*: 280
Ryōbu Shintō *Vol. II*: 43
Ryōzen Kannon *Vol. II*: 397
ryū *Vol. II*: 280
Ryu, Byung-Duk *Vol. II*: 184
Ryūjin *Vol. II*: 280
Ryūkoku University *Vol. I*: 160
Ryū Mon *Vol. I*: 129
Ryu, Sung-Tae *Vol. II*: 185, 199, 201

sacrament (of communion) *Vol. II*: 124
sacred (area/focus) *Vol. I*: 62, 87, 272 // *Vol. II*: 8, 88-9, 95, 170, 208, 228, 236, 257, 293, 324
– dance *Vol. II*: 60
– dimensions of *Vol. I*: 32 // *Vol. II*: 4
– Great Sacred Hall *Vol. I*: 58
 See also *sagrado/a*
Sacred Books of the East *Vol. I*: 59
sacrifice *Vol. II*: 280
sage/s *Vol. II*: 31, 189, 297, 324
Sagrada/o

– Área Sagrada *Vol. II*: 228
– Hinos Sagrados *Vol. II*: 234
– Solo Sagrado *Vol. I*: 272 // *Vol. II*: 236, 239
– *terra sagrada* *Vol. I*: 236
sub-Saharan *Vol. I*: 214, 248 // *Vol. II*: 133
Saigon *Vol. II*: 162-3
Saikoku *Vol. I*: 97 // *Vol. II*: 282
saint/s (various) *Vol. I*: 95, 141, 162 // *Vol. II*: 70, 112, 210, 230-1, 272, 343
– Latter Day Saints (Church) *Vol. I*: 102 // *Vol. II*: 143
Saionji, Masami *Vol. II*: 174
Saita, Kátia Metran *Vol. II*: 231, 239
sakaki *Vol. I*: 88 // *Vol. II*: 271
Sakamoto family *Vol. II*: 207-9, 215
Sākyamuni *Vol. I*: 120-4 // *Vol. II*: 259
salvation *Vol. I*: 35, 99, 123 // *Vol. II*: 5, 20, 40, 45, 51-60, 120, 234-5, 260, 322, 367
– proximate *Vol. II*: 57-60, 92, 223
– ultimate: *Vol. II*: 57-60
– universal *Vol. II*: 19, 28, 51, 151, 163, 172, 174, 224, 235, 238, 320, 323, 362
Sam Po Kong *Vol. II*: 299
-sama (honorific suffix) *Vol. II*:
– kami-sama *Vol. II*: 93, 231, 236, 239
– Kannon-sama *Vol. II*: 278-80, 282, 283
 See also, Benten, Inari, Masami, Meishu
saṃgha *Vol. II*: 53
Sami *Vol. II*: 362
samurai *Vol. I*: 155
saṃvṛti satya *Vol. I*: 254, 259
sanctification *Vol. II*: 16
sange *Vol. II*: 82
Sangha *Vol. II*: 17-18, 25, 53, 325
sanjiao (*sānjiào*) *Vol. I*: 111, 136, 138-40, 142-3, 170, 202, 243, 267 // *Vol. II*: 155, 245, 288-91, 293, 295-6, 300, 305, 346, 357
San Y Chiao (*sānyījiào*) *Vol. II*: 291

Sankōkan *Vol. II*: 233, 239
sankyō Vol. II: 357
Sannō Ichijitsu Shintō *Vol. II*: 43
Sanskrit *Vol. I*: 159, 165, 246 // *Vol. II*: 36, 243, 278, 295-6
Sansom, George B. *Vol. I*: 158
Santa Maria *Vol. I*: 82, 253
Santo Antônio *Vol. II*: 231
sānyījiào Vol. II: 291
São Jorge *Vol. II*; 231
São Paulo *Vol. I*: 175 // *Vol. II*: 218-9, 235-6
Sarasvatī *Vol. II*: 278-9, 281, 286
Sarvāstivāda *Vol. II*: 120
Satan/ism *Vol. II*: 66
satori *Vol. II*: 38
Satow, Ernest M. *Vol. I*: 158
saviour *Vol. II*: 56, 322
Sawai, Yuichi *Vol. II*: 57
sazuke Vol. II: 57, 59, 229
Scandinavia *Vol. I*: 42, 183-4, 186, 189, 194
Scheele, Paul-Werner *Vol. II*: 74, 76, 87
Schicksalsdeutung Vol. I: 32, 275
Schimmel, Annemarie *Vol. I*: 250
schism *Vol. I*: 59, 203-4 // *Vol. II*: 25, 141, 364
Schlang, Stefan *Vol. II*: 111, 116
Schleiermacher, Friedrich *Vol. I*: 32, 36, 221, 248, 269 // *Vol. II*: 23, 87, 121, 349
Schmidt-Leukel, Perry *Vol. II*: 368, 375
Schneeberger, V. D. *Vol. II*: 328, 341
schools *Vol. II*: 172, 313, 376, 378-9, 381, 385, 387-9, 393
– of tradition/thought *Vol. II*: 154, 211, 244, 385
– history of religions school *Vol. II*: 348-9
– religion and religions school *Vol. II*: 349
Schrimpf, Monika *Vol. I*: 263, 275 // *Vol. II*: 101, 402, 414
Science of Happiness *Vol. II*: 173, 208-9, 215, 227-8 See also Kōfuku no Kagaku

science of religion/s *Vol. I*: 32-3, 38, 42, 46, 50, 51, 93, 112, 115, 125, 141, 144, 146, 148-9, 150-67, 179-82, 212, 214, 224-6, 252 // *Vol. II*: 15, 32, 127, 138, 205, 220, 227, 266, 347-8, 352-3, 355
science/s *Vol. I*: 3, 15-16, 25, 162, 236 // *Vol. II*: 292,
– behavioural *Vol. I*: 4 // *Vol. II*: 80,
– cognitive *Vol. I*: 20, 89, 217 // *Vol. II*: 79-80, 86
– cultural/human *Vol. I*: , 193, 249 // *Vol. II*: 32, 40, 257
– educational *Vol. II*: 378,
– natural *Vol. I*: 154, 188
– philosophy of *Vol. II*: 135,
– political *Vol. I*: 17
– social *Vol. I*: 2, 9, 17, 20-21, 50, 68, 86, 142, 182, 184, 189, 191, 193, 217, 230, 237, 250 // *Vol. II*: 99, 265, 348
sciences religieuses/des religions *Vol. I*: 48, 181 // *Vol. II*: 87
scientific study of religion/s *Vol. I*:3, 34, 37-9, 45-7, 103, 112, 116, 231, 244, 248, 251-2, 253-4, 260
scientific (methods etc) *Vol. I*: 5, 13, 15, 20-21, 30, 33-4, 36-40, 43-4, 47, 50-51, 59, 64, 73, 86, 89, 95, 102-3, 112, 116, 137, 146, 182, 194, 214, 220, 224-5, 227-8, 231-2, 236-8, 243-4, 248-54
Scientific Atheism *Vol. I*: 227-8, 232
Scientology *Vol. I*: 88 // *Vol. II*: 161, 356
scripture/s *Vol. I*: 247 // *Vol. II*: 182
– Buddhist *Vol. I*: 150, 218 // *Vol. II*: 35
– Won Buddhist *Vol. II*: 182, 185, 187, 197-8, 200
scrolls (hanging) *Vol. I*: 60, 62-3, 68 // *Vol. II*: 283, 368
séance/s *Vol. II*: 163
sectarian/ism *Vol. I*: 121 // *Vol. II*: 42-3, 48, 97, 159-60, 177-8
sect/s *Vol. I*: 68, 127, 137, 203, 240, 258 // *Vol. II*: 20, 48, 91, 117,

125, 133-4, 145, 148, 151, 154, 157-9, 177, 194-5, 284, 364, 384
secular/ity *Vol. I*: 2, 44, 49, 59, 80, 81, 114, 161, 170, 203, 239, 262, 269 // *Vol. II*: 262, 285, 316, 322, 339, 353, 378-81, 374, 384, 387-9
secularisation *Vol. I*: 137, 184, 187, 204, 273 // *Vol. II*: 30 ,48, 63, 97, 276, 315, 334, 339, 363, 368
secularism *Vol. I*: 83, 254, 259
seichi Vol. II: 236
Seichō no Ie *Vol. II*: 172, 218-20, 226-7, 230-2, 236, 239
Seidel, Anna *Vol. I*: 159
Seiwert, Hubert *Vol. II*: 159, 161, 178, 319, 326
Sejm *Vol. II*: 332
Sekai Kyūseikyō *Vol. II*: 95, 172, 218, 220, 226, 229, 231-2, 234-7
Sekolah Minggu Buddha *Vol. II*: 298
self *Vol. I*: 120, 139 // *Vol. II*: 12, 17, 24, 53, 70, 82-3, 111, 114-5, 175, 189, 211, 218, 223, 226, 322, 346
– non-self *Vol. II*: 172
– self-power *Vol. II*: 226
– self-understanding (of believers) *Vol. I*: 25-6, 30, 72, 88, 91-3, 99-100, 104, 116, 118, 123, 190-1 // *Vol. II*: 43, 54, 57, 83, 92, 110, 114-5, 142-3, 146-7, 157, 159, 161, 175, 181-3, 185, 193-5, 244, 250, 257, 266, 275, 281, 329, 344, 383, 385, 399-400
Semarang *Vol. I*: 176-7 // *Vol. II*: 299, 392
semiotics *Vol. I*: 22, 230, 234, 242
Semitic consciousnes *Vol. II*: 250
Senhor da Luz *Vol. II*: 235-6
Senhora: see Nossa Senhora
Sensōji *Vol. II*: 21
senzokuyō Vol. I: 96
Seoul *Vol. II*: 184-5
Serbia *Vol. II*: 324
Serbo-Croat *Vol. II*: 319
sesshin Vol. II: 230
Setsuhei *Vol. I*:118, 127

Seven Gods of Good Fortune *Vol. II*: 279
SGI *Vol. II*: 171
shamanism *Vol. I*: 69, 88, 94, 166, 188, 193, 227-8, 235, 237-8, 242 // *Vol. II*: 57, 97, 109, 154, 162, 270-1, 273, 275, 362, 385
Shap Working Party/Calendar *Vol. II*: 382-3, 389
shape
– of discipline *Vol. I*: 216, 220-1
– of religion *Vol. I*: 12, 14, 136-7, 175, 201-7 See also morphology
Sharma, Arvind *Vol. II*: 371, 375
Sharpe *Vol. I*: 41, 49, 148, 170, 214, 216-7, 221 // *Vol. II*: 3, 10, 348, 351
Shcherbatskoi, Fedor *Vol. I*: 229, 231, 232, 243
Shèngmŭ *Vol. II*: 296, 301-2
Shichifukujin: see Seven Gods of Good Fortune
Shichimen, Mount *Vol. II*: 170
Shi'ite Islam *Vol. I*: 87, 192,
shikishin funi Vol. II: 96
Shikoku *Vol. I*: 97 // *Vol. II*: 397
Shimazono, Susumu *Vol. I*: 163 // *Vol. II*: 55-56, 60, 168, 203, 216
shimenawa Vol. II: 89, 271
Shimozuke *Vol. II*: 93
Shin Buddhism (Shinshū) *Vol. I*: 40, 96-102, 159-60, 272 // *Vol. II*: 8-10, 82-3, 169, 219, 226, 233, 235, 355, 363-8, 370, 399 See also Shinshū
shinbotsusha Vol. II: 397
shinbutsu bunri Vol. II: 304
Shingon *Vol. I*: 57, 62, 97 // *Vol. II*: 93-9, 208, 211, 223, 230, 270-1, 273-4, 279, 283
Shingu *Vol. I*: 272
Shingyō *Vol. I*: 62 // *Vol. II*: 273
shinjin Vol. II: 83, 233
shinkō Vol. I: 274 // *Vol. II*: 214, 374
shinkōshūkyō Vol. II: 156, 178
Shinnyoen *Vol. II*: 218, 220, 230
Shinran (Shōnin) *Vol. I*: 98-100, 106, 270-1 // *Vol. II*: 8, 10, 169

shinshinshūkyō Vol. II: 156, 172, 222
Shinshū (Jōdo Shinshū) Vol. I: 57, 97, 159, 160, 273-4 // Vol. II: 8-9, 169, 223, 227, 367, 372, 374 See also Shin Buddhism
Shinshūkyō Renmei Vol. II: 168
shinshūkyō Vol. II: 222
Shinsō (Zhēnzōng) Vol. II: 131
shinsōkan Vol. II: 227
Shintō Vol. I: 35, 48, 52-3, 60-2, 65, 87-8, 109, 111, 116, 118-9, 126, 128-9, 157-8, 161, 163, 165-6, 168-9, 264 // Vol. II: 5-6, 10, 20-21, 26, 35, 40-50, 54, 62, 64, 68-70, 86, 88-9, 92-6, 101, 111, 116, 124, 140, 143, 154, 173, 194, 200, 206-7, 215, 217, 221-5, 229, 231-2, 236-7, 245, 251, 258-61, 269-75, 278-84, 286, 304-5, 321, 323-4, 326, 356, 361-2, 378-9, 384, 397-9
Shōfuku Benzaiten Vol. II: 284 See also Benzaiten.
shōguns Vol. I: 155
Shōkokuji Vol. II: 280
Shōmu (Emperor) Vol. II: 281-2
shōten Vol. I: 93
Shōtoku Taishi (Prince) Vol. I: 162-3, 168 // Vol. II: 18
Shōwa Period Vol. I: 145, 154 // Vol. II: 284
shrine/s (various) Vol. II: 222, 290
– Shintō shrines Vol. I: 52-3, 60-3, 65, 68, 88 // Vol. II: 5, 21, 44, 46-8, 88-9, 93-5, 143, 221, 224-5, 229, 270-5, 278-85, 304, 321, 324
– Shrine Shintō Vol. II: 42-3
See also Chichibu, Ise, Kumano, Meiji, Tsubaki and Yasukuni shrines
Shroud of Turin Vol. II: 343
Shugendō Vol. I: 62, 68 // Vol. II: 92-4, 263, 270-3, 277
shugyō Vol. II: 93, 211
shūkyō (religion) Vol. I: 113, 145-6, 162-3, 247 // Vol. II: 61, 153, 208, 375

Shūkyōgakkai Vol. I: 145, 169
shūkyōgaku Vol. I: 144, 162, 168, 170, 269 // Vol. II: 352, 374, 378
shūkyōminzokugaku Vol. I: 169
Shūkyō Nenkan Vol. I: 257
shūkyōtaiwa Vol. I: 269 // Vol. II: 374
shūshin Vol. II: 379
Shutsujōkōgo Vol. I: 117, 126-31, 133-4 // Vol. II: 353
Siberia/n Vol. I: 70, 74, 77, 166, 188, 193, 227-8, 233, 235, 238, 242 // Vol. II: 327, 340
Sikh/ism Vol. I: 5, 101, 180, 251, 254 // Vol. II: 62, 136, 379, 384-5
Siktivkar Vol. I: 238
Simon, Pierre J. Vol. II: 163, 178
Simon-Barouh, Ida Vol. II: 163, 178
Singapore Vol. II: 287, 290-4, 298, 394
Sino-Japanese Vol. I: 113, 168 // Vol. II: 211, 385
sinologist/s Vol. I: 129 // Vol. II: 159
sisters
– Sisters of Charity Vol. II: 75
– See also Dharma Sisters
Sitz im Leben Vol. I: 191
skilful means Vol. I: 45, 48, 123-4, 141, 263, 266 // Vol. II: 36-7, 39, 146, 243-4, 300, 371, 374
– skilfulness in means Vol. II: 146
See also *fāngbiàn, hōben, upāya, upāyakauśalya*
Slater, Peter Vol. I: 113, 225
Smart, Ninian Vol. I: 10, 23, 32, 38, 49, 180, 211 // Vol. II: 4, 10, 52, 60, 78, 320, 326, 359, 367, 375-6
Smith, Joseph Vol. II: 143, 343
Smith, William Cantwell Vol. I: 116
social aspect/dimension Vol. II: 16, 17-18, 22, 69, 139, 145
socialism/ist Vol. II: 63, 155, 329-30, 332-4, 336, 340
social scientist/s Vol. I: 52-4, 64, 237, 251 Vol. II: 3, 98-9, 244
Société Ernest Renan Vol. I: 184, 186, 217
Society of Friends Vol. II: 82, 396
Socrates Vol. I: 159

Söderblom, Nathan *Vol. II*: 320, 349
Soeharto *Vol. II*: 298
sohak Vol. II: 164
Sōka Gakkai *Vol. I*: 58-59, 102, 167 // *Vol. II*: 18, 83, 91, 100, 155, 168-71, 176, 181, 194, 220, 228, 230
Soka Gakkai International *Vol. II*: 228
sokushin jōbutsu Vol. II: 96
Solar Temple *Vol. II*: 396
Solidarnosc *Vol. II*: 331, 334
Solo Sagrado *Vol. I*: 272 // *Vol. II*: 236, 239
Sòng dynasty *Vol. I*: 131 // *Vol. II*: 158, 160
Song Kyu *Vol. II*: 186
Song To-Sŏng *Vol. II*: 186
song/s *Vol. II*: 190, 234, 383
Sonoda, Minoru *Vol. I*: 160-1, 163, 170 // *Vol. II*: 44
Sonshi *Vol. II*: 210
Sonten *Vol. II*: 221
Sot'aesan *Vol. II*: 167, 179, 182-4, 186-7, 189-91, 197-200, 343
soter Vol. II: 322
soteriological *Vol. II*: 5-6, 21, 51-2, 54, 56-60, 68, 70-1, 85, 87, 92, 95, 101,150, 320-2, 324, 361
Sōtō Zen *Vol. I*: 87 // *Vol. II*: 382, 400
soul/s *Vol. I*: 94, 162 // *Vol. II*: 12, 75, 77, 170, 228
Soviet Union *Vol. I*: 51, 180, 188, 192, 223-6, 238-42 // *Vol. II*: 325, 330, 334-5, 338-9
Spain *Vol. I*: 42, 81-2, 175, 184, 186, 245, 248 // *Vol. II*: 394
Spencer, H. *Vol. I*: 217
spirit/s *Vol. II*: 41, 64, 82, 95, 155,163, 174, 190, 208, 222, 227-8, 230-1, 237, 248, 280, 297, 343, 362, 380, 397, 400
– Holy Spirit *Vol. II*: 81, 120
spiritism *Vol. II*: 162-3, 177
spiritual/ly *Vol. I*: 97, 123, 162, 259 // *Vol. II*: 53, 88, 210, 256
spiritual *Vol. II*: 22, 27, 34, 36, 52-3, 75, 77-8, 80, 85, 87, 89-90, 95-8, 101, 153, 156, 171, 186, 193, 197, 210, 212-3, 222, 224, 233, 236-7, 255, 322, 333, 381
spirituality/ies *Vol. I*: 162, 203, 272, 274 // *Vol. II*: 10, 23, 37, 55-6, 98-100, 142, 218, 222, 291, 364
Sri Aurobindo *Vol. II*: 143, 384
Sri Krishna *Vol. II*: 293-4
Sri Lanka *Vol. I*: 101 // *Vol. II*: 162, 213, 228, 324-5
SSSR *Vol. I*: 241
Staal, Frits *Vol. II*: 73, 87
Stalinism/pre-Stalinism *Vol. I*: 75 // *Vol. II*: 330
Starbuck, E. D. *Vol. I*: 217
Stcherbatsky: see Shcherbatskoi
Stegerhoff-Raab, Renate *Vol. I*: 263// *Vol. II*: 402
storia delle religione Vol. I: 181
stotra Vol. II: 83
Strenski, Ivan *Vol. I*: 41, 49
structuralism *Vol. I*: 186
Studia Religioznawcze Vol. I: 187, 239, 242
study of religions. *Vol. I*: *passim* espec.1-6 // *Vol. II*: *passim* espec. 3-9 See also *Religionswissenschaft*, religion/s (and cross-references)
stupa *Vol. I*: 131 // *Vol. II*: 207-8
subway gas incident *Vol. I*: 102
Sudan *Vol. II*: 316
Sufism (Sūfī) *Vol. II*: 56, 84, 123
sui generis *Vol. I*: 17, 48
Sukuma people *Vol. II*: 140
Sumeru, Mount *Vol. I*: 123
Sundén, Hjalmar *Vol. I*: 183
śūnyatā *Vol. II*: 37
supernatural
– agents *Vol. II*: 70, 80, 98
– beings *Vol. II*: 73, 77, 80, 83-6
– powers *Vol. I*: 122 // *Vol. II*: 212
superseding *Vol. I*: 118-9, 124, 127 // *Vol. II*: 151, 187
superstition *Vol. I*: 103, 259 // *Vol. II*: 157, 189-91
Susanoo *Vol. II*: 46
sūtra/s *Vol. I*: 61-2, 64, 101, 118-20, 124, 128, 157, 159-60, 165 //

Vol. II: 25, 28, 34-6, 39, 73-4, 82-3, 100, 158, 169-72, 209, 211, 223, 227-8, 230, 273, 279-80, 343, 382
– *Sūtra of Buddha Names Vol. II*: 83
– *Sutta Nipata Vol. I*: 256, 261
Suzuki, Daisetsu *Vol. I*: 166
swamis *Vol. II*: 210
Sweden/ish *Vol. I*: 76, 87, 187, 215, 228, 237 // *Vol. II*: 220, 349, 376
Switzerland *Vol. I*: 86, 186
swords *Vol. II*: 336
Sydney *Vol. I*: 197
syllabuses (RE) *Vol. II*: 377
symbiosis *Vol. II*: 268
symbol/s *Vol. I*: 27, 34, 75, 79, 82, 87, 136, 259 // *Vol. II*: 27, 43, 69, 82, 89, 115, 142, 161, 163, 190-1, 196, 220, 223, 230, 244, 250-1, 259, 297, 316, 322, 327, 334, 337
symbolic/ally *Vol. I*: 78, 80, 87, 91, 160 // *Vol. II*: 14, 24-5, 89, 98-100, 139, 148, 161, 176, 187, 203, 261, 272, 274, 279, 288, 310, 317, 319, 369-71, 386
symbolise *Vol. I*: 159, 233 // *Vol. II*: 25, 89, 185, 191, 197, 297, 305, 333-4
symbolism *Vol. I*: 82 // *Vol. II*: 48, 221-2, 230, 274, 321, 386
synagogue/s *Vol. II*: 77, 382
synchronic/ity *Vol. I*: 206 // *Vol. II*: 6, 319, 325
syncretism/istic *Vol. I*: 5, 12, 30, 37, 75, 85,137, 139, 141-3, 190, 262-3, 267-8 // *Vol. II*: 9, 18, 28-30, 39, 107, 114, 123-4, 127-8, 140, 146-8, 151, 155, 163, 176-8, 180, 200, 220-1, 225, 232, 241, 243-6, 248-9, 251, 253-78, 285-9, 290-2, 294-6, 298, 300-6, 310, 332, 351
synthesis/t *Vol. I*: 139, 141-2, 202, 267 // *Vol. II*: 114, 123, 143, 148, 176-7, 200, 221, 244-5, 264-76, 287-9, 297, 304-5, 332, 346-7
Syrian Orthodox Church *Vol. I*: 215
tablets
– ancestral *Vol. II*: 291, 302
– votive *Vol. I*: 60 // *Vol. II*: 280
taboo *Vol. II*: 88-9, 92, 100, 253
Taesan (Daesan) *Vol. II*: 184, 186, 188-9, 197, 200-1
Táiběi (Taipei) *Vol. II*: 301-3
Taiheiki Vol. II: 259, 263
Táinán *Vol. II*: 301-2
Taipei (Táiběi) *Vol. II*: 301-3
Taiping (movement) *Vol. II*: 155, 160-1
Taisekiji *Vol. I*: 59
Taishakyō *Vol. II*: 324
Taishō Period *Vol. I*: 154
Taishō Tripitaka *Vol. I*: 160, 168
Taiwan *Vol. I*: 85, 228 // *Vol. II*: 153, 158-9, 177-8, 246, 287-90, 292, 294-6, 298, 300-4, 306
Taiwanese *Vol. II*: 287, 300-3
Takagi, Hiroo *Vol. II*: 156, 168, 178
Takakusu, Junjirō *Vol. I*: 159
Takanawa Buddhist University *Vol. I*: 160
Tamaru, Noriyoshi *Vol. I*: 145, 162, 167, 170, 250
Tamil *Vol. II*: 325
Tanabe, George *Vol. II*: 90-91, 101
Tanaka, Hōsui *Vol. II*: 284
Taniguchi, Masaharu *Vol. II*: 219
Tannishō Vol. II: 233
Tantrism *Vol. I*: 49 // *Vol. II*: 211
Tanzania *Vol. II*: 140
Taoism *Vol. I*: 48, 126, 132 // *Vol. II*: 154, 223, 291 See also Daoism
tapu Vol. II: 88
tariki Vol. I: 99 // *Vol. II*: 23-4, 226
Tartu *Vol. I*: 230
Tay Hong Yong *Vol. II*: 290
Tay Kie Ki *Vol. II*: 290-291
Tay Ninh *Vol. II*: 163-4
Taylor, Romeyn *Vol. I*: 139-40, 143, 257, 262 // *Vol. II*: 155, 178, 289, 302, 306, 347, 351

temizuya Vol. I: 89, 93
temple/s (general) Vol. I: 58-64 // Vol. II: 366, 382,
– Buddhist Vol. I: 58-64, 67, 96-98, 100, 104, 149, 159-60, 230 // Vol. II: 20-21, 224-6, 229, 270, 273, 279-80, 282-3, 367, 397 See also the following
– Chinese (various) Vol. II: 287-306,
– Japanese (various) Vol. I: 58-9 // Vol. II: 171, 221, 234,
– Korean (various) Vol. II: 167, 185, 187-8, 190-1, 197,
Tendai (Buddhism) Vol. I: 62 // Vol. II: 221, 223, 273
Tenji Period Vol. II: 281
Tenrikyō Vol. I: 58, 93, 137, 164 // Vol. II: 6-7, 51-2, 57, 59-61, 72, 90, 136, 153, 168, 171-2, 218, 220, 229-30, 233-4, 239, 361, 363, 367, 369, 376-9, 383-4, 388
Tenrikyōten Vol. II: 61
Tenri University Vol. I: 164 // Vol. II: 367
Tenshōkōtai Jingūkyō Vol. II: 46, 172, 218, 220, 226-7, 230, 237
te-odori Vol. II: 171
Teoh Kon Seng Koon Vol. II: 292
terra sagrada Vol. II: 236
texts Vol. I: 21, 29, 61, 118-9, 124, 165, 191, 210, 230-1, 242 // Vol. II: 157, 182, 199, 211, 233, 243, 291, 343, 346
textual (studies etc) Vol. I: 9, 20, 36, 51, 86, 119, 146, 157, 161, 234, 251 // Vol. II: 164
Thailand Vol. II: 325, 387
theism/istic Vol. I: 38, 192, 199, 237 // Vol. II: 65, 79, 110, 126
theocentric Vol. II: 25
theocracy Vol. II: 16
theologians (various religions) Vol. I: 12, 18, 115, 178, 188 // Vol. II: 7, 12, 15, 23, 33, 38, 67, 72, 110, 112-3, 118-9, 147, 214, 253, 257, 264, 266-7, 311, 328, 355, 359, 369

theology/ical (various religions) Vol. I: 4, 9-11, 25, 31, 36-7, 47, 72, 92, 94-5, 115, 147, 164, 173, 175, 180-2, 185, 188-9, 199, 201, 203-4, 214, 217-8, 239, 250-1, 256 // Vol. II: 7, 12-13, 32, 35, 38-39, 57, 60, 63-4, 75-8, 86, 97, 99, 105, 110-1, 113, 117-9, 125, 128, 140, 146-7, 205, 230, 232, 243-4, 251, 253-8, 266, 311, 315, 317, 327-9, 337-8, 348-50, 352-3, 355, 359, 363, 367, 369, 371, 373-4, 378, 392, 394
Theologische Literaturzeitung Vol. I: 235
theory Vol. I: 1, 3, 13, 22, 24, 29, 33-4, 35-42, 43-8, 91-2, 111, 117-9, 123-4, 127-8, 134, 136-8, 140, 142-143, 170, 187-190, 202-203, 242-3, 245, 249, 261, 266-7, 271 // Vol. II: 9, 17, 25, 29, 32, 38, 49, 81, 106, 109-10, 113-6, 118, 125-7, 130-50, 155, 157, 194-5, 201, 220-1, 247-9, 252, 258-9, 261, 263, 275, 277, 346, 354, 359-60, 364, 373, 396
– theories Vol. I: 22-3, 29-30, 33-5, 37-43, 45-9, 72, 89, 92, 114, 120, 136-7, 170, 188, 193, 206, 253, 262, 269 // Vol. II: 48-9, 81, 121, 125, 132, 136, 144, 248, 318, 374, 394
– theorists Vol. I: 45, 88 // Vol. II: 135
– theorizing Vol. I: 202
theos Vol. II: 65
Theosophy Vol. I: 150, 169 // Vol. II: 123, 212
Theravāda Vol. II: 17, 20, 82, 100, 162, 211, 301, 385
Thomism Vol. II: 42
three refuges Vol. II: 52
Three Treasures Vol. II: 260
Thrower, James Vol. I: 227, 239, 243
tiān Vol. II: 291-2, 294, 296
Tiananmen Square Vol. I: 259 // Vol. II: 161
Tianjin Vol. II: 159
Tianlijiao Vol. II: 171

tianming (tiānmìng) Vol. II: 159, 165
Tiānshàng Shèngmǔ Vol. II: 296, 301-2
Tiāntái Vol. I: 87
Tibet/an Vol. I: 149-51, 169-70, 213, 230, 234, 240 // Vol. II: 77, 210, 211, 229, 325, 385
tiger god Vol. II: 296-7
Tikopia Vol. I: 209
Tillich, Paul Vol. I: 35-6 // Vol. II: 12
Ting (Bishop) Vol. II: 329
Tinsley, John Vol. I: 94
Tlaxcala Vol. I: 77, 81
Tochigi Vol. II: 74, 174
Toda, Jōsei Vol. II: 170
Tokarev, Sergey Aleksandrovich Vol. I: 230, 243
Tokugawa Period Vol. I: 117, 148, 154, 156, 158 // Vol. II: 35, 156
tolerance/toleration Vol. I: 81, 214, 262, 269 // Vol. II: 262, 285, 324, 336
Tominaga, Nakamoto Vol. I: 48, 109-11, 113-7, 123-8, 130-5, 141-3, 149, 157, 160, 165, 167, 170, 190, 194, 218, 246, 261-2, 265-6 // Vol. II: 35, 244, 289, 347, 351, 353, 357, 374
Tomsk Vol. I: 228
Tonantzin Vol. I: 81, 245, 253, 261
Tonghak Vol. II: 155, 164-6, 187, 194, 198
Tongilkyo (Tongilgyo) Vol. II: 155, 166, 181
Torah Vol. II: 16
torii Vol. I: 87 // Vol. II: 89, 272, 283
toritsugi Vol. II: 229
Towler, Robert Vol. II: 91, 101
Tōyō University Vol. I: 159-60 // Vol. II: 168
transaction Vol. I: 62 // Vol. II: 85
Transbaikalia Vol. I: 233
transcendence Vol. II: 5, 38, 52, 57, 60, 69, 189, 212, 325
transformation Vol. II: 7, 88-100
transmission Vol. I: 34, 118, 131, 137, 209 // Vol. II: 15, 27-28, 35, 44, 105-109, 136-137, 141, 145-6, 193, 215, 218-20, 222-38, 243, 355
transplantation Vol. I: 272 // Vol. II: 60, 107, 141, 178, 218, 220-1, 224, 227-9, 239, 241, 243-4, 247-52, 261, 263
transposition Vol. II: 123-5, 248-9, 251, 255, 260, 279
treatise/s (various) Vol. I: 111, 120, 140, 124, 139, 202, 257 // Vol. II: 83, 86, 289, 346
Tribhakti (Vihara) Vol. II: 296-7
Trinity (Holy) Vol. I: 95
Tripitaka Vol. I: 160, 169
Triplett, Katja Vol. I: 28, 32, 63, 68, 263, 275 // Vol. II: 94, 101, 132, 280, 286, 311
Troeltsch, Ernst Vol. I: 41, 45-6, 48, 109-10, 113-4, 203, 217, 244, 257, 261, 264, 266, 274 // Vol. II: 9, 11, 31-6, 38-39, 105, 112, 116-129, 137, 217, 349, 374
truth/s Vol. II: 6, 13, 38, 109-10, 118, 142, 151, 179, 187, 196, 210, 250, 260-1, 317, 325, 344, 349, 357, 362, 386
– two truths Vol. II: 37, 254
Tsubaki Grand Shrine Vol. II: 221, 399
Tsukuba University Vol. II: 11, 168
tsutome Vol. II: 57, 59, 383
Tǔdìgōng Vol. II: 290
Turkey Vol. I: 88, 199
Turku Vol. I: 15-16, 76, 183, 186, 238 // Vol. II: 131
Turner, Victor Vol. I: 217
Turner, Harold W. Vol. II: 44-45, 49
TWB factor Vol. I: 101-5 // Vol. II: 142, 183, 354
Tyloch, Witold Vol. I: 68, 125, 169, 180, 193-4, 224-5, 242-3, 266-7
typology Vol. I: 20, 23, 27, 29, 37, 92, 203, 205, 266, 272 // Vol. II: 3-8, 40-49, 51-60, 62-70, 73-86, 90-92, 96, 101, 111, 116, 124-5, 127, 150, 238, 310, 318, 320-1, 323, 361, 364, 400

Uchimura, Kanzō *Vol. I*: 161
Udo, Tworuschka: *Vol. II*: 237, 239
Ueda, Shizuteru *Vol. I*: 146, 170
Ugajin *Vol. II*: 280-282
Ui, Hakuju *Vol. II*: 35, 39
ujigami Vol. II: 47
ujiko Vol. II: 47
UK *Vol. II*: 316, 342, 398
Ukraine *Vol. II*: 327, 339
Ulan-Ude *Vol. I*: 233
ultimate *Vol. II*: 26, 38, 64, 120, 197, 261
– soteriology *Vol. II*: 5, 57, 59-60,
Umbanda *Vol. I*: 35, 253 // *Vol. II*: 143
understanding *Vol. I*: 123, 191, 229 // *Vol. II*: 12, 14, 27, 109, 110-1, 134-5, 353-4, 377-8, 380, 382, 391 (general usage excluded)
– hermeneutics etc. *Vol. II*: 29-38, 255-6
– self-understanding (of believers) *Vol. I*: 25-6, 30, 72, 88, 91-3, 99-100, 104, 116, 118, 123, 190-1 // *Vol. II*: 43, 54, 57, 83, 92, 110, 114-5, 142-3, 146-7, 157, 159, 161, 175, 181-3, 185, 193-5, 244, 250, 257, 266, 275, 281, 329, 344, 383, 385, 399-400
UNESCO *Vol. I*: 196, 200
Ungaran *Vol. II*: 296
Unification Church *Vol. I*: 201 // *Vol. II*: 166-7, 181, 360
Unitarianism *Vol. II*: 67, 145
United States *Vol. I*: 43, 175, 255 // *Vol. II*: 63, 197, 329, 392, 396
universal/ism/ist
– scientific universality *Vol. I*: 33
– universal/ist religion/s *Vol. I*: 163, 206 // *Vol. II*: 4, 18-9, 21, 26, 28-9, 45-6, 48, 51, 67-9, 150-1, 163, 197, 221, 223-4, 229-31, 238, 266, 320-5, 362, 384, 397, 399
– universal (widespread data) *Vol. II*: 88, 154
Universalist Unitarian Church *Vol. II*: 67, 145

universe/s *Vol. I*: 11, 44, 159 // *Vol. II*: 36, 189, 230
universities (various named, not presses) *Vol. I*: 10, 61, 63, 86, 144, 146, 156, 159-62, 164, 174, 178, 180-3, 187, 190, 196-7, 225, 228, 235, 237-9 // *Vol. II*: 8, 11, 32, 51, 65, 84, 87-8, 90, 108, 111, 131, 168, 170, 181, 184-5, 188, 191, 219-20, 233, 321-28, 352-3, 367-9, 376, 391
Upanishadic Hinduism *Vol. II*: 56
upāya Vol. II: 36, 243
upāyakauśalya Vol. II: 243 See also skilful means
uposatha Vol. II: 17, 20, 322
Uralic *Vol. I*: 228, 238, 242
Urban, Hugh B. *Vol. I*: 41, 49
urban *Vol. I*: 82, 84, 117, 163, 254 // *Vol. II*: 48, 162, 218, 230, 302
US-Americans *Vol. II*: 219
USA *Vol. I*: 236, 244, 255 // *Vol. II*: 161, 221, 235, 398
Usarski, Frank *Vol. II*: 219, 233, 239
uskonto Vol. I: 247
USSR *Vol. I*: 227, 232, 243
uta Vol. II: 233-4 See also *Mikagura-uta*
Utah *Vol. I*: 255
Uttar Pradesh *Vol. II*: 317

van Baaren, Theo *Vol. I*: 183
van der Leeuw, Gerardus *Vol. I*: 25, 92, 183, 266 // *Vol. II*: 9, 41, 49, 105, 117-29, 217, 247-9, 251-2, 255, 260, 263, 266, 269
van Gennep, Arnold *Vol. I*: 217 // *Vol. II*: 19, 31
Vansina, Jan *Vol. II*: 114, 116
variable/s *Vol. II*: 257, 319
Vatican *Vol. II*: 249, 331, 364
Vedantic Hinduism/monism *Vol. II*: 64, 67
Vedas *Vol. I*: 101, 120
vegetarianism *Vol. II*: 158, 163, 293, 295
Venice *Vol. I*: 183-4
Veracruz *Vol. I*: 77

Verenigde Oostindische Compagnie *Vol. I*: 218
Verschiebung Vol. II: 124, 255
Viaje, el Señhor de la *Vol. I*: 77
Vietcong *Vol. II*: 164
Viet Minh *Vol. II*: 164
Vietnam/ese *Vol. I*: 141, 143, 259 // *Vol. II*: 143, 152-5, 162-5, 177, 181, 194
Vihar Maharaj *Vol. II*: 210
vihara/Vihara *Vol. II*: 288, 295-9, 301
Vihara Dewiwelasasih *Vol. II*: 296
Vimalakīrti *Vol. I*: 120
Vinaya *Vol. I*: 120
violence *Vol. II*: 228, 317, 322, 339, 393, 395-6
Virgin Mary (various designatons) *Vol. I*: 81-2, 88, 93-4, 219, 253, 261 // *Vol. II*: 183 See also Mary, Maria.
virtue/s (Confucian) *Vol. II*: 292
vision/s (religious) *Vol. I*: 81 // *Vol. II*: 160, 275, 382
voidness *Vol. II*: 157 See also *śūnyatā*
voluntarism *Vol. I*: 255-6
von Brück, Michael *Vol. II*: 368, 373
von Eckhardt, Hans *Vol. I*:185, 194
von Grunebaum, G. *Vol. II*: 112, 116
von Stietencron, Heinrich *Vol. I*: 250
Voortrekker Monument *Vol. I*: 75, 210-1 // *Vol. II*: 310
Vos, Frits *Vol. II*: 164-5, 178, 180, 201
votive (tablets etc) *Vol. II*: 280, 295
vow *Vol. II*: 74
– of Amida(Amithāba) *Vol. I*: 99 // *Vol. II*: 24, 356
Vrouemonument *Vol. I*: 210

Waardenburg, Jacques *Vol. I*: 25, 32, 38, 41, 49, 91, 106, 216
Wach, Joachim *Vol. I*: 158 // *Vol. II*: 14, 75, 121, 349
Waco *Vol. II*: 396
Waddell, L. Austine *Vol. I*: 149-50, 170
Wakimoto, Tsuneya *Vol. I*: 162
Warburg, Aby *Vol. I*: 217

Warsaw *Vol. I*: 50-51, 68, 75, 179-81, 186, 193, 225, 228, 237 // *Vol. II*: 327-8, 331, 333-6
Wasim, Alef Theria *Vol. I*: 176-7, 271, 273-5 // *Vol. II*: 373, 392, 400, 410, 412-4
Waterhouse, Helen *Vol. II*: 212
Waterloo Street *Vol. II*: 292
Watsky, Andrew *Vol. II*: 282, 286
Way-ism *Vol. I*: 67
– Great Way *Vol. I*: 67
– Way of Heaven *Vol. I*: 140 // *Vol. II*: 164
– Way of ways *Vol. I*: 126, 130, 133-4
Weber, Max *Vol. I*: 30, 40, 92, 136, 203, 217 // *Vol. II*: 91, 125
wu-wei Vol. II: 163
Wei King (of Amoy) *Vol. II*: 290
Weller, Robert P. *Vol. II*: 178
Weltanschauung/en *Vol. II*: 178, 333
Weltreligionen Vol. II: 384-5
Werblowsky, Zwi *Vol. I*: 215, 250
Werner, Karel *Vol. II*: 38
Wesen (essence)
– of religion *Vol. I*: 11, 45 // *Vol. II*: 41, 121-2,
– of a particular religion *Vol. I*: 12, 109 // *Vol. II*: 33-4, 36, 112, 126, 137
Westerlund, David *Vol. I*: 153, 170
Westermarck, Edward *Vol. II*: 112, 116
westernism/ist *Vol. I*; 33, 43, 47, 49, 112-4, 247, 262, 269, 270 // *Vol. II*: 374
white (Shintō etc) *Vol. I*: 52, 87 // *Vol. II*: 89, 280, 284
White Lotus movements *Vol. II*: 157-9, 178
White Light Association *Vol. II*: 173
Widengren, Geo. *Vol. II*: 253, 263
Wiebe, Donald *Vol. I*: 21, 31-2, 194, 225, 265
Wijsen, Frans *Vol. II*: 140, 151
Wiles, Maurice F. *Vol. II*: 98, 101
Winch, Peter *Vol. I*: 38
Winchester *Vol. II*: 264
Winnipeg *Vol. I*: 112, 197, 236
wisdom (various) *Vol. II*: 6, 51, 172, 174, 234, 279

Wittenberg *Vol. II*: 337
Won Wŏn (wŏn) *Vol. II*: 144, 153, 179-201
Won Buddhism *Vol. I*: 87, 102, 106 // *Vol. II*: 106, 144, 149, 166-7, 176-9, 228, 312, 394-5
Wonbukkyō *Vol. II*: 184
Wonbulgyo (Won Bulgyo, Wŏnpulkyo) *Vol. II*: 153, 166-7, 179, 182, 185-7, 197-8, 200-1
Wonkwang University *Vol. II*: 181, 184-5, 188, 191, 352, 391, 395
Wŏnpulkyo: See Wonbulgyo
Woo, Hairan *Vol. II*: 180-2, 198, 201, 311
Woodward, Peter *Vol. II*: 383, 389
World Congress (IAHR) *Vol. I*: 208, 250 See also congress/es (IAHR)
World Congress of Faiths *Vol. II*: 311, 342, 360
World Council of Churches *Vol. I*: 256
World's Parliament of Religions *Vol. I*: 166, 249
worldview *Vol. I*: 242 // *Vol. II*: 317
worship *Vol. I*: 100 // *Vol. II*: 47, 64, 77, 160, 190, 231, 259, 278-9, 282, 284-5, 291, 296, 301, 362, 381-2
worshippers *Vol. I*: 88
Worsley, Peter *Vol. II*: 134, 151
Wrede, William *Vol. II*: 349
Writings of an Old Man *Vol. I*: 117-19, 122, 126
Wyszynski (Cardinal) *Vol. II*: 331

Xié Tiān Gōng *Vol. II*: 294
Xīnzhú Chénghuáng Miào *Vol. II*: 301, 303

Yakutia/n *Vol. I*: 227 // *Vol. II*: 362
yamabushi *Vol. II*: 94, 260, 263, 271-5, 277
Yamaori, Tetsuo *Vol. II*: 214
Yampolsky, Philip: *Vol. II*: 34, 39
Yanagawa, Keiichi *Vol. I*: 162, 167, 170 // *Vol. II*: 44, 168
Yang, Heriyanto *Vol. II*: 299

Yàoshīfó (Yao Shi Fo) *Vol. II*: 296, 304
Yasukuni Jinja (Shrine) *Vol. I*: 270 // *Vol. II*: 43, 379, 389, 397-8
Yggdrasill *Vol. I*: 245
Yi Kŏn Huŏng *Vol. II*: 186
Yiguandao *Vol. II*: 159, 165
Yinger, Milton *Vol. I*: 203
yoga/is *Vol. I*: 233 // *Vol. II*: 97, 210-11, 230, 382
Yogācāra *Vol. I*: 127
Yogyakarta *Vol. I*: 176-7 // *Vol. II*: 295-7, 299, 373
yōkigurashi *Vol. II*: 171
yomatsuri *Vol. I*: 161
York/shire *Vol. II*: 312, 377
Yoshino *Vol. II*: 272
Younghusband, Sir Francis *Vol. I*: 149, 170, 213
youth studies *Vol. I*: 242
Yudono, Mount *Vol. II*: 94
Yuga Treatise *Vol. I*: 120
Yugoslavia *Vol. II*: 324, 339
Yuiitsu Shintō *Vol. II*: 43
Yūshūkan *Vol. II*: 398 See also Yasukuni Jinja

Zaire *Vol. I*: 138
zamek *Vol. I*: 76
zazen *Vol. I*: 96 // *Vol. II*: 82, 382-3
Zen *Vol. I*: 87, 96-7, 99-102, 133, 146, 168, 170 // *Vol. II*: 22, 24, 29, 169, 193-4, 223, 226, 233, 280, 344, 371, 378, 382, 397, 400
Zhang, Xinying *Vol. I*: 143
Zhèng Hé *Vol. II*: 299
Zhēnzōng *Vol. I*: 131
Zhongyi *Vol. II*: 159
Zimbabwe *Vol. I*: 153, 174, 196-7, 202, 221, 268 // *Vol. II*: 318
Zinser, Hartmut *Vol. I*: 178, 194 // *Vol. II*: 127, 129, 238
Znak (ZNAK) *Vol. II*: 332-6
zōngjiào *Vol. II*: 153
Zoroastrianism *Vol. I*: 95 // *Vol. II*: 89, 92

www.ingramcontent.com/pod-product-compliance
Lightning Source LLC
Chambersburg PA
CBHW071655170426
43195CB00039B/2200